Bernini is Dead?

Bernini is Dead?

ARCHITECTURE AND
THE SOCIAL PURPOSE

John Burchard

McGRAW-HILL BOOK COMPANY

New York   St. Louis   San Francisco

Düsseldorf   Johannesburg   Kuala Lumpur   London   Mexico   Montreal

New Delhi   Panama   Paris   São Paulo   Singapore   Sydney   Tokyo   Toronto

BERNINI IS DEAD?:
Architecture and the Social Purpose

This book was set in Palatino by Monotype Composition Co.
The illustrations were printed by Lehigh Press.
It was printed and bound by Von Hoffmann Press.
The designers were John Horton and Elaine Gongora.
The editors were Thomas Quinn, Marie Longyear, and Michael Hennelly.
The copy editor was Sylvia Warren. Gabriele Wunderlich was the
picture editor. Joe Campanella supervised the production.

Library of Congress Cataloging in Publication Data
Burchard, John Ely.
  Bernini is dead?

  Bibliography: p.
  Includes index.
    1. Architecture and society. 2. Architecture—
Psychological aspects. I. Title.
NA2543.S6B78   720'.1'9   74-31263

ISBN 0-07-008922-1

123456789   VHVH   79876

*Dedicated to the memories of my
old friends and teachers, now
all departed, who have most
influenced the thinking of
this book*

JOHN O. SUMNER

CATHARINE BAUER

SIGFRIED GIEDION

WALTER GROPIUS

WILLIAM WILSON WURSTER

CONTENTS

LIST OF ILLUSTRATIONS

ix

Endpapers
FRONT: St. Peter's and Piazza San Pietro, Rome/*Jack Marco from Omikron*
BACK: New City Hall, Boston, Massachusetts/*photo by Anthony Taro*

ACKNOWLEDGMENTS

The illustrations used in this book were obtained from the following sources and used with their permission:

Walter Aguiar: Pl. 131
Edward Allen: Pls. 4, 70–71, 132
Alinari: Pl. 368
Austrian National Library: Pls. 351–353
Austrian State Tourist Department, London: Pl. 350

Berris Barrow/Omikron: Pl. 245
Belgian National Tourist Office: Pls. 255, 260, 288
Bildarchiv Foto Marburg: Pls. 53, 56, 202, 356
Lee Boltin: Pl. 120
E. Boudot-Lamotte: Pls. 361, 364
British Museum: Pls. 160–161
British Tourist Authority: Pls. 287, 310
John Burchard: Pls. 61–64, 99, 127, 130, 144, 147, 163, 171–172, 182, 190, 195, 220–221, 225, 251, 257, 264, 268, 278, 289, 292, 333, 354, 380

Caisse Nationale des Monuments Historique: Pls. 10, 339–340
Chamber of Commerce, Boston: Pl. 376
Bodo Cichy *The Great Ages of Architecture,* trans. Susan McMorran (London: Oldbourne Press, 1964): Pls. 49, 93–94, 157, 199, 204–205, 334–338
Circadian/Omikron: Pl. 344
City of Montreal: Pl. 378

David Davis/Omikron: Pls. 234, 306
Department of the Environment, Hannibal House: Pl. 74

Encyclopedia of World Art, vol. 10 (New York: McGraw-Hill Book Company, 1963): Pl. 117

Finnish Tourist Board: Pl. 385
Banister Fletcher *A History of Architecture on the Comparative Method* (16th ed.), (London: Athlone Press of the University of London, 1961): Pls. 2, 8, 12–20, 22–23, 28, 32–40, 45–48, 50–51, 137, 148–156, 170, 176, 181, 236–239, 242, 284, 298–301
Fondation Maeght: Pl. 388
Fremdenverkehrsband Nordbayern: Pls. 357, 359
French Cultural Services: Pls. 11, 222, 305, 311
French Embassy Press & Information Division: Pls. 213, 232–233, 246, 263, 342, 345–346, 384
French Government Tourist Office: Pls. 55, 203, 209, 215, 235, 241, 244, 267, 270, 279, 347
R. S. Friend/Omikron: Pl. 291

German Information Center: Pl. 313, 375
Sigfried Giedion *The Eternal Present* No. 6 in the A. W. Mellon Lectures in the Fine Arts, Bollingen Series XXXV, vol. II, *The Beginnings of Architecture* (copyright © 1964 by the Trustees of the National Gallery of Art, Washington, D.C.), photograph reproduced by permission of Princeton University Press: Pl. 110
Government of India Tourist Office: Pl. 96

Den Hanna/Omikron: Pls. 119, 208, 216, 230
Hedrich-Blessing: Pls. 1, 3
Mark Hewlett/Omikron: Pls. 6, 7, 253, 262, 272, 358
Hirmer Fotoarchiv: Pls. 84, 111
Lester Hult/Omikron: Pl. 355

Intourist: Pl. 197
Italian Cultural Institute: Pl. 297
Italian Government Travel Office: Pls.
81, 164, 167, 174, 194, 211, 217, 362,
369
Italian State Tourist Office: Pls. 175,
183–184, 186, 365–366

J. Jangais/Omikron: Pls. 275, 282, 290,
341, 343

Kersting, A. E./Omikron: Pl. 348
*Key Monuments of the History of
Architecture*, Henry Millon (ed.)
(Englewood Cliffs, N.J.: Prentice-
Hall, n.d.): Pl. 307

Landesbildstelle, Berlin: Pl. 374
Landesbildstelle, Hanover: Pl. 201
Lange-Hirmer: Pl. 142

Fosco Maraini *Meeting with Japan*
(New York: Viking Press, 1960),
copyright © 1959 by Hutchinson &
Co. Ltd. Reprinted by permission of
The Viking Press, Inc.: Pl. 65
Jack Marco/Omikron: Pl. 363
Media Features: Pls. 75, 77, 79, 89,
97–98, 106–107, 125, 146, 158,
165–166, 249, 259, 283, 303, 315,
373, 381
Mexican National Tourist Council: Pls.
118, 121–122, 124, 371
Ministry of Tourism, Egypt: Pl. 136

National Tourist Organization of
Greece: Pl. 86
Walter Newman/Omikron: Pls. 296,
360

Omikron: Pls. 5, 25, 41–42, 44, 52, 68,
76, 78, 83, 85, 87–88, 95, 100, 104,
109, 129, 133, 145, 159, 162, 180,
187, 189, 196, 224, 243, 250, 258,
265, 276–277, 280–281, 308–309,
314, 316, 319, 321, 349, 377, 379,
383, 387

Robert J. O'Reilly: Pl. 198
A. Orlandos/Athens: Pl. 21

J. Powell/Rome: Pl. 128
Tatiana Proskouriakoff *An Album of
Maya Architecture* (Norman, Okla-
homa: University of Oklahoma Press,
1963): Pl. 123
Roger-Viollet: Pls. 72, 103
Jean Roubier: Pls. 210, 219, 261
Benjamin Rowland *The Art and
Architecture of India* (Baltimore,
Md.: Penguin, 1956): Pl. 105
Royal Commission on Historical
Monuments (England): Pls. 54, 73,
227–229, 231, 240, 266, 285–286

Henry Saylor *Dictionary of
Architecture* (New York: John
Wiley & Sons, 1952): Pls. 92, 312
Scala/New York, Florence: Pls. 295, 372
Hans C. Scherr-Thoss: Pls. 322–332
Spanish Tourist Office: Pl. 252, 320
St. John's University, Collegeville,
Minn.: Pl. 386
Grace Swayne/Omikron: Pls. 134, 168,
188, 191, 207, 214, 247–248, 382

Tod/Omikron: Pls. 9, 24, 29–30, 80,
82, 90–91, 101–102, 108, 126, 135,
138–141, 143, 169, 173, 179, 185,
192–193, 200, 206, 212, 218, 223,
226, 254, 256, 269, 271, 273–274,
293–294, 302, 304, 317–318, 367,
370

Yoshio Watanabe: Pls. 66–67, 69
*World Architecture: An Illustrated
History*, Trewin Copplestone (ed.)
(New York: McGraw-Hill Book
Company, 1969): Pls. 26–27, 43,
57–60, 112–116, 177–178

Paul Zucker *Town and Square* (New
York: Columbia University Press,
1959): Pl. 31

FOREWORD

Over the last half century, first by chance, later by design, and always with a good deal of luck, I have visited most of the interesting areas of the world in a more than casual way. Because of my central professional interest in architectural affairs, I have made a serious point of more than superficial visits to the major architectural monuments as I went by and have "bagged" all but two or three, together with an enormous number of less notorious but often quite as interesting "minor" examples. Without these, the masterpieces would be much less fully understood.

In thus "squandering" these many years, I have happily looked also at scenery and people, at costumes and animals. I have savored cities in many more terms than architectural. I have sampled and relished a large variety of gastronomic and oenophilitic experiences. I have waded on coral reefs, gone to corridas, experienced Australian football, Japanese Kabuki and Noh theater, Osaka puppets, and indeed almost anything vulgar or aristocratic which offered itself as an experience, though I have not seared my feet on genuine hot coals, pondered Buddha in a Tibetan monastery, or tried to see what it would be like to be a cannibal. I have even tried, with scant success, to acquire a bargain or two or to see a genuine kermis, and I have especially enjoyed scrambles in the mountains. I am writing this when my wander years are spent. It has been an almost irresistible temptation to try to write everything down—to share all these delights with people I have never met, whose tastes and backgrounds I do not know. But I have concluded that I must limit the narrative to architecture and leave all the other rich sensual pleasures to my memories.

Those who stay with me will note from time to time that I have something close to contempt for the superficiality and phony camaraderie of most of our current travel guides. The great old Murrays and Baedekers were less folksy and more thorough and more reliable. Of them there are sturdy remnants for some countries in the Muirhead series. The green Michelins are excellent for France and of some help in Switzerland and Italy and no doubt elsewhere. One or two of the motoring Baedekers help in their way. If you can read Italian, the detailed series of the Touring Club Italiano are as admirable examples of what a good guidebook should be as the guides of the American Automobile Association or the oil companies are examples of what a mediocre guidebook is like. Of course, personal observations are helpful if they are written by perceptive people—people like Fosco Maraini, Sacheverell Sitwell, James Michener, and Mary McCarthy—but they are necessarily selective and cover only a small part of all the terrain. Since I have been able to advise, with some success, individual friends about their voyages, it was tempting to try a travel guide of my own. But I have resisted the temptation. This book is not intended to be a book of travel or a travel guide—not even a complete guide to architectural travel, though it may be of some help for that alone.

Another consideration which I have had to deal with is that of terminology. Architecture teems with technical terms, many of which are unknown to the general reader. Most of these cannot be turned into useful circumlocutions without serious damage to the flow of the text. The small dictionaries contain too few of these terms and define others badly. Only the largest standard dictionaries (*Webster's* and *Oxford*) offer any hope for the reader who is unwilling to glide over the unknown, and these unabridged works are, of course, very bulky. It is therefore tempting to provide a glossary in a work such as this. Indeed I had prepared one when I came upon the new, 1972 edition of *The Penguin Dictionary of Architecture* (see Critical Bibliography) which does the job better than my version would have. Accordingly I do not publish a glossary here but instead urge the serious readers of my book to arm themselves with the paperback edition of the Penguin *Dictionary* which is of convenient size and reasonably priced.

My book could more easily be taken to be a try at architectural world history, but it is not even that although I feel quite strongly, as a matter of fact, that there is practically no first-class world architectural history available for the general reader, for the following reason. Architecture is a social art. To understand the architecture of any time and place, one needs to understand the terrain, the climate, the available materials, the known building skills, and the purposes of the building. Decent architectural history usually does include at least this much. But it is not nearly enough. It is probably also necessary to understand the economics, the politics, the morals and the mores, the faiths and the knowledge, the painting, the sculpture, the poetry, the theater, the music, the dress, the transportation of the time in which an architecture is made. The genesis, the prototypes, and so on, of the architecture itself are not without interest and significance—somewhat more interest and significance as a rule than the names and biographies of specific architects and their patrons—but it is the entire cultural climate that needs most to be understood. There are a few works which come close to filling such a prescription about a single period but not even very many of these, and they are quite specialized as to a time, a place, or even a single building. But I would not seek to underestimate the difficulties of telling architectural history "like it was," in the terms of Ranke, of owning a personality which is capable both of sober mining and of human understanding.

Unfortunately, the training of scholarly architectural historians has generally placed a greater premium on accurate pedantry than upon human values or significance. In consequence most of the architectural monographs are in fact damnably dull even to the professionals who *have* to read them. And the great syntheses remain to be done. I wish I were man enough to do one. But I am not, and I have learned this by experience. I do not know enough and I have not enough time left to learn enough. And even if I did know enough, I am not sure I would have the skill to put it together. So this is not a stab at world architectural history, although there will be a good deal of history in it, now and then.

Though I have carefully tried to avoid gross errors, I want equally carefully to make it clear that this does not pretend to be a scholarly work or a contribution to scholarship. I have read, I think widely, I think discriminatingly, and I know carefully. I have faced the buildings themselves in their physical reality and have examined them seriously, extensively, lovingly, and certainly thoughtfully. Since I am suspicious of anyone who writes about buildings he has not visited, I began with the intention of never doing this myself. In the working out of this I have had to waver in a small handful of cases because the unvisited buildings were simply too important to my argument to leave unmentioned.

So this writing, however personal, is not an autobiography; it is not a travel guidebook, not even an architectural travel guide; it is not a comprehensive architectural history; it is not a contribution to the scholarship of architectural history. What in heaven's name then is it?

I hope it is more than the adventures of my soul among masterpieces. The masterpieces are there, but the soul is not large enough to justify such an account. At one level it is trying, I suppose, to show some people quite unknown to me, how they, too, might, in time, and on their own terms, acquire the memory of the happy day on happy day which I have spent in walking the corridors of the great architectural past. But I hope it is a little more. I hope there are concealed metaphors for my own day; and I know that more than once I have elaborated such hints and made them explicit.

This is all the "relevance" I will claim. I have no interest in trying to *prove* relevance or in defending my prejudices against attack. Those who find this work irrelevant or prejudiced can lay it aside.

Beside the self-imposed rule of trying not to talk of things I have not experienced, there is another one. I have said little or nothing about some very important archeological sites, such as Nineveh, Mohenjo-Daro, Taxila, Chan-Chan, and so on. This is not because they are unimportant in the study of the development of architecture. Some are very important. But they ask of the visitor who goes to them more understanding than his eyes alone can give him on the site. In a sense, of course, this is true of all architecture, even of those rare buildings of which every original stone is intact, but it is doubly true of ruins. One could not move very much in historical architecture if he excluded all ruins. But there are ruins which are extensive enough so that a good eye and a reasonable imagination of a nonprofessional sort can fairly reconstruct them. This is so of Karnak, and Chichen-Itzá, of some Greek temples, and of things like the Colosseum. It is marginally true of Hadrian's Villa and perhaps not quite true of Trajan's Forum or the Baths of Caracalla. It is clearly not true of places like Taxila or the Golden House of Nero, and these I am leaving out.

Of course they are not all I am leaving out. This discourse cannot be comprehensive. It is something more than the Best 100 Buildings according to Burchard and considerably less than a compendium of all the great architectural achievements of all time.

I should note in passing that I emphatically *do not* fear to use the words "monument" or "masterpiece," however unfashionable these words may be today. Whether the current hesitation to talk of monuments because they are associated with power or to proclaim masterpieces as such is the result of a reaction to earlier overemphasis, or of an attitude which cannot tolerate extravagant beauty surrounded by mediocrity or squalor, it is a denial of an important and an uplifting part of life and can result, at best, if accepted operationally, in a dreary pseudo-Utopian plateau.

It is perhaps an indictment of our times that our great buildings are so seldom created for major social needs, but that does not mean we should settle for bland mediocrity at any level. I am not ashamed to be able to enjoy the ordinary life of the street and the modest aspirations of the "people" without concluding that there should be no new masterpieces or that we should cover our eyes when we go by the old ones.

If, as I will, one deals mostly with masterpieces, he is likely also to deal much of the time with clichés. For this, too, there need be no apology. Hagia

Sophia, the Great Pyramids, the Parthenon, the Pantheon of Rome, Chartres and Amiens, to name only a few, *are* the greatest examples of their species. It is absurd to ignore them for fear of being cliché-ridden and to rush about the world seeking fascinating discoveries that no one has found before, or that previous discoverers have left unsung because they were too insignificant. This book revels in clichés.

It must have become painfully apparent by now that this book is written in the first person. When I was a boy, we were warned never to be guilty of writing first-person accounts, since it smacked of egotism. My teachers and my parents were, of course, quite wrong; the greater arrogance is the use of the third person to give the impression of universality to statements that are, after all, nothing but personal opinions. Besides, writing as I might talk allows me to avoid the pitfalls of bad style which trap generals—and social scientists. So I shall say "I" whenever I ought to, and let the accusations of conceit be leveled as they may.

Even by hefting it, you will also know that it is a long, possibly even a garrulous, book. This would not please many generals—or the Nobel prizeman Dr. Albert Szent-Gyorgi, who boasts in his own recent book, *The Crazy Ape*:

> It is a revolutionary book because it's only 40 pages—it can be read in two hours. The trouble with books is that they cannot be read. Who the hell has time to read 300 pages? There is nothing you cannot say in two hours if it is essential.[1]

I can only hope you have more time than this man. I hope you have more tolerance as to what is essential or more interest in the nonessential than he seems to have. I can only say that expansiveness seems to *me* the right way for *me* to deal with *my* material.

Naturally I am indebted to many more people than I can reasonably list. My general obligation to writers in the field is presumably paid by footnote citations and by the bibliography.

More deeply I am indebted to five professors of my youth who pointed me in the directions I should follow: Colbert Searles, Robert Rogers, John O. Sumner, Henry Seaver, and Dean William Emerson; and to a group of friends now departed with whom I had frequent productive discussions: Sigfried Giedion, Walter Gropius, Catharine Bauer, Sir Richard Livingstone, A. Lawrence Kocher, and Ludwig Mies van der Rohe; and among the living: Alvar Aalto, Albert Bush-Brown, Gyorgy Kepes, Spiro Kostof, Martin Meyerson, Lewis Mumford, Walter Netsch, and Steen Eiler Rasmussen. These are the people who have probably most influenced my thinking as often by disagreement as by agreement.

I should never have found the time to write the book or the freedom to travel save for a very generous grant from the Carnegie Corporation of New York made in 1964; and I never should have got the writing done save for two stays at the Rockefeller Foundation's Villa Serbelloni above Bellagio, totaling 4½ months and divided between the summer of 1969 and the autumn of 1970, under the sensitive suzerainty of Charlotte and John Marshall; and to make these productive I needed also the generously liberal interpretation of what my

[1] As quoted by Robert Reinhold in the *New York Times*, Feb. 20, 1970.

postretirement half-time duties at M.I.T. ought to be, decided by Howard Johnson, then M.I.T.'s president, and James R. Killian, then chairman of its Corporation.

It is not for convention's sake that I offer a salute to my wife Marjorie, my most difficult critic and my more than friend of forty-seven years, who has been through most of the experiences with me and often helped me to see more clearly what it was I really wanted to say and what it would be better to leave unsaid. What I have left in that I should have taken out is my fault, not hers.

JOHN BURCHARD
Boston, Massachusetts

CHAPTER ONE

ON TRAVEL IN GENERAL

Travel, in the younger sort, is a part of education;
in the elder, a part of experience.

Francis Bacon
On Travel

WHY TRAVEL AT ALL?

Writers are always urging us to travel—or almost always. Few resemble the melancholy Pope:

Happy the man whose wish and care
A few paternal acres bound
Content to breathe his native air
In his own ground.[1]

They tell us to travel to see things for the first time; to drink life's full cup; to restore one's self; to form one's youth. There are more good reasons than these. An important benefit lies in memory.

One of the most sensitive travel writers who ever lived speaks of this. Having remarked that all experience burns away, he goes on to say:

To be able, or seem to be able, to fix the forms
of a few of its momentary flames, to fall in love
with them and hug our own vision of their
beauty and give that image a place in the abiding
dream about ourselves, . . . provides the calm

[1] Alexander Pope, "Solitude."

that we need, as well as courage and pride, in order to work while yet it is light.[2]

There are other things to accumulate from travel beside its memories. Indeed, the purposes of pleasured travel are manifold and none of us is capable of finding equal interest in all. One might wish to collect exotic objects; one may simply wish to follow the tennis players or the skiers or the sun; one might be curious about the differences in the presentation of a horse race at Melbourne, Epsom, Auteuil, and Churchill Downs, or of automobiles in Monza and in Indianapolis; one might want to shoot an ibex above Baltit, a tiger in Bengal, a polar bear in the Arctic, and a crocodile in Cape York, whether by gun or arrow or camera, and whether or not trophies are brought home; to collect people or to observe them more seriously, studying, for example, how one grows up in Samoa, or the ceremonial exchanges of the Trobriand Islanders, or why all the young people desert a village in the Vaucluse. Who has a right really to say which of these purposes are the more serious, the more worthy? I at least do not claim that privilege. I shall simply stick to architecture.

There exists a good deal of amusing and informative writing about travel that is more directed to personal conveniences and inconveniences, such as Lady Mary Wortley Montagu's letters, than to architecture. Among those who did write of architecture there were naturally large differences of opinion. Nowhere is this more clear than in the views of Rome held by two great eighteenth-century writers who were essentially contemporaries, Stendhal and Goethe. Each made Italian journeys (as have so many others) to look and write, in part at least about Italian art and architecture, and both came to Rome—Stendhal many times. But how different their stances! You can scarcely believe you are reading about the same city.

Stendhal did not approach travel lethargically, however stuffily and chauvinistically he may have reported the conclusions of his many "Voyages dans Rome." Coming there on the ninth of August, 1817, he wrote as a contemporary American tourist might that despite the extreme heat they were starving to see everything, moved about incessantly, and came home every evening horribly worn out. He declared French painting superior to that of Michelangelo, disdained the stones of Rome, especially travertine, and thought the Romans would have done much better had they had the stone of Lyon, Edinburgh, or Dalmatia.

Yet the Colosseum had a prodigious fascination to him for all the wrong self-centered reasons. He was upset by the contemporary activities going on in the ruins not because they desecrated an historic place but because

[2] C. E. Montague, *The Right Place* (Garden City, N.Y.: Doubleday, Page and Company, 1924), p. 166. This book has been a happy companion of mine ever since publication. Montague was proudly romantic and sentimental and his style reflects it. "Romance" and "sentiment" are pejorative nouns today, but it is we who are wrong and not romance and sentiment. Montague had great sensitivity to time and place and a balanced modern view about change.

they interfered with his reading from his works to a few friends at dusk. And he could even dispense with the friends, remarking that if he had the power he would close the Colosseum for his exclusive use while he was in Rome.[3] How many of us in these days have felt the same about the Sistine Chapel, if for different reasons!

Goethe, on the other hand, realized that you can really comprehend the Amphitheatre in Verona only if you can see it complete and full of people. Stendhal wanted the Colosseum to himself and preferably in ruins, because when intact it was no more than a theater, while now it was, he said, the most beautiful vestige of the Roman people, who, like Napoleon, were criminals but great ones.

But like all observers of genius and near genius, Stendhal offers *aperçus* which atone for his romantic prejudices. Do not try to take in all of St. Peter's at once, he advises. The wise traveler will avoid indigestion brought on by stuffing. Stendhal at least was fortunate enough later on to be in Rome often so that there was no "necessity to see."[4]

What a marvelous thing it is to be in London or Paris for the tenth time—with no obligation to visit any great reminder of the historical past because one has visited them all before. It does not mean that this lucky person will do no revisiting, only that he can now be thoughtful and selective with no "necessity to see." But there has to be a first time, and perhaps in the beginning it is permissible to voyage widely and quickly lest the second voyage should never happen—or the third or the fourth.

Goethe was quite a different man of course. He was less cynical, less anxious to prove Rome inferior to his own country (indeed he leaned the other way). I sense he had marginally better taste and a much wider spread of interests—in science, in completing the writing of *Egmont*, in ruined castles, in painting, in nature, in architecture, in pleasant ladies and learned talk, and he leapt from joy to joy. He was a German romantic before he was a German scientist, but he could not avoid laying out a program which would be hard to follow.

> I shall never rest until I know that all my ideas are derived, not from hearsay, or tradition but from my real living contact with things themselves. From my earliest youth this has been my ambition and my torment.[5]

He looked at architecture more with a painter's eye than an architect's:

> The stadium of Caracalla is largely in ruins but still conveys an idea of immense space. To draw it, a person should place himself at its left wing,

[3] Marie Henri Beyle [Stendhal], *Rome, Naples et Florence, en 1817*, texte présenté et annoté par Roland Beyer (Paris: Editions Julliard, 1964).
[4] Ibid.
[5] Johann Wolfgang Goethe, *Italian Journey* (New York: Random House, Inc., Pantheon, 1962), p. 343. Translated from *Italienische Reise, 1786–1788*, by W. H. Auden and Elizabeth Mayer.

where the charioteers used to start. . . . if he has any architectonic imagination, he will have some faint idea of the *hybris* of those ancient times. A skilful artist could make a pleasant picture, but it would have to be twice as long as it was high.[6]

There were more profound *aperçus*. In an August "retrospect" in Rome he commented sagely on fashions in the arts and of the replacements in critical esteem of Raphael by Michelangelo and Leonardo but could not resist falling into the trap (which entices us all) of universalizing a personal taste. "All this pointed towards the coming predilection for an earlier school of painting, a taste which a dispassionate observer [i.e., Goethe] could only regard as a symptom of mediocre and unoriginal talents." It sounds like Henry Adams! But he recovered the Olympian view soon enough to continue.

> It is so difficult to comprehend one great talent, let alone two at the same time. To make things easier for us, we take sides; that is why the reputation of artists and writers is always fluctuating. Now one rules the day, now another.[7]

And, again:

> The observation that all greatness is transitory should not make us despair; on the contrary the realization that the past was great should stimulate us to create something of consequence ourselves, which, even when, in its turn, it has fallen in ruins, may continue to inspire our descendants to a noble activity such as our ancestors never lacked.[8]

It is with this belief of Goethe's that I begin my work. I hope I may also keep in mind another thing he wrote on the road in June, 1787: "When a journey is over, the traveller himself remembers it as an unbroken sequence of events, inseparable from each other. But when he tries to describe this journey to someone else, he finds it impossible to communicate this, for he can only present the events one by one as separate facts."[9]

ARCHITECTURE AND NATURE

One reason for traveling, not completely unrelated to architecture, is to view natural scenery. To me, at least, the mountains are more interesting than the prairies or the sea. The desert stands somewhere between, notably because of its light; but between the undulant desert of the shifting dunes

[6] Ibid., p. 430.
[7] Ibid., p. 378.
[8] Ibid., p. 143.
[9] Ibid., pp. 326–327.

and the punctuated desert of Ship Rock I prefer the latter. No one can deny the feeling of combined awe and repose that comes in a great stand of trees whether or not the cathedral metaphor is well conceived. But I am happier above tree line where the ridges, the gullies, and the peaks are indeed architectonic as are the sculptured Badlands of South Dakota or the towers of Arizona. Something similar is to be found in certain caves, but the torch and the electric bulb are inadequate for bringing out the best in architectural forms. There is no substitute for the slanting rays of sunrise and sundown, as benevolent to much great architecture as they are essential to the presentation of mountain relief. High noon is a bad time to look at architecture or scenery, however good for a sheriff's confrontation.

At its most majestic, great mountain scenery makes any architecture seem trivial. So indeed may a truly great stand of sequoias or cryptomerias, somewhat in the way that the ocean exceeds the fleets that borrow a little of it for a little time.

Fortunately for both architecture and nature the occasions are rare when the two need to be combined under some condition of parity. The few examples probably occur in certain cityscapes where a majestic site is covered with a great deal of building, a site like San Francisco, Sydney, Wellington, or Rio de Janeiro. The special problem this raises involves a detour too long to take here.

In the mountains, at least until recently, men have been willing to subordinate their buildings to the mountain scape—men of simple needs, subordinate to their environment and possibly affected by a genuine, if unspoken, love and understanding of it. Thus there is a common harmony and grace to be found in much peasant mountain or forest architecture throughout the world from the Finnish lakes to the Alps to the high towns of the Karakoram and the Himalaya. These buildings have a striking similarity which does not demand an elaborate theory of multifold migrations to explain. The common problems of terrain, of weather; the naturally available common building materials; the modest and common needs working on simple people uncontaminated by slogans ("Nature imitates Art") or by fashion make it natural to put things together in a direct and harmonious way, undisturbed by any speculations or assertions as to whether they are or are not in tune with nature or the times. Indeed they may even respect and fear nature too much to aspire to being at one with her. They are doubtless content if she will leave them alone, at least to the extent of not drowning them in the snow of a great avalanche, or burning them up in a fiery forest.

Her minor petulancies they learn to deal with. Unlike contemporary Californians they usually avoid ludicrous sites (such as ravines which in dry weather act as chimney-traps for deadly fires, slopes whose soil and angle are such that they will inevitably slide away sooner or later), although they must brave the almost unpredictable avalanche. They find flat stones to support their posts and to offer some protection against rodents and rot. They cap the posts for the same obvious purposes, not to make a decorative element. They chink the walls against the wind and find out how to hold the roofs down with stones. In evolved forms all these elements may mature into the sophistication of the temple of Ise or the Parthenon. But the mountain man with little time or drive toward embellishment or conscious refinement is content with some simple wood carving, some simple painting, representational or purely decorative. Almost anywhere you go in the mountains, you find these buildings to be much alike, barring minor differences; you find them to be simple, sensitive, altogether appropriate.

Where I sit at this minute above the lake of Como I can look at gentle hills backed by great dolomitic cliffs. The foreground hills are accented by Lombardy poplars and cedars and dotted with stuccoed houses and uniform red-tiled roofs to produce the harmonious Italian landscape which is so easy to love and which, save for the industrial cities, is so slow to change with time. The buildings add to the terrain and the terrain to the buildings, and it all recalls the peace of Utrillo or Cézanne. And so it is for the Greek villages climbing part way up the *akropolei* like Arkanglos on Rhodes, or much of the Cotswold countryside, or those villages a few miles from the sea in Provence.

There are exceptions. There are dreary, unforested, arid mountains where the terrain is more forbidding, where the available building materials are more limited, more refractory, and less ingratiating than in the places we remember with pleasure. Here the people are so desperately poor, the struggle for survival so unrelenting, that there is no compelling inducement to any amenity at all. Such places are to be found on the dry side of the Pyrenees or on much of the Altiplano of Peru. Stone is almost the only possible building material and the resultant shivering, gray, windswept shelters are much less friendly than the chalets of Saas-Fee or of Tibet. But even these have their rightness.

What does not have much rightness is what happened architecturally to the mountains of the United States. It is not all disaster. There are the little white villages of New England, especially those nestling in the tight, small-scale valleys of Vermont, and there are individual triumphs of

Pl. 1

sensitivity by men like Frank Lloyd Wright or Richard Neutra among the dramatic red cliffs of Arizona. But mostly it has been disaster. All the ingredients for good mountain architecture were there—save only the human disposition. The early builders of the West in America may have been simple-minded but they were neither peasants nor mountainmen. Settlers they seldom aspired to be. They were not there to lay a physical foundation for their grandchildren, to build an establishment where their offspring might graze the offspring of their cattle and sheep into the tenth generation. Instead they came to loot the hills and streams—of the coal of West Virginia, of the gold of the Black Hills, the Rockies, and the Sierra.

They came to cut and sell the great trees of the Northwest and to leave the detritus for others to mourn and to try to repair if they could.

These enterprising conquistadores had much the same ultimate aims as their Spanish predecessors. Having struck it rich they planned to take the richness elsewhere to enjoy. Almost anything would do for the moment between poverty and wealth. The consequence was not very different from Lead to Cripple Creek, to Aspen, to Grass Valley. Some of these towns yearned toward elegance, founded on weak memories, real or imagined. They imported a piano or an opera house—and occasionally a Baby Doe Tabor aspired to being a Mme. de Sévigné. But the architecture never became a genuine mountain architecture. It has no beauty, it has no repose, it is seldom more than a false front. Now and again a single building in an imported style may prompt a small nostalgic tear, the verandahed wood hotel at Volcano, California (recently burned down), the brick Elks Club in Columbia, perhaps the opera house in Central City, Colorado. The charm, where there is any, arises not from intrinsic merit but by comparison with the low level of the rest, and a romantic notion of a frontier that never was, the imputed queenliness of some miner's wife, the exaggerated nobility of the outcasts of Poker Flat—not sentiments to be scorned but merely to be understood for what they are and not to be applauded for what they are not. The arcades of Dodge City were not the peers of those of the modest bastide Monpazier or medieval Münster.

As buildings become more pretentious, I can think of few exceptions to the rule that they are defeated by the mountains. At large scale, the only example to the contrary I can easily recall is the Potala in Lhasa.

But despite this there are unhappily an increasing number of buildings which *try* to compete architecturally with the mountains. Without any effort to be monumental this can be seen in any of the twentieth-century rush towns where the gold is found on the ski slopes.

Despite these unhappy examples, in preparing to examine architecture go first to the mountains for two purposes—to see what magnificent mass can really be, and to note the virtue of honest simplicity in certain peasant buildings, closing your eyes to hotels and condominiums from Cervinia-Breuil to Aspen.

And go to nature now and again—to see how important it is that the building and the site be in harmony; the tall spire of Heiligenblut under the Grossglockner, the backwater canals of Venice, the miracle of Le Mont St-Michel, Frank Lloyd Wright's Falling Water, the minarets of Istanbul, or even lower Manhattan as it was only a few years ago. There *are* examples to demonstrate that sensitive and skillful interplay is, despite the more frequent failures, possible. All architects profess to believe this; Wright was almost the only one to practice it. Most great architecture, let us face it, is antinatural. For one Greek temple sited in the valley of Segesta or on the precipice of Lindos there are dozens of distinguished

Pl. 3

city buildings which have made such landscape as there is out of an unimpressive stream or lake shore. Most great architecture is urban. Most great cities are on sites where nature was undramatic or could even be tailored to the needs of the city as were the hills of Rome or the banks of the Parisian Seine. Urbanism itself may well be at bottom antinatural though this conclusion does not lead me to the further conclusion, which I consider a nonsequitur, that no nature should be let into the city, that the distinction between city and country should be positive, even rigorous, as advocated, for example, by Steen-Eiler Rasmussen.

Though travel to nature and travel to architecture may reasonably be joined in an enriched travel experience, and I have usually managed to arrange it so, it is just as well to remember that they are separable things and so can be enjoyed independently.

Indeed the greatest experiences are likely to be isolated and pure, mountains or city, not mountains and city. The great mountain experiences of the Fairy Valley part way up Nanga Parbat or of the clouds lifting higher and then higher and then incredibly higher before the true summit of Rakaposhi comes into view—these experiences of the distance as well as the grass and lichens and moss in the foreground come in the absence of any architecture at all; in contrast, the cathedral of Chartres, the Alcazar, the Kremlin, the great Square of St. Peter's at Rome, or the Taj Mahal—these great architectural moments—are devoid of any serious competing natural scenery and are the stronger thereby. Nonetheless great architecture and great nature are not inevitably incompatible, though I would be hard put to cite a convincing example to support this statement.

It may have occurred to you, as it does to me, that the notable exceptions are generally associated with the level horizon line provided by a body of water or with quite gentle hills rising from that horizon. One of the reasons why great oceans are as permissive to impressive architecture as great mountains are not may be that building can occur only at their edges. And the edge of an uncliffed sea or even a cliffed one is quite different and much more precise than the edge of the mountains where the last foothills dissolve into the plain. There is also the lack of a natural dominating vertical scale.

Many observers have felt a need to decide which of the final two experiences, the natural or the architectural, was the greater. Most have ended on the side of nature.

Goethe was typical of this view. He was well aware of the power of architecture. "St. Peter's has made me realize that Art, like Nature, can abolish all standards of measurement."[10] But in the end he came down on the other side: "Nature is indeed the only book where every page is filled with important content."[11]

[10] Ibid., p. 123.
[11] Ibid., p. 187.

But a different argument can be made and different conclusions drawn:

That works of architecture as things of man's creating are inferior in
interest, in excellence of design, and in perfection of workmanship, to the
humblest of Nature's works outside humanity, has often been the
burden of the moralizing of theologian, naturalist, and astronomer.
But in this reflection lies a fallacy which is fully exposed to those who can
discern in the successive intellectual works of man the part of the
human spirit, and who regard them as manifestations of Nature, of which
he forms a part. A spiritual element marks off the work of man from
that of animals; it is here that architecture begins. Building, whose end and
aim is the fulfillment of material wants, remains building and, whatever
be the nature of the material want, differs in no essential from the
work of the lower animals; but if to this be added an element of aspiration
involving the exercise of a higher kind of design, there is the distinction
that makes the difference.[12]

Fortunately we do not have to resolve this question here, though, in
my own opinion, the works of nature are infinitely superior to those of
man.

[12] William Bell Dinsmoor, *The Architecture of Ancient Greece* (London: B. A. Batsford,
1902, rev. 3d ed., 1950), p. xv.

CHAPTER TWO

ON ARCHITECTURAL TRAVEL IN GENERAL

Stone cutters fighting time with marble, you foredefeated
Challengers of Oblivion.

Robinson Jeffers
To the Stone Cutters

Even when we seek out architecture with no concern for nature, there can be many motives. Without asserting one reason to be better than another, one might engage in architectural travel for purely hedonistic or exotic or associational reasons; to search for quintessence; or to seek documentation for other aspects of history. And with more directly architectural reasons one might want to explore the relations of architecture to the other visual arts; to examine the engineering skills of the past; to indulge in a little architectural detective work of one's own; to advance one's own architectural professional skills; or some personal combination of these.

There is hardly a "bad" reason for traveling with the examination of architecture as the central purpose unless it be for the practice of "one-upmanship." No one of us, save perhaps the specialists in archeological or historical research, will be motivated by a single reason—and one might hope, even after conceding much evidence to the contrary, that at least some specialists have a lighter side. No one of us, too, will give equal weight to the multiple reasons which motivate him. Each of us may find something to deride in another's reasons or tastes in an area where expertise is grudgingly conceded, as compared, for example, with expertise in atomic equations. I, for example, regard the love of ruins for their own sake or the determination to see the Taj Mahal by full moon as bordering on absurdity. But it would be wrong to be too censorious about such things in others on the one hand, or to fear censorship in putting together one's own bouquet on the other.

THE MOTIVE OF HEDONISM

The most common reason for architectural travel, the hedonistic one, may in fact be as good as any. Here are beautiful things to be enjoyed simply for their beauty and quite independently of their time, place, or erstwhile purpose. This is naturally quite unintellectual and not highly approved of in the universities where so many scholars of the arts seem quite incapable of any sensuous reactions at all. And it can easily enough be a cover for a lazy attitude toward the arts. "I like what I like" is a perfectly respectable defense of what one chooses to see, or it would be, had it not so often been invoked by those who, by all appearances, have not taken the trouble to like or see anything very much. And it always does require at least a little trouble. One does not happen to be on the Athenian Acropolis completely by accident.

Even when we take this relaxed view of why we are somewhere looking at something, there are perplexing questions to be asked. No one can see everything and somewhere along the line there will be choices to be made. For example, if we attach our architectural viewing to some dominant other purpose, such as a business meeting in Torino, then we will have to catch what there is to catch, such as an hour at the Stupenga, and we will be lucky if the meeting is in Cairo, Egypt, rather than in Cairo, Illinois.

THE SEARCH FOR THE EXOTIC

Another reason for architectural gadding about is to seek the exotic, Coleridge's "damsel with a dulcimer." It is not exactly hedonistic save in its irrationality but it may have hedonistic aspects. I imagine long analyses could be provided as to the psychology which impels people always to be anxious to go over the hill into Erewhon with the expectation that things will be very different over there—perhaps better, from which one might derive stimulus, or worse, from which one might derive solace, but certainly different. Why do so many of us want to emulate Dr. Livingstone or Captain Cook, provided that the American Express Company script does not cause us to be lost or killed by cannibals? Why do most of us want to bring back new things for our *wunderkammer*, which is usually in the attic now and not in the parlor as it once was? Why does each of us think that when we photograph a rhinocerous or a giraffe, or an elephant with his ears flapping, or a pride of lions sleeping after a gorge, our slides will be so all-fired interesting to our friends? Most of us by now must have come to look upon the animals of the African veldt as Gertrude Stein wrote about roses or a governor of California is accused of having spoken of the noble redwood. Indeed I fancy there is one particularly old and motheaten rhinoceros whom I have come personally to know without ever having sat even for a moment in a treetop in Kenya; and one particular leopard, speaking of treetops, who never leaves his tree while there is a lensman around.

How long can anything be regularly displayed by too many people to too many people? It is not the animals of Africa who have lost their freshness but we. Yet the consequences are the same.

Similar things have happened to travel. Westminster Hall, the Cathedral of Notre-Dame de Paris, almost even the Piazza San Marco, the Parthenon, St. Peter's are old-hat now. People do not bring back slides of Salisbury Cathedral or Stonehenge any more, although there are more possible unexplored ways of viewing these monuments with a camera than are available, say, for the backside of a zebra.

Even when the old and the famous and the Occidental are accepted as still of consequence, they are too "banal" to be given more than quick checklist attention. Venice in a half day happens to more people than you would like to believe. So we have it that the traveler who has never been anywhere and never seen any of the great landmarks of our European background is avid to get as soon as possible to something more "interesting" and more "unusual"—the headwaters of the Nile not the pyramids; Roman Africa not Rome; the troglodytes of Anatolia, or the trulli of southern Italy, not Sabbioneta or Gubbio. But even these are not far enough away or strange enough. So it is off to Cambodia, or Tahiti, or the Camerouns, and now the Antarctic or even the western cwm of Mt. Everest. *Pl. 4*

The objections to such choices are personal, subtle, and not necessarily well founded. There could be no more interesting tribal area to visit than the Camerouns, from an architectural point of view at least, and no doubt from other points of view as well. There is much to admire and much to learn. There is great variety and frequent beauty in the villages and huts. I am sure it could be an enormous experience if enough time were spent to achieve some real understanding. But a fly-by with quick drop-ins, say, at Fort Lamy, Mofou, Mousgoum, Moundang, Tikar, and Baya in two or three days of safe and relatively comfortable travel can produce an excellent Kodachrome evening but less understanding perhaps than a serious reading of *L'Habitat au Cameroun*.[1] It seems sad to me that a Western architectural traveler should be bemused by the carving at Les Bamileke, interesting as it may be, when he has never seen the sculptures, say, of the French Romanesque churches which are fully as

[1] *L'Habitat au Cameroun*, Publication de L'Office de la Recherche Scientifique Outre-Mer, Éditions de L'Union Française, Paris, 1952.

vigorous, as primitive if you like, have considerably more variety, and to a Westerner are also more comprehensible—though there is still more than enough mystery if that is what you crave.

Primitive villages and "indigenous, anonymous" buildings do offer food for thought to the architectural traveler, and pleasure too. No one should deny the impact of the great Oriental architectures or attempt to assess them as inferior. Given this, it would be wrong to berate the architectural tourist because as a matter of conscious choice he has ranged afar and been blind at home, either to widen his total experience or because he thinks or knows that he prefers the strange. Nor would it be right to criticize the Westerner who makes this choice before he has experienced the great Western adventures in architecture—provided his reasons are sincere and in some decent currency, and not merely a matter of architectural one-upmanship.

In the end, of course, the serious architectural traveler to whom I am trying to address myself has every good reason to go to Iran and India and Pakistan and China if he can get there, to the now only partially exotic Japan or pre-Hispanic Mexico and Peru or Egypt, to chase the Roman ruins of Africa (after he knows Rome), to look up remote Greek temples (after he knows Athens). It is quite as legitimate as collecting the variations on Romanesque churches, as I like to do. The only thing one could object to in either choice would be if it were made for the principal reason of being "different." How sad such a posture can be and how well the fallacy was caught by my old friend C. E. Montague:

> These leaders of the march of taste seemed always to have just
> discovered some quintessential new essence of charm, some real right thing
> which we ought to have heard of already, but hadn't. They used to
> leave us standing, just when we thought that we had all but caught up.[2]

So we have to say that it is the motivation which matters in judging whether any kind of quest of the exotic is good. I should not have sought so many out-of-the-way places and I should not have written about some of them here had I not thought them good. But I think I was fortunate to have had a large experience with the architecture of my own background before the opportunity arose to have gone further afield—and to have been able to escape the limitations of the cruise and the guided tour. The great guides like Vergil do not wear uniforms. And calling on such practical help as one may sometimes need, there is no substitute for the control of one's own travel destiny.

There is, of course, the exotic in one's own backyard, a kind of strange sometimes wild exaggeration, extrapolation, or deviation from the going tradition. We think at once of Strawberry Hill of Walpole, Mad Ludwig's Castle near Garmisch, the Royal Pavilion at Brighton, or even

[2] Montague, *The Right Place*, op. cit., p. 77.

W. R. Hearst's San Simeon on the shores of the California Pacific. Each of these had a kind of macabre interest in their day and San Simeon and the newly refurbished Royal Pavilion still do. They are exciting things to visit and to look at, but they are social and not architectural commentaries. San Simeon tells us more about Hearst and his times, the Royal Pavilion more about the young prince of Wales and his architect John Nash at the time of the Congress of Vienna, than they do about architecture. Both are stage sets. Neither is close to being in the mainstream, although the Royal Pavilion is at least in the spirit, if not the style, of Regency architecture. And it has marvelous fantasies quite missing at San Simeon: the chinoiserie, the bamboo chairs and the water-lily chandeliers, the enormous wall paintings of Chinese landscapes in scarlet, gold, and yellow lacquer, the pianos with brass inlays in rosewood, the fantastic candelabra and sideboard dishes in the banqueting room, the domed ceiling painted like an immense palm tree, the gilded dragons attached to the central chandelier, the domical and minareted royal stables (now a concert hall), the north gate in the Mogul manner, and especially the great kitchen with its bronze smoke canopies and lanterns, its revolving spits at the fireplace, and its columns made of cast-iron palm trees. It is an exotic experience, set in an English seascape, an hour from London.

Pl. 6

Pl. 5

Less-commendable excursions into the architectural exotic are those made by the lovers of ruins and of moonlight. (They usually go together, for the passions of the Hudson River School and of the followers of Fuseli are by no means all laid to rest.)

The exploration of ruins as a guide to appreciating the architecture of the past is, of course, not only permissible but absolutely necessary. However, when that is your purpose you may regret the ruin. Who could honestly prefer to see the Parthenon as it is to the Parthenon as it was in the late fifth century B.C.? It is one thing to wish the ruins of Knossos back into ruins so that the overzealous restorations of Sir Arthur Evans do not limit or cripple your own insights. It is quite another to claim that you prefer the Colosseum the way it is, assuming that you could have the Colosseum as it was without the intervening hand of a misguided restorer.

Yet there are a good many people who do feel that way. Many literary men have written such things—many artists have liked to draw smashed monuments (Piranesi) with what sentiments or far-reaching symbolism I do not know. The cult of ruins for their own sake, the sentiments of "The Lion and the Lizard Keep" are never far removed from the cult of the moon.

If we are to think of architecture as something once built by users for users we will soon realize that moonlight was not the light by which most architectural monuments, or perhaps any, were intended to be viewed, excepting perhaps the twilit gardens of Shalimar, where the climate indicated a vesperal use. Great architecture was built for and can stand all lights, but especially the light of day. If it is at its best only by moonlight, it is almost certainly not great architecture.

There are a limited number of exceptions. The dark pre-Gothic churches needed the candle-lit altars and the altars of the processionals which could be nearly indifferent to the hour, and it is with mixed emotions that we see the new and unquestionably effective spotlighting of the interior of Notre-Dame de Paris. As I have noted, gardens like Shalimar in Lahore are at their best at dusk and were not designed for the midday sun. The great palace interiors of the Bourbons were most entrancing when all the candled chandeliers were alight, and even the terraces and the parterres of the nearer gardens could profit from the slant of the moon, as they did from the display of fireworks. And there is very little architecture, at least little modeled architecture, which is not, like the mountains, more impressive during the slanting lights of morning and evening than at high noon.

It is true that in modern lighting there is a resource for architecture of considerable power just beginning to be well exploited. Floodlighting is mostly a way of continuing daylight in a different and less attractive color than the sun. It has an advantage in that it can be focused on the dramatic spots and thus atone in part for designing inadequacies, and a disadvantage in that the shadows, deep or shallow, so essential to most architecture remain fixed and do not continuously change as the sun processes through the heavens or as clouds obscure it for an hour or for a day. Few buildings are designed with floodlighting as a condition from the beginning though some fountains and plazas have been and sometimes to their advantage. (One wonders how Bernini would have made his fountains in the Piazza Navona had floodlighting been available to him.) The reverse opportunity of presenting the building to the street as lighted from the *interior*, the revelation of transparency, is, I think, the greater one.

But I am not setting out here to talk about opportunities for contemporary work. As to moonlight viewing there may be occasions when it should be done, just as there might be one for ribald singing in the Roman Forum or the Theater at Orange, but night viewing as a profession is one which could better be left to the night birds.

In general I feel the same way about seeking the exotic in architecture. If the architecture is important enough the fact that it is exotic is insignificant. If the search is for the exotic qua the exotic, it is not a compelling reason for architectural travel. Other artifacts are more exotic, and, saving rhinoceros, easier to bring home.

THE KILROY EFFECT

Gently related to hedonism and even more to the exotic is what I would like to call the Kilroy effect. It stems in part from the sensible realization that buildings without people are fairly meaningless and the historical desire to restore the right historical people to the historic building. It can be a serious effort. It is in its degenerate form that I call it the Kilroy effect.

Let me give a single example. To think of Versailles with no feeling for Louis XIV diminishes the understanding of Versailles. But Notre-Dame de Paris is provided no further illumination by knowing the names of the heads of state who assembled there to pay their final respects to General de Gaulle. In this respect, the great Frenchman was a Kilroy.

Although the phrase "Kilroy effect" is one I invented, I did not, of course, invent Kilroy. He was, I think, an actual person and a soldier of minor rank, in the Eighth Air Force as I recall, who, sometime during World War II, began writing his name on walls to announce "Kilroy was here." Soon it became a popular pastime and the writing multiplied. It was an engaging idea that an obscure and unknown human should have taken the trouble to let the world know that he had passed by.

My formulation of the Kilroy effect was a consequence of the realization that every man, no matter how great his fame, can at times be no more than a Kilroy. George Washington, for example, was a Kilroy when he simply went to bed and slept somewhere. The room or the bed achieved no special merit simply because he was alleged to have slept in it once—even when the allegation was true. The Kilroy effect in architecture occurs, then, when a building is noticed simply because a general or a great lady, a pope or a saint, has or is reputed to have stood or even been murdered in its doors. Indeed, insofar as architectural matters are concerned, the Kilroy effect remains even if the noted passerby *has* done something important in the building or has had something important done to him. There is no reason per se to give *architectural* attention to the building or town where Garrison first published the *Liberator*, where Cosima Wagner was born, where Thomas Mann wrote *Buddenbrooks*, or where Charlotte Corday killed Marat in his bath.

Evidently one can easily enough slip into the Kilroy effect when one departs from peopling a building with a faceless public and begins name-dropping about some particular important gentleman who is alleged to have sat there one day.

Verona offers examples. Are you to make a better looking building out of number 23 Via Capella because it may have been the Capulet house complete with Juliet's balcony? In the Via del Pontiere is a modest complex of a cloister and Romanesque church, San Francesco al Corso, and in its crypt a plausibly old sarcophagus. Are they enhanced by the claim that this is the tomb of Juliet? Does the Emilei Palace gain any dignity because Bonaparte lived there during the Italian Campaign of 1796–97?

Anyone who makes the search for Kilroys a major part of his architectural journey will get what he deserves.

Yet the people do matter and that is what is so frustrating. The frustration comes from the fact that architecture is, in the end, for people, and it does matter to the building who they were and what they did in the building and what they wore when they were doing it.

Certainly a great Gothic cathedral is more impressive when the highest of masses is being celebrated with the maximum of celebrants and the richest of vestments. Since one of the main purposes of the cathedral is the celebration of the mass, the vestments cannot be irrelevant to the architecture. Fortunately for us the liturgical implements are often the old ones themselves or sufficiently like them. There are as yet, unhappily for a modern cathedral, few vestments by Matisse. What we cannot so easily do is people the nave with the folk of the Middle Ages, easy as it is to conjure up the bishops.

And in trying for the folk it is all too easy to slip into a world of never was. If we are to understand the medieval church as it really was, we shall have to understand who saw the vestments, especially in the English or Byzantine cathedrals, and under what circumstances.

Given the enormous difficulties of information and understanding, it is on the whole easier to invent. If we cannot use much imagination in our recall of the appearance of Mr. Pickwick or Sherlock Holmes because their illustrators were so explicit, we are safer with Henry VIII and Anne of Cleves (save for the curbs laid on us by artists like Holbein). But when we get to medieval crowds, or Roman crowds on the Capitoline, or the Argives following Agamemnon back through the frowning gates of Mycenae, we have less constraints. More often than we would like to believe these pictures come out as false as the charming notion of the Piraean heroine of the film *Never on Sunday* that in the end all the great tragic heros—Medea and her children, Helen of Troy, Oedipus, Orestes, and all the gallant rest—would join in some marvelously Greek version of a clambake on some marvelously beautiful Aegean beach.

It does not have to end in such ecstatic mists.

In his own prideful account of the building of the Abbey Church of St-Denis, as quoted by Temko, the Abbot Suger goes to great pains to tell us the names of the great who attended the consecration:

Nineteen prelates, led by the Archbishops of Reims, Sens, Rouen, and
Canterbury, took part. So did the King, twenty-four-year-old Louis le Jeune
and his beautiful and temperamental Queen, Eleanor of Aquitaine; the
Queen Mother; peers of the realm, diverse "counts and nobles from
many regions," and "ordinary troops of knights," who, Suger remarked
with an Olympian air, were too many to be counted. And, of course,
there were the common people, pushing to enter the church with such
force that the King and the nobles personally kept them back with
sticks and canes. . . .
Suger hoped the moment might never be forgotten:
    "You might have seen . . . how so great a chorus of such great pontiffs,
    decorous in white vestments, splendidly arrayed in pontifical miters and
    precious orphreys, held the crosiers in their hands, walked round and
    round the vessel (*vaisseau*) and invoked the name of God so piously

that the King and the attending nobility believe themselves to behold a chorus celestial rather than terrestrial, a ceremony divine rather than human." [3]

In his own log, and this is not quoted by Temko, Suger mentions at length those who were not there and essays to explain why. Yet this is *not* a Kilroy effect. With all his name-dropping and excitement over who was there, Suger is pointing to a larger truth. A sense of the occasion will add to the understanding of the Abbey Church of St-Denis when we finally stand before it in a way that few of the antics of the many who happened by Canterbury will really do (save perhaps Thomas à Becket). But the sad thing to report, which you have probably noted already, is that very little of such events are to be read from the stones of St-Denis or Notre-Dame de Paris, not even from the numerous inscriptions with which Suger plastered his abbey church. They have to be gleaned from other sources.

There is, to be sure, a considerable yield to the historian from artifacts, including architectural artifacts. But this is a technical matter with which I do not propose to deal extensively here. It offers for some people a substantial reason to visit architecture—indeed the main reason—but it is not the reason for the architectural tourist. For him the peopling of the building or the city with significant historical events, anonymous or personalized, is useful for the understanding of the building or the city, not the other way around.

THE SEARCH FOR QUINTESSENCE

It would be reasonable for you, after knowing that the world had produced a finite and rather small range of architectural styles, to conclude that a good way to start would be to look at the quintessential building of each style. The idea is a fata morgana. In all architectural history there are not many quintessential buildings. The characteristic and correct conclusion is the one voiced by a most distinguished scholar of Gothic architecture, Paul Frankl:

> I have avoided setting up a standard for the style as a whole, such as
> Amiens cathedral, so as not to give the idea that the value of every Gothic
> building is to be measured against this standard and that it is
> regrettable that this cathedral was not created simultaneously with the
> Gothic style, to be followed only by copies. [4]

[3] Allan Temko, *Notre-Dame of Paris, The Biography of a Cathedral* (New York: Viking, 1959), p. 105; p. 82. Copyright © 1952, 1955 by Allan Temko. Reprinted by permission of The Viking Press, Inc.
[4] Paul Frankl, *Gothic Architecture* (Baltimore: Penguin, 1962), p. xv. Copyright © 1962 by Paul Frankl.

Testimony to a similar conclusion can be summoned almost without end. There are characteristic forms and they will identify a building as Romanesque, for example, quite readily to one who takes but a little trouble to learn. There is an underlying spirit for which it takes only modest sensitivity to develop a feeling. But there is rarely sufficient uniformity to produce an archetype even when the controlling forces are quite clear. In the French Romanesque, as Henri Focillon clearly describes,[5] very strong linkages were created by the pilgrimage routes. They passed through towns. Despite the leveling influence of this continuous exchange of information, "Each town acted as a focus and magnet of its surrounding countryside, distilled its qualities, and concentrated in itself the peculiar local traditions and experiences."[6] Local taste was dominant despite the influences of trade, the copied identity of local statutes, the interpenetration of localities by the uniformities of monasticism, their "fine-meshed net over all Christendom," the particular influence and power of Cluny, the great informed and sophisticated taste of many of the abbots, and the powerful effect of the pilgrimage routes they organized.

Thus there is simply no building that summarizes the Romanesque of Italy, the Rhineland, France, England, and Spain in one neat and informative package. But matters are worse (or better) than that.

In France alone there are palpably different Romanesque churches as between Normandy, Burgundy, Aquitaine, the Auvergne, and Provence to name only five of the more important regions. Saint-Etienne at Caen has little that is obvious in common with St-Nectaire in Auvergne, or Ste-Foi at Conques in Rouergue, or St-Trophîme in Arles. Indeed the differences are so clear that we are very likely to establish favorites between the great regions. I opt for Burgundy, Auvergne, and the special church of Ste-Foi at Conques. But those who care for severity and clearly proto-Gothic types will lean to Normandy, and those with a predilection for domes to Aquitaine.

Yet even a provincial selection will not provide us with an archetype. Caen is not Jumièges in Normandy. In Burgundy, Tournus is not Paray le Monial is not Cluny is not Vézelay, and even Cluny cannot be designated as the epitome of Burgundian Romanesque. There is more in common among the domed churches of Aquitaine, or the Auvergnat churches clustering around Clermont-Ferrand or the especially homogeneous region of Roman Provence (Provincia Nostra), but even in such small areas it would be difficult to reach consensus as to an archetype.

It is not different for Italy. Who is to say that San Miniato al Monte, Santa Maria in Trastevere, Sant'Ambrogio at Milan, the Abbey of Pomposa, San Nicola at Bari, and the Sicilian churches built by the Normans

[5] Henri Focillon, *The Art of the West in the Middle Ages*, vol. I, *Romanesque Art*, Jean Bony (ed.), (London: Phaidon, 1963), pp. 62–99.
[6] Ibid., p. 63.

under strong Byzantine and Islamic influence are the most characteristic of the "Italian" Romanesque?

Although this absence of a distillate, an apex, is perhaps most apparent in the architecture of the European Middle Ages, it is probably almost always so. The pyramids are not the epitome of Egypt; the Taj Mahal is not a *summa* of Mogul architecture; the Pantheon and the Pont du Gard do not say all there is to say about Rome; or Hagia Sofia about the Byzantine. Renaissance palaces tend to look more alike, but the man who knows them well might be loath to say, "Here is the essence of the Renaissance," or even "Here is the essence of Roman Renaissance or Florentine or Venetian." Ise does not summarize the Japanese shrine.

Salisbury, having been built all of a time, is the consistent epitome, on the whole, of a moment in the course of English Gothic. (I happen to think not the greatest moment, but there are certainly many who do so think.) Elias of Dereham, the king's clerk, and Nicholas of Ely, the master mason, built the Lady Chapel between 1220–1225, the choir between 1225–1237, and the great transept and nave between 1237–1258. So the main elements were all made by the same people in a period of thirty-eight years. This was possible because the cathedral was built on an unencumbered site; there was no need to make reference to existing buildings or maintain services while building since the city was removed 2 miles from the mound of Old Sarum to the shores of the Avon.

Thus the main elements at Salisbury are all in one style, Early English. The central tower and spire,[7] which add a great deal to the first glance, were, to be sure, a century later—and in the Decorated Gothic style—and the unusual west front and the magnificent cloisters by Richard Mason were made in a slightly different manner in the eight years after completion of the nave and the cloister in 1263–1284.

Fortunately the later efforts of Wren to strengthen the spire left no important scars and the nineteenth-century depredations of the ruthless and often ignorant restorer, Sir Gilbert Scott, were minor at Salisbury. In consequence the cathedral has an unusual clarity and consistency. It may be cold as well and more ingenious than beautiful—saving the spire.

Yet, as I said, Salisbury can be taken as an epitome of only a *moment* of English Gothic time. It offers no memory of the powerful Norman nave of Durham or the stern and beautiful Norman transept of Winchester; or any premonitions of the lierne vaults of Norwich, or the

---

[7] An enormously bold and even dangerous undertaking due to the fact the original squat tower had not demanded of the pier and foundations as much as the new tower needed. Details of this venture in sufficient amount to satisfy most needs can be found in Canon A. F. Smithurst, *The Pictorial History of Salisbury Cathedral* (London: Pitkin, 1965), pp. 14–16, and in William Golding's splendid novel, *The Spire* (New York: Harcourt Brace & World, 1964), which examines in a work of imagination the possible consequence of this overweening and even arrogant ambition on those who participated in the venture, willingly or unwillingly.

magnificent ceilings of King's College Chapel at Cambridge or the Henry VII Chapel in Westminster. In the end you will have to make your own composite quintessence from what you observe—at Wells, Salisbury, Lincoln, York, Durham, and Westminster, to say the least, and perhaps several more, for there are different voices at Norwich, Peterborough, Southwell, Winchester, Hereford, Gloucester, Ely, and so on.

Very likely Greek experts would wish to say that there is no quintessence for Greece either, but it seems to me that the Parthenon almost alone among the world's great buildings comes close to being a quintessence, a perfect model, an apogee beyond argument of a major period in architectural history.

In the great classic time of Greece perfection in architecture was more desired than change—and the perfection was more abstract than human. Regional differences were thus limited, even as to the order chosen; and the orders flowed easily over regional boundaries. Either the Corinthians and the Athenians were more alike than the Burgundians and the Poitevins or they guarded their *aesthetic* boundaries less carefully. So the differences in the classic Greek temples, though existent and significant to scholars, are much less apparent to the educated but unspecialized eye than the differences between Tournus and Notre-Dame-la-Grande at Poitiers. Given this and the fact that the Parthenon was built at one of the few clearly critical apices of time, the possibility that it may be quintessential emerges.

But even so it remains generally true that the search for a galaxy of quintessential forms is bound to resemble the pursuit of the will-o'-the-wisp. This is surely no reason for despair to any save those who are content only if they have made, so to speak, a Linnaean classification of architecture and have observed and checked off each genus, each phylum, and perhaps each subphylum.

Nonetheless this hard fact does offer some problems to the viewer of architecture. Shall he still try to come to grips with all the styles by multiplying the examples of each he must explore before he can feel that he has covered the matter? Shall he abandon trying to cover all styles in order to achieve a greater mastery of a few or even one? And if he elects such a course shall he let his soul carry him off on the unbalanced course which will be prescribed by his unbalanced instinctive preferences?

It might as well be accepted right now that, scholar or not, he will be unable to rid himself of these instincts and that it is not altogether a bad thing. Much may depend, however, on how he has arrived at his "instincts" and their consequent preferences.

ARCHITECTURE AS DOCUMENTARY

Another purpose of architectural travel may be to gain a larger sense of time, place, and people. What this comes to for the scholar is perfectly clear. Dinsmoor has stated it: "Architecture might be called the sheet anchor of history, which without the everlasting testimony of the monuments would certainly become fluid and unstable."[8] We must not take this to be any very simple piece of detective work. For early periods of prehistory, the artifacts may be the only clues to the past; and for many of these periods the architectural artifacts do not remain. In happier situations the architectural remains do provide useful clues, but only in rare situations do the architecture and art to be seen *in situ* offer even a glimmering of the state of the human past to a layman unassisted by any other kind of historical guide.

The dilemma of the historian in the face of small evidence will be part of your problem too and will remain even when there is a good deal of evidence. It rests in the nature of historical time. Jean Bony has pointed this up brilliantly in his preface to Focillon's *The Art of the West*.

The good historian may not limit himself, as we can here, to the moments of most creative activity. As Focillon taught in one of his last essays, history is a combination of *tradition* (how the past collaborates in the present, often with fundamental reinterpretations or even distortions); *influences*, which are exchanges between different contemporary environments, often received quite passively and even as alien forms; and most importantly, the *experiments*, successful or not, which "bite into the future."

Thus when we deal with the history of the arts we have to think both of simultaneity and actuality. "History is not the Hegelian state of becoming." All the environments of a moment are not living in the same moment so that the present is primarily an interplay of discords, in which decadence, achievement, and experiment exist side by side and are moving at different rates.[9]

And we must realize always that our views of ancient cultures are defective, one-sided, even prejudiced. We take a Jewish view of Egypt, and an Athenian (not Spartan, Corinthian, Persian) view of Greece, for that is how we were taught.

The first difficulty for the lay viewer is, no doubt, that the single building ought not to be divorced from its urban environment. The quarter in which the medieval cathedral stood was relevant to its appearance as well as its performance. When it has been stripped away, and it usually has, you can no longer say it is the same.

We simply have to face it that we cannot experience the London of Chaucer, or of Ben Jonson, or of Inigo Jones save in a confused mind's eye, much less the Paris of Saint Louis and François Villon. It is perfectly natural to make the effort, but, unhappily, there is little material stuff for the physical eye to see. There are exceptions, as, for example, the Bayeux tapestry.

[8] Dinsmoor, *The Architecture of Ancient Greece*, op. cit., p. xvi.
[9] Paraphrased from Jean Bony's Preface to Focillon, *The Art of the West in the Middle Ages*, op. cit., pp. xix–xx.

No one could seriously wish this different. A living city is not, cannot, and should not be a museum of architectural history. It may be fun to visit Williamsburg, Carcassonne, Rothenburg on the Tauber, and the few other places where a conscientious effort, and occasionally a reasonably serious unanecdotal effort has been made to restore, recreate, or invent a whole city as it might plausibly have been, but as a total experience it is bound to fail. There are many too many people in Williamsburg all the time, and even those in wigs are not Colonial Virginians. It is not practical that Williamsburg's streets shall be muddy. Even if Williamsburg were more authentic than it is, the boy in the stocks being photographed in Polaroid color is just some twentieth-century American's kid who will be released as soon as the shutter has clicked. Our stocks are elsewhere and less picturesque. It is harder in the mind's eye to efface the presence of the tourists of Williamsburg than it is to repeople the ruins of Trajan's Forum in Rome with ancient Romans.

So we are left with individual landmarks devoid of much of their earlier surroundings and clearly devoid of the people who made and used them. Some, like the Roman Forum, are unused ruins, which in some ways are the easiest to reconstitute even for the half-educated layman. But when we come to historical buildings which have survived intact, give or take a certain amount (and usually a much larger amount than we imagine) of restoration and repair, the problem becomes a different one. Some from Monticello to Versailles have been made into special kinds of museums attempting to appear faithfully as they were *at a given moment of time*, and these, when well done, are perhaps the easiest to come to grips with. Some like the Louvre or part of the Castello Sforzesca in Milan have been amended to become art museums, and in these, no matter how skillfully the transformation has been effected and no matter how meticulously the decoration of the old palace or castle has been kept, the repeopling with those who used the place when it was pristine is more difficult. It becomes still more difficult when, as in many European cities, a distinguished architectural monument is being used for a new and private purpose, say as an embassy, a bank, or a bureau. In these cases some of the rooms are not available to the tourist at all, or only by special arrangement. A characteristic modest example would be the Palazzo Clerici in Milan where the Galleria degli Arazzi on the first floor has a superb frescoed ceiling by Tiepolo. This can almost always be seen unless the room is being used for a conference. To put it back into its early eighteenth-century context, however, your mind must remove its contemporary conferential furniture and make it again a pretty ballroom or salon, must refurbish all the approach rooms, must take out the elevator.

The adamant fact is that we enter any building in the here and now and not on the day when, for example, Joan of Arc crowned the Dauphin at Reims. The churches of God in the West, and I suppose the temples of the East if we knew their histories better, come the nearest to offering the living past. On the face of it the Christian cathedral seems to be used for much the same purposes in the twentieth century as when it was begun in the thirteenth century; but even this is only partly so.

Though it seems to me indisputable that the Church offers the best example of living architectural history, when I next go into Canterbury Cathedral, if ever I do again, I will not go into the Cathedral of Thomas Becket either physically or spiritually. I am a man of my generation and not of 1162, and, as Focillon says, I live in the presence of ancestors of my own choosing.[10]

The physical building I seek to comprehend at Canterbury is the building of 1970. Through Archbishop Ramsey it has experienced a round hundred of archbishops since the consecration of Saint Augustine in 597. One of these, Laud, was beheaded, one resigned, two were "deprived," one "restored," fifty-three have been buried in the Cathedral. Their names tickle the memory—the Latin names, the Saxon names, the Norman names, the English names—Dunstan, Aelfric, Lanfranc, Anselm, Becket, Langton, Cranmer, Pole, Laud, Temple, Lang, and so on. Thirteen were sainted. A great many laid their hands on the fabric of the cathedral in one way or another. Of whose archepiscopacy, of whose cathedral are we talking?

Pl. 2

The plan is of enormous complexity. (See Plate 2.) It starts simply enough at the west with a single entrance at a narrow portal dwarfed at once by an eccentrically placed south porch. The nave with two narrow side aisles proceeds straightforwardly enough toward the transept and choir but then confusion breaks loose; the axes tilt—the west transepts melt into a variety of steps and the northwest one wraps around the *martyrium* with its site at the ancient Altar of the Sword's Point. There are fifteen such ancient sites strewn all over the edifice. The northwest transept spans awkwardly into the cloisters and more straightforwardly into the Lady Chapel of Prior Coldstone I, but the southwest transept twists into St. Michael's Chapel where the Buff's Memorials are. The north and south aisles of the choir are not of the same width or the same east-west direction and are not reached by the same steps. Order seems to begin again at the presbytery and east transepts but is soon confused by the multiple stairs leading everywhere, the change in direction of the Trinity Chapel and the irregularity with which various chapels and memorials and monuments have been added to this Christmas tree of English church history—to the 50th Regiment, to the Buffs, to the composer Orlando Gibbons, to the Lancers, to the Black Prince, to Lady Margaret Holland, the Earl of Somerset, and the Duke of Clarence. There are additional appendages: the chapter house, the library, the Biblioteca Howleiana, squints from the Prior's Chamber, the original and present positions of Saint Augustine's chair, the original and present positions of the High Altar, the site of Archbishop Becket's shrine. You will study this plan for

[10] Focillon, op. cit., p. xxii. The quotation is from Focillon, *Vie des Formes*, and is cited in Jean Bony's Preface.

a long time before you will bring order out of it, if indeed you can. Canterbury in its disorder is, of course, a better representation of history than orderly Salisbury, but that thought does not help much.

The construction history is no less complicated. There are a few quite homogeneous parts but never for long. Almost everything shows the hand of history and the violence of man.

In the *martyrium* where Becket was murdered on December 29, 1170, in what is now almost a wholly reconstructed transept, one can only conjecture whether the stonework in the lower walls did or did not witness the murder—a small stone marks the spot where perhaps he died. The shrine containing the top of murderer Richard Le Breton's sword, and named the Altar of the Sword's Point, witnessed a vigil by the penitent barefooted Henry II, but it was broken up in 1528 when Henry VIII ordered Saint Thomas Becket to be called Bishop Becket and all images of Thomas were destroyed. The famous jewel of the shrine, the Regale of France given by Louis VII, was carted off to decorate the enormous thumb of Henry VIII and later the collar of his daughter Queen Mary Tudor; then it disappeared forever. All this peopling unaccompanied by visual realities is then one of ghosts.

The choir—vaulted by the brilliant arches of William of Sens, following the burning of the original Norman choir in 1174 which in turn had replaced another choir after its burning in 1067—witnessed the first service at Easter in 1180, ten years after the murder of Becket. During the building, William of Sens was crippled by a fall from the scaffolding and had to go back to France having pushed the choir as it now is as far as the transepts. The work fell to another William, the Englishman, who built the transepts, Trinity Chapel, Corona, and the crypt. Later Trinity Chapel was given over to the effigy of Edward the Black Prince, victor at Crécy (died 1376).

The old crypt of Canterbury is Norman, built about 1110, and has fine capitals of that time. This crypt was ceded as a church to French refugees in the sixteenth century. The cloister was remodeled in 1400; the chapter house was remodeled in the early fourteenth century and greatly heightened later when covered by a vast barrel vault of Irish bog-oak, making it the second-largest wooden roof in England; only Westminster Hall has a larger. The original Norman nave was pulled down toward the end of the fourteenth century and rebuilt in the early Perpendicular style by Yevele, the King's master mason, architect of Westminster Hall. The central Norman tower, the Bell Harry, was built anew in 1472–1494 by John Wastell, who, in addition to providing "the queenliest tower in Christendom," was responsible at least in part for King's College Chapel at Cambridge. The fan-vaulted lantern of this tower came along in the early sixteenth century. The font given in 1639 by John Warner was demolished during the Commonwealth and built anew by its donor. The Christ Church Gate which leads from the Butter Market to the Cathedral close was built in 1517 to replace another of 1200 which in turn had replaced an earlier gate. The Puritans tore down the wooden doors of this gate in 1642. They were replaced in 1660 by Archbishop Juxon, who, when he was bishop of London, had stood in 1649 on the scaffold at Whitehall to comfort Charles I at his execution. The library, destroyed by the Luftwaffe in 1942, was rebuilt in 1954.

Here then is this Mother Church of English Christendom, a parade of the chief English Gothic styles marred by and reclaimed from the desolation of fires, wars, angry kings, bigoted protestants, the scene of villainy and heroism, a place through which most of the great men of England passed after 1066 for 900 years but in which few, save the religious, are interred, a place in whose history saints, singers, scholars, and ignoramuses have been equally involved.

Which Canterbury is it then that you see when you enter this *wunderkammer* of history? What you see can be stated; what you think will depend upon what you bring with you in your memory bag. The actual stones will not provide you with much information if your vision is not accompanied by memory.

I have produced this brief exposition of the Cathedral Church of Christ Canterbury as an exaggerated example of the problem that confronts you when you meet any major cathedral of France or England, or indeed any other important historical building. The problem would be vastly simplified if all the people, big and little, could be left out—if we simply were to look at the columns and the vaults, the mosaics and the glass, and the progression of a contemporary service for contemporary people on a Sunday morning this autumn. But somehow this does not quite seem like enough. If we erase the present-day worshippers and look only at the architectural appearances, no matter how professionally, it will seem even less like enough. But when we begin to repeople the church with the men and women of history, we do begin to repeople it with ghosts and we cannot provide ghosts we have never heard of. Catherine Howard will not flee the corridors of Hampton Court Palace for us, running away from the murderous king's wrath, until somebody has told us about her. The corridors do not proclaim the horrid event.

Goethe's Verona position that you can not understand the Colosseum save when it is full of people can be taken about architecture peopled by a faceless and anonymous crowd, and no identified Caesar or procurator or local prefect needs to be lugged in to personalize the scene. This might be possible also for other great architectural scenes, for instance a papal appearance to a multitude in Bernini's Square of Saint Peter. Here again it is the crowd which counts and possibly the papal vestments and retinue but not usually the name of the pontiff.

But even in these cases, and without the aid of books or paintings by such men as Bellini or Canaletto, architecture itself is but a clue to or more often a reinforcer of historical conclusions drawn from other sources.

Though it can often add an important clue or a new insight, it cannot be the main source of what we know. As architectural travelers we should bring what we know of history to add to our enjoyment of architecture rather than seek to learn our history from the mute and often altered stones of architecture.

THE INSOLENCE OF MORAL JUDGMENT

One other pitfall to be avoided in the general examination and enjoyment of architecture is the rejection of some buildings or some periods of architecture because one cannot stomach the morality of those who built or used the architecture. Yet this is a common trap.

Many observers have been moved or seem to have been moved to their choices by an overzealous morality. The ease with which Ruskin was able to reject the Renaissance because of his indignation at the moral behavior of many of the Renaissance princes, as quoted by Geoffrey Scott, is perhaps the best-known example.

> I might insist at length on the absurdity of [Renaissance] construction . . .
> but it is not the form of this architecture against which I would plead.
> Its defects are shared by many of the noblest forms of earlier building
> and might have been entirely atoned for by excellence of spirit.
> But it is the moral nature of it which is corrupt. . . .
>
> It is base, unnatural, unfruitful, unenjoyable and impious. Pagan in its
> origin, proud and unholy in its revival, paralyzed in its old age . . . an
> architecture invented as it seems to make plagiarists of its architects,
> slaves of its workmen, and sybarites of its inhabitants; an architecture
> in which intellect is idle, invention impossible, but in which all
> luxury is gratified and all insolence fortified; the first thing we have to do
> is to cast it out and shake the dust of it from our feet forever.[11]

Ruskin was not the first to indulge in moralistic criticism of the arts; critics on this ground include Plato and Savonarola. The taste for it has persisted and will persist despite such skillful demolitions as those provided by Geoffrey Scott.[12] It is no doubt intellectually correct that "ethical criticism is irrelevant to art," but few of us are so intellectual when we cross the threshold of taste. An extended consideration of Scott might help us to be more balanced as we near the threshold—or at least to a temporary suspension of judgment while we try to see how well the

[11] John Ruskin, *The Stones of Venice*, vol. III, chap. II, p. 4; chap. IV, p. 35. Quoted in Geoffrey Scott, *The Architecture of Humanism* (Garden City, N.Y.: Doubleday Anchor, 1954), p. 97.
[12] Geoffrey Scott, *The Architecture of Humanism* (Garden City, N.Y.: Doubleday Anchor, 1954), chap. 5, "The Ethical Fallacy." First published in 1914, this distinguished treatise is very durable and should be high on the first reading list of those who are preparing for the enjoyment of architecture.

builders of any time succeeded in accomplishing whatever it was they were trying to accomplish.

Take the Villa Rotonda (or Villa Capra) in Vicenza, for example. It has been praised for its form many times, and even Goethe bubbled over, at least for a moment, though he was upset when he read the inscription on the door and learned of "the owner's ambition to leave his heirs an enormous fidei-comiosum and a tangible memorial to his wealth."[13] And certainly if great architecture is more than the great realization of inconsequential purposes, the Villa Capra is a complete success. It was built admittedly to perpetuate Capra's name, but its fame has far outrun its owner's, as has its longevity. It has to be admired, if not loved—except by the moralist who demands further that great architecture shall be the great realization of great purposes.

Who was Capra to think himself a king or that there was any nobility in mere riches?

One might have quoted Epictetus to him.

> If a horse should be elated and say "I am handsome" it might be
> endurable. But when you are elated and say "I have a handsome horse"
> know that you are elated only on the merit of the horse. What then
> is your own?[14]

A house is not quite a horse. You need money to buy either and taste to know that what you buy is good. But you cannot really cause the great horse to be made, not even by an army of Blue Grass breeders, though you may increase probabilities. In building a house you may go further, having the taste to select a good or even great architect and the restraint to be a good patron. But should this buy you immortality?

The absurdity of judging the Villa Capra by the absurdity of its owner's ambitions is evident even if it is the only way in which the apparent absurdity of the plan can be justified. To Palladio it gave, regardless of reason, a chance to realize a perfect theoretical piece of architecture and that should be enough. Do not scratch it from your list because you do not approve the ambitions of its patron. After you have seen it, like it or not as you will (I have never cared for it much, despite its skill, but this disaffection began long before I knew how it had come to be what it was).

There is a different sort of moralizing which can best be called aesthetic. It may be even more stultifying. One form of it is a kind of purism which demands that only the simple will do. The archetypal contemporary example of this might be the epigram attributed to Mies Van der Rohe that "less is more." It rejects ornament as vulgar. It may encourage an aesthete to go to Japan and examine with ecstasy the stones of the Zen temple at Ry-o-an-ji while professing to ignore or endeavoring to erase

[13] Johann Wolfgang Goethe, *Italian Journey*, op. cit., p. 50.
[14] Epictetus, *Enchiridion*, 19, vi.

from his perception the dragon screens behind. It can lead to an insistence that the Noh drama is superb while Kabuki is unworthy even of looking at once. It can make one say that the Tokugawa shrine at Nikko is all right if you confine your attention to the cryptomeria trees. A man is happier I think if he does not feel it necessary to shrink *a priori* from either Ise or Nikko, from Bassae or the Golden House of Nero. In the end, of course, each viewer will have to and indeed should make his own conclusions and determine for himself the range of what he can admire. If one is a creative architect or critic, he may impose a morality; he will try and sometimes succeed in convincing others to follow his convictions. There is nothing evil in this—indeed it is the only honest way. The bad thing, if there is any bad at all, is to arrive at these conclusions prematurely, without having even been willing to experience the alleged "bad" as proclaimed by some architectural guru whom you adore, at least momentarily; in being unwilling to indulge even for a moment of youth in what Coleridge called the "willing suspension of disbelief."

Such blinders have been notably present in the fairly common adoption of what Geoffrey Scott called the Mechanical Fallacy, which rests on the assumption that architecture first and foremost is "construction." In this view its essential characteristic, as an art, is that it deals, not with mere patterns of light and shade, but with structural laws. In judging architecture, therefore, this characteristic, which constitutes its uniqueness as an art, must not be overlooked; on the contrary, since every art is primarily to be judged by its own special qualities, it is precisely by reference to these structural laws that architectural standards must be fixed. That architecture, in short, will be beautiful in which the construction is best, and in which it is most truthfully displayed! And in support of this contention, the scientific critic will show how, in the Gothic style, every detail confesses a constructive purpose, and delights us by our sense of its fitness for the work which is, just there, precisely required of it. And he will turn to the Doric style and assert the same of that. Both these great styles of the past, he will say, were in fact "truthful presentations of a special and perfect constructive principle, the one of the lintel, the other of the vault."[15]

This doctrine is not completely true even with respect to the two architectures cited. The Greeks sometimes used concealed iron bars to reinforce their lintels. The Gothic builders had frequently to introduce tie rods to keep the piers of a central tower from spreading too far.

But even if it were completely true for the Greek and the Gothic, it does not follow that other architectures in which the display of structure is less blatant or in which structure seems to have been totally ignored are *ipso facto* inferior. Yet the doctrine has been strongly if spasmodically influential in the judging of architecture.

[15] Scott, *The Architecture of Humanism*, op. cit., p. 83.

When Michelangelo designed the dome of St. Peter's,[16] he realized he had set himself a very difficult problem. The base is nearly 250 feet from the floor and rests only on four massive piers instead of on an almost continuous circular wall. He did indeed strengthen the piers which had already been built to support Bramante's quite different dome. But he did not anticipate the totality of the problem and in the end the piers were not up to the challenge. At various times no less than ten different chains have been inserted to keep the dome from spreading.

When I was a young student we were taught to believe this a scandal. We were steeped in Ralph Adams Cram and the Gothic grail. We praised structure for structure's sake. So bemused were we by the insistence on "structural honesty" that we could overlook the manifest ugliness of the scissors ribs inserted as a necessary afterthought at the crossing at Wells because they were exposed, and therefore were "truthful," while berating the concealment of the chains at St. Peter's.

This sort of doctrine was reiterated for a time in the school of Gropius and may be turning up again in the patently cross-braced skyscrapers designed by Skidmore, Owings and Merrill in Chicago and San Francisco.

There is certainly a value, in some situations, in revealing the structure, but to take it as an essential ingredient of architectural truth I now see to have been absurd.

The truth of architecture has to be that it serves people well. If illusion is needed there is nothing wrong with illusion. The component of architectural truth which has to do with a sense of visible credibility is that the appearance shall *seem* reasonable. The reaction to an architecture should be first immediate, sensuous, even irrational. The first gasp of delight or awe is more important that the more esoteric pleasures of detailed analysis. Architects should design to people's emotions and not for the praise of their colleagues or the critic's circle.

If the new bracing is visually convincing, it is right; if it can be enjoyed only after elaborate explanation, it is wrong. There would be nothing "dishonest" about concealing it; what would be dishonest would be to flaunt it for its novelty if, in fact, it were not really necessary.

If there was a fault in the chains of St. Peter's, it was not because they were concealed but because the design was inadequate; and by this measure the scissors vaults of Wells are no more admirable simply because they show. But both should probably be forgiven as expedients to salvage the work of designers who dared too much. In architecture as in other matters it is doubtless better to soar too near the sun like Icarus than never to soar at all.

Thus the preestablishment of nonarchitectural values by which we

[16] At the age of seventy-two. He lived to see the completion of the drum and left models for dome and lantern which were used by Giacomo della Porta and Domenico Fontana in completing the work.

decide what to look at and what not to look at is at the least crippling. I am not proposing that in the end each architectural viewer, or even historian, shall not have preferences and even strong ones. What I am asking is that the preferences be established after some experiments in visiting and not before the visits are made.

Shall you decline to consider the Villa Capra because you disapprove of a man's desire to leave his heirs a tangible memorial to his wealth? Should Ruskin delete the Renaissance because of its immorality or Charles William Elliot cast out the Gothic because of its associations with Catholicism which he believed to be "idolatrous"? It is too easy to see the mote in another's eye, too hard to find the reflection in one's own. There is a vast and possibly overstressed judgment of this sort in Malraux.

Here is the first civilization [our own] capable of conquering the whole earth but unable to invent either its own temples or its own tombs.[17]

It is true. Yet, will future young men decline to look at our architectural works because we have been less than brilliant with churches and tombs and because they do not approve of office buildings, schools, and factories?

In the name of faith, of morality, of national pride a great deal of marvelous art has been destroyed or despoiled. It is a pity to decline to examine any part of the residue on its own terms—especially since, as anyone with a sense of history knows, in the end almost every bigot has turned out to have been wrong.

This may be a note particularly important to sound in a day when there is so much prejudice and so much self-righteousness about, and no effective satirists to counterbalance them. If one were to let moral judgments be his only guide, he might conclude, for example, that contemporary architecture is not worth thinking about since it does not confront or have a meaningful dialogue with any of the truly critical problems of the day; or that, even if this were not so, the glorious past of architecture is of no relevance whatsoever. If one, then, made the argument that it is, in any event, a source of delight, the answer could then be that it is not only idle but positively evil to think of delight at all when so much of life is undelightful for most of us and none of life is delightful for many of us. Obviously, if I accepted this, I could not bother to write these essays at all.

If we are to enjoy architecture in a healthy way, then I insist we must begin by trying to understand its premises—and judging its success on how well it lived up to them rather than trying to reform the premises or disdaining to experience the architecture because we detest the premises. This is by no means the same thing as implying any acceptance of the premises for our conduct or aspirations today, but only that if one cannot

[17] Free translation of André Malraux, *Antimémoires* (Paris: Gallimard, 1967), p. 11.

achieve some such attitude he is unlikely to find pleasure in much world architecture, given the slave-driving necrology of Egypt, the pagan sacrifices of the Greeks, the sybaritic lives of the Persians and Moguls, the bloodthirsty Moors, the obscene sculpture of the Hindus, the acquisitive Christian Crusaders, the worldly ambitions of men like Abbot Suger, the inquisitors of Spain, the venal men of the Renaissance, the Baron Ochs' of the Baroque, the insensitive views of Marie Antoinette, the slaveholders of Tidewater, Virginia, to say nothing of the Aztecs, the Incas, the Mayas, the samurai, the shoguns and the mandarins, and the principal clients of today. What is left after a pogrom eliminating all these architectures will not be worth much of a look.

CHAPTER THREE

ARCHITECTURAL TRAVEL WITH PARTICULAR ENDS IN VIEW

The relation of the other visual arts to architecture as an art is intimate and important. This art may be sculpture or painting, but it includes as well liturgical vessels, furniture, and even purely decorative elements. Until not very long ago it was almost impossible to find a single architectural monument in which sculpture or painting or both failed to form an integral part of the concept. Such art could not be removed from the architecture without fundamental loss to both. Yet some of it has been moved for a variety of reasons, sometimes perhaps to preserve it from destruction or deterioration, and more often perhaps for the less noble purpose of acquisition.

A case in point is the Panathenaic frieze of the Parthenon. This was carved along the top of the exterior of the *cella* wall which it completely surrounded, being carried across the east and west ends above the columns of the *pronaos* and the *opisthodomos*. It was meticulously designed and carved in greater elaboration than any previous relief over its entire 524 feet.

Pl. 159
Pl. 161

The frieze was an important part of the Parthenon but as time went on the building suf-

35

fered an unusual number of vicissitudes. Some of the damage was by design, some by accident, some by neglect. The Parthenon was converted into a Christian church with an apse at the eastern end; it later became a Latin church, then a mosque. In 1687, when the Venetians were capturing Athens, it was damaged by a shell which fell into part of the building being used as a powder magazine. When the Turks got it back they injured it further. At the end of the eighteenth century various foreigners came to the Parthenon. The Count de Choiseul-Giriffier brought back to France a piece of the frieze and two metopes which were lying in the debris. But according to the French guide books, the Englishman Lord Elgin was the principal marauder. The *Guide Bleu* for Paris, for example, after enumerating the pieces taken, ends by saying that he left to Greece "only its irritated Gods."[1]

Indeed the usual view is that Lord Elgin "stole" the sculptures. This is unfair. Not only was Elgin armed with properly negotiated legal documents, he took great care not to damage any of the pieces; he eventually allowed the British Museum to buy the sculptures for much less than he had spent. He did not foresee and it is hard to see how he might have imagined that Greece would ever become independent and stable enough to prevent the almost total destruction of these great works.

Piracy or not the facts about the Panathenaic frieze are as follows: Of the original 524 feet only some 334 remain at all. The western frieze, excepting three original figures, is in its original position; most of the north, south, and eastern sides is in the British Museum, while the rest, except for eight pieces of the eastern frieze, is in the Museum at Athens.

It is not easy to decide what to think about this. Certainly the ideal thing would be to have the Parthenon as it originally was, complete with frieze, standing on the Acropolis intact. History has, of course, made this impossible. Even with the most scrupulous attention to truth and the unlikely return to Athens of all the parts wherever they may now be to be incorporated in the new building, it is hard to believe that the rebuilt Parthenon would be infused with life. Yet only by such a lively reconstruction would it be possible to make a meaningful display of the Panathenaic frieze on the Acropolis and to reproduce some of the conditions under which an Athenian of the fifth century B.C. would presumably have experienced it.

Some advantages accruing to us from Lord Elgin's "foray" are: First, there is vastly more of the frieze left than probably would have otherwise been the case; moreover it is vastly easier to see. The new rooms in the British Museum are elegantly and simply designed for the display of these great works of art, carefully arranged, beautifully lighted. The sculpture is at eye level and there could not be a better arrangement for viewing the

---

[1] M. Collignon, quoted in *Athènes et Ses Environs, Les Guides Bleus* (Paris: Librarie Hachette, 1960), p. 174.

details as a work of art, unrelated to architecture, seen as no classic Greek ever saw them, although in a situation where the differential depth of the relief demanded by the original location is quite inexplicable to the eye and brought to the brain only by an intellectual effort.

The Parthenon is less without the Panathenaic frieze; the frieze is less without the Parthenon. At best the mind needs to do some imaginative shuttling no matter which spot one is at. If one is concerned only with sculpture as sculpture, it is easy to accept without reserve the present arrangements.

If you care more, however, about sculpture-and-architecture or about architecture of which sculpture is an integral part, then there are more dilemmas. Evidently most architecture is somewhat too large to be moved into a museum with any success, although there have been efforts with a few smallish pieces such as some of the Catalonian apses on display in Barcelona, or small Egyptian mastabas in a few Western museums, and even one or two attempts to build a museum around a piece of architecture, usually a ruin, generally not a very fruitful idea.

It is possible, however, that we will see an extension of these ideas in the future. If we do not learn soon to curb urban air pollution, to the point of making urban life modestly salubrious, the continued and accelerated erosion of the important architectural monuments which are in cities (and this means most of them) will continue. Is it idle to think of enveloping the greatest of them in Buckminster Fuller's geodesic domes, properly conditioned inside as to temperature, humidity, and light? They need not be automatically transformed into museums thereby. It might well be the best use so far contrived for this beautiful, imaginative bubble whose beauty and ingenuity have up to now so far exceeded its utility. But I confess it is not an idea which appeals to me.

But this distracts from the question at hand. If the architecture cannot be moved to the museum, should the sculpture be moved back to the architecture? In many cases, notably the medieval buildings, the fabric carefully maintained over the years would not need massive rehabilitation, as in the Parthenon, before the replacing could begin. It would probably be a good idea in all cases where the two arts had inextricably been interwoven. Fortunately, save in a few big cases, the divorces have not been so drastic as with the Panathenaic frieze.

The ancient wall paintings are on the walls of the caves and not in the Louvre; though there are sample mastabas and later tomb paintings in a few of the great museums, most or enough of the best are to be found at Saqqara or Thebes. The Hindu temples, the Mogul forts and palaces and mosques, the abstract art of Isfahan or Granada, the Buddhist temple art of Japan and China, all these are largely *in situ*, though many are unhappily deteriorating rapidly in our contemporary conditions.

Though a good deal of medieval sculpture and painting is to be found in museums from the Cluny down and though some of the great churches of the French Romanesque and Gothic suffered intolerable indignities from the religious zeal of the Huguenots and the military zeal of the Germans in World War I, there remain very extensive and moving expressions of the full range of medieval sculpture and glass from Moissac to York. After the Middle Ages there was, in the first place, less art that was central to the building and to which the building was in turn central, and less disposition to move it, save in cases of extreme emergency. We take it for granted that to see the frescos of Giotto we need to go to Padua or Assisi, that the Michelangelo ceiling will be in the Sistine Chapel (whether or not we approve of the cleaning that has taken place at Padua). The big divorces have, on the whole, been made for those cultures whose sites have been most damaged by time, in particular the great Mesopotamian arts of Assyria, Babylon, and Persia. And the set of the world now is clearly against the looting of the art of one culture to titillate the lives of those of another and possibly richer one. It is increasingly hard, thank goodness, to remove even a modest bark painting from Australia, a Maori utensil from New Zealand, or a genuine pre-Hispanic object from Mexico or Peru.

Yet for the student of architecture, even for a traveler to architecture, there remains the obstinate fact that in a few situations he is going to have to use the museum as an adjunct to architecture. In almost every case the museum can help him, and sometimes, as with the Parthenon, it is essential. Fortunately there are, I am certain, but a few cases in which the dispersal of the art has been so marked as to require a close collaboration between museum and building to achieve a reasonable understanding. The *Isenheim Triptych* by Grünwald, for example, was more significant than any building which has housed it.

Sometimes paintings have become orphans and have had to be located far from home. An example is Mantegna's *Triumph of Caesar,* commissioned by the Gonzagas for no particular place in Mantua, which after many vicissitudes, both Italian and British, rests now in the Orangery at Hampton Court Palace outside of London, though it was originally intended by Charles I (more appropriately) for the Long Gallery in the same palace. Paintings on canvas after the Renaissance were more prone to such fates. Unlike the pediments of the Parthenon, the western tympani of the Gothic churches, the walls of Uxmal, they were at home anywhere—or nowhere. (A later exception is the *trompe l'oeil* painting of the Baroque.) *The Triumph of Caesar* is an important painting, and there would be nothing wrong in the attitude of a lover of painting who went out from London to see it without bothering to visit any other part of Hampton Court. It is less likely that a sensitive architect would be disinterested in painting. But he, too, might elect to visit Hampton Court without ever seeing the Mantegna, since the Lower Orangery is of no great architectural significance. This would be a pity, but no crime against the purposes of architectural travel.

It is true that a good many famous paintings are hanging in solitude in the chapels of great or little cathedrals, commissioned after the building or presented by an affluent and grateful donor. And there is every reason for a traveler who is traveling to examine painting to visit such places, ignoring the architecture if he likes, looking at the building as a sort of museum, just as there is no reason for the traveler who is traveling exclusively for architecture to look them up at all—unless they happen to be in a building which is also of architectural importance. This is often enough the case to justify the detours even for one whose interest in painting is tangential or thin-spread. They are often disappointing because of their bad placement or poor lighting ("the sacristan will illuminate for a shilling") and they could be seen better in a modern gallery if only they could be removed there.

There are, of course, many cases in which the art has *not* been removed from the architecture and which demand on larger grounds that the art seeker must look at the architecture and the architectural student must not overlook the art. This is the case, for example, of the reliefs on Queen Hatshepsut's temple at Deir-el-Bahri and the columns of the hypostyle hall at Karnak; of the mosaics of Antioch, Istanbul, Ravenna, or Monreale; of the rounded sculpture from the Last Judgment Tympanum at Autun to the prophets of the North Porch of Chartres; of the stained glass of Chartres and York; of the sculptures of the ninety-six Avatars of Vishnu drawn from incidents of the Ramayana and Mahabharata and carved onto the pillars of the hall north of the mandapams of the Dravidian temple of Varadararajaswami at Little Conjeeveram (Kanchipuram) near Madras; and many, many more. Fortunately few of these are easily removed, and the thought of removal has become less popular now than it might once have been.

Among these—standing on shakier, but still, one would hope, firm ground—are the great frescos of Italy: of Piero della Francesca in the chancel of the Chiesa di San Francisco in Arezzo; of Simone Martini in the first chapel of the lower basilica of Saint Francis; of Cimabue and Giotto in the upper basilica of Saint Francis, all at Assisi; of Fra Angelico in the Convent de San Marco or Masaccio and Ghirlandaio in Santa Maria Novella at Florence. There are also the paintings of Tintoretto, the fifty-six canvases of the Scuola San Rocco, and Carpaccio in the Scuola di San Giorgio degli Schiavoni. Canvases are a little easier to move than frescos, though modern technology is up to either. They are a little less definitely linked to the architecture since it is not necessary that they have been painted in place; but each of them has a partnership with architecture that almost demands they should be visited both by those who are more in love with paint and those who are more in love with building. In most of the Renaissance cases cited, the painting is superior to the architecture, and this is even the case for the frescos of Giotto in the Scrovegni Chapel in Padua. But it is not the case for such famous things as Donatello's crucifix in the Church of Santa Croce, or for the Cellini statue of Perseus in the Loggia dei Lanzi, both in Florence, where the art and architecture battle to a draw as they probably do also in the contest between Ghiberti's doors and the Baptistery as a whole. And the architecture is clearly superior to the art in other cases, such as Brunelleschi's portico to the Ospedale degli Innocenti whose corners are decorated with the touching medallions of children by Andrea della Robbia—or almost any baroque work after Bernini. But this is not the kind of competition which should be argued. The works complement each other to the extent that it would be an indignity to either to allege that it was the superior.

Since, though, such buildings will be the common meeting place of followers of the arts and followers of architecture, it is not amiss to suggest to both that they consider a silly remark of Goethe and try not to repeat his mistake. It was made about the Sistine Chapel, where Goethe went on February 18, 1787,

> . . . for the ceremony of the blessing of the candles. This upset me
> very much and I soon left with my friends. I thought to myself: These are
> the very candles which for three centuries have blackened the frescoes,
> and this is the very incense which, with sacred insolence, not only wraps the
> sun of art in clouds, but also makes it grow dimmer each year and
> in the end will totally eclipse it.[2]

Who but a protestant sceptic and a German tourist could imagine for a second that the chapel and its frescos were designed, not for the worship of God in accordance with the accepted rites of those who commissioned it but instead to be preserved clean and pristine as a kind of museum for unbelievers who placed the skill of the artist above the prayers of the devout? It is the same insensitivity that complains that he cannot see the deepest interior of a Shinto shrine, the Ise shrine, after it has been consecrated, or the inner spaces of Hindu temples which are barred to non-Hindus.

When it is possible it is certainly better to be in the Capella Palatina in Palermo when all the mosaics are aflame with the candles of a great wedding than to be there alone—or at a high mass in a great cathedral than wandering around, Baedeker in hand, identifying statues, even by Peter Lombard. The action will distract somewhat from the art but it will add something to life. Life is not a trivial part of the total architectural experience; and I suppose life is what art is all about.

ARCHITECTURE AND ENGINEERING

Another purpose of architectural travel might be to study engineering methods and their development. It would be a limiting study but not

[2] Goethe, *Italian Journey*, op. cit., p. 160.

disreputable. Engineering stands as the base of most all if not quite all architecture. It is more needed for the understanding of architecture in a practical physical way than art, but, just as art does not tell the whole story of architecture, so engineering does not.

We could begin at the beginning—with ancient stone, enormous stone, cyclopean stone. The engineering questions are interesting enough: Where did they come from? How were they raised? But they are hardly as interesting as the question, the more architectural question, Why? What for—accident? design? These questions throng upon us when we go to one of the great megalithic centers such as Avebury or Stonehenge. Avebury in many ways seems the more interesting one to me but Stonehenge is clearly the more spectacular even to the point of seeming ominous in some lights and some weathers. That it was designed becomes quite evident when one looks at a plan or an air view showing that it is composed of concentric circles, enclosing two series of standing stones each in the shape of a horseshoe. *Pl. 7*

The engineering interest is limited to the precision of the layout at so early a time and possibly the speculative relations of the whole arrangement to the astronomy of the day. But there are other and greater engineering wonders at Stonehenge. The outer and more monumental stone circle, the Sarsen, is 97 feet in diameter. The stones are 10 feet apart center to center, 7 feet wide, and stand 13 feet 6 inches above ground. The bases of the stones are buried from a depth of 4½ feet to a depth of 6 feet. There were 30 lintels and enough of them remain so that we know they were cut to a curve "held onto the upright stones by a knob or tenon fitting into a hole or mortise at the under side of the lintel." The stones on line with the axis and of the U facing roughly northeast are a foot further apart than the average. The lintel was thicker (which may have been because the span was longer, or for architectural emphases, or both). Then to get the upper surface line level with the others the undersurface of this stone was cut away at the ends where it fitted onto the uprights to allow its top to come to the right height in a form reminiscent of some Inca masonry work.[3]

In the enclosure of the Sarsens are the trilithons of the inner or bluestone circle. These are enormous; the largest, of a still different kind of limestone, contains a monolith of ninety-odd cubic feet!

Where did the Sarsen stones come from? What was their route? Where did the bluestone come from—Wales? It seems established now that most of them came from Pembrokeshire. What was their route? There are several different theories.

The erection of the stones is also conjectural—most opinion favors the idea that a ramp was built and then removed after the stone had been

---

[3] R. S. Newall, *Stonehenge, Wiltshire,* 3d ed. (London: H. M. Stationery Office, 1959), p. 5; some quoted, some paraphrased.

rolled up it, all sounding easier than it is. The ramps seem to have been made of wood since there is no evidence of chalk in the soil or any dump of it.

Surely the engineering questions of Stonehenge are interesting enough. How were these great stones found, wrenched from the earth, dressed, transported, erected on a layout so precisely made by men of the Late Neolithic and Early Bronze Ages, in remote Britain, so far from the already established achievements of earlier Egypt and Crete or contemporary Mycenae and Tiryns?

But do not the engineering questions fade when we ask the deeper question, Why? Was its purpose to celebrate some great festival at the winter solstice? Was it connected with sepulchral netherworldly rites? We simply do not know; except that it was *not* Druidic. But the question is more important than the question of how it was all managed technically.

The big stones continue into history. There are the Egyptian stones, older and larger but better understood than those of Stonehenge. What extraordinary skills it took to cut the enormous stones of red Aswan granite, to get them from the quarry to the Nile, to barge them to a downstream site to erect them in forms as sensitive, say, as the obelisk of Hatshepsut at Karnak! These stones often weighed many hundreds of tons; the largest, still lying unfinished in the quarry at Aswan, weighs over a thousand tons. There is more than one speculation as to how the Egyptians may have quarried them, how they slid them into barges in Nile dry docks lifted by the river in flood. We do know that it took 17,000 laborers in 1950 B.C. to propel 60 "modest" sphinxes and 150 statues of "medium size" from the Wadi Hammamat to Coptos, a distance of about 50 miles. But again it is the beauty and purpose of the obelisk that matter more than the skill of the Egyptian engineers. This is true also for cyclopean architecture, which involves the excavation and the movement of enormous stones. It is to be found in many parts of the world—at Mycenae and Tiryns, on the walls of the platform of Darius at Persepolis, at Roman Baalbek, and in the walls of the Inca in the high Andes. Egyptian obelisks have had a peculiar allure for the many conquerors who ravaged the Nile, and they have been removed from Egypt in all periods. Assurbanipal took two of them to Nineveh. The Roman emperors carried many to Rome and Constantinople. Nineteenth-century Europeans took many more, sometimes as loot, more often as gifts. Thus, though there are only a handful of obelisks still standing in Egypt, there must be more than fifty which were spawned in Egypt but now adorn public squares of European and American cities, twelve in Rome alone.

The brilliance of Egyptian engineering becomes evident when we consider the difficulties encountered by the more sophisticated and better-equipped European engineers when they moved Egyptian obelisks in the nineteenth century. In 1829, for example, the Egyptian viceroy gave one of the obelisks of Rameses II at Luxor to Charles X of France, whose regal enjoyment of it did not materialize since it did not arrive in Paris until 1833 in the reign of Louis Philippe. The work involved in disembarking and setting it up in the Place de la Concorde is commemorated on two sides of the pedestal where are represented the various machines used by the naval engineer Lebas, who received high honors and much acclaim on the completion of the task three years later. It is 77 feet high. The obelisk of Hatshepsut at Karnak, 20 feet higher, bears an inscription which says it was made in seven months!

The obelisk *in situ* at Karnak has a greater impact than the transplanted obelisks of Central Park, the Victoria Embankment, or the Place de la Concorde, where they really have no credibility. Some of this is no doubt due to the scale of the surroundings and the activity that swirls or does not swirl around the monument. But does it not again speak, if mystically, about that part of the object which transcends engineering?

Big stones, however, made no more than walls or simple trabeated (post and lintel) construction, however refined it may have become. Let us skip by the enormous skill of the Greeks and the refinements in the art of stone dressing and wall construction they perfected to consider a second, much later development.

This is the Pantheon at Rome, a culminating engineering and architectural experience. Behind it lay years of experiment with masonry, first tentatively in the dome and then gradually in more and more adventurous spans; coupled with it was the discovery or invention of a new building material, Roman concrete based on a local volcanic stones, *puozzolana*. Of all this evolution I do not wish to speak here or even to speculate in this place as to *why* it was the Romans and not someone else who achieved it.

William L. MacDonald has reported all this beautifully in his book, which ought to be read and not paraphrased or abridged.[4]

The Pantheon is structurally very ingenious and a great leap from the much smaller earlier domed rotundas (Albano) or the similar techniques of brick-faced concrete used, for example, in the earlier markets and baths of concrete. The problems of height, weight, and stability were of a very different order of magnitude, not to be solved by mere extrapolation. The ingenuity of the foundation ring, of the way in which internal arches were used to lighten the construction, the presumed intricacy of the domical carpentry are truly engineering marvels, and, of course, the Pantheon can be visited with an eye to the wonders of its engineering. But it is much more.

Pl. 8
Pl. 9

The arrangement of the portico and the rotunda to which it leads provides one of history's most brilliant examples of a building which manages to launch you almost instantaneously and without preparation

[4] William L. MacDonald, *The Architecture of the Roman Empire*, vol. I, *An Introductory Study* (New Haven, Conn.: Yale University Press, 1965), pp. 97 ff.

into a monumental inner space, although when it was built, the avenue approach offered some introduction.

Evidently the architectural arrangements alone add a second dimension to the Pantheon far greater than that afforded by the engineering alone. But there is even more to it than that, and more than the shadow of a great emperor, Hadrian, who built it to mark forever the age that was to be his. Of transcendent importance, it was to be a temple to the Roman universe.

The Pantheon was also a *templum deorum omnium*. Here the mysteries of planetary forces once identified with the several gods were merged somehow into the suggestion that all of this merger was a metaphor for the Roman state and its eternal symbolism.

As Dio Cassius, the fourth-century biographer of Hadrian, said, the key to the matter is the symbolism of the heavens, which were both the abode of the gods and the canopy of Empire. The seamless circles around and above the great interior can be taken to describe both the cosmos and Roman rule.

> Because of its forms the Pantheon is an activated, light drenched place, expanding and revolving, visibly connected with the heavens through its cyclopic eye. It has preserved intact the essence of one of the great creative moments of Western and Mediterranean art. . . . It lies at the heart of an age of architecture and embodies and expresses the accumulated experience of a way of life.[5]

Similar conclusions though different in terms might be drawn from Hagia Sophia, built 400 years later in Constantinople by another great emperor, Justinian the Byzantine. Its purposes were different and so was the engineering, which was even more fanciful—simple yet bold, extraordinarily hazardous yet surprisingly resilient.[6]

> Defying all laws of statics, shaken by successive earthquakes, collapsing at its weak points, and being repaired, the Hagia Sophia stands by sheer miracle. Experienced master builders of 537 must have stood aghast at the disregard of sound building practices by those two non-professionals to whom the Emperor had entrusted his greatest building. True, Anthemios and Isidorus went to the very limits of what we call the safety coefficients [or safety factors—jeb]. In building the first, flatter, dome, they even went beyond and it collapsed within twenty years. Yet, at the risk of failure, they had to employ hazardous techniques— techniques which were the necessary tools for developing the design they meant to create. Perhaps they could envisage both design and

[5] Ibid., pp. 120–121.
[6] For a clear exposition of the details, see Richard Krautheimer, *Early Christian and Byzantine Architecture* (Baltimore: Penguin, 1965), p. 156. Copyright © Richard Krautheimer, 1965.

techniques only because they were not professional architects [or engineers—jeb].[7]

Yet here again the fantasies of the engineering have more than engineering significance. In its fecklessness there is more than a hint of Byzantine irresponsibility. Unlike the Pantheon, the great space does not read all at once; other spaces interpenetrate—the eye is drawn in and out by galleries, arcades, conches, half domes.

> The principle of a design which rests upon statement and denial, acts with equal force throughout the building. . . . Light seems to flood the interior from the outside, yet it seems generated inside as well. The structure is solid, yet it engenders a feeling of insecurity. The columns perform in a choral dance, the piers are sheer mountain peaks. Vaults seem to float, the dome seems suspended from heaven. Vistas change and yet the spatial shapes follow each other in a clear sequence. Statement and denial are at the basis of Procopius's description just as they are at the basis of the architect's design.[8]

Yet the final understanding of the miracle of Hagia Sophia transcends the engineering and the architectural space and relates to the complex mysticism of the Byzantine priests, who not only held much of the celebration of the Eucharist out of sight of the laity but conceived the very design itself as a symbol of the cosmos. The vault

> expands like the heavens and shines with mosaics as the firmament with stars. Its soaring dome compares with the Heaven of Heavens, where God resides, and its four arches represent the four directions of the world, with their variegated colours like the rainbow. Its piers are like the mountains of the earth; its marble walls shine like the light of the image not man-made, the Godhead; . . . In short . . . the building represents heaven and earth, the apostles, the prophets, the martyrs, and indeed the Godhead.[9]

We cannot know whether the full distillation of this symbolism, whether that of St-Denis, of Rome, or Byzantium, came afterwards at the hands of critics and poetic interpreters, or whether it was clear at least in the minds of patrons such as Abbot Suger, Justinian, or Hadrian and filtered from them to the architects of the buildings, but it is certain that much of it is not the result of later imagination and that it infused the building of St-Denis, the Pantheon, and Hagia Sophia in a way that nothing has infused the making even of such a fine contemporary building as the Seagram Building in New York. We are simply talking of a different world, in which the skill of the engineer is but a way to a much larger

[7] Ibid.
[8] Ibid, p. 158.
[9] Ibid., pp. 159–160.

purpose, a transcendental purpose scarcely to be found in the office building of people who make whiskey.

Engineering by itself is not architecture even though its materials and methods are essential to a full understanding. The structural technique, admirable as it may be, is the servant of the imagery.

That is why in the end Hagia Sophia is more important than the Walls of Constantinople, the Pantheon than the Pont du Gard, Notre-Dame de Chartres than the Cloth Hall at Ypres, impressive as all may be. It is possibly the explanation of why it is harder to say the same thing of the Seagram Building when compared, say, with the San Francisco Bay Bridge or a cyclotron or a space module.

It is, in any event, clear that, as in the case of sculpture and painting, a very considerable journey could be made to the architecture of history prompted only by an interest in the engineering. However, it is not a focus I have chosen here, and if you want to make such a journey you will have no difficulty in finding better guides than I. In the buildings for which I care most the engineering is sometimes of very great importance, sometimes of almost no importance at all.

THE ARCHITECTURAL TRAVELER AS AMATEUR SCHOLAR

Another thoroughly respectable reason for visiting architecture is to seek out clues for the forging of links with its past—one form of scholarly detective work. For the professional this is certainly a desirable, even an essential pursuit. From such studies may come more general works which will help us who are not this sort of scholar better to understand what it is we are looking at. But we are not thus specialized ourselves and the question we need to ask is how much of this sort of thing we need or want to know.

On most Romanesque churches and especially those of France there is a rich sculpture dealing with many religious subjects. The sources of this iconography are manifold: some are drawn from quite explicit Biblical tales; some are prompted by readings in Pliny's *Natural History;* some originated in older Spanish manuscripts such as those of Beatus of Gaul, often going back to early Syrian or Arabic sources; some are closely connected to a variety of ancient and Oriental ideas, by no means all Christian; most are heavy with symbolism. Later on in the Gothic this iconography expands enormously, consonant with such important works as the *Speculum Majus* of Vincent de Beauvais which dates from the middle of the thirteenth century.

There are large differences in the iconography of the two centuries. Both involve an interpretation of the Old Testament as symbolic of the New. Both are devoted to the cult of saints. But the iconography of the twelfth century is predominantly apocalyptic and full of fearful visions of monsters, of the beasts of Revelations, of seas of glass, of Christ the Judge enthroned in glory. That of the thirteenth renounces the visions and the monsters, becomes "evangelic, human, Western, and natural."[10]

Now if you were to stand before two of the great tympani comparing them, you would notice at once that there are enormous differences. Let us take, for example, the tympanum over the south portal of St-Pierre at Moissac from about the first third of the twelfth century and the Pl. 10 tympanum over the central door of the west facade of St-Etienne at Bourges a century or so later. Leaving aside the sculptural techniques and Pl. 11 the styles of representation, whose differences leap to the eye, it will be evident that the subject matter is markedly not the same although the central figure, the Christ Judge and the two angels supporting him, dominates both. The Christ of the earlier tympanum is less benign, less forgiving. He occupies at least two-thirds of the height and completely controls the scene. The rest is drawn from the Apocalypse. The other two important elements are the twenty-four elders of the Apocalypse, each quite personalized, each craning his neck to see the Judge so that those immediately beneath the Christ have twisted their heads almost at right angles to their bodies, and all eyes lead to the central figure; and the four beasts of the Apocalypse—the winged man, the lion, the calf or bull, and the eagle which identify with Saints Matthew, Mark, Luke, and John, respectively. This is the characteristic judgment of the eleventh century. It is to be found and each time in a highly original version at such other places as Vézelay and Autun sometimes coupled with the Pentecostal mission.

On the other hand the subject matter of Bourges is quite different. The Christ still sits in majesty at the top of the tympanum but the four beasts of the Apocalypse have disappeared and Christ is supported instead by more angels. The old men of the Apocalypse have been relegated to the voussoirs for we are now concerned with a more specific judgment. On the bottom level of the tympanum the dead rise from their tombs naked as they should be before the Lord, some apprehensive, some sanguine of how they will fare. In the middle layer Saint Michael weighs a soul, the devil waiting eagerly to tip the scales. Those who have been judged well move off to the left into the lap of Abraham, that is, Paradise; those who are condemned are pushed by satanic imps toward the jaws of Leviathan, that is, Hell!

When you examine either or both of these how much do you want to know? I am not suggesting by this line of questioning what you ought to know but asking what you want to know. Do you care about the identities of the man, lion, bull, and eagle? Do you care who the twenty-four old men were? Do you wonder about the sea of glass? Would you like to read the appropriate verses of the Book of Revelations? Would you like to compare other works of art which deal with the same topic?

[10] Focillon, *The Art of the West in the Middle Ages*, vol. II, op. cit., p. 72.

Before the Last Judgment are you concerned about why the souls are naked? What is to be your reaction when you find one where they are clothed, or at least bear signs, such as the miser's purse, which indicate what they were up to in life? Will you notice on some Last Judgments that only the poor seem to go to Hell while later on queens and bishops can be identified? Do you want to ask why the mouth of Leviathan? Why Abraham's bosom? Why no Purgatory? Do you care or do you find it upsetting when you go to Chartres and find that the Moissac Apocalypse is repeated there on the west front a century later though in much more gentle and sophisticated forms; or to Conques and find the Last Judgment of Bourges a hundred years earlier though in more confused, more archaic, more frightening, and possibly more effective terms? Do you ask what this does to generalizations about twelfth- and thirteenth-century French sculpture? Or even more cogently about general attitudes in the two different centuries?

The Amateur Scholar and Christianity

A very loose and fairly reliable memory might speak to you as follows when you stand in the nave of Notre-Dame de Paris. After Christians got out of catacombs or upper rooms or wherever they worshipped when they were being suppressed, they took over some Roman basilicas and moved the judge's bar from the side to the end to make an altar—then they took Roman barrel vaults and noted that when they intersected at right angles they formed four ridges meeting at a peak, called groins. They put ribs on them and this made a rib vault; they gradually made these vaults steeper into something called ogives. They developed some side aisles and galleries with arcades; they "articulated" the whole business. They learned how to lighten the buttresses by making flying buttresses, opening up more wall to accommodate the desired stained glass. Simple and at many points deceptively wrong. I do not propose to put it all right here but merely to point out some of the early errors and then to ask, At what point do you sign off?

In the first place a good many present-day scholars might suggest to you that basilican architecture of the early Christians was not really a Western development at all but should be looked on "rather as the final expression of the architectural concepts which were dominant in the Eastern Mediterranean centres and coastal areas of the late Roman world."[11]

If you were to look at this carefully, you would have to understand how much freedom the Romans of the first to third centuries A.D. offered to alternative religions or even to private worship so long as it did not publicly contradict the official cult of the Emperor. You would have to learn how Paul, severing Christianity from Judaism, built a policy which

[11] Krautheimer, *Early Christian and Byzantine Architecture*, op. cit., p. xxiii. From the same book much of what immediately follows is drawn.

might be "subversive" to Roman social and political demands. You would have to know how few the number of Christians, how loosely organized the congregations, how important the itinerant preachers, how simple the ritual, and why this did not demand an ecclesiastical architecture but could be celebrated almost anywhere, even in a private house.

You would need to observe how this changed so that by 250 A.D. some Roman Christian congregations numbered 30, but one counted 5,000. You would have to realize that among these congregations were wealthy and influential Romans, whose defections from official religious demands could not be ignored; that the congregations were more formally organized, engaged in activities such as public charity, cemetery tending, education, proselytizing, which could not be hidden in a quiet upper room; and perhaps above all that a hierarchy of professional, ordained clergy had evolved from amateur bishops, elders, deacons to the point where there were even metropolitan administrative and spiritual centers, not only in Rome, but in Carthage, Alexandria, Ephesus, Antioch.

You would then see what new structures were required for the cult of the dead, for extramural cemeteries, for *martyria*, funeral banquets, for assembly, administration, charity, for service of a rich and codified liturgy in which the common meal had become symbolically embodied in the communion, and physically the *agapai* were meals occasionally offered to the poor.

You would need to realize the distinction drawn in the service between the Faithful and the Neophytes and what this required of the plan; what the elaborately developed ritual of baptism required in the way of physical surroundings.

By such understandings and more, you could comprehend the evolution from private house to *domus ecclesiae* or *titulus*, and how in this stage it was ideologically desirable and politically prudent to be inconspicuous so that the desirable facade was that of domestic middle-class architecture. You could understand how ludicrous it is to think that the catacombs could ever have seriously served the needs of regular services.

> Needless to say, no catacomb was even intended or used for holding regular services in hiding from persecution. The idea of Roman Christians, thousands strong by 220, marching to the catacombs for Sunday services unbeknown to the police is preposterous. Moreover the catacombs were damp, dark, intricate and the largest *cubiculum* would take not even 50 people. Only memorial services were held in catacombs and if attendance exceeded a bare minimum, even they and the accompanying funeral banquets had to be held above ground.[12]

It was only after the victory of Constantine over Maxentius in 312 at the Milvian bridge, his subsequent conversion, and his occupation of

[12] Ibid., p. 10.

Rome that the civic and religious climate favored the expression of Christian concepts in the language of the official architecture of late antiquity.

By the Edict of Milan at the beginning of his reign, Constantine had recognized Christianity and given it official standing. Then by word and deed he made the Church the dominant religious power in the Roman Empire, wedding Empire and Church in close union, radically changing the social as well as the political position of the Church, tightening her hierarchic organization to parallel that of the Imperial Administration.

Now many aristocrats joined, Christian officials were numerous in the court, many civil servants embraced the new religion as the wise or "in" thing to do. The basic lines of the liturgy, now standardized over the Empire, still contained the two masses, one of the Catechumen, one of the Faithful, the rite of the oblation, the separation of congregation and clergy, the presiding position of the bishop. But Christ was no longer the God primarily of the poor and the humble, the miracle worker and Savior. Instead he was the Emperor of Heaven.

Inevitably the liturgy changed, became a ceremonial performed before the Lord, or his representative, the bishop. It picked up an increasing number of features from the analogous ceremonial of Roman officialdom and the Imperial Court. The bishop, clad in the garments of a high magistrate, entered the church in a solemn procession, preceded by insignia of official rank, by candles, by book. Flanked by his presbyters he was seated on a throne, the *sella curulis* of a Roman officer.

Along with this strengthening of the hierarchy went a corresponding reduction in the role of the laity. The altar had been a simple wooden table easily carried in for the mass of the faithful. Now it became a stable structure often covered with gold and precious stone, occasionally accompanied by a *fastigium*, i.e., an arched and pedimented lintel colonnade like the one under which the emperor revealed himself to his subjects at court.

All this called for a new plan. The sanctuary for the mass and for the assembly of the clergy had to be architecturally distinguishable from the place of the laity; ecclesiastical architecture had to be differentiated from ordinary building. The vocabulary had to correspond to that of the highest class of public buildings, such as palaces and temples. As the graves of martyrs became the object of solemn cults and pilgrimage, the venerated cult sites had to be clearly separated from the regular assembly spaces. A forecourt (*atrium*)[13] or precinct court had to be provided and to be accessible not only to postulants but to nonbelievers.

[13] The complexity of this sort of study and the traps which lie waiting for the generally well educated are illustrated by the term *atrium*, which most of us who recognize it at all will think of in terms of the enclosed inner main room of the Roman house. But it comes to the Christian church from the Greek word meaning "area under the open sky" and no one is sure where catechumens and others excluded from the Mass of the Faithful really repaired.

The old *domus* simply would not do; it was too anonymous in appearance. The once-desirable protective coloration now became undesirable, unworthy. It was too badly situated, too often in the slums, too small for the large number of new Christians, too cramped to provide space for the new functions.

The desired building could not evolve from pagan temple architecture for ideological as well as practical reasons. The new cults which did work with congregations as opposed to images and in this sense resembled Christianity, whether they were Mithraic, Neo-Pythagorean, whether they worshiped Baal or Isis or the Great Mother, generally had congregations of no more than twenty to thirty. Their buildings were too small to provide a prototype even if the idea had been otherwise acceptable.

Lacking a new architectural invention the Christians turned to one of the existing public forms, the *basilica*, a type which had been built for quite other purposes all over the Roman world since the second and first centuries B.C.

The term *basilica* as we now use it has one meaning which is canonical. Such a basilica, *which may be of any architectural type*, confers special liturgical privileges. Some basilicas are *patriarchal* and have special papal altars. Minor basilicas do not have papal altars but any basilica has hierarchical priority over any other church save the cathedral. Hereafter I shall not use the term in this sense save as the proper title of a given architectural monument.

The other major use of the word is in architecture and it bears a quite firm meaning—it is a building divided into a nave and two or more aisles. The nave is ordinarily higher and wider than the aisles and is lit by clerestory windows.

The Roman basilica from which the early Christian church evolved was rarely of this type. In the simplest form it was an aisleless hall occasionally subdivided by supports for the roof. In more elaborate forms an aisle or aisles and galleries above them enveloped the nave; the aisles and galleries might be doubled all around; they might run only parallel to the long sides of the nave instead of around it. The clerestory might be high or low. The entrance might be on a long side or a short side or there might be entrances on both. The tribunal rose on a plain dais either inside the nave or in the aisles, or in an apse of rectangular or semi-circular plan. The apse, if any, might project from the long or short side. The number of apses might be doubled or tripled. The roof was normally of open timber work which could be exposed to the nave or have a ceiling hung from it.

By 300 A.D. there was an enormous variety of secular basilican plans. Quite in contrast to the temple form, which was dead, having completed its evolution, the basilica was alive and prone to change its plan according to use. The Basilica of Maxentius, for example, had a huge *vaulted* nave flanked by niches very much resembling one of the big halls of a public bath. Throne basilicas in palaces sometimes had central plans. Sometimes, though rarely, there might be an open area surrounded by porticos. But by the end of the fourth century the most common, if not the prevailing, type was a longitudinal, timber-roofed hall, without aisles, terminated and thus dominated by a raised apse. Huge windows in single or double rows along the flanks lit the interior. The exterior of such a building was dominated by plain stretches of wall of brick or stone. The interior might be resplendent with marble revetments, and gilded capitals and ceilings.

However, the Romans used the word *basilica* to apply to the function rather than the form, and the generic function was that of a large meeting house. The *forum basilica*, found in any Roman town, was but a covered extension of the adjoining market place—a hall in which to transact business, to exchange gossip and news from the empire, a *souk* to display and sell wares much like the *galleria* in many modern Italian towns. On a dais, the *tribunal*, a magistrate and his assessors, might sit in court—above this a shrine sheltered the effigy of the Emperor in whose presence, alone, law could be dispensed and business contracts validly concluded.

Pl. 12

In large cities basilicas became more specialized as stock and money exchanges, clothing bazaars, florists' arcades, special law courts. Riding and drill basilicas were provided in army camps; baths had basilicas. They served a number of different religious sects; one was a funerary college; many were audience halls where the Emperor would solemnly appear in the apse. None was really completely bereft of religious connotations, of images of Godhead or Imperial head (much the same thing). The borderline between the secular and the religious functions of the basilica was fluid throughout late antiquity, and the wide variety of purposes which the buildings served fluctuated between these two poles.

We will probably be near enough the useful truth if we look on the early Christian basilica merely as another monumental public hall with religious overtones. By A.D. 300 there were a few features which had become characteristic of the majority of pre-Constantinian basilicas. There would be:

A longitudinal axis for an oblong plan

A timber roof either open or concealed by a flat ceiling (a vault, such as that in the Basilica of Maxentius, was unique for a long time)

A terminating tribunal, rectangular or apsidal

The nave with side aisles, the high large-windowed clerestory, were preponderant but remained optional

Then all this had to be modified to meet the demands for greater dignity and monumentality laid down by the new Constantinian spirit, adapted to specific liturgical requirements, to financial means, to local building practices. The Catechumens withdrew in different places, to the atrium, to the aisles, to a separate building; the clergy might sit in the apse or in front of it; the offertory table might be near the altar in an adjoining room. There were many different locations for the altar; there might or might not be an atrium; the wall materials might be dressed ashlar, large stone, random small stone, bricks, either alone or in combination. At least until 350 one could not say there was such a thing as *the* Christian basilica.

And we are not really able to see an unmodified example today or even one that has not been greatly changed, whether it be the Basilica of Constantine, now San Giovanni in Laterano, or old St. Peter's.

The latter was completely replaced between 1505 and 1613. We cannot learn about it from an architectural visit although scholars agree that a clear picture can be derived from excavations, old descriptions, drawings, and paintings. After we have mastered that it may be discouraging to learn that this particular church, no archetype, had a double function, congregational and funerary, and that the church was atypical. It may have been primarily a burial place and a hall for funerary banquets; the shrine is a tomb, it had no permanent clergy; mass was not regular, for a resident congregation, but sporadic, for pilgrims' gatherings. Indeed it was outside of town. Only scant fragments remain of the Golgotha Church in Jerusalem, and the basilica at the Grotto of the Nativity at Bethlehem built as early as 333 was replaced in the sixth century by the present structure and our bequest from the old one is only some excavations of foundation walls and mosaic.

Pl. 15
l. 14

What with destruction and rebuilding, in the end what we can understand of these early basilican churches is largely based on scholars' drawings based on what they make of literary, graphic, art, and archeological fragments. Our understanding is not simplified when there was another competing type round or octagonal in plan, often domed, beginning probably as a *martyrium* but not always ready to play that role, originating in a different part of the world, deriving from a different source, playing a somewhat different but still Christian role and represented by such splendid existing churches as Santa Costanza, the later and now much overlaid baptistery at the Lateran, and San Stefano in Rome, together with the well-preserved San Lorenzo in Milan. Even a modest architectural history would have to take these fully into account but this is not a comprehensive history, and I mention them here only to show how little of the surface has been scratched in this narrative.

Pl. 20
Pl. 19

What we can see more clearly is what happened when the early Christian basilican church began to draw on the entire repertory of late classical Roman designs of the second, third, and fourth centuries, especially during the incumbency of Pope Sixtus III (432–440), which Krautheimer calls the *Sixtine Renaissance*. To understand this development at least in superficial terms it may help to look at some comparative plans:

Pl. 21

an early Christian basilica at Sagalassos in Asia Minor which is almost a diagram of the fundamentals—a nave, separated from two side aisles by a row of columns, an area which has only the slightest suggestion of transept and might have had none, and an apse at the eastern end of the nave; an isometric reconstruction of the Church of the Nativity in Bethlehem as in 333; the Church of the Acheioropoeitos in Salonica of about 470, which brings us back to a basic basilica with galleries; Hosios Demetrios of the late fifth century, also in Salonica, to show a cross-transept basilica at its best.

These are the main changes which were rung on the early Christian basilican theme, although many other combinations were possible and were used. It should be clear by now what the central elements of the basilican church were and what you would look for if you were trying to identify a church as basilican. But understanding a plan and having a sense of what a building is really like are quite different things. The question then becomes, Where can I experience a genuine basilica today? The answer is disappointing.

Of the churches so far described only one is physically extant in anything like its original form and most do not exist at all. Hosios Demetrios, though faithful as to plan and section, is a reconstruction and impoverished as to the materials used.

What might we expect to find nearer to hand? Perhaps the best free-standing example of a Roman apsed basilica (not, however, a church) is the Basilica at Trier which was the palace hall of Constantine. It was built about 310 A.D. by Constantine as a throne hall over an extensive old palace. Like almost any building we will see in Europe built prior to the Renaissance and not frozen as a ruin, it has undergone so many vicissitudes that we cannot be sure just how it was. But here some physical visualization remains possible.

Though quite stark now as compared with the Constantinian days and though surrounded now by small white automobiles, the basilica creates a massive impression. It is a long rectangular mass, entirely of brick, with a large apse filling almost the whole north wall. (Excavations now reveal a probable transverse construction with apse to the west suggesting a most unusual T-shaped plan.) The walls, nine feet or more thick, have two tiers of windows enframed by monumental high-rising arches. The handsome brick was probably once plastered. There were evidently wooden galleries which once went completely around the exterior.

Here the emperor sat in his throne looking down the 275 feet of the nave made to look longer by the architectural tricks of putting the upper windowsills of the apse about four feet lower than those in the side walls and by narrowing and lowering the windows of the apse toward its middle, thus forcing the visual perspective. This much we can sense even now, though the hall no longer has its magnificent black and white marble floor, its marble wall panels, its pilasters "adorned with geometrical ornaments made of coloured cut stones and with golden glass mosaics with garlands in the niches of the apse."[14] At least the basilica as it now stands, and barring such errors of reconstruction as may have occurred, does not deceive us by the countless accumulations of time.

This is unhappily not the case for the great basilican churches of Rome where the development reached its peak under Pope Sixtus III, and *Pl. 13* you have to do a good deal of imagining when you go to the contemporary *Pl. 18* but originally old basilicas such as San Paolo fuori le Mura. *Pl. 16*

I suppose the nearest we shall come is at Santa Sabina, also in Rome, *Pl. 17* sometimes called the "Pearl of the Aventine." It was built by Cardinal *Pl. 24* Peter of Illyna (422–432) on the presumed site of the house of a sainted Roman matron, Sabina. It was restored in 824 and again in 1216, disfigured in 1587 by Dom. Fontana, and restored by Munoz in 1919 and by Bertier in 1936–1939. Except for a few tombs and the baroque Elci Chapel, it probably comes closest of any of the Roman churches to resembling those of the fifth century, especially inside.

Now where does this relatively simple, if lengthy, excursion leave us?

One thing it clearly says is that though the architectural artifacts even in the relatively simple case of the basilica do offer substantial evidence or confirmation of other evidence, in this case, of the early evolution of Christian meetings, this evidence does not spring obviously to the untutored eye but has to be teased out of other tissue which can be irrelevant or even deceptive. This is what the scholars do for us and what we can rarely do for ourselves. So for us I am afraid it is the knowledge we gain from other sources which enriches our encounter with the basilica rather than the other way around. In short, a visit to architecture for the purpose of reconstructing the past of architecture is fraught with danger if the visitor is ignorant, and perhaps even more if he is half-informed. All I have been telling about Christian evolution explains the basilica more than the basilica will explain Christian evolution to you and to me.

Questions of origin, of communication, of development are of central importance to scholars of architectural history. To resolve them even tentatively requires skill in the reading of ruins, of documents, in the weighting to be given to apparently contradictory evidence. To acquire this skill and to apply it is a full-time job or very near to it. Moreover, if the work is to be reliable and profound, the scholar will have to concentrate on a rather small period or style of architecture and let the rest more or less go by.

How much of this shall you need to know or care about when you stand in front of and then inside Sant'Ambrogio or Santa Sabina? The "happening" school might say "nothing." You arrive in Milan by accident, you start rambling the streets at random, you happen by Sant'Ambrogio,

[14] Wilhelm Rauset, *Treveris: A Guide through Roman Trier* (Trier: Paulerius-Verlag, 1962), p. 30.

something about it catches your eye, you go into the *atrium* and then into the nave. You notice a vault, a tower, a sarcophagus, a cloister. You know nothing about world history, Italian history, Church history, the history of Milan, or even who Ambrose was. You know nothing about the ritual of the church for which this building was contrived. You know nothing about structural principles or their history and are spared any awe at the deeds of your predecessors. But a warm glow is there, you are doing your thing, today is today, and tomorrow you will not remember the building or the town.

Or with a little more sense you may come to the building either as a devotee, or as one who understands, sympathetically if not believingly, the liturgy and the meanings of contemporary Catholicism, and you may look at the Church in order to wonder whether this building as it stands today in the here and now serves well or ill the needs of the Church of here and now. If this is your purpose, then you may achieve it without worrying about the evolution either of the ancient liturgy or the old architecture.

At the other extreme you may approach with the concentrated curiosity of the scholar, which, depending on your interest, the number of examples you have to consider, and maybe pressure of time, may force you to overlook peripheral or certainly irrelevant details of the building and possibly whole categories of other buildings. You may have to ignore human values in order to know enough of engineering values. Very little scholarship is in fact as limited as that; and not all scholars resemble Carlyle's Dry as Dust—but some do. More of their reports do, first because of the limitations of space which do not permit drastic excursions away from the subject at hand, second because of fear by the authors of error if they wander where their steps are unsure, third because of fear by the authors of criticism by their peers for having been too general. As a result many of the most reliable books will require more devotion to a question and more concentration on a subject than you choose to give. Consider the dilemma of Jonathan Swift on his voyage to Brobdingnag. You will recall he praises the man who can make two ears of corn grow where only one did before, as being more deserving than the "whole race of politicians put together." But it can be overdone, and when Gulliver visits the scholars floating around on Laputa he notices the absurd.

> He had been eight years upon a project for extracting sunbeams out of cucumbers, which were to be put in phials hermetically sealed, and let out to warm the air in raw inclement summers.[15]

There is the chance in such a project, not only that the thing will not work, but that the researcher in the process may have lost all pleasure in the taste of the cucumber, the beauty of sunlight, and the caprice of a summer's day.

[15] Jonathan Swift, *Gulliver's Travels*, part III, chap. V.

Furthermore, the reports of scholarly investigation in architectural history vary enormously in their importance for the understanding of the architectural artifacts we see. A few are very important indeed—many more are trivial, a consequence of our unholy system of graduate education and of promotion in academic ranks. But important or not to you and me, it is doubtless true that there are great rewards which come to all but the most dismal scholars who are untouched emotionally by the cadaver of architecture or art they are dissecting: the positive pleasures which come to the researcher; the hunch which leads him to look into something in the first place; the intuitive inspirations entertained while finding an avenue of approach; the aesthetic delight of working over the problem in a particular way; and the triumph of a conclusion, perhaps even joy in the conflict which will swirl around the conclusion if it has any real salt in it. This is of course the pleasure of a private world, but there is no reason why it is one which needs to be enjoyed only by the full-time professional scholar.

It is a world which you can enter if your temperament is suited to it. You might therefore elect to indulge in architectural touring as an amateur scholar. There is nothing automatically demeaning about the word amateur if we take it to mean only that you do not indulge in architectural scholarship as a primary source of livelihood. It would be demeaning only if you were not to adhere to the standards of reputable scholarship. It is entirely possible for an amateur thus defined to do better work than many professionals—and to experience the same joys.

I suppose if one were to think of becoming an amateur architectural scholar, he might pick a building or a style which he loved most and read widely in the journals to find out what scholars have said about it. He could thus decide whether this did in fact interest him or not, and if it did, whether it prompted him to some type of investigation of his own.

The pleasures will be great for the suitably disposed; but there are prices. There will be a demand for much work in documents as well as on the site, and also a requirement that there be some concentration—causing thus at once a widening and a narrowing of the totality of one's experience. There will be the cost, probably, unless you are very quick, of limiting the number of types of architecture you know (or even care) much about, but the gain will be some of the special joys of involvement, of discovery, of argument which you otherwise would not have enjoyed. It is probably not the way most of you will wish to go about.

Between these extremes there is an enormous middle ground. It is inconceivable to me that a fully pleasured enjoyment of historical architecture can be based on an understanding of the political, social, economic, art, engineering, and evolutionary history of the architectural artifact less slender than the sort of detail I have provided for the selected cases in the preceding pages. And this amount can with concentration and purpose be arrived at within the time bounds possible for an intelligent person whose main interest has focused elsewhere. It is probably not to be achieved merely by consulting even the best and most detailed travel guides unless you have an enormous skill at quickly relating one set of facts to the larger tapestry of history. And it certainly cannot all be achieved in the bus on the way to the site, or by listening to the explanations of the local custodian, even when they are more accurate than they usually are, or least of all by wandering through the monument, guidebook in hand, reading as you go. None of these is really completely out of bounds providing they do not block from view the larger sights and meanings and turn the trip into a diary checklist of things seen but not remembered.

However, how much you choose to know, or how little, is something no one else has the right to prescribe for you. The most another might properly do is indicate the nature of what you may find if you elect to follow this or that path. Then the choice will and must be yours and one can only wish you good luck. There were, after all, many roads to Rome although every road did not lead there.

THE EDUCATION OF THE ARCHITECT

One of the significant justifications for architectural travel has been that it will help to educate the architect himself. What the result of this ought to be has been the subject of differing opinions, especially over the last fifty years.

When I was an architectural undergraduate back in the early twenties a number of things were taken for granted. It was assumed that the Beaux-Arts methods of attack on an architectural problem, a tightly organized and highly disciplined approach, were unchallengeable. The student was assigned a problem of which the requirements were explicit and complete. This was in effect a pronouncement that the client know exactly what he wanted and where. I remember vividly my first assigned problem, "An Orangerie in a Park." We were told exactly where the park was, the exact latitude and longitude, the length of the storage season, when the tubs were to be brought in, how they were to be brought in, how many there were and so on. Today an architectural school problem will generally ask the student to do his own "research" on the conditions which will often lead to a quite different program. This attitude is based on the assumption that a particular client may really not know what he wants, at least in much detail (an assumption which is often justified); or that he is not really *au courant* with the latest advances either in the technology of the events for which the building is being erected or in the latest appropriate technology of construction. This is even more likely to be true. So it is then expected that the architect ought to learn how to contribute to the formulation of the program for the building instead of embarking on a design in the blind confidence that the client knows not only what he wants but what he ought to want which obviously may not be the same thing.

This broader view of the architectural mission has on the whole, I think we must say, been beneficial. It has led to some serious travesties of function to be sure, such as Frank Lloyd Wright's Guggenheim Museum, but on the other hand it has produced Marcel Breuer's much more efficient and equally impressive Whitney Museum on nearby Madison Avenue or J. L. Sert's magnificent Fondation Maeght in St. Paul de Vence.

But it is one thing for an architect to press the client very far as to what he really wants and quite another to take on the role of being wiser than the librarian, the priest, the museum director, the *regisseur*, and the chemist as to what a library, a fane, a gallery, a theater, a laboratory ought to be. On balance and despite some egregious and arrogant blunders, our contemporaries do not lay as heavy a hand on the users of a building as was laid years ago, for example, by the distinguished architect Charles Follen McKim when he built the beautiful Italian Renaissance palace which serves uneasily and falteringly the technical needs of the Boston Public Library, or when the effectiveness of the Sterling Library at Yale was crippled by casting it in the mold of a stirring Gothic tower. On the whole, we do much better now, although there are still those who would say that the architect (librarian) is the librarian's (architect's) worst enemy, and more than one disgruntled client can be heard to mutter (especially if his architect has been a big name) that all the architect was really interested in doing was leaving a monument to himself.

However the program was arrived at, the design in the not-so-good old days would then require the provision of a plan which would be based on having identified the major elements correctly, and then having arranged them efficiently with respect to each other and with great clarity as to the circulation between them. Since the general attitude of the day (not particularly to be blamed on the methods of l'Ecole des Beaux Arts) called for symmetrical arrangements and a certain degree of monumental relations or at least clear hierarchies even in small buildings, there had to be some forcing of the plan. This became much more severe under the American interpretation of the Beaux Arts which in effect assumed that the style of the architectural envelope was also predetermined. Now the plan became forced indeed. If you had a program which called for the arrangement of elements such as had never been found in the Farnese Palace and if, at the same time, you were determined to cast your building in the form of the Farnese Palace, a substantial conflict was almost certain to arise unless the program was also that of a palace. Now the prototype as to form but not function could be twisted around only within a very limited range before its proportions would be irreparably damaged, and in such a contest it was the program which would get pushed around. It was the form of the Farnese Palace that would emerge the victor and the library which would emerge the defeated. This philosophy was really accepted by most, perhaps all, of the American schools until at least the end of the first quarter of our century. It is not wholly abandoned yet. Most good architects would assert and even believe that the form of the building should not be predetermined but should flow from an intelligent provision for the needs in the plan and structure. In practice it is not quite so simple as that. I know of many buildings where distinguished architects have conceptualized a form, not at the outset of a design but possibly in mid course, and thereafter have been unable to deviate very much from the expression; once this Rubicon is crossed, it is inevitable that subsequent maneuvering will be aimed to preserve the expression even if some of the functions have to be as distorted as they became in McKim's Boston Public Library. Though they would heatedly deny it, the fact is that most of our best-known and most highly regarded designers do practice what Paul Rudolph preaches (and practices): "Function follows form."

There is a difference between this and the attitude of the early twentieth century. Then the architect had an extant and specific example in mind which he began to try to fit the program into—usually, if not always, a Renaissance or early Baroque palace. He might toy with the details somewhat and perhaps even invent some. He understood the form principles of the buildings he was imitating well enough so that he could do his own details quite in the spirit of the model, though scarcely ever quite as well. But he also understood the style he was using well enough so that he knew he could not indulge in gross manipulation of the proportions, the rhythms, the scale. (Later on when the architect, still eclectic, had less sensitivity to scale he distorted Georgian architecture, for example, into multistory buildings, thus denying the Georgian, if perhaps serving the Harvard program a little better.) These limitations severely cramped the program from the outset.

Today most of the best architects of whose methods I have any inkling do not freeze their idea of the envelope at the outset. They do manipulate flow diagrams, and ultimately more detailed and alternative ways of satisfying the program. But since three-dimensional form, which springs from the plan and from structural skeletons and utility networks, cannot be postponed to the end and put on like a suit of clothes, elevations and perspectives and rough three-dimensional study models do begin to emerge long before the client sees anything. They have to exist before the client sees them because no first-rate architect wishes to offer his client four or five alternative choices as he would be offered a number of necklaces, discreetly displayed for comparison on a jeweler's counter. He wishes to go to the client with one proposal that he believes is the best— hoping the client will agree. If not, then he will go back and amend his first proposal or present a quite new one depending upon the circumstances and the depth of the first rejection.

As these study models and alternate plans develop, there comes a day when the designer has developed a clear front-runner in his own mind. It does not matter here how much the decision is rational and how much irrational. Thereafter, barring a disastrous and obvious planning blunder which forces a reconsideration of the basic envelope, minor discrepancies will be accepted in favor of the greater good of the convincing envelope and will even be rationalized as not being defects at all.

This process differs from the old one in two important ways. First, the preconception of the envelope is delayed. Secondly, when it is formed it arises from the conditions of the plan and not from the image of a specific precedent building which is now to be copied as closely as possible.

Of course there will be major influences from the work of others but it will be mainly from the work of contemporaries and not from historic figures. The shadow of the skeletons of Mies, of the plastic forms of Le Corbusier or of the honeycombs he used in his various Unités d'Habitation, the brickwork of Alvar Aalto, will have a major effect on the taste of the individual designers, even those who are trying hardest to be independent innovators. But it will be the spirit of the system which lies in reserve and not the recollection of Seagram's Building, Ronchamp, Eveux, or Saitsauna. This is quite different than starting with the idea of imitating the Ricciardi Palace, the Ca d'Oro in Venice, or the Butter Tower at Rouen. Insofar as these two attitudes provoke a desire for travel, most of the reasons for and probably most of the specific targets of the architectural itinerary will be different.

Returning to that first problem of my school days, the Orangerie in a Park, I recall that one of my friends and colleagues, now dead, had a remarkably rational and simple solution to the problem. The orange trees ought to be easily got into their winter storage. There was no requirement in the program that they be available for viewing as they might be in a conservatory. The temperature and the humidity ought to be nearly constant. This could be most economically provided in 1920 by having the storeroom or rooms sufficiently far underground—sufficiently far did not imply an impossibility or even an absurdity. To reach the rooms he then provided ramps of comfortable slope on four quadrants of the compass. He paid skillful attention to the architectural problem of the meeting of the side walls of the ramps with the ground plane but with an undecorated straightforward geometry. He topped the storage room with a very flat truncated stepped pyramid of a few steps.

His grade was F. What the faculty had expected every child should know was that the solution shrieked for an imitation of an adequately sized wing of the Petit Trianon or perhaps a diminished Orangerie from Versailles. Though it did not say so, what the program was asking for was a well-rendered copy of a first-class Renaissance or Baroque building of appropriate size with a fleeting side glance at the orange-tree tubs. This was not explicitly in the program presented, but we soon enough got the message.

The first problem then was the selection of an appropriate style, normally Renaissance, or some other version of classic, commonly enough Georgian or Romanesque or Gothic, only rarely Byzantine, Islamic, Japanese, and only in extreme cases Cambodian or Egyptian. The genius of Henry Hobson Richardson had left many monuments of the 1880s before our New England eyes by 1919 right in Boston, but the going interpretation was that this was a gigantic reinterpretation for modern needs of some of the visual if not the structural and functional expressions of the Romanesque. I am by no means convinced today that this was not a truer analysis than the spate of later literature which has set Richardson up as the great anticipator of the modern revolution. As Trinity Church with its recollections of Arles stood at one corner of our vision from the Rogers building on Boylston Street where we studied, so McKim's Renaissance palace of the Boston Public Library stood in the center, and in the other corner, the modestly Italianate campanile of Old South Church.

Downtown there were excellent Federal things—the State House by Bulfinch, Faneuil Hall, and others, which, together with some of the older buildings in the Harvard Yard and Peter Harrison's churches, King's Chapel downtown, and Christ Church in Cambridge, represented the only historic style in which America had then had a chance to participate in anything other than a revivalist way. Farther afield were the fine historic wooden houses which adorned and still do adorn the peripheral towns. Just across the way there were intimations of new ideas in Despradelle's iron-skeleton, terra-cotta clad, large-windowed Berkeley Building, which was really as prescient of the future as the flashier Hallidie Building done in San Francisco by Willis Polk in 1912. Boston's was a goodly environment, one scarcely to be matched anywhere else in America where there was a leading architectural school unless it were to be at Columbia in New York and Pennsylvania at Philadelphia, both of which were then presided over by staunch supporters of the Beaux Arts and supported, as were M.I.T. and Harvard, by well-known imported French critics.

But the environment was naturally not so rich in prime examples as were to be found in Europe, especially in England, France, and Italy, which were at that time the main ports of call for architectural travel, although Spain had been rediscovered by Ralph Adams Cram (Granada and Burgos, but not the Barcelona of Gaudi). The Low Countries always had tagged along in Gothic connection to France, especially in respect to mourned ruins of the World War I such as Louvain, the Belfry of Bruges, or the Cloth Hall at Ypres. Baroque was not held in high esteem, Rhenish Gothic considered inferior, the Bavarian Angst was thought corny, and the north brick architecture of Lübeck, Königsberg, and Bremen was largely unknown. Germany stood low on a list on which the Scandinavian countries did not stand at all. Greece was a sentimental journey; Italy was the mine of the Renaissance. The European tour had to be made then to find the examples to be copied. With respect to all styles preceding the

Georgian, there were no originals to be found at home; but it was generally conceded, usually though not always correctly, that the best examples even of Georgian were to be found in England and not at home. The shift of affection, just before the cataclysmic revolution, was going away from the Renaissance to the Gothic, admired for its romantic appearance and for its structural "honesty," but for many building types the Gothic envelope was so clearly unsuitable that the Renaissance could not be emptied from the bag. Though the finest Renaissance was certainly in Italy, the finest Romanesque and Gothic were believed to be in France. The French Classical Baroque would do in a pinch. Given deans who had studied in and loved France, French critics, French food, French wine, World War I, the Lafayette Escadrille, the boulevards of Paris, and so on, it was inevitable that however widely it might extend, the architectural hub was France.

Among the practicing architects there was a difference of opinion about the scope of eclecticism. There were those who thought the architect should be able to design in any style, according to its appropriateness and the client's taste. They had to range from Cordoba to Venice and from Rome to Durham. There were others who felt that an architect of sensibility and conscience could not love all styles equally and that a man could understand and design well only in the styles he loved. They became Renaissance specialists or Gothic specialists and later "Spanish" specialists, and you selected your man at least partly in terms of the architecture you wanted to get. This was reasonable and it is still valid. You should not expect Lou Kahn or Marcel Breuer to produce a Kevin Roche or Gordon Bunshaft or I. M. Pei building for you or vice versa. But your choice now is much more personal and only loosely related to vaguely defined current "styles" such as Brutalism. On the whole the best buildings of the eclectic period were made by the men who had chosen a side and not by those who insisted that eclecticism should not be selective.

But these were the practitioners whom our teachers discussed in varying degrees of awe or reverence. Some of us, already discontent, were off on different tacks, looking at the Stockholm City Hall, the Dutchmen like Deklerk or Dudok, more uncertainly at Le Corbusier, very dimly in 1920 at Gropius but with considerable respect for the state capital at Lincoln by Goodhue. Later we were all fired up because Eliel Saarinen had won only the second prize in the Chicago Tribune Tower Competition. As I reflect now, we had a very mixed-up idea that something was wrong with eclecticism and a suspicion that someone somewhere had the right new "message." But we did not know who or where.

Still if an American student were going to move ahead at all in that moment, he was unlikely to think of rushing off to Bauhaus or even to Taliesin. He complained, he joined conspiratorial seances, he was sassy to the younger conventional critics, he made fun of the professor of architectural history who misread Le Corbusier, and the other one who had never heard of Alvar Aalto; he succeeded in getting a few new periodicals into the library, he grabbed Paul Nelson or Frederick Kiesler or Antonin Raymond if they were near. He did not have the written word of Giedion or the spoken torrent of Bucky Fuller, much less the ideas of McLuhan and Robert Venturi, to lead him ahead or even astray. He still hoped and prepared for the Grand Tour, which was not really to follow a different path from that of his predecessors. He knew that he, and indeed most of us, would manage it, some on lush traveling fellowships, won by the flashiest presenters who were more often than not the most brilliant if not always the most thoughtful designers. The rest of us would make out as best we could and most of us made out. Meanwhile there were the plates.

All decent architectural school libraries, as well as the libraries of the larger architectural firms, were crammed with enormous and handsome photographs and drawings, often measured drawings, of the noteworthy European architectural monuments, and a few of other monuments, especially Oriental ones. In addition to that there were huge files of mounted photographs and drawings, one per mount so that a group could be assembled at will. These were frankly expected to serve a much more concrete purpose than simply as a resource through which one might browse in search of a general atmosphere or a serendipitous inspiration.

Indeed when the designer got down to the brass tacks of his envelope, in office or in studio alike, you would usually find a selection of plates littering his board or tacked up before him. And when we went to Europe one of the major pragmatic results that was anticipated was a collection of sketches, not for exhibition or sale but a kind of personally collected notebook of visual data that might conveniently serve in a very practical way on some later occasion.

I think that this use of architectural history and architectural artifacts as a mine of details to be lifted and inserted into whatever of the new architectural fabric was your own was a very wrong-headed use which could even be called immoral if one felt happy about such terms in relation to the arts.

This is in fact exactly what the revolution found it to be. The revolution moved with great speed after the Hitler-provoked diaspora, after some of the great Europeans settled here and others came frequently to build, to talk, to teach. At the time it seemed to all of us who were working, each in his own way, to bring it about, that it was moving very slowly and indeed might not prevail at all. But things were softer at the core than we believed, and so in retrospect the shift now seems to me to have been very fast indeed. I do not intend to talk here about the revolution, its fits and starts, its consequences, but only upon one detail of it that is related to architectural travel.

Affronted by the damage the wrong use of history seemed to have done to architectural thinking, the new skippers abolished the history courses, in some cases completely. Distressed by the wrong use of the plates as ore from mines instead of general background, they literally destroyed or at least threw away thousands of well-nigh irreplaceable plates; they consigned many of the great tomes to the pulp mill or at best to deep storage. They acted in all this with the best of intentions but with all the unhappy zeal of the Jesuit priest who immolated the Mayan codices, or the Hugenots and the Cromwellians who tore the saints' statues from the church facades as high as their ladders would reach.

In the beginning travel for architectural reasons was gently discouraged, although the leaders were forgetting the enthusiasm with which Le Corbusier had saluted the Acropolis. This phase did not last long, but the routes of the travel were drastically changed. The roads of the pilgrims now led to Finland, Sweden, Denmark, Germany, to the places where the best examples of the most contemporary architects' work could be seen.

If it was all right to see the new models and to be influenced by them, even to using clips from the latest architectural journals instead of the unlamented vanished old plates, it was still contended in some quarters that the young and impressionable should not make the European journey lest they realize how impressive the old work was and be discouraged from being architects since they could never hope to equal it in contemporary terms! This was, of course, nonsense. Courageous contemporaries have not been discouraged from composing because of the stature of Bach, Beethoven, and Mozart, or of writing because of the achievements of Chaucer, Shakespeare, and Milton. Only the brave should enter the lists of the arts anyway.

Gradually we have crept back to sanity. History has been restored to the architectural curricula; travel is no longer discouraged or limited to Scandinavia though there may be a slight bias in favor of Vällingby in Sweden, Tapiola in Finland, and the New Towns of England. Gradually and at considerable cost and difficulty, we are restoring photographs of old work to the looted library files.

But the purposes of travel have been changed and we may hope beneficially. Here and there Japanese or Mayan patterns may seem to have crept into a design; of two "name" architects in America, unkind observers have suggested that they may have sat too long in the moon before the Taj Mahal. But where imitation remains, it is usually imitation of some revered contemporary, such, for example, as Lou Kahn, and this is no different from what happened in the days of the High Renaissance or the High Gothic or the High Baroque when a few men rang the changes and many worked in the same vein and as well as they could.

How long this may continue it is idle to try to predict. What values can we say there are in architectural travels for those who are also architects, nascent or matured? It is not to find explicit solutions hidden away to cope with a contemporary problem. It is not to find explicit art or decoration which can be applied to a new building. It is not to find any forms beyond the most basic which are so fundamental that they appear in every architecture and could be rediscovered now if we did not see them in the past. It is not to learn how to arrange modern space or how to connect modern spaces though here some questions do arise. If the space of the Piazza San Marco is conveniently "human," can we safely double all its dimensions, the human size being constant, and expect a similarly happy outcome in Washington, D.C.? If the Champs Elysées is a pleasant street, what will be the case for an avenue in Brasilia which is much wider, much longer in uninterrupted vista, defined by much taller buildings? The old will not answer such questions but it can reasonably raise them.

It has never hurt any artist to be reminded from time to time that there were brave men before Agamemnon. The vague but central purpose of such travel has to be to understand, to venerate, perhaps to love; to be impelled not to imitate but at most to emulate the great builders of the past by seeking as high standards for the employment of our materials and our technology in achieving our goals as they did in achieving theirs.

The architecture of the past may not serve us well at all in our functional problems. We have no such clear priorities as to what is important as we think the men of most other times did have. We are a little like the men in Cowper's *Conversations* who "built God a church, and laughed his word to scorn." We have a wider stretch of needs. A commercial society may well feel an urge to be in constant state of seeking novelty. But explanations are not defenses. We might as well face the fact that most of the contemporary architectural confections which we oh and ah at and which serve as conversation pieces in so many circles are of no interest whatever to people in Harlem or Watts, the laboring people, to country-folk, or to most of our disenchanted young. This is so much the case that sometimes social critics have been led to wonder whether Architecture with a large A is even relevant to our times. Although we have a number of incipient Bernini's in our midst, vying for public acclaim, is it possible that we do not need them at all?

Let us not be carried away by this in our rush to find a "people's" architecture, something that no previous society, save perhaps the Greeks, seems earnestly to have sought, and they only in public buildings.

The more we search architectural history for an architecture of the poor relevant to our times, the more despairing we shall become. The poor were always there, and the Egyptians for example uttered pious sentiments about them, but not much was done for them. There are no examples of great public housing save perhaps for the little *Fuggerei* of Augsburg, or a few special small towns like Freudenstadt, but there are many infamous examples such as the *insulae* of Rome or the tenements of Crassus. The Middle Ages occasionally produced a *hôtel-dieu*. And churches may have offered the poor a chance to see great art which they could not view in private palaces. (Indeed the church itself was in part an architecture for the poor, although in all too many instances they were not allowed in the shrine or even to observe what was going on in it.) The Egyptians let them witness the great processions from Luxor to Karnak. The Greeks encouraged their participation in the Panathenaic processions and provided them some good seats in the theaters. The Romans gave them doles of grain, put on great shows for them, and afforded them access to the public baths. But even after Marie Antoinette's possibly apocryphal remark about eating cake and her subsequent beheading, little changed until the beginning of this century, when the *Siedlungen* were conceived in Germany, Switzerland, Austria, and a little later in Scandinavia—good but too little and too late. Otherwise what architectural history will show is various versions of keeping the people quiet, of *panem et circenses*, of different kinds of opiates. Historical architectural travel essentially offers no informing precedents about what to do about one of the pressing problems of our time.

The obvious conclusion is that the performance has never been good enough in the past, not even in some alleged and nonexistent Golden Age, and that it is certainly not good enough now in an age which none of us should have the temerity to call Golden. In our time the architectural performance in behalf of the poor is superior to that of the United States in such semisocialized nations as Finland and Sweden and also in the Federal Republic of Germany, but even there barely good enough. How we here are to do better as we must do is less easy to say. It will not, in my opinion, be done by achieving consensus of *the People* or by grasping for will-o'-the-wisp innovations such as Habitat '67 or geodesic domes or the complexes of Paolo Soleri, but, if at all, by a major change of national priorities and among first-class architects as to which things come first. And it is more than possible that it cannot be achieved at all by Architecture but only by architecture in which the role of the architect is to produce a comfortable and decent but neutral environment which will permit the occupants to provide their own embellishments, together with a system of incentives for them to do so and, above all, a management whose instinct will be to say "yes" rather than "no."

This is because while architecture has always had to be measured in part by its social significance our definitions of what is socially significant have changed. In his recently published tome, *Ekistics*, Constantinos Doxiadis has stated the situation with clarity and modesty.

> New architecture is a necessity for everybody whereas in the past it was needed only for the well-to-do classes, and even earlier only for monuments, only for kings and gods.[16]

This is a very important statement and each of us needs to decide where we stand on it. Sitting among the monuments of the past, the archi-

---

[16] Constantinos A. Doxiadis, *Ekistics* (New York: Oxford, 1968), p. 7.

tect will not find answers to such questions, but he may have time to reflect upon them. Did his great predecessors overlook the real problems of their day? What did the Pantheon or Versailles have to do with the important things of life? Should the earlier architects have neglected the other problems? How might they have done otherwise than they did? Are the problems Doxiadis states as transcendental as he makes them sound? Does the phrase mean anything in the end? Is our architect, brooding on the Acropolis or in the nave of Chartres, guilty? Is there anything he ought to do about it? What?

If we carry our desire for new social architecture to the extreme we might agree with Matthew Arnold, who called history "the vast Mississippi of falsehood."

The old stones will not act like Sibyls, providing even cryptic answers. But somehow they can provoke the questions as the hurly-burly of 42d Street or the peaceful executives' lounge in a world airport may not.

André Malraux tells how in 1934 Paul Valéry told of a discussion he had had with Gide.

> I am fond of Gide, but how can a man accept young people as judges of what he thinks? ... And, then! I am interested in clarity, not in sincerity.[17]

One might not like to put it so cynically. Surely it is not necessary to put sincerity aside in order to achieve lucidity. But in the name of sincerity there is a good deal of muddy thinking. Our times have no monopoly on morality or sincerity whatever youth may think or assert. Surely we who are older have no monopoly on lucidity. Contemporary architects are, if anything, nearer to being sincere than clear. It is not certain even that success may not have clouded some of their sincerity. Perhaps extended architectural travel might restore both to them.

Why should you care what architectural travel might do for architects since you are not one? Because the architecture is made for you, not them, and because, as so often has been remarked, a society will get the architecture it deserves.

Out of other people's reflections or positions we may derive our own similar or opposite ones. If you are bent toward sad thoughts, do the tombs and the churches you meet on your architectural voyage cause you to lament rather about your own times? When Goethe reached Venice and admired the mosaics of the Basilica San Marco, he wrote:

> The art of mosaic which gave the ancients their paved floors, and the Christian the vaulted heavens of their churches has now been degraded to snuff boxes and bracelets. Our times are worse than we think.[18]

---

[17] André Malraux, *Antimémoires* (Paris: Gallimard, 1967), pp. 12–13.
[18] Goethe, *Italian Journey*, op. cit., pp. 79–80.

Or you may be as pessimistic (or as foresighted) as Henry Adams:

Adams more than once sat at sunlight on the steps of the Church of
Santa Maria de Ara Coeli, curiously wondering that not an inch had been
gained by Gibbon—or all the historians since—towards explaining
the Fall. The mystery remained unsolved, the charm remained intact.
Two great experiments of Western Civilization had left there the
chief monuments of their failure, and nothing proved that the city might not
still survive to express the failure of a third.[19]

Gather your quotations where ye may and indulge in reverie or not
as you choose. If you do choose to reflect, join Verdi if you will in thinking
that to look for progress means that you must look to the past or add
to the thought of Focillon that it is the experiments of history "that, bite,
as it were, into the future," the hope that the best experiments are
yet to be.

Make architectural travel purely as a matter of pleasure, for the
greater understanding of people, of the other arts, of the evolution of
building engineering; for reasons of scholarship, professional or amateur,
for professional architectural education or architectural inspiration; as a
form of curiosity about the exotic; or as a stimulus for reflections on our
own times. Put these motivations together into your own mix. This will in
considerable measure determine where you go and how you go. To make
such a mix will require some deliberation, but those who cannot face it are
condemned to flop around, privately or on tour buses, clinging to perhaps
charming but surely inadequate private conceits. But even if you are
going merely to flop, it is time to start.

[19] Henry Adams, *The Education of Henry Adams* (New York: Modern Library, 1940),
pp. 90–91.

CHAPTER FOUR

ON WHAT TO LOOK FOR AND WHERE TO FIND IT

You were made for enjoyment, and the world was filled with things which you will enjoy, unless you are too proud to be pleased with them, or too grasping to care for what you can not turn to other account than mere delight.

John Ruskin
Stones of Venice
vol. I, chap. II, sec. 2

ON WHAT TO LOOK FOR

What will we look for when we come face to face with some building we have chosen to meet? Surely we need to know something of why it was made and what it was for and this we ought probably to sense before we get there. Then we need to know *how* it was made, at least in general. It is interesting if you care about it to study the economics of architecture—how could they possibly afford it? What did it cost them to make it? What did they give up to achieve it? And if one cared to avoid moralizing about how other people have elected to spend their money, it might be rewarding. It is interesting to look at the sociology of architectures. Were the workers free or slaves? Innovative or routine-minded? Did they sing at their work? Did they have pride? But you do not need to know any of these things to take delight in a building.

To see how a building was made we need to know first how to read a plan and a section so that we have working graphic guides. We need to know in general the structural problems that existed and how they were met since the engineering necessity

71

always limits what a building may be, though not necessarily how it expresses itself.

Then we can begin to examine the building itself, first as to its main elements—its front, its sides, its back, the impression of mass it provides, if it does. We can go in and sense the nature of the space it suggests, if it does. We can move from the largest space to the smaller elements of space, of structure, that help to define and negate or emphasize the space. And since great buildings generally are connected to important sculpture and painting and ordinarily have details that themselves are interesting, we can pursue this into however small minutiae we finally elect to observe.

Now no one goes at a building quite that methodically I would suppose or holds his emotions under so iron a discipline. The eye will wander, the mind will wander. The light is not as you want it, the weather is unfavorable outside (or overly favorable). The building is not peopled, and so you cannot envision it as you ought, or it is overly peopled with the wrong people, which has the same result. Or your feet hurt, or time has run out, or something is locked and the sacristan has gone away, or a big section is under renovation and covered with scaffolding or closed, or you may just not be feeling well. Then you have to be flexible and put things together as best you can until another day. That is the reality of visiting an actual building. On paper we can be somewhat more systematic.

But how to be systematic? One dreary way would be to talk about many approaches, many facades, many interiors, all in bunches in a sort of colloquium on comparative architecture. I think this is not very useful.

What I propose to do instead is first to provide some preliminary pedagogy: What is a plan, a section, an elevation? What are the programs? What are the main building materials? What does each offer of advantage and disadvantage? How have the disadvantages been minimized and the advantages been exploited, especially in terms of the structures which emerged?

Of architecture, the epigrammatic Le Corbusier once asserted that "the plan is the generator." This is very nearly true but it may be elliptical. A good plan will be a satisfaction of the program, and from it surely springs the architecture. But in the beginning and before there is the plan, there must be the program. The program, then, is the generator and the plan the first offspring—the sire so to speak which, married with the structure, engenders the building.

The Program

Few, if any, important works of architecture have been designed with no purpose at all in mind—and on the whole very few have been designed with frivolous purposes. If the building is a successful one, the program may be clear from the plan and certainly should become clear when you visit the building even without a guide. This at least should be true for a contemporary building. If the visitor knows his own times and can guess pretty well at what was reasonably needed, and if the architect has done well and has not sacrificed the working of the plan to some other objective, then the contemporary and perceptive stranger should be able to move without much or even any direction, at least to the principal spaces, and to understand why they are where they are and approximately why they are what they are.

A building in which a visitor seeking only to understand its architecture can get lost or can miss something truly important without a thicket of signs to tell him where he is and keep him going straight to where he wants to go is a bad building and is the consequence of one the following: an accumulation of expedients appended over time as in the rabbit warrens of the Massachusetts General Hospital or, for that matter, of Canterbury Cathedral; or an accumulation of a range of activities inside a flexible shell, in which no one has been able to assign clear priorities on the plan; *or* a failure of the architect to achieve mastery over the necessities and the emphasis of his program. I cite no examples here because you can find them almost everywhere you look in a world where clear and forceful buildings, such as the new City Hall in Boston, are the exception and not the norm.

When we come to an historical building, although its statement may be and usually is clear, it is by no means so obvious how well it satisfied its purpose. That is because we are not ancient Romans or Greeks or Incas and nothing can make us so. We cannot understand a mosque even in a superficial way if we understand nothing of Islam, of Mahomet, of the Koran. We cannot even do well by more recent ancestors of what was possibly our own blood and certainly in our own line of political and religious evolution. You will not make much of a Greek or Roman temple if you can think of architecture only as enclosed space or of religion only in congregational-pastoral terms. You cannot make full sense out of a closed Gothic choir if you think religion begins and ends in a New England meeting house.

So if architectural viewing is to go beyond the ohing and ahing stage, the need to know something about the program becomes pressing—and as we move further back into history, the pressure becomes greater.

I do not mean by this to make light of the ecstasy of ignorance. There are a few monuments in the world—in Isfahan, say, or Agra, or Istanbul, the Pyramids of Gizeh, or the Pont-du-Gard near Nîmes—which are capable of casting a magic spell on almost anyone. But like other works of man, few works of architecture have achieved such a transcendental power. For all the marvelous rest, sheer basking in their effulgence is likely to be limited in its rewards.

Yet the problem of transporting one's imagination over the centuries to another time and therefore a different place than the one in which we now stand to examine, say, an early Byzantine church, is very difficult in anything other than intellectual terms. The hardest thorn to grasp is surely that which involves symbolism. Consider, for example, the relation of Byzantine symbolism to the very plan itself, so well described by Richard Krautheimer.

> As early as 630, Maximus the Confessor presents an interpretation of the church building and of the liturgy it houses. The entire church is an image of the Universe, of the visible world and of man; within it the chancel represents man's soul, the altar his spirit, the naos his body. The bishop's entrance into the Church symbolizes Christ's coming into the flesh, his entrance into the bema, Christ's Ascension to Heaven. The Great Entrance stands for Revelation, the Kiss of Peace for the Union of the Soul with God; indeed every part of the liturgy has a symbolic spiritual meaning.
>
> About 700, Germanos the patriarch of Constantinople, summed up ideas presumably current for some time and which continued as late as the fourteenth century. The church building to him was the Temple of the Lord: the sacred precinct, the Heaven where God resides, the sacred cave where Christ was buried and whence He rose, the place where the mystical sacrifice is offered. The chancel, in particular, and the altar (the two are used interchangeably) was viewed as the Seat of Mercy. They were the manger of Christ, His tomb, and also the Table of the Last Supper. Equally, they were seen as the Heavenly Altar on which the hosts of Angels offer the eternal sacrifice. The apse was a symbol of the Cross; the seats of the clergy were the raised site and throne where Christ sat among His disciples. They foretell His second coming and the Last Judgement. The columns of the templon revealed the division between the assembly of the people and the Holy of Holies where the clergy gathered; the architrave over these columns symbolized the Cross. The canopy with its four columns stood for the site of the Crucifixion, and also for the four ends of the earth. Finally, the dome represented Heaven. . . .
>
> [No] . . . doubt, only a small group of laymen was fully conscious of all this sophisticated symbolism. The general ideas, however, permeated to a wider public. In entering the church, the average believer was aware, we may be sure, that he entered Heaven; and he saw, in the procession of the clergy, the angelic host about to offer the sacrifice on the Heavenly altar.[1]

We are obviously already in quite deep water, deeper than you may wish to wade in. But the hard facts are that the symbolism is of serious importance in the understanding of these churches—and that it does not spring out at you when you enter the church unprepared. It is obscure or even meaningless without more explanation than the building itself can

---

[1] Krautheimer, *Early Christian and Byzantine Architecture*, op. cit., pp. 212 ff.

offer you. Yet if you know about it, it adds immeasurably to your understanding—yes and appreciation—of the building.

The problem of the symbol is only a little less difficult when the symbol is stated fairly explicitly in concrete visual terms, as in Romanesque and Gothic iconography. You can look at an aspic cowering beneath the feet of Christ on a French cathedral as nothing more than a skillful if meaningless piece of carving, sufficiently rewarding if it is graceful or even charming. You can look at the pained face of a prophet of the Ancient Law on the north porch of the cathedral of Chartres simply as a great portrayal in stone of medieval Jewishness, or in a more general way of human suffering, anguish, or wonderment. But surely something is added when you know *why* Christ is standing on the aspic; or what the aspic is telling us when he presses one ear to the ground and curls his pointed tail in the other so that he may not hear unwanted words; or when we know why Ezekiel is on the north porch instead of the south, what the planned parallelism between the prophets of the Ancient Law and the apostles of the New is, how the entire Old Testament is construed as offering analogous portents and precursors of the events of the New, how the Flood, the lions of Daniel, the whale of Jonah, the pelican who pierces her own breast, all prefigure the Resurrection; and perhaps most of all, how the whole is wrapped into that early ecumenical promise, so often since betrayed, of the Nouvelle Alliance. All this was part of the program.

Obviously there is a great deal here that the building alone cannot reveal to the untutored eye. Surely one can know too little about a building he is about to visit; very likely he can also know too much. There is a fine knife edge on which to walk, and the discussion of this warrants some serious treatment. But let us defer it until later.

The summary is that a building may be enigmatic even when you might fancy that it is not. I repeat, architecture cannot escape the necessity of purpose; it is the real or the presumed purpose that has allowed the plan to be the generator, the structure to be the implementer, the elevations and the details to be the emphasizers. If we try to imagine a Panathenaic procession in terms of an Inaugural Parade; if we whip up some notion of the Great Pyramid simply as a monumental statement of power squeezed from the bloody backs of slaves; if all our views of all these buildings start from a WASPish, a Jewish, a black, or some other bias, we will miss most of the architectural experience. It does not matter much which the prejudice.

I do not mean to propose that some untutored hearts may not leap up simply on viewing the blue glass of Chartres, or the tiles and mosaics of the Maidan Square, or the ruined temples lining the ridge at Agrigentum. I do not even mean to insist that it really matters very much what any one of us may choose ignorantly to conclude, so long as we realize we are indulging in fantasy. In the matter of architectural viewing I am confident that the reality is fantasy enough, that no Camelots or Xanadus are necessary as props.

Although there are classifiable types, such as the Gothic cathedrals of the Île de France, the mastabas of Thebes, the Greek temples of the Aegean, within which the major elements of the program are the same, in a limited sense every piece of architecture has a unique program. But over all architectural history, a few classifiable types of general programs have been dominant at least among the buildings which have survived. Though there are many accidents involved in architectural survival, it is a safe generalization that the buildings which survived were usually of the more durable materials and that the use of durable materials suggests that the builders thought the buildings to be important.

Between 4000 B.C. and A.D. 1800 there were some 700 architecturally distinguished buildings still extant. Most of these can be found in the Index, severally and under their styles; in large cities they will also be found listed under that rubric, e.g., Rome.

Suppose we were to try to classify these into rough groups according to purpose. The fringes of some of the classifications are bound to be fuzzy, but the number of examples in the fringes are not enough to affect the general conclusions.

The overlaps may be most noticeable in villas and palaces; a princely building may in part have been a place of business or a place of government or both; a Mogul "fort" was many things, including a mosque; a monastery might also be a hospital or a school.

Certainly too there were ups and downs locally and in time. One might even find moments such as a century or two in Imperial Rome where the weight in public service or amusement could be comparable to that of today, or in the Netherlands Renaissance when the commercial building loomed as large. But I am not trying for trends here or even a refined analysis. The breakdown given below is a fair account of the past. We can be confident what the emphasis of human aspirations in architecture has been through most of architectural history. Before 1800 the distribution would have looked like this:

Building Distribution Before 1800 (percent)	
Religious	
Churches, Temples, Mosques, Shrines, Precincts, Monasteries	59
Tombs	3
Total	62
Government and Power	
Forts, Castles, Walled Towns	6
Royal Palaces	5
Monuments	2
Total	13

Building Distribution Before 1800 (percent)	
Civic	
Public Squares, Town Halls, Hospitals, Schools	10
Theaters, Circuses, Baths	2
Bridges, Aqueducts	1
Total	13
Private	
Houses, Villas, Manors, Unfortified Chateaux, Palazzi	11
Commercial	1
Total	12

Religious architecture accounts for about three-fifths of all significant architectural remains of the period between 4000 B.C. and A.D. 1800. The other two-fifths are divided about equally among the architecture of government and power, the architecture of civic affairs, and the architecture of private persons and of commerce.

But after 1800 and especially after 1900 there occurred a marked change in emphasis. A distribution based on a list of about 200 major buildings from 1800 to 1969 looks like this:

Building Distribution After 1800 (percent)	
Religious	
Ecclesiastical	8
Memorials	3
Total	11
Government and Power	
Government Buildings (used by government other than services)	10
Palaces	0
Total	10
Civic Services	
Public Amusement and Recreation (Theaters, Galleries, Exhibitions, Parks, however financed)	16
Transport (Stations, Airports, Hangars)	6
Bridges, Power Stations, etc.	4
Education (public and private); Hospitals	15
Total	41
Private	
Residences (private)	11
Collective, however financed	7
Office Buildings	11
Factories	3
Commercial	6
Total	38

A comparison of the two tables is startling:

	Pre–1800	Post–1800
Religious	62%	11%
Government and Power	13	10
Civic	13	41
Private	12	38
Total	100%	100%

So much for programs. As we look at buildings together, or as you later look at them for yourself, we should try to keep in mind what the desired program was. It should help us to understand its offspring, the plan.

The Plan
What is a building plan? It is the drawing of the main elements you would see if you were to cut a horizontal slice through a building and then look down upon it. If you know how to read it, it will be a powerful tool in the understanding of a building before you come to it, and in reflecting upon it after you have come away. Indeed it is not too much to say that you will achieve very little knowledge of architecture if you have not mastered the simple art of interpreting a plan.

This plan map will help you to anticipate, to get around, and to remember. It will explain many things but not everything. It may ascend to sheer geometric beauty as a thing in itself; and when it is looked on that way it will not matter perhaps if it is the plan of a building which was never built, or if it promises pleasures beyond those which the actual building provides. But this is an aesthetic which derives from architecture, and is incidental to it, and it is not of central importance.

For the architect the plan is something more. In some architectures of the past when traditions of building were well established, when craftsmen were skillful and eager partners of an architect who may have been no more than the senior man among them, when there were no questions of competitive bids or "fair competitive prices," and no pretense about trying to save money for the public weal (since the public weal was not construed mainly in fiscal terms), there may have been very little in the way of formal plans. A few lines scratched in the sand may have sufficed to start the builders, and the architect standing constantly by would have corrected deviations or even modified ideas as the structure rose. Later on in the Middle Ages, when the architect wore gloves to show he no longer did the physical mason's work, it may have been enough for the master masons to know the spacing of the columns and the desired heights of the bay. This was especially true in the fully developed Gothic where there was an accepted and understood relation between the horizontal and the vertical geometry. If one lacks that understanding, the interpretation of the visual appearance of a Gothic building solely from its plan is more difficult, say, than "reading" the Romanesque. Even as late an architect as Henry Hobson Richardson (1880s) could go to his buildings and change things for the better as the building grew, even though by then there were plans and drawings. These were often unusually handsome, as the specimens of the work of Richardson and Frank Lloyd Wright reveal.

Today things are much changed even in the conceptual stage. Architects, at least the most talented, still draw free sketches early on principally as messages to themselves and their close colleagues, though perhaps less masterfully and less commonly than in the days of Erich Mendelssohn. In studying the problem, however, they do many things their predecessors did not do. This is not so much the case for churches, houses, and the like, but for buildings which are technologically complicated or sequentially oriented, such as hospitals, airports, city halls, factories, universities. They make flow diagrams before they make plans; they make sketch plans, not all of which are seen by the client; they prepare preliminary plans and other drawings which will more or less explain to the client what he is probably going to get; and after he has approved these, the architect makes numerous other plans. These plans are often overlays of "tradesman's work"—heating and ventilating, power and lighting (electrical) fixed equipment, special services (piping), plumbing, as well as the numerous details for finish, and the like. These are accompanied by voluminous specifications drawn as carefully as possible to ensure that all the contractors who bid competitively will be bidding on precisely the same work (which, in fact, they never quite do).

The architectural plan we are talking of here, however, is different from the plethora of plans of a contemporary building and the nonplans of early buildings. It is a diagram by which we can begin to "read" the building, and it will not be much different in scope whether it is of the Choragic monument of Lysicrates in Athens in 335 B.C., or Eero Saarinen's Kresge Chapel in Cambridge, Massachusetts in A.D. 1954. In addition to the horizontal "slice," a plan may also show the mosaic design of a floor or a "reflected" ceiling to show the vaulting. It cannot, of course, show both simultaneously, but if the plan is a regular one this too can be done by devoting one-half of it to one subject, the second half to the other.

It will be evident immediately that this plan is not providing all the necessary basic information. It shows, for example, the shape of the openings where the horizontal plane has been cut. But how do we know that the windows are rectangular and not oval in elevation? How do we know how high above the ground their sills are and their lintels? How do we get the same information about the door? The plan does not tell us about an arch above the lintel.

To get this basic information without hundreds of horizontal sections, we need one or sometimes two additional pictures of these cuts made by vertical sections. The one along the longer axis will be called the longitudinal section; the one along the shorter axis, the transverse section. If the building is symmetrical to both axes there is of course no longer a definition by dimension, but usually one axis or the other is more dominant in its interior arrangements (e.g., an altar, throne, etc.), and this principal axis we will call longitudinal. If we combine drawings of the horizontal cut (plan) with those of the two vertical cuts (longitudinal and transverse sections), we will begin to get a good deal of information.

Evidently we need all three (and sometimes more) if we are going to study a building in advance or retrospect. A multistoried building, for example, will require plans of each floor for the builder or mason, but whether we as observers of the architecture need these will depend on how much variation there is from floor to floor and how fundamental this variation is. It is likely, for example, to be very noticeable in domestic or palatial arrangements and less so in multistory office buildings, where we do not really care too much about the distribution of secretaries, general managers, and chairmen of the board, but may care about the auditorium, the refectory, and the library, if any.

The plan is insufficient in another and even more important way. It tells us very little about the vertical shape. The same elemental plan, for example, emerges from any rectangular height. A circular plan might support a cylinder, a cone, or a dome. We must leave this information for sections or elevations.

An accessory drawing appearing occasionally but perhaps not often enough in expository books on architecture consists in adding to, say, a transverse section a projection either isometric or perspective of what lies beyond the plane where the section was cut. A good and familiar example is the speculative reconstruction of the old basilican church of Saint Peter in Rome (see Plate 15). If one combines this with a plan, he can learn possibly much of what he needs to know, although, naturally, a drawing of the exterior carries us still further.

There is no doubt then that in *studying* a building we need the guidance of more maps than the plan. Sections and elevations are important enough to justify treatment of their own. But if, for the moment, we limit ourselves to the study of the plan, we can be comforted by knowing that it is the space, the elevations, and to some extent the sections which we *see*; it is the plan which, as earthbound mortals, we lay our feet upon and through which we move. Thus the plan remains the generator not only of the architecture but of our movement through it.

Pl. 22 Let us start with the simplest possible examples of plans—the idealized forms, say, of two Greek temple types. The first shows us quite clearly what the building is: a rectangular room surrounded by unbroken walls, entered by a single door at one end. The side walls project beyond the room and enclose on two sides a porch. The outer edge of this porch is supported by two columns and these columns are reflected on the lateral walls by pilasters. The whole rests on a platform (thin outer line) which is called a *stylobate*. This is called a temple *in antis*. The second plan is only a little more complicated. The room is longer and narrower. It still has only one door. The side walls project at both ends to provide two porches *in antis*. The whole is surrounded by a single row of columns and the platform now has three steps, which became the usual convention. This is called a peripteral temple. Now to be sure these do not tell everything one would need to know, but given also an understanding of the general principles and proportions of classical Greek temples it is not difficult to imagine the rest. Nor are the variations hard to distinguish from the plans.

Pl. 23

Pl. 25

Such plans can also do much to give us a quick understanding of major differences, as we can see if we place side by side the plans of the typical Greek temple, the temple of Aphaia, and the typical Roman temple, the Maison Carrée at Nîmes.

Pl. 27
Pl. 28
Pl. 26

Trajan's Forum in Rome offers an apt example of a very orderly hierarchical design. An individual element of the complex, such as the basilica, offers few difficulties. One sees the simple monumentality of the whole. There is the great central entrance from the Forum with two flanking entrances on each side, some approached by steps, and the two at the ends leading directly from the colonnades of the Forum; there is the double arcade running around the room (the plan does not tell us it was two-storied); there are the conventional two tribunals at the ends, each raised and reached by steps, the judges and assessors arranged around the hemicycles on a dais with the characteristic altar in front where the sacrifice was offered before transacting business. Then, going further, three passageways lead to the end building which contains a large central, almost open area with two flanking buildings and, in the center, Trajan's Column. The plan does not tell us that Trajan's Column was built to depict and memorialize his victories over the Dacians. It does not tell us of the brilliance of the spirally located carving, that the column was entirely of marble, that it contains about 2,500 figures, that it was about 115 feet high; it does not tell us that the columns separating the nave and the aisles of the basilica were of red granite from Syene, with white marble Corinthian capitals; it does not say that the galleries were only over the side aisles and that above them was a conventional and characteristic clerestory and timber roof. It does not inform us that one of the libraries was for Greek manuscripts and the other for Latin, or that the libraries were probably the only buildings in the Forum complex made of brick— or why.

When we look at the whole plan of Trajan's Forum, of which we now can observe that the basilica is only an important central element, the larger plan also seems to read with great clarity. We can make out the triumphal gateway, the great rectangular court with something in the middle (it was a bronze equestrian statue of the Emperor); we can see long porticos on each long side, and to the right and left of these, separated from the main court by avenues, two immense hemicycles (the plan does not tell us that these were several stories high and accommodated shops and offices). Then we note the Basilica Ulpia at right angles to the axis of the Forum and slightly raised above it. Beyond we see the third important element, a generous enclosure for a large Roman temple.

The plan will impress by its orderliness, its directness, and its relatively simple arrangement of what could have become unduly complex. It will also suggest that the whole thing was fantastically large. The paved open space measured but a little less than 300 by 400 feet, and the total length of the basilica (slightly more than 500 feet) was 1½ times that of the Parthenon.

We can intuit from the plan that by now the Romans of the Empire were quite prepared, even anxious, to interrelate sacred and secular building elements. The plan will not say why. It will not remind us that the temple in Julius Caesar's Forum had been dedicated to the family goddess, Venus Genetrix. It will not explain that it was taken for granted that after his death the Emperor Trajan would himself be worshipped as a god in the temple in his Forum, or that thus, "the temple itself became a glorification, not of religion but of imperial power." It will not tell us for all its persuasiveness as a plan that it was archaic in its engineering, remaining trabeated, while the markets that Trajan was building alongside his Forum were employing the new vaulting techniques. And since I have omitted the plan of Trajan's markets here for clarity, it will not give us any idea of the importance of these markets, one of the great Roman achievements in architecture and urban planning. The markets are much harder to show in simple plans and to talk of them here would be distracting, but they are worth a great deal of study and no better introduction can be found than in William MacDonald's *The Architecture of the Roman Empire*.

So the reading of a plan will not do everything for you but it is an essential start in preparing to understand a building or a congeries of buildings. And with a plan as elaborate as that of Trajan's Forum we can begin to understand some other things.

The powerful impressions of a climax of room sequences evident from the plan of Trajan's Forum has been well understood in most hierarchical architectures from Rome to Kyoto. It has offered greater ideological problems to democracies where leaders must pretend to be humble and seem not to be leading. It is the difference between the triumphal procession of Radames and a furtive advance on an elevator in the Inland Steel Company by a contemporary tycoon, or a university president sneaking into his office by a back door.

An examination of the plan of Trajan's Forum has some advantages over treading the site as it reveals itself today. Only on the plan is it possible to conceive the extent of the dovetailing of the elements. But here again the plan offers a limited experience, not giving a strong enough impression of changes of level and scale, as in the earlier-cited examples, and, especially, of the superhuman scale of the space.

Of course even this cannot be totally experienced on an ancient site. Ruins destroy scale to some extent and space even more and we are prone to conjectures which may err on either side of the reality. The hypostyle of Karnak without its roof is too light inside; the sun shining through demolished walls of the Parthenon may be great for color photography but is deceptive as to how the temple appeared to the Greeks; the great marches of *Aïda* do only a little more for us in the arena at Verona.

A confused plan may not always be evidence of ineptitude, although we tend to think so today. Aristotle praised the confusion (the *labrys*) of the streets of Athens because it was of such great assistance in time of war to the defenders who knew their way around and so confounding to attackers who did not.

This advantage may have seemed worth cultivating in some great palaces of antiquity which were themselves cities and forts as well and therefore might have to be defended from time to time. The palace of Knossos in Crete offers a pat example. It does have a great central court, a principal north entrance, and a general orthagonal arrangement. Yet the overall impression is one of confusion, and the details are hard to remember. The outcome was not axial planning or symmetry—and we cannot know whether it was or was not the consequence of a well-considered program.

We cannot know what the buildings were like before their upper stories were destroyed; we can barely penetrate the complexity of the ground floor. If it was called the Labyrinth by the Greeks, the name was apt whether it was a matter of accident or of design, say by Daedalus for King Minos.

Emily Vermeule goes further to say there may have been spiritual as well as practical reasons for the Minoan disorder. Flat roofs permit a plan to straggle; earthquakes and repairs after them could account for much. It appears to her that the Minoans had no innate objection to disorderly planning as such. They seemed to see no fundamental advantage in symmetry. They may have loved the accidental and the picturesque whatever the consequences; her judgment is that their architecture like their other arts showed little or no sense of form.

By the time a visitor had threaded narrow corridors to the heart of the palace, walking past shadowy walls where lifesize painted figures seemed to move with him, he would feel lost in a maze. Each segment had its logical order, but connections between them seemed haphazard; recesses, stairways, dark passages, light wells, doors opening into hidden places. Partitions muffled the sounds of life—soft voices, bare feet padding across

plaster floors, the chuckle of running water. Glimmering pools offered relief
in hot weather.... Drains running under the floors mingled their
murmurs with the chatter of green monkeys, the song of caged birds,
the slithering of house snakes, the distant bellowing of the sacred bulls.
It must have been a relief to reach the sunlit central court. Here there
could be no secrets or monsters, only ordinary people passing by or
leaning over balconies and the excitement of the royal bull games.[2]

As one travels to Knossos and Phaestos today, one will see very
little of the chaos of the reconstructed plans. Too much is still on the
ground or lying beneath it, too much has been overzealously restored by
Sir Arthur Evans, and so on. But the plans probably do not lie.

It must have been a pleasant place to be lost in if Dr. Vermeule is to
be believed and there is no reason to think she should not be. But perhaps
the natives, the residents, did not get lost and knew all the alternate paths
without a map, just as we in Boston can go unerringly to streets we cannot direct strangers to. Perhaps our strictures about unreadable plans
should be modified. Except in expositions, buildings are not usually made
for strangers.

Comparative Plans
The study of the plan as an introduction to a specific example is the main
reason I introduced it here. It does have other uses, some historical,
some not. Once you can read them, an array of plans will provide you,
for example, with a quick view of the sort of variants that have occurred
within a style depending on regional and other factors; or it may offer
you a quick synopsis of stages in the evolution of a style, say from the
ideal Christian basilica to the Abbaye aux Hommes at Caen or even to
the Ste-Chapelle with certain detours along the way; or it may entrance
you with the evolution of a particular form such as English vaults from
Durham to the King's College Chapel in Cambridge.

Comparative plans can be used for simpler and naturally also more
complex purposes. Consider, for example, the case of the best six examples
of the Auvergnat version of French Romanesque architecture. The smallest
of these is St-Saturnin, the largest Issoire, and between these in ascending
order of size are St-Nectaire, Orcival, Notre-Dame-du-Port at Clermont-
Ferrand, and the ruined Mozat. They were all built at about the same time
and in a radius of less than 25 miles from Clermont-Ferrand. Their sites
vary considerably; some are much more dramatic than others topogra-
phically, some much more tightly integrated than others to the towns
they serve. The building stone varies from place to place depending on
extremely local geology; and hence the colors vary. Some of the builders
used more decoration than others; in some of the churches the carving is

[2] Emily Vermeule, "The World of Odysseus," in *Greece and Rome* (Washington, D.C.:
National Geographic Society, 1968), p. 65.

interesting, in others it is sterile or even nonexistent. In consequence it is easy to have personal favorites even among these churches of a small area.

But it must be recognized that the differences are really slender—less, for example, than between the canvases of Braque and Gris. Generalizers will call the Romanesque of Burgundy rich, elegant, colorful, exuberant, and that of Auvergne austere, rigorous, solid, and say that even Tournus seems rich compared to Orcival. And this is partly true.

But great as these Auvergnat churches are, they cannot be said to define or even to epitomize the style of a province which is more than 125 miles long. The crow's flight distance between Issoire at the south and Mozat at the north is about 25 miles. Indeed those interested in exceptions need only travel 20 miles from the nave of St-Austremoine of Issoire to St-Julien at Brioude.

But among the churches in question and barring exigencies of geography, materials, and funds, the similarities are remarkable. There are no technical evolutions to be observed; all alternate the pillars; there are almost the same number of colonnades along the ambulatories. They were not by a single architect but they all possessed the marvelous plan of a sanctuary with an ambulatory and radiating chapels—they are all quite small. Issoire, 216 feet long, does not seem much more monumental than the tiny St-Nectaire.

When the plans in outline are laid over each other to the same scale, there are differences in the widths we may notice and these are significant enough to affect the spatial sense (as of course does the height). There are greater differences in the lengths. Orcival and St-Nectaire have four bays in the nave, Notre-Dame-du-Port has five, and Issoire has seven. All have a narthex of one bay. All have transepts. All have one apsidal chapel at the north and south sides of the east wall of the transept. Saint Saturnin has a single apsidal termination; St-Nectaire an ambulatory with three radiating chapels; all the rest have an ambulatory with four radiating apsidal chapels to which Issoire adds a rectilinear one on the main axis. These are the principal differences.

Two plans can be set one beside the other for comparison of "archetypes," for example, the "typical" English Gothic as represented by Salisbury and the "typical" French Gothic as represented by Amiens. Here one will see that the English transepts project boldly while the French project slightly if at all; the English even will add a second transept. One would conclude that lateral chapels were rare in England (true for churches not designed for the laity, that is, most of the cathedrals) and numerous in France, where they were used both for worship of minor saints and the intoning of special or private masses. The beautiful apsidal east end of the French developed into the chevet by the ambulatory and the radiating chapels is replaced in England by a square end, although in both cases a processional could usually go around the choir. English aisles are almost always single but often double in France, although Amiens does not show this. Other differences do not show clearly on the plan, such as the importance of the western towers in France and the central one in England, the emphatic flying buttresses of the French and their infrequency in England. The great height of the French churches provides their most important interior effect, while the English interiors have elaborately complex piers, triforia, clerestories, and soon enough go over to complex lierne and fan-vault ribs.

Thus, though the comparative plans do not tell the full story and may encourage overgeneralizations, they do again serve quickly if not quite at a glance to fix some fundamentals which are not easily forgotten.

They can be used gingerly for a tentative examination of a part of the tricky question of "prototypes" and "evolution," and this is done in many books. I forego it here.

Finally, if less direct to our purpose, well-drawn plans can be looked at simply as handsome things in their own right, and I offer you a nosegay of these. See, for example, the reflected ceilings on the plan of the mosque of Yldirim at Bursa, the plan of the theatre at Epidauros, the reflected plans of lierne vaulting at Norwich, or the fan vaulting at the Henry VII Chapel at Westminster Abbey, or the "net" vaulting of the late Gothic hall type churches in Germany.

Pl. 31   The same thing can be said of the ideal city plans of the Renaissance, such as those proposed by Scamozzi, Perret, or Filarete, or the handsome plan of Sforzinda.

I have repeatedly emphasized that the plan cannot tell us all we need to know about the physical aspects of a building, though it will prepare us for what we can see through the study of what we really cannot see, and if the plan is good we will sense it as we walk around. Despite its limitations, the plan is the hub of architecture. It is conditioned, to be sure, by the structural skills which are available and by the materials, but they exist to make it possible and not the other way around.

So a discussion of a building without the presentation of plans is sterile. To engage a building without an understanding of its plan is to leave too much to chance. Even when they are adorned with profuse and ingratiating details, great buildings have dominant and unforgettable spaces of one sort or another. These cannot be experienced in absentia or vicariously through photographs, much less through words. They also have simple plans and elevations. One of the best tests you can make of whether you have come to grips with a building and understand it is to see whether you can draw (the skill of draftsmanship is unimportant) a quick line sketch which shows what the fundamentals are.

If you cannot do this, the chances are you will soon forget the important things about the building *as architecture*, however handsome your slides and movies. So get yourself to the *plan* and then add something to it by consideration of the sections and the elevations.

Sections

After we have learned to read plans, the encounter with sections will be easier. Sections are something we see in real life little more than we do plans. After all there is an occasional opportunity to look down from the air on a city square or a quite ruined building. Only occasionally even in a ruin can we get some visual notion of a section as, for example, when you look west at the abbey church at Glastonbury, or stand in the Basilica of Maxentius in Rome.

Of the two major sections, the transverse will normally be the more revealing of structure, at least of rectilinear buildings, since generally an attempt is made to span the shortest way.

The transverse section can reveal the elevation of anything set beyond it. This appears in the cross section of the Hephaesteion at Athens, which shows the east portico both in section and elevation; or the section may be quite strictly structural as in the one of the Temple of Aphaia at Aegina. It may become a little complicated to read when it cuts half the section at one point, the other half at another, as a compact and economical way (possible where sections are symmetrical) of showing what things are like both in the Naos and the Parthenos of the Parthenon at *Pl. 32* Athens. It can tell you about the arrangement of more than one level as in the section of the Cathedral at Aachen. It can reveal very clearly what happens in a Gothic cathedral, such as the one at Peterborough, England, where the roofs are of wood and exert no thrust; or how the thrusts of the vault ribs are taken up at Reims. Or it can clearly expose how the cortile worked in the Renaissance palace of the Strozzi in Florence (as indeed a longitudinal section would also do).

Longitudinal sections, on the other hand, may say more about what the interior looks like. They will not say very much because they will offer no sense of space, of color, of light and shade, of texture, or of change as we walk along. They are completely static. They offer us, back of the things actually sectioned, a map of the interior wall. It is a true map but not one we can often see, except in this diagram, since inside a building we can hardly ever get far enough away from any wall to see it as a flat area or in undistorted curvature if it is flat. We have to scan the wall so to speak, to pan it with a motion-picture camera, to use wide-angle lenses and other devices to tame the problem, and the results with the camera are never really convincing if one tries for more than a few bays. So the longitudinal section does stand us in good stead to provide a partial view of what the inside of the building is and it may be extraordinarily useful if we want to compare various buildings of the same general school. This is particularly true of Gothic cathedrals. In these the design of the bays of no two of the great churches are identical—indeed they are not often identical in more than a part of a particular church, but this is largely a phenomenon of the time of building.

The comparative study of bays is a rewarding exercise in itself.

Consider, for example, the internal bays of Amiens, Chartres, and Paris when all drawn to the same scale. They will give you clear understanding of the enormous differences in height, in arcading, in fenestration, and so on of these three essentially contemporary cathedrals of France.

Pl. 37
Pl. 34
Pl. 33
Pl. 36

Or if you are looking for some sort of hallmark of the progression of the English Gothic styles, you could do much worse than to get a few of the longitudinal sections together before you all at once as you never can do in the field. You cannot do this in a glance, but a little reflection will fix these things quite permanently and make it much easier for you when you go around. It is a fair test of your architectural sensitivities as well because by now you not only ought to care about the blatant differences but be able to detect them as well.

Pl. 35
Pl. 38
Pl. 39

Longitudinal sections will, it must be said, do a lot more for you than this rather specialized initiation. You will get a fairly sharp notice as to how the progression of experiences might be at the Temple of Amon-Mut Khons in Luxor, or the Treasury of Atreus in Mycenae, or Hagia Sophia, or the interior height and length spectacle of Amiens.

This examination is also a useful accessory to preparation. I am sure many people wander through a series of Gothic churches with no attempt to notice these differences and no instinctive awareness of them. They will remember rather a special clock or map or other minor feature. There is nothing wrong about the clocks or the maps—or perhaps even about having a greater curiosity about the gargoyles of Notre-Dame de Paris than about its greater features, but it is something different from the observation of architecture. Just as the examination of the cross sections of Gothic piers may have led you to be interested in and indeed see the colonnettes when you are actually in a cathedral, so preconsideration of the Gothic bay as revealed in the longitudinal section may lead you to a greater awareness when you make your visit.

The Gothic example is a specially clear one, but the study of sections in other styles will usually offer comparable rewards.

Elevations

The elevation is a diagram of something you actually can see when you come to the site.

We ordinarily think of the facade as the front of a building, but there are in fact as many facades as there are detached sides. The simplest of circular buildings, such as the Temple of Portunus (Vesta) in Rome, may present the same facade all around—and the facades of Palladio's Villa Rotonda are alike. The facades of a Gothic cathedral are most unlike due to the nature of Gothic construction as well as the elongated plan. The west front or main entrance, and the east elevation, whether or not apsidal, are almost inevitably greatly different from each other. The lateral (north and south) elevations could be identical in theory but accretions and nonsymmetric additions, such as cloisters or chapter houses or new portals, have generally caused them to differ.

It is also true that not all buildings have a full set of elevations. An urban building will not have facades on all sides unless it occupies the entire block. If it owns a half block it will have one long and two shorter visible elevations; if a corner, only two; and if it is put in the middle of a block it may end with only one as is true today for the Chiesa de Santa Maria in Assisi, formerly the Tempio de Minerva, as well as many contemporary minor urban buildings.

Let me distinguish between an elevation and a facade. The elevation in the sense I am using it here is a line drawing of a facade. It will show *Pl. 40* the parts in such detail as the purpose of the drawing requires and its size permits, whether or not dimensioned. It is useful for the builder, in fact, essential for him, and in modern practice dimensions are usual; it is valuable to us for the understanding of the main components and how they relate to each other and for comparison with other buildings. And it is a perfectly reliable memory tool, since the actual facade will look enough like the drawing to permit easy recognition.

But it is *not* a facade. It lacks color and texture; most of all it lacks depth. There have been only a few moments in the passage of great architecture where the play of light and shade was not a major element of the appearance of a building, and a line diagram of an elevation does not provide a reading of this. It can be made to suggest it by a device—called "casting shadows"—more popular some years ago than it is now. This is done by assuming that the sun is falling on the building at an angle of 45 degrees to the horizontal plane and 45 degrees to the longitudinal vertical plane. Though this is not an incidence enjoyed by many buildings much of the time, it has the metric advantage that the shadows thus shown can be measured to reveal the actual overhang and/or outthrust of the element casting the shadow. It has the minor advantage for the draftsman that it requires only one drafting triangle and is the easiest to draw.

This conventional representation can then be blacked in for contrast or left itself as a diagram. It still falls short of being a true representation. Unless subtly done, it does not take account of the fact that reflected light reduces the intensity of some shadows. When the shadow is cast on a circular surface, for example, this is particularly noticeable. In the Beaux-Arts days of the great presentations through renderings, people became extremely skillful at the art of delineating shades and shadows within the 45 percent convention, so that what the client or the competition jury saw in the *rendu* was a fair statement of what might be seen at least once in a while, in daylight.

But there is a more important way in which the cast-shadow rendered elevation is unfavorable to the reality. Quite aside from the solstice there is the matter of the cloudy day and the sunny day and the time of day.

You will not really have seen the west front of St-Pierre at Angoulême, for example, until you are there on the late afternoon of a sunny day—the east chevet of Bourges, always dramatic, is at its best in the morning. In planning short visits to architectural masterpieces, it is reasonable to make some effort to find the best time to be there even if in the end you may not manage the optimum. It is better to have seen the Acropolis in a downpour than never to have seen it at all. But there are better times.

As in the case of the plan, you can make a simple test of whether you really do or do not remember the elevation of a building. Can you, even with minimal drawing skill, sketch from memory the main components of the elevation of a building you have just visited? The fewer the basic elements you have been able to reduce it to without omitting anything important, the nearer you will have come to clear observation and basic truths.

This is all that really needs to be said here about the elevation as map. There are other problems of the facade which we will need to recall when we start touring a building. It is perhaps an unhappy thing that the facade is usually what we remember most about a building—only rarely its mass as might be the case at Mont St-Michel, for example—and even more rarely its interior, which would surely be the case in the Roman Pantheon or Hagia Sophia or any of the great German Baroque churches. As time has gone on, this has influenced some architects, one might even say too many architects, to indulge in what is often scornfully called "facade" architecture.

The criticism is leveled in different ways. Years ago the then librarian at Yale was so upset about the damage being done to the library services of the future Sterling Library by the architect's preoccupation with pseudo-Gothic details that he is said to have asked that the inscription read, "The library is inside." In this case overconcern with an external architecture was being allowed to destroy or handicap function. Whether this is serious or not will depend on the nature of the function. A mortician's objections to the disposition of the coffins in the Taj Mahal would scarcely be given much weight. The Yale librarian stood, of course, on firmer ground, as might a scientist in some of the laboratories produced by some of our more famous contemporary "form makers."

Another criticism, more theoretical in nature, has to do with what is "truth" in architecture. It is generally but not universally true that architecture which has been universally or almost universally admired has tended to reveal by its exterior appearance both how it was built and what went on inside. But there are countless brilliant exceptions to either rule of which the dome of St. Peter's might be cited as one type of example and the false fronts of some of the main mosques of Isfahan as another.

In the Middle Ages if the Thomist theories influenced design in the way that Panofsky has suggested, the relations between the inside and the outside were supposed to mesh tightly, but the fact remains that few of the great rose-windowed west fronts of the Gothic do much to tell us how the roof of the nave is made; while at Notre-Dame de Paris only three portals on the west front lead you to the five aisles of the church. On the interior this is made plausible enough by the intervention of a narthex between the front and the nave, but the fact remains that the facade is not a straightforward guide to the interior. As we shall see later, there were even more flagrant failures in correspondence in the Baroque.

Such deviations tend to bother devotees of the "truth" theory. But what is any of us to say of the University Club in New York: here McKim needed a different number of floors inside for the use of the members than the demands of Renaissance composition would easily accommodate themselves to on the exterior. He could not sacrifice the exterior appearance. The consequence is that one of the handsomest eclectic buildings in New York is one of the most architecturally deceptive. I doubt that it bothers very many members; I am sure few passersby even think about it; I know it bothers me a little but I do not know whether it ought to bother you. I think, though, you ought to know the facts just as you ought to know that some of our leading contemporary "brutalists" are making columns and overhangs much bigger than they need to be in order to magnify the power of the monumental pools of light and dark. Then you can make up your mind where you want to cry halt and the degree to which you can accept the fact that all architecture is in a sense an overly permanent stage set.

There is no degree of moral indignation which would justify ignoring the facades as an important element of architecture and getting super-refined about them. But it is well at the same time to remember that even when it is a very important element of the architecture (and sometimes it is not), the facade is seldom the only important element. Many of the Italian Renaissance palaces seem to be most memorable for their facades. In some there seems to be only a front either because there actually were abutting buildings or because the side elevations faced such narrow streets that there was really no place from which the elevations fronting them could be seen. In many Renaissance buildings the facade was even designed by a different architect than the rest of the building. In some periods of Chinese art some of the most beautiful carving was reserved for the bottoms of inner boxes and other places where it would seldom be seen. But this has not been the spirit of the West, so it was not surprising that the Italian architects of the cinquecento went so far in downgrading the lateral facades as to build them of inferior materials—and to carry the important frontal cornice only a little way around the sides.

But if we look at the plan and sections of such palaces or can find an interior uncontaminated by offices or by parked cars, we will see that

Pl. 304

the three-story inner court (cortile), an enclosure of space by a three-leveled walk around, which also provides access to the peripheral rooms, is in fact the principal design element. Its treatment was more important to the users than the street front which people went by, much as families like the Rucellai may have cared to enhance their public image with the beautiful facade by Alberti. One does not need to look long at Roman palaces in this way, such as the Cancelleria or the Farnese or Florentine palaces such as the Strozzi or the Riccardi, to realize this. How the cortile and perhaps the monumental inner stair were handled is more important than the facade even in less conventional layouts, such as the palaces of the Pitti, of Pietro Massimi, of Farnese Capriola, or even the Villa of Pope Julius.

Space

The plan, the walls, the structure, the transverse and longitudinal sections, the elevations—which do so much to help us to differentiate one building from another—are tools for the definition of space either within the architecture or around it.

The definition of space is subtle and elusive and not to be approached very successfully through diagrams. It is very difficult to draw, to paint, to photograph, or to film; it has really to be experienced physically to be understood. Yet we must try to say something about it in this program of explanations of what to look for and how to be prepared to look for it. If we are to understand and enjoy architecture, we must continually sharpen our awareness of space.

Space, of course, serves function even in such pedestrian things as modern bathrooms and kitchens, which, having been made into machines, are no longer spacious, beautiful, or luxurious whatever Madison Avenue may boast. Space serves function of larger magnitude when it offers the interior of Hagia Sophia, St. Peter's, the Pantheon, Amiens, and less surely when it is less certain of purpose and its defining walls are translucent as in a geodesic dome. Such great spaces are clearly related to associations their patrons wanted made—and this is equally true of the unroofed urban living rooms provided by the Renaissance and the Baroque squares. All of these are enclosures of space; people of other times, for various reasons, preferred to surround buildings by space rather than to enclose the space by buildings. Now and again there have been valiant efforts to be limited to neither but to have the space flow around and in and through. The fashions in these things change and we need to look at architecture with a considerable sense of the fashions of its builders and a considerable setting aside of our own fashions. The present fashion is to declare most interior space too expensive to indulge in and to overdo the scale of exterior space.

There are tricks by which space may be made to seem larger or smaller than it is by the use of forced perspective. (Causing buildings to deviate from parallelism will deceive if we expect the normal convergence of perspective.) If the street flares out, its sides will *seem* to be converging more slowly so an object at the end will seem farther away than it is and hence larger; if the street closes in, it will seem to be converging more rapidly, and the object will seem nearer and therefore smaller. And similar tricks can be achieved by making an object of an expected size larger or smaller than it ought to be. A low rail will make the building behind it seem larger, a high one smaller. Then there are ways of arrival which emphasize or diminish space. You can explode into it from small approaches or fall down into it by large ones or not be aware you have arrived at all if the preparatory areas are of the same size as the climactic are. At one extreme is the considerable preparation of St. Peter's, first the street and bridge approaches, then the great elliptical piazza, then the open forecourt with its diverging arms and the imposing facade, the generous portico, the enormous nave, until the high altar, the rotunda under the dome, and St. Peter's chair are reached. This is in marked contrast to the way in which we are precipitated almost without warning into the great half sphere of the Roman Pantheon. Space may be used as simply and directly as in the Pantheon or as a sort of continuous dialogue of affirmation and denial as in such large and notable Byzantine examples as Hagia Sophia. It may be viewed as an art in itself, as a symbolic device, or in more pragmatic terms.

However it is viewed and wherever you turn, you will find that space is a major consideration of architecture.

So long as architectural space is enclosed in a building, we are on fairly familiar ground since we have experienced it, good and bad, in most of our Western places of congregation. When the space is that of an urban square, it is still enclosed and the problem of sensing that space is not fundamentally different. Paul Zucker has expressed this as clearly as anyone I know.

> Artistically relevant squares are, however, more than mere voids; they represent organized space and a history of the square actually means a history of space as the subject of artistic creation.[3]

As the walls surround the inside of a building, so the buildings surround the square, and it is the relations between their form and surround which define the square—how uniform they are, how varied, their absolute dimensions, their relative proportions to the width and length of the enclosure, and their location inside or among other three-dimensional elements.

We perceive this space by visualizing its limits through a kinesthetic experience, sensations of movement. The surround, the volume, the scale

---

[3] Paul Zucker, *Town and Square: From the Agora to the Village Green* (New York: Columbia University Press, 1959), p. 2.

may exert pressure and resistance, may stimulate and direct reactions. The floor and the ceiling are important definers of the space in a room; outdoors where the ceiling is the sky, the texture of the pavement, its levels, even its slope, as in Arezzo, define space.

As I have hinted before, people of different times have had quite different views as to how space ought to be organized. The Greeks "were interested in unlimited views with the landscape in the background." The classic Greek *acropoli* did not organize space on their eminences but "concentrated on perfection of form and design of the individual volume," whether building or sculpture. The Romans, on the other hand, always wanted a final visual stop; "it is this continuous alternation between expansion and confinement which makes the spectator conscious of space as such." But by the Middle Ages all this was changed again. Sometimes there was essentially no parvis around the cathedral. "In Strasbourg, Freiburg im Breisgau, and Ulm, for instance, the houses around the cathedral left just distance enough to admire the magnificent sculptural decor of the west portals and of the entrance to the transept." Things are even more cramped in Bourges. Such churches might be said to have no parvis at all. The space was inside!

Even when it did exist the medieval parvis was functionally an expansion of the Early Christian, Byzantine, Romanesque narthex, or entrance hall, a place for mystery plays soon degenerating into an unintended market square.

But by the Renaissance the wind shifted again. The Renaissance sought a parallelism between inner and outer space, an unromantic clearcut visual articulation between volume and space. The cupola becomes the center of attraction; development in depth becomes important, creating spatial counterpoint. "Hence the lateral houses, colonnades, or arcades represent merely framing elements for the dominating structure and a stage effect is achieved. Whereas the medieval parvis as space element is *subordinated* to the church, anticipating the spatial directions of the interior, the Renaissance, and baroque parvis creates a *coordinated* void in contrast to the controlling architecture."[4]

Baroque space went further. The architects sought for illusions of infinity, for unnoticeable transitions, for fluidity and yet also for a space which arrested movement while seeming to move. In its decline they were quite prepared, as in the Spanish Steps of Rome, to produce a great elegance of plan and of the steps themselves, which yet approach nothing of great importance.

When we go around looking at buildings of different times, it will not take us long to perceive that the town spaces are saying the same things as the buildings, each in a voice which one has to assume was consonant with the received opinion of the day; some in voices and languages which

[4] The quotations are from Zucker, ibid., pp. 29, 61, 65, and 12, respectively.

we have difficulty in comprehending, or sympathizing with, today. To get the most out of these journeys, we must, for the moment at least, suppress our preferences and prejudices; and since in most historic towns we are likely to meet architecture and public areas from several periods, we have to become skillful at gear shifting too. The shifting must occur in our minds and not our bodies since the physical tools we have are little changed over time—our successful angle of vision is still about 60 percent horizontally and perhaps 27 percent vertically. The human scale, the size of the human body, still remains the primary measuring rod, and this offers problems for contemporary designers of titanic plazas.

Of space I despair to say anything more enlightening than to remind that if we are to understand and enjoy architecture we must sharpen our awareness of it. To remain unaware may not be a sin, but it will make it hard to derive either pleasure or profit from architectural travel.

It need be emphasized again that the observer of space will be confronted with enormous variety—the space-enclosed Egyptian pyramid; the dark and narrow ranks of the hypostyle hall at Karnak; the buildings enclosed by space which is itself enclosed by the boundaries of the Greek *temenos*; the vast vaults of the Roman baths; the unroofed ellipse of the Roman arenas; the explosive entrances to the Roman Pantheon; the multiple bubbles of Hagia Sophia; the dark mystery of Norman Durham; the light-infused nave and transept and choir of Chartres; the undulant exteriors and interiors of the Baroque; the internal interpenetrations of San Vitale and Hagia Sophia; and the final effort at the dissolution of space through the transparent walls of Mies van der Rohe and Buckminster Fuller, which, unlike the colored transparencies of the Middle Ages, cause the wall almost to disappear. If you care enough about history, you can relate each of these and variations of them to the spirit of a particular time and you can safely indeed think in terms of "Greek space," "Roman space," "Gothic space," "Baroque space," and so on and then try to see what the space ideas are, for example, of Americans of the late twentieth century. But even if you elect none of these exercises, the space is there to be experienced. You can hardly be oblivious to the space effects no matter how much you may try; but you will derive more pleasures and profit from the experience of space if you are consciously and conscientiously aware of it.

Materials and Structure

Much is being currently written in overpraise of the computer as a designer of cities and of their buildings. The computer can be of great help in framing the program for either. It can accept the data that is fed into it and return it in a variety of combinations far beyond the powers of seven architects with seven mops sweeping for half a year. If all the significant factors can be quantified, it can then help to determine the probability of success as between various possible combinations. As such it represents an enormous potential for better understanding of the choices which are available and therefore a powerful tool for programming. It may even take some of the labor out of actually drawing up alternatives. Some day it may do more—but not yet.

Because of these powers it has proved and should have proved fascinating to young architects, especially socially minded architects, especially architects who desire to be of the contemporary world. It has unhappily led some of them to absurdities. In the end a building is an *artifact*. It may begin as an *idea*, it may gestate as a *program*, its potentials may be revealed by a *plan*, but it is not the idea, the "process," the program, the plan which is the architecture. Architecture is and must always be the palpable encloser or the enclosed—and often both. As the painter Kepes has said, "if your head is cold you don a hat not a process." No computer's printout can legitimately be called architecture any more than Maxwell's equations can properly be called poetry in anything other than a metaphorical sense. No, it is the artifact which is the architecture and the city, however important as a preliminary may have been the *idea* of the architecture, or the city, or the computer's contributions to the *program*.

I see no evidence that this is ever going to be different. Talented designers may find their talents freed by the computer or they may not; but as a maker of architecture the computer must remain a failure without the talent of the designer; and it cannot and will not guarantee a fine design from the hand of the incompetent, the clumsy, or the unimaginative.

Something analogous can be said about the building. A building is realized as an *artifact*—as opposed to an *idea*—only when the space is defined, the program is working, the plan is the support of building materials. Without materials there is no building, there is no artifact, no matter how many invisible screens of hot air some inventor may promote to take their place.

Materials do not leap full-blown into enclosures. Not even balloons do that. They have to be put together into a combination which will stand up at least for a while. (One of the great arguments of our day is how long that "while" should be; how desirable durability versus ephemerality?) This combination is, among other things, a structure. A structure is essential to architecture, though honest structure does not guarantee wonderful architecture. No structure can be made without materials. So materials are central. They determine what kind of building can actually be realized. Frank Lloyd Wright and Alvar Aalto are among our near contemporaries whose respect for materials (and every decent architect must have this respect) extended into love for materials (and this is felt perhaps only by the greatest). Love is more than affection and respect. It will not let you misuse a material as affection might; and it will not hinder you from asking as much as you can of the loved one, as too much respect might.

I shall, therefore, treat materials and structures together but get at them through talking of the nature of the materials rather than the nature of structures.

Differences in requirements and properties being what they are, there is no single universally useful material, and we have had to learn to combine what we have and to minimize their antagonisms. But there is almost always a primary material in a given building which characterizes its major structure as well as its appearance. The choice of this major material is a first determinant of architecture, though the word "choice," I am afraid, suggests greater freedom than really exists.

Over all architectural history up to now at least and certainly with respect to all extant buildings there have been really very few major materials. The whole list is as follows:

Wattle and daub

Pisé de terre or rammed earth

Brick, sun-dried and kiln-burned

Timber

Stone

Metal frames and enclosing sheets

Concrete, and especially reinforced concrete

Other materials have collaborated for calking, for fastening, for protection, for decoration, and here we would have to call the roll of glass, of lead, copper, zinc, and gold, of tin and bronze, of nonstructural ceramics, of paints, of asphalts, and so on, even to plastics of our day. Sometimes these materials have emerged as important not only to the working of the building but to its appearance. But it is the primary materials which are responsible for the architecture and always have been. Of the seven, regardless of how many lesser buildings may have been made of wattle and daub, of woven grass, and even of rammed earth and sun-dried brick, the architecture which has come down to us out of the past[5] is the architecture primarily of stone, secondarily of burned brick, and thirdly of wood.

All these three were by no means available to the builders of a given place and a given moment of historical time. Conditions of topography and geology and climate might make one material hard or impossible to procure and another much easier. The technology of transport and its economics, even in slave states where this resource was really not limitless, might determine which of the available materials could really be brought to the site. Though there are notable exceptions, such as the granite of

---

[5] Though metal frames with skins, and reinforced concrete, dominate the building art of our day, they are achievements made almost entirely in the last century.

Aswan floated 200 miles down the Nile to Thebes, and the Roman imports of marble from all parts of Africa, and possibly the transportation miracles of Stonehenge or Cuzco, the fact remains that most of the great buildings of history had to be contented with materials from nearby. In the short radius of 25 miles from Clermont-Ferrand a half dozen Auvergnat Romanesque churches built to the same programs and essentially the same plans and structures differ nonetheless very substantially in appearance for this reason.

Because they had to use local stone, the Greeks made temples to the same plan of tough granite, elegant marble, or shell-filled sandstone, depending on where they were built. Even the ambitious and energetically persuasive Abbot Suger, who wanted to build St-Denis with the finest of imported stones, had to settle for the sandstone of nearby Pontoise.

The Peruvian situation is representative of what occurred in many parts of the world. Garcilaso reports, probably faithfully, that the only big trees in Peru were of wood so heavy and hard that even canoes could not be dug out of them and that resort had to be taken to rafts of a very thin and light wood. Something like these can be seen on Lake Titicaca even today.[6]

He also reports skiffs made of bundles of reeds of a type which may not have been very different from those still to be seen on Lake Titicaca and describes bridge structures of reeds at Apurimac and elsewhere. Given the scanty and not very workable timber supply of the upper highlands, it is not surprising that the Incas turned to stone. So much is obvious enough. Why they were so concerned with large stones and with dressing them with a precision not demanded by the necessities is a mystery.

Other mountain men, whether in the Alps or the Karakorum or the Himalayas, where both stone and timber were available though more or less at different altitudes, have opted for stone only when it could be picked up locally and laid into place more or less at random like New England stone fences and for superstructures, and often most of their buildings preferred the no more available but much more easily workable wood.

In other areas of the world, notably in dusty areas where stone too might be hard to find or hard to manipulate, it was not surprising to find some form of adobe or mud brick, the common building material of the Indus, of Mesopotamia, of our Southwest, and of the Pacific shores of Peru. Unless there is never much rain, or unless the tops of the dirt walls are protected by wide overhanging eaves, these adobe constructions weather away all too easily and tend to melt, so to speak, down into the terrain. Thus we find the many-layered remains of ancient cities of the Middle East. It now seems quite clear that many of the Peruvian sites

[6] Garcilaso de la Vega, *The Incas*, Alain Gheerbrant (ed.), (New York: Avon, 1961), p. 96, pp. 106–107.

which must have been most impressive in their day were on the coast where the usual building material was adobe or mud brick.[7]

We know little about these great cities because weathering has so often destroyed the form of buildings in this material beyond recovery. The best example may be the difference in what we are able to see of the buildings of Mesopotamia as compared with contemporary ones in Egypt. And so it is in Meso-America where the stone buildings even when fallen leave evidence from which successful reconstructions can be made.

Now if you are building in your own time and are concerned with the present and not with what posterity may know about you, you may accept the ceaseless task of repair and rebuilding imposed upon you by adobe as necessary when stone is scarce or missing, or as acceptable when stone is hard to work. But durability has generally appealed to men of all times before ours. The great Chavin peoples, two millennia before the Inca, for example, made their pyramidal platforms of conical adobes or rubble set in mortar down on the coast, but when they erected the massive terraced platforms at Chavin itself at an altitude of 10,000 feet, they opted for stone. There may have been other than practical reasons for such choices. Some speculate that the Inca edifices prior to the Augustan regime of Inca Pachacuti were mainly sod and clay.

It would be easy to multiply the examples. Well before their great civilizations developed, the timber supplies of Crete, the Aegean Islands, and the Greek mainland were inadequate both in quantity and quality. The tight ranges limited the amount of flat land which was therefore too precious for silviculture; the near slopes were so heavily grazed as to discourage the maturing of anything but scrub, and transportation of large logs across the mountains seemed to the Greeks a labor too immense to be worthwhile, although in a different cultural milieu the Japanese concluded to the contrary. In consequence the Greek use of wood was sparing and even then in shorter pieces than would have been desirable for serious building. Also their woodworking tools may have been too crude. Tools certainly are significant but it is not clear that they come first. Had the Greeks wanted to work the timbers, they might well have developed the tools as they did for the more difficult manipulation of stone.

The Greeks, however, also experimented with adobe and found it would last fairly well when they waterproofed the top and kept the base dry. Projecting eaves cared for the first necessity and a single course of stone was generally enough at the bottom. All that remains now of their older buildings is the base course or the base courses, since sometimes the stone was run up several feet.

Since stone *cutting* was seldom attempted in the Bronze Age, the Greeks, like others before and after them, went about picking up pieces

---

[7] See, for example, G. H. S. Bushnell, *Peru* (New York: Praeger, 1957), p. 110, which gives a description of the important coastal city of Chan Chan.

that were lying suitably to hand, assisted by the fact that several limestone formations in parts of Greece will split into more or less rectangular blocks when exposed to the weather. The interstices were packed with mud or preferably clay. So a stone tradition was born in the natural quality of a local stone and then matured and was perfected with the aid of tools to manipulate the stones which did not come so conveniently prepackaged by nature.

The Romans, on the other hand, had more options both as to resources and as to developed technologies, and they were much bolder both with timber trusses and stone arches and vaults—actually, with every material:

> The old Roman architect had skill with the dark, soft stone of the volcanic regions of Central Italy, the hard, grey limestone of the Appenines which gave them also the fine lime for their mortars and plasters, with local clays for brick and terra cotta, with timber . . . . But these materials "evoked no necessary visible expression." It was on the dynamic surfaces of mass or volume that the architect spent his effort and depended for his effects. Hence while stonework might be profiled, jointed, or finished to be seen for its own value, it might equally well, like walling of brick, or rubblework be hidden by stucco, trimmed or painted. Hence the visible surfaces of timber might be carved, painted or shielded with plates of terra cotta.[8]

There have been few societies which, before our own, have enjoyed such freedom of selection among materials. On the whole it has not been demonstrated that this freedom is necessarily conducive to the finest in architecture. There may be something to be said in architectural materials for the "freedom of necessity."

The ubiquity of the major materials can quickly be seen from an analysis of the same large list of noble buildings I have previously used for other purposes. It needs of course to be noted that we are not talking about the materials used for *all* buildings in these earlier civilizations. We are talking about the materials used in the buildings of which we have substantial remains. How long a building lasts is partly a matter of luck of course. A few wooden buildings have escaped fires and insects for centuries—but not many and only those which were zealously protected. Naturally then the buildings of the most durable materials are those which have tended to remain. As I have previously suggested, it does not seem unreasonable to conjecture that the most durable materials were chosen for the buildings which their builders thought most important. Hence after all allowances we may find the figures significant, especially as they are so dramatic.

Assume then that men have crawled out of their trees, their caves, and the holes in the ground they have dug for themselves, and have begun

---

[8] Frank E. Brown, *Roman Architecture* (New York: Braziller, 1961), pp. 15, 16.

Primary Building Material (percent)

Pre–1800				
Stone	80.0	}	Masonry	95.0
Brick	15.0	}		
Wood	4.5			
Concrete	0.5			
Metal Frame	0.0			
Post–1800				
Stone	12.0	}	Masonry	32.0
Brick	20.0	}		
Wood	2.5			
Concrete	35.5			
			Metal Skin	2.5
			Base	4.0
Metal Frame	30.0	{	Masonry Skin	10.0
			Glass Skin	13.5

to fashion these same materials into the artificial forms we call Architecture. They take the wood from the tree, but they do not achieve a structure of roots and trunk and branches and leaves no matter how they may try. They bend the willows and they plait the grasses and they tie the poles together always leaving nature a little farther behind and finally achieve a wooden architecture. They deposit the sediments or chip away at the rocks and put them together again in ever more skillful ways, the craggy steles of the dolmens, the precariously balanced slabs of Stonehenge, the refined lintels of Athens, the majestic domes of Rome, the slender skeletons of Amiens. They do not make Ship Rock or the Matterhorn; yet the achievement is miraculous enough. Of the three primary materials, which came first, the wood or the clay or the stone? Who can say? Perhaps it was a matter of where the men built. Of the oldest buildings we call architecture, the work of Mesopotamia was of clay and the work of Egypt was of stone, and it was the stone which survived. But let us start with wood. For most of us, at least of the north, it will seem to be the warmest and most "human" material. We may end in awe of stone, but we are more likely to be in love with wood—at least those of us whose ancestors, centuries ago, were children of the forests and not of the barren rocky highlands where even the Krumholz and the scrub bend to the blasts and where the birds chirp rather than sing.

ON WHERE TO LOOK FOR IT

Where shall we go to find our finest examples—whether of wood or stone or brick? It would be folly to try to say much about where an unknown person ought to go to satisfy his architectural curiosities. There is no number-one tour. No large consensus exists as to the "greatest" buildings, the "musts." Even so few as five current authorities can agree unanimously on but eighty-odd buildings in such a category. This is a distinguished shopping list, naturally, but too small. The buildings listed in the Index include all the buildings I think deserve an amateur's visit—and even these may be too many for your taste or desires. However, it is not a sure-fire list for anyone else—some would certainly want to add and many might have to subtract.

Some travelers will prefer to follow a style through its many national variations, some to follow a country through its many stylistic switches; others will want to proceed in a more random way, some relying merely on places suggested by friends they trust, or on places which are world-famous.

CHAPTER FIVE

THE ARCHITECTURE OF WOOD

The groves were God's first temples.

William Cullen Bryant
A Forest Hymn

INTRODUCTION

There are areas of the world where wood can never be a primary building material, deserts where no wood grows, the higher parts of mountains where either there are no trees or the tormented alpestrine growth is quite unsuitable for building. (It is easier to slide logs downhill than it is to snake them up so not many alpine wooden constructions will be found much above timber line.) To these naturally unforested areas men have added others by their imprudent and ruthless exploitation of sylvan resources for immediate advantage. The great stands of cedar in Lebanon were mostly carried away to meet the desires of ancient Egyptians; from Queen Elizabeth to Samuel Pepys the great forests of England fell to supply the victorious British ships of the line. The roster of once-wooded lands now bereft of great trees runs from Greece to China, and many parts of the United States have met the same fate while other parts continue to be threatened, so great is man's selfishness despite all we now know about the consequences of deforestation and the useful technologies of silvi- and arboriculture.

In the areas where trees were either abundant or sufficient, a seemingly endless variety of opportunity was open to the imaginative builder. But this apparent plethora of opportunity was largely a mirage.

In a world list there must be thousands of types of wood, the number depending on how fine a screen one uses in discriminating among examples in the genera, the species, or the subspecies. Using two sources—Henry Saylor's admirable but small *Dictionary of Architecture*, and a more general and much larger, though unhappily an uneven general dictionary[1]—we find some forty-two different types of wood under the letter *a* alone. Obviously larger and more comprehensive reference works would increase the numbers enormously. Only seven names are common to the two cited works under the letter *a*.

This variety has not produced as much freedom of architectural choice as the mere numbers would suggest. For example, consider the seven listed in both sources: acacia, alder, amboyna, arucaria, ash, avocado, and avodire; of these the acacias are little used commercially; amboyna, avocado, and avodire serve only as veneer or cabinet woods; alder seldom appears even in interior work; ash and arucaria, though having multipurpose potentials, are of only minor significance to building. Thus the list quickly whittles itself down.

Some two dozen of the woods listed in Saylor are modestly common in architecture. Of the 175 others most are not generally familiar even to many architects; all have been used almost exclusively for decorative veneers, inlays, wood mosaics, furniture, cabinet work, and occasionally flooring, and generally in earlier years.

The general failure to use most of the 175 has been the consequence of several forces—sometimes acting singly, sometimes together.

The supply may have been too scant to justify its development on anything other than the most parochial basis. The forest may have been too remote or the means of transportation to building sites too limited or too costly. More important limitations have been set by the properties of the trees themselves. Some are too slender or too squat to offer adequate sizes of lumber. Some are so gnarled that they are hard to cut into desired straight pieces without inordinate waste. Some are too hard to process comfortably; some too gummy; a few too soft.

Then there are limitations set by the properties of the cut lumber. Some of it is difficult to cure. When it is dried, even in the most carefully controlled modern kilns, it either warps too much or checks too easily and too frequently. Moreover careful kiln-drying processes were a late development in the technology of timber, made long after wood had ceased to be an important structural element for major buildings. Some woods are too brittle and chip too easily; some are too eager to give off splinters; some are too prone to split along the grain, which makes the problem of connection very difficult; some are too easily destroyed or damaged by erosion, by boring animals, by dry rot, fungus, or other diseases. Some are too limber.

[1] *The American Heritage Dictionary of the English Language* (Boston: Houghton Mifflin, 1969). This dictionary is unhappily a weak source for an architectural reader. Apparently its architectural editors and consultants, though eminently qualified, were insufficiently zealous.

If we leave out the redwoods, which, despite their current popularity in northern California, were not much known to important historical architecture, the significant *structural* woods come down to the other conifers, especially cedar, fir, larch, pine, and spruce, and one broad-leaved hardwood, oak. Historically the range was only a little greater. Chestnut was once common but is now too worm-ridden. Hickory and hemlock were more common once than now. The important *exterior* woods, used because of their good weathering properties, are cedar, cypress, and spruce. The most durable and handsome *floors* are made of maple, oak, and teak, although softer floor materials are common and satisfactory if zealously maintained or used as underflooring. A much wider variety has proved attractive for furniture, cabinet work, and for interior finishes and veneers. I omit inner concealed sheathing for which lesser woods are possible since it was not common in the great days of timber architecture and when used, say as a support for roofing materials, seldom was a significant element in the visible architecture.

There can be little doubt as to the human qualities of wood as a finish material—its goodly odor, how it feels to the touch, the range of textures and patterns and colors it offers even before it is manipulated by men into mosaics, or treated with enamels and other finishes which protect it and sometimes heighten its gloss. My own taste prefers the naturally aged rough gray of a cypress shake to the fanciest inlay in all India or Italy, but that is a matter of taste. But if all these beauties were limited to the finishes of buildings, wood—though remaining an important building material of the order, say, of tile or glass—would not be one of the few major building materials. As in the case of the other major materials, it was in its exploitation as a structural material that it became important.

THE STRUCTURAL PROPERTIES OF WOOD

Something like steel and quite unlike stone or brick or unreinforced concrete, wood has about an equal resistance to being stretched or compressed. This is a major determinant as to how it can effectively be used.

The common problem of all architectural structures is to pick up the weights that rest on floors or roofs, and the weights of the structures themselves, and to carry them down to the ground and on to some sort of geologic base that will not settle too much at the outset or over time.

This involves, at least in the simplest form, two types of components: one horizontal or diagonal, stretching across or spanning some amount of open space; and one vertical or essentially so, transmitting the loads of the spanning elements to the ground and perhaps providing wall closure as well. Let us start with the vertical.

The crudest way to provide this vertical support in wood would be by a continuous wooden wall. One might arrange a set of logs vertically and touching each other, possibly driving them into the ground as a palisade is built (and as log cabins were built in French Colonial America), or one might lay the logs horizontally one on top of the next somewhat as one would lay a stone wall. There is evidently a fundamental difficulty. A stone wall built this way has no great tendency to roll away but the logs do. One way to correct this would be to cut the cylindrical log into a rectangular timber which would lie flat on the timber below as dressed stones would do, but to reduce the logs to this shaped timber obviously wastes a good deal of material, and a better solution is to notch the logs into each other at the corners of the building whereby they brace each other from rolling off. Thus the first important device of structural wood technology appears in the cutting of timbers to hold together.

As for the horizontal spans, they can, in the crudest examples, be achieved the same way—by laying the logs side by side and resting them on the walls. But again this is not the most efficient way to use the log and of course does not provide a surface to be walked on if there is a second story.

Here it may be desirable to understand one or two simple principles of beam action. Let us lay a rectangular shape of something across two supports and put some loads on it. It will try to fail to do its task of carrying the load in three ways. Nearest the support where the load on the beam is the heaviest, it may try to break simply by slicing itself in two. This is called *transverse shearing*. It is important to design against in some unusual situations where the loads are very large and the spans very short. Resistance is directly proportional to depth.

Secondly, when the beam is loaded it will *bend* between the supports. This has two potential effects: the material at the top of the beam tends to be shortened and thus compressive forces develop and need to be resisted, and at the bottom, the material tends to be elongated and hence the resistance must be to stretching or tensile forces. If the material is weak in compression or in tension, it will break under this bending. Wood is about equally resistant to both these forces and hence makes a good spanning material. Resistance is proportional to the square of the depth.

Not only does a beam tend to break near the center under either tension or compression or both, but it is also possible that it may bend a great deal without breaking. The degree of sagging is called *deflection*. If the deflection is too great it may be visibly displeasing or even frightening, it may harm collateral materials, or in extreme cases it can be so great as to cause the beam to slide off its support. Resistance is proportional to the cube of the depth.

The resistance of a given material to transverse shear, to bending stress, and to deflection depends both on its tensile and compressive strength, on the frictional resistance of adjacent planes (shear), on its stiffness (modulus of elasticity), and on its dimensions. In timber construction some woods have to be ruled out because they crush or tear too easily or because they are too limber. The ones which pass these tests are naturally the ones which have remained in use.

Now we might make a floor by placing beams edge to edge but it would be wasteful since if we used such timbers only deep enough to carry the load without breaking, the floor would be too limber; and if we made the depth enough to be stiff, we would be wasting a good deal of material. It almost always pays to make a wooden construction with deep beams and thin flooring.

For only slightly different reasons, then, it soon proved better to make walls the same way rather than of uniform logs or even planks. Thus the important wooden architecture of the world is a framed architecture, whether it consists of simple posts, lintels, sills, plates, bearers, girts, girders, beams, rafters, and purlins, plus whatever diagonal bracing may be needed, or of more advanced and complicated forms for longer spans such as the variety of trusses which have evolved over time.

A frame construction is almost certain to offer problems of connection of one element to another. One of the weaknesses of wood at the connection point is its tendency to split (weakness in longitudinal shear) if you try to place a connector too near the end of a timber. Anyone who has tried to drive too big a nail or screw too near the end of a board has experienced this.

In earliest times no doubt the connections were made by lashings using various fibers or ropes as was, for instance, the Inca practice. But with the improvement of tools carpenters learned many ways to connect one piece of wood to another. In the simplest forms they merely cut one piece into another (rebating or rabbeting) or divided the responsibility by cutting both pieces. Seeking more positive connections or sometimes more elegance of finish, they learned to cut a tenon which would fit into a hole in the female member, or to make a secret mitre dovetail, or to connect two parallel pieces with a butterfly dovetail, and many more even more complicated devices. We need not try to describe the whole range here but will simply remark that as one wanders around in wooden architecture, observance of the variety of the devices and the skill of their makers is not trivial or the least of the pleasures.

Another method was to bore holes in the pieces to be connected and to insert dowels, usually round, and often accompanied by glue. The dowels might show, as in the justly famous pegged floors of England and New England or the wooden pegs to be seen in many old trusses, or they might be used blind as was often done in furniture old and new. The development of iron, nails, screws, connector plates, brackets, and stirrups added efficiency and ease to the carpenter's job. It is not, I think, mere nostalgia or antiquarianism to feel that preiron carpentry remains the most beautiful and that *early* iron-wood combinations far exceed the results produced by contemporary carpenters, except perhaps in Japan where traditional methods have not quite been extinguished.

Although timber beams were capable of considerable spans, they could not by themselves do everything that was needed. For one thing, the supply of trees tall enough to provide really long beams was sharply limited. Even when there was a supply, as in the mountains of Japan which provided some 200-foot timbers, it was often remote and it was very hard to bring the log or the finished timber to the site. Moreover on too long a span the effective depth needed to be augmented. An invention was needed and two or perhaps three were made.

In the first place, one might try to shorten the actual span by brackets or corbels of wood. Some of these, one piled upon another, became very ingenious, especially in China and Japan. But there are limits to this technique and the more powerful invention was that of the truss. The design of trusses took quite a different direction in the Occident than it did in the Orient, and to avoid complication, we will postpone the description of Chinese and Japanese trusses until we come to talk of their marvelous wooden architecture.

The Western truss in essence rests on a simple principle: When members are arranged in a triangular disposition they are rigid, and otherwise they are not. If you put four members together in a square, it can easily be pushed into a parallelogram or even almost flat, depending on what rigidity you can introduce into the joints (which in wood is not very much). But if you introduce a diagonal member, you cannot distort it at all so long as the diagonal member is able to resist the compression or the tension which is introduced by the effort to distort it. A Western wooden truss starts then by being a combination of triangles.

In a true truss, members are supposed to act only as compression members or tension members,[2] and the loads are put on the truss only at the panel points. In many cases the bottom chord could be only a tension member, but in wooden trusses which support ceilings as well as roofs or floors, this is often not the case.

I cannot recommend that you try to remember the variety of trusses which have evolved or to spend much time trying to figure out how each works and what are its relative advantages and disadvantages. For Western timber architecture, however, it is important to note one further and beautiful development, a combination of brackets and corbels and trusses with both curved and straight members (not arches) called the hammer-beam truss, about which I shall offer more details later.

Similar developments occurred in the post and bracing of the wall frames, expressed most visibly in the early English churches and especially in the stave churches of Norway and later in different guise in the elegant half-timbers of England and of northern Europe, especially France and Germany.

---

[2] An oversimplification but good enough for our purposes.

EARLY WOODEN ARCHITECTURE

We will move rapidly by very early manifestations of wooden architecture, of which examples can be found almost anywhere where there was a supply of timber, for much the same reasons that we skip the circular huts of reeds of the tropics, the small domed grass huts of Swaziland, the snow blocks of the Arctic, or the pile houses of Borneo.

So too we will only wave at the vertical log cabins of the French American colonists or the Swedish horizontal log cabins adopted by the American pioneers, or the more elegant wood slab houses of old New England farms, and the still more refined log constructions of Saas Fee in the Valais of Switzerland.

No doubt many peoples whose architecture became one of brick or stone began with wood. We know this to have been so in Mesopotamia, Egypt, Greece, and Yucatan; this is shown by archeological research; moreover the later stone architectures often have vestigial details such as the triglyphs of Greece, the stone-carved canes of the Mayans, or the capitals of later Egypt so obviously derived from the palmetto or the papyrus. Again, although the earliest major architectural effort of the Muslims [Muhammed was still alive (d. 632)] was undertaken in wood by an Abyssinian carpenter from a wrecked ship and in his native style, essentially all the important subsequent architecture of Islam is in brick and stone.[3]

The wooden tradition in some of its most primitive forms persisted for a long time in the more remote parts of Russia. Eighteenth-century wooden storehouses there look like dilapidated Swiss Alpine log cabins. An eighteenth-century tavern between Kostroma and Yaroslavl bears some resemblance to the old stave churches of Norway. But as a contemporary lithograph reveals, it also used half-timbering, a ship's keel roof, and a little bit of everything. The church of St. Nicholas in Panilovo, built in 1600, had an octagonal plan with log walls, a pyramidal roof with an onion-bulb top, and a ship's keel gable. Stairs under the gables led from outside to the raised nave floor.

Such buildings contained the primary elements, however crudely stated, that were translated into stone in the later great churches. While the transition was going on, the northerners of Novgorod were derided by the Ukrainians of Kiev as "carpenters." The first masonry church seems to have been built in Kiev after the adoption of Christianity by Vladimir in 938. It was dedicated in 1037.

The most striking shift from wood to stone, with at the same time the most durable vestiges repeated in the new material, is no doubt to be

---

[3] The only important exception might be those deriving from the aisled basilica. Many of these continued to have triangular truss-beamed roofs of wood, as in the Great Mosque at Damascus begun in 1707.

found in the classic Greek temple. All the evidence and the speculations are too complex to recount here.

Carpenters were evidently recognized as serious craftsmen in Greece, even after the major shift occurred, and still worked on timber supports for use in construction for various construction engines and, of course, for roofs, but we shall not find joyful and loving use of wood in classical Greek or Roman building or really anywhere around the Mediterranean.

Among the Greeks when dressed stone replaced the old brick-and-timber construction, it was not treated as a major innovation calling for other kinds of expression. The general system of structure was unchanged, and so was the system of ornament, so that each traditional feature was Pl. 158 conscientiously reproduced in the new material, the *triglyphs* for the wooden beam ends, even the *guttae* which started as tapered wooden pins driven through the *taenia* to hold the beams on the *architrave*.

It is in Japan where we can see the most convincing contemporary continuation of an ancient wooden tradition. The first Japanese buildings were probably of forest materials—timber and bamboo frames covered with thatch. These frames were lashed together with twisted or braided ropes and naturally had no metal connectors. One type, which resembled a tent in appearance, was probably built over a pit so that the gable started at ground level. The other was a development of the tent roof into a low-walled hut on stilts, or later a platform such as may still be found in the coastal or river areas of southeast Asia. These dwellings laid down the lasting elements of Japanese architecture: the wood frame, no load-bearing walls, the platform on stilts suitable for building on a damp or rocky or steep hillside site. The ridgepoles and battens were also an early feature. The temples of Ise are but a perfection of this, but this simple statement is a deceptive synopsis of the careful siting, the cultivation of the landscape, the studied simplicity, the refinement of proportion, of detail and of workmanship, the control of the plan through the modulus of the *tatami* mat.

The Western European experience was different both from the Greek and the Japanese. As in Greece the ultimate great material for great architecture in Europe became stone, but the wood tradition was persistent in the north—from the stave churches of medieval Norway to the great wooden trusses of England and the half-timbers of England and the Continent. Up to this point there was an affection for wood which might have led to a continuation of the wooden tradition along different lines to parallel that of Japan. But it did not work out that way. Indeed toward the end of the period of the great wooden architecture of England, the carpenters were making woodwork to look like stone vaulting! This was the precise opposite to the Greeks, who kept the forms of the old material in the new; skillful English carpentry was used in a decadent way to shape the old materials in the form of the new.

Thus we have three quite different examples of the early use and early abandonment of wood (Islam, Russia, and Greece), of a long but ultimately decaying tradition in wood (northern Europe), and of a tradition in wood which has remained beautifully alive for a millennium (Japan and to a lesser extent, China).

Stave Churches

The oldest examples in the West of distinguished wooden architecture still to be seen in our day are stave churches, once abundant in Scandinavia, but the only original ones still extant are in Norway. In England, for example, despite her many early contacts with the Scandinavian peninsula and its peoples, there is very little evidence of pre-Conquest timber buildings. A sole survivor is a part of Greensted Church in Essex, which dates from about 1013.

The Norwegian churches are Christian and any vestiges of paganism are to be seen only in the sculpture. Christianity was introduced into Denmark when King Harald Blaatand (Harold Bluetooth) was christened in 950. He soon built a small stave church in Jelling, Jutland, 36 feet long and 20 feet wide with a 6-foot square choir at the end. This church, of which only fragments remained, has now been reconstructed in Jutland.

And although there must have been many stave churches in Sweden, the only one now preserved there is at Hedared in the woods of Västergötland, all the rest having been replaced by stone. One has been reconstructed at Skäne. Hence if you want to see stave churches as originals, you will have to go to Norway. How many of these buildings still exist there, all dating from the twelfth and thirteenth centuries, seems to be a matter of considerable disagreement, but the authorities hover between 20 to 30 out of an original 500 to 600. What is certain is that there are a number eloquently worth visiting, for example, at Borgund, Urnes, Lom, Heddal, Torpo, Hylestad, Røldal, Rødberg, and Vaga, plus one which, originally at Gol, has been rebuilt in the Folklore Museum at Bygdøy, which is reached by ferry from Oslo. Moreover, there are remnants of beautiful portals of churches now destroyed, such as that of Ål in the Hallingdal or the famous portal of Hylestad, to be found in such museums as the Oldsaksamling at Oslo University.

Pl. 41

Of the standing churches it must be said that though they have common features, they also have substantial differences. There are single-aisle versions, and basilican types with more than one range of interior wooden posts, and though they are obviously related to the contemporary stone Romanesque churches to the south, they are by no means the same thing with a mere substitution of wood for stone. The same must be said of their decorative and sculptural elements, seemingly borrowed also from Romanesque stone, so that Urnes reminds us of Souillac so far away in the south of France (Périgord) without being at all the same thing.

They vary noticeably in their verticality. The roofs of Borgund pile up outside around the spire to produce an effect comparable to but not at all like the multiple apses of the French Romanesque. Urnes has fewer roofs and they are less clustered so that the effect is more that of a linear projection of three stepped-down roofs; its tower spire, an octagonal form rising from a square base, rests on the ridge at the high end of these roof stairs and not in the center.

Pl. 44

Of the churches, Heddal is the largest, Urnes in my opinion the most interesting, Gol or Borgund the most beautiful. But you had better go and see for yourself.

Although recent excavations at Urnes show traces of an older building constructed on piles which may be taken as a forerunner of the later stave church construction, the bulk of these churches in Norway were presumably built in the Middle Ages, most of them in the Romanesque period from 1050–1180. They never became large as architecture goes and the earliest, such as the Holtalen in Kinsarvik, were very small and also very simple, the plan consisting only of a small rectangular nave and a tiny projecting straight-ended choir.

The main elements of the plan resemble those of the contemporary stone churches in the rest of Europe, having a main room for the congregation and a chancel at the far end, but the cults of saints and martyrs and the consequent pilgrimages were rare in the north, and so did not lead to later apsidal and ambulatory developments to be found in the south. Moreover the main area or nave was nearly square in plan, so that the church seems to open up not along a longitudinal horizontal axis but rather along a vertical axis stretching toward the capping pyramid. This verticality of the nave is quite different from that, say, of the elongated nave of Amiens. Why the churches developed this way, I have no idea. Though it was possible to build this way with the materials at hand, these materials by no means dictated such a construction.

The materials were wood—sometimes oak and chestnut but more usually the array of long resinous timbers prevalent in the Scandinavian forests.

The frames had vertical timbers or posts to which the horizontal members were jointed with the joints strengthened by wooden pins (later nails) and diagonal braces. The same principles applied without regard to the size of the building, which never became big enough to make them awkward to apply. In the simplest types, four vertical posts (staves) were fixed to a bottom frame of logs which in their turn rested on an internal frame of logs laid on stone foundations. Up at the top the staves carried horizontal members which supported the roof. The closure was by wall boards pushed into sockets carved into the posts and rafters. The sloping parts of the roof were braced by horizontal tie beams and cross members. The most elementary but rarest roof was a simple span repeating the principle of a ridgepole supported by a king or queen post resting on the bottom chord, but more frequently trussed rafters made of pairs of rafters without a ridgepole were used. Here the outward thrust was contained by horizontal collarbeams at the level of the wall plate, or by braces or collar-beams halfway up the length which allowed more height and headroom. Sometimes the rafters were connected by curved timbers to form what is called an arched trussed rafter.

When the church was built on a basilican plan, there was a low and wide construction, within which rose the higher construction to offer clerestory windows. The choir was usually long and narrow, and if terminated by an apse it might be either semicircular or orthagonal.

One diagram, a cross section of Borgund, will tell more clearly than many words how this worked out.

Pl. 43

The exterior effect is spectacularly pyramidal in the finest examples, where the steep shingled roofs at many angles rise over the various interior spaces from the outer aisles and porches to the spire.

The exteriors owe most of their effect to the contrasts of planes and wooden materials and there is relatively little sculpture, save for a cross on top of the tower. But often on the eaves and at the upper gables are dragon heads which look much like the figureheads of the old Viking ships. On the latter at any rate they were supposed to drive away evil spirits, and the Fodor guide suggests that on the churches they existed also "just for safety's sake," as a kind of hedge in the event that Christianity turned out to be a booby trap after all. This may indeed be a reason. Nevertheless the only rich ornamentation on the exteriors is at the portals, and these too contain motifs that could be interpreted as pagan, going way back in form at times to the rune stones. But the *art is* Christian art despite its zoomorphic nature, which seems to rely more on the Bestiaries, for example, than on the Gospels, the Mirrors of Vincent of Beauvais, the Apocalypse, or the countless other more specifically Christian sources to be found, for example, in France. Fronds, animal designs, fighting dragons interlace as they might have in earlier Norse or Celtic periods, but they have attained a Christian symbolism just as they have at Souillac.

Pl. 44

Inside, the capitals are often richly carved with the same motifs and these sometimes also turn up on the pews, as at Lom. Occasionally there are human figures, as in the famous twelfth-century portal of Hylestad, now in the Oslo University collection; still less frequently one finds an extremely high quality of human carving, as in the head of a monk from Urnes.

But despite the spots of elegant decoration, the interiors of the stave churches, like the exteriors, owe most of their appeal to the combinations of positive and negative planes, to the piling up of structural motifs, and to the power and subtle skill of their carpentry.

The European Tradition—Roofs and Trusses

As we go around looking at the wooden roofs of the West, we will encounter many forms: the one-sloped lean-to; the typical V-shaped gable; the hipped roof where the gables are cut off diagonally at the ends; the

Pl. 49

mansard which has two pitches, a steeper one at the bottom and a flatter one at the top; the pyramidal, especially for spires; the conoidal for the same situations; more complicated forms of these, such as the rhomboidal and the folded rhomboidal; and the curious bulbous or onion shapes which we associate with Russia though they may have an Islamic origin. Wooden structural systems might have been and indeed were used to support all these types, some of which required very complicated if generally concealed carpentry—but the great development of the wooden truss as a visible and important architectural motif, principally in England, occurred almost exclusively in connection with the simplest of all the symmetrical roof shapes, the gable.

The use of the truss unconcealed to support the roof was old enough. It was common in the early Christian basilicas. It appeared in the old basilican church of St. Peter and in San Paolo fuori le Mura at Rome. There is an open roof truss at Romanesque Monreale. Even as late as the Gothic period in Italy, such churches as the cathedral in Orvieto or Santa Croce in Florence were curious Gothic versions of basilican churches retaining open timber roofs. But these seem to have been considered merely utilitarian devices, and if something "finer" was desired, as in the Romanesque nave of Peterborough, the trusses were boarded in. Here a tie-beam roof (see page 115) is ceiled under with boards, in panel form, running the length of the nave. The outer rows are canted where they meet the top of the clerestory wall. The boarding of the panels is diagonal and thus produces a handsome lozenge-shaped pattern. Though the painting was much renewed in the fourteenth century and later, it is still considered typical. Webb says this is the only surviving example in Britain of a timber roof in a Romanesque building of the first order.[4] The nave ceiling at Ely, which looks similar, was actually boarded and painted in the nineteenth century and the original roof appears in engravings as of open trussed rafter construction. Such applied ceilings are handsome enough at times but lack the mystery and the elegance attained by the best of the later open truss work. The most famous of Romanesque painted wooden ceilings is St. Savin-sur-Gartempe near Poitiers in France.

Trusses were also used in more utilitarian and concealed ways *over* the *vaults* of the Gothic cathedrals, to support the tile or leaden roofs which kept off the rain which would otherwise have seeped through the vaulted masonry. When we look at the interior of a vaulted Gothic cathedral, for example, we are often not looking at the form of the roof. The fan vaulting of King's College Chapel in Cambridge, for example, is surmounted by simple hammer-beam trussing. Such light covers are found almost everywhere—from Autun, where the truss work is simple, to St. Stephen's in Vienna where the roof of the transepts soars so high above the vaults. In most of the French cases, however, the umbrella is as compact as the roof pitch will permit.

[4] Geoffrey Webb, *Architecture in Britain: The Middle Ages* (Baltimore: Penguin, 1956).

But these are mere practical matters and I am concerned here with the exfoliation of the truss as a beautiful thing in its own right, qualified to take a high position in ornamental architecture. To follow this we must, I am afraid, go back to a description of the various potentials.

Open timber roofs were carried to a far higher degree of development in England than anywhere else in the West, and this development may be said to have culminated with the elaborate hammer-beam varieties of the fifteenth century, often gilded or painted in gay colors or both. But it would be wrong to think of this as an evolution from the simplest forms to the more complex. Unlike the march of stone vaulting from the barrel to the ribbed arch and flying buttress, all the principal wooden types, except possibly the hammer beam, seem to have arrived at about the same time and to have been used indiscriminately, the choice being more conditioned by the desired pitch of the roof than by the popularity of a given truss type. Fletcher has proposed four classes of roof in addition to the hammer beam, which I would like to treat separately, the tie beam, the trussed rafter, the collar beam, and the aisle.

Tie-beam roofs were the simplest of these types and possibly the earliest. Two rafters were butted against each other and held together at the bottom by a tie beam which thus contained any outward thrust. They were common in the Norman days but persisted throughout the Middle Ages. Samples can be found in Trinity Chapel in Arencester Church and St. Martin's in Leicester. Early on, the beam was pinned to the wall plates, as were the rafters, and the tie was not connected directly to the rafters. As time went on, some changes were made in the interest of harmonious design. The tie beam might curve slightly upward toward the center. In steep roofs the space above the tie beam could be filled with posts and carved tracery (Outwell, Norfolk). Curved braces might connect the tie beam to the wall, producing a frame that was shaped like a four-centered arch.

Trussed rafter roofs, as at Stow Bardolph Church in Norfolk, may have begun as Fletcher suggests to give room for pointed vaults beneath, but, when visible, they did look higher and more impressive and might have been chosen over the tie-beam type for this reason. Each rafter now had a collar stiffened by braces. Sometimes these would pass through the collar (Lympenhoe, Norfolk), or they might stop at the underside (Stow Bardolph, Norfolk). Since the rafters rested on the outer portion of the wall, an unsightly ledge was left on the inside, though it was partly concealed by upright struts which helped to stabilize the rafters. Fletcher suggests[5] that the triangle thus formed was the origin of the hammer beam, but this, though plausible, is conjecture. A trussed rafter roof might be given an arched form by using curved timbers to connect the rafters and collars (Solihull). Again these might be lined with boards to form a pentag-

[5] Sir Banister Fletcher, *A History of Architecture on the Comparative Method*, 17th ed. (New York: Scribner, 1961).

onal ceiling, whether or not with ribbed and bossed ornaments. Such roofs, no longer open, are called *barrel roofs*.

Collar-beam roofs, of which St. Mary Magdalen at Pulham is an example, can be regarded as a simplification of the elegant hammer beams. Here the arched braces, as thick as the rafters (as they were not in collar-braced types), were carried to the ridge without the intervention of collars. They served both to strengthen the trusses and to carry the outward thrust lower down on the wall, thus reducing the tendency to tip it over. A roof of this type can still be seen in the great hall at Stokesay Castle, really a fortified house, in Shropshire. It is well to remind you here that not all the examples cited are still extant and that a serious traveler will need to do his own current checking as to their availability and the amount and quality of restoration, since faithful restoration and contemporary active church requirements are not always fully compatible even in the roofs (for example, the church at Sompting in England).

Aisle roofs need not play an important part in this account. Examples such as those of New Walsingham or Ixworth in Norfolk usually began as a simple continuation of the nave rafters, but trusses were soon introduced to support purlins, and then the tie beam of the aisle truss might be carried through the nave wall to supply a corbel for the wall piece of the nave roof.

You can spend a good deal of pleasurable time in tracking down these simple structures, as I have, but in the end you will I think agree with me that the glorious flowers of all this burgeoning are the *hammer-beam trusses*.

How early these began is not a conjectural trail I ask you to follow. There is a drawing in Villard de Honnecourt's famous sketchbook of about 1240, but the hammer beams never became really current in France or in England before the fourteenth century. Webb says the earliest known *dated* example is Westminster Hall, which was begun about 1394, but adds that so perfected an example could hardly have been the earliest of its type.

Pl. 47

Also I think it idle here to wonder whether it did really evolve from the triangle at the foot of the trussed roof. What is clear is that its purpose is to get the weight and thrust of the roof as low down on the supporting wall as possible, thus reducing the tipping tendency. Each truss has two principal rafters and hammer beams with struts, curved braces, and collars, all of which may vary in quantity and in shape. The hammer beam itself is a lengthened sole piece. The projecting part is supported from below by a curved brace reaching from the wall. It supports a vertical strut which helps to support the rafter. All this system is tenoned and pinned to form a rigid structure. It does exert some thrust on the walls, which was sometimes resisted in Gothic designs by an exterior stone buttress. The hammer-beam trusses were not always used throughout and might be alternated, for example, with beam trusses.

Once invented, such trusses offered possibilities for enormous variations. Little Welnetham in Suffolk combines the hammer beams with struts, collars, and curved braces. At Wymondham and Trunch in Norfolk the collar beams are left out and the curved braces are carried up to a wedge-shaped strut at the ridge. At Palgrave in Suffolk these curved braces go all the way to the ridge. At Capel St. Mary, and Hampton Court Palace, the hammer beams are short and the struts are replaced by curved braces with collar beams above. In Eltham Palace and Westminster Hall, an arched rib springing from the wall piece to the collar gives additional rigidity. At Knapton a second range of hammer beams is used further to stiffen the principals and adds to the elegant complexity. This double hammer was a magnificent development, most practiced in East Anglia. The lower brackets project from the clerestory wall to support via posts and curved struts a second set of brackets projecting from the *middle* of the principal rafters—thence arched braces mount to collars. Some of these alternate with plain arch braces or tie-beam trusses, and they are often decorated profusely with polychromed bosses and especially with angels who seem to glide into the room on outspread wings.

Pl. 45
Pl. 46
Pl. 50
Pl. 48

The buildings already cited have probably given sufficient evidence that these great wooden trusses were as common in secular buildings as in clerical. It is possible to cite countless examples in such hospitals as St. Mary's in Chichester, almshouses as at St. John's, Northampton, barns such as the Tithe Barn at Bradford on Avon. They served the bar well at Gray's Inn Hall or in the Middle Temple. And they were very common adornments of great halls in "castles" such as Stokesay or manors such as Little Wenham Hall, Suffolk, Penshurst Place, Kent, or even the banqueting hall at Haddon Hall in Derbyshire. The greatest of them all, miraculously spared from Nazi fire bombs, and now being protected from a more steadfast enemy, the deathwatch beetle, is Westminster Hall, whose hammer beams cover an area of half an acre with such an elegance of curved braces, carved figures, and period tracery that it is hard to understand why the style was abandoned for the more difficult and scarcely more elegant perpendicular tracery and vaulting in stone. It is probably the finest example of the style to be found anywhere.

Pl. 51

Now I may have imposed on you a longer discussion than you care to have encountered. But first I have a particular affection for these things, and secondly I wanted to offer some intimation of what you might get into if you get serious about any one of many developments in architecture, even one which seems minor. You can do this with vaults, or buttresses, or Last Judgments, or stained glass, or classic column details, or little mosques, or almost anything that strikes your fancy. It is a recreation highly to be recommended, offering not only its internal pleasures, comparable to those enjoyed, I suppose, by the serious collector, but also, I believe, a better understanding of or at least sympathy for the richness to be found in types of architecture which you may not have had time or inclination to pursue.

Though a great deal of this particular collecting can be done without ever leaving East Anglia, the trusses are richly available in other parts of England as well, and if I have turned your fancy in this direction you could not do better than to engage yourself with the thorough and interesting and completely authentic series[6] by Nikolaus Pevsner, whose paperbacks, shire by shire, cover the historical architecture of England so completely. It is a treatment of architecture which is unique.

Some other examples of the monumental English timber construction which began at the end of the thirteenth and the early fourteenth centuries are quite different. There is the roof of the Chapter House at York covering an octagonal space with an internal diameter of 59 feet. This dates from 1300. A quarter century later it was followed by what many regard as the most remarkable of all English timber building, the *Pl. 52* roof and lantern tower of the Octagon at the eastern crossing of Ely Cathedral. Ely has much other wood, including the much-decorated transepts with fifteenth-century hammer beams. Here the angels are doubled, their bodily postures are different, and each bears a different symbol. These lead to the lantern of the crossing.

The stone Romanesque lantern tower of this eastern crossing fell in 1322, and Alan of Walsingham conceived the idea of replacing it in wood. One bay of each of the four arms of the church was devoted to the crossing space to form an irregular octagon of which the cardinal sides were defined by the arches of the choir, transept, and nave from the eight points of the stone octagon. Elaborate timber brackets of great size carry eight massive oak uprights 63 feet high which form the angles of the central octagonal lantern. A model shows the construction most clearly.

Now, however, function was abandoned. The underside of the timber brackets was ceiled with boarding but this was not enough. Ribs were added to give the appearance of stone vaulting over a 70-foot-diameter space.

Here is the first sign, despite its remarkable quality, of an unwillingness to let wood be wood but to make it seem like stone. Ultimately this trend brought about the demise of the great tradition of carpentry. But not right away. The execution of Ely was by William Hurley, the King's Master Carpenter, founder of a great dynasty of timber engineers who, two generations later, indulged in no such folly of imitating stone when they built the trussed roof of Westminster Hall.

The hammer-beam trusses of the Great Hall at Hampton Court Palace were built between 1531 and 1536 by Henry VIII to replace the modest hall of Wolsey's house. But this marked the end of the great and honest hammer-beam tradition which from Westminster Hall to Hampton Court had a span of about a century and a half. Even a year before the Great Hall was finished, the same capricious monarch lavishly embellished the

---

[6] Penguin Books, Baltimore, various dates; a few are in cloth; perhaps a few are out of print.

Chapel Royal built originally by Wolsey with a new fan-vaulted ceiling, carved and gilded pendants, and a blue vault powdered with stars all looking like stone but in fact executed in wood.[7]

Thus the tradition of the great English wooden roofs came full circle. Later there were the wooden vaults at St. Alban's Abbey, then the Octagon at Ely, and finally the woodworking ended as it began at the Chapel Royal. It is probably true that the ceiling of this chapel is "one of the most remarkable pieces of joinery ever achieved."[8] But when you visit it, I wonder if you will find the Chapel Royal as unhappy as I do. Surely it is hard to see the ceiling against the intrusions of the painted designs between the windows and the oak reredos demanded by Queen Anne, designed by Christopher Wren, and carved by Grinling Gibbons—good work in an inappropriate place.

But somehow I think it is possible to expunge the later corruptions from the mind and still see that the ceiling lacks the quality on the one hand of the true wooden expression of Westminster Hall, or on the other of the true stone fan vaulting of King's College Chapel in Cambridge or the Chapel of Henry VII in Westminster Abbey finished twenty years before the Chapel Royal was undertaken. The artisans were surely not at fault—their work could scarcely have been better. Was it because the designers were dull—or because nobody can make a lie, even an architectural lie, seem beautiful? This is a decision you should make for yourself. I used to know what I thought. Now I am less sure and in no mood to impose my uncertainties on you.

Half-timbering

Another development of medieval timber architecture, which should not be shrugged off as merely picturesque, is the half-timbering which is to be found in different manners in England, France, and Germany.

It was traditionally made of squared oak timbers connected to each other by the usual joinery of wooden pegs or mortises and tenons. This produced a frame only, and the wall was completed by filling in between with straw and mud or brick, sometimes carelessly, sometimes with care approaching elegance. Though the extant examples are mostly to be found in Western Europe, it was a natural way of doing things. It was once common enough in China and Japan; there are many remains at Pompeii of houses whose upper floors were built this way. The origins in Europe were doubtless simple "cruck" houses of which a few examples still remain, such as the end of a cottage at Sutton Bonington in Nottinghamshire.

Despite the paucity of Anglo-Saxon remains, it is possible to deduce that the West Germanic races in England were familiar with half-timber

[7] *Guide Book Hampton Court Palace* (Ministry of Works, London), pp. 14 and 20.
[8] Webb, *Architecture in Britain*, op. cit.

construction. Early stone buildings again reflect a vestigial influence of wooden details, since the strip-patterning of wall surfaces produced by the wood technique was copied in stone where it had no functional significance. An interesting example of this is to be found in the Saxon west tower of Earl's Barton. Here the stone strips, structurally irrelevant, are arranged in zigzag patterns and vertical rows as a surface decoration. Their monotony is generally regarded as characteristic of Saxon design. Such linear decoration, still further modified from its original inspiration, is used with more refinement in later English Gothic, but in these cases the half-timbered source is quite forgotten.

Whether coming from cruck houses or stave churches, this wooden architecture seems to have appeared all over Europe where the influence of Roman stone architecture was slender and where most of the people were of Germanic stock. It was a style that could thrive only where the climate suggested it, where the woods were suitable, and where there were skilled carpenters. The best examples are certainly medieval, although the style lasted into the seventeenth century. Probably many of the best ones go back as far as the twelfth century, though until the fifteenth century the remains are sparse and hard to date closely, thanks to many alterations and additions.

Almost everywhere the country units were rambling, made up of the addition of one unit to another. In the crowded towns, however, the buildings tended to be narrow, had steep gables, and rose to heights of six or seven stories. In earlier times the upper stories projected from the lower. The reason may have been military but this is dubious. The projection did add a little space to the upper floors and did provide a little protection to the doors below from rain or slops. But most likely these were advantages incidental to an important structural consideration: The beams, thus cantilevered, counterbalanced to some degree the loads carried on the full spans. The construction, though mainly interfilled with solid materials in early days, offered all sorts of opportunities to the panels; shutters, louvers, or bars appeared, and as life became more secure and glass technology improved, the spaces began to be filled with leaded glass windows.

The carpentry obviously offered many options to the whim of the designer. The exposed ground posts might be carved with images of the proprietors, the craftsmen, or the patron saints. Other framing elements might or might not be enriched, but as time went on generally were. The carving became lavish, and fanciful wooden members were added apparently with structural purpose but actually with none. The filling panels, first of earth, were later built of brick in careful herringbone array or the plaster was molded or incised with floral and other forms or might have inlays of stone or colored tiles. But it was the arrangement of the structural members themselves which really and properly dominated the design, and here again there was a wide range of legitimate choice. If the verticals were set very close together and the bracing omitted or concealed, a pronounced vertical rhythm was achieved. Though this was a favorite device in France, it existed on both coasts of the Channel well into the Renaissance, and one of the most pleasant examples is the President's Lodge at Queen's College, Cambridge, of about 1540. *Pl. 54*

But especially in England as the Western world moved into the Renaissance, square panel forms became more popular, more timber work was exposed, crisscrossed bracing became common beneath the windows, and elsewhere the panels were broken by cusped shapes or chevrons which produced brilliant contrasts of black and white, particularly in some of the west counties such as Cheshire or Lancashire. For a long time German designs were simpler, stronger, perhaps even cruder, laying heavy emphasis on the angle bracings, curved or straight. These might run across many vertical strips; though characteristic, it was not uniquely German, as, for example, Swaffham Prior, Baldwin Manor, built in Cambridgeshire in the first half of the sixteenth century, attests.

Though there were generally national characteristics, they can only be called characteristic and not defining, since all the patterns of disposition of the posts, the sills and ledges and the braces, diagonal or curved, flowed easily across national boundaries. Indeed there were even more localized characteristics also not confined to the region they dominated. In German Franconia the timbers tended to be quite wide-spaced, as in the attractive town hall at Michelstadt, but in Saxony they tended to be close together. *Pl. 53* Moreover, as in the splendid sixteenth-century Knockenhauern-Amtshaus of Hildesheim, which was destroyed in World War II, each timber sprung from one of a row of handsome corbels which supported the overhanging storys. Alsatian and Swabian designs emphasized the windows by projecting their frames outward from the corbels. The great, almost fantastic one is the Kammerzellschen Haus (Maison Kammerzell), a large house of 1580 *Pl. 55* just around the corner from the cathedral in Strasbourg.

The picturesque patterns made by dark timbers and light interfills might be thought to supply decoration enough, but more elaborately minded patrons or designers demanded wooden carvings, often painted with stucco (Hildesheim) or painted decorations (Kammerzell) between. It was fairly common in all the countries that the ground story should be of stone but sometimes the building rested on sturdy open trussed porches as at Michelstadt or the Market Hall at Ledbury in Hereford where the *Pl. 56* open porch has sturdy posts and knees to support the upper stories, most of whose timber is chevroned except in the gable.

Though you can make an excellent tour of half-timbered buildings in Germany, the largest number of good examples now are probably in England. In the west of England it was common to divide all the outer surfaces into regular compartments which might be patterned differently on each story. The Feather's Inn at Ludlow in Shropshire of 1603 is an example.

The Architecture of Wood 121

Here there are three stories and three gables, and the horizontal window bands have diamonds at the first floor level and cusps at the second. The windows here are very large, forming essentially continuous horizontal elements interrupted only by thin mullions and by their leaded-glass panes, and a balcony at the first floor adds to the memorable confusion. Bishop Percy's House (1580) at Bridgnorth, on the other hand, also with three stories, alternates cusped panels under the windows and a combination of cusps and curved diagonal braces between them at the second story but goes to herringbones and cusps at the third. A well-known timber-framed building at Pitchford, Shropshire (1560–70), though rambling in plan, presents only an orderly array of herringbones with simple verticals beneath the windows, and at the ground floor bays at the end of the projecting wings. This geometry, free from curves, nonetheless offers a tendency toward one of the simpler confusions of op art. The additional variations seem endless, such as the Butcher's Row in Shrewsbury, Leycester's Hospital in Warwick, or Little Moreton Hall in Cheshire, whose courtyard (1550–59) reveals a great deal of glass.

In the eastern counties, as I have said, the tradition followed that of France, stemming no doubt from the Normans. Thus there are close resemblances between the sixteenth-century Maison Quatrans in Caen and the Middle House at Mayfield in Sussex, although the former has intermediate spaces halved together to form a series of crosses, and the latter adds cusps to the verticals. The common principle was that the strips of wall between were barely wider than the posts themselves. The vertical accent was common in the east of England in buildings such as the Old Wool Hall at Lavenham in Suffolk, or the Paycocke's House, 1500, at Great Coggeshall in Essex. It was common too in London before most of the old buildings were swept away by the seventeenth- and twentieth-century fires, and we can see a good example in a photograph of the Staple Inn built at Holborn in 1581, which is now gone. But it spread westward too, so that an etching of Bramhall Hall in Cheshire of the fifteenth century shows a ground story in the vertical style while the upper stories and the gables belong to the western tradition.

Evidently the half-timbers of England and Germany offer as rich and varied an experience for the collector of architectural specialties as the open roof trusses do. But it is a collection which should not be postponed too long, since the deathwatch beetle, fire, urban redevelopment, and war are not extinct and work almost as inexorably to reduce the supply of noble wood examples as industrial smog does to erode the stones of the cathedrals from Milan and Mexico City to London.

The half-timber tradition was tenacious and in places continued even into the nineteenth century, but it lost its elan after the days of Elizabeth and James. It came to the United States undiluted as to structure with the New England colonists, but the rigors of climate soon enough caused the settlers to cover the timbers with boards, and so the exterior appearance vanished.[9] When it reappeared in college and suburban Tudor, it was entirely fake, with thin boards applied to or sunk into plaster appearing to be the structural members they were not.

With the discontinuing of the open trusses and the half-timbers, the great days of wood as a primary material in Western architecture were over. I know that aficionados of American architecture will be offended by this statement. They will point to Colonial New England houses, to the mansions of Charleston, South Carolina, to Downing's board and batten style of 1842, to the Newport shingle style as exemplified by the Watts Sherman house in Newport of 1874, or the California redwood work of a succession of house designers from the brothers Greene and Bernard Maybeck to William Wilson Wurster and Harwell Harris, ending, if not culminating, at the moment with the stovepipe, Sea Ranch style fostered by such designers as Charles Moore. All of these save the last seem to me to have charm at various levels, as do the wood details of Alvar Aalto. But let us face it—however attractive some may be, they are not architecture at the level of importance occupied by the stave churches, the hammer beams, and the half-timbers.

Wood As Accessory

Of course wood never disappeared from American domestic architecture. And it was and still is used elegantly as interior finish material, simple or complicated, so that until great Western wooden sculptors and cabinetmakers became scarce, it remained important, though in minor ways.

The flèche, the slender pyramidal spire over the crossing of French Gothic cathedrals, was often made of wood. There were magnificent wooden doors well into the Renaissance. Choir screens of wood in the Flemish style were remarkable, and I have a particular fondness for the sometimes serious, sometimes humorous, sometimes pious, sometimes symbolic, sometimes vulgar, sometimes just indecent miserichords of many a medieval choir stall.

These stalls provided a row of hinged seats in the chancel for the clergy and the choir. They were hinged so that you could be supported during an interminable stand and also so that if you nodded into sleep it would slap you awake. Support for the occupant was provided by a small bracket. This was called the miserichord, and it was frequently carved, grotesquely or charmingly. I have squandered many an hour turning the seats up and down, fighting off a tiring back, a suspicious verger, or an overly reverent fellow tourist.

There are the splendid Spanish wooden retables and balustrades; oriel windows such as the one at the town hall at Krems in Austria, even though the architectural form is now overshadowed by the emphasis on

---

[9] It did not disappear so rapidly in the French and German American settlements where there were faithful copies of the Continental models being made even to the middle of the nineteenth century.

decoration. There is the great wooden screen of King's College Chapel of 1530; the ceilings of the galleries of Francis I and Henri II at Fontainebleau, or the Great Chamber of the Chateau de Blois of the sixteenth century; the Golden Room of the Rathaus at Augsburg of the early seventeenth century, many of these combined with stucco, paint, and gilt; the mirror frames of Versailles, the restrained decorative use of wood in the Renaissance interiors of England, especially in the Georgian Period as, for example, at the Banqueting Hall in Whitehall Palace by Inigo Jones, where wood is presented in modified classic stone forms. All of these and many more, some extending quite late into our own time, are examples of intelligent and often affectionate uses of wood to be examined and relished as one encounters them in a building. Though they are not the centrality of the architecture, without them the architecture would be diminished.

THE WOODEN ARCHITECTURE OF THE ORIENT—CHINA AND JAPAN

I have not been able to visit the great Chinese monuments on the mainland, and though I promised not to talk about many things I have not seen, I now need to fudge the promise a little because the Chinese and possibly Korean underpinning of Japanese architecture is of importance. It is possible I think to do this without aesthetic judgments which would really be permissible only to the visitor.

Like the Japanese, the early Chinese builders often had access to pine or cedar timbers of great width and girth and were perhaps more limited by problems of transportation from the mountains than by the size of the trees which grew there. There were differences between the north and the south as to the size of available timbers, with some effect on buildings, but this is a distinction that need not be labored here. The same is true of the fact that there were stylistic differences in the upturn of the eaves, or that the southern upturns were more extravagant, or that the northern quieter tradition was generally dominant.

The Chinese also had good stone or bronze to provide bases for the columns which would protect them from the damp. But despite the generous size of some of their timbers, the Chinese builders, like those of the West, soon reached a point where they wanted to span a space longer than their timbers would reach or where the excess of the span became so great as to cause undue deflection. In the solution of the spanning problem, the West chose the truss, essentially a rigid triangle above the column level, an excellent system but one which inhibited expansion and was not very flexible. The Chinese, on the other hand, shortened the span by corbels and brackets, and by superimposing on the first layer of corbels short vertical members to sustain a second similar system and so on, built up a sequence which seemed to lock together endlessly. Each increasing projection was carefully balanced on the one below, sometimes in one plane, sometimes in two, at right angles to each other. Thus the place of the wooden arch or truss was taken by a system of beams of diminishing length as you moved toward the peak of the roof.

Such a beam-frame system is obviously capable of great expansion in every direction. Transversely (in the direction of the span) the Chinese could increase the number of beams, could add columns, could provide for veranda bays or inner spaces of almost any desired width. Longitudinally, as in the West, the building could be extended by repetition. Upward the heights of different parts of the cross section could be varied almost at will so that low verandas, for example, could be combined with higher internal rooms, clerestories were easily arranged, mezzanines and upper stories could be inserted.

Pl. 57

Even greater freedom was afforded the design of the roof line. This was controlled by the relative position of the purlins, and these could be positioned as desired by the use of struts. Thus the Chinese could easily build a wholly straight or a wholly curved roof line or any combination of these. Each of the forms appeared on appropriate occasions. Humbler or more utilitarian roofs were usually straight; buildings of ceremonial or other importance were usually curved, including a dramatic form which reversed itself and swept over the apex curved like a wave without the appearance of any ridge at all.

This great balancing act had another influence on roof design. A cantilever is a special kind of balancing which the Chinese understood very well; they used it to provide large overhangs at the eaves. They were able to do this in several ways, but the main way of carrying the rafters out well beyond the columns was a cluster of brackets called *tou-kung*.[10] Such brackets were also used for internal cantilever supports.

Pl. 58
Pl. 59

The extended eaves had more than visual importance. These buildings had an open plan, sometimes even without walls at the end, they were made of wood, and they needed the weather protection provided by the eaves.

Pl. 60

Above this beam and bracket system were longitudinal purlins commonly round in section; these in turn carried round bamboo rafters, running transversely, to which boarding was fixed. On the boarding was an insulating layer of clay; above that two layers of finishing segmental tiles. Given the fact that the roofs were at will gabled, half-hipped, half-gabled, hipped, or pyramidal to many different degrees of pitch and curvature and that the tiles might be grey, purple, blue, green, or yellow with or without glaze, it is evident that even before any wood carving was indulged in, the Chinese architect had a large potential palette.

The same range was open to him in the planning. He might leave the roof timbers to be seen—or he might fix on or suspend from a chosen

---

[10] One special form, which developed under the Sungs, used very high raked brackets called *ang-tou-kung*. They were independent and asymmetrical, and with them structures of great elegance were achieved.

level of crossbeams a wooden ceiling intended entirely as decoration or visual confinement of space. These ceilings were most often of square frames in panel or coffer form.

He had the same flexibility in subdivision. His walls and his partitions were screens not structures and even the end walls of buildings did not carry loads. They might then be sloped back so that the upper brackets and the roof could be seen. Thus he had no need to make cornices. Internal partitions, framed in timber, could be put almost anywhere and were often not carried up to the crossbeams.

All these features can be seen in Japanese architecture with some differences in taste which are of considerable importance.

For example, Chinese design seems to have regarded the whole building as an exercise in color quite as important as the exercise in form. It may be, as Andrew Boyd suggests, that this was very uncommon in architectural history, although certainly something comparable is to be seen in the great Iranian examples of Islamic architecture as well as in the Chaldean ziggurats.

> The functional basis was the protection of the timber members from decay and parasites; the aesthetic aim was that the timbers played a major part in a totally polychromatic building. The actual colours varied according to time and place. Their general distribution was: enclosing walls and base walls, if plastered and not left in natural materials, one colour, often red, also white, yellow or black. Balustrades on top of such a wall or podium, with their steps and ramp, one colour, if painted at all and not left natural, e.g., white marble. Columns one colour, often red. Beams, brackets, rafters, eaves members and ceilings, a range of vivid colours and patterns. Roof, one colour throughout, including the decorative and symbolic ornaments at the ridge and eaves.[11]

Sometimes this painting could even be pictorial. The long gallery of the Summer Palace (1644–1911) has scenes of the palace painted on the beams of each bay.

Although the Japanese did use painted screens to great effect in their interiors, and although some *torii*, bridges, and even pagodas, as well as Shinto shrines like Kasuga, are painted in brilliant vermilion, and the *Pl. 62* deeply undercut Momoyama reliefs were polychromatic, the Japanese use of wood was generally far more restrained, which is consistent with their higher standards of craftsmanship and less exuberant temperament, betrayed only occasionally in such ostentatious "baroque" displays as the Tokugawa mausolea at Nikko. The Japanese seldom painted or treated the wood but preferred to exploit its natural characteristics of texture and color.

This much of Japanese prototype seems worth remembering. Fossil remains now make it clear that Japan was once joined to the mainland of

[11] Andrew Boyd, "Chinese Architecture," in Trewin Copplestone (ed.), *World Architecture* (New York: McGraw-Hill, 1963), p. 86.

Asia. Even after the geologic and geographic separation, birds, seeds, and the like—and no doubt some humans—moved freely across the waters. The Japanese culture was never totally isolated from the continent. Very old artifacts bear what scholars believe to be clear traces of influence from Greece, Iran, and India as channeled through the Korean Peninsula and China.[12] We can take this for granted and not try to sort them out further, interesting and complicated as the detective work might be. We can examine how these prototypes turned out after they were affected by local environmental factors, primarily and sequentially centered on Asuka, Nara, Kyoto, and Edo (Tokyo), without stopping to wonder what here is Greek, what Indian, what Chinese, what Korean. The problems of comprehension are difficult enough without adding this complication which is of scholarly-historic importance but which for most visitors without an equal exposure to Chinese work will add or subtract very little to or from the delight of a visit.

The Japanese followed the Chinese principle of making a space larger by the multiplication of additional units in a continuous row. This is what Kojiro calls the provision of unity through the process of continuation, expansion, dilation.[13] Though the Chinese or Japanese roof can be made to cover a considerable space and was so used, for example, at the hall of the Great Buddha, the *dai-but-su-den* or main image hall of the To-dai-ji temple precincts in Nara, it is not the preferred way, and this we can see as we go around.

The grand Kasuga shrine at Nara, for example, is dedicated to the protective deities of Ko-fu-ku-ji, a group of four militant Shinto gods whose cult was transferred from eastern Japan. But the four deities are not enshrined in a single building; instead each has his own structure, built side by side and with adjoining roofs. A single large roof would have offered better rain protection, but the pavilions serve the standard of the human scale better and the line formed by the four roofs offers the point for the pillars of the deities.

In quite another time and for quite a different purpose, the Katsura Detached Palace in Kyoto was built continuously in a diagonal direction so that the old study hall, the middle study hall, the music room, and the new palace are connected at the corners.

> [The same] geese formation [avoids] the overpowering feeling one gets
> from a large roof. The formation creates deep shadows again and again
> where warmly human subtleties gather. A painted scroll is unrolled from
> one scene to another, which in turn welcomes the following scene;
> and this continues; moreover, each and every scene is complete as a
> fully realized picture in itself. To the upper hemstitch the lower one is added,

[12] Noma Seiroku, *The Arts of Japan, Ancient and Medieval*, 2d ed., vol. I (Tokyo: Kodansha, 1968), p. 12. Translated and adapted by John Rosenfield. Photographs by Takahashi Bin.
[13] Yuichiro Kojiro, *Forms in Japan* (Honolulu: East-West Center Press, 1965). Translated by Kenneth Yasuda. Permission to reprint granted by University Press of Hawaii.

which the next one follows in a linked poem, yet each verse is an independent verse by itself; and the content flows from verse to verse while the rhythm repeats itself again and again. Forms in continuation are boundless rhythmic movements that know no end.[14]

It is even easier to see the magnificent and subtle craftsmanship and the joinery. There are the vertically extended latticework, the palisades of joined split bamboo. There are the many forms of joining, such as the "well-head" or "crosshatch"; originally this was simply two pairs of wooden planks placed crosswise over each other over the mouth of a well.

Pl. 61

Developed in three dimensions, it may support the high wooden terrace of Ki-yo-mi-zu in Kyoto or provide a turret.

There is the elegant bracing *nuki* when a wooden beam is run horizontally through upright members to form the lintel of a gate or a more complex structure. There is the clear unconfused carpentry of a small curved roof; the dramatic strength of simple round posts; the subtle rail, the plain battens and beams of the rear end of the Main Sanctuary at Izumo; the careful joinery and hardware of the door of the West Treasure House of the Ge-ku (Ise); the deeply incised horizontality of the timbers of the Imperial Storehouse (Sho-sho-in) at Nara; the *torii* at the bridge at Ise which an American might compare with embarrassment with his analogous form which marks the entrance to many a western ranch, or the more refined first *torii* across the U-ji bridge astride the main path leading to the inner precinct; the elegant crossing of the gable members projecting well out from the roof and called *chigi* at the west gable of the main sanctuary of Ise; the beauty of the round billets holding down the ridge; the treatment of the round posts and their caps; the way the beam ends are protected by metal; and so on almost without end. All this can be seen and appreciated and at least partially understood.

One may even go further, and after some careful looking and thinking establish in his mind certain basic and unfamiliar principles of Japanese architecture. These have been summarized as they appear to the distinguished contemporary Japanese architect Kenzo Tange as follows (the statements are paraphased and abridged and some of the more mystic expression removed):

Japanese civilization was the only one to build exclusively in wood right down to modern times. (Other materials are now used in larger buildings, especially concrete—jeb.)

Because of the limitations of ancient iron tools, straight-grained cypress was the most esteemed material. From this developed a special construction, avoiding diagonal structural members and resulting in "Mondrianesque" patterns.

The soft texture of cypress encouraged an appreciation of plain unadorned surfaces of wood.

[14] Ibid., p. 22.

A taste for straight lines encouraged patterns of horizontal surfaces and vertical lines. The religious tradition of the forecourt led to still greater emphases on horizontal surfaces and gave rise to the peculiarly Japanese interpenetration of interior and exterior space.

If you rely on straight lines, warping and noticeable sagging become unpermissible thus leading to solicitous attention to workmanship.

The architecture is a union, now with greater emphasis on one and now on the other, of somewhat contradictory requirements of dispersal for space according to function and for modularization (standardization of timber and *tatami* dimensions, with the *tatami* mat acting as the ultimate module).

There existed an ability to add and subtract units almost at will.

Regeneration was accomplished by such simple devices as repapering a *shohji* movable partition, thus changing the light; or recovering of the *tatami* mats to provide the "faint clean smell of rice straw."

The buildings and the rebuildings are reminders that it is not a matter of life being short and art eternal but rather "to know that it is art, in truth, that is short and life that is eternal." [15]

Evidently there are more things in Japanese architecture than spring readily to a Western eye or are easily stored in a Western mind. Some of this comes from our feeble knowledge of Japanese history and some from our uncertainties as to the architectural requirements either of Shintoism or Buddhism; but most elusive of all are questions of mystique.

The historical questions are difficult enough. Vague as the memories of most of us may be of the parade of peoples through Paris—the Celts, the Franks, the Romans, the Merovingians, the Carolingians, the Vikings, the Burgundians, the Capetians, and later the English, the Bourbons, the Communards, the Bonapartes—they should have some connective value for all of us. So somehow we can put together a line of Western political and architectural change which makes some sense and is more or less true. But with our skimpy educational background, what are we to say of Jomon and Yayou, of Kofun and Asuka, of Nara, and Huan, of Fujiwara and Kamikura, of Muromachi or Ashikaga, of Momoyama and Edo and Mei-ji?

What shall we think of as the medieval times of Japan beyond the glimpses of samurai in Japanese cinema? When did Japanese art cease to be the redoubtable handmaiden of religion? What happened in the sixteenth century so that in art thereafter the common man did not need to be "mystified, awed, frightened, ridiculed"—or is this even so?

If the political history is so remote from our experience, we may sketchily connect it at least to the nature of Japanese castles, palaces, and

[15] Kenzo Tange and Noboru Kamazoe, *Ise: Prototype of Japanese Architecture* (Cambridge, Mass.: M.I.T. Press, 1965), pp. 200–206.

tombs. But though these are important, they are far less so in Japanese architecture than is temple architecture, whether Shinto or Buddhist. Can we comprehend the religious history of Japan, more complicated even than the feudal history? Can we relate details of temple or other architecture in terms even of the simplest events if we are told, for example, and accept it as true that in the eleventh century Buddhism lost its ability to make spiritual inquiry meaningful; that the priests lapsed into a pleasurable and aristocratic life which, to be sure, included ritual but also encouraged the cultivation of priestly armies which had finally to be broken by force when in the twelfth century changes in military strategy brought an end to divisive patrician disputes? What were the consequences to architecture of the Zen priests of the thirteenth and fourteenth centuries who tried to tell people that all truths were not in appearances; of the interminable wars of the fifteenth century; of the sixteenth-century emergence of belief in the minds of the influential that a man might be able to control his own destiny; or of the consequent destruction of the military power of the Buddhist organization by Oda Nobunaga?

It helps when you are wandering around Nara and Kyoto to know that in the eighth century one impelling reason for relocating the capital 25 miles northwest of Nara in Kyoto (794) was that the political leaders were nervous about the increasing power and arrogance of the monks of Nara and the intrusion of the Buddhist clergy into political affairs. But why did the great Buddhist temples not accompany the court? Why were new ones built in the Heian-Kyo (Kyoto)? Why were the monasteries which were to be most representative of the new aesthetic and religious attitudes built not in the cities but in the mountains, often in very remote sites and amid grand scenery? Does it add anything to your comprehension or feelings about To-dai-ji when you enter its Nara precincts to know or to believe that its sheer physical splendor was, to the new monks who moved to the remote mountains, a sure sign of the corruption of the court and the capital?

Can you detect for yourself in the new temples of Kyoto that one of their reasons for being was perhaps that the court hastened to support the new sects of Esoteric Buddhism,[16] perhaps as a way of opposing the ancient Buddhist institutions of Nara?[17]

It may matter more than it seems. The mountain sites, with their rugged contours, forced the abandonment of simple symmetrical temple and precinct layouts on a single horizontal level. The ambiance of great trees soon evoked a new sense of architectural beauty and its relation to natural surroundings. The easily obtained cypress bark and shingles

[16] Called Tantrism in India and Mikkyo in Japan, it was a sort of strange marriage of Buddhist and Hindu creeds, emphasizing magical charms, incantations, ritual gestures, and private meditation, all aimed at producing a state of religious exaltation. It was called esoteric because the inner mysteries could be revealed only by a select to a select group of initiates.
[17] The very action of acceptance by the court may have been the first step in the degeneration of Esoteric Buddhism into a religion for the aristocracy.

replaced on the roofs the gray rounded clay tiles which had descended from the Sino-Korean tradition. The forests abetted the desire for mystery by almost forcing darkness and gloom in the ceremonial halls. This time of reformation and renewal denied the previous colorful opulence, called for locking away many of the images in tabernacles whence they were withdrawn on special (and rare) occasions.

You will not find much emphasis on these mountain temples in brief surveys of Japanese architecture, on guided tours, or in short guidebooks. And within my scope I can say little more of them either. Many of them have suffered severely from fires and earthquakes. Koya-san in its forest 2,000 meters above sea level has been burned over and over again. Not a single one of the ancient buildings of Jingo-ji is still standing. Yet the path to it up the slopes of Mount Takao a few miles north of Kyoto is beautiful, especially in the autumn foliage, crossing a torrent in a narrow ravine and then winding up the steep slopes on a path which is said to be considerably older than the streets of Kyoto.

The best single one to visit I suppose would be Muro-ji, whose buildings of the late Nara period, absorbed by monks of the Shingon sect when they abandoned urban Buddhism, are very much as they were in antiquity. The path soon joins a mountain stream and parallels it—"an avenue of seclusion and quiet." Then you cross a bridge over the Muro River and wind up the steep slopes to find the compact and small-scale halls, spaced irregularly so that each may take advantage of a narrow stretch of level or leveled grounds. The stone bases offer a unity with the mountain site and appear again in stairs and retaining walls. The cedar shingle roofs and the faded paint of the brackets and posts accord with the landscape. The towering cryptomeria trees form pools of darkness and filter the light. In some of the halls there are ferocious Tantric images, in others none. This was a monastery temple which welcomed women, and Noma Seiroku feels that "the gentle curves of their shingle roofs are almost feminine."

You can make yourself an unusual and rewarding Japanese holiday, if you go in the right seasons and are a stout walker, by collecting mountain temples. In my opinion it might be more rewarding than spending much time on the giant Buddhas of Kamakura and Nara or the overly ornate Tokugawa shrines at Nikko. It would require only a little research to make a shopping list. But I am not going to do it for you, and it is past time for us to return to our muttons.

So there is some lower limit of knowledge about the religion which a temple or church is designed to serve, below which your understanding and even appreciation of the building will be seriously diminished. But what is the lower limit in Japan for Westerners?

Surely we need to know that Japan is hospitable to two major religions, Shinto and Buddhism, and that many Japanese practice both. Is it too superficial to regard Shinto as animistic (which it is) and the practical religion whereby one asks the gods to care for one's health and prosperity? How much farther does it take us to know that you solicit the gods by prayers and presents so that after you have entered a Shinto shrine beneath the *torii* (a gate erected exclusively before a Shinto sanctuary) and have come to the *haiden*, you are in the worship hall? Here you as a devotee face the deity's sanctuary and offer prayers or presents in advance or toss a few coins later as a reward if things have gone well. You must know too that beyond the *haiden* is the *heiden*, where as a rule you will not be permitted to go and certainly not without being purified. In the *heiden*, which is the offering hall, the clergy present food and other gifts to the deities enshrined in the *honden*, which is the main sanctuary building where the deity is supposed to dwell. This will help you to understand why a Shinto precinct is often such a lively place as, for example, at Inari, where marriage ceremonies and country dances and hundreds of hucksters vie with the shrines for the attention suitable to the premises of a worldly religion. But when you encounter the austere peace of Ise, you will realize that there is another side to Shinto. At Inari you will see a marvelous sculpture of a fox prominently displayed; at Kasuga an array of hanging lanterns, gifts of the grateful. And now and again there are confusions. Hachiman was certainly a martial Shinto god. But by the eighth century he has been absorbed into Buddhism. The throne has been built for him in the three-story pagoda and two of the most popular Buddhist sutras concern him. He has become the guardian of the temple at To-dai-ji. His cult is at least as much Buddhist as Shinto.

Pl. 63

Out of all this it may be possible to spin a fair or rudimentary understanding of what Shinto architecture is all about, and perhaps all the terms you need really to remember are *haiden*, *heiden*, *honden*, and *torii*. Of course you may also want to know that *Jin Ja* is a designation of the standard Shinto shrine, of which there are about 80,000 altogether, and that *Jingu* designates a Shinto shrine which is ranked above the ordinary; and you might even try to sort out which is which. I myself would not bother.

But if Shinto nomenclature seems deceptively simple, the glossary of Buddhism is quite another matter. A minimal glossary related only to the parts of a temple and the religious terms directly concerned with them would amount to from 85 to 100 unfamiliar words. Of these the architectural terms are not so many but still difficult to remember. A Buddhist temple of any consequence is made up of a number of buildings. The terms applying to these number twenty-five or more, but many of these merely designate that the building applies to a specific sect or purpose. Leaving these out, we have the following:

Butsuden is the word for a hall which enshrines Buddhist images.

The *Chumon* (central gate) was one of the standard parts of early Japanese temples, the entry into the colonnade which enclosed the core of the compound; it often houses statues of guardian gods on either side.

A *Dai-but-su-den* is a hall which encloses a Dai-but-su, an ancient word for a "great" Buddha, who may have been Vairocana, Rushana, Amida, or some other.

An *en-do* (circular hall) is usually octagonal and normally was built at least in part as a memorial to distinguished men. If located at the north it is a *Nan-en-do*; at the south, a *Ho-ku-en-do*.

A *Hon-do* is the hall for enshrinement of images of the major deities, similar in function to a *Kon-do*.

Karamon gates, perhaps of Chinese style, are named for their form with gables over the entry and sides, a little like a helmet. They were common during the Momoyama period in castles as well as temples.

Kari-Sansui (dry or withered landscape) defines a garden, common in Zen monasteries, of which Ry-o-an-ji and its nine stones is a very well-known example. Sand and rocks replace ponds, rivulets, verdure. All reflect "the austerity, even the limited and metaphysical attitude of Zen toward the arts."

A *Ko-do* (lecture hall) is one of the basic parts of a Japanese temple, a hall for the ceremonial reading of sutras and sermons, and for other gatherings of monks, replaced in Zen by the *Hat-to*.

A *Kon-do* (golden hall), another standard part like the Hon-do, houses images of the chief deities of the place.

Sammon is the main ceremonial gate of a Zen temple, and is usually behind a smaller and more modest general gate or So-mon.

A *stupa* is the Sanskrit name for the Buddhist pagoda which evolved into the towerlike form prevailing in East Asia from the Indian solid hemispheric mound with a sacred relic at the summit.

Pl. 64
Pl. 68

There are other buildings in a few precincts; treasure houses; the *tatchu*, a small independent group of dwelling and meditation halls within the walls of a large Zen monastery; or the *Yu-me-do-no* (hall of visions), an octagonal building in the To-in at Horyugi on the site of the former palace of an emperor Shotoku Taishi who was said to have had a religious vision there.

Now even if you memorize the whole list or selected parts, you will have little idea of the surprising variations within a general type. Consider for example the *torii*.

Every Shinto shrine has at least one, some have two, most have three. They are not gates in the sense of being an opening through a wall or fence. Often you can walk around them, although you should not since to walk under them is a form of purification and preparation during the passage to the shrine itself.

The idea is very old, and similar gateways for comparable purposes exist in India, China, Korea, and Siam. The Japanese have various poetic theories about the origin. Was it perhaps at first a perch for sacred birds now long forgotten; or is it explained by episodes in the solar myths? What sorts of associations do three *torii* have with the cockcrow at dawn?

As the cock is the announcer of the passing of night and the coming
of day, so do the three torii prepare the heart of a pious worshipper for
his purified appearance before the god. His passing under the
god-gate expels the darkness from his heart just as the darkness of night is
lifted at dawn.[18]

Pl. 65

Torii are not to be confused with the gates to Buddhist temple precincts, which are almost always more complicated and more Chinese
looking. In its simplest form the *torii* is something almost any peasant
could build by erecting a pair of logs (*hashira*) and lashing a horizontal
one (*shimaki*) across the top. He would probably tilt the uprights a little for
stability, thus producing the appearance of a flat-topped letter A without
the crossbar.

Since there are perhaps 100,000 Shinto shrines in Japan, the *torii* are a
prevailing feature of the Japanese landscape.

Torii like crucifixes or church towers or steeples in the Christian world,
or *chortens* and pagodas in Buddhist countries are symbols of a
civilization. The universal presence of the *torii* in Japan is, I think,
comparable to the sound of church bells in the West. I used greatly to
miss the sound of church bells here; Buddhist temples have a bell, it is true,
but it is rung rarely, and with long pauses between each stroke.
But then I realized that it was sufficient to use the eye instead of the ear,
for there were the *torii*, particularly the small, bow-legged country torii,
covered with moss and lichen. You catch sudden glimpses of them from the
train, see them on promontories on the coast, at the turn of a path
on a mountaintop.[19]

They are by no means all alike. Almost all of them have two horizontal members quite close to each other. The top one (*shimaki*) runs across
the post (*hashira*) and projects well beyond them, an essential element to
the form of the *torii*. The lower one (*nuki*) braces between the posts only.
This produces the simplest *shimmei* type. But the columns may be round
or square and so may the horizontals, though the latter are more often of
rectangular section. The spacing between the two horizontals is not open to
much variation before the proportions are damaged. But the details of
how the horizontals and verticals are connected matter. The top member
may or may not be beveled to shed rain and change appearance by intro-
ducing a line at the beveled edge; the ends may be chamfered; there is
considerable latitude about the thickness of the lower horizontal and also
its depth. The verticals may be perpendicular or lean inward.

This is, of course, but the beginning. You might let the lower horizontal member pass through the posts (the *kashima* type). You might add

[18] K. Yamaguchi, *We Japanese* (Tokyo: 1952). Cited by Fosco Maraini, *Meeting with
Japan* (New York: Viking, 1960), p. 133. Copyright © 1959 by Hutchinson & Co. Ltd.
Reprinted by permission of The Viking Press, Inc.
[19] Maraini, *Meeting with Japan*, op. cit., pp. 133–134.

a block at midpoint (*gakusoku*) between the horizontals and use two timbers at the top, the upper extending beyond the lower (*shimaki* and *kasagi*). This gives you the *hachiman* type. You might put the posts on bases (*kifuku*), tilt them inward, and cap them (*taiwa*), and then curve the *shimaki* and the *kasagi* concavely upward, transforming the *hachiman* type into the *myojin*. Of course to those who like to overdesign, excesses are possible such as shown in the remaining two fundamental types, the *sanno* and the *miwa*.

And you can treat the materials differently: alter the carpentry, especially the joinery; add metal, even ornamental metal to cap ends of timbers; allow the timber to weather into a handsome gray or paint it a flaming and ultra-noticeable vermilion. You can even cast the whole form in concrete, a recent and spreading development—practical and regrettable.

But once you have learned the terms, and perhaps even some of the variations of a single form, you have only begun. You have the names of a few buildings and roughly the purposes they serve. But what are the prayers and the meditation about? Whom do the major and minor statues represent?

How long will you have to study Japanese Buddhism before you can identify its three kinds and clearly distinguish between the "small vehicle," *Shojo Bukkyo* (Himayana); the "great vehicle," *Daijo* (Mayahana); and the esoteric, *Mikkyo*, and its two sects, the Shingon and the Tendai? Where does Zen fit into all this?

How many different Buddhas are there and how different are they? They certainly do not all represent the same thing—Amida, Vairocana, Yakushi, Miroku, Nagorai, and Shaka, or the others. To make it harder, each of them has several alternative names.

Can you tell a Raikan or an Arhat from a Bodhisattva? And if you can, do you know that there are at least twenty-five Bodhisattvas with all sorts of different qualities—Fugan, Bosatsu, many Kannons, Gakko, Jizo, Monju, Seishi, Shuho-o-Bosatu, and so on? How many can you expect to recognize on the street—or in the temple? How about the five Myo-os, people like Fudo and Gundar, the fierce Bodhisattvas, manifestations of Vairocana's wrath against evil? They usually appear in sets of five but you cannot count on it. What are you to make of the twelve divine generals, the four deva kings (Shitemmo), the two guardian kings (Ni-o) who often appear at the doorways, or the Yakishas, the animistic deities, guardians of Shaka, who are more commonly portrayed in India than in Japan? It certainly appears to a Westerner like a more complex assortment of gods than those of Christianity or even of the Greek and Roman pantheons.

It seems clear enough that to understand Japanese temple architecture very well from an historical and a religious point of view would require more work than you (or I) are probably prepared to spend on it.

But this is still only a beginning because there is in Japanese aesthetics a mystical poetry which is hard for us to grasp but which I sense as genuine.

Ise has it, Ry-o-an-ji garden has it, Katsura may not, and Nikko certainly does not.

It is what Yuichiro Kojiro means when he says that "Japanese culture cannot be explained satisfactorily in terms of wood, bamboo, and paper or the cleverness of Japanese hands although these are real."[20]

> For the Japanese a pillar is the symbol of support. In the European
> stone house the weight of the roof is evenly distributed to the walls,
> but in the wooden house of Japan the weight is all concentrated on the
> pillars which support it. Faith in the holy pillar, the heart of
> structures styled like grand shrines, or faith in the pillar of the God of
> Wealth seen in the commoner's house, probably has come from the
> supportive strength of the standing pillar which receives the force
> concentrated on it. The pillar, exceeding its function as a support for
> weight, comes to be regarded as a prop for the human heart. As the pillar
> that supports weight becomes a prop for the human heart, so in this
> form of support man's volition is most strongly involved. In those pillars
> that resist the pressure of compression many are in the form of curves,
> as if they were legs planted in the ground even when a frog crotch placed
> against a small building wall has become such a decorative element that it
> actually supports no weight at all, still it takes the form of outstretched legs
> that stand firmly; and to us who look at it, it appears beautiful only if
> it is in a form which resists the weight from above; but it looks ugly if it
> seems to sag. Those forms that resist the force that pulls and
> stretches emphasize a taut, outstretched symmetry. We make the cord
> of the hanging ironware appear proportionately lengthened to enhance
> the form itself. Hooking, suspending, hanging, there are many forms that
> respond to the force of pulling and stretching. On the hoisted temple bell
> there is always a design similar to a Flemish knot. Is it, I wonder,
> that the heart that had the bell hung and supported there remains
> as an adornment?[21]

Surely we could not have deduced all this by ourselves. And obviously the various temples have many things in them—architectural, sculptural, and emotional—which are responses to things we probably can never understand. Does this mean we had better stay away from Japanese architecture altogether? Certainly not. But in the end I fear your experience and mine have got to be at a higher than intellectual level. One of the arts of understanding architecture is the art of suspending knowledge and letting the senses take charge. It may be better to feel Ise ignorantly than to *understand* the Seagram building.

The only sensible way to proceed is to look at a few examples and see how they affect us.

At this point then let me supply a condensed chronology of important

[20] Kojiro, *Forms in Japan*, op. cit., p. 15.
[21] Ibid., p. 94.

Japanese architecture, including many things you may wish to look for but which I shall not discuss here.

Summary of Japanese Calendar

4000–250 B.C.	Jomon	
250 B.C.–A.D 250	Yayou	
250–552	Kofun	Tomb of Emperor Nintoku
552–646	Asuka	Ise
		Izumo
		Hory-u-ji 607
646–710	Early Nara (Hakuho)	
710–794	Nara (Tempyo)	Ya-ku-shi-ji 717
		To-dai-ji Buddha 747
		Dai-but-su Consecration 752
		To-sho-dai-ji 759
		Ko-fu-ku-ji eighth century
		Kasuga eighth century
794–898	Early Heian (Kyoto)	Founding Ki-yo-mi-zu-dera 798
898–1185	Late Heian (Fujiwara)	Dai-go-ji pagoda 952
		By-o-do-in 1053
1185–1333	Kamakura	To-fu-ku-ji 1236
		Kamakura Dai-but-su 1252
		First Mongol Invasion 1274
1337–1573	Muromachi (Ashikaga)	Conversion of Sai-ho-ji to Zen 1339
		Tenru-ji 1340
		Golden Pavilion 1397
		Five-story pagoda Ko-fu-ku-ji 1426
		Ry-o-an-ji 1450
		Silver Pavilion 1490
		Arrival of Portuguese 1543
1586–1615	Momoyama	Matsumoto Castle 1597–1607
		Hi-me-ji Castle 1608
1615–1867	Edo (Tokyo)	Nikko Mausolea (Tokugawas) 1617–1636
		Katsura 1620
		Ni-jo Palace 1626
		Shu-ga-ku-in garden 1656
		Ohara Kurashiki late seventeenth
		American/Russian ships at Nagasaki 1804
1945		Atomic bombing of Hiroshima and Nagasaki

In our time and among most aesthetes who know anything about Japan, there is general consensus that the most beautiful and most moving architecture to be seen in Japan are its oldest extant monuments, the Shinto shrines at Ise. Not in fourteen centuries since their creation have Japanese architects been able to design their equal. The only other architectural work in the world that is similarly unchallenged is the Parthenon of Athens. Both emerge from house architecture and both elevate it to the highest pitch of simple refinement and sophistication—but the all-meaningful physical approach to the temple and the totality of emotions of nature enveloping man are even of a higher order at Ise than at Athens.

There is certainly a greater *degree* of emotion surrounding a visit to Ise than most people will find at Istanbul or Persepolis or Agra; and the nature of that emotion is directly related to trees and water and peace of soul. It is not that Ise cannot stand up firmly enough to intellectual and critical analysis; it is rather that in its presence the zest for such analysis is muted.

It would be hard to say how much of this emotion in a Westerner who is neither Japanese nor a believer in Shinto is the consequence of the actual experience and how much the consequence of the reading about it ahead of time which is practically unavoidable. Of all this reading nothing is superior to the recent book by Kenzo Tange.[22] Let me quote from the Introduction I was privileged to write:

> The Ise Shrine is not hard to reach physically [by] early-morning
> express train from Nagoya and . . . a two-decker "pilgrim express" equipped
> with vista domes and head phones by every seat. . . . When you detrain
> [at Ise city] . . . a few miles in a taxi and a half mile or so of walking in
> towering cryptomeria groves will take you either to the third-century
> Naiku Shrine of the Sun Goddess, Amaterasu-Omikami, or to the
> fifth-century Geku Shrine of Toyouke-Omikami, Goddess of Farms,
> Crops, Food, Sericulture—a Japanese Ceres. . . . The Ise Shrines are
> *not* hard to reach physically. The spiritual journey is longer. It is longer
> at least for most Westerners.
> Every Japanese should make the pilgrimage to Ise if possible, at least
> once in his lifetime. Hence, the precincts are full of Japanese most of
> the time.
> The precincts are very old, pre-Buddhist, and pre-Chinese. They are
> very holy. Even now very few people are admitted to the inner sanctums.
> The precincts have been very Imperial, and the high priestess is
> usually a daughter of an Emperor. . . .
> The buildings at both shrines are very old and very new. They are very
> old because they are identical with the ones that stood there at least as
> early as 685. They are archaically pure. They are very new because they are
> ceremonially rebuilt every twenty years. Carpenters in spotless white
> repair to the sacred forests on the Kiso Mountains to cut the
> new timber. They bathe frequently; if blood should fall on any stick,
> it would be rejected.

[22] Tange and Kawazoe, *Ise*, op. cit.

138 *Bernini Is Dead?*

Two alternately used enclosures stand side by side. In the empty one the
new group of buildings is made in the image of the existing ones.
At the night of change the simple symbols of the godly presence are
transferred to the new shrine. Then the old buildings are dismantled and
their sanctified materials put to good work somewhere else. . . .
The buildings themselves have what Fosco Maraini called a "heroic
simplicity." They are made of plain cypress, cedar, and thatch with a
few metal ornaments. There are no great sculptures, no great polychrome,
no intricate spaces to fathom. There are great refinements, but they
are subtle. You can observe the shrine in a five-minute glance, or it
might take you five years. But even then you would have to look and
think and feel harder than most of us want to do most of the time. . . .
When Walter Gropius visited Japan he quoted Zen to the Japanese
architects: "Develop an infallible technique, and then place yourself at the
mercy of inspiration." Ise is pre-Zen. As it is renewed now in the
ceremony of *sengushiki*, which [was] in 1973 . . . , the mercy of inspiration
was bestowed long ago, and we are left only with infallible technique
and memory. Yet they are enough.
Ise has many lessons for contemporary architects. There is surely the
lesson of devotion, and of craftsmanship, and of infallible technique,
all of which seem to have become so slovenly these days. But there is,
I suspect, an equally important if more elusive message. Sixty years ago
Lafcadio Hearn visited Ise and wrote, "There is nothing imposing
but the space, the silence, and the suggestion of the past." Even if
suggestions of the past may not be much valued today, and certainly
are not to be valued in new buildings, Ise recalls the priceless
ingredients of any great architecture anywhere—repose, serenity, and
silent space. Perhaps these can be fully achieved only if one believes
in something very much—and if the something is greater than architecture.[23]

But what is that something? There is a cluster of legends about
ancient kings and priestly princesses; there is a cluster of ceremonies so
old they may now be performed mostly as habit; there are interesting relations between the buildings and the less refined farmhouses extending back
into antiquity and still to be seen on many parts of the Japanese landscape;
there are the details of the physical approach to the shrines, the kind of
mental and spiritual conditioning by physical environment, characteristic
of many Shinto shrines but outstanding here. Some similar sensations arise
in the great redwood groves in California and Oregon; but at Ise there is
also the architecture, which includes the gates, the precincts themselves,
and finally the materials and the structure—and then there is the matter
of the ceremonial rebuilding which has already been mentioned.

The survival of the spirit of a design through countless tumultuous
and frequently antagonistic periods is surely somewhat of a cultural
miracle, as is the fact that though there has inevitably been some refinement and simplification in the sixty or so rebuildings of 1,500 years, there

[23] John Burchard, Introduction to Tange and Kawazoe, *Ise*, op. cit.

has been so little change. A photograph of the Inner Shrine taken about 1900 shows the east and west treasure houses directly flanking the main sanctuary while now they have been moved forward nearer to the south side of the innermost fence. This is obviously a considerable change in plan and in the resulting space, at least as important as changes in carpentry or ornamental details would be. But it is not of the same order as the changes in the main hall or *honden* at equally old Izumo. The present building there, dating from 1744, rises a 78 dramatic feet, but according to shrine tradition it was originally at least twice as high.

Even in the Nara period when old Japanese culture was brutally overridden by the culture of T'ang China, the culture of Ise somehow escaped. Now as then there is a ceremony at each dawn and each sunset in which the foods of mountain and sea are offered to the gods of the shrine in a ritual as archaic as the buildings.

The relation to the farmhouses will occur to anyone who goes about Japan with his eyes open. It is not of course an extraordinary relation but a logical one repeated in Greece, in Yucatan, in England, and I suppose practically everywhere in history where the style of a foreign invader was not imported to supplant the native evolutionary tradition. But whether it is manifested in the heavy thatched gables, the obvious stressing of the horizontals, the reveals, the platforms, the ridge construction, the stair, the *chigi* or the billets, you will find the relation all over central Japan but especially in backcountry along the northwest coast of Honshu and in Ishikawa Prefecture north of Nagoya. Indeed the collecting of Japanese farmhouses from cold Hokkaido to the suave tiles of Nara is another pleasant experience for those who enjoy detours.

It is not surprising to find the same early farmhouse types introduced at the two most ancient and revered of the national Shinto shrines, Izumo and Ise, in their archaic if refined forms.

Of these Izumo may be the older though the dating of these traditional Shinto shrines is not unimpeachable. Of Izumo I will say little here.[24] What stands now is mid-eighteenth-century rebuilding, which, though it looks primitive, has lost much more of its archaic purity than the Ise shrines and whose compound is symmetrical with an elaboration suggestive of Chinese monumentality.

At Ise there are in fact two shrines, the Outer, or Geku, and the Inner, or Naiku, not next to each other but actually a few miles apart. The outer is dedicated to the goddess Toyoriki-Omikame, the patroness of harvests; the inner, to the founder of the Imperial Line, Ameratsu Omikami, the goddess endowed with the virtue of the sun's rays.

Let us pass with Maraini up the road to Geku through this "area of wooded hills and clear streams that runs glittering along channels of bright stones."

[24] There are good descriptions in Robert Treat Paine and Alexander Soper, *The Architecture of Japan* (Baltimore: Penguin, 1955), pp. 165ff.

After passing the first of the three gateways [torii] normally to be
found along the approach to every Shinto shrine, we found ourselves in a
wood of marvellous antiquity and stupendous vigour. A gently winding,
gravelled avenue was flanked on either side by cryptomerias, which are
similar to cypresses, but of a size no cypress ever reaches. There were
many people, almost a crowd: mothers with children on their backs,
leading by the hand other children, with balls, dolls, bags of sweets;
peasants in all sorts of clothing, from pure traditional to impure western
style, with every conceivable variation in between. . . . students and
school children; old men with young *mekake* ["pendants from the eyes,"
i.e., mistresses], and geishas with wealthy patrons; serious business men
from Osaka, the Japanese Manchester; learned professors and distinguished
civil servants, looking a trifle pompous and starched, as was appropriate in
such a place; and every now and then a priest passed in his ancient
robes of bright, plain colours.
Where were all these people going? Where did all these avenues lead?
What should we find hidden in the wood? We were in the east,
and should be prepared for the strange, the fantastic, perhaps the
monstrous. Would there be a terraced hill covered with sculpture,
as at Barabudur? Or a temple in the form of a huge human face smiling
enigmatically, as at Angkor-Thorm or Bayon? Or a padoga [sic!]
from which two vividly painted eyes look at you as at Gyantse in Tibet;
or two rows of impressive statues of real or fantastic animals, as at the
Ming tombs? Or caves carved out of the rock and painted with disturbing
pictures as at Ajanta? Or pinnacles interwoven with marvellous and
terrible visions of metamorphoses, couplings, strange, symbolic
voluptuousness, as at Tanjore? Should we find a palace, a column,
a tower, a monument?
We found none of these things. Instead the object of supreme veneration to
nearly 100 million Japanese at work in the fields, at sea, in the air,
in the mountains, in the docks at Yokohama, in the factories of Kawasaki
or the laboratories of Osaka, in the big shops along the Ginza, in the
universities, the mines, banks, offices, and all the other departments of
modern industrial life, is a small, bare, and unadorned thatched edifice
built of cypress wood in pure prehistoric style. . . .[25]

Before speaking of the buildings more specifically, let us walk again
with Maraini now to Naiku, the Inner Shrine.

We got out [of the car] crossed the river Uji by a handsome bridge,
passed under the first torii and soon reached the spot where everyone
goes down to the stream to wash his hands and rinse his mouth as a
token of purification.
After the second torii we came to another avenue flanked by huge
cryptomerias. The farther we got from the road, the farther the everyday
world, the world of noise and motors, receded, the farther back we
seemed to be moving in time, and the more we were seized with the magic

[25] Maraini, *Meeting with Japan*, op. cit., pp. 130, 132.

Pl. 66

of the place. We passed a number of pavilions, including the Kagura-den, the place of the sacred dances, rounded a bend, and came to some crude stone steps. We were now at the edge of the clearing where the sacred buildings stand; the Sho-den, the principle [sic!] shrine, where the sacred mirror is kept; the two Ho-den or treasures, and the Mi-ke-den where offerings are made morning and evening of rice, water, salt, fish, birds, vegetables, fruit and seaweed. [The Mi-ke-den actually is not in the final enclosure but in the northeast corner between the first and second fences; see plan—jeb.] The architecture with which we were faced was of the most heroic simplicity, the most absolute purity; the structural elements are unpainted wooden pillars, and rafters supporting thatched roofs. All the lines are straight, except for the slight curvature of the roofs; the surfaces are completely devoid of decoration and ornament. [Well, they are almost devoid of decoration; see for example the west gable where the decoration is only the vestigial dowels and the metal on the *chigi* or projecting rafters; there is somewhat more on the Main Sanctuary at the Geku but still very little—jeb.]
There has been no secondary treatment of the raw material. A big silk curtain hangs across the entrance; only the Emperor, a few members of his family, and envoys who represent him on certain occasions are allowed to pass beyond.
In accordance with ancient custom, everyone . . . stood to attention for a moment, bowed slightly and clapped his hands twice. . . .
At the conclusion of their brief moment of prayer, people turned and walked cheerfully away. There was not the least sign of strain or tension in the relation between man and the higher powers. For the great majority of Japanese, of course, a visit to a Shinto shrine is less a religious experience in our sense of the word . . . than a moment of poetical communion with the past, with the roots of the nation and its civilization.[26]

The experience of Ise, whether at Naiku or Geku, is multiple. There is the presentation of nature as only the Japanese can do it, almost but not quite leaving her alone, so that she seems more herself than when completely untended. There is the hierarchy of the progressive experience, the array of gates or *torii*, the development of fence within fence, each surrounding a more important enclosure, the ultimate enclosure of which we can see only the tantalizing roofs of the sanctuaries lifted above the fence; there is the direct, simple, and clear unity of the structures themselves; and then the beautiful design and the loving and skillful craftsmanship of each of the details. Photographs tend to emphasize the latter—but they are only a refined passage of the refined whole. None of them can clearly be described in words.

Of the natural habitat and of the paths through it I have perhaps hinted enough. The supreme experience is one of hush broken only by

[26] Ibid., pp. 134–136.

delicate sounds, the plash of water, the fall of a leaf, the filtered light. Then each successive *torii* offers a new message.

One follows an orderly path in approaching the main sanctuary: a *torii* at each end of the U-ji bridge; a right turn on to the main approach, a short flight of steps, the first *torii*; a curving around until almost at right angles, the second *torii*; a long almost sinuous path past the outer hall for ritual dances; storehouses, stables, resting places for visitors such as the Emperor; until again a right-angle turn near the river and up the steps to the plateau on which are the four fences each one inside the other until the enclosure of the main sanctuary and its two treasuries is reached.

At the Ise shrines the *torii* are appropriately simple examples of the simplest fundamental form, the *shimmei*.

The round posts lean in slightly—the upper surface of the top beam is beveled and its ends chamfered. Neither beam is as thick as the column but the lower beam is thinner than the upper. It is further braced to the column by simple wooden wedges. Then color arrives by the simple weathering of the structure. These are the *torii* at the east and west ends of the U-ji bridge.

The first *torii* along the main path toward the inner precinct gives the impression of being wider and of being slightly concave at the top when seen through the trees but not when viewed looking backward from the *matarashi* or place of water purification where shallow stone steps lead down to the Isuzu river.

The second *torii*, the *torii* at the bridge leading to the Kazahinomi shrine (wind god), is not in any serious way different. The *torii* at the south or main entrance of the inner precinct, set in the outermost of the four fences, boasts of two top members. The *torii* between the second and third fences are much the same. So are the *torii* at Geku, the outer Ise shrine. There is in this a beautiful simplicity. The hierarchy of the journey does not need and does not get the punctuation of increasingly complex or ornate *torii* as might tempt a vulgar designer.

At either Geku or Naiku the paths and their emphasizing *torii* will lead you at the end to the inner precincts and their array of surrounding fences.

No detail is of indifference to architecture and though fundamentally bad work cannot be promoted to good by fine details, fundamentally good work can be seriously degraded by bad or slovenly detail. There are not many but there are a few architectural situations in which a surrounding wall or fence is an important element of design (the serpentine brick walls of Jefferson's Virginia). Nowhere, though, are they more significant than the wooden fences of the Ise shrines.

Both Geku and Naiku have four fences; they are rather more closely spaced on the sides at Naiku than at Geku, as the plans show, but about the same amount of forecourt is afforded in both. The more elongated shape of the Naiku complex produces an inner precinct which is much

The Architecture of Wood 143

more rectangular than the almost square one at Geku, but since the treasure houses are behind the main sanctuary at Naiku and in front of it at Geku, the distance from the south gateway of the innermost fence to the porch over the entry or the stairs to the main sanctuary is about the same.

There are differences between the details of the fences at Geku and at Naiku which are interesting and which you will want to note if you go there but which are too involved to mention here. Let us speak only of the fences of Naiku.

Pl. 69

The array of the fences is of great interest. The outermost one is of solid planks laid horizontally against heavy posts. The inner three are of spaced vertical boards, each carefully tailored but of quite different spirit. The differences are related to the height, the spacing of the boards, the amount of horizontal emphasis provided, depending on the organization of horizontal rails from the almost complete horizontality of the outer fence; the great horizontality of the second fence, achieved by using quite short vertical boards and letting a prominent horizontal plank near the top speak clearly thanks to the substantial void between it and the paling; the beginning of verticality and suppression of horizontality at the third by putting the top horizontal member very low down; and the final almost complete lack of visible horizontal members at the innermost fence where they can be seen only from the inside. It is all very clear and very sophisticated and very elegant.

After you have circumnavigated the fences so to speak and peeked as well as you can, you can come back to the main gate and get as far in as you can which is unlikely to be very far. Most people are stopped at the first gate while as a rule only members of the Imperial Family pass the second. If you pass the first gate at either shrine, you will observe at your left a guardhouse. If you get through the gateway of the second fence, at your right will be the *Yo-yo-den* or hall for ceremonies in bad weather. It is simply impressive, four square to the ground, a wall of board only halfway up and then open to the eaves and to a similar height at the gable ends where the heavy wood carpentry is clearly revealed. The thatch roof is impressive, thicker at the eaves than at the ridge, held down by heavy cylindrical billets of wood (*katsuogi*) at the ridge; the gables have the characteristic crossed rafters (*chigi*). All of this is reminiscent of some of the main forms of the principal sanctuary but with less elegance and much less employment of finishing details in metal, and so on.

Between the third and fourth fences is a more elaborate gateway—the Ban-gaki; and if you pass the fourth gateway through photographs or were to look in from a helicopter, if you could, you would see the main sanctuary flanked by two treasure houses—in front of it at Geku, behind it at Naiku. The treasure houses are up on stilts, or rather heavy round posts; a narrow platform leads to the only door, and the steps to this are steep and narrow or there are none. The walls are solid planks, and at the gables a cylindrical column stands free of the building and rises from the ground to support the ridge. The roof materials, the crossed rafters, the billets all resemble those of the other buildings but now there is more refinement— tapering of the billets toward their ends, ornamental metal here and there. If you look closely, you can find further subtle differences between the two shrines.

The treasure houses face north on the Geku, south at the Naiku, that is, in the direction of the main sanctuary. In the Geku the treasury roofs have five *katsuogi*, in the Naiku, six.

The differences are somewhat greater between the two main sanctuaries to which we must now come despite the interest in several other collateral buildings which are easier to see. The differences are not fundamental and it surely does not matter much that there are eleven steps up to the platform at Geku and ten at Neiku. The greater differences rest in the opulence of the detail and it is sufficient so that almost anyone who compares them ends up by having a decided favorite.

Kenzo Tange, for example, says:

> I personally recognize in the Geku a primitive strength lacking in the Naiku. I refer not only to the design of the main sanctuary but also to the spatial depth created by the placement of the Geku buildings.[27]

It is a view which, so far as I can tell, I share, and maybe because Geku, though younger, having escaped more fire and disasters, may have better preserved its original shape and had fewer embellishments at various times of rebuilding.

Either one certainly owes some of its form to older raised-floor storehouses, but this has to be deduced from the construction elements rather than from written records—and the same thing has to be said for some stylized elements believed to derive from imperial palaces. Let us not go into these problems of genesis today, much as they might interest others— and if they interest you, any source book will provide the main lines of the debate, especially if it contains a record of the researches of Dr. Toshio Fukuyama.[28]

What we would see is perhaps most clearly shown by line drawings, say of the front and sides of the main sanctuary of the Geku. There is a platform supported by strong simple round posts. (The roundness cannot be read from the line drawings.) The platform is reached from one side only by broad steps occupying about one-third of the width of this facade. From the platform rises a simple rectangular structure made up of strong infrequent posts with boards between them. This rectangular space is girdled by a walkway resting on the platform and protected by a hand-

Pl. 67

[27] Tange and Kawazoe, *Ise*, op. cit., p. 47.
[28] Toshio Fukuyama and Noboru Kawanoe, *Nihon no Yashiro—Ise (Japan's Shrines— Ise)* (Tokyo: 1962). Not translated.

some wooden rail. There is only one door to the inside placed on axis with the steps. The room is capped by an enormous roof which more than over-hangs the balconies, both on the sides and the ends, and which is the dominating feature of the whole design, characterized, like the other elements, by simplicity and forcefulness. The roof has several unusual features. At each end the overhanging ridgepole is supported by a free-standing pillar, notably tapered, rising from the ground through the balcony to the ridge. (It is called *munamochi-bashira* or ridge-supporting post.) Across the ridge are the billets, much refined, slightly tapered, bound with metal rings at the ends—nine billets at the Geku, ten at the Naiku. At the ends of the walls the rafters cross each other to form the characteristic *chigi* cradling the ridgepole. Holes are cut through them, perhaps to reduce wind pressure or for lashings, but the reason is lost in time. From each side of the barge-board there is a row of long pegs, closely set, square in cross section but with rounded ends. Decorative as they are, they have lost whatever function they had and this is unremembered. The roof itself, which is of thick thatch, is not curved like a Chinese roof and I like it the better thereby. It is remarkably and subtly beautiful, offering deeply slant-ing reveals at the eaves, at the same time achieving, by reducing the thick-ness of the thatch as it rises, a certain convex curvature.

That is all except a wooden post not to be seen, called *shin-no-mihashira* (sacred central post) standing under the middle of the floor in each of the main sanctuaries, and not found elsewhere. The holy mirror of Naiku is in a cylinder of cryptomeria resting directly above this post.

> The *shin-no-mihashira* are a secret of secrets, and although there is no way of knowing for sure, they are said to be posts of plain wood, about seven feet in length, the lower half buried in the ground and the upper standing free, not touching the floor above. Many layers of silk are reportedly wrapped around the posts, into which branches of the *sakaki* tree are inserted. Clay tablets are then heaped around, and the whole is protected by a wooden fence. All we can see of them are these wooden fences under the raised floors of the two main sanctuaries and in the middle of the alternate sites; in the latter they are covered by small roofs resting on top of the fences.[29]

There are many differences between the two sanctuaries besides those already mentioned. The thatch at Naiku is substantially thinner and more fragile-looking than at the Geku. The *chigi* are cut off vertically at the Geku and horizontally at the Naiku. There are two slots in the *chigi* at the Geku and three at the Naiku, the end one actually being cut across by the horizontal end. The rail details are quite different. Especially the amount and the elaboration of the metal ornamentation are far more ex-uberant at the Naiku than at the Geku.

[29] Tange and Kawazoe, *Ise,* op. cit., p. 42.

It is clear that some of the main elements of these magnificent buildings are vestigial much in the sense that the *triglyphs* and *guttae* of the Parthenon are. The *katsuogi* were originally weights laid across the ridge to hold it down against the wind but were long ago made into stylized symbols of an imperial palace. The *chigi* originally projected because when the rafters were bound together with ropes of straw, the crossing and projecting were very convenient, but now they serve only to lend grandeur by their projections. The doors of the storehouses were at the end and the projecting eaves served as protective cover. It needed to be a large projection, more than a cantilevered ridge could manage, and hence the prop, the "ridge-supporting post," the *munamochi-bashira*. When the door was moved to the center of the long side, the gable projection shrank and could have been still shorter, but the *munamochi-bashira* remains. No one of these important visual elements is therefore any longer functionally necessary. But as Tange says:

> They became indispensable elements for the support of the balance of the Ise form, and it is impossible to imagine that form without them.[30]

Some Other Examples of Japanese Wooden Architecture

If this were a guidebook of Japan or a comprehensive story of its architecture, its wooden architecture, the marvels of Ise could be only a beginning. (But in nobility it is a sufficient beginning and a sufficient end.) The tourist will of course desire to visit additionally at least the enormous Buddhist monastery of Ho-ry-u-ji, outside of Nara, almost contemporary with Ise, and its complex arrangement of halls on a quite different plan. He may wish to collect the pagodas of Ho-ry-u-ji, Ya-ku-shi-ji, Dai-go-ji, and others, to note how little storage space these pagodas really offered and to wonder how they ceased to be the most important monument of the ritual and lost their central location in the precinct to the *kon-do*; or the nunnery of Chu-gu-ji and its gentle wooden sculpture of Siddartha in contemplation; the severely impressive *kon-do* at To-sho-dai-ji; the crowded, noisy, but still magnificent Dai-but-su-den at To-da-i-ji. He might wish to stay longer at romantically sited Ki-o-mi-zu or the phoenix temple of By-o-do-in in the Fujiwara style, but most of all perhaps at Kasuga, Katsura, and, regretfully, Nikko.

In all these visits there are surprises. At Ya-ku-shi-ji the visitor would specially notice the eastern pagoda, the remainder of a pair. It practices a marvelous deception by which its mere three stories are made to seem like six; with a result that its contrapuntal roofs offer a lively contrast to the simple and direct and more monumental taper of Ho-ry-u-ji.

If you toil further up the hill of Nara beyond the Dai-but-su-den, you will come to the more peaceful Shinto shrine of Kasuga. It is much affected

[30] Ibid., p. 47.

architecturally by the Buddhist building of Nara but is still Shinto. The four shrines arrange their curved gables and their curved veranda roofs in a connecting series. The roofs are far clumsier than those of Ise, but the buildings lie skillfully on the slope of the mountain and offer colorful displays of white, red, and green on walls and woodwork. One comes up to them on walkways lined by over 1,200 stone lanterns given by grateful supplicants. Along the porches and walkways hang another 1,000 metal lanterns. All around are spotless white gravel corridors, and all the 2,200 lanterns are lighted in February for spring festival and in August for the Buddhist all-souls day.

There are pleasant little excursions on these hills too: the gallant *torii* of the My-o-in type at the little Wa-ka-mu-ja shrine, whose posts have a careful entasis and all of whose members are painted red except the Shimaki which is brown; and higher up the hill the Ni-gat-su-do, set on a side hill with a heavily bracketed balcony all around, a curved hip roof, the whole in brown except for the white stone lanterns that line the flanking stairs and the gray tiles of the roof. It was founded in the eighth century, and on the twelfth of February it too has a torchlight procession of a sort which has been threading its galleries now annually for more than a millennium. A little lower down there is another and very different temple founded in the same quarter century—the San-gat-su-do. Here there is still the balcony though much lower, a more complicated curving of the roofs and the same brown-gray color scheme except that now the areas between the posts and brackets are filled in in white so that their structure is very explicit in a planar way but much less mysterious in its third dimension.

Nor can we stop long here in the gardens of Japan, justly famous and varied as they are, whether the terraces and the downhill walks of the Shu-ga-ku-in or the 200 mosses of Sai-ho-ji, or the famous nine stones on the raked sand of the Zen temple of Ry-o-an-ji which has elicited so much audible reverence from so many famous modern architects and artists and their sedulous imitators, or the equally but differently moving dragon screens, or the high rushes in the canal of the same temple. In all of these cases as well as the Gin-ka-Ku-ji Temple of Kyoto, happy as the ambiance, it is no longer the architecture which is the main thing, and save perhaps for Katsura the architecture is in fact quite inferior.[31]

But there is one more stop we must make before we leave Japanese architecture. We stop there not because it is better than the ones we have glossed over but, in fact, because it is worse. I am speaking of the Tokugawa mausolea at Nikko.

---

[31] This probably dismisses Katsura too cavalierly because of my devotion to the Ise shrines as more important in their purpose and more perfect in their realization. You can decide for yourself by visiting it, or if this is impossible, by looking at another outstanding book, also by Kenzo Tange: *Katsura* (New Haven, Yale University Press, 1960).

A fast express train will take you there in just over two hours from Tokyo. You can drive the 90 miles in some four hours or a little more. There is an excellently comfortable hotel at the end of the line, and the tourism is alas all too well organized.

The landscape is superb—a dramatic composition of valleys, peaks, forests, of waters, rocks, and trees. The Tokugawa shoguns knew how to choose a burial site as flamboyant as their courts but they may have been the first Japanese really who did not know how to marry buildings to a site, although they still did better than the Chinese. They were vulgarians of the highest order, these managers of the Japanese seventeenth century— dictatorial, mean, jealous, confusing pomp and luxury with taste, sparing no funds to collect all the most expensive artists.

Ieyasu had tried to make sure while he was alive that his monuments eclipsed those of his arch rival Hideyoshi—and would not even let Hideyoshi's *reibyo* be rebuilt after it burned about 1610. His grandson, Iemitsu, along about 1634, continued this posthumous rivalry with Hideyoshi but could think of no way to do it save through the flamboyance and the extravagant use of materials and men. Over ten years he is said to have used 1,600,000 carpenters, 23,000 gilders. The place is full of statistics instead of art, 2½ million sheets of gold leaf for gilding which would have covered nearly 6 acres. The timber extended would reach about the length of the famous Tokaido Railway between Tokyo and Kyoto (330-odd miles). There are no such statistics for great architecture like that at Ise—and it took Napoleon, not Chephren or Sneferu, to think that it mattered how big a wall the Great Pyramid might have made. Nobody ever tried to exceed Nikko afterwards and this is certainly more than just as well.

As one approaches the mausolea, the first impression is good. There is a large and simple gray *torii* leading to a splendid gradual climb through the end of a majestic cryptomeria forest which even now contains some 16,000 trees and extends for 23 miles along the roads.

But once one reaches the architecture, the groves are downgraded and soon denied by buildings which are overly eclectic, overly decorated, and overly bracketed, so that their forms are hard to make out (this is often merciful). The structural repertoire has been elaborated out of all shame. The lintels and the cornices, the pillars and the doors, crawl with foliage, birds, scrolls, dragons, often in many colors, while blue and ivory and red and gold are everywhere. For a time after the first portal, the trees hide things and we are spared a full exposure to the excesses and the eccentricities of these "lacquered harridans" of buildings, one of which stops every tourist because it has the original of the notorious three monkeys who closed their various senses to evil. But after the big gate the trees no longer extend thus.

Nikko is one of the nineteen most popular parks in Japan and that means it is very much visited indeed. Fortunately there are lakes and streams and modest mountains to climb, as well as fishing and camping,

The Architecture of Wood 149

so that one is not always and perhaps not even ever at the mercy of the memory of the Tokugawa shoguns.

Fosco Maraini has summed up Nikko.

> The fact that Nikko was built only a few years after the Katsura villa gives an idea of the heights and depths between which Japanese art is capable of moving. . . . Nikko is old age, weariness, feebleness, bad aesthetics, trying to redeem itself with money, gold, size. Nikko, in other words, stinks of death.
> Ise, Nara, Kyoto, represent only one aspect of Japan; there is another, which is attracted by the opposite polar force—wealth and display, silver and gold (as against simplicity, purity, nature). Nikko is the embodiment of this second pole.[32]

I suppose if you go to Japan you will and probably should go to Nikko. But hurry back to Ise before you leave.

[32] Maraini, *Meeting with Japan*, op. cit., pp. 358–359.

CHAPTER SIX

THE ARCHITECTURE OF STONE

The hand that rounded Peter's dome
And groined the aisles of Christian Rome,
Wrought in a sad sincerity;
Himself from God he could not free;
He builded better than he knew;
The conscious stone to beauty grew.

Ralph Waldo Emerson
The Problem

STONE AND ITS USES

We have already noted how much of the most important architecture of the world is made of stone.

The stones that have proved practical to use in building are of three general geologic classes. The sedimentary rocks which have been widely used are limestone and sandstone, and more rarely shale. The metamorphic rocks that have served best are marble, slate, schist, and serpentine, especially marble. Some so-called marbles indeed are really limestones, but it is not a distinction that need bother us here. Finally a very important and beautiful building stone is igneous; granite at its best may indeed be the most elegant of all building materials although not very versatile. Fine-grained igneous formations such as lava and volcanic tufas have served well in places; and more rarely coarsely crystalline igneous rocks, such as basalt, porphyry, or onyx.

The degree to which these various stones have been used has varied in place and time. The choice, like the choice of woods, was not enormously wide in any one place. In Saylor's *Dictionary*, to which I have previously referred,[1] there

[1] See page 104.

are some 175 terms relating to stone materials. Of these 18 are general and another 10 concern various ingredients of stuccos, plasters, and cements. Of the rest 70 are marbles, 45 are granites, 28 are sandstones, and 17 are limestones. Two are travertine (a calcium carbonate of special texture related to limestone), and two are serpentine, a hydrous magnesium silicate which is used much like marble. One each is obsidian, basalt, and porphyry, and one is alabaster, a translucent form of gypsum.

This distribution is not decisive statistically. There are, for example, more textures and patterns in marbles than in the other stones, which encourages a wider listing. Moreover the quantities used are not necessarily indicated by the number of names cited. Though marble, granite, sandstone, and limestone are almost certainly the four most important stones of all architectural history, the chances are that the quantities used would appear in almost reverse order.

The limestones are easy to quarry and easy to work, and most of them are of quite even color and texture and weather well.

The sandstones are often but not always softer and even easier to work. But though their colors do range from white through buff, red, and brown, most of them are in the darker range and even tend to look muddy. A special variant, bluestone, is bluish-gray; having a fine texture, bluestone is a good material for paving, coping, and stair treads. Some of the sandstones are quite porous and thus let in water and may spall—and some are overly friable and are damaged by wind and dust.

The word granite is used loosely if inaccurately to define most light-colored, coarse-grained, crystalline igneous stones. It is harder than the lime and sandstones to get out of the quarry and harder to work with tools, but very weather-resistant. When it is brought to a high polish, it often has magnificent color—and under brush hammering or even simpler treatments it reveals its sturdiness. In my opinion it is the king of the stone materials. And it has a wider range of choice than most people tend to think.

Granite usually has a rather coarse grain—but the grain may be in fact fine and uniform, medium, or coarse. And though we think of it as a gray stone, it has a larger range than that. Some is almost black when polished; some is so light as to be almost white, although when polished it reveals a pinkish tinge. A uniform gray exists but is rare, since the gray background is more normally veined, speckled, or clouded with deposits of mineral salts. There are a few blues, even an unusual azure. More often the gray is tinged with green or brown or with black marks. Among the most beautiful are those in the red spectrum—pink, black, and pearl gray; red with broad dark veins and clouds of red, pearl, gray, and even blue; a deep pink mottled with black like Cordova pink; a coarse-grained rich red, and especially the magnificent red granite of Aswan on the Upper Nile.

If granite is the king of the stones, marble is the queen, and she permits herself a greater range of display. Since marble is a calcium carbonate with many kinds of deposits, including shells in various stages of deterioration or fossilization, it has a wide range of softness, of workability, of weather resistance, and particularly of veining and of color combinations. Though common in many parts of the world, it somehow seems Italianate, so that the word *parmazzo*, which suggests brilliant, even wild patterns, is often taken by us thoughtlessly as a description of all marbles. The range is much wider than that.

Many architects and sculptors and perhaps the better ones seek from marble the chaste forms. So the Greeks preferred the pure or almost pure white Parian or Pentelic marbles, without grain when they could get them; so the marbles of Carrara have long been famous; and in the United States some of the marble of Colorado, some of the marbles of Vermont or of Alabama are much desired, although the latter is creamy or even gently bluish.

At the other extreme of purity are the much rarer, nearly grainless blacks, such as lucullite, or the Nero Antico of ancient Greece. To get grainless stones may require a good deal of culling.

The blacks are more often found with veining, sometimes spectacularly of gold. Thus the Island of Tino in the Gulf of Spezia yields a stone with a jet background and chain veining of old gold color; while in Arizona, where almost every color of the spectrum may be noted, there are spectacular black and gold combinations bearing such endearing names as Navajo gold, Apache gold, or Geronimo gold! Veined networks can sometimes be found on rich cream grounds as in the best Italian *cremo*, although much of this is lower grade and debased by red and green spots or by thicker veins of the gold which loses quality as the filament widens. One of the most spectacular of the simple combinations is French *grand antique* where large and small black fragments are juxtaposed in sharp contrast.

Beyond this almost anything can be found and used: buffs, richer browns, light coffee colors with still lighter cream patches, slender undulating veins of golden brown and barely noticeable veins of whiter calcite, brownish creams with clouds of still darker browns and hairlike veins of yellow.

There are many reds, close-textured creams tinged with yellow and flecked with rose and sometimes gray, dark grays of a reddish tinge, with white veins and small red marks, reds with rose or violet spots, old roses or deep pinks combining with greenish black and greenish gray veins. Some are downright red, brilliant reds with white blotches, or have bold swirling masses of red, cream, and rose, deep reds with white and black markings.

Next to the white and black marbles the greens are probably the most popular, especially the serpentines which are actually magnesium oxides and carbonates and not marbles at all. Some are brecciated serpentine so that the deep and light green colors are threaded with undulant veins of calcite, which appear white. Another is generally green, about the color of copper patina, but splotched with buff. *Maryland verde antique*, another serpentine, is among the most beautiful. It has a mottled grass-green ground while the veins are lighter green.

The blues are less common and generally less popular. But some *are* used, for example, one whose grains resemble flowers, or another, the blue background of which is laced with thin, almost straight, pure white veins suggesting twig layouts. Still another has large and small bits of gray-blue and white emphasized by golden red veins but manages to appear bluer than any other marble. Even purple is approached by *griotte*, a Pyreneean marble.

Less appreciated are marbles in which shells and fossil traces are still clearly visible. The most famous of this type are the English Purbeck marbles, dark blue-green, marked by many fossils, which perhaps *faute de mieux* were used with such gusto for clustered piers in Early English Gothic churches and cathedrals.

Of the other stones travertine is certainly the most important, especially around Rome but also with contemporary architects. It is a light or creamy-colored compact type of calcium carbonate formed like the stalactites and stalagmites of caverns but less porous. Its irregularly shaped voids give it an interesting texture when finished as they are irregularly spaced and vary in size almost at random from pinheads to eggs. Not every observer has been enamored of it. Stendhal, for example, was openly contemptuous.

Alabaster, because of its translucency, was important in architectural history before window glass was common and practical—and provides a light which interests architects enough so that Gordon Bunshaft, for example, wanted to use it in the windows of his recent Beinecke Library at Yale University. But the stone is rare these days and its use this way must now be looked on as a tour de force.

Evidently if the whole palette of stones were available to an architect in one place, he would have an almost frightening freedom of choice as to physical properties and appearances. But even in the most opulent of times (and for architecture at least ours are far from being the most opulent of times), this much choice has never been possible. In some parts of the world stone was hardly available at all!

This was the situation in lower Mesopotamia, rich in alluvial muds and clays but devoid of stone or wood, so that the development of a brick architecture was almost inevitable. In the Assyrian mountains to the north there was stone, but the Assyrians chose to imitate the conquered Babylonians and limited their use of stone to facing their interiors with alabaster or limestone carved in low relief. The only serious exception in the Middle East was the Persians, who used hand-colored limestones at Persepolis.

Later on the people of Byzantium had no good building stones; they imported some finish marbles but otherwise relied on brick; and during the Middle Ages the people on the North German plains had little stone and so developed their interesting and very special version of Gothic architecture in brick. For some less clear reason the Lombard builders in Italy, where stone was not far away, chose to make the romantic Lombard Romanesque of brick; finally and almost a sport the Gothic fortress-church Ste-Cécile at Albi and indeed the whole city in the south of France is a rosy brick monument among many nearby of stone.

Even when stone was plentiful nearby, it was not always the desired kind. The Egyptians, for example, had excellent limestones in the Mokaitman Hills in the north, and sandstone in the central districts, but preferred the beautiful red granite or syenite of Aswan to the south. They governed themselves accordingly except that the northward-flowing Nile made it possible to use the Aswan granite over a wider radius than might otherwise have been possible. The great pyramids of Gizeh and Saqqara had prototypes of brick but were themselves built of local limestones. Most of the temples of Luxor and Thebes were of the local sandstone but some of the obelisks were imported from Aswan. The Egyptians, though, tended to decorate main walls with stones they had hewn from special quarries so that the temple of Rameses at Abydos, for example, combined yellow sandstone from Gebel Silsileh, white limestone from Tura, gray and pink granites from Aswan, quartzite from Gebel Ahmar, and alabaster from Middle Egypt. They learned, miraculously, how to carve and polish even the hardest stones with copper or bronze (not iron) chisels.

The Athenians in their heyday loved the fine-grained white marbles of Hymettus and Pentelicus of the islands of Paros and Naxos, and used them on their Acropolis. But the Greeks could not find their equal at Agrigentum in Sicily, where they had to settle for a stone with visible shells, fossil plants, and aqueous weeds. At Paestum too in Italy they could do no better than travertine; while the great temple of Alphaia at Aegina had to be made of soft yellow limestone. Each of these they faithfully stuccoed though most of the stucco is gone now; while in the rocky pass at Bassae in the Peloponnesus they used a hard gray limestone for the Temple of Apollo Epikourios. Today it is softened by pink lichens, but it must have seemed quite dour to a fifth-century Athenian who wandered into perilous if pastoral Arcady.

The Romans had countless marbles around them and so loved their ostentation that they imported even other varieties from Africa. They also had travertine, which they evidently held in less esteem than we do, and tufa, and excellent bricks. But they had no aesthetic philosophy which required them to let the building materials show for themselves, and so they had no qualms about stuccoing and/or painting over all or parts of even the finest stones as fancy struck them. Thus their greatest contributions to lithic architecture perhaps rest in their development of *pozzuolana*, an Italian volcanic sand which, when pulverized and mixed with slaked lime, forms a hydraulic cement of great strength, so that many of their greatest works are owed to concrete rather than stone, even if they did not discover the art of reinforcing.

The early Christian buildings had copious quarries supplied by ancient Roman edifices. But there were not enough of these in Gaul, so when the Romanesque and the Gothic developed they depended on local stones. In Auvergne local volcanic types were used, but in northern France the builders had the good fortune to discover Caen stone, a fine-textured material of Normandy which was soft when quarried and thus open to sharp carving and which hardened with exposure. There was enough of this not only to provide for the cathedrals of northern France but to permit exportation to England at least as far as Canterbury and Westminster.

Once when Napoleon I was resisting the idea of building the Pont des Arts out of iron and was being baited with the English prowess in iron, he remarked rather loftily that the reason for this was that the British Isles did not have good stone and were forced by necessity to solutions which the French with their great supplies of beautiful stone need not resort to. It was a canard. In addition to the modest marbles of the Isle of Purbeck and the flints of Norfolk and Suffolk already alluded to, the English had a fine oolitic firestone often called freestone, and very hard granites in Cornwall and Devonshire and sandstone in Yorkshire, and the history of the use of local stone in England goes back at least to Stonehenge. In this history Caen stone would play a very minor role.

The subcontinent of India also had rich supplies locally limited—fine pink marbles in Rajputana, trap and granite in the Deccan, and volcanic stones in Halebid. Thus, though the early Indus settlements were of brick and wood, and the wooden forms, as in so many other parts of the world, are perpetuated in early stone buildings—even when they have become altogether vestigial—by the middle of the Epic period, say toward the middle of the first millennium B.C., stone begins to dominate the architecture, even to the extent of imitating wood construction. Indeed the rock-cut sanctuaries of western India beginning in the second century B.C., although barrel-vaulted, are really imitations—often very literal and including small details—of earlier wooden constructions.

In the Netherlands, on the other hand, although there were marbles in the Ardennes, the clays and the beach sands had more appeal and the architecture was significantly one of brick.

So all through the ages stone had first to be found; then it had to be extricable from quarries depending on the tools available, and this was for a long time related to whether or not it lay in natural beds. If it could be removed from the quarry, it had to be possible to transport it to the building site, often with primitive machines which limited its practical range of influence; when on the site it had to have the necessary properties, neither too hard nor too soft, too heavy nor too light. It needed to be resistant to abrasion, to freezing and thawing, to shock and other destructive forces depending on the climatic conditions of the site. And finally there was the matter of appearance, which assumed importance as soon as the minimal technical needs were met.

Although one need not make a fetish of structural "honesty," I think it is fair to say that the heyday of every building material has been when the structure was best developed and when the material was part of the structure and not merely a covering for something else which was really doing the work. On such an assumption the apogee of stone occurred, in my opinion, in the high Gothic of the thirteenth and early fourteenth centuries in France.

But between then and the Egyptian pyramids, the temples of the Nile, the Greek trabeated construction, there was a long period, several millennia, of experiment and change. During all this time the builders were confronted with one very hard fact: however other properties of stones may differ, all have one serious flaw—they are exceedingly weak in tension.

In the beginning this may not have mattered much. Men crawled into natural caves and used them as they were; they learned to cut into the caves and mold them into something more nearly resembling architecture but without, save by accident, breaking into the totality of the rock. Even when they began to pick up stones, they were not involved in the weakness of stone so long as they were content to build only stele or walls. (There are some problems of tension even in walls but to introduce them here will only be confusing.) The real problem began to emerge when the builders wanted to roof their structures with stone. They always had the alternative where wood was available of building stone walls to support wooden roofs. But wood was not always available. When it was, it had a bad habit of burning up. So in the end the builders faced up to the problems involved in using stone to span horizontal voids. From their struggles with this emerged some of the great glories of historical architecture—the arch, the vault, the arcade, the ribbed vault, the flying buttress, the dome.

There have been, to be sure, some works of architecture where the problem of large spans did not exist, or even the problem of spanning at all. Stonehenge, for example, required neither a complete peripheral enclosure or a roof—even its lintels may have been ceremonial and surely carried no weight beyond their own. Again the apparatus of enclosure may have been provided by nature or carved by men cutting into a rocky cliff or hill. Though most of these were early, they did not always precede structures whose walls or columns had to support a roof. But when this has been so, they were off the main line of architectural development and it will be clearer to ignore chronology for the moment and to dispose of all these types first.

MENHIRS AND DOLMENS—STONEHENGE

A *menhir* is a prehistoric monument, usually a single stone, standing tall in the countryside. It is found in many parts of the world, and menhirs are especially common in Brittany in France. A *dolmen*, also prehistoric, also especially common in Britain and France, is a burial chamber made minimally of two upright stones and a lintel, though it can be more com-

Pl. 70
Pl. 71

plex, like a cave standing above ground. If architecture began, as I think, when men began moving materials out of their natural location and, whether or not also shaping them, putting them together into a new synthesis, then both menhirs and especially dolmens qualify as architecture.

Stone architecture then begins, not in caves, but with dolmens, menhirs, cromlechs, and especially with places like Avebury and Stonehenge. They are the result of conscious acts, and are indeed part of the beginning of architecture even if we expand our definition to say that architecture is a self-conscious organization of human spaces, usually a building but not necessarily so, usually an enclosure of space but also legitimately enclosed by it.

The relation between places of burial and places of worship, between the tomb, the shrine, and the worshipper's hall, has always been complex. Now the emphasis rests here, now there. But in the earliest architectural forms, the stones of Brittany and Cornwall and down at least through the Egyptian mastabas and pyramids, it was the necrologic element which dominated, although the architectural artifact was not always the tomb itself, but often only something related to a burial mound or tumulus or "long barrow."

The reasons for the existence of Stonehenge remain at least in part in controversy.[2] For whatever purpose the great stone rings were used, we can understand the *design* quite readily if we remember that it consists principally of two concentric circles of which the inner enclosed two series of standing stones, each in the shape of a horseshoe.

Pl. 74

The plan, which is quite clear from a drawing or even from the air, but especially from a drawing, is by no means so evident when you stand on the windy grounds in the driving, almost dreary, dusk, full of grog from a Salisbury pub and confused by speculations, spectators, and the unexorcizable Druids.

Pl. 75

One ought to start I suppose from the outside, but the description is more easily made the other way, beginning with the inner of the approximately concentric circles. Called the Bluestone Circle, it is less regular than the outer or Sarsen circle but probably had sixty stones around its 76-foot diameter, while the larger 97-foot diameter circle had only thirty stones.

Twenty stones of the smaller circle either stand or lie on the ground. Four of these in two pairs are of thyolite, the rest spotted dolerite, but the unusual ones are in no special position, for instance, flanking the entrance. If there were sixty stones to start with, the average spacing center to center would have been about 4 feet. Since the stones are thick, the average spacing face to face near the entrance is about 2 feet, but the two

[2] R. S. Newall, *Stonehenge, Wiltshire,* 3rd ed. (London: H. M. Stationery Office, 1959) and R. J. C. Atkinson, *Stonehenge and Avebury and Neighboring Monuments* (London: H. M. Stationery Office, 1959), to say nothing of the theories of Hawkins.

These two books, published in the same year and under the same auspices, differ seriously even as to the sources of the stones and of course as to prototypes elsewhere.

stones seeming to mark the entrance (49 and 31) are set back from the inside of the circle by about their own thickness and are about 5 feet apart, which puts them very near the next stones. There is no evidence that these stones were spanned by a lintel.

The outer 97-foot-diameter circle was of thirty stones, about 10 feet apart center to center. They are genuinely large, 7 feet wide, 13 feet 6 inches high above ground, and 4½ to 6 feet more below grade. The uprights were spanned by lintels and each of the thirty was *cut to a curve.* *Pl. 73* They were held onto the upright stones by a knob or tenon in the upright which fitted into a hole or mortise cut at each end of the soffit of the lintel. Six are in their original position now; two or parts of two are on the ground; twenty-two are missing and nobody knows if they were even put up. Five of the uprights of this circle are missing. There is an entrance here so that its flanking stones 30 and 1 are on the axis of the inner circle entrance and of the horseshoe. They are a foot farther apart than the average and their lintel was thicker, possibly for structural necessity (longer span) or possibly for emphasis (monumentality at gate). To get the upper surface of this thicker lintel in line with those of the other lintels, the soffit was cut away at the ends where it fit onto the uprights to allow it to sink down to the correct height.

In this there are touches of human error such as a misplaced dowel hole in the lintel above stone 2.

If you look through the gap furnished by these "gates," you will see a large standing stone 256 feet from the center. Its top seems nearly level with the horizon. This is the heelstone or sunstone, and on the longest day of the summer solstice the sun is supposed to rise "very near" its peak. It is a large undressed stone, quite naturally pointed at the top and it does lean inward, but you need not be bemused by the sometimes expressed notion that it is bowing toward the monument.

If you walk from the center a few paces toward the Heelstone, as far, say, as the inner or bluestone circle and turn around and face the tallest stone, you will be looking nearly southwest, the direction of the midwinter sunset. Here the tallest stone 56 at the right was matched by a left-hand stone 55 now fallen with its lintel lying athwart the altar stone. This was the central of five trilithons of which the left-hand ones 51/52 and 53/54 are essentially intact. Of the right ones one pair and the lintel are fragmented and the second right-hand one was reerected in 1958, having fallen outward in 1797. We need always to remind ourselves in ancient places that other people have been there from time to time and may or may not have been willing to leave things unchanged.

The trilithons increased in height and span of lintel from the ends to the center. In front of them were nineteen tall slender stones, the tallest either side of the center about 8 feet high, the shortest at the ends 6 feet. These are of the same bluestone as the stones of the inner circle.

At the foot of the great trilithon is a big stone called the altar stone but probably so named only for its position. It is 16 feet long, 3 to 4 feet wide, 1 foot 9 inches thick, must weigh about 30 tons, and is of micaceous limestone from Pembrokeshire.

Outside these main stone arrays are several rings of holes, a bank, and a ditch, all of which can be studied in order to arrive at guesses as to how accurate the layout was and how and why; or as to their exact purpose—for example, to celebrate some great festival at the winter solstice or to give some netherworldly sepulchral significance. We shall, however, leave such speculation to the detailed monographs.

The best dating now seems to say that Stonehenge I—the bank, the ditch, the holes, the heelstone, and the central feature—was about 1800 B.C.; the double bluestone circle about 1600; the trilithons and the Sarsen circle about 1500; and that it all ended by 1400 B.C. Thus it is Late Neolithic and Early Bronze architecture.

What shall we say of Stonehenge? Certainly it was designed and certainly it took more than a little effort to put it together. It has no roof. Its space is defined by the sky, and the horizon and the obviously planned arrangement of the elements which, drawn from nature, have nevertheless been shaped by man within the power of his tools (and no one can say whether, given better tools, he would have elected to shape them more precisely) moved by men over considerable distances, erected there at what, until yesterday, would have been enormous effort, in a place to which they were not indigenous, in a highly ordered array and clearly for a purpose. Without knowing anything really of what it was like to be a Neolithic Briton, we can guess Stonehenge had a symbolic purpose. Further, we can sense its power with our eyes without any symbolic understanding of our own.

By the time Stonehenge was made, people in other parts of the world had built greater enclosing walls, had cut and moved bigger stones over bigger distances, had fabricated more refined and elegant posts and lintels. But not in Britain. Time is not the same everywhere all the time. It is constructed at least in human affairs by the nature of communication. At Stonehenge we move beyond natural caves, beyond stone monoliths stuck in the ground, beyond a pair of stone uprights and the casual slab of a dolmen to something far more purposeful, far more contrived. There are the lintels of the Sarsen circle and the trilithons. But, though these have mystic symbolism and though they frame space, they are not asked to carry any physical load beyond their own weight. That became the purpose of masonry walls and columns.

WALLS

Once we begin to think of roofed structures we have to think of what their support shall be and then how the roofs shall manage to hold themselves up from support to support. Over history the wall has been the principal form of basic vertical support. Indeed much of architectural history might be read as the story of how supporting structures were freed from the limitations of the wall.

It was natural enough to build a wall where stone was common even before there was much of a building in mind. A low one could serve to keep herds together, to shelter animals or men from the wind with or without a cover. For such simple purposes a man might pick up whatever stones were lying around, glaciated boulders, for example, and without dressing them at all simply pile them together with such skill and patience as he could muster to select those which nested well. Anyone who has seen, repaired, or tried to make a typical country New England stone fence will understand the process. It took only a little better selection of stones to permit corbelling, which would roof crude small huts, like the conical shielings of early Scotland.

Whether or not these were put together with mortar is unimportant once we understand what mortars will and will not do. They are not really glues. They are seldom so strong as the stone they "bind" in compression and usually weaker in tension. What they do do is serve to hold things together while the walls are "settling down" and to bind small stones to larger ones and of course to keep wind and rain out of the cracks. When masonry became more sophisticated and stones were dressed to flat surfaces, the mortar could be dispensed with altogether if the dressing was accurate enough, but it was generally retained to serve as a bedding into which stones could be laid and leveled and by which flaws in the dressing could be compensated for.[3]

Masonry put together this way of rough irregular stones bedded in mortar and not laid in regular courses is called *rubble masonry*. More than other stone building it profits from through courses, that is, by the laying of some stones across the wall. Rubble naturally falls apart more easily than dressed stone masonry. It abrades more easily at the surfaces. And to most viewers it appears less handsome than more contrived stonework. For all these reasons it tended to be used behind faces of stone that were more carefully dressed. This was a custom much employed by the Normans in building their great Romanesque piers where mass was the main thing desired. Rubble was easier to put together and would serve perfectly well if it was contained by sturdier exterior stone surfaces. And so it has served for nearly a millennium, though now it is often deteriorating in many English cathedrals, requiring extensive repairs.

The device was so natural as to be common throughout the world. Partial reconstruction of the northern building facade at King Zoser's com-

[3] In brickwork it plays a rather more important but similar role to which I will return when we talk about brick.

plex at Saqqara in Egypt shows a combination of dressed stone exterior and rubble interior in what was one of the earliest known advances from brick building to building in hewn stone (2800–2700 B.C.).

Of course, if an easily available stone had characteristically flat surfaces, it might be laid more easily, and now and again a wall of what might be called first-class rubble can be found. Something of this sort can be seen in the lower walls of the Kato Phournostholos tomb from Mycenae of the late fifteenth century B.C., and a more characteristic rubble in the interior of the Epano Phournostholos of the same period. You have doubtless seen more recent examples, for example, in houses in New Jersey where there is a stone which beds thus conveniently.

Cyclopean Walls—The Incas

Some of the most spectacular stone walls of the next development were produced not by trying to cut the stones into shapes which would fit well together at relatively small scale but by moving enormous stones over considerable distance and difficult terrain to build formidable walls. This sort of masonry laid without mortar is called *cyclopean*, and it too appeared very early. The large rough stones at the beginning were simply selected as well as they might be and smaller stones were wedged into the interstices. Why the transport of such large stones was chosen over quarrying smaller ones nearer at hand is hard to say. It can hardly have been a lack of tools. Possibly the enormous stones were more resistant to attack or thought to be more so than a wall of comparable thickness built out of smaller stones, and certainly most of the cyclopean monuments are in one sense or another fortifications. But they are impressive in another sense, and there is no reason to suppose that their builders were unaware of this.

Examples are to be found in many parts of the world. From Mycenae in the thirteenth century the North Gate reveals a great deal of irregularity although the touching faces fit well, and this is generally the situation in the walls of Tiryns. At the more important Lion Gate, also in the walls of Mycenae, the almost cyclopean stones are much better fitted, although the setting is still crude as compared with the masonry of Inca Peru. In Peru the stonecutters seemed to take the greatest pleasure in dressing stones to fit around and interlock with each other, and the skill of the cutting, perhaps not always necessary, is at least the match to their size as a cause for wonderment whether they line a street in Cuzco or furnish the wall of the great outlying fortress of Saccsihuamán.

Pl. 72

I suppose if you asked me to select the most impressive piece of cyclopean masonry to visit, I would send you to Peru to see this fortress of Saccsihuamán above Cuzco and the walls of the great Temple of the Sun in the city itself, even though there are bigger stones elsewhere, and the Egyptians and Romans used stone with more variety and imagination. The Peruvian trip is full of other nonarchitectural values, from the

Pl. 76

Pl. 77

Pisco sour to the llamas and alpacas, from the great museums in Lima of other and older arts than Inca to the snowcapped mountains and the desolate reaches of the Altiplano or the Indian market at Pisac. Not much of this is Inca. If great walls made great architecture, then we could say that Inca architecture was great; but all we have to see is the walls and all the rest is hearsay, and perhaps not very credible hearsay at that. Aside from the walls my conclusion as to Inca architectural remains is that they are only of marginal interest.

According to Rowe, the Inca dynasty began in Cuzco about A.D. 1200. All of its big masonry dates from a great and relatively peaceful period in the fifteenth century.

From the colorful but unreliable writings of Garcilaso de la Vega,[4] one might be led to think more highly of Inca architecture than present visible evidence would justify. Garcilaso, himself part Inca, son of a conquistador and a highborn Inca mother, left Peru while young, shortly after the conquest, and after fifty years in Spain wrote his memoirs from gossip about things he had never seen and some youthful memories. They tell us, for example, of phenomenal and unnecessary feats of stone transport. In one place he talks of dragging some of the cyclopean stones over 1,200 miles of mountain and gorge road! "And yet I give my word, I who am also an Indian, that Pedro de Cieza's informers did not lie but told him the truth." It takes no more than a look at the terrain, and the fact that stones of the same size and kind were available much nearer to the sites, to realize the absurdity. It may indeed be the lack of restraint in his language that makes his work so appealing. He quotes Cieza with approval. "All I could say of the royal palaces of the Inca would not be enough if I wished to make them appear more marvellous than they were. . . ." He speaks for himself. "The royal mansions of the Incas were second to none in the grandeur, opulence and majesty of everything that pertained to the service of these princes, and one might even say that certain of them, as we shall see later, outshone all the royal and imperial palaces in the world!" Garcilaso was not much traveled; he did not in fact see the Inca palaces until long after the Spaniards had looted them.

There were of course notable Inca achievements, and some of these were like those of the Romans: the generous assimilation of conquered neighbors; brilliant and demonstrably useful engineering works; an excellent communications system through the high mountains for the transmission of "useful" messages; a careful distribution to all of food and clothing. It was a society which asked for craftsmanship, but also a system which repudiated innovation and indeed took steps to prevent it; a system which could not deal with abstractions even in its spoken language and probably did not want to, a system which kept its people happy with coca and alcohol. A society may have efficient management

[4] Garcilaso de la Vega, *The Incas*, Alain Gheerbrant (ed.) (New York: Avon, 1961).

and excellent supportive engineering without important poetry, art, or architecture.

Would this all have been different if, as some Incaphiles such as Hiram Bingham imply, the Incas had been luckier?

> It is indeed a great pity that the Incas never had the opportunity, as did the Greeks and Romans, to come in contact with a people like the Phoenicians who were clever enough to invent an alphabet.[5]

Maybe so, maybe not. For all we know they might have rejected the alphabet as subversive. We have to take their society for what it was. It was not a society which demanded much from architecture, nothing more than terraces, roads, granaries, temple motels, rest houses, small private palaces, fortresses, and a public square which might be an open field where large meetings could take place once in a while. It got no more than it demanded.

I must assert again that there have been few societies which have produced a great architecture in the absence of other great arts, both precedent and contemporary. I myself can think of none, though the architects and artists of our own time are trying hard to prove otherwise. The intimacy with which the other arts embrace the architecture has, to be sure, varied with historic taste, but actually and until now the embrace has been general though not always so intimate as, say, the iconography of the French Romanesque and Gothic churches. If one wants to argue the Romans as a spectacular example to the contrary, one can only say that the most interesting Roman achievements were the inventions and developments they made in vaulting and the dome or in such nonarchitectural structures as the Pont du Gard.

But in any event it does seem relevant in trying to understand Inca architecture to think of other Inca art. In the architecture of the Incas, art clearly played no seminal role and was hardly ever invoked, save for the decoration of inner rooms by the overlay of gold sheets. Decoration qua decoration is unhappily not a major role for art and is not likely to demand or produce major art. The Inca builders asked no such help from the artists; and if they had I suggest they might not have been able to get it, even from the conquered and imported Chimus.

At any rate what we can see in Inca building is mainly the great stones and the skill with which they were artificed. It looks as if the Incas had no desire to cover wide spans, but if they did, it was with wood or cantilevered rushes, which are gone. Short spans they covered with slabs of stone; slightly larger ones with small wooden purlins. It was with these few inventions that they managed all the recorded innovations—the stone pegs bonded into gable walls to tie the thatch onto, and the perforated slabs Bingham calls "eye bonders" to which the purlins were tied.

---

[5] Hiram Bingham, *Lost City of the Incas* (New York: Atheneum, 1963), p. 17.

Neither of these can be called spectacular. To cover the roof the Incas turned only to crude thatch, not dressing stone for this purpose, or cutting wood into shingles, or burning ceramic tiles. It was, of course, the easy way, but it seems a careless way to roof untold treasure.

They were short of useful metals other than copper and tin. Gold they did have and a great deal of it despite all the Spanish disappointments and after all the long tales have been thoroughly discounted. But gold has little virtue as a building material; soft as lead, it may or may not have been used as a kind of mortar in some buildings as the eulogists say, though no trace has ever been found which in turn suggests an unbelievable thoroughness on the part of the Spanish gold-pickers; it was certainly used and sometimes in profusion as banded ornament outside or as the walls of the cells of some of the temples, though these rooms were seldom more than 12 feet on a side. And since the rooms were so small, it is not hard to conjecture the limited effect this opulence could in fact have.

In the end, and save for gold decoration, the building mastery the Incas displayed went into the erection of walls of great size, sometimes of cyclopean dimensions. The admiration for this has to stem mostly from the fact that it was done with no pulleys, no wheels, no cement, no shaping tools other than stone. The Incas obviously had great manual skill with such simple apparatus as the backstrap loom, but all this skill, even when coupled with a boundless and patient labor supply, still leaves the result to be marveled at more than to be admired.

Their masonry may best be described as of three types: The dramatic type, which generally causes all the ohing and ahing, is megalithic, made of large, sometimes enormous, perfectly fitted, polygonal blocks and is used for the retaining walls of terraces and for large enclosures. A second variety, called cellular, is of small polygonal blocks and was also used for small buildings and higher up on some bigger ones. A third type, coursed ashlar (of which more below), is less common and quite beautiful though not so spectacular because we are more familiar with it. These rectangular blocks generally have a somewhat convex surface with sunken joints and are used in buildings. Finally, a variant of the last used for a few important buildings was smooth ashlar. It appears that even the hardest stones, such as granite or syenite, were pecked into shape with stone mauls. Beautiful examples are to be seen on the streets of Cuzco, notably in the substructure of the convent of Santa Catalina which was formerly the Accla Huasi or House of the Chosen Women. It invokes reminiscences of some of the fine rusticated masonry of the Italian Renaissance palaces, which, incidentally, were essentially contemporaneous.

The big megalithic stones are real. In Tiahuanaco, Father Joseph de Acosta reported that he measured a stone 38 feet long, 18 feet high, and 6 feet wide, and he added that some of those at Saccsihuamán were much bigger than that. Here one does not need to rely on Father de Acosta's memory. Anyone who goes can see the stones. They are magic enough without the hyperboles of Garcilaso. Gradually the claims of hauling over long distances of arduous terrain have been whittled down. Even the friendly Bingham, who wanted to believe the best about the Incas, rejected them in favor of their having been brought from sites little more than a mile away, moved over an inclined plane by levers. The more recent archeologist Valcarcel reports that three kinds of stone were used to build the great fortress, and that the two gigantic types were found on or very near the site. The third (black andesite) used in the inside came from quarries the nearest of which were 9 and 22 miles from Cuzco. And with regard to the very greatest blocks of the outer wall he remarks that there is nothing to prove that they were not simply hewn from a mass of stone existing on the spot. Even with this amount of deflation the rest of what Garcilaso says rings true to anyone who has stood before this wall. It *is* so well fitted that it is hard to slip a knife blade between the stones. Such fitting, given the lack of precision instruments, must have required trial and error involving moving the stones up and down apparently, as noted above, without cranes or pulleys.

They did make minor inventions to help them. They left protuberances in the stone against which levers could apply; and surely they knew how to raise stone lintels, for example, by the use of ramps of dirt which could be removed after the lintel was in place. Nonetheless they did no more of this than they had to, sharply limiting the number of doors, windows, and even interior wall niches to a usable minimum. All of these were usually shaped like those of the Egyptians with the bottom wider than the top.

There is no doubt that the masonry is often spectacular and even magnificent at times. But in the absence of interesting plans, of dramatic spaces, of an elegance and refinement in anything save the precision of the masonry and its occasionally overwhelming scale, in the absence of collateral arts save what may have been achieved by the lathering on of gold, this is not enough to make great architecture, which is more than masonry.

Pl. 78 Before we leave Incan "architecture," we ought perhaps to look briefly at two rather famous examples. Of Machu Picchu much ecstatic writing has been done. It is an ecstatic place to visit, scenically superb, approached in a dramatic way, and it does provide a rather complete layout of some kind of a village, most probably one of a chain of forts against Amazonian invasions, which must have cared for 1,000 people or so. No one believes any more that it is really the last Lost City but this does not matter much. It is a fine place to observe the quality of Inca terraces, conduits, stairways, domestic construction, and the smaller kinds of stonework. There is also a semicircular small building with finer stonework which may have been a temple and a dramatic example of the Intihuatana or sundial stone where at the winter solstice the astronomer high priest tied up the Sun, ostensibly to prevent his departure, in reality to mark the beginning of his return, as usual carved out of a solid stone but in this case remaining undecapitated. So Machu Picchu is a great general adventure, but it is not so overwhelming architecturally as Chichen-Itzá or Uxmal, as Thebes or Luxor, as Persepolis or Epidauros or even Mycenae, although whether Mycenae would look so impressive to anyone not steeped in Homer and Aeschylus and their tales of the horrible adventures of the House of Atreus, I am not prepared to insist.

I do know that anyone who visits Machu Picchu will have a much more rewarding experience if he stays overnight at the comfortable inn there instead of trying to do it all in one long day from Cuzco. The place improves once the train and its passengers have left, even on Christmas Eve, which we once spent there. There is now a much larger and modern hotel which may spoil everything just as the one at Sounium in Greece does.

Finally, what of the Temple of the Sun, which is being restored within the Convent of Santo Domingo in Cuzco? It was no doubt the largest building there. The stone walls are reported to have been completely covered with beaten gold or, in the case of the Chapel of the Moon, with silver. But only three Europeans ever saw this temple in its heyday—Hernando de Soto and two followers—and they left no record. What one can see now does not tell much and what one can read is very speculative.[6] Generally this has been the fate of the Inca remains in Cuzco, a wall here, a wall there, the Plaza of the Nazarenas built on the ruins of the ancient building of the House of the Teachers. Pleasant trips can be made to Tampu Machay where some of the Incas are supposed to have come to bathe and where fountains still trickle, or to a fascinating shrine built around a natural stele, called Kenko.

Pl. 79

Was there really much more? Yes, if you believe Garcilaso's descriptions of palaces and temples he never saw, walls plated with gold, all delicately embossed with figures of sheep, birds, butterflies, mice, snakes, all very naturalistic and highlighted in silver; a solid gold seat for the Inca; bathing suites in every mansion with basins and even waterpipes of gold and silver.

Most of this nobody has seen who can provide a reliable account. Perhaps it is true as Pedro de Cieza de Leon told that all these palaces and temples which had been built to stand the ravages of the centuries were destroyed in a few years by the Spaniards. It remains nonetheless curious that so little was left when so much was left everywhere else. Other cities have been thoroughly ravaged and traces have been found.

Inca work offers two lessons to young architects. One is that it is possible to overcome great difficulties. The other may be not to try to do deliberately worse than your technology permits through some mysterious notion that the crudeness of the peasant hand is superior to the precision of the machine, or as a protest against the countless ways that precision may be misused. The Incas never made that mistake.

[6] G. H. S. Bushnell, *Ancient Arts of the Americas* (New York: Praeger, 1965).

ASHLAR MASONRY

Cyclopean walls are things of great monumentality and sometimes even of beauty. They are always sources of wonder—how were they quarried, how were they transported, how were they erected in a time when stone tools were the hardest available and metal tools, when existent, were soft and unreliable? All these are perfectly natural and legitimate questions. They are human questions. But as we have said, they are not centrally architectural. In any case, such walls are an extinct form.

Pl. 80

Once men began to have skill in the dressing of building stone, they had some choice as to where to do the dressing and some choice, consequently, in respect to the means of transportation. They had other choices, too. Occasionally, though not often, they elected to arrange the stone in polygons. There are samples of this in Inca work and again at Delphi in the sixth century B.C. or Cnidus in the third or second. But the more practical choice was for stones of rectangular shapes, and this masonry, which is called *ashlar*, has dominated stone masonry through most of its history.

Ashlar is a masonry made up of trimmed rectangular flat surfaces with squared edges. It did and still does offer an enormous potential variety. The stone itself may all be of uniform size or the thickness of the courses may vary. The thickness of the joints may be changed. The vertical joints may all line up with each other or may be staggered; colors may be changed; different stones may be employed for contrast. Quoins may be put at the edges of the wall to emphasize corners. And among other things when a great show of power is desired, the joints may be rusticated. In rusticated masonry the beds and joints of the stones are squared but the surface is left rough, or made so artificially.

Much of the best simple stonework is to be found, not surprisingly, in military architecture. We can think of such examples as the interior of the tower near the Arcadean gate at Messene from the middle of the fourth century or at smaller scale in an Attic frontier fort of the third century at Aegosthena. One would expect to find more refined forms in temples and so we can, for example, on the wall of the Temple of Athena Nike, on the Athenian Acropolis of 425 B.C., or even better at the inner porch of the Propylaea, 437–432. The Romans, who often treated stone more as a decorative material than as a structural one, except in their aqueducts and bridges, and once their exploitation of concrete had matured, were fond of depressing the joints between alternate broad and narrow courses to create a very stylish effect, as in the early Temple of Portunus in the Forum Boarium at Rome in 31 B.C.

Wall Faces

It remained for the Romans, too, to demonstrate that what you see on the face of a wall is not necessarily all that is there. Three of their best-liked ways of facing concrete walls involved the appearance of stone. These were *opus incertum*, whose small irregular-shaped stones were embedded in the face; *opus recticulatum*, which used small squared stones set with the joints in continuous diagonals to produce a netlike appearance, hence the name; and *opus spicatum*, where roughly rectangular stones were set diagonally in alternate directions to form a herringbone pattern.

But this takes us in the direction of decoration, the play, for example, of colors of opposing stones as in the later Pisan bands, or of the side walls and tower of the Cathedrals at Siena and Lucca, or the reticulated facing of red and white stone slabs on the gatehouse of the Abbey of Lorsch, circa 770, first squares, then diamonds, then hexagons; it takes us much farther afield than we ought to venture right now.

It was the architects of the Renaissance, however, who carried the art of careful design of the facade wall to its highest level. They used other elements, indeed, besides the simple ones of stone sizes and shapes and finish and joints, but there are great lessons to be learned from these especially if we can learn to exclude in our imagination the cornices and the pediments and the pilasters and the urns and the statues.

At the Palazzo Strozzi in Florence (1489) we can see a very steady use of rustication throughout. It is actually later than Michelozzo's Palazzo Medici Riccardi (1430), where the heaviness of the rustication is diminished and finally disappears as we ascend the stories and move from the solid fortalice of the street to the living quarters above. *Pl. 82*

Raphael's Palazzo Vedoni Caffarelli in Rome seventy-five years later keeps the rustication, now in alternating thick and thin bands, only on the lower story, while Giulio Romano's Palazzo del Té in Mantua only a few years later (1525–1535) shows how the meaning of rustication can disappear in the hands of a Classical Mannerist where it is used not as a designator of strength but merely as background ornament behind a classical order.

The most refined and elegant of all these Renaissance city street facades is, I believe, the Palazzo Rucellai built by Alberti in 1446 in Florence. Most of the rustication is omitted. Not only is the Roman use of orders, tier on tier, revived, but also some of the elegance of the stone arrangements of almost a millennium and a half earlier in the Forum Boarium. In the Rucellai the artistry is so careful that the module (half the width of a column or pilaster) controls all the measurements of the facade including the stone jointing. As in the much later work of Mies van der Rohe it clearly pays off when the results are compared with the work of lesser men. *Pl. 295*

Structural Notes on Walls

In a strictly structural sense the top of a wall can be thinner than the base since it does not have to carry the weight of the wall itself. Moreover insofar as stability against tipping over is concerned, it is better to have more of the stone near the bottom, that is, to have a wider base. When the wall encloses a building, the floor loads begin to be more important than the weight of the wall and to reduce the load-bearing significance of the taper. Moreover for buildings there may be reasons to want an orthogonal surface both inside and outside. Nonetheless the slope of a wall or a pier upward and backward from the perpendicular, that is, its batter, can be a forceful expression of the wall in architecture.

The batter is expressive in a notable way on all sides in the gate pylons of Egyptian temples such as the temple of Horus at Ed-fu (third century B.C.); or at the ends as in the temple of Hathor at Dendera (fourth century B.C.); or on the great wall of the fort at Peshawar; or on the wall of the Nijo Palace in Kyoto; and more subtly in many other places than you would suspect where it may add to appearance without even calling any explicit attention to itself.

Pl. 83

The buttress is another quite common functional addition to a wall. We are most familiar with it as an abutting pier to help a wall to take the thrust of an inner arch, but it was used as a general reinforcement long before there were any arches to do any thrusting. Although the remains of the great sun-dried brick cities of Mesopotamia are not easy for us to understand without the aid of models reconstructed by archaeologists and therefore out of bounds for much discussion here, it appears that such monumental constructions as the Great Ziggurat at Ur (2350 B.C.) were a marvelous combination of powerfully battened walls and strong regularly spaced buttresses, and enough of this can be seen on the site to prove it. The buttress also serves a decorative function in addition to its structural purpose. It breaks up the wall by projections which permit the play of light and shade, in constantly changing rhythms. This is not essential to architecture, as the short reign of glass skin buildings has demonstrated in our time, but it is a common element of almost all, perhaps all, the greatest architecture of all times. It may or may not be a fundamental canon of design but it is very near to being one at the least. Even in our own day we have begun to turn away from the architecture of reflecting surface back to the architecture of shades and shadows.

The movement of light on a wall can be achieved in many ways, by indentations as well as projections, by setting back of whole pieces of wall, by applications of pilasters or the hollowing out of niches, by quite unfunctional things as well as originally functional ones, such as buttresses.

Pl. 84

This was discovered soon enough by the Egyptians. When King Zoser built his complex at Saqqara in 2800–2700 B.C., his talented architect Imhotep provided an important single entrance. Here, although the building was of stone and though buttresses were unnecessary, the architect broke the surface by almost equal vertical indentations and projections. Though these were doubtless influenced by earlier buttressed mud brick walls, they were executed in such a beautifully mannered way that it might be impossible to say whether we are dealing with projections or recesses were it not for the fact that the door opening is recessed and that the plane of the wall at the top is the plane of the projections and not of the recesses. Thus we have here a wall treatment of great beauty, provided, so to speak, by buttresses in reverse.

Rhythm and the play of light and shade on walls can also be provided by openings through them where the reveals of doors and windows provide shadow lines, and this became very important in later architecture. But in earlier construction the problem of spanning these openings was difficult enough to limit them to the barely necessary, while so long as most buildings needed also to be defensible, the desire to open up the wall was naturally limited.

One way to reduce the span of the stone lintel, and incidentally to brace the wall at the point of penetration, was to taper the sides inward as one went up. There are handsome examples of this many places in Peru and nowhere better than the trapezoidal so-called Palace of the Nusta or the "Three Windows" at Machu Picchu. The next step was the corbel, which provided relief in the loading of the lintel, and of which the notable example is the Lion Gate at Mycenae. The corbel might further be used not to relieve a lintel but to provide a very interesting element, almost a monumental corridor, through a building as in the Governor's Palace at Uxmal, which is certainly one of the most beautiful monuments I have seen in America. The steep triangulation, most unusual, might be taken by some as a lack of courage in the corbeling, but I take it on the contrary to be a highly dramatic statement of the true nature of the corbel, which could only be more true if the stones had a stepped profile; either the steps or the chamfered triangle are in my opinion more excellent than the rounded, almost arch—but really apparition of an arch—at Labná, although this itself is handsome enough.

It must be evident by now that the wall is such an important element of architecture that the connoisseur will never neglect it.

In some situations it will be impossible for him to overlook it. This is the case certainly for great fortification walls such as those at Aigues Mortes, Avila, Carcassonne, the Krak des Chevaliers, or the Château of Pierrefonds. Aigues Mortes has a simple, businesslike rectangularity. It is in strict contrast to the heavily merloned and heavily machicolated walls and towers that were built in the fourteenth century to surround the papal establishment at Avignon; or the circuitous walls of Carcassonne rising in double rank, climbing up and down the contours whose every gate and tower has its own individuality; or the longer, often straight stretches of Avila where the round towers are so many and so large as to make the wall seem only a connecting membrane; or the piled-up citadel of the twelfth-century Krak des Chevaliers whose towers are still more dominant; or the bristling towers of Pierrefonds connected by a wall which is

Pl. 85

Pl. 86

Pl. 87

Pl. 89

Pl. 88

Pl. 90

The Architecture of Stone 171

now also the closure of a chateau and whose top, dating from about 1400, is beginning to suggest signs of peace. For all such types the wall cannot be ignored; it speaks firmly for itself; indeed it is the architecture.

Nor can the wall be ignored when it impresses us with an enveloping form or by its very shape as do the great undulant church facades of Vierzehnheiligen at Banz (1744) or the Abbey Church of Ottobeuren (before 1766). Such Baroque walls, though much ornamented, sing through the ornament because of the positive impression of their undulant forms.

Walls are also very noticeable if they have been adorned with powerful statuary at their gates, such as those of the warrior in high relief on the outer jamb of the Royal Gate at Boghazkeuy or the winged bulls at Gate A of the Citadel of Khorsabad or the winged genius at the same gate. These are, to be sure, primarily sculpture, but they are so architectonic and so certainly placed for architectural emphasis that they punctuate the wall itself.

Pl. 91

Even less architectural adornment will cause the wall to shout at us. We have only to think of the stone patterns of the facades of the Duomo in Florence, or Santa Maria Novella or San Miniato in the same city; of the more ornate apse of Monreale, of the carved scallop shells poking out well over the surface of the Casa de las Conchas in Salamanca (1514) or of the painted stucco walls adorned with horses and figures of the Casa Rella in Trento or the many similar wall treatments in Bavaria or the Tyrol.

Sometimes these treatments of the wall may run too wild. This is very nearly but not quite the case for some of the Mayan buildings, such as the great frieze accounting for more than half the height of the Governor's Palace at Uxmal or the dramatic use of the superimposed masks of the rain god at the Nunnery Quadrangle, showing the eyes, the ears, the mouth, and the nose of Chac. At Uxmal these do not cover the whole facade but are grouped so as to form accents to the wall and not to cover it up. We should remember that the main walls were of rubble and lime while the finely carved blocks of the facade are a purely decorative skin. This carving does lend extraordinary distinction to the architecture of Yuacatan and you may or may not agree with Ignacio Bernal that

> . . . this utilization of the faces of the gods simply to ornament its palaces gives the impression of a culture which—while not neglecting its religious principles—attaches more importance to the decorative aspects of these images than to their value as objects of veneration for the faithful.[7]

Be this as it may, it becomes clear that this adornment is a dangerous game. With the Mayas it appears in another Puuc city, Kabáh, not far

[7] "Kabáh Codz-Pop" in Ignacio Bernal, *Ancient Mexico in Color* (London: Thames and Hudson, 1968), p. 70.

from Uxmal. Here the decoration of the facade of the palace of the Codz-Pop is overpowering.

Every square foot of the front and even the sides are overcrowded with enormous masks, entirely reminiscent in an unhappy way of the same excess in Hindu architecture. In these situations the wall tends to disappear altogether.

But to this a Mayan might cogently have replied, "We are more interested in Rain than in Walls—or Architecture. The only critics we heed are the Gods."

But though obvious walls may demand they not be overlooked and underscore this demand by various devices, the sensitive architectural viewer will always want to consider the wall, even when it is wearing its most modest clothes. Sometimes it will be the primary element of the architecture, sometimes very deferential. But it will never be trivial.

THE COLUMN

Obviously a masonry wall may perform one or two different functions or both together. The functions can be separated, and this appears most clearly in relatively modern times. On the one hand the wall may be the actual supporting structure; on the other it may be the closing element. But in modern steel-framed buildings there is no need for stone to carry the loads. This is done by the metal ossature. The problem of closing the building is, then, a separate one.

In antiquity there were times when closure was not needed or even desired, and yet stone was the best available building material. This led naturally to the elimination of intermediate walls and the collection of the bearing loads on pieces of walls, that is, piers or, later, columns with beams spanning the voids between the columns. This sort of construction, called variously post and lintel, or post and beam, or columnar and trabeate, or just trabeate, is the second great way of building. It has been responsible for many of the major achievements in architectural history. As in other uses of stone the column was not without vestigial instincts to retain things learned from wood. It is not uncommon in wooden architecture to find columns whose taper is downward. The reasons for this are arguable. Was it because the original posts were driven into the ground; or, as Dinsmoor conjectures,[8] was it because the rain would more readily drip off? Whatever the reason, this downward taper has appeared in many parts of the world.

Now when the column is made of stone, such logic as there is suggests that the column shall, if anything, be thicker at the bottom than at the top. It needs a somewhat greater area, for instance, to hold the

[8] William Bell Dinsmoor, *The Architecture of Ancient Greece*, 3d ed. (London: Batsford, 1950).

additional weight imposed by the column itself. This is not, however, a large factor and unless the load-carrying designs are stretching much nearer the limit than they really ever are, the upper cross section should be quite capable of carrying the marginally larger loads imposed on the lower cross section.[9] This is at least true for most architectural columns; it may not be true for very tall ones, such as obelisks, where we might feel some alarm if the base were palpably smaller than the top, for here the taper is expressing visually the facts of the load, and a visual denial of these facts would seem strange. There is a comparable problem with the fenestration of towers to which I shall return later. Again if there is any great tendency toward tipping, the column will be more resistant with a broader base. And finally, whether the column is a monolith or made up of drums, it is easier to put it up if the narrower part is at the top. But all these functional reasons are marginal and not sufficient to demand that the column taper upward if there is any good reason for it to taper downward. For a time the sufficient reason was that of habit, so vestigial tapered columns of stone are to be found here and there not only in Crete but in the Festival Hall of Thothmes III at Karnak.

As much could be said of the visual qualities of columns as I have said about walls. From the simple piers of the early Egyptians to the tapered carefully proportioned Greek columns or the twin-horsed capitals of Persepolis is a far cry. But how the column was developed visually in various forms of trabeate architecture can be more clearly exposed in discussion of the various examples of that architecture.

Walls required means of spanning the distance between them—not an easy problem in stone. The column added the additional problem of spanning between the columns. A parallel problem arose in a wall where a very wide window or door was desired and the normal horizontal lintel was inadequate.

CORBELS

Once you are trying to span an open space either from a wall or a column, you begin by thinking of a beam. For our purpose here, a slab can be thought of as a group of beams laid face to face. The same things happen with a stone beam as with a wooden one. As it is loaded, it begins to bend. As it bends, its upper material is compressed and stone can stand this very well. But the bottom part begins to stretch. And stone can hardly stretch at all. Its tensile strength is only about a thirtieth that of most woods and a four-hundredth or less than that of steel. So it soon breaks in bending. The way one tries to accommodate beams to make them

[9] This will be evident if you realize that there are many perfectly satisfactory round stone columns of a uniform cross section and that they look very well and raise no questions in most minds; while when the round sections are replaced with rectangular ones, the question of taper does not often arise.

stronger is to make them deeper. This works well with wood or steel. It works miserably with stone, which is so heavy in comparison to its bending strength that if you make a stone beam deep enough in an effort to increase the span, it may break under its own weight without any superimposed load at all.

The failure of stone to "shape up" as a transverse material affects everything you might want to do to make a building of stone more useful unless you are willing to settle for timbers for long spans. If you want windows and doors in a wall, it sharply limits how wide they may be with stone lintels (only a few feet). If you want to make a room with a stone slab running from wall to wall or a set of stone beams running from post to post, the room must be very narrow; and if the structure is columnar (trabeated), that is, made up of posts and beams, the columns will have to be very close together. This is what happened in Egyptian temples, and for that matter in Greek temples if they were roofed in stone, and always at the colonnades and peristyles of Greek temples where only stone was permissible and where Greek efforts to stiffen the horizontal stone architraves by inserting metal bars permitted only marginally better results.

A first effort to get a wider space can be made with a *corbel*, which is not to be confused with an arch. A stone corbel is made by laying one stone on top of another and pushing the upper one somewhat into the desired span so that it is cantilevered a little over the lower one. It will evidently tip off if you push it out too far. And of course successive layers of corbels will reach a point where the top one will certainly tip off. This is prevented by applying additional counterweight from masonry above. In the end the corbel from one side meets the corbel from the other and the cover is made. Such corbels may simply go from post to post or from rectilinear wall to rectilinear wall or may, with a little more complicated geometry, start from a circular or other vertically enclosing form.

In any event though a corbel buys something, it does not buy very much. Each successive stone (or brick) cannot project enormously from the one below it. The consequence is that the corbel tends to exact a considerable amount of height, often too much height for the free span it allows. This may not cause too much difficulty when it is used to relieve the weight on a lintel. For instance if you wished to push a fairly wide gate through a wall, you might find a stone capable of carrying its own weight if that is all it had to do. You might then relieve it of the additional weight above by corbeling the wall so that all the load was carried down to the sides. If then you did not want an open hole above the lintel, you might fill it with a light slab. This is essentially the construction of the famous Lion Gate at Mycenae.

Here, so long as the wall is high enough to accommodate the pitch of the corbel, there is no problem. But when you are trying to make a room it is not so simple, and corbeled rooms or corridors are likely to be much too high for their width, which introduces not only practical problems but visual ones and an impression of undue narrowness. Thus the through corridors of the Governor's Palace at Uxmal in Yucatan, though they look quite impressive on the facade, are in fact wastefully narrow. Moreover, the corbel is fundamentally unstable. The Mayans, looking at times for a somewhat more monumental span than came readily to a corbel, tried to help out with a burnt lime cement they had and sometimes with wooden tie rods.

Corbels can naturally be smoothed out by cutting off the useless underparts of the projections. Then they may look like arches or vaults or domes, but they are not. The corbel works on an entirely different principle from an arch, a vault, or a dome. And it has so little potential for greatness (even in the bracketed wooden corbels of high Chinese architecture) that had no further inventions been made, many of the greatest achievements of stone architecture would not have been realized. The notable exceptions are the corbeled brick domes of Iran.

ARCHES AND VAULTS

The spanning problem of the *arch* is the same as the problem of the corbel. How are we to get from support A to support B across a distance which is greater than a stone lintel can manage without using a different material? The problem is solved by taking a number of wedge-shaped stones or bricks called *voussoirs* and arranging them so that they support each other and the imposed weights by mutual pressure. The familiar half-circular form will illustrate the point well enough. Starting with the apex or keystone, it is trying to fall to the ground. It is prevented by the two adjacent stones. But since these support the keystone at an angle (and they can do it no other way since, if they were vertically side by side, the keystone would simply slide by), the force they apply is at right angles to the joint, and hence partially vertical and partially horizontal. Both these pressures accumulate as the arch moves toward its springing from the wall. There is a vertical force downward and there is a horizontal force outward (thrust). Another way to imagine it is to think how you might keep the central stone from sliding down if the adjacent stones were vertically jointed. You know you cannot use glue. The other way would be to clamp the stones, in other words, to apply strong horizontal pressure. In reverse this is the thrust. Or you might think of the arch as wanting to flatten itself out and you can prevent this only by applying horizontal pressures. Think, for example, of how a straight wooden bow can be bent by pushing from the ends.

Now when these forces of the arch reach their springing on the wall (or column), the vertical component is readily carried to the ground through the natural compressive strength of the stone. What are we to do with the horizontal component? We might use a tie rod at the springing, but it will always be unsightly and space-encumbering and it will be very hard to manage as a tension member before we have iron. If there is only one arch in a very long wall, the problem does not exist. The sheer mass of the flanking masonry will be sufficient to resist the overturning tendency and contain the thrust.

But to have only one such opening in a wall, however monumental and majestic, will not satisfy us long if we have a building with rooms separated by walls and want rather free access between, say, the aisles and the nave. Here we can combine a range of arches to form an arcade. The thrust of the intermediate arches will counterbalance each other and so we can spring them from rather narrow piers or columns if we desire. But the end arches have no such counterbalance and their thrust must be resisted by larger pieces of wall or buttresses or more sophisticated devices if we can think of any.

I have made this analysis on the basis of a half-circular arch (*plein-cintre* in French), but many other shapes are possible, a few more efficient, most not but adopted for other reasons. Arches of steeper pitch may or may not result in less thrust for vertical load carried, and arches of flatter pitch may present more thrust for vertical load carried, but there is no way in which thrust can be made not to exist, and much of the ingenuity of masonry design has rested in the devices employed to contain it.

Some of the most common arch forms are: Pl. 92

Flat
Round
Horseshoe
Trefoil
Segmental
Pointed (equilateral)
Pointed (lancet)
Ogee
Curtain
Tudor

Shift our problem slightly now. Instead of trying to get an opening through a wall, we are trying to get a stone covering over a rectangular space. We can do this by building a barrel vault. You can think of a barrel vault as a series of arches which are laid face to face. Each one then has its thrust and there is continuous thrust all along the walls which receive the vault. Within rather narrow limits such thrusts can be compensated for by arcaded supporting walls provided the piers are substantial and some cross buttressing is available, thus limiting the freedom of motion in the aisles and tribunes. The barrel vault was much used by the Romanesque builders and has a marvelous sense of solidity and strength, but it is not open to much penetration.

The Romans too had used barrel vaults and had gone further. If two

Pl. 93

barrel vaults of the same shape and height intersect at right angles (as might be the case in the transept of a church), they have definite edges called groins at the intersections. Such a geometry not only permits the vaulting of intersecting rooms but answers the problem of containing the thrust at the ends of the arcade at the crossing (though not at the outer end of the arcade where a buttress was still needed, and was often supplied by a tower).

The next step was a Gothic step. It rested on noting that the edges of the groins were natural lines for *ribs,* so that a sort of arcuate stone framework could be made concentrating the loads (and the thrusts) in the ribs and allowing the rest to be filled in. The great rib vaults, the most beautiful in structural terms, were perhaps, as is so often the case, the earliest. They were *quadripartité;* that is, each vaulting bay was divided into four parts so that two transverse ribs connected the columns across from each other and two diagonal ribs connected diagonally opposed columns and met in the center of the bay. The arrangement might call indifferently for sharply pointed ribs or flatter ones. It is the arrangement in most of the twelfth-century French vaults, such as Rouen, Chartres, Amiens, and Reims, and is certainly the most direct way of going about it. But in a few cases, notably at Paris and Bourges, sexpartite vaults were used. Here every other column was connected across the nave only to the opposite column by a transverse rib, while the diagonals went from alternate columns thus providing the intersection of three ribs rather than two at the center and a bay which had six vaulting panels instead of four.

The concentration of the vertical loads in the ribs made it natural that the columns should be articulated to each rib; and the concentration of thrusts opened up the way for systems of buttressing which could count more on skillful counterpressures than on mass. Thus the flying buttress was developed as a quadrant arch to transmit the oblique lateral thrusts of the ribs over the roof of the aisle to an exterior vertical buttress, which in turn was made more slender through the skillful addition of weight to resist tipping over.

These arrangements opened the walls of the Gothic cathedral so that they became sanctuaries of light instead of caves of darkness. The development, both symbolic and engineering, raises the question whether it was the desire for light that prompted the invention of rib and flying buttress or the engineering innovations which instigated the cult of light. If I had to choose, I would bet on the latter, but the alternatives are probably not as sharp as stated.

The apogee of stone masonry construction had, I suppose, been reached by the end of the thirteenth century but not in a decorative sense. The masons went right on piling beautiful absurdity on beautiful absurdity into the sixteenth century at least. They added intermediate ribs to the quadripartite vaults in the form of tiercons (these start from the intersection of two ribs), ridge ribs, and liernes (subordinate ribs other than the ridge rib which do not start from the springing of the vault compartment) to produce a star-shaped pattern generally given the name of stellar vaults. The tiercons were supposedly inserted to give additional support to the panels, the ridge ribs to resist the thrust of the tiercons, and so on, one unnecessary invention demanding another. Stellar vaults can be seen in Gloucester, Canterbury, Wells, Ely, and Norwich. The increase in rib intersections led to a multiplication of bosses, which, originally acting as structural keystones against which the ribs abutted and as covering for awkward mitering at the joints, soon became a major ornamental feature of the late English Gothic ceilings.

Late in the English Gothic the English developed a special form, the fan or conoidal vault, in which all the ribs in each vaulting bay radiate, fanlike, from the same point and equidistant from each other. These are certainly elaborately unnecessary for any structural purpose save the vaulting of a round room from a central column as in a chapter house, but even when unnecessary, at their best they are very decorative and pleasant indeed as at the Henry VII Chapel in Westminster Abbey or King's College Chapel in Cambridge, as long as one looks at the pendants and the bosses and the ribs and does not worry about the enormous problems of geometry and stereotomy and craftsmanship. These problems were not always thoroughly solved, as in King's College Chapel where the sides of the conoids had to be cut off and offered awkward transverse intersections; or were resolved by "fakery," as in the Henry VII Chapel where hidden transverse arches above the vault support pendants from which the conoids spring, thus reducing a rectangular space from an oblong to the necessary square. These are noble achievements enough and it is carping to downgrade them too much because they were after all in a decorator's cause. So was practically everything else in Tudor times. They were no longer the times of Durham or Chartres.

Even less important perhaps but still amusing are the net vaults common in late German Gothic hall churches. Here the pattern is a complicated net of curved ribs making no pretense at function and serving nothing but decorative purpose. Such vaults, which almost deny the structural purpose of the ribs, can be seen in churches like St. Lawrence, Nuremburg, or St. Barbara, Kuttenberg, or deduced from a typical plan.

Finally the brick Gothic builders of northern Germany developed a special honeycomb type where the surfaces between the ribs were folded to form individual cells.

DOMES

The other major spanning device is the dome. In the simplest terms you can think of a dome as an arch rotated around its vertical axis. The geometry raises some different or at least slightly different problems, but the principal problem is similar. The horizontal thrust, now circumferential, must be contained—the vertical loads more or less take care of themselves. The thrust might be held in by a circumferential chain if you had one. Or all the walls might be made thick enough to resist over-turning; or large buttresses might be built at intervals not so large that the intermediate walls could not carry the thrust to them, or built in support of ribs which have collected the thrust of the dome; or the main dome might be supported on smaller peripheral ones and so on; and it will not be hard to understand these as you go about if you are looking for the thrust and how it is contained. And though the logical dome shape is hemispherical, it will not surprise you to find flatter ones as at Hagia Sophia, more pointed ones as in Parma, or ones which have a stilted springing as at San Giovanni degli Eremiti in Palermo, or ovoid stilted ones as in the Sassanian palace of Firuzabad in Iran, or the great variety of Islamic or Byzantine external shapes until the bulbous Muscovite forms are reached. Their analogues you have seen in the forms of arches; and it is not always a matter of efficiency which is in question. Nor will you be surprised especially as you move toward the Renaissance and Baroque where no more nonsense was preached about structural "honesty" to find that the dome you see outside is not like the dome you see inside, that there is a double dome in the chapel at Versailles and a triple one in St. Paul's, London. This is no more serious (perhaps?) than the fact that the Italian Gothic builders of the Duomo in Florence used the domical ribs but did not elect to build the rest as a Gothic structure so that the appearance, as in much other Italian Gothic architecture, was mere window dressing.

Another point about the architecture of the dome is worth noting. In essence it should start from a circular wall or, failing that, a bay which is nearly a square or a regular polygon. Domes may be combined to cover rectangular spaces: as in many mosques; as in the side aisles of the cathedral at Palermo; as in the nave (three domes) and crossing (double dome) of the "Romanesque" Angoulême Cathedral (1105–1130); or as in the whole cathedral of St-Front, Périgueux (1120), whose Greek cross plan reminiscent of that of San Marco in Venice is essentially a Greek cross with each arm and the center topped by a dome. (The domes of St-Front are almost semicircular, those in Venice flatter and capped by enormously higher stilted semicircular domes.)

But in all cases the base of any one dome is as indicated. If it is circular, as at the rotunda of the Roman Pantheon, the springing geometry is not too difficult. But when the plan is a decagon, as at the Minerva Medica in Rome, or an octagon, as at San Vitale in Ravenna, there is a problem of transition from the polygon to the circle. This is at its most acute when the transition is from square to circle, and the devices used are seen with the greatest clarity there.

There are at least three ways. When the diameter of the dome equals the diagonals of the square, you can cut away the portions of the hemis-phere outside the square, thus yielding four spherical triangles, which are called *pendentives*. They merge into the dome above.

Pl. 94

If the diameter of the dome equals the side of the square, then you begin with pendentives until you have defined a circle which can be exactly inscribed in the square. This is called a dome on pendentives.

Or you may throw an arch or a system of concentric arches across the corners of the square to turn it into an octagon, or repeating into some other regular polygon on which an octagonal or other almost but not quite circular dome may be built. The system of arches is called a *squinch*.

Combinations are possible. A decagonal ribbed dome was built on pendentives in the Minerva Medica in Rome; a dome was erected on an octagonal base in the Baths of Caracalla.

You can derive much pleasure among the domes by observing how each gets from its base to its summit. And especially in Islamic work and particularly in Isfahan it is a pleasure to see the joy with which the mosaicists and the tile setters and the masons set about adorning the pendentives with so-called stalactite decoration, filling the squinches with pieces of blue and green, or working up their honeycomb vaults into an ecstasy of elaboration.

Before we set out on our stone journey, there is one more thing we ought to know. As a masonry building or tower (whether brick or stone) gets higher, the walls have perforce to become thicker. At some point the construction can reach a height (16 to 18 stories for pure masonry) where the bottom floor has to be nothing but masonry. At this point there is naturally no use in going higher save for ritualistic or symbolic reasons. There are ways in which this truth can be cleanly expressed in architecture. The best example I know is the tower of the Abbey of Pomposa not far north from Ravenna on the Adriatic. It happens to be of brick, but the point would be the same if it were of stone. Notice, if you will, how skillfully the architect has displayed the truth through his windows— at bottom a mere slit, then doubled, tripled, widened as you ascend until the top is nearly all open. It puts to shame the absurdity of the more famous Torre Magnia in Siena which rises brick on uninterrupted brick so high that the ultimate machicoulis are too high to be of much defensive value. The tower is a landmark all around Siena and it certainly has its beauties, although they are less forthright than and represent a different value scale from those of the tower of Pomposa which I suspect may be the handsomest Romanesque tower in the world.

CAVES

Before we make an orderly progression into the development of architecture based on the principles just discussed, which is indeed the mainstream of architecture, we should make two important detours and dispose of the cave and the pyramid.

We can be quite certain that men used natural caves very early in their history as places of shelter from weather and refuge from animals including their own kind. But at first they did little if anything to modify what nature had provided and we cannot call this architecture.

If you go in for speleology you can find handsome arrangements of cavern walls, of stalactites and stalagmites often architectonic in form, but these, too, are not architecture.

PREHISTORIC CAVES

Some caves, of course, were habitations, and somewhat similar caves were used by early humans for various human purposes. There are, for example, the enormous piles of tools and bones of prehistoric men to be found in the many caves of the nearby valley of the Vézère in the region of Les Eyzies-de-Tayac—Magdalenian men, Aurignacian men, and so on— all now beautifully organized in the national museum of prehistory installed in the eleventh-twelfth-century castle of the barons of Beynac. It is interesting to see the caverns briefly and especially to visit the museum. But this is the pursuit of anthropology and not of architecture.

Some of the caves of Les Eyzies in France contain splendid wall paintings of bisons, horses, mammoths, reindeer, and Cervidae; these, along with those of Altamira in Spain, were considered the finest of this kind in the world but are now known to be surpassed by those of the nearby Grotto of Lascaux.

In these spaces we pass into a half-world of magic and art. That the art had significance to fertility and to hunting, there can be no doubt. The absence of tools and bones suggests that these halls were not domiciles but more sacrosanct than that, in some ways analogous to temples but perhaps in no very literal way. The painting is, it goes without saying, both magnificent and moving. It stirs deep-layered emotions—even atavistic recollections. It has suggestions to artists and to architects how art, freed of the gallery frame, might again work with architecture to the advantage of both and even what the absurdity is in visual matters of thinking of everything in terms of upside down or rightside up. But these caves are still not architecture. Nor are the magnificent and much later mortuary paintings in the caves in the Valley of the Egyptian Kings at Thebes or the Etruscan wall paintings in the tombs of Tarquinia.

The architecture of caves begins when men set out to modify the natural form of the cave in some way or other, or even to make caves of their own.

ROCK CUTS

Spiro Kostof has recently published an interesting book, *Caves of God*, which deals primarily with the Byzantine cave architecture of Cappadocia but ranges more widely in the process. After a colorful description of the topography of the "earth sea" of the Anatolian plateau, its sculptured tufa, rock folds, shifting colors and the frequency of the cones on this landscape, the *peri bacalari* or fairy chimneys, as the peasants call them, and the legends that swirl around them, he describes the cutting of the caves in terms which are susceptible to wider generalization.

> Not the least incentive to legend-making is the knowledge that the cones and pleats of stone have from an early time been used for shelter, burial, and sanctuary. The tuff [sic] is easy to carve. As water and wind freed the larger shapes from sheets as thick as 4500 feet at places, so human hands burrowed in for small protective hollows to serve as homes for the living and the dead, and to ensconce divinity. The practice of scooping out an environment from natural features is a primeval one. At its simplest, advantage is taken of hollows in the earth like natural caves; but often too, and even in the most advanced of cultures, rural folk communities will make these hollows by cutting into natural matter usable shapes, mostly hidden from view, which are the exact opposite of much architecture as we have come to know it. They stress not *constructed* form, built up in defiance of the law of gravity, but rather form that is dug, i.e., created, with interior space as the main objective. Columns and vaults, when they exist, are no more than structural symbols, liberated from natural matter in the same way a sculptor liberates the human form from a slab of limestone or marble. To speak of the columns as "holding up" entablatures, or of the vaults as "resting" on walls, is only to demonstrate the tenacity of the traditional view of architecture which centers on burdens and supports.[10]

This is an interesting position weakened a little because most of the famous rock-cut creations are postarchitectural rather than prearchitectural; that is, the forms were in fact in existence in precedent buildings and were imitated in this inverse technique so that almost no innovation is to be detected.

> Instances of this sculptured architecture, so to call it, are numerous, and the practice of making it universal. Written sources record excavated environments that we have lost. Agatharchides, a Greek geographer of the third century B.C., spoke of the rock dwellers of the Red Sea; Herodotus of Ethiopia, and Xenophon, of Armenia. In the vision of Obadiah, the Lord admonishes the land of Edom, "Thou that dwellest in the clefts of the rock, whose habitation is high." (Obad. 3) And the Koran, in one of its several mentions of the wicked city of Thamoud, refers to its people as those "who hewed out their dwellings among the rocks of the valley." But we have, of course, also actual remains. Rock tombs abound in the Near East. Those of Petra in the south of Jordan are famous. In Sicily, whole towns

[10] Spiro Kostof, *Caves of God: The Monastic Environment of Byzantine Cappadocia* (Cambridge, Mass.: M.I.T. Press, 1972), p. 18.

are rock-cut; Siculiano, Caltabelotta, Rafadalle, Bronte, Maletto. Further afield, in the *loess* belt of China, a large area comprising the Honnan, Shansi, Shensi and Khansu provinces, about ten million people live in dwellings hollowed out of the silt which has been transported and piled up by the wind.[11]

But though there are whole villages of sculpted architecture, including the pair in Cappadocia from perhaps the third century A.D., the important architectural rock-cut monuments are generally tombs or temples.

The oldest are certainly Egyptian. The Egyptians had been building rock tombs for at least a millennium before this kind of work culminated in the great funerary temple of Hatshepsut (1504–1483 B.C.) at Deir-el-Bahri in the XVIIIth Dynasty, a temple which has emerged from the rock wall and is only partially cut into it.

The royal tombs always played a more than regal role in Egypt, since the identification of the king with Osiris and therefore with God was persistent. For the kings and for royal functionaries in less degree the tomb had two parts. One, the burial chamber, usually at the bottom of a shaft, was the dwelling of the deceased where his mummy was deposited and also the objects, often beautiful and valuable treasures, which he would need in his afterlife; the other was a funerary chapel where he could enjoy worldly pleasures, where priests came to perform the repeated funerary cults, and where the marvelous magic pictures of the royal deeds were sculpted or painted. Sometimes the spaces were widely separated as in the days of the pyramids, sometimes combined as in the mastabas. The rock tombs with which we are concerned here were tunneled into the desert cliffs at almost every period, at Giza in the Old Kingdom, at Beni Hasan and especially at Thebes in the Middle. Generally a single corridor was cut into the cliff or hill almost horizontally (or it might be a series of rooms) and at the end a burial shaft was sunk down to the burial chamber. Usually there was an artificial grotto, an open part decorated with reliefs or paintings, except for the royal tombs of the New Kingdom in the Valley of the Kings and the Valley of the Queens. These are much concerned with the highest elements of the religion, the regeneration of the solar god, and were completely closed. Before the pillagers did their work, these tombs held the treasures and the remains of the great New Kingdom Pharaohs from Thutmose I to Rameses XI as well as many important unregal figures. The mummies and their sarcophagi are now mainly in the museum at Cairo; the brilliant undisturbed treasure of Tutankhamen, and of Prince Mahepre, and the stripped furni-

---

[11] Ibid., p. 18. Cave architecture is even more widespread than Kostof indicates. Apparently at least as interesting and as easy to reach are the rock churches in the Ethiopian highlands, such as those at Lalibala, which Kostof does mention, Qorqor, etc., also Byzantine. [See George Gerster in *National Geographic*, CXXXVIII (December, 1970), pp. 856ff.]

ture of the parents-in-law of Amenophes III are all in Cairo too. Pieces of dissipated but recovered treasures are in many other museums. What remains in the tombs are the splendid wall paintings which reveal almost every aspect of Egyptian life from the ritual night journey of Osiris to duck shooting in the reeds. Of the sixty-one or more tombs known to exist, many are, as Strabo said in 27 B.C., "an excellent work—worth a visit."

In the VIth Dynasty (2420–2258 B.C.) rock-cut tombs were made by cutting rectangular chambers parallel to the walls of the cliff; later they penetrated deeply into the rock. A notable example of the first type can be seen from Aswan. Crossing the Nile and advancing over a stone causeway well up a steep slope, one comes to two rooms unseparated by a wall. They belonged to two governors, a father, Sabeni, and his son, Mekhou, who completed his father's tomb and then built his own, a funerary chapel alongside it. Sabeni's chamber has three rows of six round columns; Mekhou's, two rows of four rectangular columns, all cut out of the living rock. The entrance to Sabeni's chamber is particularly impressive, with the distinct horizontality of the layers of differently colored sandstones, with the general austerity unrelieved by decoration, with two uninscribed steles flanking its threshold.

> These dry facts cannot do justice to what was here accomplished, for in these tombs with their infinitely wide outlook the relation of death with the cosmos can be sensed more powerfully than usual. From their position halfway up the steep cliff wall that rises abruptly from the banks of the Nile, nothing limits the view to the east. Stepping out from their entrances, one is embraced by the cosmic vault. We of today seem to gaze out into an endless void, but for the Egyptians the heavens were peopled. From the east the celestial bark emerged, its passengers renewed to life.[12]

The much more famous temple tomb built at Abu Simbel by Rameses II a millennium later (1330 B.C.) is vastly inferior.

Pl. 95

It is, of course, very big, one of the most stupendous and impressive of the massive works of this oversized man who also built the Ramesseum at Thebes and the hypostyle hall at Karnak as well as many other gigantic monuments eulogizing his memory.

There were in fact two temples cut into the rock, one for Rameses and an adjacent smaller one for his consort Nefertari. An entrance forecourt led to the imposing facade 119 feet wide and 100 feet high formed as a pylon carved with four seated colossal statues of the Pharaoh which were bigger than the Colossi of Memnon. Behind there was a vestibule

---

[12] Sigfried Giedion, *The Eternal Present*, vol. II, *The Beginnings of Architecture* (New York: Pantheon, 1964), p. 407. No. 6 in the A. W. Mellon Lectures in the Fine Arts, Bollingen Series XXXV (Copyright © 1964 by the Trustees of the National Galley of Art, Washington, D.C.), reprinted by permission of Princeton University Press.

flanked by eight Osiris pillars, also very large, and vividly colored wall reliefs. Eight small adjacent chambers were probably to store temple utensils and furniture, and beyond this was a small hypostyle hall 36 by 25 feet. In this hypostyle was the frequently portrayed panorama of Rameses' victory over the Hittites at the battle of Kadesh, which he celebrated monotonously on the pylon in front of the temple at Luxor, at the Ramesseum, and in one of the longest texts in Egyptian literature. Behind the hypostyle was a long narrow chamber off which was the sanctuary with an altar and four seated figures of deities.

The "small temple" was even more graceless and not much smaller. The facade was 90 by 40 feet; six recessed colossal statues of Rameses and Nefertari, 33 feet high, were separated by buttresses, carved with coarse votive inscriptions. A narrow entrance door surmounted by Rameses sacrificing to Amon and Horus led through a vestibule to the sanctuary.

If outward show and colossal scale were enough for architecture, this temple might command respect. The craftsmanship was degenerate, the style bloated and arrogant, the technological virtuosity, extraordinary. Indeed the latter may be equaled only by that displayed recently in moving it high up on the cliff above the sands of the site which gave it its only justification for being, in order to save it from the level of the Nile to be raised by the new dam at Aswan, a case of badly misguided sentiment for preservation at all costs.

It was, of course, very exciting to its European discoverer, John Lewis Burckhardt, who, following local clues, came upon it from above on March 22, 1813;[13] and to Giovanni Balzoni, who cleared the entrance four years later. It positively sent the Victorian Englishwoman, Amelia B. Edwards, a vigorous promoter of Egyptian archeology. In her book, *A Thousand Miles Up the Nile*, she describes sunrise at Abu Simbel when the temple was in its original location:

> Every morning I waked in time to witness that daily miracle. Every morning I saw those awful brethren pass from death to life, from life to sculptured stone. I brought myself almost to believe that there must sooner or later come some one sunrise when the ancient charm would snap asunder; and the giants must arise and speak.
> It is fine to see the sunrise on the front of the Great Temple; but something still finer takes place on certain mornings of the year, in the very heart of the mountain. As the sun comes up above the eastern hill-tops, one long, level beam strikes through the doorway, pierces the inner darkness like an arrow, penetrates to the sanctuary, and falls like fire from heaven upon the altar at the feet of the Gods.
> No one who has watched for the coming of that shaft of sunlight can doubt that it was a calculated effect, and that the excavation was directed

[13] John A. Wilson, *Signs and Wonders upon Pharaoh* (Chicago: The University of Chicago Press, 1964), p. 23.

at one especial angle in order to produce it. In this way Ra, to whom the temple was dedicated, may be said to have entered in daily, and by a direct manifestation of his presence to have approved the sacrifices of his worshippers.[14]

Well, if the men of Stonehenge could do it, the men of Egypt could have done it had they wanted to. Decide for yourself whether or not they wanted to. The temple remains a brutal one and in its new site the alleged phenomenon can no longer be tested.

Rock-cut buildings or parts of buildings can be found in so many parts of the world that one might, if he chose, become a collector of them. The collection might well be interesting but it would scarcely be first-class. Taken solely as architecture I know of no rock-cut creation outside of India which can be placed in the top rank and is not to be missed at any cost. If the temple of Hatshepsut at Deir-el-Bahri were to be cited, it would have to be remembered that most of it and surely the most interesting part of it architecturally is not rock cut; and if the unquestioned merits of the Indian achievements at Ajanta and Ellora were to be called in witness, we would have to ask whether they would rate so highly were it not for their painting and their sculpture.

However, some further examples must be cited. Anyone who is in Iran will scarcely wish to miss Persepolis, the great ritual city of the Achaemenid kings who had more elements of grandeur than pro-Greek historians have encouraged us to believe. The city was begun by Darius I in 518 B.C. before the disasters of the Greek wars and was continued by Xerxes and Artaxerxes until about 460 B.C. About four miles north of Persepolis, at Naqsh-i-Rustam high up on the cliff, are four rock-cut tombs for Artaxerxes I (465–424), Xerxes I (486–465), Darius the Great (521–486), and Darius II (424–404) (only that of Darius the Great is positively identified by inscriptions). There is a great deal of soft information about these. One story is that Darius I was prompted to emulation by having seen the Egyptian royal tombs at Thebes when he was there with the expedition of Cambyses. This may be true, but if so the tombs were for vastly different purposes. The Achaemenids were Zoroastrians. They built no temples but rather fire altars under the open sky. Generally they exposed their dead to the sun and the vultures on platforms above the plain. The tombs were small, even the mausoleum imputed to Cyrus at Pasargadae. But the burial needs were not aniconic.

And in the reliefs of the royal tombs at Naqsh-i-Rustam . . . the dead king appears in the act of adoration, before a fire altar and under sun and moon, while standing on a bare stepped platform.[15]

[14] Quoted in Ibid., p. 70.
[15] Henri Frankfort, *The Art and Architecture of the Ancient Orient* (Baltimore: Penguin, 1955), p. 224.

The facades of the four tombs are about the same size, 75 feet high and 60 feet wide, widespread along but not quite uniformly on an irregular rock face 500 feet long by some 200 feet high. Each has a door in the center, two columns on each side capped with conventional double bull heads supporting an Egyptian type of cornice, a frieze, and then a panel above it. The panel in turn is carved in two parts—on the lower, two rows of envoys of vassal tribes support the king's throne. He himself is standing in an attitude of prayer on a prayer platform before an altar, holding his bow in the left hand and raising the right in adoration, engaged in worshipping the sun god whose image appears above.

In the heyday of the Achaemenids the tombs were probably not to be reached by any permanent construction. Today you can climb up some modestly difficult steps, helped by an iron rail, to discover that the unimpressive inner rooms are empty, though you will be told that they were undoubtedly richly decorated in their time. But you will note also that the facade has no relation of significance to the interior. Indeed, it may be rather sculpture than architecture.

Thus though the rock-cut tombs at Naqsh-i-Rustam give us a good idea of what Persian architecture was probably like in the time of the Achaemenids, they are no more architecture or scarcely more so than the huts carved in the frieze of the south building of the Nunnery Quadrangle at Uxmal in Yucatan—and much less so than Abu Simbel or Ajanta.

In some recent years the rock-cut city of Petra in Jordan has attracted tourists bent on finding places which everyone has not seen whether or not they are as significant as those many have seen. If you can brave the glares of the Jordanians and you are not depressed by the incessant whine of Israeli jets aloft, then go if you wish. If you do, you will find some rock cuts dating back to the sixth century B.C., showing Egyptian influence early and Greek and Roman later. And perhaps most typically you will encounter the Roman tomb of "El Khasne," dating from about A.D. 120. But this facade, 65 feet high, is as decadent in its way as Abu Simbel is in its—and more vulgar in an architectural if not in a human way. The lower story has a hexastyle Corinthian portico of which the central four columns align with a reasonable pediment. From this, central and side doors lead into tomb chambers, and up to this point the whole affair is acceptable if not brilliant. But atop this, the designers have applied a second set of columns of which the lateral pairs support a broken pediment and the central ones a circular affair with a conical roof topped by an urn! If I were you, I would respect the Israeli jets, ignore Petra, and settle for something which is better known and more visited for the best of reasons: because it is better. However you may feel about East Indian architecture and it is hard to be neutral about, you should not miss Ajanta and Ellora and perhaps some of the other cave temples of India, almost all of which are to be found within a radius of about 200 miles of Bombay.

I am simply offended by most East Indian culture, and this accounts for the little attention genuine Indian architecture gets in this work. It does not apply to the work of invaders, such as the Moguls, whose forts and palaces and tombs from Agra to Lahore are much to be admired. It stems partly, for example, from an aversion to overproliferation of decoration, so that while I find the *torii* at Ise and even at Nikko beautiful, I find the East Gate of the Great Stupa at Sanchi very near to being offensive.

There is certainly a thin line to be drawn here. Why is a Last Judgment on Bourges West Front a reasonable thing to me, the saga of Trajan on his Roman column permissible, and the Great Departure at the East Gate of Sanchi somehow wrong? It is not because of the quality of the *Pl. 96* sculpture, because the movement and the variety of the detail of the Indian work are fantastic and interesting and brilliantly composed. This may be because the ideas of the sculpture, dimly understood, repel me, but I suspect it is because while at Bourges, and in the French Romanesque churches as well, there is a good deal of lively carving, the sculptors have left large spaces alone to the benefit of both the architecture and the sculpture. But the Indian sculptors knew no such constraint, and the result is that their buildings literally crawl with people and animals and vines to the utter destruction or near destruction of the forms whatever the style. This applies with essentially equal force to the Mahabodhi tower at Bodh Goya, the Lingaraj Temple at Bhuvanesvar, the temples of *Pl. 97* Khajuraho or Gwalior, the Shore Temple at Mamallapuram, the Rajarajesvara Temple in Tanjore, the Gopuram of the Great Temple of Madura, or the Hoysalesvara Temple at Halebid.

The prejudice goes deeper I suppose. I am definitely unenthusiastic about enormous melon breasts, about legs and arms akimbo, about gods with many arms, about overt demonstrations of fecundity. I have found nothing whatsoever to admire in Hindu temple compounds, save isolated sculptural details such as the individual deeds of Rama on the columns at Kanchipuram. Buddhism is a different matter, but regardless *Pl. 98* of its origins, it seems to me to have been much more successful aesthetically in China and Japan. *Pl. 99*

Given these feelings, which are much stronger than those I feel against any other architecture, I cannot be expected to do very well by any part of the building in India (except the Mogul). But if I were to, it would be easiest to say words in praise of the cave temples—beginning with an early *chaitya* hall, such as the one at Bhaja perhaps of the first century B.C., and extending through Karli (A.D. 120) and Ajanta to the *Pl. 100* last great if declining achievement at Elephanta (eighth or ninth century A.D.). One of the anomalies of these is that, though the early ones are Buddhist, the last is Hindu (Temple of Siva).

A cave temple we must begin by remembering is not a modified natural cave.

These entirely man-made recesses are among the most sophisticated examples of religious art in all Indian history.[16]

Surely there were precedents all around. Though Indian sculptors may well not have been aware of Abu Simbel, their encounters with Naqsh-i-Rustam are much more likely even though the physical appearances and indeed the purposes of their rock-cut sanctuaries were far different from those of the Achaemenid tombs.

They hollowed their temples out of the almost sheer rock of the Western ghats. It was a sculptural rather than an architectural achievement and involved indeed a procedure antithetical to the methods of architectural construction, beginning with the roof ("vaults") and digging down around stone left in place to form columns until the floor was reached.[17] Nonetheless the appearances are essentially exact replicas of pre-existing structural forms and "in almost every one the reminiscences of these prototypes are carried to the point of having many parts of the model fashioned in wood and attached to the rock-cut replica."[18]

The term *chaitya* sometimes applied to these halls is simply a term applied to any holy place. Despite the proliferation of buildings to serve special functions found in the later Buddhist precincts, such for example as the one at Ho-ry-u-ji in Japan, the earlier requirements were simple, at first being only to meet the needs for the retreat of single holy men or ascetics; by the time of the rock-cut temples the minimal requirement had been enlarged to take care at least of a monastic organization and thus to provide a place in which there might be a procession around a *stupa* (altar) and a space for a "service." (It was also desirable to furnish a place for the monks to live, called a *vihara*. This might be at most a large rectangular space off which the monk's cells clustered. There are remnants of these in many parts of India and they served any monastic faith— Jain, for example, quite as readily as Buddhist.)

Returning to the religious hall, it is not surprising, then, that the plan is reminiscent of the plan of an early Christian church. The early *chaitya* hall at Bhaja, for example, has a central nave framed by columns, two narrow side aisles, and an apse with an ambulatory centered around the stupa.

Though Bhaja is important chronologically, most visitors will find the much larger and later hall at Karli more interesting. It still is Himyana Buddhist "Small Vehicle" (A.D. 120). The plan is much the same, but there are additions. There is a sort of forecourt, *atrium*, or narthex. Two enormous columns, more or less *in antis*, once stood free at the front; one re-

Pl. 101
Pl. 102

[16] Benjamin Rowland, *The Art and Architecture of India* (Baltimore: Penguin, 1953), p. 63. Copyright © Benjamin Rowland, 1956.
[17] This is the majority view of how they were made. A Swedish architect, Bernard Lindahl, proposes that the masons chiseled from the main entrance through the nave to the altar, proceeding from the bottom up.
[18] Rowland, *Art and Architecture of India*, op. cit., p. 64.

mains, still revealing its steeply tapered, arissed shaft, and its enormous lotiform capital, which in turn supports lions. These no longer carry the massive metal wheel they were designed to support. The walls of the entrance are elaborately carved, seeming to rest on elephants which originally had metal ornaments and ivory tusks.

When you enter, you come into a large space, 46 feet wide, about the same height, and 124 feet long. But it is not enormous and you can be deceived by statements such as that of one very distinguished authority: "[T]he scale of the shrine is that of a Gothic church."[19] Of some Gothic church no doubt, but if so, a small one. Even such a little Romanesque church as St-Andoche at Saulieu is the same width, a sixth longer, and a third higher!

The columns of the nave are enormous, squat, sixteen-sided affairs resting in what look like stone water jars. Both the bases and the enormous and ugly lotiform capitals are ill proportioned to the shafts. Above the capitals are inverted stepped pyramids supporting very fancy elephants ridden by people of both sexes. These are so deeply carved and are so close together as indeed are the columns that capitals and elephants seem effectively to form a frieze and the interpenetration of space between nave and side aisle goes quite unfelt—in sharp contrast to a Gothic or indeed even to a Romanesque church. The "barrel" vault seems to have "ribs" but these bear no such patent relation to the columns below as do the Thomistic sinews of the French Gothic or the much later ribs of one of Pier Luigi Nervi's concrete domes. The *stupa* around which the apse is formed is large and also, in my view, extraordinarily ugly. The facade screen, intact, is of carved stone except that there is a teak framework to the lotus window which roughly corresponds to the rose or lancet windows of the Gothic Western facades and which filters in such light as penetrates the interior.

[It] gives us some idea of the original effect these cathedrals produce, with the light streaming through the timbered rose window to illumine the interior with a ghostly half-light, so that the very walls of the rock seem to melt into an envelope of darkness and the sensation of any kind of space itself becomes unreal.[20]

The darkness, of course, was implicit in the choice of excavation as a way of building. Here is another of these hen-and-egg questions. Did the cave temples produce their mystic darkness from desire or because the choice of the cave made it almost inevitable? One would like to hope the former, and it has some plausibility in early Buddhist theories of preserving Buddhist law through the bad times by going into the bowels of the earth.

[19] Ibid., p. 66.
[20] Ibid., p. 67.

The choice may then not have been too difficult for these early Buddhist cave cutters. How different it must have been for the rock cutters of Cappadocia in Byzantine times. Spiro Kostof has written beautifully about this.

> Being part of the empire, albeit a marginal part, Cappadocia could not of course be completely isolated from the precipitous extravagance of ancient Delphi. It should go without saying, though perhaps we have gone too long without saying it, that a Middle Byzantine church in such settings as these will not inspire the same appeal of faith as the cross-in-squares of sere, rockbound Goreme. But within? We admire justly the clean classic look of Daphni, the exquisite complexity of Hosios Lukas. Yet how much of their effect is a gift of light! The crown of windows in the drum of the principal dome setting aglow the image of the Pantokrator; the banked windows that flood the apse with brightness; and that profusion of subtly placed perforations in the fabric of the building, windows divided by slender colonettes into two lights or three and screened, filtering daylight to the supple interior, across the narrow ring of aisles and narthex and into the openness of the central baldachin. It is this insinuating film, as much as the delicate proportions of the supporting members that dissolves any weight the architecture might have and transforms walls and vaults into texture, especially since they have already been sheathed with applied marbles and gold-backed mosaic.
>
> Now it is clear that by denying himself the use of natural light the carver-architect of Goreme has forfeited dematerialization. What light is allowed in through the entrance or an occasional small window cannot conjure away the sense of obtuse matter nor bring the images of the upper reaches, domes and vaults in particular, to exist in an aura of muted radiance. Liturgically the least important images—saints, donor portraits and the like—having the lowest emplacement [the arrangement could hardly be reversed owing to the hierarchic relations to Heaven—jeb] will be most emphasized by the light from the entrance, while the true realm of Heaven further up will remain lackluster, obscure. And since it is to shafts of light that our eyes are drawn in enclosed spaces, the worshipers' awareness of iconic priorities will be sharply curtailed. The primacy of the Pantokrator dome cannot be appreciated unless it is dramatized by something other than mere height.[21]

Indian rock-cut sanctuaries persisted under Mahayan, a "Great Vehicle" Buddhism, in sanctuaries of the Bombay region, even in the Gupta period (A.D. 320–647), which many observers consider the great period of Indian florescence and fullfillment. The most notable examples are at Ajanta. There can I would suppose be no argument at all as to the brilliance of the paintings in this remarkable set of caves, and frequently their beauty as well, their skillful treatment both of religious and of secular subjects, their quality as iconography and of painting qua painting. It would be foolish to deny that

[21] Kostof, *Caves of God*, op. cit., p. 136.

they constitute one of the main attractions to a tourist in India. As architecture there is somewhat less to be said. Many of the constructions, for example those of Cave I, are quite overwhelmed by the paintings; and indeed the square hall with its roof supported by simple pillars which themselves were once painted seems to have been designed with paintings in mind and to be subordinate to them.

It is otherwise at Cave XIX, which can be said to be more "architectural." It is a more magnificent accomplishment than the hall at Karli Pl. 107 but the architectural vocabulary is little changed—the same basilican plan, the same apse, the same close spacing of the capitals to give the effect Pl. 103 of an almost continuous frieze, the same lighting from the facade only. The porch entrance is somewhat different; there is what would be a clerestory in a basilica, but here containing niches to hold Buddhas standing or sitting. The *stupa* is even larger in respect to the ambulatory, carved more luxuriantly. But the principal differences, nearly all advances, are in the complexity and variety of the iconography imposed by the new anthropomorphic concepts of Buddha and his many manifestations, and the greater skill and taste of the sculptors. But the advances are essentially all those of the artists and not of the architects.

Finally, if conditions are unfavorable for a visit to Ajanta, and they often are, one might reluctantly settle for the easier and less rewarding trip across Bombay Harbor to the cave temple on the Island of Elephanta. Dedicated to Siva, it was probably built no earlier than the eighth or ninth century and is the last of the big Indian architectural sculptures. Though much damaged by the Portuguese in the sixteenth century, though much coarser and imperfect in its geometry than Ajanta, though lacking any sense of unity in its plan, the gigantic carvings of the legends of Siva cannot fail to impress. But again it is a sculptural result and not an architectural one.

It remained for the Indians to produce the *reductio ad absurdum* of sculptured, rock-cut architecture. You start by whittling a rock down from within to produce the *appearance* of an interior architecture and are still left with the enclosing rock. Why not carve the whole rock into the *appearance* of an external architecture? This is exactly what the Pallava architects did south of Madras on the seacoast during the Mamalla period (625–674). What they produced there are five fairly small rock-cut temples at Mamallapuram (Seven Pagodas) called *raths*, carved entirely out Pl. 104 of granite outcrops into forms which duplicated those of contemporary structural buildings.

> The term rath means a chariot or a processional car used to transport the idols of the Hindu gods on festal days. Its use to designate a type of temple probably stems from the concept that the sanctuary was a reproduction of the celestial chariots of the deities.[22]

[22] Rowland, *Art and Architecture of India*, op. cit., p. 170, footnote 20.

There is considerable variety in these architectural absurdities. The Dharmaraja *rath*, a Siva temple, 27 by 29 feet and 35 feet high, has crude open porches on the sides of a square supporting a three-terraced pyramidal *sikhara*, perhaps a model of stories added to a Buddhist *vihara* to care for increases in the monastic population. On top is an ugly bulbous finish which is repeated many times at smaller scale on the terraces. Bhima's *rath*, the largest—48 by 25 feet and 26 feet high—also with a sort of colonnade, has a barrel roof ending in the semidome of an apse; only part of the hall has been excavated. Draupadis *rath* has an 11-foot one-story cella in a three-story building with a curved roof, and it resembles some contemporary Indian huts.

All of this is naturally a considerable achievement for its time and a curiosity which ought to be visited if only to know that one need never go again. The beach at Mamallapuram (or Mahabalipuram) is pleasant as Indian beaches go, and if you like to see columns rising from lions' backs of greater antiquity than those of Venice and Lombardy, you can find them at the *raths*. Also, between the Drapaudi and the Arjan *raths* you can find an attractive monolithic lion and an elephant, while east of it is a fine Nandi bull. These were the vehicles (*vahanas*) of the god Indra, the goddess Durga, and the god Siva, and probably were meant to be before the shrines. But most of all you will want to visit the great rock-cut bas

Pl. 109

relief—96 feet long and 43 feet high—depicting the Penance of Arajuna or the Fall of the Ganges from the Himalayas, a very lively sculpture, very plastic, and no doubt the greatest work of the Pallava sculptors.

One might regard the *raths* as local playthings were it not for the

Pl. 105

Pl. 106

Kailasanath temple at Ellora. Altogether on this famous site are twelve Mahayana Buddhist cave temples, seventeen Brahman, and five Jain, all carved in the Deccan trap rock. The conditions were different from those either at Mahabalipuram where the *raths* were made out of outcrops, or at Ajanta where the temples were cut into a cliff that was nearly perpendicular. At Ellora the excavations are in a sloping side so almost all of them have natural courtyards. But the enormous Kailasa Temple, dedicated to Siva, is nearly free-standing, as a pit has been excavated almost around it, and it can be said to be the largest *rath* in history and is often acclaimed as the noblest Hindu monument of ancient India.

The rock here is black volcanic. The back wall of the pit is over 100 feet high, and the court itself is 276 feet long and 154 broad, which is something like the area of the Parthenon and one-half again as high.

You enter through a rock screen near which are two gigantic elephants. You ascend to a great podium 25 feet high. Here, after passing a Nandi bull court and going over a bridge, you find a porch, a spacious central hall, and a dark *cella*. The hall, 57 by 55 feet, has four groups of massive square columns with broad cruciform aisles between the groups. A sort of ambulatory leads all round the shrine and to five chapels.

There are two very impressive things about this temple but neither is the architectural form. The place literally crawls with impressive stone carving, the Ganges and Jumma acting as guardians of the door to the shrine, the niches containing deities, the scenes from the Ramayana in relief on the bridge and staircases, the rock-cut gallery opposite the porch with statues of the seven great goddesses and Ganesh. Most spectacular of all are the deeply carved plinth of the podium where lions and elephants, and monsters of immense size are projected from its walls, or the lesser sanctuaries of river goddesses and other minor members of the Hindu pantheon which run almost all the way around the circumference of the great pit in which the temple was carved.

There is no question that this is all very spectacular, even stupendous. It may well be one of the remaining wonders of the world. It leads one to wonder at the enormous vitality and skill the carvers must have had to have wrought what they did with the modest tools they had, and to speculate about what they might have done had they been possessed of power drills like those Gutzon Borglum used to mar innocent Mount Rushmore and at the same time to thank Krishna that they did not have the power drill!

When you come back from India today after an energy-sapping summer stay, Istanbul will seem to you like a comfortable Western city and the Istanbul Hilton like a sophisticated, even elegant hotel. In the same way we can happily leave Indian rock-cut architecture and come back to more familiar ground where we can find architectural monuments which are intrinsically interesting qua architecture and not because they are a reminder that men can do a great many extraordinary things when only they put their wills to it.

PYRAMIDS

The other important but unusual type of stone architecture we should note is the pyramid. Of the three pyramidal architectures I mean to discuss, only the Egyptian is technically and truly a pyramid. In a purely geometrical sense, a pyramid has polygonal bases and its faces are defined by triangular planes which meet in a point at the apex. The Mesopotamian ziggurats were really a series of stepped-back platforms. Had they been projected to a point, they might have been "stepped pyramids," but they were not and can at most be called truncated pyramids. Most of the Meso-American forms had rectangular or square bases and might have sloping or stepped sides to produce a genuine truncated pyramid or in many cases a truncated step pyramid. But some had more complicated bases and, if these were oval, they resembled truncated cones. It is a distinction we need not press here and from now on let us call them all pyramids.

Such constructions are to be found in many parts of the world.

Often made of mud or sun-dried bricks, such artificial hills may have quite lost their geometric shape or have been made to look like anthills by overzealous gold-seekers or amateur archeologists. Many are covered with foliage now and are not easy to separate from natural hills if the area boasts any. They can be found in China, in Cambodia (Khmer), at Etruscan Cerveteri; in many parts of the Peruvian coastlands, near Trujillo, at Chan Chan where the chroniclers called them *huaca*, at Pachacamac, the greatest religious center of Old Peru a dozen miles south of Lima. There they *may* have been built by the government seated in mountainous Cuzco to impose the sun cult in situations where the Inca did not want to risk destroying the imputed sanctity of the old oracles. The largest of these pre-Inca pyramids are at Trujillo, the larger 755 feet long and 131 feet high now, having once perhaps been 164 feet. In high Bolivia the Acapana stepped pyramid, in the Tiahuanaca style, is faced with dressed stone.

These pyramids and mounds may have served many purposes. Often, but certainly not always, they served various burial customs. Sometimes perhaps they were for fortification, or rather military observation posts. Most often they served religious purposes, with or without necrological contexts. They may sometimes have had multiple functions. The terraces of Huaca del Sol near Trujillo in Peru are, for example, early A.D. 400–1000. They are reminiscent of faraway Copán in the western edge of Honduras or of Monte Albán near Oaxaca in Central Mexico where a series of broad terraces rising from a long rectangular platform provided space for many purposes—for houses, porches, halls, accommodation for guards and priests, and, incidentally (or perhaps not incidentally), to supply an impressive and sober stage setting for ceremonies, secular or religious or often both. Finally they were certainly symbolic. How symbolic has been the subject of much dashing conjecture, not very often backed by much direct hard evidence, except perhaps in Egypt. Most of the time we cannot find accounts to rely on and must fall back on art, the degree of whose abstraction is often uncertain. But even when the mystique is open to some certification and therefore comprehensible intellectually, it is quite another problem for a man of the twentieth century to "be with it." As Giorgio di Chirico has said:

> One of the strangest feelings left to us by prehistory is the sensation of omen. It will always exist. It is like an eternal proof of the *non-sequitur* of the universe. The first man must have seen omens everywhere, he must have shuddered at each step.[23]

Probably so, but can we shudder with him at least under the same omens? Of the many examples that might be cited, I have chosen three of the most important, two of which have very substantial remains. The older

---

[23] Quoted by George C. Vaillant, *The Aztecs of Mexico* (Baltimore: Penguin, 1955), p. 7.

two are from Mesopotamia and Egypt, respectively; the third is from Meso-America.

In all three examples and particularly in the Mesopotamian and Egyptian examples, we need frequently to remind ourselves that, however isolated they may now seem, they did not stand alone in their contexts when they were living monuments. The ziggurats of Ur and Babylon were part of an enclosure which could probably be called a city without too much misunderstanding. The greatest of the pyramids of Egypt, the step pyramid of Saqqara, was inside an enormous necrologic and ritual complex, the complex of Zoser; while the later and larger ones of Giza were the terminal and climactic points of a path of valley temples, causeways, and pyramid temples. In Peru at Chan Chan long before the Incas, each urban ecologic unit was separated from the others by thick walls entered by a single gate and each had its mound, artificial hill, or pyramid (*huaca*). Later on the Mayan pyramids were elements of a larger congeries and not always even the most noticeable element. These congeries too could be called cities, although they may have been limited to ritual functions. The platforms of Teotihuacán were carefully arranged with other constructions along a great avenue. To think of pyramids as big monuments standing alone in some desert or in some swamp is to misconceive them altogether. We cannot neglect the ambiance, though we may have to imagine it when we are looking at the extant pyramids.

MESOPOTAMIA

At the beginning I promised not to take you to sites where the eye alone could not provide enough material for a reasonable mental reconstruction of at least the physical nature of the architecture visited. Now I must waver briefly, for the ziggurats of Mesopotamia are too important in architectural history and thought to be casually laid aside.

Though more than one scholar is likely to say that history began at Sumer, to find more inventions there than in any other one place, to declare its art more dynamic and ergo superior to that of its contemporary, Egypt, I am afraid most of us today have extremely misty notions of the area which is now mostly contained within the boundaries of modern Iraq and even less of the succession of cultures which dominated it over the two millennia or more before the Persian conquest of 539 B.C.

The term Mesopotamia means "between the rivers," and the rivers were the Tigris and the Euphrates. The area involved extended from the foothills of the Armenian Taurus in the northwest to the effluence of the rivers on the ancient shores of the Persian Gulf and was bounded on the west by the steppes of the Great Syrian desert and on the east by the Zagros Mountains.

The upper part of this region was the land of Carchemish on the Euphrates and of the Assyrians on the Tigris. The lower part, the black alluvial plain south of modern Baghdad, contained Babylon in its north and the civilizations of Sumer and Akkad with their cities of Ur, Nippur, and Lagash in its south.

What is left for us to see if we visit these parts does not carry us very far. The general impression was well summarized by Giedion.

> The ziggurat of Ur arose in the midst of the highest culture then existing. It was not completely isolated. Even today the ziggurats of Eridu and Al'Ubaid are within view from its summit. It stood in an urban and an agricultural landscape, well irrigated by numerous canals; a scene past imagining today, when nothing can be seen on the journey from Eridu to Ur save swarms of locusts clattering against the windows of the car.[24]

The step trench excavation of Tell Judeidah, an ancient city of Syria, reveals the problem. The *tell*, or mound of debris, grew there from the sixth century B.C. to the early Christian era. The buildings were mostly of mud brick and they crumbled and settled around the walls of the town. The debris preserved the bases of the walls and added to the height of the pile. New buildings of the same sort were built on top of the pile and the process went on and on.

A similar process must have occurred at Ur until, at a date not fixed, a new race came into the valley, perhaps from the Indus or further, bringing with them a civilization already well formed. These were the Sumerians. They rebuilt the old hill village into a town made of more permanent burnt brick, enclosed it in strong walls. Woolley conjectures that the Sumerians more or less reserved the citadel for themselves and consigned their predecessors to mud huts at the foot of the slope outside the walls; nonetheless, the *acropolis* of Ur grew ever higher as the refuse accumulated until at last the Flood came.[25]

Or did it? It does not matter here, for Ur survived. "After the Flood, Kingship again descended from heaven" say the Sumerian annalists.

At any rate what we can see of these great buildings is extremely limited, whether it is at Eridu; Aqar Quf, where the tower, though well preserved, looks little different from a nature-made Ship Rock in Arizona; or at the site of Etementanke, the tower of Babel, where now only a stagnant pool remains.

Pl. 108

The ruins of Babylon betray little more to the uninitiated, though they may be richly informative to the archeologist-stratigrapher. At Ur Nammu you can see a *restored* ziggurat. But on the whole the only remains that will say much to you and me are those at Ur; and even they will not say much without substantial preparation and preferably an archeologist-guide

---

[24] Giedion, *The Eternal Present*, vol. II, *The Beginnings of Architecture*, op. cit., p. 221.
[25] See C. Leonard Woolley, *Ur of the Chaldees* (New York: Norton, 1965), p. 20. By permission of W. W. Norton & Company, Inc. Copyright 1965, All Rights Reserved by W. W. Norton & Company, Inc.

if one can be found. Given the eternal hostility of the countryside and the present hostility of the people who live in Iraq, it is not a pilgrimage which can be recommended to many. But that does not lessen the importance of the ziggurat.

Whatever you may have heard of ziggurats, they were *not* tombs. Certainly the Mesopotamians did have burial places but not in the elaborate sense of the Egyptian mastabas, pyramids, and rock-cut tombs. They seem never to have had a highly developed mortuary cult and looked upon the afterlife as a sort of gloomy continuing gray experience much like that of the Sheol of the Hebrews or the Hades of the Greeks. It is true that the kings who were semidivine in Sumer were accompanied to their graves by a whole series of court officials, servants, consorts, and other women who were privileged to continue their service in the next world. The ordinary grave was a simple rectangular pit. In it they laid the body, either wrapped in matting or in a coffin of wood, wicker, or clay, and with the body a few personal belongings might be interred.

The royal tombs did contain a wider range of objects, more beautifully wrought, more obviously costly, but, except for the immolation of a whole group of people surrounding the lord, the royal tombs were not different from the humble save in size and magnificence of artifacts. Neither required an architecture; neither required a great mural and sculptural art.[26]

I have emphasized the separation of the royal tomb from the ziggurat because of its importance in understanding what the ziggurat was.

We are talking here of the great days of the Third Dynasty, about 2300–2180 B.C., when Ur was the capital of the Sumerian Empire, and about a construction begun by the founder of that dynasty, Ur-Nammu, who "seemed to build for all time and shrank from no amount of labour to that end, and it is no wonder that his reign of eighteen years did not suffice for the completion of all he planned,"[27] including a rampart of unbaked brick 77 feet thick, around a space three-fourths of a mile long and half a mile wide. His dynasty was contemporary with the VIth dynasty in Egypt (Pepi II) during a period in which the power of the Egyptian kings was declining, about 300 years after the architect Imhotep had built the great complex for Zoser at Saqqara and well after the completion of the great pyramids of Cheops, Chephren, and Mycerinus at Giza. From this period about twenty-five ziggurats have been found and identified, but there must have been many more.

The neo-Sumerian period was probably responsible for two new struc-

---

[26] The generalization is probably good despite the famous mosaic, *The Standard of Ur,* found in the largest of all the stone-built royal tombs. Its two panels, each 22 feet long and 9 feet high, and two triangular pieces forming the ends do show aspects of the life of the king and royal family in peace and war which resemble in subject if not in style some Egyptian tomb wall paintings. But it was probably something carried on a pole in processions. "We actually found it lying against the shoulder of a man who may have been the king's standard bearer." (Woolley, ibid., p. 84.)
[27] Ibid., p. 113.

tures—the ziggurat and the low temple or *Tieftempel*, which was not erected on a terrace.[28] The ziggurat was in essence a series of terraces with a sloping or a stepped exterior ending in a flat platform on which the high temple stood dedicated to the *current* divinity of the city,[29] which was reached by steps or ramps. It is not clear whether these were the expression of a new religious-cultic idea or merely a somewhat automatic enlargement of early structures whose rebuilding resulted in the raising of the platform. In any event the truncated pyramid had no interior spaces and it was the approach to the platform and the platform itself that mattered. Why?

Sumerian cosmology was quite different from the elaborate daily sunrise and death of the Egyptians, evolving out of earlier Mesopotamian notions. In its simplest terms it conceived of an original chaos that produced sky and earth, united at first in the primordial cosmic mountains. These are taken by most observers to have been symbolized by the structure of the ziggurat. It is an idea which we shall find repeated in different guise in the pyramids of Meso-America.

Woolley calls to mind that the Sumerian origin was probably in hilly country, that the animals pictured in their art are often mountain types, and so on. From this he concludes:

> People living in a mountainous land nearly always associate their religion with the outstanding natural features of that land and worship their gods on "high places," and this would seem to have been true of the Sumerians. When they moved down into the alluvial plain of the Euphrates, they found themselves in a country where there were no hills meet for the service of a god, a country so flat that even a private house, if it was to be safe from the periodic inundations, had to be raised on an artificial platform. The latter fact supplied a hint as to how the former difficulty could be solved; the platform had only to be built high enough, and there, made by man was the high place which nature had failed to provide; and so the Sumerians set to work to build—using "bricks instead or stone, and slime (bitumen) had they for mortar"—a "ziggurat" whose name might be called "the Hill of Heaven" or "the Mountain of God." In every important city there was at least one such tower crowned by a sanctuary, the tower itself forming part of a larger complex.[30]

Note that such a platform need only be higher than other things around and does not have to scratch the sky. That does not mean that the largest ones, such as the ziggurat at Babylon, now entirely destroyed, were not big. But the Great Ziggurat of Ur, the best preserved of all these monuments, is about 200 feet long and 150 feet wide and was originally some

[28] There are earlier prototype ziggurats as at Wurka of the Protoliterate Period (3500–3000 B.C.).
[29] Or several, one for each platform.
[30] Woolley, *Ur of the Chaldees*, op. cit., pp. 118–119.

70 feet high, only one-fifth as wide and one-seventh as high as the Pyramid of Cheops at Giza, and less than one-half the size and one-eighth the volume of the Pyramid of the Moon at Teotihuacán (the Pyramid of the Sun there is still larger). It was, however, fairly close to the size of Toltec El Castillo, the late pyramid at Chichen Itzá, about half as tall as the tallest at Tíkal but generally in the same order of size as the Mayan pyramids.

This was perhaps because, though the ziggurat could be ascended, it was more of a ladder to help the god from heaven than a ladder to help man from earth. The temple did serve as a sort of altar, but the primary purpose was to provide a suitable home for a god who had originally lived on a mountain top and had followed his people down to the plains.

Herodotus described this. He was talking of the ziggurat temple in Babylon during the Assyrian hegemony.

> In the middle of the precinct there was a tower of solid masonry, a furlong in length and breadth, upon which was raised a second tower, and on that a third, and so on up to eight. The ascent to the top is on the outside, by a path which winds round all the towers. When one is about half way up, one finds a resting place and seats, where persons are wont to sit some time on their way to the summit. On the topmost tower there is a spacious temple, and inside the temple stands a couch of unusual size, richly adorned, with a golden table by its side. There is no statue of any kind set up in the place, nor is the chamber occupied of nights by anyone but a single native woman, who, as the Chaldeans, the priests of this god, affirm, is chosen for himself by the deity out of all the women of the land.
> They also declare (but I do not believe it) that the god comes down in person into this chamber, and sleeps upon the couch. . . .[31]

But there are difficulties if one takes as fact the idea that every ziggurat was simply the artificial mountain platform to provide a temple, a house, for a displaced mountain god. There are no traces of temples to be found on some of the ziggurats. The ziggurat is shown as a high altar in one important Assyrian relief. There are signs of burnt offerings here and there. If there were any rituals in the Sumerian ziggurat temples, we do not know what they were. A much later Seleucid text may indicate what they were if one believes that Mesopotamian rituals changed slowly and that new ones would not be invented in a dying culture. In that case a great feast was laid on a gold table for the god and his consort and the seven planets, with very careful instructions as to the meat, the fowl, the beer and wine, the fruit, honey, spices, and the seven golden incense burners. Some think the ziggurat to have been in effect a symbolic moun-

---

[31] Herodotus, *The Persian Wars*, I, translated by George Rawlinson (New York: Modern Library, Random House, 1942), pp. 181–182. The translator's word "tower" would be less confusing architecturally if it were "terrace" or "platform."

tain, a link between heaven and earth or that each of the terraces had a different planetary connection.

However you interpret them, ziggurats were there. And they were very simple compared with all the complicated theories as to *why* they were there.

The ziggurat in general, this form of artificial holy hill, was not planned to provide any internal chambers. It was constructed with a core of sun-dried brick set in mud and then outer faces were hammered into the wet brickwork, perhaps hundreds of pottery goblets, perhaps a facing of baked brick set in bitumen, while the surmounting temple might be covered with blue glazed tile and the roof gilded, even the colors being symbolic.[32]

It was thus exclusively a brick construction and in a more orderly treatise might not belong in a section on stone, but the relation to other pyramids has seemed to me more useful to preserve here than the consistency of the material.

More specifically the ziggurat at Ur stood in a court of the lower temple of Nannar, the Moon God. The core was as usual of unbaked brick, and the face, about 8 feet thick, was made of baked brick set in bitumen. The walls of the terraces had a very pronounced batter and their surfaces were relieved by shallow buttresses. The first terrace was reached at a height of about 50 feet—then the succession of progressively smaller stages began providing narrow walks along the sides and wider ones at the ends.

> [B]ut the stages are curiously unsymmetrical, so that there are three storeys at the northwest end of the building and four at the southeast end, all communicating by flights of brick stairs; on the topmost storey, which was virtually a square, stood the little shrine of the god.
> On three sides the walls rose sheer to the level of the first terrace, but on the northeast face fronting the Nannar Temple was the approach to the shrine. Three brick stairways, each of a hundred steps, led upwards, one projecting out at right angles from the building, two leaning against its wall, and all converging in a great gateway on the level of the second terrace; from this gate a single flight of stairs ran straight up to the door of the shrine, while lateral passages with smaller flights of stairs gave access to the terraces at either end of the tower; the angles formed by the three main stairways were filled in with solid flat-topped buttress-towers.[33]

Woolley, being a Sumerophile, went further, concluding that the Ziggurat at Ur had deliberate slight curvatures for optical effect similar to the entasis of the Greek builders of the Parthenon. Whether or not this is so, it is hard to dissent from his more general judgment.

[32] That is, blue = heaven; gold = sun.
[33] Woolley, *Ur of the Chaldees*, op. cit., p. 120.

Indeed, the whole design of the building is a masterpiece. It would have been so easy to pile rectangle of brickwork above rectangle; and the effect would have been soulless and ugly; as it is, the heights of the different stages are skillfully calculated, the slope of the walls leads the eye upwards and inwards to the centre, the sharper slope of the triple staircase accentuates that of the walls and fixes the attention on the shrine above, which was the religious focus of the whole structure, while across these converging lines cut the horizontal planes of the terraces, the division of the building which they effect being emphasized by zones of colour.[34]

So far so good, and these broad lines can be made out even in the present state of affairs. But there may have been more to it. There is, for example, the matter of the weep-holes, tall and narrow slits, at regular intervals and rows, piercing the brickwork, running all the way through the outer casing and well into the mud brick where they are loosely filled with shards. They are real enough and they are obviously meant to drain something. But what? After dismissing many possibilities, Woolley deduces that they were connected with irrigation of trees planted in the soil of the terraces.

Thus we have to imagine trees clothing every terrace with greenery, hanging gardens which brought more vividly to mind the original conception of the Ziggurat as the Mountain of God, and we shall recognise how much better the sloping outer walls harmonise with this conception, rising as they do like the abrupt bare-sides of some pine-topped crag, than if they had been uncompromisingly vertical, the walls of a house of man's building.[35]

Whether this is telling it like it was or whether it is the poetically licensed rhapsody of an archeologist, you could never know from a journey to Ur today. It is a trip which most of us ought to want to take vicariously through books and pictures and museums and models, but a trip to the site can be recommended only to architectural tourists with a special sense of dedication.

This, however, is certainly not the case for the necropoli of Memphis, the capital of the Old Kingdom (Dynasties III to VII) in Egypt.

EGYPT

A visitor to Cairo in days long gone could usually see the pyramids of Giza on their limestone plateau so large were they and so clear was the air. They have not changed in size but the air is now so smog-laden that they are seldom to be seen until you have come quite near.

---

[34] Ibid., pp. 121–122. In addition to the gold roof and blue tile of the temple, the lower stages of the ziggurat are presumed to have been painted black for the dark underworld, the upper ones red for the habitable earth.
[35] Ibid., pp. 124–125.

They were one of the seven wonders of the Ancient World and now they are the only one left. Gone are the Pharos of Alexandria, the Colossus of Rhodes, the Mausoleum of Halicarnassus, the Hanging Gardens of Babylon, the Statue of Zeus Olympus, and most of the Temple of Artemis at Ephesus. But the Great Pyramids of Cheops (Khufu), Chephren (Khafre), and Mycerinus (Menkure) continue to excite the attention of men, as they have done for millennia.

The whole area from Cairo out to the west of the Nile is an enormous cemetery or necropolis of the kings of the Old Kingdom, near Memphis. Memphis of the "White Walls" was once a foremost city of Egypt. It was the defensive fort with which every invader had to reckon; it was a producing center for weapons and ships; it received traffic from all the branches of the Nile, and Herodotus was fascinated by the array of foreign merchants he saw there. Today there is little of the ancient urban glory to be found—a handsome alabaster sphinx, impressive ruins of the white wall in brick and rubble, some ruins of the temple of Ptah, a fallen colossus—little really to establish in the eye the memory of a great city except for the fact that adjacent to its flat, depressed, palm-shaded site there is one of the largest necropoli in the world and certainly the most imposing of any known from antiquity, a site studded with ancient mastabas, and later pyramids, the tombs of royalty and of many lesser ranks of the royal establishment. It can be divided into five areas, of which I shall say something of Saqqara, Dahshur, and Giza, in that order.

Memphis, the link between Upper and Lower Egypt, was perhaps founded by a legendary, almost symbolic, King Menes, the first king of the first Thinite Dynasty, who united Upper and Lower Egypt about 3000 B.C., but it became a great city only under the rule of the "big dynasties" of the Old Kingdom, the IIId to the VIIth from about 2780 to 2280 B.C.[36]

The great days began with King Zoser and his minister Imhotep at Saqqara, continued through the reigns of the IVth Dynasty (Sneferu, Cheops, Chephren), began to peter out with Mycerinus, and broke apart into provincial autonomies and revolutions under the Pepis of the VIIth Dynasty.

It was a period of great expansion in the arts, in engineering, in mining, in trade (with Phoenicia, Somaliland, Nubia, Sudan), in techniques of government and administration.

> The Old Kingdom appeared as the most perfect flower of the Pharaonic civilization . . . splendour, order, peace and beauty . . . a classical pyramid: at the top an autocratic king.
> He was expected to care for his subjects as though they were his own family, and to shower upon them the blessings of his own divinity. Though

---

[36] All Egyptian dating wavers somewhat with the authority. The date cited is Posener's.

he personally lived in splendor and had a large and privileged bureaucracy, this was probably acceptable to the workers.

The small peasant in the marshes and in the fields went about his own work; he must have found the burden of the 'pyramid' heavy but he knew that his own life could not continue without the royal magician.[37]

What remains of this for us to see outside of museums is the remains of a vast city of the dead.

A vast city of the dead was not in Egyptian terms a vast dead city. Work was going all the time, new tombs being built, older ones being maintained or refurbished. A horde of workmen was busy building walls, sawing timbers, while sculptors and painters were always at work. Through them threaded the endowed priests performing rites for which they had contracted over many years. At night there were the jackals and the thieves—and perhaps even furtive lovers.

Any cemetery is influenced by the current cosmology. In the Egyptian world every morning, the sun, the divinity Re, the solar disk, was born of the sky goddess (Nut) and undertook his celestial crossing in his daytime bark, accompanied by a cortege of minor gods. At the end of the journey, he had naturally to get back. And it was of central importance that he did get back. This he did by sailing a cavernous river in the bark of the night, lauded by the spirits of the dead as he did so but opposed by the wily gods of darkness, headed by the serpent Apophis, who submitted him to terrible questioning. The basic legend was modified with time. Osiris begins to merge with Re; by the end of the Vth Dynasty the dead king was already an Osiris. And later on at Thebes the necessity for the dead king himself to make the nocturnal passage of the underground river had a great influence on the paintings of the cave tombs. But in the time of the great building at Saqqara and Giza, the term Pharaoh had not yet come to be used as a kingly title; the identification of the king as Osiris or Amon-Re or indeed any specific god had not been made or was very tentative, and so the influence of the cosmology upon the design of the tombs was far less important than that of the burial customs.

We know of no other people who made such great efforts of all kinds to ensure a survival of its dead and a happy one at that. What this required changed with time and indeed with social class. In the beginning and despite local variants the Egyptian views were much like those to be found in other ancient cultures. You put the dead in a grave dug in the sand or in a rock cave somewhere in the desert in the expectation that somehow sometime the dead body would live again. Inside the tomb his life would be very much like that on earth. He would need food of course and this food would have to be renewed—when pictures replaced actual food more permanence was assured and then the symbolism could progress

[37] Jean Yoyotte in Georges Posener et al., *A Dictionary of Egyptian Civilization*, translated by Alix MacFarlane (London: Methuen, 1962), pp. 195–196.

to where large quantities could be simply recorded. Meanwhile all the other manifestations of life were multiplied, scenes of harvest, of vintage, of hunting and fishing—and all in abundance. But the idea of food for survival in the tomb was central.

To this in time were added other ideas. There was the Osirian afterlife, embalming to preserve the *body* from destruction so that it could travel widely in the other world, formulas for trial and, if acquittal, entry into the Osirian paradise of the underworld—working as on earth but spared some labor if provided with substitute statuettes to do the work. Then there were the later solar-bark ideas involving purification in a tent at the edge of the desert and later solar "lustration."

> The dead man is at one and same time in heaven, in the god's boat, under the earth, tilling the Elysian fields, and in his tomb enjoying his victuals.[38]

He had to be able to get into and out of his tomb at will, remaining as a rule in the tomb by day, with occasional excursions on earth. Night was the time for the subterranean journey; dawn brought him back to the tomb.

Out of these ideas emerged such funerary cults as the idea of providing for "perpetual care" by employing a corporation to maintain tombs, to pour symbolic libations of water, to recite formulas and texts or merely the name of the deceased; and funerary customs, professional mourners, funerary barks, processions. Naturally these had large effects on the architectural requirements. For example, the cult of the dead might require, in the case of a monarch, a triple-aisled hallway through which the funeral procession would enter the sacred precinct; in time this could assume the role of a sacred grove if the aisle were decorated with a fringe of palm fronds, and these were ultimately executed in stone.

So it is too that the big pyramids are evidence of a transition from a conception of the tomb as a mere residence for afterlife, however elegant, and the mortuary precinct as a realistic stage setting for mortuary rituals, to a situation (after Sneferu) where the valley temple was greatly expanded for the embalming rites, exhibiting a vaulted-over causeway for the funeral procession, a gigantic temple of adoration very near the pyramid, and a very large pyramid tomb, all aimed at expressing the idea of divine kingship. But this will be better understood by understanding the pyramids themselves.

Before there was the pyramid, there was the mastaba, which is essential to the understanding of the pyramid.

As the function of the Egyptian tomb began to change from one of simple depository for a body to that of, among other things, an offering place, the tomb itself began to change. First there were little improvements

[38] Serge Sauneron in Posener et al., *Dictionary of Egyptian Civilization*, op. cit., p. 99.

which can be found side by side with the open-pit graves in the earliest cemeteries. The pit was lined with sun-dried clay bricks and roofed with wood and clay bricks. Slowly the shape of the graves became rectangular. They were made deeper, larger; they were subdivided; on the subterranean substructure a superstructure was added. The form of this was different in the fertile deltas of the north (Lower Egypt) and in the gravelly lands of the south (Upper Egypt) where the nomads were content with small cairns or tumuli. In the north the superstructures came to resemble rather closely the houses of the living. Built of sun-dried brick, they were made into a low flat-topped form with sloping, often paneled walls, the *mastaba*, which is Arabic for bench.

By the beginning of the Ist Dynasty the mastabas had developed extensively. Whole cities were made of them, with streets and other appearances of a living city, especially in the various sections of Memphis of the White Walls—Giza, Abusir, Saqqara, Dahshur, and most particularly at Saqqara and Giza. Such houses for the dead were prepared for a great many people in the hierarchies of the Old Kingdom. Although the types remained essentially the same, those developed for the highest nobles, especially the kings, became more and more elaborate. Then in a sort of architectural quantum jump the architect Imhotep conceived for King Zoser at Saqqara a burial complex where the actual burial place for the monarch, differentiated from that of all others, leapt from a single mastaba to what looked like several mastabas piled one upon the other and so to the step pyramid, the ancestor of the subsequent great pyramids in other parts of the Memphis region. Thereafter the mastabas were grouped around the royal pyramid and on a regular plan, almost as hierarchical as a company suburb.

Though scholars can identify many types of mastabas by their plans, by the coursing of the masonry and toward the end by whether they are made of brick or stone, it will do for us to think of a typical one. It had two separate parts, each for one of its functions. At the bottom of a customarily vertical shaft there was a burial pit containing a sarcophagus and such funerary furniture as was deemed necessary for the future life of the deceased beyond the tomb. After the interment, this room was sealed off and the shaft filled up with rubble and earth.

The upper part of the mastaba, visible above ground, had stone or brick walls with a slight batter which in the beginning simply enclosed a mound of rough building material. Then outside and on the eastern facade a small chapel was added for practice of the funerary cult. Soon it was incorporated into the mastaba, which itself began to be laid out into rooms. The chapel was to permit the living to bring food and drink for the deceased and on appointed days to burn incense in his honor.

The deceased could participate in these activities in two ways. First there was the *serdab*, a completely closed chamber except for narrow slits. In the *serdab* his statue or statues were walled, and they could breathe the incense through the slits. There was also a false door carved into the wall and through this he could pass at will although, of course, the living encountered only a wall.

Whole mastabas have been removed from Egypt to various museums and rebuilt there. You need go no farther than the Metropolitan Museum in New York to get a very fair idea of what a mastaba is like (shorn, naturally, of its ambiance, which is not a trivial shearing).

The mastaba itself has interest as a transitional architectural form for the architectural tourist, but what is probably of more interest is the decoration of the chapels, which are richly covered with bas-reliefs or paintings. These, designed to serve purposes earlier described, show life in fields, workshops, and at home; games and dancing; and an enormous array of foods. There are scenes of banquets, processions of servitors bringing agricultural produce from the estates, modes of killing, carving, and bringing beeves to table, a menu of nearly 100 dishes in a list of offerings, and a system of enumerating the quantities so that one goose, for example, might serve to represent 10 or 100 or 1,000.

The work of the Old Kingdom mastabas, amply spaced and dignified, is perhaps less exciting than the paintings in the cave tombs of Thebes but is undoubtedly a great thing to see. It can really be thoroughly enjoyed only *in situ*, and the tombs must themselves be visited before the museums come alive.

Visits to the princely tombs of the Ist Dynasty or the great mastabas, such as those of the nobles such as Ti and Mera, can offer a great deal more than pleasure at Saqqara, but they are overshadowed by the enormous accomplishment of King Zoser and his prince of architects, Imhotep, in the step pyramid and the surrounding Zoser complex there.

The whole complex is in one way difficult for a Western Christian to come to grips with because much of it is only facade architecture whose facades lead nowhere. We have constantly to remind ourselves what it was all about; and again that it was a symbolic place for the activities of a god-king shade.

Zoser reigned from 2650 to 2600 B.C. His achievements as monarch must have been enormous to have supported the power suggested by his funerary precinct. But whatever they were, they have been outlasted in memory by the precinct, and he is best known as the Egyptian king in whose reign began the extensive use of stone in building, first for Egypt certainly and first no doubt for the whole world. In many minds his fame is overshadowed not only by the complex at Saqqara but by its architect, Imhotep, the first architect of world fame.

Over time and throughout antiquity, Imhotep acquired a range of fames. He became much more than the chief architect and chief minister of Zoser. He was the patron spirit of later scribes. They regularly poured a libation to him before setting to work. His proverbs were sung for centuries. Twenty-five hundred years after his death he was the god of medicine whom the Greeks called Imorithes (Asklepios). A temple was erected to him near the Serapeum at Memphis. The priests who rebuilt Ed-fu for the Ptolemies claimed they were following his plans. His name is inscribed on a statue of Zoser and also on the enclosure at Saqqara. Never before and I suppose never since has an architect been quite so famous and quite so influential.

Ironically the great work is not quite architectural in the technical sense because of the many false fronts and nonspaces. There are, to be sure, magnificent *architectural* innovations in the step pyramid itself and in many of the details, but there is something more.

Thanks to a lifetime of faithful restoration by Jean-Phillippe Lauer you can see enough today to realize that you are standing in what would have been for its time and possibly for all time one of the great architectural marvels of the world.

It was a new architecture—the first big stone architecture. It is naturally full of tentatives. There are a few explorations of columnar architecture, and the drums, like the masonry blocks, are small. But the sense of magnificence is there. The pyramid itself, not geometrically true, was, after several enlargements, about 360 feet from north to south and about 410 feet from east to west and rose in six enormous steps on all four sides to a height of about 200 feet. But the enclosure covered something like 35 acres; the rectangular walls surrounding it rose to about 35 feet and had a peripheral length of close to a mile!

As if to emphasize the sanctuarial element, there was one and only one entrance by which the living might enter the enclosure. This was an ever-opened door made right down to the inoperative hinges of stone, not over 40 inches wide and passing through a tower. Presumably the spirit of the dead god-king could close this door any time he saw fit. As we shall see, he himself had many other doors, through which a living man could not pass.

If you go through this door and a tiny trapezoidal court, you find two more ever-open stone doors. A second short passage leads to another door *Pl. 114* and then into the first large stair hall 180 feet long, a veritable if narrow processional way whose center area is higher than the sides.[39] This way is flanked by twenty engaged limestone columns painted red. At the exit the space is enlarged by a covered hypostyle-like enclosure formed by four pairs of ribbed (bands of reeds) engaged columns connected by cross walls. Thence we emerge into a galaxy of courts which, as Sigfried Giedion rightfully notes, are not truly architectural courts as we think of them. Quite uncolonnaded, "They are in truth piazzas in the city of the Ka."[40]

Of the general layout I do not mean to say much. Many of the buildings are purely symbolic dummies, with elegant stone walls backed by

[39] The same concept on which the later gigantic hypostyles of Karnak were based.
[40] Giedion, *The Eternal Present*, vol. II, *The Beginnings of Architecture*, op. cit., p. 283.

The Architecture of Stone 209

rubble; the two "government" buildings are, for example, of this sort. Some have token fragments of inner space. Few except the storerooms and tombs were utilitarian.

This becomes possible to understand only when one realizes that the complex is an elaborate and giant mastaba, of super size and super complexity, appropriate to accommodate the many activities of the dead king. So there are shrines, altars, courts, gateways, storehouses. In the whole arrangement lived only the dead king's Ka (the vital force emanating from the god to his son, the king).

It was the king's Ka . . . who resided in the subterranean palace chambers, who issued his orders in the government building, ran his ceremonial [Heb-Sed] race in the large court on the anniversaries of his jubilee festival, wandered through the entire precinct, closing behind him the ever open carved stone doors leading to chapels and other buildings, and departed on journeys through the many dummy doors in the huge enclosure wall.[41]

The Heb-Sed festival jubilee of the king's reign was celebrated periodically (perhaps every thirty years) during his life. It was more than a commemoration of accession or a test of his physical power to carry on. It was also "a renewal of all those beneficial relations between heaven and earth which the throne controls."[42]

Toward the end of a five-day feast the living king discarded his royal garments and his scepter and ran a ceremonial race between two fixed stones. "This sprint was regarded as a dance over the 'field' that symbolized the two lands of Egypt."[43] The stones for the after-death race are still to be seen in the large Heb-Sed court in this complex.

In the general layout there were the usual and humbler tomb locations, somewhat proliferated here. The mummy was deposited in a simple tomb beneath the step pyramid. The other tomb, beautifully and delicately adorned with glazed blue tiles, has some of the best bas-reliefs of the Old Kingdom showing Zoser running the ceremonial race. This tomb is in the south wall of the complex and provides the intimate domicile of bed chamber, reception room, and nearby storage chambers for his personal needs. The *serdab* is in the final court on the north face of the step pyramid.

In addition to the majesty of the whole complex and the ingenuity in the building of the step pyramid, the first of the great pyramids, there are many minor "firsts" to be seen—stone corner posts, columns, cornices, torus moldings, papyrus bundled columns, open papyrus flower capitals, all of which played a major role in later Egyptian architecture.

When you go to Cairo, it is almost impossible to imagine that you will not go to Giza, lured by the three great pyramids of Chephren, Cheops,

Pl. 111

[41] Ibid., p. 275.
[42] Frankfort, *Art and Architecture of the Ancient Orient*, op. cit., p. 79.
[43] Giedion, *The Eternal Present*, vol. II, *The Beginnings of Architecture*, op. cit., p. 277.

and Mycerinus, by the mystery of the Great Sphinx, by the camels, by the dragomen. But it would be a great pity if this were to be done at the cost of Saqqara, which is an infinitely greater architectural experience. And of course an understanding of Saqqara is necessary for an understanding of Giza.

But it is time to examine the details of the pyramids themselves.

The evolution of the first of these, the step pyramid of Zoser, is quickly revealed by a cross section cut from east to west. Lauer suggests six stages in its development, starting with an unusually large mastaba in brick—about 200 feet square and 26 feet high. Secondly one side was extended and the whole faced with limestone from Tura. Then a further addition restored the square plan.

Pl. 113

Now the whole idea was changed and a four-stepped square pyramid was built asymmetrically over the mastaba. In the fifth stage a much greater verticality was achieved, while the sixth stage added only slightly to the size.

The whole was faced with stone, but the builders were still used to the dimensions of clay bricks and were cautious about increasing them much when they first worked in stone. Though the burial chambers of the king and eleven members of his family plus a number of other chambers and corridors are fairly elaborate and sometimes beautifully decorated, we must note that the additions to the pyramid were not made to provide any additional interior spaces. They simply acted to increase the monumentality of the tomb in an enormous way.

Pl. 112

If you are a pyramid collector, you will next want to move to Medum, about 33 miles south of Saqqara, which is often said with some uncertainty to have been built by Sneferu, the first king of the IVth dynasty (circa 2670 B.C.), who organized the high level of prosperity and power which made the late great pyramids possible. To him are credited also two pyramids at Dahshur, which is easily reached from Saqqara. Each of these is interesting to look at for a variety of reasons, which I must refrain from elaborating here. They contain the evolution of the true pyramid from the step pyramid, and the true pyramid was probably first realized in Sneferu's northern pyramid at Dahshur. No facing stones remain—the structure is made of local red sandstone—and the blocks are now much larger than at Saqqara. Though not so large as the great pyramid of Cheops, the base does cover the same amount of ground.

If you do drive across the desert to Dahshur, be careful of your car, your tires, and your driver. The hard-packed sand of the "road" offers firm driving, but the edges are not clearly marked and it is easy to get off it and become mired at once in extremely soft sand. You are unlikely to be carried away by desert nomads or die of thirst, but you might spend some unpleasant, even nervous, hours. The reason for going is that here you can see the nascence of an entirely different concept of the pyramid complex.

Gone forever are the architectural representations of daily earthly life. The smiling aspect of the Zoser complex has given place to the stern ritual necessity to transform the dead king into a living god. The essential architectonic organization . . . is here represented on the smallest scale— valley temple, causeway, mortuary temple before reaching the final sepulchral chamber within the pyramid.[44]

The burial rites have changed enormously. Perhaps the body of the king is borne across the Nile or carried to the valley temple (which is not always near the river) for some preparatory rites, even the embalming. It is then carried in solemn cortege up the causeway to the mortuary temple for the final rites. The causeway through which the funeral processions enter the sacred precinct becomes a triple-aisled hallway, which assumes somewhat the role of a sacred grove whose columns with their fringe of palm fronds resemble or even stand for trees. After the last rites the god is encased in the pyramid tomb presumably for eternity but usually only until the dynasty has weakened. For what men can build men can destroy, and few of the Egyptian tombs were proof against looters who opened them for the precious ornaments surrounding the king there.

The emergence of the new ritual was amazingly rapid for so tradition-bound a state as Egypt. The big pyramids represent the complete switch from the royal tomb as a residence for afterlife and a mortuary precinct designed as a most realistic stage setting for rituals. After Sneferu the idea instead was to express the idea of kingly divinity. The valley temple was greatly expanded, the causeway was covered, the adoration temple at the pyramid became gigantic; of course the pyramid itself became huge.

Pl. 110
Much of the surrounding building is gone now and to get some idea you have to put pieces together, for example, the Valley Temple of Chephren and the mortuary temple of Mycerinus. But you will be quite unusual and extraordinarily avid in your pursuit of the history of Egyptian architecture if once you reach the site you are able to take your mind off the pyramids and potter among the ruins of temples and causeways.

Pl. 115
The general layout can be seen from the plan of the site. Naturally, the three pyramids take on different relations to each other depending on where you stand. From the south they read: Mycerinus (much the smallest, 221 feet high), Chephren (477 feet high), and Cheops (490 feet high). Since the pyramid of Chephren is nearer than Cheops, it seems the larger, though it is not.

Khufu (Cheops), founder of the IVth dynasty, not a Memphite but a noble of a provincial town near Beni-Hasan, supplanted Sneferu and established a new and powerful line. His achievements were doubtless many, but the one that is incontestable is his pyramid, which dominates the Giza settlements. Originally it was 755 feet on a side, and 480 feet high, but is now some 30 feet less high. It has three burial chambers, only one planned

[44] Ibid., p. 306.

for use at a given moment, all entered from the north and built in successive enlargements so that the two lower were abandoned before use. The third is entered by two narrow passages, first descending and then ascending, which explode into a monumental ascending gallery 28 feet high and 153 feet long and 6½ feet wide, all faced with limestone. At the upper end is a vestibule originally blocked (after the interment), and this leads to the tomb chamber, a generous room 50 by 32 by 19 feet faced with granite slabs and holding a granite sarcophagus. Above are five relieving chambers to reduce the weight of the material.

The work itself is, needless to say, spectacular. There are many blocks in this pyramid that individually weigh more than 5,000 pounds. Herodotus reported that it took 100,000 men twenty years to build it, and the more scholarly Petrie thinks the estimate credible. The blocks were taken from quarries east of the Nile, south of Cairo, and carried across at highwater. When much of the valley was flooded, the stones could be brought nearest to the site. Even then, and whatever the engineering and construction methods, the subsequent achievement was obviously fantastic. But the work was not only enormous, it was fine in quality. The average error at the base is said to be less than one part in 10,000 in equality, in squareness, and in level, although the site itself rose so that direct measurements could not be taken from corner to corner. Some of the joints are as fine as 1/10,000 inch. The exterior was sheathed in an exquisitely fitted casing of limestone, since quarried away, which entirely concealed the place of entrance.

But all this perfection, though of vast interest and the source of much speculation, pales when we think what this was all for. The grand gallery was used once only—when the mummy of the king, lying in his wooden coffin, was carried along it to his funeral chamber. The marvelous great boat, found untouched in 1954 on the south side of this pyramid, was also probably used but once, to bear the body of the dead king from his royal residence to the valley temple.

If ever proof were needed that this architecture—sealed forever, inaccessible to all human beings once the funeral rites were ended—was created as an offering to invisible powers, whether Ka or god-king, it is here.

I do not know whether you will care to journey into the burial chamber. On a warm day when the site is full of visitors, the line long, and the ventilation stuffy, it can be quite unpleasant. But I do not know how else you can grapple with the power of the reality of an architecture which seems to have absolutely nothing to do with anything which we are likely to think real.

Although they compose well for photographs, and although Chephren's has the Sphinx, and Mycerinus, the charming combination of its three little pyramids in the foreground, the fact is that after Cheops the quality and impressiveness of the pyramids declined. Cheops was succeeded by the

Pl. 116

The Architecture of Stone 213

obscure Dedefre; then came Chephren, whose pyramid is slightly smaller than that of Cheops and inferior in workmanship. The materials were still sumptuous; the great granite from the first cataract was used for the lower part of the casing while red granite and alabaster were used in the gateway temple. We know little about Chephren's deeds, but the pyramid affirms that he must have still sat in a very powerful seat.

His successor Mycerinus was in a different position. The royal power was slipping away to the priests and the nobles. The cult of Re, which required a different sort of temple, was on the threshold. It was probably not only from modest choice that his pyramid is so much smaller or that his ruined and unfinished temple was faced with sun-dried brick and not elegant granite. Although Egyptians continued to build smaller pyramids in substantial numbers and on many sites and well into the XIIth Dynasty, the great days of the great pyramids were over almost as quickly as they began.

How are you to interpret the Egyptian pyramids, or should you even try? You can find some rhapsodist to support almost any view you choose to hold, from the most materialistic to the most mystical. You can look on them as a lavish waste of power built on slavery for the ostentation of a tyrant and see nothing but the overseers and the lashes. You can look on them as stairs to or from heaven, giant stairs to be sure, stairs for a god. You can think of their pristine state when the smoothly dressed limestone blocks might have made the pyramid unclimable by a common man—or so some mountaineers might assert. Whether the glassy surfaces would actually have defeated a modern Sierra Clubber fully equipped with pitons, ropes, carabiners, and even lassos might be disputable. In their present state they have often been climbed and taken their toll, too, of the unwary. But for the pitonless Egyptian at least only the spirit of faith could ascend them.

Or you may look on the pyramids in a quite different sense. You may believe that "the nation was literally incarnated in its king-god, it partook of the celestial privileges of his person which was simultaneously divine and human,"[45] so that the poor man participated vicariously, though the fellahin have left neither revolutions nor writing to tell us how they felt.

Perhaps you will want to put them somewhere in the middle—not only the visible and ostentatious expression of the religious magic, but also the temporal power of the monarchs expressed palpably by the very immensity.

Ladders, artificial mountains, a cone of divine (solar) light, a cosmic place, or what you will.

In leaving the tomb of Khufu our admiration for the monument . . .
should not obscure the real and final significance; for the great pyramid is

[45] Paul Gayet-Tancrède, *The Glory of Egypt*, translated by J. E. Manchip-White (New York: Vanguard, 1956). Text and notes by Samivel (pseudonym).

the earliest and most impressive witness surviving from the ancient world to the final emergence of organized society from prehistoric chaos and local conflict, thus coming for the first time completely under the power of a far-reaching and comprehensive centralization effected by one controlling mind.[46]

Today we might be more prone to judge the quality of such a far-reaching and comprehensive control by the quality of its crop control and distribution than by its monumental artifact, but this may not diminish the significance of the Breasted assessment.

Be as mystic or as pragmatic as you will; conjecture as wildly as you like. But if you will let your eye control your intellect for a brief span, it may well be when you actually stand among the pyramids that you need no explanation at all, that it is enough for you that they are there. Many works of nature and a few of man need no literary rhapsody.

MESO-AMERICA

The last of the important groups of pyramids is to be found in pre-Hispanic Meso-America. Like the ziggurats of Mesopotamia they are not true pyramids. Though important in the urban complexes of the Yucatan lowlands and the Central Mexican Plateau, they are not by any means always the most important architectural feature. But considered not only as lofty mounds but also as monumental step terraces, they become a major feature of one of the most interesting combinations of architecture and sculpture to be found anywhere in the world.

Pl. 117

Although this architecture is better known than it was, its proper place in the architectural hierarchy of the world is not yet commonly conceded. Our eyes still focus mainly on Europe with somewhat more generous side glances nowadays to Japan, China, and Islam. Pre-Hispanic architecture of the Americas occupies scant space in the most famous tomes on the architecture of the world.

Years ago, there may have been some excuse for this. Mexico and Peru were far away, difficult and even dangerous to reach. Very little of the great work had even been uncovered. The sites were remote, hard to get to, not very safe on many counts. But there is no excuse any longer. The archeological work has been extensive and good. The literature is rich. There is no finer or more elegant museum in the world to provide a glowing introduction than the Museo Archeologico in Mexico City. Ignacio Bernal's informative works have not only been put into English but have been published with beautiful illustrations mostly by Mexican presses. The major sites of Teotihuacán and Cholula can each be reached and visited in a comfortable day's round trip from Mexico City. The great Mayan center

[46] James Henry Breasted, *A History of Egypt from the Earliest Times to the Persian Conquest* (New York: Bantam, 1964), p. 119.

The Architecture of Stone 215

of Uxmal and the Mayan-Toltec complex of Chichen-Itzá both are easily visited from Merida in Yucatan where several main airlines stop in passage from the United States to Mexico City, and there are comfortable, even luxurious, accommodations both in Merida and on the sites themselves. The great Zapotec centers of Monte Albán and Mitla near Oaxaca entail no hardships to visit. Journeys to Copán in Honduras, Tíkal in Guatemala, and Palenque in Chiapas province are a little more difficult and require a little more planning, but they are not arduous.

The area involved spreads out along the diagonal of a rectangle whose sides are about 650 miles and 880 miles and whose length is therefore about 1,100 miles, starting at the north from a little west of Tampico, ending at the south at Copán, near the boundary of Honduras-Guatemala, at the west at Mezcala and the east a little north of Tegucigalpa in Honduras.

The time span was something like 2,500 years from the colossal Olmec head of San Lorenzo to the landing of Cortés in A.D. 1519. It began not much later than the building of Abu Simbel by Rameses II, spanned the Golden Age of Greece, the conquests of Alexander the Great, the birth of Christ, the fall of the Roman Empire, the coronation of Charlemagne, the entire Middle Ages, and the beginning of the Renaissance.

The geographic span lacks the unity of the Egyptian Nile or the extreme fragmentation of the tight valleys of mainland classic Greece, and there was also less tribal unity, hence more variety in the architecture.

If we think only of the two great developments, the Mayan and the Mexican, we can reach the dimensions of the geographic-climatic problem. The pre-Hispanic Maya occupied the Mexican states of Campeche, Yucatan, Tabasco, the east half of Chiapas and Quintano Roo, plus Guatemala, Honduras, and a part of Costa Rica—altogether an area of about 750,000 square miles, six times the area of France. The area was limited at the southwest, south, and east by a circle of mountains concave to the north dominated by volcanic peaks (some still active) from 8,500 to 14,000 feet high. This vast relief enclosed deep valleys, one the Rio Motagria, reaching the Atlantic at the bottom of the Gulf of Honduras, the other Rio Usumacinta at the bottom of the Gulf of Mexico.

The high part has an average altitude of 3,300 feet. The winters are dry and even cold; the rainy season, from May to November. The forest is interrupted by great prairies which dominate above 10,000 feet. The plain of the center (Guatemala and southern Yucatan) has an average altitude of 500 feet extending through the area bounded by the mountain range. It is about 62 miles long and not over 20 miles wide at the most. This plain and the hills which limit it at the north are covered with dense tropical forest. The temperatures are high especially in the dry season of February, March, April, and May; the rest of the year is very wet. The north half of Yucatan is the third natural Mayan region. Here the vegetation is much less powerful and dense. It is a low flat plain about 5 feet above sea level cut by some hills never more than 60 feet high. It is an extremely dry region with, however, much underground water, many natural wells, and a number of sizable lakes (the largest 7 by 30 miles). Thus the Mayan country was not a geographical unity, a climatic unity, or even a cultural unity; indeed there were at least six language groups, and Meso-America included also the non-Mayan high plateau of Central Mexico. On the Mexican Plateau, terrain and climate had somewhat greater unity and the area was somewhat more suitable for military maneuvering and semipermanent conquests.

Over these two areas the conquerors and the cultures came and went.

The cultures varied ethnically, in ways of making a living and of living, in religion, and indeed in everything which would condition the crafts, the art, the architecture, though most of them, at least until the Aztecs, were doubtless theocratic. Their centers were as far apart in distance as in time, though the cultures each spilled over the edges of the others and modified and were modified by them. We can gauge the complexity of the problem of understanding all this merely by rehearsing the names of the most prominently identifiable cultures and asking ourselves whether we really have even a foggy but reliable recollection of where they were located and what they stood for, from Olmec through Mayan, Zapotec, Toltec, Huastec, Mixtec, and Aztec, to Totonac. Which were around Oaxaca, which in Central Mexico, which on the Gulf Coast, which in the Mayan area? Or what confusion arises in our minds when we recall sites again in rough chronology from San Lorenzo, to Tlatilco, La Victoria, La Venta, Cuicuilco, Izapa, Kaminaljuyu, Tres Zapotes, Teotihuacán, Tíkal, Copán, Monte Albán, El Tajín, Uxmal, Tula, Mitla, Chichen Itzá, Tamuin, Mayapan, Cempoala, and finally Aztec Tenochtitlán, which fell to Spain? We can put these on a time chart and this will help us a little, but only a little.

The historical evidence is scanty, and what comes through comes through dimly.

As in Peru the evidence we have about the life of the people of Meso-America was much reduced by those ferocious Spanish evangelists, who, on the one hand acting as iconoclasts, destroyed most of the original source material in the codices, and, on the other, were so impressed with the culture that they passed on notes and sketches without which modern scholars would have had a very hard time.

Our evidence is of three kinds: the Spanish chronicles, the codices, and the carefully dated multiple inscriptions on bas-reliefs on buildings which also adorned the stelae which were ceremoniously erected on carefully calculated calendar days.

The codices were written on a paper made of fibers from a tree (the *copo*) impregnated with a natural vegetable gum and covered with a layer of fine white chalk. These were disposed in a long band of which different parts or pages were folded on each other so the whole thing could be unfolded. Only three are known to have survived from the Mayan area. Now in Dresden, Paris, and Madrid, they total some 40-odd feet in length, some 210 pages around 4 or 5 inches wide and 8 or 9 inches high, and are all really nothing more than fragments.[47] Although vividly illustrated, their topics are limited mainly to astronomy, ritual, and divination. They say little about daily life or political events. The stele inscriptions are much more numerous. About half of the identified glyphs, or some 450, have been cataloged. But these together with the codices continue to tell us more about Mayan mathematics and astronomy and to some extent religion than they do about political history, which is very speculative except as to the broadest lines, and common daily life, which is only a little better described. They are quite unlike the Bayeux tapestry.

A potential power for real resistance to white invaders developed among the Toltecs (Teotihuacán and Monte Albán). Their buildings and civilization were surpassed by their southern contemporaries only in superior development of sculpture and in the religious calendar, but they were a more militant people. Still more so were the Aztecs who conquered the Central Valley.

The Aztecs would seem by most of our standards brutal. From childhood on, the individual grew up into correct social behavior; the violator of the code met with serious consequences. There was little to harass the individual intellectually or economically. Freedom of thought, individual liberty, personal fortunes were nonexistent, but people lived according to a code that had worked well and continuously for centuries. Yet by all accounts, Tenochtitlán was a magnificent city. On November 8, 1519, Bernal Diaz del Castillo, marching with Cortés, saw the city.

> We were amazed and said that it was like the enchantments they tell us
> of in the legend of Amadis, on account of the great towers and buildings
> arising from the water and all built of masonry. And some of our
> soldiers even asked whether the things we saw were not a dream.[48]

Now this was the period of Bramante, Michelangelo, and Raphael in Italy; the guild houses of Antwerp were not yet built, nor any of the works

---

[47] I have referred before, and doubtless shall again, to the problem of keeping *au courant* with the latest discoveries and the subsequent revised conclusions about architectural history. A recent example concerns the "three" Mayan codices. The *New York Times* of April 21, 1971, reported an exhibition at the Grolier Club of a fourth and smaller codex (eleven pages) whose anonymous owner had curiously managed for several years to keep its existence secret from all but about six people. At least one of these is a scholar of good repute who is prepared to stake his professional reputation on its genuineness, although extensive microscopic tests have not yet been performed. Scholars not having seen it are bound at best to be neutral and at worst to doubt its authenticity. Later on there will be arguments as to interpretation which apparently mainly concerns how the Mayans considered the four phases of the Venus cycle. On the face of it, this would not affect any of the conclusions of my text, but sometimes stones dropped in archeological or anthropological pools initiate wider ripples than might, at first, have been anticipated.

[48] Bernal Diaz del Castillo, *The Discovery and Conquest of Mexico* (New York: Farrar, Straus, 1956), pp. 190–191.

of Sansovino and Palladio, whilst the Cathedral of Bourges was less than 100 years old, the Cathedral of Seville not yet complete, and the Cathedral of Salamanca just dedicated. This great city of Tenochtitlán fell to Cortés only two years after his landing at Vera Cruz, Montezuma's conquered allies proving to be no strong defender of their Aztec leaders.

Thus the ancient cities of Mexico are of many different periods, of many different cultures; cities of the grain-growing Maya who charted the heavens but had no wheel, who counted correctly to the millions but could not weigh a sack of corn, who seem to have been lost in the contemplation of time and eternity; of the more practical Toltecs; and of the militant Aztecs, whose militancy nonetheless was ambivalent and who could write poems whose pessimism and anguish are in sharp contrast to their vigorous and threatening sculpture.

Yet all were entangled in magic, in propitiation of a supernatural world, where questions of good and evil did not arise, whose polytheistic gods were generally ambivalent, though some were on the whole more favorable than others. Thus the goddess of life-giving water in her jade skirts was also the demon of the floods; the patroness of domestic work was also the patroness of the courtesan; each god exhibited this duality in his own way, not really excluding even Quetzlcoatl, the plumed serpent, the hero founder of agriculture and industry, who portrayed the dual function of creator and destroyer.

To tend each in his own season, ritualistically, privately, was the function of the priests who carried on their hidden rites in small temples set on pyramids high above the crowds to whom they might then report whether things were going well or ill.

So religious life dominated city life. It is temple remains which mainly provide us with gauges as to past splendor.

Indeed the remaining Meso-American city is largely a collection of temples, and some observers think it to have been only ceremonial, occupied only transitorily at feasts or markets by people who, farmers mainly, lived nearby in small villages of only a few huts settled in the woods near the fields and who had to provide the food of the chiefs and priests, the building labor, the artwork, and, above all, the tributes and offerings to the gods. They would have been little better off than slaves who were either orphans, criminals, or prisoners of war. The other two classes—nobles and priests—were hereditary. The priests were the most important. Some of them and some nobles may have lived in or on the immediate periphery of the city.

With this superficial background, let us examine a few of the greatest architectural achievements in Meso-America, Uxmal and Chichen Itzá, Teotihuacán, and Monte Albán, with cursory side glances at Tíkal, Copán, Bonampak, and Cholula.

It is pretty clear that none of the early Meso-American cultures, especially the Maya, was very imaginative about domestic animals, though they used dogs, turkeys, guinea pigs, and bees for food, insects for dies, and alpacas, llamas, and dogs as beasts of burden, and possibly hunted caribou and bison. The lack of suitable domestic animals must have limited their migrations, as compared, say, with that of the great hordes from Asia which beat in the end against the walls of Rome. The Meso-Americans were essentially sedentary.

The Chronica de la Santa Provincia del Santissimo Nombre de Jesus de Guatemala, a sixteenth-century manuscript about the Mayans, says:

> If one looks closely he will find everything [these Indians] did and talked about had to do with maize; in truth they fall little short of making a god of it. And so much is the delight and gratification they got and still get out of their corn fields, that because of them they forget wife and children and every other pleasure as if their corn fields were their final goal and ultimate happiness.[49]

The Maya probably developed their agricultural system on which the whole civilization was based in the Guatemalan highlands; their highly specialized culture originated in the interior drainage basin and reached its most brilliant aesthetic expression in the lush Usumacinta Valley lying immediately to the west; the Maya renaissance and final decay took place in the third section, the more arid northern half of Yucatan.

The great work of the so-called Old Empire may have begun at about A.D. 320 and continued to 987. It embraces such famous places as Tíkal, Copán, first Chichen Itzá, Palenque, Bonampak, Quirigua, in about that order. As time went on, urban life in these centers persisted but with a slower and slower rhythm. The collapse remains a mystery, although there are many theories; earthquakes (no evidence), climatic changes (no evidence), epidemics, external or civil wars, landslides. Smallpox and yellow fever seem not to have existed in America before the European conquest. Archeology has found no traces of foreign invasion. An extensive civil war seems unlikely. Most likely is the exhaustion of tropical lands because of inappropriate agriculture. After only three years or so of Mayan practices of land burning and tilling, the yield would have become sparse. What is certain is that at the end of the tenth century all the cities of the Ancient Empire were abandoned to the forest. Few, save Chichen, were resurrected. Here, though, around 1007, a new empire emerged under an alliance, the League of Mayapan. For a century and a half the culture was brilliant, both at Chichen and Uxmal. But Chichen and Mayapan waxed too great. In the inevitably ensuing civil war, Chichen was defeated and abandoned in 1194. The Mayapans continued an ever more tyrannical course until 1441 when their city was sacked, and all pretense at any centralized authority disappeared from Yucatan. Thereafter the Mayans were quite unable to offer

[49] *Chronica de la Santa Provincia del Santissimo Nombre de Jesus de Guatemala*, cited in Sylvanus Griswold Morley, *The Ancient Maya* (Palo Alto: Stanford, 1946), p. 2.

effective resistance to the Toltec and the white envelopment. Nevertheless there was a certain resilient toughness; the Spaniards who had landed in Yucatan in 1511 did not succeed in mopping up before 1697. They may have had no serious incentive.

The Meso-American "Pyramid"

The "cities" of Middle America had many kinds of buildings, as we now see at sites like Chichen Itzá and Uxmal; and among these are some remnants of great distinction, such as the "Governor's Palace" and the "Nunnery" and "El Castillo" (all probably deceptively misnamed) or the ball court at Chichen. Among these the pyramid was not always the largest—but it did have the highest religious significance. In a work of this length I must skip lightly by many of the other important building types and emphasize the pyramid itself. This is justified by the ubiquity of the truncated pyramidal forms and their centrality in the urban architecture.

Meso-American pyramids were always stepped, always truncated, usually but not always steep, erected on bases which were usually rectangular or square but might at times be oval. These stepped platforms served many functions. The highest were something like artificial hills or ziggurats supporting temples at the top; some were tombs, though the number of these to have been found remains small. Some were extensive platforms serving as bases for large buildings whose purposes remain generally speculative. Many were built by accretion—that is, a first pyramid was simply the base for a second larger one, then a third, or a fourth. The enlargement was straightforward and simple, since the pyramids were either designed to have no rooms at all or only trivial interior spaces.

Recent investigations show that the pyramid was sometimes funerary, but not universally so.

The whole question of Mexican burial customs needs more illumination. In early Teotihuacán the dead seem to have been cremated or buried in a simple fashion, but the later Zapotecs at Monte Albán had much more elaborate rites which led to a tremendous complex of tombs. Toward the end these became elaborate and sumptuous; sometimes very elegant facades were created only to be covered when the tomb was sealed immediately after interment. But we do not know who was buried in them, and it seems certain for all of Middle America that the necrologic was not the main or even a principal driving force creating the architecture—as of course it was in Memphis, in Egypt.

Nor indeed is the notion of artificial hills for mountain people who missed them when they came to the lowlands sufficiently explanatory, since pyramids turned up where there were already more than adequate, even impressive, hills, for example, in the Guatemalan highlands. Moreover there may have been practical reasons as well for building platforms, especially in the wet Mayan lowlands where all the edifices rested on terraces varying from 20 to 10 feet in height. Usually there was one terrace per building, but sometimes a single building had a several-stepped terrace, and in other cases one terrace supported several buildings. In places like Tíkal even the pyramid-temples started on terraces up to 8 feet high.

These trapezoidal platforms came in many forms following several distinct cultural sequences. Even a glance at a few of the combinations will show how careless it is to speak of them all as pyramids.

Though definitely monumental, the American pyramids did not usually come even close to the absolute size of the great Egyptian pyramids, which, it may be recalled, were 850 feet on a side and 450 feet high. A typical Mexican pyramid, such as El Castillo at Chichen Itzá, is 185 feet square, and its nine layers achieve a height of 80 feet with the crowning temple adding another 20 feet. The largest of the known pyramids, the Pyramid of the Sun at Teotihuacán, was 700 feet on a side at ground level, which is the size of an Egyptian pyramid, but in height was far shorter, only about 200 feet high. This height was exceeded in America only by the steep pyramid temple of Tíkal whose base is much smaller but whose platforms, 115 and 130 feet high, are surmounted by temples which, with their roof lines formed by the great cresteria or roof-combs, are from 200 to 230 feet high.[50] This is the highest construction yet found in Ancient America, and later Mayan constructions never approximated such heights.

The classic Mayan pyramids were much steeper than those of the Mexican Plateau, rising to heights three-fourths that of the base. Their upward thrust was emphasized by the flights of steep steps without landings. Sometimes the steepness reached absurdity, as in the 80-degree slopes of Xpuhil, whose stairs are quite unnegotiable. In general, the drama of the plateau architecture is one of immense horizontal tablelands; that of the Mayan pyramids depends on their verticality.

All the pyramids were stepped but the steps were usually so high as to need accessory stairs. The faces of the steps were vertical or battened inward. Sometimes the faces were plain surfaces of stone, sometimes paneled. In the Mayan pyramids the stairs were an essential architectural element, sloping as they usually did at a flatter angle than the slope of the pyramid itself, for example, 45 or 60 degrees. Sometimes the stairs rose at angles as steep as 65 degrees and were higher than wide. The early ones in Yucatan generally had stairs on all four sides (Uaxactun), but after Tíkal they were usually only on the front. The pyramid at Uxmal has two stairs on opposite sides and the later El Castillo at Chichen returned to the four sides. Sometimes the ramps were cut into the mass of the pyramid; sometimes they projected firmly from the face, and when, as at Chichen, the stair slope was substantially less than the slope of the pyramid, a fine composition was achieved where the stair projected powerfully from the

Pl. 119

---

[50] The crests were of great architectural importance in the Mayan highlands though their function is not clear. Simply elaborate screens they were often higher than the temple itself. Thus temple V at Tíkal rises 30 feet above its pyramid but the crest rises 52 feet above the temple. Very few crests remain among the ruins.

base and merged with the pyramid at the upper platform level. The stairs usually stopped abruptly at the edges of the steps but were sometimes bounded by strips. These might be plain as at Palenque or decorated as on the hieroglyphic stairways at Copán. None, however, had balustrades or handrails, and all are and were precarious to climb and especially to descend.

When one sees these in the light of the subtropical latitudes, one becomes aware of the power of this simple geometry, with its overweening horizontal and vertical symmetry, constructed at solar angles where the slightest projection can produce deep shadows. The scale is invariably enhanced by wide esplanades. As Stierlin emphasizes,[51] the impression of backward movement created by the terraces and platforms harmonizes the austere rectangles of buildings with the surrounding spaces. "The combinations of this formal syntax surprise by their simplicity." Acropoli do not cut off the buildings from the world as in Athens but form springboards for the eye. Instead of perpendicular cliffs or cleavages, there is a series of ramps. In such a system the stairs, the varying heights of the pedestals, are all in a great but subtle equilibrium, though the patterns of the complexes are not those of modern rectangular towns.

Indeed this architecture, like that of Zoser, cannot best be appreciated in terms of individual buildings but only as congeries of constructions skillfully related to one another. These were at their most geometric and formal in early Teotihuacán and only slightly less so at Monte Albán. Less firmly symmetrical in the Mayan cities, the arrangements were never so helter-skelter as they were in Ancient Greece or as they are in contemporary America. The Mayans continued to arrange the axes of their building groups to set off exterior spaces to the best advantage. Since the central cities at least were most likely ceremonial, there were no vehicles or beasts of burden, there was no need for conventional streets. (There were of course *roads* between places; a highway 60 miles long and 30 feet wide connected Coba to Yaxuma following a level gradient which sometimes demanded high embankments.) Stierlin thinks of these cities as really garden cities without fortification.

In addition the effect of the buildings was enhanced by sculpture and wall painting, used not at all or sparingly and with restraint at Teotihuacán and Monte Albán and much more profusely in the Maya area.

First to emerge from the mists of the past are the Olmecs, dwelling on the flat humid tropical alluvial plain of southern Vera Cruz and northern Tabasco. The most important excavations at La Venta, Tres Zapotes, and San Lorenzo are of a culture corresponding in time roughly to that from the fall of Troy to the fall of Athens (1000–400 B.C.). All these sites show portents of urban planning. There are mounds, presumably once topped by temples, and they are arrayed around plazas in a regular pattern,

[51] Henri Stierlin, *Living Architecture—Mayan* (London: Oldbourne, 1964).

while the whole ceremonial area is arranged along a principal axis running almost north and south. The Olmecs, although prodigious carvers of giant monolithic sculpture, rarely used stone in their buildings, which were mainly of adobe and earth. The main pyramid at La Venta, the tallest known of the period, is only about 100 feet high without the temple, which has disappeared. It rises from a 330-foot base. What we can see on the site is scarcely yet to be called architecture, and you would have to be deeply committed to understanding pre-Hispanic America before you would care to visit it at all, save to view the magnificent sculpture, some of the best pieces of which are in the museum at Mexico City.

Pl. 122

At about the same time as the Olmec development, another culture was emerging on the Mexican Plateau near modern Oaxaca. This was the first period of Monte Albán. Vertical or nearly vertical walls and large staircases without balustrades were common. The vertical walls of Monte Albán I were covered with great stone slabs placed in horizontal rows, each slab engraved with a human figure in a horizontal pose called *danzantes*. Sometimes these were accompanied by hieroglyphs or numerals. Over forty of the slabs have now been recovered, and when coupled in the imagination with the ruins of the Danzante Building, which stands on the platform of Monte Albán, they evoke the idea of an interesting building. You will want to visit Oaxaca if you care much about pre-Hispanic architecture in Middle America but not alone for this monument, since there is much other interesting architecture there from later days at Monte Albán.

The earth pyramids, like those at La Venta, had little weather resistance, so the first stone pyramid of the Plateau is of more than usual interest. It is called Cuicuilco and lies in the lava-covered area called Pedregal near the University of Mexico. Cuicuilco was long thought to date from about the time of Alexander the Great, but carbon dating now puts it before 500 B.C., when it was enfolded by a sheet of lava. Not really a pyramid, or even a cone, it was a circular set of four terraces made of large stones laid in clay on an original diameter of 440 feet and rising about 65 feet. It had a ramp and three short flights of stairs which led to the top platform and its surmounting altar or temple.

But these are only preliminaries. The first great installation emerges at about the time of Constantine (A.D. 300), when Teotihuacán became the dominant Middle-American site of the first half of the Classic era. The architecture now was no longer formative. Burnt lime plaster was used as a plaster surfacing but not as a bonding mortar. Cantilevered panels jut out from the inclined talus at the platform bases.

The axes are straight, the platforms rectangular, the proportions excellent, the scale grandiose.

The remains of the ancient American city of Teotihuacán (300 B.C.– A.D. 900) are among the most impressive in the Western Hemisphere and would stand high on any world list. They are very accessible—by automobile on a good road 30-odd miles north of Mexico City, by tour buses, by special half-hour express buses, and by cheap, slow second-class buses. One can even go by train if he is in no hurry, but this is not really much to be recommended.

The first idea one needs firmly to erase is that Teotihuacán has anything to do with the Aztecs. The great Aztec city Tenochtitlán was in a different place at a different time and was very different in style and purpose. Indeed by the thirteenth century when the Aztecs had taken control of the Central Mexican valley, Teotihuacán had long been a ruin. The Aztecs did not even know its history. They were awed by the immensity of the monumental works which remained for them to see and thought them to have been built by god-giants. Teotihuacán was a place of pilgrimage even for Montezuma, who went there at least yearly.

Some of the people who lived at different times in Middle America were peaceful; some belligerent. For all of these domestication of a staple vegetarian food supply and its maintenance was vital. Each had its pantheon, though the names of the same god would vary. An important mystic one, Quetzalcoatl, the flying serpent, was Kakulcan among the Maya. Gods of war and death or even the sun god Huitzilopochtli of the Aztecs who could subsist only on the nectar of human blood may have had greater prestige in some of the cultures than in others, as did the gods of death. But for all, the god of rain and fertility was centrally important. He was called Chac in Yucatan and Tlaloc on the Central Plateau.

The people who built Teotihuacán and other great centers of the classic era at Cholula (probably a provincial version, though current excavations may show differently) were evidently peaceful and agrarian. They certainly were among the greatest architects of pre-Hispanic America, and what they built was in no way inferior to the later achievements of the Maya, save in the matter of architectonic sculpture. Indeed in a purely architectural sense, the work of Teotihuacán may be superior to that of the Maya.

The first stage, from 300 B.C. to the first century A.D., antedates the pyramids, which were built during what is called Teotihuacán II, from the first to the third centuries A.D., that is, in the heyday of the Roman Empire. The important outlying suburbs, of which we know so little, were built during the years 400–700, and toward the end of this came destruction by fire and abandonment.

No other single city on the Central Mexican Plateau, at least before Tenochtitlán, ever attained the size and importance of Teotihuacán. By the end of the first period perhaps 30,000 people occupied 17 square kilometers; in period II there may have been 45,000 on 22½ square kilometers, and in period III, 90,000 on a smaller area. Just before the end some 60,000 people may have lived on 20 square kilometers. This was large and dense for an ancient city. The whole city had many zones, residential and otherwise, possibly arranged in some hierarchical order. These surrounded and possibly ran into the ceremonial center which is all we now see. Since very little of the vast archeological area other than the ceremonial center has as yet been opened up, as in so many other ancient places, the common life of Teotihuacán remains largely a mystery.

To accept the idea that the Teotihuacanos were great architects requires, perhaps even more than at Saqqara, a revision of our conventional architectural values. This has been well stated by Kubler.

> Our conception of architecture has been dominated for so long by the need for shelter, that we lack the sense of building as monumental form apart from shelter. As monumental form, architecture commemorates a valuable experience, distinguishing one space from others in an ample and durable edifice. It is not necessary to enclose rooms; it suffices, as in Ancient America, to mark out a space by solid masses, or to inscribe the space with a system of lines and shapes. . . . The architects of ancient America were far more attentive to the spaces engendered among the elements than their European contemporaries, and they excelled all peoples in the composition of large and rhythmically ordered open volumes. Teotihucán is the most regular and the largest of all Ancient American ritual centers with a coherent composition ordering the elements in an area 1½ miles long by about ½ mile wide.[52]

Pl. 118

The pyramidal architecture of Teotihuacán shows little iconographic or even decorative sculpture. The south pyramid, the so-called Temple of Quetzalcoatl built in Teotihuacán III and designed in a severe unsculptured style, overlays a smaller older pyramid of Teotihuacán II, that is, in the time of Christ. About half of the newer pyramid has been uncovered to reveal a central stair and panels garnished by feathered serpents whose heads spring boldly from the wall, alternated with conventionalized heads probably of the rain god Tlaloc. The heads are spectacularly adorned with shells and other marine objects associated with water. But even this much sculpture was uncommon in this place and at that time.

On the other hand mural painting was carried to a high level. The great local example is from Tepantitla, outside the ceremonial area about a quarter of a mile east of the Pyramid of the Sun. It has some unique features, being the only example yet to be uncovered where the painters ignored the religious canons which stylized so much of the other mural work. It is a representation of the paradise of the Teotihuacanos' Tlalocan, the land of the rain god Tlaloc.

Of the frescos found elsewhere in abundance, some are of priests or gods in ceremonial attire casting gifts; some are of animals, real or fancied. Some are abstract and may have had meaning or merely been decorative. A few, like the Tlalocan fresco at Tepantitla, depicting the paradise of the god of rain, are more descriptive. Bernal describes it thus:

[52] George Kubler, *The Art and Architecture of Ancient America*, Copyright © George Kubler, 1962 (Baltimore: Penguin, 1962), p. 29.

226   *Bernini Is Dead?*

It represents the paradise of the God of Rain—only certain people could attain to it—not on their merits but through the manner of their dying. Those who had died by drowning or as a consequence of the numerous illnesses which were thought to be produced by water or themselves to produce water went to Tlalocan. Thus the word "paradise" is rather misleading since there is no suggestion of a reward; the qualification is simply a fortuitous manner of death. The whole composition is divided into two parts, one on either side of the door. At the top, above both panels, a great figure of the God of Rain, sumptuously dressed, casts drops of water to earth. This is little more than another instance of the official paintings of the great gods. But the lower panels are far more interesting. To the right there is a mountain out of which runs a great river. The mountain itself is all water. What could be richer, what more desirable, than a mountain of water? Both on the mountain and in the river men are swimming amongst fishes, plants, and water animals. On the ground numerous little figurines, all masculine, are playing, talking or singing, chasing butterflies among the trees, the fruits, and the flowers. . . .
How different from the Greek heavens, peopled with beautiful men and women; how different also from the paradise of Islam! The houris, the cushions, the fountains, the perfumes, the sexual delights are entirely unknown in Teotihuacán's paradise. It is a simple heaven of almost childish pleasures, of games, of little boys. Really the central theme is the richness of nature, a richness that produces water, the scarcity of which has been the nightmare of the Mexican Highlands from time immemorial; water that will seep into the dry land and make it fertile far more efficiently than all the sweat that men in the fields can pour into it.[53]

What brought down such a civilization? Conquest, perhaps, but only after an exhaustion brought about by the fact that the crops of the adjacent Highland Valleys could not sustain so large a population for a millennium, especially as fewer and fewer engaged in agriculture and more and more in producing luxury objects. So there had to be reliance on commerce, tribute, and war with the apparently inevitable result. At least this is the usual view, though Kubler offers a different explanation, involving the overuse of burnt lime, which would make sense to a modern ecologist, since to get the lime they burned the forest cover.

When we come to the ceremonial zone of Teotihuacán today, we will soon find ourselves on the so-called Avenue of the Dead. It is badly named Pl. 120 since there are no burials along it or in the bordering structures. Moreover it is not really a street but rather a succession of long plazas connected by stairs. The site slopes about 100 feet. There were no draft animals or wheeled vehicles for which a ramp would have been more commodious. Hence the designers were able to mark off the several plazas by stairs, much more effective for ritual purposes. These stairs also delimit the empty spaces and assist in the harmonious composition of the building masses

[53] Ignacio Bernal, *Ancient Mexico in Color* (London: Thames and Hudson, 1968), p. 33.

which occasionally stand in the middle of a plaza but usually toward the back of one which flanks the street.

The ceremonial zone is over a mile long, north to south, and the avenue, 148 feet wide, runs through it terminating at the north with what is presently the most interesting structure on the site.

When you go there you will not wish to pass by, as we must here, many of the interesting structures along the way: the Cuidadella, a rectangular esplanade bordered by platforms; the previously mentioned pyramid of Quetzalcoatl; the west side temples of Tlaloc and of agriculture; and especially the well-organized museum.

About half-way up the avenue on the right is the Pyramid of the Sun, the largest structure on the site, approaching major Egyptian dimensions at its base (700 by 700 feet) though not in height (200 feet). This pyramid has five receding stories of varying height, each one battered. The uppermost platform is reached by a monumental flight of steps on its western facade. It has a grandeur of scale and produces a wonderment at the technical skill required to build so sturdily as to resist time and so imaginatively as to create an illusion of something approaching infinite time and space. But it was inaccurately put in its present form some sixty years ago when archeology was young and archeologists amateurish and naive.

Pl. 121

So the greater experience of Teotihuacán is the smaller Pyramid of the Moon, which stands at the end of the Avenue of the Dead. Though smaller than the Pyramid of the Sun, its gods must also have been important since the avenue leads only to it. This pyramid has been carefully and convincingly restored up to the top of the third section and must partly indicate some of the original magnificence. In all it has five sections formed either by *talud* (slope or batter), as in the upper stages, or by *tablero* (panels), as in the first stage of five steps. This arrangement was indeed invented at Teotihuacán and served as a later model in many places. On the axis is an enormous staircase with a low balustrade, broken at the lower level by rectangular projections on the level of the upper ledge of each section, carrying through the panel projections.

Equally important is the plaza in front with an advocatory (place of worship or altar) in the center, surrounded by a dozen symmetrically arranged low platform buildings, in a very classic form, each four-tiered, each provided with a staircase and low balustrade.

What we cannot see and can hardly imagine is that all this fine stonework, artfully put together, was covered with stucco and then painted in brilliant colors. The effect, like that of the Acropolis, was clearly far different from that produced by the gray or brown monochromes we see now. It should *not* be approached as a Son-et-Lumière experience but rather in sunlight and without electronic aids.

Pl. 122

At least as impressive as a plateau city with a congeries of pyramids is Monte Albán near Oaxaca. It was begun back in the time of Teotihuacán, which doubtless accounts for some of the irregularities of the site plan. It did not reach its apogee until the ninth century under the domination of the Zapotecs. It is an amazing temple center, no doubt the most grandiose of all the American temple sites. Here the top of a hill, standing more than 1,300 feet above the valley, was leveled to form a vast terrace visually but not measurably in the form of a rectangle about 3,000 feet north to south and 800 feet east to west. At the north and south ends hills too large to be removed stood, and these were converted into foundations for higher temples and made to appear like constructed pyramids by facing them with *taludes* and *tableros*. Also in the center a natural hill was left as the foundation for three large temples but only after conversion into architectural form.

> Thus a magnificent harmony and unity was achieved, which even the inclemencies of weather and the vandalism of man have not been able to spoil![54]

The proliferation of pyramidal platforms, all the principal surfaces of which are inclined, is finished with roughly shaped stones set in sun-dried clay. The vertical surfaces are interrupted by a variety of receding and layered planes which render a very light sense of horizontality but serve more to impel the eye upward. The surfaces as you now see them were nearly all refaced by Alfonso Caso before 1940.

Extremely important elements of the design at Monte Albán are the generously proportioned stair balustrades, which sometimes reach two-fifths of the total stair width. They appear like immense ramps, and are entirely different from the more linear barriers found elsewhere.

This is a sober architecture, even more so than that of Teotihuacán. Even in its heyday it did not go in for much profusion of detail and preferred to let the lights and shadows of its long horizontals describe the scene.

Like Teotihuacán, Monte Albán is a sharp reminder that the grouping of buildings is quite as important a factor in the appearance of an urban architecture as the excellence of design of individual edifices. It may even be a more important factor.

At the south end of the acropolis stands an asymmetrical group of pyramids, the highest. At the north end another cluster surrounds a sunken court. On the east end of the main plaza there are great stairways, at the west three free-standing temple groups—while in the center of the plaza is a rectangular platform faced with stairways and buildings "reflecting or echoing" those of the periphery.

Kubler notes that this assemblage of buildings could properly be described as a kind of amphitheater affording privacy and enclosure to gatherings whose attention was centered on a dominant stairway or temple.

[54] Ibid., p. 50.

If you poke around Monte Albán, you can come on some other things. There are a few cylindrical masonry columns *in antis* and even an early though short suggestion of a portico. We will find more of this at Uxmal and Chichen Itzá but will not make much of it even there since it is not in Meso-America that we should look for notable examples of trabeate architecture.

But if you have a feel for monumental architectural space, you should not miss Monte Albán, which is one of the great architectural experiences of pre-Hispanic Meso-America.

If you are now firmly hooked and crave a much more exotic experience, possibly entailing some degrees of discomfort, you will wish to descend to El Tajín, 125 miles north of Vera Cruz on the Gulf Coast. It was lively in the period 500–1200 and peaked perhaps around 900.

Tajín is only 20 miles from the Gulf of Mexico and is very little above sea level. The climate is hot and humid and the site is surrounded by dense jungle. Most of the buildings, though cleared of dense vegetation, are still unexcavated and so appear as green mounds. The buildings were disposed around what was probably a vast urban plaza.

Aside from the numerous ball courts, the most impressive monument at Tajín is the Pyramid of Niches. It is not large, resting on a base of 120 feet square, and is less than 80 feet high, shorn as it is of its temple. It is made up of six receding stories of equal height, each set back from the one below by an equal amount. But the design of the stories shows something local and new—unusual, whether or not beautiful. Each story has a battered base supporting an extended panel and topped by a projecting cornice which offers a considerable terrace ledge, apparently only of visual function, since there is no possible access from the great staircase to the ledges. The panels are decorated with niches of varying depth (three fewer on each side on each story). These niches were evidently never intended to hold anything, but were meant simply to model the architectural surface. Their interiors were painted dark red, their frames blue. They are all over the pyramid, even on the foundation, and especially under the 33-foot-wide stairway which conceals about half the niches on its side. In the center of the staircase there are five further groups of three niches each having no correspondence to those of the building. All the niches together, visible and invisible, add up to the 365 days of the year, a symbolism which appears again at El Castillo at Chichen Itzá.

The relatively wide balustrade has thirteen frets in relief, equaling the days of the local week presented as stylizations of the body of a serpent.

The Pyramid of the Niches at El Tajín is a considerable architectural curiosity, but I would have to know what you are like before suggesting whether you should or should not add it to your architectural game bag. Beneath the visible pyramid is a smaller one of similar conformation, of an earlier time, as was so common in Meso-American building. But you cannot see this one, and if you want to wander around in minelike corridors looking at the surfaces of earlier pyramids, you will have to do it at Chichen Itzá, or better still at Cholula.

Mayan Cities

Among the Mayas, the pyramid is still important but less dominant. Their agricultural system probably developed in the Guatemalan highlands, the most brilliant aesthetic expression occurred in the lush Usumacinta Valley lying immediately to the west, and the renaissance and decay occurred in Yucatan.

The middle development came down out of the hills at Copán in Honduras near the Guatemalan border, the southernmost important classic Maya site. It hovered there for a while, then spread rapidly into the Petén area of Guatemala where Tíkal stood at its heartland; it spread further west and a little north to Palenque in Chiapas province of Mexico. A jade Tíkal plaque now in Leyden dates its beginning at A.D. 320. The first stone corbel replacing wood appeared in the Petén about 350, though some Mexican archeologists place these dates earlier. In the century from 330 to 430 the development centered around Tíkal and Uaxactun. For the century after 430 the powerful expansion to the west created Palenque and provided at the north Old Chichen Itzá. Toward its end as it passed its maximum of grandeur and fell into decadence, there was a great final renaissance at Uxmal at the end of the ninth and the beginning of the tenth centuries.

The early important buildings in the more southerly centers are from around 550, coinciding with the Age of Justinian, while the great temples of Copán and Palenque were being built in the seventh century at about the time of the beginning of the Arab conquest of Africa and Spain and were finished by 780 not long after the decisive battle of Tours-Poitiers and the subsequent accession of Charlemagne. Incidentally, for those who are looking for Asiatic sources, it might be noted that the emergence of the Khmers in Cambodia is at least a century later.[55]

The Mayas served an enormously complicated pantheon. There were nine lower worlds and thirteen heavens superposed one on the other. Good gods produced thunder, lightning, rain, all of which were thought to favor the harvest, while bad ones originated drought, hurricanes, war. But most of the gods were ambivalent. All of them, including the god of death, were invoked and propitiated in multiple ceremonies commencing with periods of abstinence and continence, which were sometimes very long.

Although the Maya evidently believed in an afterlife, sometimes pleasant and abundant, sometimes painful and suffering, this did not pro-

[55] Hieroglyphic staircase, Copan, 545; Temple of Foliated Cross, Palenque, 536; Temple of the Sun, Palenque, 642; Pyramid of the Inscriptions, Palenque, 692; Staircase stele, Copan, 752; Palace Tower, Palenque, 783. Tikal, 320–867; Copan, 460–801; Palenque, 536–783. The founding of Uxmal is often put at 1007 but there is evidence of earlier building there.

duce any great necrologic art. The corpses were swathed, their mouths stuffed with corn. They were placed in tombs with a few clay figurines, or objects of wood or stone, and utensils consistent with the vocation of the deceased. The dead man's house was then generally abandoned. Some people of higher rank were incinerated and their ashes stored in temple vases; more rarely the body lay in a vaulted tomb (corbel) surrounded by ornaments and tools. Even more rarely the facial part of the skull was preserved and the soft parts of the face replaced by resin or chalk mortar. But none of this led to any consequential funerary architecture.

The most important god was certainly Chac, the god of rain, who appears in the codices and the sculpture alike with a long nose like an elephant's trunk and with a highly stylized pair of eyes and ears. Death, shown less commonly, was a skeleton and its accessories.

Toward the end the appearance of the gods became an important part of the architectonic sculpture of the temples, but also of importance in determining their forms must have been the cult of human sacrifice.

Rivet has described this luridly from a little evidence in the codices, a few steles of Piedras Negras, and particularly the frescoes of Bonampak. The custom was most common in the new empire and especially perhaps among the Toltecs—the painted victim and the four priestly aides, the tearing out of his still palpitating heart, his flaying, the wearing of his pelt by the *chelan* (priest) in the subsequent ritual dance, followed sometimes by a cannibalistic finale if the victim had been a brave warrior.[56]

This direct encounter with human pain and death will seem very repellent to present generations which by and large can stomach better the more abstract and remote deaths of concentration camps, of military juntas, defoliation, and anonymous bombing. And it may even be true that the Mexican ways, bred in a superstition that demanded blood that the life-giving sun might not die, are more forgivable than the sacrifices of today bred in superstitions of a different sort but no less compelling.

We do not know how often the sacrifices occurred or whether they involved youth specially reared for the purpose, honored captured enemies or aliens simply taken for the purpose, or citizens for whom the choice was a high and permanent honor; perhaps there were all these kinds.

Whatever their frequency, the sacrifices were so important that they must have conditioned the architectural layouts.

Certainly they, along with other things such as the symbolic representations of Chac, Quetzlcoatl, and other gods, were subject matter for the rich and varied high relief and incised sculpture and the earth-colored frescos at both of which the Maya were masters and which will properly engage your attention both on the sites and in the museums.

The Spanish did not go much to Yucatan. One who did was the Fran-

---

[56] Paul Rivet, *Les hauts lieux de l'histoire*, vol. IV, *Cités Maya*, Albert Champdor (ed.) (Paris: Albert Guillot, 1962).

ciscan Archbishop of Merida, Friar Diego de Landa, scarcely a totally friendly witness since he was the great burner of books and codices as works of the devil. Yet he describes the Mayan cities in language as glowing as that Pericles used about his native Athens.

> If the number, grandeur and beauty of its buildings were to count toward the attainment of renown and reputation in the same way as gold, silver, and riches have done for other parts of the Indies, Yucatán would have become as famous as Peru and New Spain have become, so many in so many places and so well built of stone are they; it is a marvel; the buildings themselves and their number are the most outstanding thing that has been discovered in the Indies.[57]

In another place he says the cities were well ordered and neat. This we cannot verify, since it is generally accepted that we can see only the ceremonial centers today.

Some general observations can be made about these cities of the Mayan lowlands. Bernal is probably right that they show much less regimented planning than the cities of Central Mexico, and certainly none appears to have been as urban as Teotihuacán. That is why they have often been believed to be ceremonial centers featuring temples and palaces which ordinary people, living in separated hamlets, would come to visit only for festivals or markets.

They do contain several types of buildings. The pyramids, though important, no longer are always the dominant thing, though more so in the early than in the late classic period. Often the buildings look more like what we would call buildings in other cultures—long, low, entered by portals, sometimes of considerable importance, though always essentially masonry wall buildings with no true columnar or trabeated development. Since the span possibilities were so limited by the limitations of the corbel, the interior spaces were meager and would not seem to us to be suitable either for habitation or assembly. This adds force to the notion that their use was transient, but it does not prove it, since our notions of "habitable" space are doubtless quite different from those of the Maya, and they may have felt that it was more appropriate to assemble outdoors anyway.

Whatever their purpose, the buildings are usually arranged around plazas, on platforms or pyramids, in a rather regular pattern, "but the Maya architect seems to have been more interested in the beauty of the facade and its adornment than in the relationship between one building and another."[58] Some of the complex decoration is wonderful, some seems excessive especially toward the end. Some of it is quite openly extraneous,

[57] Cited in Tatiana Proskouriakoff, *An Album of Maya Architecture* (Norman, Okla.: University of Oklahoma Press, 1963). Other translations vary substantially as to words but not as to sense. Proskouriakoff's drawings of the old Mayan cities as reconstructed are illuminating.
[58] Bernal, *Ancient Mexico in Color*, op. cit., p. 57.

such as the temple combs which gave more apparent height and were mainly decorative, although they may have done something to balance the corbels.

Kubler gives rather more credit than this to the aspirations of the Mayans toward urban compositions. The cities of the Petén (from Copán to Palenque) he perceptively calls "island cities" or "archipelago cities"; these consisted of many groups of platforms and buildings on knolls and shoulders of hilly land, rising above the surrounding swamps which may have been lakes in antiquity. Sometimes they were connected by causeways both for circulation and to extend the ordered space of the plazas. The connectors are gone now and all we can see are some of the isolated hillocks.

> Probably a cardinal objective of the Maya architect was to achieve differentiation by height, in many levels, marking the rank of the vague functions to which the edifices were dedicated. At the same time he was always extremely sensitive to the spaces engendered between and among edifices seeking to achieve large and rhythmically ordered open volumes. Such open volumes with storeyed changes of level are the most striking formal achievements of Maya architectural history.[59]

The Maya then habitually thought of groups of platforms and buildings rather than single and isolated units.

If the Mayas did think this way, it becomes apparent to the layman only when he looks at models of reconstructions. The sites themselves, even Chichen Itzá and Uxmal, do not give this impression unaided by non-visual knowledge. They are much less effective this way than the great layouts of the Mexican Plateau, Teotihuacán, or Monte Albán. On the other hand they are much more picturesque and much richer in diversionary detail. Yet the idea of the space designs suggested by Kubler is a very important one, only beginning to be taken seriously again by architects after a long drought of overconcern with the individual building, the individual corporate image, the individual architect's personality.

We cannot examine all the excavated Mayan cities in the detail they deserve, and it is tempting to move at once to Uxmal and let it go at that. I will simply list here Piedras Negras, Quirigua, and Uaxactún, which are hard to reach and only of specialized interest when you do reach them. Palenque, though most noted for its sculpture, perhaps best of all the Mayan, has several very interesting buildings, particularly the enormous stairway and ten-tiered corbeled vaults of the Temple of the Inscriptions, the unique tower of the palace, and the remarkable interior of the Temple of the Sun.

But there are special features of Copán and Tíkal which even a cursory account should not ignore.

[59] Kubler, *Art and Architecture of Ancient America*, op. cit., p. 123.

At Copán as a special feature you would find a primary platform, quite properly called an acropolis, covering about 12 acres and overlying an earlier village cluster of dwellings. This platform supports many secondary platforms merging in a fairly continuous spatial design of many courts on the level flood plain of the Copán river. It is a city which turned its back on the river, so to speak, building an artificial hill 100 feet or so high on the bank, much of which has been washed away by the river including the grand stairway which once formed the western bank. J. E. Thompson has called Copán the Athens, and S. G. Morley, the Alexandria, of the Maya world. Neither may be very appropriate, though it does appear to have been the scientific center of the Old Empire. The valley is a beautiful one, the hills covered with vegetation, the climate temperate and salubrious. On the acropolis are five or more plazas or courts, pyramids, the important Stairway of the Hieroglyphs, where the face of each stair is carved with an individual glyph and at the middle of every twelfth step there is the heroic figure of a brilliantly garbed anthropomorph. On some of the shorter stairs there are jaguars whose bodies are encrusted with discs of obsidian. There are also the Stairway of the Jaguars and the Temple of the Inscriptions. Though there are many excellent sculptural details, Copán is most impressive when regarded as an assembly of open volumetric spaces rather than as a collection of buildings. The large concourse platforms are studded with sculptures standing at many levels, all of which I leave you to discover for yourself, along with the greenness of the local tufa, of which so much of the enterprise was built.

Pl. 123

Tíkal was probably the largest Maya center, and here the evidence is a little clearer that it was in fact a city and that its planned center was surrounded by houses of different orders. The hills at Tíkal are very noticeable—the higher natural ones of the background wooded in dark greens, the artificial ones on the edges of the ravines covered with lush grass of a lighter green. It is certainly one of the most picturesque Meso-American sights, with the grass of the wild often running over and covering the stairways. Nine groups of courts and palaces are separated by ravines but were once connected by causeways and ramps. The pyramids are higher than in most other Mayan places—they are abnormally steep and their single main stairs are hard to traverse, while the steep angles of the sides and rear are unusually forbidding.

> The pyramids at Tíkal in Guatemala are more than twenty storys high;
> today still they emerge from the towering jungle like islands lost in a
> green sea. They are made of rock with earth filling the interstices and faced
> with limestone blocks beautifully cut and set with lime. Sometimes
> stone blocks were used in true masonry style in the Petén, whereas in the
> Peninsula a veneer set in stucco is more usual. But Tíkal and its like
> are exceptions; in most Maya monuments refinement is put before size.[60]

[60] Bernal, *Ancient Mexico in Color*, op. cit., pp. 57–58.

This brings us to what many think to be the masterpiece of Maya architecture, the last of the uncontaminated late classic style, the city of Uxmal in Yucatan. It is, however, more a masterpiece of individual buildings than of urban layout.

I am not alone in selecting Uxmal as my favorite. Morley places it as the veritable center of the Mayan architectural renaissance.[61] Kubler calls it the most beautiful of all Maya cities but adds that it is also "the least typical, having like most masterpieces transcendent properties and qualities."[62]

Located in a large valley formed by the last edges of the Petén Hills, the area is still partly forest-covered. It was probably first occupied at the end of the seventh century, although the far from complete diggings have not, up to now, unearthed any preclassic remains. Whether or not it was refounded by the Xiu, a Mexican-Mayan tribe which invaded Yucatan at the end of the tenth century, as Rivet contends,[63] it certainly had its great development in the tenth century and so is almost without exception classic Maya. In the third period, the second apogee of Chichen Itzá, when the Toltecs came there from the Mexican plateau, Uxmal may never have had a Toltec occupancy at all. In any event the architecture is pure Maya.[64]

Uxmal is easily reached in a little over an hour by automobile from Merida and there are comfortable accommodations in both places. As it now stands, the site occupies about one-half mile north to south and 700 yards east to west, but a few scattered remains lie outside this zone, chiefly to the south. A plan conjectures what it may have been like about A.D. 1000. It appears that even then, although the main buildings did have rectangular plazas, there was very little overall planning, and certainly what there was was much less systematic and regular than the layouts of Teotihuacán or Monte Albán. This is much more evident when so many of the buildings are in bad repair. The great pyramid, for example, between the House of the Governor and the Dove Cote is only a mound covered with rubble. The Dove Cote itself still awaits research and possible restoration. This is also true of the Cemetery Group, the Pyramid of the Old Woman, and the North Group, all still unexcavated, which may have been of great importance. The Ball Court, between the Nunnery and the terrace of the Governor's Palace, was probably never as important as the great one at Chichen Itzá, and even if it was, is quite unimpressive now. Indeed there are only four structures which are likely to say much to the modern visitor

[61] Sylvanus Morley in Rivet, *Cités Maya*, op. cit. It is more nearly the culmination or even the end.

[62] Kubler, *Art and Architecture of Ancient America*, op. cit., pp. 147–148.

[63] Rivet, *Cités Maya*, op. cit., p. 66.

[64] People who find pleasure in early accounts of visitors will perhaps enjoy a book with interesting steel engravings first published in 1841: John L. Stephens, *Incidents of Travel in Central America, Chiapas and Yucatan* (1841) and *Incidents of Travel in Yucatan*. Steel engravings by F. Catherwood. [Republished with introduction and notes by Victor Wolfgang von Hagen (Norman, Okla.: University of Oklahoma Press, 1962.)]

236   *Bernini Is Dead?*

who is not an archeologist. But they are more than enough to make a visit to Uxmal highly rewarding. They are the Pyramid of the Magician, the Nunnery, the House of the Governor, and to a less degree the House of the Turtles. Let us look at them in that order.

If you keep your eyes open at all at Uxmal, you will soon be aware that you are encountering two quite different styles. The dominant one is called Puuc. The name derives from a word which means "land of low hills"—specifically, the limestone plateau of Yucatan, where Uxmal and a number of other great Puuc exemplars nearby such as Labná, Sayil, and Kabáh are located. There are several characteristics of this style which will complicate our story too much to mention, but the main feature of Puuc is to make a lower story of plain smooth walls with skillful arrangements of doors, windows, short porticos, and to surmount this by a highly decorated frieze of the same or even greater dimensions. Between the wall and the impressive ornamented band is a wide molding girdling the building, called by Mexican writers *moldura de atadura* or binder molding, which may repeat itself at the top in the form of a cornice. Some scholars, like Stierlin, find that these borders to the frieze derive from the linking cords which were used to strengthen the walls of the common thatched huts. If this is true, it is another translation of construction in other materials into stone vestiges like the triglyphs and the dentils of the Greeks.

The motifs used by the Puuc sculptors for the decoration of the friezes were many. A favorite looks like a row of contiguous engaged balusters deriving possibly from logs placed upright, side by side, and lashed together. At Uxmal it can be seen in parts of the Nunnery and on the House of the Turtles.

Greek fret patterns symbolizing serpents and crosspieces of stone in the shape of Saint Andrew's crosses are also common.

But the most important form derives from the snoutlike nose and the abstract eyes and ears of Chac. This type of ornament was in fact highly stylized and appears in the other style, the Rio Bec or the Chenes. But in the latter the ornament covers the entire facade; in Puuc work, it is usually limited to the frieze. An exception is the Codz-Pop at Kabáh, where the all-invading decoration of the Puuc style has taken possession of the whole wall and thus seems like an example of the Chenes style. But the sole *authentic* example of the Chenes at Uxmal is the temple at the base of the Pyramid of the Magician, where the whole facade represents a great mask of the rain god whose mouth serves as an entrance.

Interesting as the Chenes always is, the Puuc is more sophisticated. These builders found a way to face rubble cores with veneers of thin squares of carefully cut stone. They emerged from the heavy piers of the south to square or even round columns offering more graceful entrances. Stucco was abandoned for the geometric designs of carved stones, which were not carved *in situ* but were assembled like mosaics or tiles on the friezes.

This was done with consummate skill and a kind of mass production. On the Governor's Palace at Uxmal, for example, there are some 7,500 square feet of frieze made up of stones from 8 inches to 2 feet long. There are 150 masks of Chac, each no more than 3 feet wide and a little over 2 feet high. The Greek fretlike patterns symbolizing the serpents have forty elements each. The masks of Chac have 300 eyes, 300 horns, 300 probosci, and 300 ears each formed of two blocks, making 600 pieces. In the whole composition there are more than 20,000 pieces, which have been fitted with great accuracy. An error of more than 1/3 inch per element would not have permitted the frieze to continue, while the relief decorations of the Saint Andrew's crosses based on vertical unstaggered joints[65] could have tolerated only tiny errors without disastrous results for the distribution and the proportion.

Pl. 125
When you come to Uxmal, probably the first thing to catch your eye will be the Pyramid of the Magician. It is not the most beautiful thing at Uxmal; it is not the handsomest pyramid to be seen in Meso-America, and it is not even a typical one. But it does boast a spectacularly steep stair on the west face, it is a mine of pyramidal historical development, it has an excellent example of the decoration of a Chenes style temple, and a romantic legend available in all the local literature gives it its name.

The pyramid is not typical, rising from a base which is roughly elliptical rather than the normal square or rectangle. It has a pronounced tilt to the west due partly to collapses and more to a series of rebuildings or rather additions.

The piling up of one pyramid and temple on a previous pyramid and temple was a common practice. The Pyramid of the Magician has five such stages, most of which can be seen with a little effort (climbing the western stairs, and especially descending them, is no joke); and hence it is an historical mine.

At the very bottom on the west you can see the remains of the facade of a base temple. It was once admirably decorated. There were blank sections which alternated with a group of three columns; the frieze was embellished above the doorways with great masks of Chac, and feathers; the architrave has a variety of reliefs, frets, interlacings, human figures, drums, astronomical signs, and what may be the spine of a serpent. You can see two excellently preserved masks of Chac over the central door— but the beautiful piece of sculpture called The Queen of Uxmal has been taken away, and you must now view it at the National Museum of Anthropology in Mexico City. It is a conventionalized head of a snake, from the mouth of which emerges the head of a priest with tattooed cheeks.

In due course the inner rooms of the temple were filled in with rubble

[65] Staggered joints would have required two types of blocks instead of one, i.e., a cross and a diamond, plus half blocks of each type to permit an overall appearance of crosses.

in the building of a second pyramid which reached as far as the first landing of the present staircase. On this, later, three more temples were built. The first of these at the east (Temple II) is now covered by the later pyramid, but you can reach its interior central chamber through a passage made during excavation. The original stairs to this lie under the present eastern stairs.

You cannot see Temple III at all. It was attached to the wall of the rear facade. The last of the temples at this level, Temple IV, is the most interesting of this group, for it is in the Chenes style and its whole facade is decorated. Although the rest of the temple is covered over by the later pyramid, the facade can still be seen. It is reached by the steep western stair, and here you will see the entire facade as a great mask of the rain god whose mouth is the entrance.

Finally the pyramid was carried over these temples to a new platform about 90 feet above ground. This temple could be reached from the west by the steep stairway and on narrower stairs flanking the Chenes Temple or by a more negotiable stairway from the east. I doubt if you will find the single row of rooms or the remnants of the decoration worth the climb.

From the platform of the Chenes Temple, though, you can get a good look down into the courtyard of the so-called Nunnery, one of the three important well-excavated installations at Uxmal.

Down at the south end of the main area are the ruins of what may have been one of the most important buildings at Uxmal but which is now so ruined and so little studied as yet that only those who want to be exhaustive will view it, save from afar. It is called the Pigeon Group or Dove Cote, but the name has nothing to do with its use, which is unknown.[66]

The Dove Cote belongs to a family of amphitheater courts such as we have noted at Monte Albán. At Uxmal there were barrier mounds on three sides and the fourth side had a stairway pyramid not unlike a stage. Almost none of this is now to be seen, save dimly. The most visible remain is a wall pierced by a corbeled arch somewhat rounded into a parabolic appearance and surmounted by a crest of nine triangular sections, each pierced by openings which may once have had sculptures embedded in them. It is these openings, reminiscent of a dove cote, which led to its present name.

Though evidently more complex than the Nunnery to which it has some similarity, the Dove Cote is presumably older and the Nunnery is surely an improved and more refined building, or rather group of buildings.   *Pl. 124*

---

[66] The problem of misleading names is one we must get used to on ancient sites. The Pyramid of the Magician at Uxmal did not necessarily involve a magician; the Nunnery had almost certainly nothing to do with nuns; the Governor's Palace was certainly not a palace as we conceive one and may not have related to a governor at all.

The more scientific way would have been merely to number or letter the buildings so that the titles would imply nothing about function. But names are easier for most people to remember than Roman numerals, and they do no harm so long as they do not give rise to imputed incorrect meanings.

The group lies just to the west of the Pyramid of the Magician, to which it may have had some functional connection, but the main entrance was from the south up a monumental stairway to reach a platform from which the enclosing buildings rose at various levels from platforms of various heights. The exterior facades were treated with some care, but those which front the enclosure were far more carefully designed and more lavishly decorated.

The south building is pierced at the center by a great corbeled arch on the axis of the ball court to the south, smoothed roughly to a parabolic shape, and through this we pass into the quadrangle, which is about 215 feet by 150 feet, but by no means close to being rectangular. The Mayans could have laid out a true rectangle had they chosen to; why they chose not to, we do not know.

The entrance stairway which once spanned the whole south facade is now badly destroyed, and most visitors will find it easier to make a nontriumphal entrance into the Great Court by sidling in at some corner.

But however you approach it, you are bound to find this court both beautiful and impressive, a real testimony to the architectural skill and sensitivity of the Maya, as to proportion, as to rhythm, and as to how to use detail.

Was it a palace group, a set of institutional dwellings, or merely a concourse center with surrounding chambers for official ceremonies and for storage? Or was it indeed somehow related to Maya priestesses of which the Conquistadores claimed to have found some tradition? Or was it called the Nunnery by the Conquistadores because it reminded them somewhat of the convents of Spain? You can choose what you like, and probably find some scholarly support for your favorite view.

In any case, after you have engaged yourself with the general spatial arrangements, you should begin to become engaged with the details.

The south or front building lies at a lower level than the others. You will notice that, unlike any of the other buildings, *each* of the chambers here does have direct access to the outdoors, so that half of them open on to the south side and the other half on to the patio. I hope you will notice that the facade doorways are variably spaced; the widest spacings are at the center and they diminish toward the corners. This is an architectural refinement of a considerable and deliberate order—it is missing on the important north building but fully developed on the west building and tentatively at the east. It was not invented at Uxmal, for there is an antecedent on the palace facades of Palenque, but it is well treated here and is only one of many subleties we shall discover.

The frieze of the south building, arranged as on all the buildings here in the Puuc style, that is, atop a plain first-story wall, is simply decorated. There is a general background of the Saint Andrew's crosses, which may or may not be vestiges in stone of the mats used in decoration on earlier buildings of wood and thatch. Emerging from the background over every doorway is a hut in stone very like huts still to be seen in the countryside, and above the hut is a mask of the rain god.

Had you entered the court by the great corbeled archway, you would have been facing the most impressive and majestic of the buildings, the one to the north.

The north building is the highest, built on a platform over 300 feet long and nearly 25 feet high. The great stairway which leads up to it is 100 feet wide. It is flanked at grade at the left by a curious structure not repeated at the right because of the limitations in symmetry imposed by the angle of the flanking buildings.

Pl. 124

The larger of the two first-story arrangements, the one to the west, is called the Temple of Venus, supposedly because a motif of the frieze has been construed to refer to that planet, but it is more likely that the motif was only a simplified mask of the rain god.

The decoration of the Puuc frieze calls for special attention. It runs along the whole building. But over every other one of the eleven doors huge masks extend higher. They are superimposed faces of Chac. Over the other doors there are thatched huts surmounted by two-headed snakes. Steep frets and Saint Andrew's crosses fill other spaces.

Here again you may notice a subtlety. The facades lean outward slightly, which results in a visual correction of what would otherwise be overly long horizontals. You can notice something else, which may or may not have been deliberate. The western and eastern buildings converge toward the north building, and the stair is wider at the top than at the bottom. These devices provide an optical illusion of scale through forcing the perspective. They were well known to Michelangelo, who used them powerfully in his designs for the Campidoglio in Rome. But whether the Mayas were up to this or the result was one of carelessness or accident, you will have to decide.

I find the Temple of Venus to be a jarring note. It has a four-pillared portico, a device used elsewhere much more skillfully, as, for example, in the "Palace" at nearby Sayil, where the porticos, each two-columned, with more refined piers, run across the whole facade at the first terrace level. There is the beginning of a suggestion of trabeated architecture here, but only a suggestion. It was never carried much farther than Sayil among the Maya.

Pl. 126

The west building has a remarkable frieze which should engage your interest. And though the east building is the smallest and simplest, you should examine the three masks of Chac which are carved at the corners and above the central doorway. These are a genuinely elegant version of the superimposed masks, especially when seen in profile. And they will serve you well to remember when you later go to the Codz-Pop at Kabáh and find the masks used too profusely. They afford another affirmation, this time with respect to architectural sculpture, of the famous statement of Mies van der Rohe: "Less is more."

The Architecture of Stone 241

Pl. 127

You come to the climax of a visit to Uxmal by going to the Governor's Palace. It really is imposing architecture, standing on a great platform with three levels connected by stairways. It is a much longer building than it is high, and might indeed seem too long had the architect not so skillfully divided it into two side pavilions and a wider section by corbeled roofed hallways which originally went all the way through the building. The steepness of the corbels, which offer the highest vaults known in the Maya world, and the strict geometry, which kept the profile straight-edged instead of curved, offer a note of such emphasis as to bring the whole facade into striking harmony and repose. If you look more carefully, you will note that the architect recessed the arch behind the facade, an important contribution in accentuating the separation of the three pavilions. You will also, if you choose, be able to count out overlapping and contrapuntal rhythms. The doorways are 2-7-2, the stairway 3-5-3, the mosaic decorations in the frieze 5-3-5; and the elegant frieze has several levels of rhythmic order. All told, this building is essentially without architectural flaw. It is not only the finest building we know the Maya to have produced, it is the finest building of pre-Hispanic Meso-America, and I am myself not prepared to say that it has been outdone by any other architectural design of the Western Hemisphere, past or present.

It is hard to leave Uxmal, and though anything else there is anticlimatic after the Governor's Palace, you should pause briefly at the House of Turtles on the northwest corner of the first terrace of the Governor's Palace. It is badly damaged but, again, shows a remarkably classic simplicity. It has a frieze made only of a row of small columns between cornice and architrave with turtles carved in the cornice; it also exhibits excellent workmanship, balanced proportions, and the same elegant sobriety to be noted in the Governor's Palace.

While you are at Uxmal, it would be a pity not to drive a few miles farther to Kabáh—both for the fantastic Codz-Pop crawling with rain gods to which I have already referred and for its Maya gateway; to Sayil, whose "Palace," despite the bad state of its preservation, was one of the great achievements of the Mayan architects; and to Labná, for the enormous roof comb of the Palace and its monumental archway. All of these cities were in the best Puuc tradition. All seem to have been abandoned before the arrival of the Toltecs, who so much changed Chichen Itzá.

In practice you will probably now visit Chichen Itzá, which is in the same vicinity, if indeed you have not unhappily visited it even before you came to Uxmal. But if you are pursuing a chronological line relentlessly to the end, you must first detour back to the central Mexican Plateau and Tula, the legendary capital of Quetzlcoatl. Much smaller, much less grand than Teotihuacán, it is sloppily built, probably due to the nature of its Toltec builders, who were more militaristic, less priestly. It is most interesting for its large porticos, its many ball courts, and especially its powerful Atlantean columns. Their sculpture was vigorous, and attentive to dress, to adornment, to weapons, to postures.

Their square faces, solemn and empty, suggest the hardness of the warrior on the night of victory. Their strong bodies and short legs have the rigidity and arrogance of the soldier who combines religious fervour with his profession.[67]

The most spectacular building at Tula was no doubt the great temple of Tlahuizcalpantecuhtli; it stood on a pyramid base, but four Atlantean warrior columns are now almost all that remains of the many which supported the roof of the temple. Each had four sections of tenoned drums beautifully fitted. They are all alike: a head with crown adorned with beads and feathers; a chest with a breastplate in the shape of a butterfly; a knotted belt, short sturdy legs. The right hands carry a spear thrower and the left a bundle of darts. Each stands nearly 40 feet high.

Pl. 131

In all these wrappings the knots and binders are portrayed with loving military care; the rear view is like an examplar of the knot-maker's art. . . . The fourfold repetition conveys the effect of a frightening palace guard.[68]

The plan of the temple suggests that here indeed there was a suspicion of trabeated architecture, a temple *cella* supported on columns and pilasters, and with a roof which has disappeared. The Atlantean figures are in fact like caryatids, but how different in style and intent from those of the Erechtheion!

If you go to Tula, you will naturally also visit the Coatepantli, or Wall of Serpents, with its interesting and often macabre relief. But let us not pause or longer delay our farewell to Meso-America to be paid at Chichen Itzá.

Chichen Itzá lies about 75 miles or two hours' drive east of Merida. Though its Mayan part is inferior in quality to Uxmal and its Toltec part is less vigorous than Tula, it is probably the most visited of any of the Mexican sites. It was opened up rather early (1923) by joint efforts of the Carnegie Institution of Washington and the Mexican government, which has engaged in extensive exploration, research, and restoration. It has been much publicized. It does contain a variety of historical samples and offers more buildings and more contrast than the other sites, plus romantic things like the great *cenote* or sacrificial well.

Chichen was an important town in the classic Mayan period, possibly even more important than a mere ceremonial center. During this period a number of still extant buildings were made in the pure Puuc style. Certainly one should visit them if he is there, but they are clearly inferior to the great creations of Uxmal or Sayil, and I shall say nothing about them.

At about the tenth century, the Toltecs began to filter down from Tula and brought with them their characteristic architecture and sculpture, porches and galleries of colonnades, pillars in the form of feathered ser-

---

[67] Bernal, *Ancient Mexico in Colour*, op. cit., p. 103.
[68] Kubler, *Art and Architecture of Ancient America*, op. cit., p. 46.

Pl. 129

pents, merlons on the roof, Atlantean sculpture, the distinctive Chac Mool sculpture, intertwined serpents on the balustrades, reliefs of tigers and eagles eating hearts, platforms embellished with skulls, much-enlarged ball courts, an array of Mexican deities, all of which are very noticeable at Chichen Itzá although sometimes watered down from their Mexican ferocity by Mayan memories.

If you examine a map of Chichen Itzá as it was at about the time of the collapse of the Mayapan hegemony, you will see that the Toltec remains lie largely to the north, and the classic Mayan buildings largely to the south.[69]

Of the Toltec remnants, the Ball Court, the Temple of the Jaguars, one or two of the platforms, the Temple of the Warriors, the Market, and the Castillo are the most interesting. Let us examine them in that order and not worry here about which came first and which last in the brief period of Toltec supremacy and prosperity, although the Ball Court is probably the latest and surely built after the Temple of the Warriors.

The Ball Court is truly remarkable and not typical. It is much the largest of any yet discovered, shaped (typically) like a capital I, flanked on the long sides by platforms with outwardly opening stairways. There are temples at each end, and the Temple of the Bearded Man has interesting sculptures relating to human sacrifice and fertility rites. The walls of the Ball Court are embellished with strong low reliefs, of which the strongest shows one player holding in one hand a stone knife and the other the head of the player he has decapitated. Streams of blood flow from the neck of the beheaded one, the side streams turning into snakes; the central one, into the stem of a plant which bears flowers and fruit.

Pl. 130

On the south corner of the eastern platform rising from its own foundation is the dramatic Temple of the Jaguars, the main facade facing the Ball Court. This building is a remarkable combination of traditional Mayan architecture, in its corbeled arches and the general lines of the facade, and Toltec elements, in particular a frieze of shields and walking tigers and most notably the dramatic entrance portico. The lintel is supported by two massive columns shaped like snakes whose heads squat out onto the floor, whose bodies are the columns, and whose tails fully equipped with rattles and plumes support the architrave. They are irresistibly dramatic but overly heavy so far as strictly architectural purposes are concerned and almost the converse of a statement as to what a column should be. But this is a case where Quetzalcoatl is more important than a column.

You can go around the end of the temple and descend a steep narrow stair to the east and thus see the temple in a quite different light—a temple at the base, with a portico divided into three parts by pillars decorated with

[69] The Caracol or Observatory is a curiosity standing in between. Its interest lies mainly in its shape, hence its name, Caracol (snail), and in notions of how it may have been used for astronomical observations or at least orientations. Architecturally it is far from being a masterpiece.

reliefs of the rain god. In the central opening is a jaguar-shaped throne, and inside splendid bas-reliefs in four tiers. Above this rises the truncated pyramid on which the upper temple stands.

Down in the area to which we have now descended, there are several small structures called temples but which are in reality platforms designed for open-air ceremonies and reached by stairs on all four sides, quite like the smaller platforms at Teotihuacán but extensively decorated. The platform of the eagles has plaques in low relief showing eagles and jaguars eating hearts, while snakes ascend the low balustrades of the stairs and thrust their heads out aggressively from the top.

The platform of the skulls (Tzompantli) has reliefs which represent skulls placed on poles, but here and there too are heart-devouring eagles, warriors, and feathered serpents.

Beyond these lies El Castillo, the pyramid (see Plate 119), the most prominent structure of Chichen Itzá. It was certainly not a castle, but a temple. It has been well though only partially restored. There are nine stepped sections, skillfully projecting stairs, the number of whose steps is ritualistic. The main stair baluster ends in snakes' heads at the ground. Within what you see is the older structure on which the new pyramid was characteristically built. It is possible to reach this through a tunnel and see a jaguar-shaped throne painted red, the spots designated by discs of jade.

The Temple of the Warriors and the adjacent market patios I found confusing at the time and hard to remember now. The temple is large, standing on a clumsy pyramid of several ill-proportioned steps, adorned with a Chac Mool statue, with some of the serpent columns such as seen at *Pl. 129* the Temple of the Jaguars and with serpent-bearing balusters. But the important thing is the large colonnade which stands at the facade facing El Castillo and runs over to join with the market. What this shows clearly enough is that by this time trabeated architecture had become part of the vocabulary of Meso-America. But there are better examples of it elsewhere, and it is to them we should turn.

Certainly we come away from Chichen Itzá with impressions of savagery far different from those gained from Teotihuacán, Monte Albán, or the earlier Mayan cities. It does seem somehow to reek of blood in a way we do not like to think of blood. Some of this may be due to the very uncompromising power of the architectural form. But more I think is due to the explicit statements of the iconography, the devouring eagles and jaguars, the sacrificial games, the blood changing into serpents and vines before our very eyes, the militant and severe postures of the men, the parades of skulls. Even the serpents seem more menacing than the abstractions of Uxmal, the plumed serpent more ferocious than the elephant-nosed Chac. It is a far cry from the pastoral or marsh scenes of Egypt; the array of animal-headed Egyptian gods where even the jackal Anubis carries himself well; the gay court dances of Crete; the dignity of the Olympians; the stoic integrity of the Roman death masks; even the crawling eroticism of India. Its nearest parallel may be from our times—Picasso's *Guernica*. Architecture and art do not tell all there is to know about a people; like words, as Voltaire said, they may conceal thought. So when we go to Chichen Itzá, we might better leave our morality behind, or if it insists on coming along, let us use it as a reminder to reflect on our own morality, not on that of the Toltecs, who have no more chance to atone for whatever wrong they did.

I have dealt so extensively with the Meso-American bill of fare for two reasons: one, to make some amends for what I think has been too much neglect in too many of the books; the other, to show how far you must be prepared to range if you become enamored of an architectural style, even one so limited in geography as this one. To have done this with one of the more familiar styles would have been quite impossible because of the plethora of essential examples.

MYCENAE—THE CORBEL REVISITED

Mycenae and its ill-fated House of Atreus bear a close relation to the historical development of Attica, but only a faint one to its architectural development. Architecturally it represents, in its *tholoi* or tombs, a high achievement in corbeled, rather than trabeated, architecture. Unlike the corbels previously described, however, these are not lintels or vaults but beehive domes.

The idea of edging stone into space, so to speak, never appeared in more refined form than in the passageways of the Governor's Palace at Uxmal, but there was another way to use it quite different from this or from the corridors of the Sumerians, the monumental grand gallery of the Pyramid of Cheops, or the smoothed corbel vault of Hatshepsut's Hathor Chapel.

Pl. 128

It is difficult to disentangle the fame of the Lion Gate at Mycenae (really a lioness gate) or the nearby *tholoi*, such as the "Treasury of Atreus," or the "Tombs of Clytemnestra and Aegisthus" from the names of the famous Homeric and Aeschylean characters who lived there. These remains were unearthed by Europeans steeped, as too many of us today unhappily are not, in the *Iliad* and the *Oresteiad*. The fame of Mycenae, of Agamemnon, of Clytemnestra, Aegisthus, Cassandra, Orestes, Electra was quick in their memories. When people like Schliemann or his wife came by, they naturally enough applied what they thought were suitable names, backed somewhat by the unscholarly claims of Pausanias. Thus the "Treasury of Atreus," or Agamemnon, is now dated back to about 1330 B.C., several hundred years before Agamemnon; the "Tomb of Aegisthus" is probably as old as 1500 B.C.; and that of Clytemnestra goes back to the thirteenth or fourteenth century B.C. So, though these tombs were probably those of monarchs of Mycenae, they cannot be properly given the luster of the Homeric literary association and must stand on their own architectural feet.

Similar care has to be exercised about the Acropolis of Mycenae and its gates. Obviously there were Pelopidae at Mycenae before Agamemnon, else we should not have had the bloody rivalry of Atreus and Thyestes, the sons of Pelops, and the long succession of family-blood crimes which culminated and ended with Orestes. If we stand on the Acropolis of Mycenae and peer toward the sea and try to imagine ourselves as Clytemnestra might have stood watching the beacon's light from island top to island top proclaiming the return from Troy, we may be indulging in a harmless and even entertaining reverie-lie, but we are not looking at architecture. Indeed there are very few occasions in all architectural history where this marriage of myth and literary license adds much to truth.

So when we are at Mycenae, it may be as well to send all the Homeric shades away and to look at the monuments as the product of the unidentified brave men who came before Agamemnon.

The gate itself has an impressive approach. An ascending ramp, 30 feet wide, climbs 48 feet, passes by heavy walls, so that the gate is at the end of a deep court. The lintel, covering a clear span of 9 feet, is an enormous monolith, 16½ feet long, 8 feet thick, and 3½ feet high at the middle. It weighs about 35 tons. Dinsmoor[70] thinks that it was surely strong enough to carry any weight likely to be imposed upon it, but that the corbeled triangular arch which relieves the load on the lintel was used here as a consequence either of caution or mere custom. In any event the opening provided by the corbel was then filled with a limestone slab 12 feet wide and at present 10 feet high. This was carved with an heraldic religious composition in which a central sacred pillar represents the protecting divinity.

Pl. 86

It would not be hard to seem to take in this pillar at a glance, but to anyone who cares about architectural history it should have surprising significance. It stands on what might be a pedestal, a plinth, or an altar. The shaft tapers downward like the columns of Crete and this taper is deliberate, not the consequence of erosion. The column meets the slab directly without the intervention of a base. It does have a capital, though, which has an echinus and an abacus clearly foreshadowing the Doric capital, and it is surmounted by what looks like a fragment of entablature. This has an ornament like that over the tomb doorways which is reminiscent of and may be derived from the log ceilings of primitive houses, as we have seen before in Egypt and in Mayaland.

The panel, because of its material and because of the technical skill of its modeling, is believed to be not earlier than 1250 B.C. and thus con-

[70] William Bell Dinsmoor, *The Architecture of Ancient Greece*, 3d ed. (London: Batsford, 1950).

The Architecture of Stone 247

siderably later than the cyclopean fortification walls, to be seen even more impressively at Tiryns (24 to 57 feet thick) where the masonry can be compared with that of Peru. Thus we have at the Lion Gate, in the midst of a corbeled architecture, an early intimation of a very different approach, the trabeate (see Plate 86).

Around 1500 B.C. a three-dimensional application of the corbel developed in some parts of the Aegean—to some extent in Crete but more frequently on the mainland as far north as Thessaly and particularly in the Peloponnesus with the best presently known examples around Mycenae and Argos. These were the conical or beehive domed tomb chambers known as *tholoi*. They were not true domes but instead an application of the corbel principle into an essentially conical form. Though they had no important future in architectural history, they are interesting to visit.

It was the tomb chamber itself which was new. As in other parts of the world, there had been vast numbers of chambered tombs throughout the Aegean. They were usually carved out of soft stone or in hard-pan underlying rock ledges on a convenient hillside. They were reached by a narrow artificial passage, the *dromos*, which was sometimes horizontal but usually sloped downward, sometimes so steeply as to require steps. Instead of cutting the side walls so that the escarpment diverged as one neared the surface, these walls usually leaned toward each other, and if the *dromos* were narrow, they might come so close as to leave only a slit at the top. The *dromos* ended in an entrance doorway cut out of the rock so that its jambs inclined inward to support a horizontal or arched top. The door led to the tomb chamber, sometimes irregular in plan, more often roughly oval or rectangular. Sometimes there was an additional smaller room off the main chamber. Between burials the doors were filled with rubble walls and the *dromos* backfilled with earth. In time the walls of the *dromos* were also covered with stone, increasingly well worked, and the door frames might be stuccoed and painted in stripes, wave patterns, running spirals, and the like, while at least the appearance of a lintel-relieving corbel over the doorway was preserved in paint.

But the important thing to us here is what happened inside the royal tombs. These were no longer cut out of the rock but were lined with masonry. To do this a well of the desired diameter was dug adjacent to the *dromos*. Within it a pointed "dome" (corbel) was built up in projecting horizontal courses backfilled as it rose to provide countervailing weight. The conical or near conical form was more practical than a hemispherical one, just as the triangular corbeled "arch" was more practical than the parabolic since, in the latter, the inward curvatures called for an ever-increasing amount of cantilevering as the apex was reached if the same thickness of coursing were to be preserved. The top of the structure projected slightly above grade and was then covered with a slight artificial tumulus. It is true, of course, that the generally circular plan of the *tholos* preserved the most primitive form of dwelling, the circular hut, but there were also good technical reasons for the shape. If a rectangular or square plan had been used, the resulting pyramidal form would have more quickly reduced the headroom; if an effort were made to have the conical dome form "spring" from the walls at a higher point, another invention, such as the pendentive, would have been required to supply the transition from the orthogonal to the circular plan, and although this was used in the much later *trulli* of southern Italy,[71] it either did not occur to the Mycenaeans or was not thought necessary.

Pl. 134

Over the two or three hundred years of this development, there were characteristic improvements but very little change in the matter of size. The rubble wall entrance was replaced by actual doors standing on a stone threshold. The decoration, though remaining conventional, was refined. The side walls of the *dromos* were lined with ashlar. By 1350 B.C. there was great technical skill at all points. The ashlar masonry was made of hard breccia blocks, often very large, but now precisely sawn.

The largest, most representative, and best-preserved of the *tholoi* is the already-mentioned Tomb of Agamemnon, or Treasury of Atreus at Mycenae, and it dates from about 1325 B.C. It is approached by an essentially level *dromos*, 21 feet high and 115 feet long, so that as it penetrates into the hill, the ashlar walls rise to a height of 45 feet. These walls are 7 to 10 feet thick and behind them is a thick wall of yellow mud brick to protect the stone from water. The floor of the *dromos* is paved. At the end of the *dromos* we meet a facade 34 feet high with an 18-foot door which is 9 feet wide at the bottom, contracts to 8 feet at the top, and is also inclined inward, making it reminiscent of an Egyptian pylon or a Mayan door frame. The relieving triangle is empty and no longer has its carved slabs— also what might once have been complicated decoration. But today it is hard to visualize this by putting together the now visible forms with memories of the green limestone half-columns (parts of which are now in the British Museum) and relics from other places, and I do not encourage you to try.

Instead go inside for an impressive experience. The dome itself is 47½ feet in diameter and 44 feet high, quite uncemented. Despite the gentle curvature (as compared, for example, with a parabola or hemisphere), the curvature both vertically and horizontally becomes so sharp toward the vertex that the blocks had to be cut to run back at widely divergent angles, thus becoming intensely wedge-shaped and working more like a dome thereby. This you do not see, but there is evidence of the difficulty in that they are not so carefully trimmed for fitting except at the inner face so that the interstices were filled with pieces of stone and clay packing.

Pl. 132

All the stones are chamfered to the shape of the voussoirs, and the conjecture is that this dressing down of the inner face was probably done after construction, as was the hollowing of the capstone on the underside, to continue the anterior curvature to an uninterrupted conclusion. Again

[71] About which see the interesting book by Edward Allen, *Stone Shelters* (Cambridge, Mass.: M.I.T. Press, 1969).

there was probably a good deal of interior decoration. The floor is too broken to know. Here and there are bronze nails indicating the attachment of something, but our problem is the same as in Peru—we have only the literary guidance of Homer to suggest to us.

The extant, the missing, the conjectural decoration is important for scholars seeking to trace the development of Greek columnar architecture, for example, but I think you can forget it and be impressed by the simple majesty and beauty of the stone interior. If you like it, you can visit a few other less notable examples such as the later, less ponderous, possibly more *Pl. 134* refined, but more ruined "Tomb of Clytemnestra." And you can also pursue the conoid stone forms into the more recent days of Alberobello and other parts of the rocky plateaus of Apulia in Italy, where you can see how they looked from the outside as well as the inside often in very picturesque groupings, serving now as houses for the living rather than the dead.[72] They have great visual similarity to the cone-shaped village of the Camerouns where the construction materials were entirely different.

But whatever charms it might offer, the corbel had no serious architectural future—it simply could not stretch far enough.

Though arts are not entirely evolutionary, there are trends, at least over long periods. One of the surest trends in architecture has been a constant pressure to be freed from the limitations of the wall. The wall originally had two functions, one of closure, the other of support. But the exigencies of support controlled the freedom of closure—where it had to be and what it should be when there. If the necessities for the wall as structure could be reduced or even eliminated, then the wall as closure might or might not be invoked as the occasion demanded.

This effort to free the design through freeing the structure has gone on with ups and downs through much of architectural history and is continued today in many concrete forms as well as in the more exotic dymaxion structures of Buckminster Fuller or the extrapolated "tents" of Frei Otto. But the corbel offered essentially no such promises. The first true promise came with the post-and-lintel or trabeated structure, although the realizations had to be limited so long as the horizontal parts were to be of stone and before spanning by vaults and domes had yet been taken seriously.

POST AND LINTEL—TRABEATE

Post-and-lintel stone buildings are found extensively throughout architecture; to examine them all would be both too exhaustive and too exhausting. I mean to look at only three cases: the Egyptian; the Greek, which is the

[72] Ibid.

greatest; and an interesting variant provided by the Medes and the Persians of Persepolis.

The essence of columnar or post-and-lintel or trabeate architecture is that posts are erected at appropriate intervals and that these are then spanned by beams or girders, a girder being a member which receives the loads of beams intermediate between columns and transmits these loads to the columns. The small examples we have noted, for example in the Mayan buildings, were tentative efforts in this direction in that the wall was opened up briefly to provide, for example, a small porch. But trabeated architecture did not come into full swing until the columns penetrated more deeply into the structure so that some sort of framework emerged, whether made up only of columns and spanning members or of columns, walls, and spanning members. One of the difficulties encountered when the trabeate construction is entirely of stone, we will recall, is that stone cannot carry across very wide spans so that the free space available inside is quite limited. One way to avoid this is to use other types of materials, wood for example, for the horizontal spans, and ancient builders no doubt did this when they wanted to roof fairly large and uninterrupted interior spaces. Another way is to minimize the limitation—possible perhaps if no very large interior space is desired anyway, or if it is immaterial whether the space is frequently interrupted by columns. It is hard for us to put ourselves in such a frame of mind, since we are so used to think of architecture in terms of the *enclosure* of space. So when we encounter such a forest of columns in an antique building we are likely to dismiss it as an undesirable result consequent to the inability of the builders to do otherwise. This is almost certainly an error on our part which, if we insist on retaining it, will cause misunderstanding of the architecture of Egyptian Thebes, Persepolis, and Athens alike. It is an error partly because it underestimates the skill old builders could muster when they thought the occasion demanded it and does not take into account the possibility of quite other choices for quite other reasons than any we might hold.

EGYPT

The Egyptians, for example, knew how to build modest but true barrel vaults of brick as early as the IIId Dynasty and even produced one small dome. In time the barrel vaults were made somewhat larger; but with rare exceptions, such as two halls at Medinet Habu or in the Hathor Chapel in Hatshepsut's mortuary temple at Deir-el-Bahri, they used them primarily for utilitarian structures such as warehouses, or storerooms in temples such as those at the Ramesseum. Since brick was easier to come by than big stones and since the engineering difficulties of transporting the stone at least equaled the craft difficulty of erecting vaults, it is hard to believe that the Egyptian emphasis on trabeation was not at least partly a matter of choice and not solely one of ignorance; for example, by the time the

Pl. 133

Moors built their Great Mosque at Cordova (A.D. 786) with its 1,200 many-colored columns and arches, Islamic architects were perfectly skilled at making vaults and domes and could have done so if they had wanted to. It is dangerously arrogant to look at what people have made in the past and to call it unimaginative or stupid on the assumption that it was not a matter of choice.

The column emerged as a possibility early in Egyptian architecture. There is, for example, the colonnaded processional hall in the Zoser complex, which has already been mentioned. Even more explicit and not much later is the structure of Chephren's Valley Temple, where we see post and beam in its simplest and very impressive form. The posts or piers of monolithic granite rise directly from the ground without any intervening base. They support the beams or architraves with no intervening capitals. And the beams themselves are of the same uncompromising form. Every opening is firm and chiseled. The effect is very powerful, the essence of simplicity, and beautiful as well.

When does a piece of wall become a column? It is a fruitless question. We are trained to think of monolithic columns as rare and to believe that columns are usually made up of drums skillfully imposed on each other and indeed that did become the usual way of making them. We are trained to think that they have bases, shafts, and capitals. But neither of these is essential. The columns of Chephren are true and wonderful columns.

When it came time for the Egyptians to provide drums, to fit them, to design and carve capitals, to embellish the shafts, they showed the same skill in shaping and erecting them as they had shown in building the pyramids or the complex of Zoser.

Indeed the idea of the capital appears as early as the Zoser complex on the east wall of the dummy northern building. The three columns there are engaged, that is, connected to the wall, and not free-standing, almost half-columns emerging like pilasters from the wall. The form of the capital derives from the bell-shaped cup of the papyrus flower, an emblematic plant of Lower Egypt, while the shaft recalls the triangular stem. It is very handsome, this "first capital in stone," as Giedion claims, and it justifies his assertion that it is "imbued with all the freshness and vitality of early spring."

Until the decadent end flower and plant forms dominated the columnar treatments of Egypt. They rose without bases or from simple slabs or drums. Their shafts might be round or faceted but were seldom fluted like the later Doric columns, partly, I suppose, because this was not a natural plant form and partly perhaps because the Egyptians did not like the sharp divisions of light and shade provided by the arrises of the flutes.

The columns were in fact quite close copies of the plants themselves, and were possibly derived from earlier columns of trunks, or bundles of reeds, used to hold up reed or wooden ceilings. A few forms were quite general. The *palmiform* had a circular shaft opening into a palm leaf; the *lotiform* had a ribbed shaft of collected rounded stems opening into a bud which might be either closed or open; the *papyriform* had a shaft which began with triangles where it left the base, and pointed ridges broke the roundness of the ribs. There were variations such as the *monostyle papyriform*, which had no ribs on the shaft or even any capital. Although the forms deriving from the palm, the lotus, and the papyrus with their many variations of degrees of openness of the flower dominated most Egyptian architecture and are certainly the most beautiful the architecture produced, toward the end and during the decadence of the Ptolemaic and Roman periods other forms crept in, either debasing the plant forms or even dispensing altogether with signs of plant origin in favor of Hathor heads or the excesses of the "composite capital."

Sometimes these columns stood alone as a sort of monumental pillar, analogous to the larger and simpler obelisks. But more often they were parts of the structures of a temple. Standing free to the light as ruins now often permit them to do, they are enticing objects viewed as sculpture or as isolated subjects for photography. But we should steel ourselves against this at least in part and try to think of them first as an essential ingredient of an architecture which is unfamiliar to us in purpose even more than in appearance.

The Egyptians, Giedion is convinced both from the pyramids and the temples, were obsessed with the need to create massive volumes placed freely in space, rather than to create massive spaces enclosed by architecture. The corollary of this was to suppress interior space. If a large hall was demanded, it was nonetheless filled with a forest of gigantic columns. This they did at Karnak, and a millennium later the Persians did the same thing in the 100-pillared throne room of Darius at Persepolis. Observers like Giedion or Alois Riegl[73] suggest that the great hypostyle halls of the temples were not interior spaces at all in the later accepted form. At most they were impressive corridors. In the great hypostyle hall at Karnak, for example, 134 colossal papyrus columns seem to fill the entire void, and the effect is strengthened by the fact that the column centers are staggered in alternate rows so that direct passage either by foot or by eye is made almost impossible. At Medinet Habu the bases of the columns have become so large as to almost touch one another.

Pl. 136

> The visual effect of the distant walls, ceiling and floor would have created an impression of space which would certainly have caused the Egyptians the utmost discomfort.[74]

[73] A. Riegl, *Spätrömische Kunstindustrie* (Vienna: Osterreich Staatsdruckerei, 1927), as cited by Sigfried Giedion in *The Eternal Present*, vol. II, *The Beginnings of Architecture*, op. cit., p. 508.
[74] Ibid., p. 508.

Pressed by what Riegl called their "space phobia," the eye was held by the impression of the individual columns.

Naturally this spatial or nonspatial interior had to emerge from or at least support the functions of the temple. It is enough for the moment to remember that a hypostyle hall was not an enclosed space for a congregation of believers like a Christian basilica or an Islamic mosque. It was entered only by the priests and some of the elite of the land who were often themselves priests. It was not a resting place even when it was contributing to the celebration of important rites but more like a corridor through which a god might progress from shrine to shrine. The art did not need to be seen for it was not that kind of art. The exceedingly dim lighting was an asset, not a liability.

When the columns, terminating in buds or flowers, reached the architrave or the ceiling, they were not to be thought of as representing a support scaffolding, since the hypostyle was expected to appear open to the sky, even when roofed.

We need always, as we look at buildings, to look at their natural surroundings as well. Usually, at least in the country but not always even there, these are less despoiled than the buildings. In Egypt the terrain cannot have changed greatly and the principal difference, not a trivial one, is the disappearance of the residential mud huts which probably filled the foreground of many of the important Egyptian buildings.

The scenery is one of sand and sky and sun and uncompromising limestone or sandstone cliffs spread apart by 10 to 30 miles, cliff to cliff; of a canyon or trench, the cool, life-giving river covered with black alluvial deposits and verdure. But most of the life, whether of peasant or temple, rests above it, on the brief plain or against the cliffs themselves.

Temples

Egyptian temple architecture was created for a priesthood which was all-powerful or nearly so. The king had become more and more god. The priest's duties, first those of a local noble as a part-time activity, became full-time, noble themselves. It was a powerful occupation, with the high priest standing next in influence to the king and in moments of royal weakness, being more powerful.

The great temples are clustered around Thebes, not Memphis. The pyramid builders were long gone when the temples were begun. They were built in the feudal society of the late Middle Kingdom under such rulers as the Amenomhets and the Sesostrises, but the big work was done in the Empire from Amenhotep, Thutmose I and II, Hatshepsut, through the momentary aberrations of Akhenaton (*roi du soleil*) to the Ramessids. These last were indeed imperial and all-powerful, especially the kings of the XIXth Dynasty (1350–1150), but this power had long been building and was well expressed both as to its confidences and its fears back around 2000 in the Middle Kingdom when Amenemhet I, probably a usurper, firmly established the Theban hegemony and the classic period of Egypt. The imperial pharaohs who came later did conquer much of the immediate world and made Thebes a metropolis, but after Hatshepsut, large as their architecture became, it lost in dignity and beauty what it gained in monumentality.

Moreover, in their urge to build more and more they looted the distinguished architecture of the Middle Kingdom, used it as quarries, transferred the art with new inscriptions to their own temples, and left only residues to be compared with their enormous projects, always to the latter's disadvantage.

Even as early as Amenemhet I, the god's name and some of his attributes have changed; he is now Amon-Re but he is still the sun. And the purposes of his temple are clear. They involve the common man only in the sense that the temple is devoted to the maintenance of the sun—that is, to creation. Here there is nothing of the central cosmic mountain as in Ur or Uxmal. Here there is nothing of the joyous public festivals of the Greeks; of the begging for personal worldly advantage of the Shinto; of the working for ultimate salvation of the Buddhist; there is nothing personal about it. Personal advantage does not appear. It has no lift-up function, no alleluia of chant or of vaulted nave; it is not mortuary. It is impersonalized bureaucratic management of the needs of the sun god so that all the rest may not suffer, and for this the public has only the role of supplying most of the provender and of occasionally watching a procession go by of a feast day. Thus the people seldom enter the temple at all and never progress beyond the open court behind the entrance.

Since the temples were originally conceived as houses of god, the first plans conformed presumably to the plan of a private house in pre-Dynastic Egypt and were translated later into stone.

With the translation, the private room of the god, the holy of holies (or *naos*), gradually became a shrine hewn from a single block of granite—containing a statue of elaborately carved and adorned wood from 1½ to 6 feet high. The service of the divinity was simply that of supplying him with things both necessary and luxurious that might be required by a wealthy Egyptian of high rank. These "needs" were by no means trivial—food, drink, fine raiment, music, a dance offered originally without ceremony but in the end elaborately ritualized.

Then the accretions began. Near the *naos* or in it the portable barque might be stored, on which the idol was carried from the temple in processions or at festivals. Small rooms for other accepted cults began to cluster around the *naos*; chapels or sacristies multiplied—the latter for garments, jewelry, cult objects. Rooms grew bigger and bigger as one moved out from the sanctuary to the hypostyle halls; the hypostyle halls in turn were separated from the entrance pylons by a court which sometimes contained an altar or a statue. Occasionally the people were allowed to come into the forecourt on special feast days. On such days they might even share in the food offerings, which ordinarily were eaten by the priests and temple servants after having been offered to the god.[75]

Auxiliaries were piled on, a second pylon gate, a third, obelisks to flank the gates, a sacred lake, a well, dwellings for the staff, granaries, other store houses. All these could be and often were multiplied to the point where, as at Karnak, the plan became very hard to understand. A final touch might be a quay where the barque could be moored.

Pl. 137

With these arrangements in mind let us examine three temples: the one at Ed-fu, the complex at Luxor-Karnak, and the mortuary temple of Queen Hatshepsut at Deir-el-Bahri.

I choose Ed-fu to begin with, not because it is the finest of the temples but because it is simple in plan and easy to understand, and because it is by far the best preserved even to the point of having a roof over the roofed parts.

The temple has no very spectacular location and is half surrounded by the nondescript buildings that make up the modern town. Indeed it was once so completely covered with debris that an Arab village was built on its roof. It was no doubt this mercy that protected it so thoroughly that it remains to give us the best single idea of what an Egyptian temple was supposed to be like. It was not built in one of the great periods but rather in a time of decadence; it was begun by Ptolemy III about 237 B.C. and not finished, due to intervening revolts in Thebes, until 57 B.C. It was once surrounded by many of the late-period auxiliaries such as the artificial lake, but of these only the *mammisi* have yet been unearthed to confuse the visitor, and I shall not confuse you here. Its pylon is massive and of typical tapered form but much covered with coarsely designed incised inscriptions. The bas-reliefs are of lively interest, showing the battles of Re and Horus against Seth who is in the form of a hippopotamus. These bas-reliefs were once brightly colored and streamers flew from tall masts all along the pylon. Two obelisks, now missing, stood at the entrance. The pylon was an important feature of Egyptian temple architecture and you can see its significance best here. Though some of those at Karnak may be more impressive, the 118-foot pylon of Ed-fu is majestic enough.

Pl. 135

Through the gate you pass into a very large colonnaded open court once presumed to be crowded with dedicatory statues but now dominated only by a beautiful sculpture of the Horus-hawk in the round standing to the left of the portico which fronts the hypostyle hall. The six columns of this portico are more squat and far less handsome than the great ones of Karnak, and the open portico effect is marred by screen walls between all the columns but the central ones. The column capitals alternate, there being one of simple open bud design and two more elaborate and less attractive ones on each side. You pass through the entrance into the hypostyle hall itself, where twelve columns with elaborate capitals support the

---

[75] James Henry Breasted, *A History of Egypt from the Earliest Times to the Persian Conquest* (New York: Bantam, 1964).

flat stone slab roof. Beyond this was a smaller hypostyle hall of twelve columns bearing Hathor-headed capitals, and beyond this the vestibules, smaller chambers, and the sanctuary.

Inside the hypostyle hall, given the existence of the roof slabs, you can get a good idea of the small amount of light the Egyptians evidently wanted in their inner temples.

Though more complex in plan, the details and scale of Luxor-Karnak are far more impressive.

The temples of Luxor and Karnak, a short carriage drive (or walk) from the modern city of Luxor with its beautiful palm-lined Nile frontage on the east bank, and across the river from the famous necropoli of the Valleys of the Kings, Queens, and Nobles of Thebes, were part of the great center of Thebes when it was the most important city of Egypt and one of the most important in the world. Along with Saqqara and Giza they certainly are the greatest architectural experiences ancient Egypt can now offer us. When the explorer Champollion crossed the river from the necropoli and came to Karnak, he was stirred to remark on the sublimity of the scale, "They thought in terms of men 100 feet tall."

Though a succession of kings added much and took away some so that neither complex has the clarity of Ed-fu, it is possible to make them out with a little pain. Luxor has the simpler plan and for me at least the greater charm, and Karnak, the greater majesty. Here I mean to select only a few of the more interesting elements.

Thebes began as an outpost, "the keeper of the door of the south," the protector against Nubian or other dark invasions. But as the center of power moved upstream, it became probably the most beautiful and influential city in Ancient Egypt.

Luxor was its southern suburb, the "harem of the south," and as nearly as any Egyptian building might, its original temple had some gently feminine characteristics. This was not altogether unfitting, since at Karnak Amon-Re had particularly taken the form, engraved over and over again, of the nonchalantly indecent, the shamelessly ithyphallic male god of fertility, Min—the consumer of presumably aphrodisiac Cos lettuce, the bull who served the cows, the god who was brought yearly from Karnak in state procession along the symbolic Avenue of Ram Sphinxes to visit for a few days at Luxor and then to return down the Nile in a ram-headed barge.

Luxor is certainly not as fine now as when Amenophis III (1400–1362) (1408–1372) rebuilt it at the height of the XVIIIth Dynasty of the New Kingdom with the aid of his architect, Amenhotep, son of Hapu, who was later deified and subsequently became the god of healing with a chapel at Deir-el-Bahri, all in emulation of his great predecessor Imhotep, whom we met at Saqqara. The last of Amenophis III's work, the hypostyle corridor, was finished casually by Tutankhamen, adopted successor to the heretic Akhenaton and last of the line of the XVIIIth Dynasty. Then the imperial and vulgar Ramessids came along, the succession of generals who controlled Egypt in the XIXth and XXth Dynasties, the second half of the New Kingdom. In particular there came Rameses II (1301–1235), son of Seti I, ruler for sixty-seven years, husband of five or six "great" wives, father of more than one hundred royal children, victor over the Hittites at Kadesh, builder of many new towns, erector of many colossi, proliferator of cartouches of himself, "Chosen of Re," all ostentatious, all repetitive. His taste for the grandiose created the Ramesseum across the river from Luxor, the 58-foot high, 1,000-ton red granite colossus of himself, the rock temples in Nubia. And he did not leave Luxor alone but added at the front a great court, a pylon, four modest colossi and two obelisks, all skewed from the original axis of Amenophis III, all in much less good taste.

After the despoilers by aggregation came the despoilers by subtraction. The greatest of these was probably time itself, but there were later Pharaohs who appropriated stones and even slabs of art to themselves, there were Coptic Christians, and Muslims, who built a still extant mosque in one of the courts. (In it is the tomb of an Islamic saint and during his festival the people bring in the procession the barque of Sidi Abu'l Haggaz as though it were the barque of the long gone ancient Amon-Re.) And there were the ultimate despoilers, the early archeologists, their privatepatron collectors, museum directors whose acquisitiveness and morals have not changed much yet, and khedives such as the one who gave one of the obelisks to France so that we can now see it inappropriately but familiarly sitting in the Place de la Concorde.

Yet even with all this coming and going, it is possible today at Luxor to recreate in the mind's eye what the temple was like at its heyday.

The plans even as modified by the additions of Rameses II still show a clear progression from large and open colonnaded courts through halls diminishing in size until the sanctuary is reached. Around the *naos*, if you go that far, you will find many special situations, two shrines for Amon, a special place for the solar boat, and so on, but we must ignore them here.

We face first the pylons of Rameses, not as well formed as those of Ed-fu, much damaged, fronted by one of the two obelisks, of which the mate is in Paris, and by three of the four middle-sized colossi which are anyway big enough. The central gate is gone and we peer into the court by a jagged breach in the pylon. All this is of no great interest save for amusing details, such as the eight dog-headed apes which are carved at the bottom of the obelisk, or, along the lower leg of the seated colossus of Rameses, a miniature figure of his queen (Nefertari). The Egyptians were never self-conscious about using several scales in the same representation and attributed to such changes no such satirical implications as we might feel prone to. (See, for example, the beautiful paintings in Nefertari's tomb in the Valley of the Queens.) There is a more brilliant example of this at Karnak where Rameses stands resting his hand on Nefertari's head.

When we pass through the pylons into the ruins of Rameses' double colonnaded court, there is little reason to tarry. But we can notice if observant that the axis is considerably tilted from that of the Temple of Amenophis. Was this a matter of accident or, as Giedion suggests not too clearly, a matter of following "more subtle considerations"?[76] Perhaps we do not need to care. Rameses II was not otherwise notorious for his subtlety.

But of the subtlety and grace of Amenophis and his architect, Amenhotep, you will have no doubt as you enter the temple which he left. Strip the Ramessid additions and the plan becomes very simple, though not quite standard. There is no doubt that, as Giedion says:

> [T]he architectural rhythm at Luxor flows unusually steadily. The architecture itself is powerful and yet, for Egypt, very delicate, like the outlines of the funerary reliefs of high officials on the opposite bank of the Nile.[77]

One of the elements that contributes to this flow is the long preparatory corridor which Amenophis inserted between the entrance and the forecourt. This too is not quite on axis, but the skew is so little as compared with that of the Ramessid court as not to be really noticeable visually except to the very well-trained eye [there is actually a deviation of axis (see plan)] all the way from the entrance to the main hypostyle hall to the gate.

Pl. 138

This corridor, which might be regarded as a hypostyle rotated 90 degrees from its usual position, was originally planned, it is believed, to have had three aisles of columns but was reduced to two, each containing seven papyrus-bundle columns with open campaniform capitals. It remains impressive enough and is an eloquent introduction to the masterpiece of Luxor, the inner court.

Pl. 141

This court, with its double colonnade of beautifully executed papyrus-bundle columns with closed buds fronting the four-column-deep transverse hypostyle with columns of the same design, is one of the great achievements of columnar architecture anywhere, one which Giedion believed to be the most beautiful employment of the plant column anywhere in Egypt.

We do not see it as it was. Ruined walls outline the columns against the blue sky and the shimmering river which Amenhotep would not have been able to see from the same position; the absence of roof projects capitals against the sky—marvelous for Kodachrome but not authentic. But there is enough so that we can reconstitute fairly a great architectural achievement.

This is as far as I am going to take you into the temple of Luxor, although, of course, you will want while there to look for the famous remains of Egyptian bas-reliefs. For example, there is the relief in the Birth

---

[76] Ibid., p. 541.
[77] Ibid., p. 389.

Room which shows Amon meeting with Amenophis's mother—symbolic of the divine origin of the monarch. Or the reliefs on the walls of the hypostyle showing the "beautiful festival of Opet," that is, the various stages of Amon's journey from his *cella* at Karnak to that of Luxor and back, "shown in minute detail along a 150-foot band; the king's sacrifice before the barges in the Temple of Amon at Karnak; the barges in the Temple of Amon at Karnak; the barges being carried from the Karnak Temple to the Nile on the shoulders of the priests; the journey of the barges on the Nile to Luxor, with an accompanying procession on land";[78] and so on until the return journey is completed. But it is time to go to Karnak.

A nice way to go is via the Avenue of Ram Sphinxes. The ram was naturally an important personification of the official god Amon-Re. The avenue leading from Luxor to Karnak is flanked by a thick row of sphinxes; their bodies are the bodies of lions, their heads bear the flat-shaped horns of domestic sheep (rams). The sacred barge had golden rams' heads on the prow and stern. All this is a gentler reminder of the need for fertility than the impressive and unconcealed organ of Min.

When you reach Karnak, no matter how, you are in for some confusion. This will be so no matter how much you have studied the plan or how tightly you clutch and how frequently you consult your inadequate guidebook. The plan is practically impossible to remember while you are on the ground. An air view does help and you can get a fair one by climbing to the top of the first pylon (that is, the last to be built). The incredible confusion, much greater than that of Luxor, stems from the same sources, an accumulation of generations of Pharaohs from the Middle Kingdom to the Ptolemies, and the removals by vandals from the Assyrians to us.

If we look at a plan briefly, we can see how complicated it would be even if everything were neatly in place.

Pl. 137

We would pass into the walled sanctuary grounds by the first pylon (the last one to be built, either by Sheshonq I or the Ptolemies), which was never finished and lacks the usual inscriptions and wall reliefs. We would penetrate an enormous court colonnaded on two sides, with central columns marking the route toward the sanctuary. In one corner of this court are some distinguished columns, part of a Temple of Seti I leading off the other side, and a special temple of Rameses III. We would then come to the second pylon prefaced by the gateway of Sheshonq the Libyan. This pylon by Rameses I leads into the great hypostyle hall flanked on its far side by the pylon of Amenophis III. Then a narrow but important central court, the Festival Hall of Thutmosis III, bounded on the other side by pylons V and VI, which lead toward the inner shrine; to the right successive pylons lead into successively larger courts, pylon VII by

---

[78] Ibid., p. 397.

Thutmosis III, pylon VIII by Hatshepsut, and so on, bringing us ultimately to the isolated Temple of Nut. Add the sacred lake, the remains of a tomb of Osiris, the Temple of the Child-God Khons, a Temple of Opet, the propylon of Eugertes, some Sarte chapels, an enclosure for the Temple of Mont; put these all in various states of disheveled ruinery, and you have it as it is today. It is not a beautiful nor an articulated vision, if indeed it ever was. You will surely prowl around it for several satisfying hours. Here I mean to ask you to stop in the hypostyle hall—one of the great architectural wonders of the world.

Like most important Egyptian things, its area is very large, perhaps three-fourths that of the Cathedral of Notre-Dame in Paris, and its central *Pl. 139* height is 80 feet (the nave at Amiens is 140 feet). It has 134 columns arranged in 16 rows, the two central and higher rows of six each, the flanking rows of 7 by 9 on each side, not centered on the larger ones, which flank the axial road from the great court to the sanctuary.[79] The side columns have papyrus-bud capitals; the larger ones are campaniform and supply three aisles, of which the central one leads to the sanctuary. On the cornice of the first row of columns adjacent to the big ones were pillars to support the roof over the central aisles. They were separated by stone grilles which let in a little light as a clerestory would.

These are the bare facts. They cannot describe the impression even now when only a single roof slab remains in place to shut out a tiny patch of sky. The play of light and shade remains remarkable. There are subtleties difficult to explain. But the main effect is not that of subtlety but of reasonably controlled gigantism, a restraint Rameses II never again attained, although his successor Rameses III did manage some at Medinet-Habou. It is hard to realize it, but the diameter of the columns of the main passage is the same as that of Trajan's Column in the Imperial Forum in Rome (11 feet, 7 inches). After we have put all the statistics aside, however, we are left with one overwhelming impression that anyone who trod this processional way, modestly lighted along the path, falling into almost total darkness and silence at the sides, must have remained impressed by the majestic and powerful remoteness of the god.

By now you may wish for something a trifle more human and go in search of the world-famous anatomy of Min. You can find it shrouded in gloom on almost every column and often the walls too. It is on the whole more productive to examine the reliefs on the walls of the hypostyle hall where we can see Rameses making offerings to Min (shorn of his symbol by the pious and modest Copts) on the south wall or presenting incense before the sacred barge.

But I would not like you to leave Karnak before giving homage to the magnificent obelisk of Hatshepsut. I am confident that it is the finest *Pl. 140*

[79] There are 134 instead of the 138 indicated by the above inventory due to the omission of four by the intrusion of a portal.

obelisk extant and that I am not betrayed by the admiration I built up for this remarkable woman long ago in Professor Sumner's two-year course called European Civilization and Art.

Hatshepsut may not have been as beautiful as Nefertiti, the wife of Akhenaton, famous for so long to so many from the polychrome Berlin bust and to fewer from the more beautiful quartzite head in the Cairo Museum. But as you see Hatshepsut portrayed as Osiris in the Metropolitan Museum in New York, you will not find her ugly. And she was clearly more influential and energetic and productive than Nefertiti.

A woman Osiris—a woman king of the XVIIIth Dynasty? That was the rub. She was the daughter of Thutmosis I and his "great" wife. Her half-brother Thutmosis II was the son of a secondary wife but he legitimized his throne by marrying Hatshepsut and then promptly died. Thutmosis's son, not by Hatshepsut but by a secondary wife, was Thutmosis III. Hatshepsut had the advantage of better birth, the support of the Temple of Amon. So she married Thutmosis III, made him into an unimportant associate, and freely made her own statues into male form including the royal beard. She was an impressive queen. She moved from the imperialism of her father toward a more pacific and prosperous regime; she sent large expeditions down the Red Sea to bring back exotic goods from the fabled lands of Punt. She built much and beautifully through her great architect Senenmut, the third of the famous Egyptian ones. But she made Thutmosis so angry that after she died he went all about Egypt destroying the physical evidences of her memory, leaving none of her statues unbroken, erasing the name of the queen from most of the inscriptions even at her most famous temple at Deir-el-Bahri.

Pl. 140

She erected two splendid shafts of red Aswan granite in the narrow hypostyle hall her father had built at Karnak. They stood 97 feet high; they were less busily inscribed than many and this improved their appearance. The pyramidions at the top were of pink granite sheathed with a combination of silver and gold called electrum. They were "to rise to heaven, to be seen from far and wide from both banks of the Nile and to illuminate Egypt like the sun."[80] Thutmosis III could not leave them alone either. He enclosed them almost all the way to the top in towers. One of these remains. The other obelisk we can fortunately see almost as it was. And it is beautiful.

Also beautiful is the great mortuary shrine of this inordinately vain woman at Deir-el-Bahri, which is the last of the Egyptian sites we will visit. It has a single theme—Hatshepsut.

The task she set herself and her architect was difficult and new. At Deir-el-Bahri formidable cliffs break sheer to the plain; their scale is such as to dwarf most adjacent architecture. Years before, in the XIth Dynasty, Mentuhotep had built a mortuary temple up against the same rocks. Only

[80] Giedion, *The Eternal Present*, Vol. II, *The Beginnings of Architecture*, op. cit., p. 365.

a little of it is to be seen now, but it must have been very evident in the time of Hatshepsut. It too had a good deal of novelty and it may well have contained suggestions for her architect. It had a ramp, two terraces, a colonnade. Emerging from the center of the upper terrace was a tomb pyramid.

But the days of interment in the pyramid-temple were over. Hatshepsut's father had broken the custom when he caused himself to be interred in a cave in the Valley of Kings. Hatshepsut's great achievement was then not a tomb but a mortuary temple. It called for a great processional toward a climax in the rites for the dead preserving in new form the ancient sequence—valley temple, causeway, mortuary temple, and finally the funerary chapel pierced into the rock face.

Unquestionably a great client, Hatshepsut needed, and found, a great architect, Senenmut (Senmut). As nearly as can be guessed, he was much more than architect to her. Like Imhotep in earlier times, he gained enormous overt powers. He administered all the vast estates of the Temple of Karnak. He was "Overseer of All of the Works of the King." But he was also high steward of the queen's household, "Superintendent of the Private Apartments, of the Bathrooms and of the Royal Bedrooms," guardian of the queen's daughter. But he dared so much more that his relations with the queen must have been more than formally secure. He had his portrait painted behind many of the doors of the temples. Though many of these were defaced by Thutmosis III, one revealing portrait can be seen. In some of his inscriptions he dared to couple his name with that of the queen and even with the god Horus. "Long live Horus, Hatshepsut, and Senmut." Out of protocol he had of course to be buried in a different tomb, but his sarcophagus was identical to that of the queen.

Many Egyptologists have not liked Hatshepsut, or Senenmut, as much as I do. They have berated her reign as one dominated by an architect. But her reign was one of peace, and whatever else her reign, or her love life with Senenmut, may or may not have been, this client and her great designer collaborated to produce one of the world's great architectural results.

You can see a good deal of it now, though not the approaches or all the buildings on the upper terraces. You will be able to see more later, for it is being carefully and fully restored. Meanwhile a plan helps.

The great ceremonies occurred when the wooden statue of Amon-Re was taken from his shrine at Karnak, brought across the Nile in his sacred bark, and led up from the river for his visit with Hathor, the cow goddess, the body of the sky, the soul of trees, the mother of Horus, and many other sometimes mutually contradictory things. At Deir-el-Bahri a cow sculpture in Hathor's chapel represents her in her cosmic role. Amon might also visit with Anubis, the jackal-headed lord of the necropolis, embalmer of Osiris, who had a delightful chapel in Hatshepsut's temple. And he would rest a while in his own holy of holies.

Leaving the Nile, the procession passed through an alley of sandstone

Pl. 142

sphinxes leading up from the rim of the cultivated lands and then entered the precinct, passing now between large sphinxes of red granite no longer there.[81] It then passed up the ramps and across the various terraces and past the various colonnades to reach the chapel of Amon.

What the views may have been on the way up we can only conjecture—perhaps the large painted limestone statues of the queen, fronting the colonnade of the upper terrace. All the time the shade of the colonnades must have contrasted with the glare from the cliff amphitheater as it does today. And darker still would have been the inner rooms of the shrines. Probably the people of the procession would not have paused as we will wish to do to examine the delicate painting of the reliefs behind one of the colonnades showing on one wall the expeditions to Punt and on the other the genesis of Hatshepsut from Hathor. They did not peel off to inspect the graceful proto-Doric portico of the Anubis sanctuary with the column bases, the fluting, and the four square capitals all far from the traditions of the lotus or the palmetto, or the excellent murals of the offerings in the Anubis sanctuary, or any of the other countless details, each so charming, each so well integrated to the others. By all means we need to look at and admire these details, but in doing so we should not forget the impressive synthesis or the distinguished arrangement of colonnades and ramps and terraces against their formidable God-made backdrop.

Pl. 143

I do not know of any critic who has not found this work admirable whether as masterful handling of space, adaptation to a vast landscape, or great architectural independence. It is justly praised for the way it gently but inexorably leads the eye upward, for the freedom and the delicacy of its treatments, for the firm control of the rhythm of light and shade, for the subtlety in the variant use of columns and piers, and most of all perhaps for its understanding of the basic architectural virtue of planned unity. It presents a monumentality to which no Greek temple could aspire, and an amalgamation of form and site—a rare realization of what should always be a high aim of architecture.

PERSEPOLIS

Most of us who studied classical history in school were taught on an English model, according to which the Athenians were enormously superior to other men of their times—among the other Greeks to the barbarous Macedonians, the avaricious Corinthians, and the pig-like Boeotians, and overseas, to the Persians, who were cowardly, unimaginative, and vicious.

The fact, however, is that the civilization which developed on the Iranian plateau, and the empire which resulted from the fusion of the Elamites, the Medes, the Persians, and their widespread conquests, was, in

---

[81] One reconstructed from fragments can be seen in the Metropolitan Museum in New York.

its heyday of two centuries, one of the great empires of the ancient world. Cyrus the Great consolidated it in 550–530 B.C. His son Cambyses conquered Egypt, and Darius I (521–486) pacified it within boundaries which extended from the Indus to the Mediterranean, from the Caucasus to the Indian Ocean. A revolt of the Ionian Greeks was suppressed but led to an unnecessary pair of expeditions against the mainland Greeks in which, as every schoolboy used to know, the Persians were thrashed temporarily at Thermopylae and Marathon in 490 and finally at Salamis and Plataea in 480–479. These battles were of central importance to the Greeks but peripheral to the Persians. The Persian Empire, though waning—weakened by internecine struggles for the succession and local revolts—was not overthrown for another 150 years when it was conquered by Alexander the Great of Macedon. During this extensive period there were several capitals, at Susa, the seat of power, at Ecbatana, at Babylon, and at Persepolis, which played a very special role.

The site of Persepolis is in a mountain valley of southwestern Iran, the homeland of the Achaemenid clan. Legends cluster around the origin, none justified as yet by any archeological evidence. In one legend Persepolis was the throne of Jamshid, the mythical King of Persia, sometimes even identified with Yama of the Indians; in this view Darius and Xerxes merely completed the original palaces. Whatever you believe, Persepolis was not a strictly political place of residence like Babylon, Susa, and Sardis, but was rather conceived by Darius as a ceremonial shrine, reserved mainly for celebration of the Persian New Year. This celebration did, however, have more than undertones of imperialism. Not only was the Achaemenid kingship formally renewed at that time, but men came from every part of the empire to bring tribute and render obeisance. All this is made explicitly clear in the sculpture and other decoration. The craftsmen were brought from all quarters of the Empire in an effort, as Darius and Xerxes explained in their inscriptions, to create a "Palace of All Nations." Yet if these origins were true, the craftsmen learned fast to express themselves in a standard style approved by the Achaemenids. Even the gifts of the tribute bearers are seldom local produce as should have been expected; rare are the horses from Cilicia, the balls of cotton from Hindush. Even the faces and the costumes do not express many differences; it is as though the sculptors had sought to underplay outlandish details; "no stress was laid on anthropological diversity."[82]

After Xerxes I and certainly after Artaxerxes I the great hegemony of Persia was weakening and no doubt the ceremonies of the New Year became less impressive. But the physical reminders and some semblance of court life carried on until Alexander, pursuing his conquests, came through. The tale has it that either in a fit of drunkenness or of swollen vengeance for the Persian burning of the Athenian Acropolis long ago, he burned the

[82] William Culican, *The Medes and the Persians* (New York: Praeger, 1965), p. 113.

whole city and then wept in remorse about the beauty he had destroyed. Certainly the ruins are reminiscent of those produced by some great holocaust, with individual columns thrusting their forlorn way up here and there. As Culican suggests, the flames may ironically have preserved Persepolis for posterity. The collapse of the massive timber, earth, and tile roofs formed a protective cover for the sculpture and preserved the clay tablets of the Treasury. Time would have dealt with them more savagely.

But the staircases do remain, and the sculptured walls, and beautiful inscriptions, and some 65-foot columns, and here and there a remarkable double-headed animal capital. It is not remarkable that stories woven about the ruins took them back to the legendary Jamshid. Fitzgerald perpetuated the legend in *The Rubaiyat of Omar Khayam:*

> They say the Lion and the Lizard keep
> The Courts where Jamshyd gloried and drank deep;
> And Bahram, that great Hunter—the wild ass
> Stamps o'er his Head and he lies fast asleep.

Pl. 147

When you come to Persepolis, the first and most impressive architectural experience you will have is to see from below the great platform on which it is built. It stands 40 feet above the plain, partly carved out of the rock and partly built up of local stones, some of them very big. A beautiful double stair with a handsome balustrade leads to the platform. The stair is monumentally magnificent, it is 22 feet wide and of so gradual a slope that horses could easily negotiate it. Although the masonry looks cyclopean, it is not. Instead the roughly squared boulders are held in place by iron clamps set in lead.

On reaching the top of the stairs we are aware of the enormousness of the *apadana* platform—1,500 feet by 1,000 feet—and also of almost the only architectural direction we will have. We are confronted at once by the triumphal, monumental entrance flanked by sufficiently impressive remains of man-headed bulls and massive piers glowing in glazed bricks.

Pl. 146

Guidebooks often say too much. If you were to believe the one by Azis Hatami, you would encounter "a magnificent panorama of stately portals, columns, steps, friezes, doorways, capitals, and ruined palaces." This is not quite true. The ingredients are there, and derived from many sources since Persian architects had no qualms about borrowing, but they are scattered, and it is too easy to wander anywhere at will, even skirting the *propylaea* if you like. You have really to be content with individual excitements, the wonderful legs, body, and tail of the bull on Xerxes's porch, the northern staircase leading to the higher platform of the Apadana Palace with its splendid carving but only parts of thirteen of the original seventy-two slender and graceful columns of the main audience hall. This grand staircase, make no mistake, is an important architectural detail, but it is a detail. Then there are the tripylon doors of the central palace and the most complete of the ruined buildings—the Tachara, the private palace of Darius, many of whose doorways bear effigies of the king. The most moving thing of all may be a large panel of cuneiform inscriptions.

Indeed if you look at a plan of the platform or a reconstructed line drawing axonometric, you are likely to be more reminded of a world's fair than of a city. You may quite easily be led to agree with Seton Lloyd[83] that Persepolis was essentially a nomadic concept, a grouping of tent pavilions executed in stone. It is a thoughtful conceit.

The sculpture is something else again. It is almost everywhere but carefully contained by the architecture. It is easy enough to call it monotonous, stereotyped, insipid—and as sculpture, the terms may all be justified. But it is truly architectonic, stiffened enough and formalized enough to render plasticity to the architecture without taking it over.

Pl. 145

The buildings indeed may have been, as Culican explains it, more the work of a sculptor than of an architect. There are architectural innovations—double-turn staircases, bell-shaped column bases, fluted columns, cavetto moldings—but the work is also cumbersome and the details are not careful; the structure is retrograde. Undecorated plain surfaces have crude masonry.

This is not necessarily "bad"; tent pavilions, preeminence of sculpture over architecture, may be permissible, even desirable, in a part-time shrine, and it is not surprising that the sculptures roughly portray the stages of the festival: satrapies leaving their horses, camels, bulls, chariots, wearing traveling clothes, passing through the gate, being reviewed, carrying tribute and banqueting. There are many costumes, weapons; there is Artaxerxes with his fly-swatter; there is the beautiful, if soft, heraldic device of the *symplegma*, the lion attacking the rearing bull. It is lively as it is, and we can not know how much Persepolis when living was enhanced by tapestries, metal sheets, banners, other forms of decoration.

Pl. 144

Persepolis is very interesting and the tent analogy fascinating. By all means go; I feel sure you will enjoy it, if not principally as an architectural experience. But as you look at the stereotyped, pompous parade of the stiffly vertical, "petrified" guests, all arranged in bureaucratic sequential order, you may have trouble in dispelling from your mind the image of lively relaxation of the riders on the Panathenaic frieze, which it is now time to visit.

GREECE

When you cruise the isles of Greece, as more and more people do these days, you will encounter many wonders that have no particular relevance to our present concern with trabeate architecture; marvelous Byzantine

---

[83] Cited in Trewin Copplestone (ed.), *World Architecture* (New York: McGraw-Hill, 1963), p. 27.

remains as at Hosios Loukas, and Daphni; crusaders' castles as on Rhodes; the labyrinths of Crete; the windmills of Mykonos; dramatic volcano-riven Santorini; the lions of Delos; the theater of Epidauros; the Syracusan forts and other famous battlefields; the Ear of Dionysus, the Latonian quarry, and the papyrus-lined stream of Syracuse.

Within the list of Greek temple precincts or sites you will inevitably find favorites: Delos, whose development was so much arrested when the treasury of the Delian league was transported to Athens; Kos, the site of the medical ministrations of Hippocrates, which is the favorite of Lewis Mumford; the groves of Olympia with all their athletic connotations; the dramatic steep hillsides of my favorite, Delphi, dotted with the memorial treasures of the various Greek city-states, and its oracular memories.

Among the individual temples, of which nineteen are extant, you will also find favorites: the long array on the scarp of Sicilian Akragas (Agrigentum); Segesta in its bucolic Sicilian vale; the gargantuan Selinunte; the Basilica and other shrines on the shores of Italian Paestum; the severe temple of Apollo Epikourios at Bassae on a wind-swept goat-trodden pass in Arcadia; the great temple of Apollo at Aegina or that of Athena Pollias in Pergamon. And there are picturesque fragments such as those at Sunium and Corinth and above all at Lindos on Rhodes.

All these you ought to see and doubtless will but I need not describe them all here. As you do travel you will note variations in the overall layouts, the colonnades, the column proportions and details, the entasis, the sculpture, and the stone materials used. But despite these variations you will conclude that great Greek temple architecture was so standardized that one can extract an archetype and that it is the Parthenon on the Acropolis of Athens, despite the diversions of the Erechtheion and the Nike Apteros on the Acropolis, and the Hephaesteion (Theseion) below. This is so partly because the Greeks, though so adventuresome in so many directions, were conservative in architecture—more interested in perfecting one form than inventing new ones.

The Parthenon is so familiar and so much has been written about it that I shall spend more time on the conditions which brought it about than on the artifact itself. The democracy of Athens and even of the more oligarchic neighboring city-states was turbulent and internally inconsistent. We should call this a Greek phenomenon, rather than solely an Athenian one although it may characterize any true democracy. The people who mistrusted the Greeks in other parts of the world from Priam to Cyrus the Great, to Vergil, had more than Athenians in mind. When Vergil speaks of fearing the Danae when they come bearing gifts, this is not a metaphor for Athens, although the Athenians were no doubt the ultimate distillation. Over a period of fifty to seventy years this one small city became the greatest single producer of an enormous variety of talents which the world has ever known or ever is likely to know.

The Athenians themselves boasted that they were impatient and inconsistent, more prone to action than to reflection. They were capricious in the extreme. They could debate calmly with the Melians about their fate and within a few years extirpate Miletus with vengeful fury, while at the same time lamenting the fate of the Trojan women as portrayed by Euripides. With almost monotonous regularity they ostracized their most effective popular critic, the acidulous Aristophanes, who pricked all their favorite balloons as well as balloons they liked to have pricked. This people, so praised for their moderation, executed their greatest sage, Socrates, for making "the worse seem the better cause" and for "corrupting the youth." The Socratic *Dialogues* themselves suggest that many things must have been rotten in the state of Athens, else there could not have been so much talk about them.

They loved youth for its beauty but were not so sure of its wisdom. They listened to the aged while they were alive but as soon as they were dead they wrote brief epitaphs which almost invariably proclaimed the failure or futility of what they had done.

They were ambivalent about everything, indulging in *hubris* while being wary about it, praising *areté* without always seeking it. In one sense they placed the athlete above the poet and certainly would have rated a great American professional performer above a mediocre American poetaster or one who published extensive observations of his own navel in the form of his personal laundry lists. But the sophist Protagoras quotes Euripides complaining of these same athletes.

> Now of ten thousand curses that plague Hellas
> There's none so pestilent as this breed of athletes
> For what stout wrestler, or what nimble runner or discus thrower or
>   brave jawbone breaker,
> Profits the country, gone a gathering garlands?

A work of art was more important to them than the artist; there was always the respect for those who operated in the service of the State, those who gave of their fiscal resources to embellish the city and those who did the work.

On this side of the coin it is pretty clear that most, if not all, Athenians agreed with Pericles: "Fix your eyes on the power of Athens . . . make yourselves her lovers, and, when you find her a great city, remember that men won that greatness for her." And here the Athenians did differ, say, from the Spartans. Lycurgus might scorn walls of brick in favor of the backs of brave men, but the Athenian commandment might be: "Honor the gods; help your friends; adorn your city."[84]

Though these traits led to the debacle at Syracuse, they also yielded a remarkable life—life of great poetry, great drama, great sculpture, great

---

[84] Paul MacKendrick, *The World of Pericles in Greece and Rome* (Washington: National Geographic Society, 1968), p. 140.

painting, great architecture, and great dialogues about all the principal dilemmas of man.

Whatever their confusions about morality, about barbarians, about politics, or war, the Greeks were not confused when it came to expressing ideas, whether in architecture, poetry, tragedy, comedy, history, sculpture, painting, or philosophy. They always came clearly and directly to the point. The great architecture of the fifth century B.C. has the same directness that so pervaded Athenian expression—possessed of great details to be sure, but sparse, and carefully chosen, and this explains why the contradictions of Greek life were not reflected in the Greek temple.

Yet to be able to admire simplicity here and richness there enriches one's life. Edith Hamilton is perfectly right to say:

> To be enabled not only to feel the simple majesty of a Greek temple
> along with the splendor of St. Mark's and the soaring immensity of Bourges,
> to love the truth stated with simplicity, as well as the truth set off by
> every adornment the imagination can devise—is to be immensely
> the richer.[85]

There are difficulties to surmount before we can "feel the simple majesty of a Greek temple." A. W. Lawrence states one well.

> In many ways a strenuous intellectual effort is required to form an
> appreciative judgment of Greek architecture. For one thing every building
> is to some extent ruined. The wooden portions have invariably perished,
> any metal accessories have been looted, the sculptural decoration is never
> complete, the paint has vanished. Almost every roof has fallen, bringing
> light where there ought to be shade, and causing surfaces that were
> originally polished to weather like the rest. The demolition of walls, in order
> to obtain material for re-use [or to convert the building as when the
> Christians mutilated some of the Greek temples by building apses in
> them—jeb] has often left columns standing clear which were intended
> to be seen against a background of masonry. The effect of many buildings
> has been transformed too by a rise or fall in the level of the surrounding
> ground, while in practically every case the character of the setting has
> changed beyond recognition; modern buildings stand around, or a town has
> lapsed into wasteland, or a sanctuary is overgrown with trees and bushes.[86]

But the trouble lies deeper than that caused merely by the destruction of time. Lawrence goes on to describe a society living in a world of unseen dangers, defined safeguards, omens, and oracles; a world in which the gods are anthropomorphic and have houses; a world which relies on the sacrifice of animals and the subsequent eating of their flesh by the worshippers, of the necessity of sustaining and propitiating the ghosts of ancestors; of

[85] Edith Hamilton, *The Greek Way to Western Civilization* (New York: Mentor, 1948), p. 49.
[86] A. W. Lawrence, *Greek Architecture* (Baltimore: Penguin, 1957), pp. 289–290. Copyright © A. W. Lawrence, 1957.

government in which tradition is hard to change because change may be impious and therefore dangerous.

Manifestly the effort to understand Greece is enormous and the understanding can never be complete. But I know of no one who has tried who has felt unrewarded.

Though the Greeks paid more attention to their temples than anything else and next perhaps to their theaters, which also served a religious function, they built and you can find remnants of frontier forts, fountain covers, round monuments, tombs, stadiums, gymnasiums, council houses, indoor theaters in the round (*telesteria*) or concert halls (*odea*), of arsenals, stores, baths, warehouses, mercantile exchanges, *agorae*, and toward the Hellenistic time, the planning of at least the central parts of cities, as in Priene. Many of these are interesting, but on none were lavished the care and perfection accorded to temples and perhaps to theaters as, notably, in the case of Epidauros where the theater is the most spectacular thing left of the shrines of Asklepius.

The mainland of Greece, with the islands which stride out from it, is one great barren, precipitous mountain mass of marble, riven by earthquakes, partially submerged by the ubiquitous sea. The mountains cover 80 percent of the land. They are not set out in neat ranges but cross and intersect, and the small interstices or basins are the valleys in which men lived and died. The mountains rush down to the sea, break off in cliffs, go under the water, and emerge ten miles or so away as island peaks, stretching almost to the coast of Asia Minor.

The sea's edge follows the contours of the hills. It is long, tortuous. The water is a brilliant blue much of the time and occasionally Homer's "wine-red," but it is often rough too, and a mariner can be glad that shelter is never more than a few miles away, especially if he is not much of a navigator, as the Greeks were not.

Usually strong mountains breed strong rivers, but Greece was dry and its rivers few and small. Not many were perennial and these were turbid. Others showed dry, white beds during the summer but were torrents after the rains. The Ilissus, the famous river of Athens, was but a chain of pools all summer. The Cephesus, seldom actually dry, probably never reached the sea. None of the rivers was navigable and the ports were not located at their mouths. The principal effect of rivers on the history of Greece was that when they were in flood they could upset military plans. Athens did not have its Seine, its Thames, its Danube, not even its Tiber. No Greek city did.

The mountains and the sea were, then, primary conditioners of ancient Greek life and its resultant architecture. But so was the extraordinary climate, a climate of sky, of sun, of cloud but not fog, of wind, of infrequent but torrential rain. The anemone-bedecked spring was short and the sun was powerful as early as March, held at bay by capricious north winds. The summer would have been hot save for the Etesian winds which blew steadily from the north-northeast for nearly two months; this was when the gales ruffled what was otherwise a shining sea. But by the end of July the southerly *libas*, or sirocco, sent Sahara-like blasts across the land. In October the clouds, never absent for long, began to gather in stronger array, and the Greek was warned that winter was on the way. Snow began to appear on the mountaintops, and the winter winds, almost always cold and penetrating, blew from all points of the compass so that the capricious legendary bag of Aeolus had a stout underpinning in the facts of the Greek winter. The first rains began.[87]

Zimmern says that the Greek winter life was essentially one of hibernation. The houses were draughty and cold, not well equipped for a comfortable winter home life. People in the country did have to keep on working—picking the olives, for example. In the towns the parliament and the law courts droned on, out in the open air; the plays of Aristophanes, which bordered on the subversive and were better not viewed by strangers, were generally performed in January when foreigners would not yet have braved the sea. The Greeks could stand cold when necessary but they did not enjoy it and their buildings and their activities were designed for a season that began in March and ended in October.[88]

This Greek environment of cliffs and waves, of winds and sun, of an open season and a closed one, was also an environment in which the atmosphere played an important part. The sky like the sea was always evident. Though cloudy it was almost never overcast except in the rainy season. Most of the time the atmosphere was bracing and extraordinarily clear, the light mobile and sharp like the Greek temperament. It was against such a sky that the Greek saw his buildings and against such a sky that we must reconstruct them.

The barren hills were not entirely barren but they did not yield a great variety of useful crops. On the uplands olive trees did very well and "their roots coil[ed] round the marble rocks like serpents."[89] Vines did well also so there were ample supplies of olive oil and of sour wine. But on the whole the soil was thin enough "to roll up like a rug and take away," and fit for little but the pasturage of Arcadian sheep. A number of beautiful trees and shrubs enhanced the landscape—laurels, myrtles, oleanders, plane trees, white poplars, cypresses, aromatic plants. On the higher hills there were hardwoods such as oaks and chestnuts in sufficient supply for the wooden ships and for the timbers of the buildings. Higher still there were resin-bearing conifers, and on alpine heights, alpine flora, which the Greeks left to the gods to enjoy. Green for a short season, Greece, like Australia or California, was brown most of the time.

[87] Sir Alfred Zimmern, *The Greek Commonwealth*, 5th ed. (London: Oxford University Press, 1931), p. 37.
[88] Ibid.
[89] Thomas Craven, *The Pocket Book of Greek Art* (New York: Pocket Books, 1950), p. 8.

Nor was the land very rich in other resources. In classic days minerals were little known in Greece, although Athens did have her profitable lead mines, and bronze and iron had their smaller place. There were great quantities of limestone and marble, good for building in that climate. There were good clays which encouraged the ceramic arts. That was about all.

The Greek view of nature seems unusual to us. Set amid wonderful scenery, they were sensitive to it in choosing sites, but they did not write rhapsodic nature poems like those of the English. Their art never dealt with landscape.

Their religion was like their view of nature.

> Man to him was one with Nature, and Nature was God. But Nature focused and found its true significance in man. Man was the measure of all things in very truth; the proportions of Greek architecture reduce to a module taken from the human body; landscape loses its mystery in the personification of its aspects into human terms; trees are dryads, fountains nymphs, and rivers gods. The gods themselves, as personifying a humanized Nature, are but sublimated men, subject on occasion to human limitations; a Victory on the balustrade of a Nike temple stoops, like any woman, to tie her sandal. Greek art records a time when men were at their ease with nature, and unafraid of life.[90]

Their directness led them to a view of the arts which was quite different from that of modern times. The arts were something alive, something to be used, something to be enjoyed, not something to revere.

Art was closely welded to utility. The artist could be admired for his accomplishments as an example of *areté*, doing one's best with one's talents, and art would be lavished on the right things. But this could never mean that the artist had to be handled with kid gloves. Sculptors who used mallets and others who worked with their hands could not spring from the nobility or belong to a court society. They were likely to be slaves. Pericles may have said:

> No generous youth, from seeing the Zeus at Pisa [i.e., Olympia], or the Hera at Argos, longs to be Pheidias or Polycleitus; nor to be Anacreon or Philetas or Archilochus out of pleasure in their poems. For it does not of necessity follow that, if the work delights you with its grace, the one who wrought it is worthy of your esteem.[91]

There is a Greek word, *kalós*, often translated "beauty" but really a word conveying an indefinite sense of praise, something like "fine," which could be applied to many things besides art—to speaking, fighting, various

[90] Charles R. Morey, "The Vision of Ancient Art," in *Studies in the Arts and Architecture* (Philadelphia: University of Pennsylvania Press, 1941), p. 27.
[91] Plutarch's *Lives*, Vol. II, translated by Bernadotte Perrin (Cambridge, Mass.: Harvard University Press, 1916), pp. 5–7.

personal traits—much as we now use the word "beautiful." Goodness is not quite involved in the sense of ethic that Ruskin would have it, but it is not altogether excluded either since "Fineness automatically included excellence, because what is fine must be fitted to its purpose and therefore Good."[92]

The Greek Temple

So what was to be beautiful in Greece must be fitted to its purpose. And for architecture and for the fifth century this purpose was inevitably the temple. What in turn was the temple for?

We shall go very far astray if we think of the Greek temple as in any sense a church. It was primarily and almost solely the house of the god in a literal sense, the shelter built specifically for him. Its main, sometimes its only, room was for the express purpose of enclosing his visible image, an image which was far more than a symbolic statue. Around the temple other elements of ritual developed, of course, and the temple was indeed a shrine; but it was never a church and would not have worked as one.

This was not a religion with a Bible, with a formalized priestly organization. It boasted no doctrine, no metaphysics, no creed. There was no organization in support of or in opposition to the church. There was no substantial distinction between godly and worldly things. The priests were laymen, public officials, appointed to perform certain rites.

Like so many other things in Greek life, it all arose from the peculiar Greek interest in nature and their persistent questioning of what this mysterious thing was. Starting no doubt with the cults characteristic of primitive religions, with godly explanations of unexplainable natural phenomena, with totems and taboos, it soon merged with Greek practicality to become the strange thing it was; the gods in the last analysis were cast in the image of an enlarged man. It was inevitable that the Greek with his particular attitude should conclude that nature was something like himself and proceed to personify the gods.

Thus the gods could be capricious; so was man. They could be angry; so could man. Like him, they could be propitiated; they were capable of jealousy; you could play one off against the other; and all the dealings were only exaggerated examples of dealings with men. Patience, insight, even bribery might help quite a lot. The problem this posed to a human was nothing like the problem of getting along with Jahveh or the God of *Pilgrim's Progress.*

It was inevitable in such a system that the religion should rely more on art and ritual than on sermons and dogma. The festivals were in the nature of ritual. The sacrifices were a part of the ritual, but everything was always so human that it was reasonable for the oblator to select the best

[92] Charles Seltman, *Approach to Greek Art* (London and New York: Studio Publications, 1948), p. 29.

parts of the sacrificial animal and take them home to his own dining table. But it was also not a light matter. The Athenians delayed the execution of Socrates while a ship went to Delos and back because during this particular holy period the city could not be polluted by a public execution.

When the rituals commenced in primitive times, they required only altars in the open air. Except for the altar structure itself, all you had to do to make a shrine was to dedicate a piece of ground, the precinct, to a particular deity. You kept it inviolate by putting up some boundary stones and later on perhaps a fence or a wall. The altar and the boundary were the essential elements. You could set up a statue of the deity; you could build a temple to house the statue; you could add treasuries, elaborate entrance gates, or *propylaea*. But all these things were only additions, and even in late days the simple altar might adjoin the elaborate temple.

The simplest altar was but a small mound of earth or even just the ashes of previous sacrifices. The great altar of Zeus at Olympia remained a pile of ashes to the end, albeit a great pile. But more and more the altars were made of stone, more and more they were ornate. Either altar or temple was inside the sacred enclosure or precinct. All the most important temples were built in such a precinct surrounded by a wall. The site at Athens was the rocky Acropolis and the shape of the sacred enclosure or *temenos* was predetermined; on the flat site at Olympia or on the hillside at Delphi an arbitrary shape was laid out. The precincts were not consecrated to a single idea as might have been the case with later religions. The great temple of the presiding god or goddess might indeed dominate the layout; but there could also be minor temples for other deities, treasuries, covered colonnades with historical paintings, votive monuments to heroes or even to the winners of games who were often close to heroes in the Greek eye, or to donors of sufficient generosity. The general idea will be clear if we imagine the cloistered area of St. John the Divine containing memorials to Theodore Roosevelt, Carl Sandburg, Babe Ruth, and Joe Namath, a couple of churches of minor and even mildly competing faiths, certainly a monument to Ralph Adams Cram and one to Bishop Manning, perhaps one to J. Pierpont Morgan or Andrew Mellon, to Franklin Roosevelt or Martin Luther King, plus some groves of trees which had a somewhat sacred character, some other buildings to contain regalia for state processions, and finally, semicircular seats or shallow, walled recesses (*exedrae*) on which one could sit and meditate. It seems, you may think, a restless idea, and that is a commentary about us and not about the Greeks.

Since the temple was the house of the god, it is not unnatural to suppose that it started like a house for humans. Surely the early coverings of the statues were little more than huts. There were traditions of these ephemeral temples in Greek lore. The first temple of Apollo at Delphi was supposed to have been constructed of laurel boughs, the second of wax and feathers. But the third one was more permanent and perhaps less apocryphal too, and was of bronze. We have authenticated examples of

Pl. 148

Pl. 149

bronze temples to Athena at Sparta and shrines at Olympia according to Pausanias. The transition from wood or even bronze to stone was not unnatural.

The developed temple as illustrated by the Parthenon consisted in fundamental only of the large internal room, *cella* or *naos*, containing the votive statue of the titular god or goddess. Before it there might be an antechamber, the *pronaos*; behind it and separated by a wall, a treasury or storehouse, the *opisthodomos*. The original walls which enclosed the *cella* were no doubt of mud brick exposed to the weather on three sides, protected only by eaves and by a front portico, which later ran all around, while the walls themselves became fine stone. Temples were seldom more complicated than this, but there might be an additional room off of or attached to the *naos*, designed for the oracle and called the *adytum*.

The temples were expected to face east. In point of fact, the axes of Greek temples "box the entire compass" but more than 80 percent of them do run east and west or almost so. Dinsmoor finds that they lie within the arc formed on the horizon between the sunrise directions of winter and summer solstices, and he hazards the subtle suggestion that they were laid out to face the sunrise on the actual day of their foundation, presumably the festival day of the divinity.[93] That they would face east was taken for granted, and the herald in *Agamemnon* is not making much of it, simply speaking fact, when he salutes his home.

> Hail, royal palace, roof most dear to me,
> And holy shrines, whose faces catch the sun.[94]

The temples were not enormous by Roman or even Hellenistic standards, much less by those of Berlin or of Washington. In the middle of the fifth century a temple built in a remote place such as the one to Apollo Epikourios at Bassae might be 50 feet wide and 125 feet long. The one to Poseidon at Paestum, somewhat out of the way but more prosperous than Bassae, might be larger but not so big as the two great temples of the period, that to Zeus at Olympia or that to Athena Parthenos at Athens, 100 by 230 feet. Either would take up no more room on an American football field than a very big marching band.

The largest of the Greek temples of the classic time was that to Zeus at Akragas or Agrigentum, 173 feet across the front and 360 feet long, but this was in almost every way atypical. Akragas (Agrigentum) was a city famous for its extravagance. Plato said of its citizens that they built "as if they were going to live forever and feasted as though they were to die on

---

[93] Dinsmoor, *Architecture of Ancient Greece*, op. cit., p. 49. Scully has a quite different theory, appearing frequently in Vincent Scully, *The Earth, the Temple, and the Gods* (New Haven: Yale University Press, 1962), and especially on pp. 44ff.
[94] *Agamemnon*, 11 519 520, translated by George Thomson in *An Anthology of Greek Drama*, C. A. Robinson, Jr. (ed.) (New York: Rinehart, 1949), p. 17.

the morrow." Grinnel quotes Diodorus as saying that "their luxury reached such a point that during a siege of the city a decree was issued limiting the sleeping equipment of the guards on duty at night to three covers and two pillows."[95] The largest temple in Akragas was characteristic of the people.

The entablature was so heavy, the distance between the columns so great, that architrave blocks could not be cut and placed long enough to reach. So stone giants (Atlantes) were used as supporting figures between the columns. These were nude males some 30 feet high which stood on horizontal members between the columns. Iron reinforcement was also used. All the columns were engaged so that there was a wall around the peristyle and a second one around the *naos*. It shows that the Greeks as well as the Egyptians could nod.

If the processionals were outside the temple, if the sacrifices took place at an outdoor altar, if the small size of the building obviously prevented it from accommodating many people, how were these buildings used? It is not far from the truth to say that they were used as the private habitation of the god. Perhaps, as Dinsmoor suggests, "the interior of the temple was open to privileged persons only . . . ," and

> [T]he one view which most people had of the god (except perhaps
> at festivals) was from the open doorway to the east; and one can under
> such circumstances have some idea of the awe and sense of mystery
> inspired among them by such a view of the image of Zeus or Athena.[96]

Each city might have its patron god or goddess, and to this deity the best temple would normally be dedicated. In return it would be assumed that the deity would find this temple its favorite dwelling place and pay more attention to it than to the temples provided for it in other towns. But the rights were not very exclusive. Zeus was the leader at both Olympia and Dodona, Hera at Samos and Argos, Apollo at Delos and Delphi, Artemis (who was particularly Asiatic) at Ephesus and Sardis. But there would be temples to the others in many of these cities and also to Dionysus, god of wine and drama, Poseidon, manager of earthquakes and the sea, Hephaestus, patron of fire and metalworking, and Asklepius, worker of miracles in his role as patron of medicine. Even nymphs and lesser mythological characters such as Aphaea and Herakles and Theseus could have temples, too.

The principal temple had as its function the housing of the votive statue of the principal deity. Such a statue was large, and lavish in its execution. The Greeks would have wanted it so whether or not it was in the interest of religion. They were impelled to express symbolic meanings, personality traits, past deeds of their gods in the sculpture, but they had

[95] Isabel Hoopes Grinnel, *Greek Temples* (New York: Metropolitan Museum of Art, 1943), p. 22.
[96] Dinsmoor, *The Architecture of Ancient Greece*, op. cit., p. 49.

also to provide a totally rich environment. Their motivations in this must have been echoed in part by the motivations of some of the great medieval builders like Abbot Suger, but I mean only that element of religion which says that only the best is worthy of the deity. Usually what the Greeks did in this matter was out in the open for everyone to see. There were few concealed devotions, little art made for love and not for show. Possibly the nearest exception to this is the Panathenaic frieze around the *cella* of the Parthenon, which was not in the full light of day, and so high up that it was not easy to see.

But the votive statues in the Golden Age represented the best efforts the Greeks could put forward. The statue of Athena Parthenos, for example, standing in the *naos* of the Parthenon, was about 40 feet high, including the pedestal. It was one of the greatest works of Pheidias. It represented the titular goddess fully armed with her spear, her helmet, her banner, her shield. She supported a winged victory in her right hand. It was chryselephantine, that is, it was made of the most precious materials, of gold and ivory. The gold plates which formed the drapery, armor, and the like were hung on a wooden core in such a way that they could be removed if the temple were in danger, a typical example of the practicality of the Greek. The face, the hands, and other exposed parts of the body were of ivory, the eyes of gems. And so it was for the other great votive statue, Zeus at Olympia. The Greeks had been working in ivory and gold for a thousand years but in small scale. It was reserved for Pheidias to achieve what must have long been the ambition of Greek artists, the development of this technique on a colossal scale.

This statue was impressive enough and important enough, but it was not to be treated with the same kind of devotion that ought to be rendered to the statue of the Virgin of Chartres, which, as Malraux suggests, for a long time could not be regarded as a statue at all but as the very personification of the Virgin. There is little doubt that the votive statue of Athena Parthenos standing within the Parthenon, quite as much as the statue of Athena Promachos standing outside, was also a symbol of the power and glory that was Athens. It is inconceivable that a resident of Paris, Chartres, or Bourges of the thirteenth century could so completely identify the Madonna of his cathedral or even the patron saint with the eminence of his city, but it was otherwise in Greece.

> The undoubted emotion which stirred the breast of an Athenian at the name of Athena or the sight of her chryselephantine statue may best be understood by noting the identity of the names, as close as that of Britain and Britannia.[97]

It was a patriotic as well as a religious emotion.

But the treasure of the titular goddess was not entirely inviolate. It

[97] W. K. C. Guthrie, *The Greeks and Their Gods* (Boston: Beacon, 1955), p. 255.

could be borrowed as long as one undertook to return it. When Pericles summed up the resources of Athens for the war with Sparta, he included the gold ornaments of Athena herself as a matter of course. And if a city fell, the temples were the property of the conquerors.

With such a complete intermixture of godly and human interest, it is not surprising that the Attic festivals had the same complexion. Recreation and religion were joined together in a happier way than Puritans have ever been able to manage; the Panathenaic festival has but a feeble shadow in the basket social, a block party, or a ticker-tape parade.

To build their temples the Greeks used trabeate construction. At first everything was of wood, later more and more of the materials were stone. This was all right since the Greeks had no need to span large openings and were moreover unduly timid as to the capacity of stone even when used in this relatively unfavorable way. They preferred to set the columns close together even in large buildings. The columns were ordinarily heavier than they needed to be. As a result the distance between columns in a truly Greek structure is seldom much more than the diameters of the columns, sometimes even less.

Once in a while they tried some expedients to get longer spans or to support unduly heavy masses. Thus the marble ceiling beams of Bassae were hollowed to reduce their weight, the Doric friezes of the Propylaea were cantilevered. Occasionally and sparingly iron beams were used but always concealed. In the Parthenon the Greek builders set flat, wide iron bars, cantilevered out from the stone to support the heaviest statues of the pediment so that their weight would not come directly, and perhaps adversely, on the cornice. Even bigger ones were used in the Propylaea and in the big temple at Agrigentum. It would not have occurred to the Greeks to call this structural dishonesty, any more than the refinements they introduced for visual purposes would have seemed to them to demand justification on "organic" grounds. They were much too sensible to be taken in by any such dogmatic ideology, and would have laughed at anyone who proposed it. Their construction to the end remains the simplest and most direct exposition of post-and-lintel or trabeate construction, at least until very recent days.

Greek walls were made of solid blocks of stone held together by metal clamps without mortar. Thus the joints had to be effected with great accuracy and the wall surface had to be polished smooth by a great deal of hand labor. Where marble was not sufficiently abundant to make all the walls, a local soft and coarse-grained limestone called *poros* was used, and this was often faced with a marble stucco which could take on a polish comparable to that of the solid marble walls. Sometimes the walls above the lintels were made hollow to reduce the weight on the stone beams; this was done in the frieze of the Parthenon, for instance. Openings were square at the top and spanned by a stone lintel. The roofs were carried by wooden rafters resting on the *naos* wall and the colonnade. These rafters were covered externally with thin marble slabs, and similar slabs served as the paneled ceiling material of the colonnades. The pediments or gable ends took their slope from the slope of the roof. Even the downspouts and gutters were of stone.

Athens

Admirers of the Greeks have not always agreed about the high point of Greek history. The selection of a "best" time may say more about the selecter than the time. The flowering of all the arts is seldom synchronous. But occasionally this almost happens. There *are* high clusters, there *are* nodal points in history, and we can select Athens in the fifth century B.C. as one such without any doubts, despite the human appeal of the earlier archaic. Not typical of all Greece, the Athenian fifth century was nevertheless typical of what Greece could do at its best.

Economic prosperity will not in itself produce a great art but it seems to be a necessary condition for such production. The Athenians had this prosperity partly because of their own trading efforts and partly because of the treasures which poured in from the members of the Delian League. These treasures always were supposed to be a form of taxation for the common defense and not a sort of tribute to Athens, and for years they were kept in the treasury at Delos—indeed, from the founding of the League right after the Persian victory in 477 to the fateful year 454 when the treasury was removed to Athens. It was this move which on the one hand brought to fruition all the latent talent of the Athenians and at the same time brewed all the jealousies which were in the long run to bring about the Peloponnesian War and the downfall of Athens. The significance of this transfer cannot be doubted. The temple at Delos which was started with great éclat shortly after the removal of the treasury might have been a Parthenon. As it was, construction languished, detail was impoverished, and it took more than a century to complete, while the Parthenon was finished in nine years except for the sculpture.

In 431 when the Peloponnesian war began, the hill of Lykabettos, 1,100 feet high, overhung the city of Athens but was outside the defensive walls because of its unfavorable shape. A visitor would note the strong hills inside the walls, the oblong Acropolis with its 500-foot sides, all perpendicular except the one to the west. He would see the Aeropagus and the Pnyx and the Hill of the Nymphs, each perhaps a hundred feet lower. He would see the Acropolis, perhaps noting that the Athenians regarded it as an important religious precinct rather than as an important fortress. Most other Greeks might have wondered at this, not aware of the principle which Aristotle would advance later, that "An Acropolis is suitable for oligarchy and monarchy, level ground for democracy."[98]

The Acropolis may not have been so pure as it has been described by Fougères.

[98] Aristotle, *Politics*, vii, 10, 4.

Below was the buzz . . . of the life of labour, business, industry and politics; above, the serenity of a supraterrestrial atmosphere, where the gods reign alone among the smoke of sacrifices and the murmur of prayers; while a handful of soldiers scan the horizon from the heights of the ramparts.[99]

Down below the Acropolis there was not a great deal to wonder at. Much of what Pausanias later catalogued was yet to come. The Persians had done a thorough job of destroying the Agora and it had been slow rebuilding. The *tholos* was there, that famous circular building which served as the dining club for the presiding section of the Athenian senate. The music hall or *odeion* was there, that *odeion* later mentioned by Plutarch, with "many tiers of seats and many pillars, and which had a roof made with a circular slope from a single peak they say was an exact reproduction of the Great King's pavilion. . . ."[100] Pericles himself had put this up and had introduced rehearsals and musical contests as early as 446. But the new *bouleuterion*, the great colonnaded *stoa*, and most of the temples were yet to come. The Agora was not the great array it was later to be. As for the residential parts of the city, they were nondescript; most of the houses were simple, even to the point of meanness; the streets confused and narrow and probably dirty.

Nor were things around the outskirts much more exciting. The stadium was to come a century later. There were three gymnasiums, but these were not particularly impressive. Five thousand citizens could meet in the Pnyx, which had been built against the hill by Cleisthenes three-quarters of a century earlier, but this offered little more than natural rock-slab seats in a natural amphitheater with a back wall and an orator's platform, and it would be a hundred years before the great *tour de force* of turning it around against the hill was to be essayed.

Athenian tragedy was at the height of its fame, but the theaters were still not remarkable. Some time after 498, when the wooden scaffolding had collapsed in the Agora in the midst of a performance, the Athenians had removed the theater to the precinct of Dionysus south and a little east of the Acropolis. But in the time of Pericles it was still simple; the architecture pretensions were to come later when the tragedies themselves were no longer great. For now it was just a circular orchestral terrace behind the stage, a scene building, or perhaps only a flat wall, with some temporary seats for spectators at the sides.

And even on the Acropolis, there was less to see than our reconstructive imagination provides, an imagination which puts the buildings of all the ages together on a single site at a single time. The only buildings of

---

[99] G. Fougères, Selinonte. Quoted by R. E. Wycherley, *How the Greeks Built Cities* (London and New York: Macmillan, 1949), p. 37. Wycherley regards this as an exaggeration but says the brillant development of the Acropolis of Athens was exceptional, not in type but only in its excellence.
[100] Plutarch's *Lives*, op. cit., vol. III, p. 43.

importance standing at this moment were the Propylaea which was just being finished, that majestic gateway to the sanctuary itself, and the Parthenon, on which sculptors were possibly still carving the last representations, painters applying the last blue and gold. The old temple of Athena had been desecrated by the Persians and pulled down. The little temple of Nike Apteros was not to be finished until 426 and the Erechtheion, not until 420, both in the uneasy truce of the War.

If the Acropolis was not yet as full of buildings as it was to be later (though it was never very full), it literally swarmed with statues. Most conspicuous, no doubt, was the 30-foot bronze figure of Athena Promachos, fully armed, whose spear and helmet shimmered at every vessel rounding Cape Sunium on the way to Piraeus. But she was not alone. There was the statue of Athena Hygeia erected by Pericles in memory of the slave who had been hurt while helping to build the Parthenon. There was the large bronze image of the Trojan Horse. There was Myron's group of Marsyas. There were statues of Xanthippus and Anacreon and many others besides.

But if the diversions of the lower town and the sun's reflections on the helmet of Athena Promachos might have attracted a visitor's attention for a time, that attention must finally have rested, as did the Athenian attention and as must ours, on two of the buildings which rose from the Acropolis. Here the great walls of the north, south, and east, completed by Cimon, raised the impressive platform on which Pericles was now completing his magnificent structures, war or no war. Here from the west the steep ascent led to the Propylaea, which, popular as it was with the Athenians, was but the prelude to one of the greatest buildings men have ever built, the temple of Athena Parthenos, Athena the Virgin.

In later days the direct Romans were to build a blunt and monumental approach to the precinct, but in its Greek heyday the stairs and ramps to the top of the Acropolis zigzagged up the hill. From a distance an Athenian could have seen the great front porch or vestibule of the Acropolis, called the Propylaea, and some intimations of the temple of Athena the Virgin, but as he came nearer and ascended along the parapet and finally became enveloped by the flanks of the Propylaea, he could look only up and was finally confronted only by the west facade of the latter.

A *propylon* meant to the Greeks simply a gatehouse to an enclosure, usually a sacred one, but also the entrance to an *agora* or a palace. In its simplest form it would be a porch containing a gate with the columnar support of the roof extending both outside and inside the gate. If it were more complex and monumental, the plural term *propylaea* would be applied.

About Greece there were many such precincts, many such walls, many such gates guarding the enclosures which were ordinarily open only between sunrise and sundown. There were particularly interesting examples at Epidauros, Sunium, Eleusis, Priene, but there was none finer than the Propylaea at Athens. Like the Parthenon it introduced, it was Doric.

Although the Propylaea was never completed, its essential purpose *was* consummated and it is not impossible that the structures which would have served subordinate or actually irrelevant purposes were better left unbuilt. In any event the actual situation does permit us to concentrate on the Propylaea's main function, which was to serve as a gatehouse.

As we ascend from the west, we are confronted then by a simple *Pl. 150* facade which can be technically described as follows. It is a Doric hexastyle portico of Pentelic marble; its pediment and metopes are undecorated; the regular intercolumniation is interrupted at the center where the column spacing is proportioned to the regular spacing as 3:2. This is essentially a complete description; it can be so brief because the classic proportions had rules which had been so thoroughly worked out by the time of this building that each of the terms stands for something quite explicit. A more precise statement would be needed only if one were interested in minutiae. But what do the terms mean to those of us who are not experts in the classic orders?

Almost all the Greek buildings of importance, certainly all those with which we are here to be concerned, were of trabeate construction, that is, composed of flat horizontal lintels, not arches. These lintels or beams were supported vertically by masonry walls or by columns. Ordinarily the inner part of a temple, which was fully enclosed, was surrounded by a solid wall of stone which, of course, supported the beams of wood or stone. The whole building (or its front and rear) was then enveloped by a porch or portico, the outside lintels of which were supported by columns, the inside by the wall. Usually there was but a single row of columns, but more complicated arrangements of two or three rows were also made. There are technical names for all these things. If the portico is on the front and rear only, the building is said to be amphiprostyle; if it surrounds the building, it is said to be peripteral. A single row of columns is taken for granted; if there are two rows, the building is dipteral, and so on. The number of columns across the front is designated by a suitable term. Thus if there are six, the building is hexastyle; if eight, octastyle; and so on. The number of columns on a facade was almost always even, although there were five at the temple of Apollo at Thermon of the late seventh century and seven at the fifth-century temple of Zeus at Akragas. Six was by all odds the prevalent number; of twenty-one of the most important temples built between the last part of the seventh century and the middle of the fourth century, sixteen were hexastyle. Of the other five, the temple of Artemis at Ephesus and the Parthenon at Athens were octastyle; the temple of Athena Nike at Athens was tetrastyle; and there were the two with an odd number of columns already cited. We will speak of the lateral arrangement of columns when we get nearer to the Parthenon.

How the columns were proportioned, how they were spaced, how they rose from the base of the building, how they ended under the lintels, how the lintel was disposed—all these things were clearly defined once the order of the design was stated. In the classic era there were really but five major orders, the Tuscan and Composite, which were Roman additions; and the Doric, Ionic, and Corinthian from the Greeks. The Doric and Ionic were essentially contemporary with each other; the Corinthian came a little later. As a general matter the Doric column was the shortest and thickest, the Corinthian the longest and thinnest, and the profusion of detail increased from the Doric through the Ionic to the Corinthian, but this was not true at every point. The orders can be clearly differentiated by their proportions, by the bases and capitals of the columns, by the arrangement of the entablature, which is the superstructure of the temple resting on the columns and is made up of the architrave, the frieze, and the cornice. But other things were different too, even the number of flutings on the columns. The simplest quick recognition for those who do not have a trained eye for proportions is to be found in the capital, the simple set of moldings and the echinus of the Doric, the shell-like volute of the Ionic, the acanthus leaves of the Corinthian.

Pl. 154
Pl. 155
Pl. 156

It was characteristic of the Ionic columns that they were more slender than the Doric, and the Corinthian, more slender still. The architraves, friezes, cornices, and the column bases were correspondingly modified to suit the different proportions and the greater amount of ornament. Vitruvius, who lived in the time of Augustus, wrote some very practical things in his ten books on architecture and a good deal of nonsense as well. Here is what he said of the Doric and the Ionic.

> The Doric column, as used in buildings, began to exhibit the proportions, strength and beauty of the body of a man. Just so afterward, when they desired to construct a temple to Diana in a new style of beauty, they translated these footprints into terms characteristic of the slenderness of women. . . .Thus in the invention of the two kinds of columns, they borrowed manly beauty, naked and unadorned, for the one, and for the other the delicacy, adornment, and proportions, characteristic of women.[101]

Of the Corinthian Vitruvius says that Callimachus invented it at Corinth. But Pausanias says that Callimachus made a golden lamp for the goddess Athena Polias in the Erechtheion and a bronze palm tree reaching to the roof to draw off the smoke. Certainly the details of the early Corinthian capitals do suggest a bronze origin. Also Corinthian bronze was celebrated in antiquity. So the title may mean the material of the prototype rather than an invention at Corinth. A very early single Corinthian column at Bassae dates at least a century before the campaniform "composite" caps of leaves in relief of Egypt, and hence a claim of Egyptian origin is not very convincing.

The Greeks would, on occasion, use more than one order in the same temple. Bassae's Temple of Apollo Epikourios, possibly designed by the

[101] Vitruvius, *The Ten Books on Architecture*, translated by Morris H. Morgan (New York: Dover, 1960), pp. 113–114.

great Ictinus, was essentially Doric, but on the inside of the *cella* Ionic capitals were used, presumably to dispense with an architrave at midheight, falsely suggesting a gallery, and with the necessary second tier of columns, had the shorter Doric order been used. At Bassae there are even a pair of Corinthian columns and an isolated one between them at the southern interior possibly suggesting "Apollo's tree." But this was unusual and the Doric appealed much more generally to the classic Greeks, while the Ionian, and especially the Corinthian with its wide potential for increasingly ostentatious vulgarity, gave the Romans more pleasure.

In this discussion I shall say nothing more about the Corinthian and Ionic orders. The important thing is to recognize that any one of the orders in their day was quite sharply defined and that the variations permitted were subtle ones. Later on the Romans created their own distortions, and our own eclectic architects who had selected Greek as a basis tried to express their personalities by bringing changes on the Greek proportions. They were men of no large originality themselves and inevitably failed to improve the Greek forms.

So when we have said that the west portico of the Propylaea was Doric hexastyle, we have said that it had six columns. What more have we said by calling it Doric?

A Doric building normally stood on a slab of three steps called the stereobate; the upper step, the stylobate, formed the direct support of the column. The column rose without any intervening forms directly from this base. It was relatively thick. The height, including the capital, might be anything from 4 to 6½ times the diameter at the base, with a classic average of 5½. But even the thinnest of these was thick when compared with a typical Ionic column whose height was at least 9 times the base diameter.

We will easily notice about the Doric column that it had a smaller diameter at the top than at the bottom. The west-front columns of the Propylaea, for example, were a little more than 5 feet 3 inches across at the bottom but just under 4 feet across at the top. The central columns of the Parthenon, which were larger in all respects, were only slightly less attenuated, being about 6 feet 2 inches at the bottom and just under 4 feet 10 inches at the top. But in either case this was no simple tapering of the shaft such as might be proposed by a thoughtless or careless designer. On the contrary the Greeks recognized many other principles of optical illusion. They knew that columns with straight sides might appear concave so they experimented early with ways to produce a profile which was slightly convex. Their conclusion was to make the shaft go up straight for about the lower third of the height and then to curve it gently to the desired smaller diameter at the top. This profile, called entasis, was sometimes too obtrusive, as in the Basilica of Paestum, but it was no mannerism, as the static impression of Corinth, which has no entasis, will demonstrate. Like most other things in Doric design, it reached its supreme expression on the Parthenon and its accompanying Propylaea.

This is the first of the many refinements which the Greeks gave to their great monuments and which stand as one of the characterizations of their best work, differentiating it from less discriminating architectures.

We will then notice of the columns that they had flutes running through their height right up to the capitals. There are many theories as to how this process of grooving or fluting the columns came into being. It is argued, for example, that square columns were the primitive form. If you had close-spaced square columns, there were not many unimpeded diagonal views you could get. So you chamfered the edges of the squares, producing octagonal cross sections. Having done this and having found it an improvement, you continued to increase the number of sides of your polygon, thus approaching the shape of a circle. Each of the angles of the polygon produced a sharp projection. Then you carved grooves between these projections and thus produced the flutes. Anyway, the Doric order always cut its flutes so that the corners of the polygon left to separate the flutes had sharp edges called arrises. Indeed, one of the differentiations between the Doric and Ionic orders is that in making an Ionic column, you flattened off these separating edges.

But there was more to a Doric flute than that. The Doric designers held fast to a theory that projections should be placed one over another. The top member of a capital of the round Doric column was square and its edges were parallel to the edges of the building. One of the arrises should therefore line up with each of the corners of this square. But the column would look better if, as you examined it head on, you saw at its center line not an arris but rather a flute. You could achieve this if you had only four arrises, one under each corner, and one great flute going from corner to corner. You could achieve it if you put an arris at each corner and three flutes between, resulting in a total of twelve flutes for the whole capital. You could also achieve it with twenty flutes and with twenty-eight. A column with twelve flutes has too few to give a good appearance. A column with twenty-eight is already beginning to look too busy. So twenty became the classic number from which no deviation was desirable. To be sure, the temple at Assos had only twelve flutes, and a few, such as those at Sunium (sixteen), Pompeii (eighteen), or Paestum (twenty-four), broke the rule altogether, but these were clearly undesirable exceptions.

The Doric column ended at the top with a simple capital. First there were from three to five simple horizontal fillets or annulets which served to stop the arrises and flutes of the shaft. Then there was a swelling out by way of a molding, which has come to be called the echinus. The word is Greek for sea urchin and may have been applied by Vitruvius because the profile looked something like the shell of that marine animal. In early temples the projection was quite full and curved almost like a parabola (temples of Ceres and Poseidon at Paestum, for example); later on, as in the Parthenon, the projection was much less and the curvature approached that of a straight line or the curve of a hyperbola. The final member was a square slab called the abacus.

On top of the columns rested the horizontal structure, the entablature. First there was the principal beam which carried across from column to column. This beam, called the architrave, was quite deep, and for the Doric Pl. 157 order resembled a single member in that its vertical face was all in one plane. In the Ionic and Corinthian orders, on the other hand, it usually looked as though it had been built up in laminations, ordinarily consisting of three planes. Most people believe that both these forms were carried over in stone from the shapes they naturally had when all the framing of the temple was in wood. Above the architrave was the second large horizontal member or frieze. The Doric frieze occupied the area where the crossbeams of wood had once rested on the architrave. Thus it was not unnatural to preserve the appearance of their ends, and these forms, usually grooved, are called triglyphs. The spaces between the triglyphs, which, when they were wooden beams, might have been empty, were called metopes and were sometimes decorated.

Between the architrave and the Doric frieze was a smaller horizontal band called the *taenia*, and beneath it and also beneath the triglyphs was a series of protuberances called *guttae*, looking like pegs, which may well have been the stone vestiges of the wooden pegs that once held in the wooden beams.[102]

Finally, above the frieze, was the top member of the entablature, the cornice, which had a horizontal component, the *geison*, and a sloping one corresponding to the roof slope.

If you look at the triglyphs with any care, you may notice something strange about their centering. A beam would normally rest over a column and it is not surprising to find a triglyph directly over each column. Nor is it surprising to find a second triglyph between those over the columns since beams could naturally also rest on the architrave. This is the usual Doric arrangement, one triglyph centered on each column, alternating with a triglyph centered between the columns. But the end triglyphs offered a problem.

It was one of those major problems of architectural design which come up in almost every period with a genuine solicitude for the right

---

[102] We must recognize that such questions of source are usually highly controversial. For example, there are some who insist that the triglyphs, *guttae*, etc., could not have been derived from wooden forms and adduce some practical reasons why that could not be so. But most opinion seems to lean to the position I have stated. The matter is not without importance. For if the triglyphs and *guttae* and the *mutules* were replicas in stone of an obsolete form in another material, this might not render the same praise to Greek purity as a theory which held that the triglyphs, like the flutes, had a strictly optical purpose. The more pedestrian interpretation could also be said to give aid and comfort to those who would like to defend modern impurities by pointing out that the Greeks were also impure in much the same way.

forms in the right places. We shall encounter it again when we learn what trouble the Gothic builders had in locating the rose window. For the Greeks the trouble was that if you centered the triglyph on the end columns, you had a small space at the edge of the frieze which was flat and unsightly and weak. So the natural thing to do was to try to move the triglyph over to the edge of the frieze. This was no serious offense against structure since the eccentricity of the beam axis from the column axis was not large. But it produced other troubles. For if this triglyph were moved and nothing else were done, then the end metopes would be perceptibly longer than the others, and this too would be an aesthetic offense. You could and usually did let them be a little longer than the others, but not too much. There was one more thing you could do: you might keep the metopes the same size or nearly so and let the position of the end triglyph determine the edge of the building. But you could not center the end column this far in, for obvious reasons. Then the distance between the end column and the one next to it would have to be less than the distance between the columns in the middle of the portico. Here you might have shaved a little both ways, made the end column a little thinner, the spacing a little less, and perhaps it would not be noticed. But this was not the Greek way; on the contrary, their temper would insist that the statement be clear and unmistakable. So characteristically the end columns of the Parthenon are thicker than the intermediate columns although they carry less load, their bases measuring 6 feet, 3⅛ inches, while the intermediate ones are 6 feet, 2 inches; the intercolumniation at the end reduces to 5 feet, 9 inches, while that in the middle is 7 feet, 11½ inches.

There were many more refinements, of which we may pause to note but one or two. The long horizontal lines of the stylobate or the entablature would seem to sag so they actually were given a slight convexity with respect to the ground wherever this was practicable. It was practicable on the Parthenon for both entablature and stylobate, at the Propylaea only at the entablature.[103] The entasis I have already mentioned; the column axes were given a slight inclination toward the center, the small vertical upper surfaces slanted slightly toward the outside.[104]

Some modern psychological experiments have attempted to demonstrate that the optical illusions which these refinements were supposed to correct would not have occurred. But Dinsmoor says this does not matter, for

> [W]e have nevertheless definite evidence that the ancient Greeks
> believed that such illusions required correctives and, in consequence,
> must admit that such was the primary purpose of their employment . . .

[103] Because of the difference in levels of the floor between the east and the west and the necessity for carts to pass through the middle.
[104] Other refinements involved tapering the walls in sympathy with the column inclinations, inclination of the door and window jambs, inclination of the abacus of the capital to parallel the inclined axis of the column.

all entailed a mathematical precision in the setting out of the work and in its execution which is probably unparalleled in the world.[105]

But there are dissenters. Rhys Carpenter is particularly caustic about attributing too much refinement to the Greeks:

It needed the archeologist to discover that there was no single material aspect of the classic civilization which could endure a really close scrutiny and still maintain its calm poise of assumed impeccability.

A measuring-stick and a scrupulously attentive eye can work strange havoc with the perfection of a Greek temple. Identical parts refuse to reveal identical dimensions: some are over size, some under, others are miscut and patched; errors of computation vie with errors of execution; outright miscalculation betrays itself under a guise of last-minute improvisation.[106]

The intercolumniations at the corners were, as I have said, narrowed somewhat in order to have a harmonious spacing of the triglyphs and metopes. The corner column was thickened to give emphasis to this development. The reduction of the spacing between columns at the end had another powerful effect. Viewed from most angles the space between the corner column and the next one is perceived against the clear blue sky of Greece, the spaces between the other columns are perceived against the background of a yellow or white or very pale blue stone wall. Against the strong sky background a space may seem wider than against the lesser contrast of the stone background. Many people look at Greek colonnades with no realization that this substantial difference in dimensions exists. Worse than this, modern architects who have rejected history have neither learned the visual lesson as a dogma of history nor achieved it as a matter of intuition, so they build modern colonnades surrounding walled buildings against the bright sky of California, in many ways so Greek, with no understanding of what they are doing and occasionally with unpleasant results.

The Doric facade was not a stale and fishy white. Color was added as reinforcement though mostly to the nonstructural parts. The Greeks understood that you could diminish the importance of structural elements by coloring them and paid enough tribute to firmness not to wish to do this. On the other hand, they also knew that the right colors would seem to reduce the weight of the nonstructural parts. What these colors were and exactly where they were applied, I must leave until later.

Between the sloping member of the cornice and the horizontal member was an area called the tympanum. All the roofs were of about the same pitch and quite flat by northern standards. A triangular area is hard to

[105] Dinsmoor, *The Architecture of Ancient Greece*, op. cit., p. 165.
[106] Rhys Carpenter, "The Vision of Ancient Life," in *Studies in the Arts and Architecture*, op. cit., pp. 16–17.

decorate with sculpture, especially if it is to be generic, objective, and story-telling as the Greek sculpture almost always was. In such a space the figures in the center are likely to be of superhuman size, but in the corners they will be either pygmies or be forced into strange positions, such as a reclining one. Finally, the decidedly central axis posed further limitations, almost insisting upon a balanced design. Not every people would have tackled this problem.

Pl. 160

Most of the great Doric temples did have decorated pediments[107] and many had carved metopes,[108] though this was not general. Some of the temples which did not have sculptured pediments or metopes were in provincial areas where both artists and funds may have been scarce;[109] in others the absence of remnants of the carving does not prove that there was none; sometimes perhaps the temples were never finished. The pediments and the metopes of the Propylaea are not carved, but we cannot tell whether this was deliberate choice, to lend more force to the culminating brilliance of the Parthenon, or merely the consequence of the Peloponnesian War, which we know to have prevented the completion of other elements of the original design.

The final thing we have to note about the west front of the Propylaea is that the central columns are farther apart than the others, so that there are two triglyphs between the column centers in contrast to the usual one. This is most unusual for a Greek structure and resulted from the need to provide a wider opening through the gate for the passage of ritual processions and also building materials for new buildings or for repair of the Parthenon.

As we approach these columns, we will note two smaller Doric porches at right angles in front of the flanking buildings, but we will neglect them and pass at once into the vestibule.

Pl. 151

Pl. 152

Pl. 153

When we enter the vestibule, we will notice that our passage to the precinct is obstructed by a wall set about two-thirds of the way through and pierced by five openings roughly corresponding to the openings between columns. It was this wall that contained the gates so that when the pilgrims needed to wait they might wait under cover within the large vestibule. The doorways were of different heights, diminishing at the flanks. In the vestibule the ceiling span was too great to be carried without interior columns, and so the central passage was flanked by three columns on each side. On this spacing Doric columns would have been too short; one group might have been superposed on the other, as was done in the Parthenon, but these could not have been properly terminated in the Propylaea, and so the designer chose the taller Ionic order to flank this

[107] Notably those of Apollo at Delphi, Aphaia at Aegina, Zeus at Akragas, Zeus at Olympia (which some think to have been finer than the carving of the Parthenon), the Theseion or temple of Hephaestus at Athens.
[108] Including those of Apollo at Thermon, Hera at Selinus, Hephaestus at Athens. The metopes of Zeus at Olympia were not carved, or at least there is no evidence that they were, although the general level of execution of the temple might make this strange.
[109] Probably this is what happened at the temple of Poseidon at Paestum.

290   *Bernini Is Dead?*

passageway. The interior was highly colored and decorated by the finest artists of the day as a further preparation for the visitor who would emerge into the light of the precinct as soon as he had passed through one of the gates and through the eastern portico, which, in all essential respects, resembled the one at the west.

But if the visitor were interested in Greek subtleties, he might note one more thing about the Propylaea. All the time, you remember, we have been climbing stairs toward the shrine. Indeed, we do so even within the Propylaea. Now if you climb stairs toward a portico, always looking up at it, the proportions will appear differently than if you are descending and looking down at it. Mnesicles, the architect, took care of this problem too and we find that the columns of the east portico of the Propylaea were slightly more slender than those of the west portico to compensate for the difference of viewpoint. We also have to admire the skillful way in which he has managed the problem created by the fact that the eastern and western pediments were to be of essentially the same size and yet one had to be at a higher level than the other.

An Athenian temple was made of Pentelic marble. The mountain of Pentelicus, about 2,600 feet high, stands on the Athenian plain overlooking the battlefield of Marathon. From its quarries came the stone for almost all the buildings of the Athenian heyday. The stone itself was white with blue veins and a little translucent, but when exposed to air finally assumed the rich yellow color with which we are acquainted. When they were built, most of the Greek temples presumably were white except for the color applied to the sculpture and upper moldings.

The first thing we will notice when we come through the Propylaea into the precinct is that the axis of the Propylaea from which we are emerging has no brutal or obvious relation to the axis of the Parthenon. The Parthenon is not right in front of us, it is off to the right side. Its axis is not even parallel to that of the Propylaea, although nearly so. It is inevitable, then, that we will first see the Parthenon not as a facade, as is so often our experience with buildings, but as a piece of three-dimensional sculpture, something to be viewed in the round. And this is an important characteristic of Greek temples from which we can learn much. They are not part of streets, they are not just fronts, they stand alone. We can walk around them. We are expected to walk around them. They are expected to present a pleasing aspect from every angle and at every distance. And they meet this expectation, until you get too close to a corner. Try to think of very many other buildings of which you can say so much. It is a trying test of the competence of a designer, a test many would fail.

The Greeks were helped to some extent by a few simple rules which they had worked out themselves, it may be noted, and not taken from books. I have already spoken of some of the canons of the Doric order. There were many more relations, almost fixed between all sorts of other proportions.

Indeed, the extent of the possible dimensional relationships which can be traced in a classic Greek temple is such that it has encouraged many people to try to establish theories of proportion based on various absolute numerical or geometric relationships. Even if I believed in any of these, which I do not, it would not advance our thinking to present it here. The chief point is that there was a large number of general understandings about appropriate proportions and appropriate visual refinements, so many in fact that most modern artists might find them very restricting of individuality. The fact remains that the Greeks were able to work enormous changes on these sharply iterated fundamental themes so that all the Doric temples look alike to a casual eye and have enormous and pleasurable differences to the eye which has learned how to see. Order is always present but it is never rigor; discipline is there, but not chains.

Next we will realize that we are not looking at the front but at the back of the temple when we gaze on the west facade of the Parthenon, which is the nearest to us. This might also seem extraordinary and we might seek for different reasons. We might, for example, hazard a practical one. Greek temples we know were expected to face east. If the Parthenon had to face east and if the slopes of the Acropolis were so steep except upon the west and perhaps a little on the south where Cimon built his retaining wall, possibly this arrangement was a matter of simple practical necessity.

But then we have to realize also that it was not important that one should see the front of the temple from the gate of the precinct for the rear also had important functions. And again it might even be an advantage to extend the walk to the front.

As we stand before this building, our emotions will be more aroused than our intellects. If we have any sensitiveness at all, we will feel the exquisite proportions without having to measure them to confirm the fact that they exist. But they do exist. The ratio of the axial spacings of the columns to the column diameters is as 9:4. The building is nine axial spacings long and four wide; the ratio of the height of the elevation to the width of the stylobate is also as 4:9. We could multiply such observations many times.

The columns are of the classic Doric proportions, 5½ diameters high. The echinus of the capital has a stiff hyperbolic profile, just right. And when our eyes meet the metopes, we find still another refinement. Here there is a repetition of the perspective illusion so carefully presented by the angle contraction of the colonnade. Here there is a careful gradation of the widths of the metopes from very wide ones at the center to quite narrow ones at the corners, offering a maximum difference of a little more than 4 inches and of course having the result that no triglyph is exactly centered above the corresponding column. By now the triglyph has become admittedly vestigial and barefacedly decorative. All these metopes are carved. For the most part they represent battles, fights between Lapiths and Centaurs on the south, gods and Titans on the east, Greeks and

Amazons on the west, scenes from the siege of Troy on the north. They are usually composed about a central polygon, the sides of which are the bodies of the paired contestants. Their aesthetic has been much debated. Take them as you will, these metopes are exciting individually and impressive collectively; we must remember that they were to be seen from the ground at least forty-five feet away so that it is right they should be two-figure compositions showing great physical exertion through the use of line, surface, and pattern.

From the metopes our eye moves naturally to the pediment. Here we will notice that the face of the tympanum is quite deep. It has in fact been recessed 8 inches behind the plane of the architrave to allow the sculpture greater relief.

The subjects of this pediment and its opposite one on the east are quite different from those of its competitor in the temple of Zeus at Olympia. There the tales are those of a great trilogy exalting Herakles, Zeus, and Apollo, and might be interpreted as having some elements of faith or mystery. Not so for the pediments of the Parthenon. At the west Athena and Poseidon contest for the supremacy of Athens while legendary figures look on—". . . the gods performing their magic for the favour of mortals."[110] And at the east end we see the birth of Athena, springing full-panoplied from the brain of Zeus, a symbol perhaps to the average Athenian that he is "a citizen of the most enlightened of all cities."[111] If we were to pause for more than the impressive overall architectural effect, we would note the molding of the draperies, how clinging and transparent they are, and we might remark how well the sculptor, by using reclining and sitting figures in the corners, has managed the difficult geometry of this flat isosceles triangle.

At the corners of the gable we would note that the *akroteria* and *proteria* placed there as accents are colossal openwork designs of marble about 9 feet high, made up of stems and tendrils which rise from acanthus leaves and end in palmettos.

At about this time, had we been there when the Parthenon was in its prime, we would have become aware of the color. The important structural members remained in the natural white of the marble, and indeed the whole peristyle was white below the capitals. The incision under the necking of the columns was blue the annulets, red and blue; the triglyphs and *regulae* and *mutules* were blue; the *taenia*, red with a gold meander; the *regulae* had a gold *anthemion* on their blue ground. The *guttae* were white and so were the metopes, except that details of the sculptured figures were colored. And there were similar colored arrangements on the sculptures of the pediment. Finally, looking inside, we could have seen that the interior moldings were gold, green, and white.

[110] Charles Seltman, *Approach to Greek Art* (New York: Studio, 1948), p. 68.
[111] Ibid.

This color emphasized the design of the building, affected the view from afar as well as from near, and was not done to court the realism of which the Greek designers are so often accused. The purpose of the paint was one of decoration, of design, and not of portraiture. If the design happened to need blue at the point where a man's head appeared, the artist would not hesitate to paint the beard and hair blue, although he would leave the flesh in the unpainted marble.

It took a long time for the Western world to realize that Greek architecture was not white. Very few great architectures, if any, have been. Bright and formal colors were used by the Sumerians, the Egyptians, the Greeks, the Romans, and the people of the Middle Ages. It was the Renaissance scholars, who began to dig up Roman copies of bleached Hellenistic statues, who led us astray.

But now we step inside the portico of the Parthenon and find ourselves confronted by a second porch of six columns raised on two steps.

The inner portico is also Doric. But on the architrave the triglyphs have been replaced by a continuous Ionic frieze. This frieze running all around the inner building was a distinct innovation. It was topped by a decorative cornice, which in turn was repeated on the inner face of the main entablature to form the transition to the marble ceiling of the peristyle.

The frieze was a remarkable thing. It is like a long filmstrip, a narrative of Athenians marching in a Panathenaic festival, winding to its climax over the east door in the presentation of Athena's *peplos* to her priest while the gods as invited guests look on. Not the least remarkable thing about this frieze is that it was in an obscure position and difficult to see and certainly hard to appreciate. The artists did what they could. The riders, the chariots, the graybeards, the musicians with plodding tread, the young men with animals and the maidens with vessels, all move along carved in very low relief a little deeper at the top than at the bottom in recognition of the visual problem. In the scant space of a panel 3 feet, 4 inches high, 525 feet long, and only 1¼ inches deep, the sculptors have managed their planes, their carving, and their applied color to maximum effect, so that at times many horses seem to march abreast. We cannot see much of it now in Greece; the west frieze, except for three central figures, is in the original position; most of the other three sides were carried off to the British Museum where they did not belong, though they are beautifully displayed there. There are a few fragments in the Louvre and the Athens museum.

But all this, even the scene of Athena and the peplos, and the gods over the door, was but a prelude to the chryselephantine statue of Athena which we would then have seen, towering its 40 feet high within the *naos*. Of the statue I have already spoken. The builders of the Parthenon took good care that she should be seen in fitting surroundings.

Pl. 149 Inside the *cella* is another colonnade forming a U facing the door. This is made of ten Doric columns on the sides and five at the rear. They carry an architrave which in turn supports a second upper colonnade. Perhaps there was a balcony to allow privileged travelers to walk around; perhaps at any rate the lower level could be used by such people as Pausanias as an ambulatory so that they might view the statue from all sides. The double colonnade of the *naos* offered an unexpected contrast and an unusual majesty and scale to the votive statue. There was no structural need for the double order. But the use of one-storied columns and their consequent size might have diminished the importance of the statue which was consistently intended to be the focal point once you were within the temple.

There have been many disputes as to how the statue was lighted. Some think there was a skylight; some think the double-tiered columns permitted a side lighting through a clerestory; some think the roof may have been hypoaethral, that is, open to the sky, but this is dubious; some think all the light the statue got came from the door and this simply made her more mysterious. We probably will never know. But regardless of how it may have been, we can have no doubt that the Greeks managed it well. They did not build up to this climax to let the devotee down at the last. And the emphasis which the pediments, the metopes, the first portico, the second portico, the climax of the Panathenaic frieze, all give to the votive statue of the goddess as fine an example as we could seek of the unity and wholeness which are the supreme quality of the Greek temples.

To say more of the Parthenon is anticlimactic. There was another room at the west end called the *parthenon*, or chamber of the virgin, a name which the temple as a whole may not have acquired until the late fourth century. This was a smaller room and the superposed orders would have been absurd in such a shallow space. So here the roof is supported by four Ionic columns set symmetrically in the room.

The Parthenon is exciting in restoration, clumsy as it may be, magnificent in ruin where our imagination may, if it likes, take us astray into a Greek world that never was. The majesty of this great and almost perfect conception has survived the shields that Alexander the Great applied, the dissolute residence of Demetrius Poliorcetes, the robberies of Lachares, the fires, the inscriptions of Nero, the intrusion into the *naos* of a statue of Hadrian, the addition of an apse to make it first a Greek and then a Roman Catholic church, the addition of a minaret to make it a Turkish mosque, the explosion of the Turkish gunpowder stored there, the rape of the western pediment by the Venetian leader, Morosini, the looting of Lord Elgin, and subsequent good and bad reconstructions. It remains to us the purest and most exciting architectural example from one of the great times of history.

> When old age shall this generation waste,
> Thou shalt remain in midst of other woe
> Than ours, a friend to man, to whom thou say'st,
> "Beauty is truth, truth beauty,"—that is all
> Ye know on earth, and all ye need to know.[112]

[112] John Keats, "Ode on a Grecian Urn."

ROME

The nearer we come to our own times, the more uncertain generalizations seem. We had to be careful about the Greek city-states, even the single city-state of Athens: What was Athenian amid the contradictions of Melos and Miletus, of Pericles and Alcibiades? How much less shall we be sure of classic Rome! Rome of the Republic, Rome of the Augustans, Rome of the Flavians, Rome of the Antonines, Rome of the Huns; is it the Rome of Seneca or Nero, of Cato or Agrippa, of Marcus Aurelius or of Apuleius? Is it even the Rome of Latium or the Rome of some place far to the north, the south, the east, or the west?

Thus we might not be able to speak of a prevailing Roman geography or a Roman climate were it not for one thing. The empire did include the far-flung islands, plains, deserts, and coasts of the bland Mediterranean, the foggy British Isles, the icy central Europe, the burning North Africa. The local Italian climate in which it began was benign most of the time and has been long praised by travelers.

This Italian terrain and climate determined Roman Imperial architecture. Italian geography encouraged an easy absorption of the local city-states which had been denied to Hellas. The Italian peninsula provided abundant and varied natural materials and resources so that Roman building had a good start before Romans ever took to the sea. The Italian climate was variable enough to prepare the Romans for life in other places. And the Romans were much like the British when they went abroad. They carried their version of the dinner jacket and the afternoon tea with them wherever they went. They were not above borrowing but they loaned more than they borrowed. They might, to be sure, use a local stone in Syria or Egypt, but they usually supplanted the local building techniques with their own. You find buildings most suitable to the climate of Latium appearing with essentially no modification in Baalbek below the dry hills of Lebanon, Nîmes in the Mistral Zone of France, Philae on the hot middle Nile, Byzantium on the breezy Golden Horn, Segovia in arid Spain, Aachen in frosty Germany, Timgad on the sparkling North Coast of Africa, or enduring the fogs of Silchester, Dover, or Bath. As it aged, the Roman State drew few of its citizens and even fewer of its leaders from Italy, let alone from the Roman campagna. Yet it was the climate and the resources of the campagna which determined the architecture and most of the ways from Baalbek in Lebanon to Hadrian's Wall close to the boundaries of modern Scotland.

ROADS, BRIDGES, AND AQUEDUCTS

The wayward hills of Greece were unlike the regimented mountains of Italy, set like a spinal chord, taking off from the Alps, hugging the Gulf of Genoa then striking east to parallel the calf of the leg of Italy, bending toward the middle above Rome, then running inexorably to the toe. There was no nonsense about this. And the Roman roads had the same temperament, marching straight ahead from point to point, uphill, downhill, seldom conceding a contour to the slope of a hill or the swell of a stream. They cut their way straight across the countryside, marching up and down and seldom around, built of bricks or stones or even concrete, built so well that many still exist and some are still usable. They built the roads to let the legions pass with unmuddied feet, to speed the path of messengers needed to keep the ever-growing mass of citizenry together. The first, the Via Appia which you can still ride out of Rome, was built by Appius Claudius from Rome to Capua in 312 B.C. Julius Caesar was able to do 800 miles in ten days on such roads; one courier is reported to have gone 360 miles in 36 hours; an ordinary horsecart could average five to six miles an hour. The Romans kept building roads almost to the end. These roads followed and supported the Roman conquests. They spread the Latin tongue. They did not always lead to Rome. They might stop for a while at the Alps or the heel of Italy, but in the end they also took you to London, to Palmyra, to Lutetia, to Timgad, and finally to the Roman boundaries wherever those might be.

When the roads came to the rivers, there was little swerving. Whatever temporary materials the Romans began the crossings with, they soon came to the stone arch. An anonymous bridge from Spain shows the masonry arch in its most direct and aesthetically most powerful form. The large wedge-shaped stones clearly exert force and counterforce upon each other. The thrust of the ends is clearly contained by the wall through which the arch was pierced in the first place. Hundreds of years later Henry Hobson Richardson used the same theme with equal power at the Allegheny County Court House and Jail in Pittsburgh.

But this Spanish span was very short and the stones, however dramatic, are unnecessarily large. Soon the bridge spans became longer, although intermediate piers had to be placed in the widest rivers. The masonry arches of the Pons Aemilius were built as early as 142 B.C. on 18-foot spans. In 109 the Via Flaminia was brought across the Tiber two miles north of Rome over the 60-foot spans of the Pons Mulvius. Forty years later, in 62 B.C., the Pons Fabricius spanned 80 feet. The last two were typical of their class. The main arches joined the piers, but smaller arches were placed on the piers themselves to save material and reduce the weight and perhaps to speed the flow of water when the river was in flood. Of the Pons Aemilius there remain only the foundations in the present Ponte Rotto. But the Pons Mulvius, now Ponte Moele, is in excellent condition.

Such bridges were fully intended to be utilitarian and there was no attempt for example to make the piers more slender for appearance's sake. They stood foursquare, making little concession to the flood save for modest cutwaters on the piers of the Pons Mulvius. And they continued to do this into the Empire so that the bridge of Augustus, the best-preserved Roman bridge in Italy, but in A.D. 14–20 over the river Marecchia at Rimini, is of the same mode.

As time went on, greater and greater bridges were built throughout the Empire where the rivers were often more powerful and the terrain more spectacular than in Italy. The Romans seldom tried to decorate them. They were designed to fit their particular situation and almost always achieved harmonious proportions even on complicated terrain.

When possible the Romans made their piers of uniform cross section. But the contours of ravines are seldom orderly, and thus the piers might have to be placed at irregular intervals which, in turn, produced uneven spans. But all the arched spans were bridged by semicircular arches. So if the spans were different, either the half circles would have to spring from the piers at different heights or the curves would have to be modified from the basic half circle. Usually the former choice was made so that sometimes one arch sprang from a higher point on a pier than the other, actually an asset when sensitively done.

Many of the later bridges had amazing spans. One of the greatest of the survivors is in Italy, the Pont St.-Martin between Ivrea and Aosta, leaping nearly 117 feet in a single span. Surely the most handsome is the one crossing the Tagus at Alcantara (Moorish for bridge) in Spain. This bridge, made entirely of granite blocks without mortar, was built during the reign of Trajan (A.D. 98–117) with the contribution of eleven Lusitanian communities. In six bounds it carries a level roadway 600 feet across the valley. As the valley rises, the piers naturally become shorter. To achieve a uniform result, the Romans reduced the spans so that the ratio of width to height was maintained. Here the Romans faltered from their general principle and placed a triumphal arch across the bridge at the central pier more than 200 feet above the river, but this does not seriously detract from the whole.[113]

After roads for their soldiers, the Romans needed roads for their water. It was of course no new trick to bring water to cities by aqueducts. The Greek Eupalinos had, after all, tunneled Samos for water for the tyrant Polycrates. But the Roman demand for water was greater than anything seen before.

If you look at a map of the ancient city of Rome, you will be struck by the many aqueducts which slash across it. The Roman baths and fountains made incessant demands; perhaps as much as 350,000,000 gallons of water poured daily into Rome through the eleven principal aqueducts, which in Imperial days must have been one of the most impressive sights in the Campagna.

---

[113] Occasionally they placed triumphal arches at the ends and this was usually less successful.

The Roman water, unlike the Roman soldier, could not march up much of a hill. So the Roman engineers had to design a proper system of downgrades from the hills to the towns. The ravines that separated the undulations they could not tunnel were spanned with the aqueducts. Even then the topography sometimes prevented a straight line; thus the routes of Roman aqueducts in the hills were inevitably more circuitous than the Roman roads, but on flatter ground they ran in a beeline only slightly tilted downhill to provide free flow.

Like the roads, the Roman aqueducts did not all lead to Rome but were built throughout the empire. The earliest, the Appian, built in 312 B.C., carried water underground for 11 miles. The Marcian, of 144 B.C., was one of the first to carry parts of the conduit above ground and later served the Baths of Caracalla. The arches of the Claudian aqueduct of A.D. 38 to 52 were raised so that water might be supplied even on the top of the highest hill in Rome.

Spain boasts two aqueducts higher than any in Italy, but the finest extant Roman aqueduct is in France: the Pont du Gard near Nîmes built *Pl. 166* in the first century A.D. It stretches 882 feet across the valley of the Gard. The river is not in the center of the valley, the slopes are not of equal steepness, but these problems merely inflamed the Roman imagination, which was further stirred by the immense height needed, 180 feet above the river bed. Three tiers of arches were imposed on one another. The upper tier was made of twenty-five smaller arches, each with a 14-foot span. These ranges of arches, as Ferguson says, give "to the structure the same finish and effect that an entablature and cornice gives to a long range of columns."[114]

Like the Roman bridges, the hill-country aqueducts have a remarkable beauty, resulting in part from the fact that the builders usually omitted all the ornamental superfluities of which the Romans were normally so fond. If they had been the final statement of the Roman aesthetic, it would rate higher than it does. Unhappily, however, the Romans were unable to exercise the same restraint when they passed to structures not primarily or even exclusively utilitarian. We can even sometimes see the effect when they tried to embellish their aqueducts at "important" places such as where they crossed the city gates.[115] In such situations they added pilasters, entablatures, niches, and pediments to bad advantage. American bridges have often suffered from the same compulsion.

Noble as bridges or aqueducts may be, they will not quite meet all the architectural needs of a society. It is the fountain or the bath which calls for the aqueduct; the forum for the Appian Way. Forum, bath, basilica,

---

[114] Cited in William J. Anderson and R. Phené Spiers, *The Architecture of Greece and Rome*, 2d ed. (London: Batsford, 1907), p. 277.
[115] As at the Porta Maggiore.

and colosseum imposed requirements that could not be met by engineering alone. The architectural genius of the Romans or of any other people cannot be judged exclusively by the skill and purity with which they have contrived their most utilitarian works. People invariably essay nobler things as well, and it is by their solutions to such problems that they come finally to be judged.

We must not imply that Roman engineers did not bring the same imaginative techniques to the great edifices of Rome. We must not even think that the power of the engineering solutions did not often break through the ornamental incrustations. Their engineering also was not limited to the arch and the vault and the dome. Elie Faure could properly say, "The Roman wall is one of the great things of history."[116] They built post-and-lintel structures over longer spans and with greater daring than the Greeks. They were inordinately fond of the Corinthian order. But they were fond of it not only because the moldings and capitals were florid, not only because the capital shape was easier to adjust to round buildings, but also because its thinner shaft was better engineering.

They used their arches, not only semicircular ones but sometimes forms which were quite flat, to support other things than bridges and aqueducts, such as arcades, to provide buildings with much wider intercolumniations than simple horizontal beams of stone or concrete would have permitted.

THE BOUNDARIES OF ROMAN BUILDING

Within the boundaries of the Imperium, new cities and magnificent structures arose—all in emulation of Rome.[117] Roman work in Africa and other well-known places outside of Italy is now very popular with cruise arrangers on the dual assumption, probably valid, that many travelers have by now "checked off" the longer-known marvels and have exhausted their interest on a first and superficial visit. For those who know the Roman homeland well, the fascination, particularly of Africa, is real. It impressed the ancient Romans who, like Pliny the Elder, announced that "Africa always offers something new." There the Romans built scores of miniature Romes and occasionally a theater or temple surpassing anything in Rome. But to visit these for reasons other than that of the picturesque, one should first know Rome well. Then they become exciting. An African site such as Leptis Major may be more obvious than the Roman sites; and the sky and the sea more brilliant. But the plus in a real comprehension, based

[116] Elie Faure, *History of Art*, vol. I, *Ancient Art*, translated by Walter Pach (New York: Harper & Brothers, 1921), p. 296.
[117] For a beautiful presentation of many of these combined with an excellent text see Sir Robert Eric Mortimer Wheeler, *Roman Africa in Color* (New York: McGraw-Hill, 1966).

on more than literary data, is that the Romans did push so far to build the magnificent gateway, the Porta Nigra, at Treves (Trier), the bridge of Alcantara in Spain, the Temple of Jupiter at Baalbek in Lebanon, and the theaters, amphitheaters, and markets of North Africa. So there are values in walking the boundaries of Rome, so to speak.

It is true that there are no aqueducts left in Italy to vie with the Pont du Gard and the aqueduct at Segovia in Spain. There is no single temple to compare with the Maison Carrée at Nîmes. The theaters at Sabrata, Leptis, Aspendos, or Orange may let you understand the Roman theater better than the Theater of Marcellus in Rome will. The six great columns of the Temple of Jupiter at Baalbek perhaps fling themselves more grandiosely against the western sky than the three of the Temple of Dioscuri in the Roman Forum. The amphitheater at Verona is nearer to being in working order than the Colosseum, and so on. But most of the greatest work is in Rome itself. The triumphal arches of Provence are inferior to those of Titus and Constantine in Rome; the markets of Leptis do not hold a candle to those of Trajan; there is no bath anywhere to match the Baths of Caracalla; the Basilica of Trier, though more complete, does not begin to compare with the Basilica of Maxentius and Constantine; no other triumphal column compares with Trajan's; no villa with Hadrian's; no mausoleum with the Castel Sant' Angelo. There was no Pantheon outside of Rome. The mosaics in the Piazza Armerina in Sicily or those in the museum at Hippo Regius are more extensive and better presented than those in Rome, but not more elegant than the fragments to see there. In general the architecture of the peripheries ought to be the dessert and not the entree of the Roman feast.

ROME IN A.D. 200

Imagine a traveler coming down from Tuscany to Rome at the end of the second century A.D. As he neared the city, he would enter the valley of the historic Tiber which came tumbling down from the high Apennines. He would notice the prominent alluvial deposits forming the plains and valleys of the left bank; and the nine or ten hills and ridges of tufa, sand, and ashes left from volcanos which were but recently extinct. Around some of these hills, such as the Janiculum, he would observe the remains of an old sea beach of fine golden sand and gray potter's clay, looking still very much like an ocean. Such a man might well not know or care that the Roman Forum and the Campus Martius were on sites that had once been impassable bogs or pools, drained by the great *cloacae* which were one of the most important architectural works of his early predecessors. He certainly would not sense in this achievement any foretaste of the architecture of the Imperial City.

He might have been told that the famous hills of Rome, still fairly forbidding, had once been more so. Each had once supported its own separate tribal fort. But later on these protuberances had become a nuisance to a city which always sought symmetry, vistas, and monumental scale. So the tops of the hills had all been leveled, their ridges filed off, their cliffs smoothed down into gentler slopes.

The Rome he approached was a complicated city and even a native would have found it difficult to describe in his own time. The Imperial City is much more difficult to describe. It was obviously not a composite of all the buildings ever built in the Republic and by all the later emperors, for the Romans did not hesitate to tear down in order to build more grandly. Nor was it a clean-cut sample of Roman town planning of the day. The methodical Roman soldiers adopted for their camps the grid plan of intersecting streets aligned with the cardinal points of the compass like the schemes of Hippodamus. This direct layout became the Roman standard when new towns were to be built.[118] But Rome was not a camp or a new town, its hills could not be leveled entirely, and so for the plan of the greatest city of all the Romans had to put aside their affection for axial symmetry and mechanical regularity.

The Tiber wandered by at the west, curving sinuously as it passed. The great roads approached from all sides. But they did not all penetrate to its center. The Via Flaminia, coming in from the northwest parallel to the river, ran straight until it stopped near the Forum. The Via Appia and the Via Latina joined shortly after they passed their respective city gates at the south and then ran northwest until they met the Via Ostiensis at the horseshoe of the Circus Maximus. Then, barred by the Palatine Hill, they turned north to end at the Flavian Amphitheater which was also the terminus of some of the great roads from the east. Here the hills and the complex of buildings permitted no clear plan. So although "all roads led to Rome," they did not all lead to the Forum, the heart of Rome, which was the eventual destination of most visiting Romans.[119]

It will not help us here to try to unsort this confusion. Rome of the second century was a clutter of temples, theaters, amphitheaters, baths, and arenas, some enormous, surrounded by islands of tenements. The tenements really dominated the town, but the big edifices of pleasure created the first impression.[120]

---

[118] Ostia, the port of Rome, for example, had a camp or citadel laid out along these lines as early as the fourth century B.C. When the town expanded later, the *decumanus* was lengthened and provided the main street; the forum grew on the south half of the *cardo*. See also Timgad, etc.

[119] The Romans were not kind enough to archaeologists to inscribe the names of all their streets on stones. We cannot even be quite sure of the position of the important Via Sacra which probably ran from the Colosseum along the Palatine and under the Arch of Titus.

[120] The Colosseum oval, for instance, was 500 by 600 feet and had a canopy to cover the whole. The arena itself was the size of an American football field, measuring 200 by 300 feet. It could seat perhaps 45,000 people. Lest this sound unimpressive, it must be considered in terms of the size of Rome at the time of its building. To be comparable, Soldier's Field in Chicago would have to seat 135,000 instead of the 102,000 it does.

Of all the colonnaded streets and areas, none was more magnificent or orderly than the series of forums which successive emperors had added to the original Forum Romanum. The greatest, Trajan's, we have described earlier (pp. 81–82). These linked one magnificent plaza to another still more magnificent until they ran all the way from the old and original *agora* to the Campus Martius under the Quirinal Hill. Each of these enormous squares was axial and symmetrical. Most were surrounded by colossally high walls isolating them from the nearby streets and from the beetling cliff of the Quirinal. All were encircled by porticos. But we must not think of them as clean-cut like the theoretical *agorae*, say of Priene. Rather, like the rest of Rome, they were cluttered up by additions. Scale competed with scale, commemorative column with commemorative column. It was such a high honor to have a memorial statue erected in such a place that many coveted it—and gained it.

Now, although the quick impression of Rome may have been one of munificence and monumentality, the average of Rome, like the average of New York or even San Francisco today, was something majestically shabbier. Much of the city consisted of block tenements like the Insulae Feliculae which rose higher than most of the buildings of modern Europe from streets which were usually 10 and seldom more than 17 feet wide.

> Near the Capitol the roofs already reached to the level of the hill-saddle. But always the splendid mass-cities harbour lamentable poverty and degraded habits and the attics and mansards, the cellars and back courts are breeding a new type of raw man—in Baghdad and in Babylon just as in Tenochitlán and today in London and Berlin. Diodorus tells of a deposed Egyptian king who was reduced to living in one of these wretched upper-floor tenements of Rome.[121]

Cicero said there were more tenements than private houses in Rome. Sulla lived on the ground floor of one as a young man. A poor poet of the empire reported he had to climb 200 steps to his lodgings. Earthquakes and fires wreaked havoc and death, especially in the upper wooden stories. Crassus used to go around to buildings near those which had recently burned and buy them cheaply from frightened landlords. Augustus promulgated a code forbidding buildings more than 70 feet high, but there were already a great many. They were frequently the butt of Juvenal.

But these observations need not deter us from examining the greater monuments, for unhappily they can be said of every city in every time, and it is by the monuments and not the slums that we unwisely make our picture of a society's architecture, even of a society's worth.

ROMAN MATERIALS

To achieve their buildings the Romans had a plethora of materials and were daring and lavish in their use. We should not forget this because I

---

[121] Oswald Spengler, *The Decline of the West*, vol. II (New York: Knopf, 1928), p. 101.

emphasize here concrete, arcuate, and domical construction. Their clays made fine bricks whether sun-dried or kiln-baked. They laid these with skill in many bonds. In the kilns they also fired terra-cottas and more elegant ceramics. The nearby hills abounded in useful volcanic remnants. Tufa, ranging from a warm brown to a yellow or grayish green, did not last well in the weather but was excellent when protected by stucco. Nearby Tivoli furnished a better stone, travertine, a hard gray limestone with a characteristically handsome worm-eaten look. Statuary marbles, granites, basalts, including a red one called porphyry, were brought, according to Pliny, from all parts of the world to wharves specially built to receive them.

But the material which the Romans particularly developed themselves, and which was never again well exploited until recently, was concrete. This too they owed to the volcanos. Pozzolana, a red sandy earth, lay in thick strata in and under Rome. When it was mixed with lime and water, it formed an exceedingly cohesive, hard, durable cement.

The Romans did not make refined concrete such as we now know, of carefully selected and proportioned and relatively small aggregates and finely ground cements with careful attention to the amount of water used. Instead, they mixed the pozzolana with large pieces of stone or brick, often as big as a man's fist. Such a concrete did not come out with a clean surface and a fine texture, so it had to be sheathed with marble or brick mosaic or plastered with stucco. Thus it was very different from the homogeneous marbles of Attica.

Also, the Romans did not develop the art of reinforcing concrete so it would be good in tension, although pozzolana was more cohesive than masonry. Thus when they went after their big spans, they had to follow the principles of the masonry arch, the vault, or the dome. Unfortunately, pozzolana also tended to flow while it was still wet, and to deal with this the Romans devised brick frameworks which remained in place and provided a sort of reinforcing—though it was nothing like the tensile reinforcing provided today by steel.

Since their concretes were often so rough, their building stones so friable, it is not surprising that the Romans developed a fine stucco of pozzolana, lime, and finely pounded bricks or shards which they plastered onto their walls in three, four, or even more coats, building up the thickness to as much as 5 inches. They also made a fine finish coat of marble aggregate which they applied thinly to produce a smooth white stucco nearly as hard as marble.

The Augustan architect Vitruvius devoted a whole chapter to concrete, but, since he was an arch conservative, he did not really examine its potentials, the external use of the orders being his principal concern, as indeed they were to his patron, Augustus, who most admired the Hellenistic envelope. The great days of the vaults and the domes were to come later; the arch was acceptable somewhat earlier.

After the aqueducts and the bridges, arcaded construction had been used on the exteriors of buildings, as in the Tabularium of 78 B.C., though not much inside. Tentative barrel vaults also appeared early, but the intersected (groined) vault, not until the second century A.D. It was the invention of the groined vault that opened up the great Roman architecture of interior spaces, which is the finest characteristic of Roman architecture, but for the time being the Romans relied most heavily for important buildings on trabeated construction and, save for the Pantheon, they never really abandoned columnar systems when a temple was involved.

THE CORPUS OF ROMAN BUILDINGS

However, for larger buildings the Greek columns lost their functional purpose and were soon reduced to the role of decorative elements, as were the entablature and the cornice.

Among the orders Roman taste ran unerringly toward the ornate, and even among the simpler forms Greek refinements were soon lost. They did not hesitate to combine forms or proportions from different orders. The early Roman version of the Doric order and its simplified form, the "Tuscan," were usually too severe for the Roman taste, and even the Corinthian order was "souped up" in the composite. The original Greek significance was gone. Pure and often vulgar ornament replaced architectural decoration.

Almost from the beginning the Romans developed a system of superimposing the orders, the lowest Doric, the second Ionic, the upper Corinthian. This was an elaboration of some Hellenistic ideas and had some rationale. In any event it soon became a tradition, and this tradition characterized Roman columnar architecture, thus establishing what was really the precedent for the Renaissance, which owed more to Rome than to Greece. An early appearance was in the Theater of Marcellus (13–11 B.C.). It appears in full dress form on the Colosseum (A.D. 80), whose arcades became a decorative motif, framed with engaged columns carrying an entablature. Here the usual hierarchy of Doric, Ionic, Corinthian was capped at the fourth story, wall and niche, by Corinthian pilasters.

Pl. 162

It may at this point be clarifying to supply some simplified chronological tabulations.

The table shows more or less reliably how the trend of building need and building taste developed in Rome. After the aqueduct and the bridge came temple and theater—then the beginning of more attention to enormous places of congregation, forums, or entertainment, enlarged theaters as at Sabrata, new kinds of entertainment as in amphitheaters and baths, imperial signs such as triumphal arches or commemorative columns, mausoleums. The pleasant citizens' villas of old Pompeii become the palaces on the Palatine, the Golden House of Nero, Hadrian's Villa in Tivoli. The simple temple becomes the imperial Pantheon; the basilica attaches itself

Roman Architectural Highlights

Republic 509–27 B.C.	Mostly Etruscan-Hellenistic. Aqueducts, bridges, theaters, basilicas, temples. Brick and concrete begin to be common.	Pons Mulvius 109 B.C. Amphitheater Pompeii 70 B.C. Temple Portunus 31 B.C.
Empire 27 B.C.–A.D. 306 Augustan 27 B.C.–A.D. 14	Intense activity—conscious return to style of Classic Greece. Marble, stately massive forms, structural stability, unabashedly derivative.	Maison Carrée 16 B.C. Theater of Marcellus 11 B.C. Tomb Caecilia Metella 10 B.C. Theater Orange A.D 50
Flavian 70–96	Vespasian, Titus, Domitian. Classic severity abandoned for richer, more derivative.	Pont du Gard ca. first century Colosseum 80 Arch of Titus 81 Temple Jupiter, Baalbek First century Flavian Pal 96
Antonines	Trajan, 98–117; Hadrian 117–138. More rigid classicism, but also baroque.	Aqueduct, Segovia A.D. 100 Forum of Trajan 113 Trajan's Column 113 Pantheon 120–130 Mausoleum of Hadrian 135 Temple Antoninus and Faustina 141 Column of Marcus Aurelius 180 Temple Vesta, Rome 200 Baths of Caracalla
	Antonines decline in craftsmanship.	Temple of Jupiter-Baalbek Porta Nigra- Trier 300 Theater Sabrata Third century Palace of Diocletian 300

Post-Constantine	Constantine 306–337 to Justinian 527–565.	Basilica of Maxentius 313 Arch of Constantine 315

to a separately conceived market and then turns itself into a church. Evidently Rome offers an enormous number of building types to examine. The amphitheater, whether as complicated as the Colosseum or as simple as the arena in Verona, requires little explanation. One of the most important buildings in Rome, offering an excellent display of domical and spatial arrangements, was Nero's Domus Aurea, but, though you can wander into some of it, it is mostly an archaeological treasure trove. Here I think it best to refer you to the excellent, scholarly, and readable exposition of it provided in MacDonald's splendid work.[122]

THE TRIUMPHAL ARCH AND MEMORIAL

Triumphal arches begin by being interesting as arches. The earlier examples had a moderate simplicity as in the arch of Titus at the foot of the Forum Romanum or the originally defensive Porta Nigra at Trier, but as they developed under successive emperors, they become more and more ornate.

The Arch of Titus is no longer a true gateway but a symbolic monument, not often even a processional gate. As Roman arches go, it is fairly direct: deep coffers in the barrel vault of the arch, large piers on both sides of the arch, framing engaged columns on the piers (the earliest known composite style), simple if heavy entablature with a plain frieze and then a balancing "attic" story bearing the dedicatory inscription. The proportions of this arch shorn of decoration have a monumental dignity. The bas-reliefs showing the victory of Titus over the Jews are about as good as Roman narrative art offers. This arch was surely the prototype of many Christian west fronts, although there was of course a transfer of the symbolism of triumph from Emperor to Christ.

Pl. 164

The Porta Nigra at Trier, on the contrary, was not triumphal but was much more than a mere postern let into a wall. It shows how by the end of the third century A.D. either the Romans were contemptuous of their enemies and looked upon fortifications as mainly symbolic or had become careless. This gate had two arched passages opening into an open square court. Above the two entering arches were two stories of open arched ramparts with purely decorative three-quarter-engaged columns between

Pl. 165

[122] William L. MacDonald, *The Architecture of the Roman Empire*, vol. I, *An Introductory Note* (New Haven: Yale University Press, 1965).

the arches. At the flanks were towers one story higher than the center. These were rectangular but had semicircular projections on the exterior. The arcading of the towers and the double ramparts was carefully articulated. As some sort of gesture of defense there were no openings between the engaged columns of the ground level. The scale of this gate is impressive and the proportions unusually harmonious but obviously much more complicated than the older arched entry to the Forum at Pompeii or the monumental archway built in the first century A.D. at Palmyra.

If you want to pursue the degradation of the triumphal arch—more arches, more fancy materials, more complicated details—you can find in Rome examples such as the arches of Septimius Severus or of Constantine.

A more profitable excursion would be to become aware of how the Romans loved to use the elements of trabeated construction essentially only as decoration (save for the temples, where the problem was slightly different and to which I shall come soon). Note, for example, the relatively simple application at the Flavian Amphitheater or Colosseum, the comparable one on the even earlier Theater of Marcellus (11 B.C.), and then move along in time to the overdone Temple of Bacchus at Baalbek only about a century later than the Colosseum. The residues of triumphal arches, imitated down nearly to the present, and the notion of applied orders as decoration, with use in new buildings at least as late as 1925, have been among the most durable if not the most admirable architectural legacies of Rome—and thanks to the booster shot from the Renaissance are perhaps the most extensive of all the legacies to be found in the West.

The Romans were almost as given to boasting of triumphs as the Ramessids. Their great columns were adapted from an Eastern custom. The most famous, dedicated to Trajan's victories over the Dacians, was *Pl. 163* erected in A.D. 114 adjacent to Trajan's basilica. It is a Roman Doric column over 115 feet high with Trajan's tomb in the pedestal; it is now surmounted by a statue of Saint Peter, but originally boasted one of the Emperor. The most interesting feature undoubtedly is the bas-relief story unfolded over a spiral band a little over 3 feet wide and 800 feet long. Here with field glasses and patience you can make out the more than 2,500 figures and the many incidents of military campaigning, including such realistic bits as the legionnaires piling timber for fortifications (the original panel is now in the German Archeological Institute at Rome).

This bas-relief was presumably much easier to see when the open colonnaded court surrounding it had many balconies at different levels. Today if you want to read the scroll in detail, you might prefer to consult the full-sized plaster reproduction in the Victoria and Albert Museum, although the sensation is by no means the same. One thing to think about when you look at Trajan's Column, which looks so big standing alone in the ruins of the Forum, is the matter of scale. When you arrive at the exterior of the Cathedral of St. Peter, you might care to remember that the

Corinthian half-columns and pilasters there are only 7 feet less in height than the column of Trajan, although their environment makes them seem much less large.

The successors to Trajan continued the tradition of memorializing triumphs. Antoninus Pius built one in A.D. 161, but only the pedestal remains standing in the hemicycle of the Giardino della Pigna of the Vatican. The column of Marcus Aurelius in the Piazza Colonna (A.D. 174) commemorates his campaigns north of the Danube against the Marcomanni and the Sarmatians. It is very like Trajan's, but though a little higher, seems smaller, and the carving is less distinguished and less interesting. Here also the statue of the emperor and Faustina on top was replaced (in the reign of Pope Sixtus V, A.D. 1589), in this case by a statue of Saint Paul.

Emperors with their eyes on posterity did not forget memorial tombs either. The system derived rather directly from sepulchral tumuli of the Etruscans, which placed the burial chamber under a circular drum, which in turn was covered by a conical mound of earth. An early one, 10 B.C., on the Via Appia Antica, was devoted to Caecilia Metella and had the same general form, except that the cylindrical drum now stood on a high square podium. In 1299 the Caetani converted it into a fort by adding a castellated superstructure, and it is best examined now in Piranesi engravings. Augustus, too, had a mausoleum modeled after the Etruscan form but on larger scale. Its remains are of only modest interest.

The largest of the mausoleums was built for Hadrian in 135–139. Except for the high podium, 300 feet square, and the immense circular tower, 240 feet in diameter, it offers little of its original aspect, but now as the Castel Sant' Angelo it remains very noticeable on the Roman skyline. You can no longer see the white marble facing of the podium, with equestrian groups at the corners, the marble and porphyry peristyle of the drum, 150 feet high, the stepped conical marble dome planted with trees, crowned by a quirigua, or the marble lining of the tomb chamber, and so it cannot be rated high on a list of current architectural experiences of ancient Rome, although it is full of Kilroy associations from Hadrian to Tosca and Baron Scarpia and the museum has many amusing things.

THE TEMPLE

Although not to be compared with the Greek temples and although not the most important creations of Roman architecture, the Roman temple should not be dismissed too lightly.

The general practice of ritual by the Etruscans and the early Romans was not in principle different from the Greek. The true temple was not the building at all but the open space before it. Here around an open altar a highly stylized act was performed involving both offerings and prayer. The Romans may have been a little more likely than the Greeks to define the space by a curbing or a parapet enclosing a terrace. At any rate the temple building, which was really the house of the god or his image, was the generator and definer of the space, standing at the back of the precinct area, overshadowing it. Following Etruscan practice and unlike the Greek, the house of the image was raised high on a podium, accessible only by monumental stairs, drawing the eye to the ritual act.

Thus even in Republican days, the temple was more ordered than the Greek, the axis more pronounced, the image less personal and more remote, expressing, even before the gods became state gods, the idea that Rome did have a moral order of values and attitude. The form was solid, sure, uninnovative, competent.

The best example in Rome was the Temple of Fortuna Virilis (40 B.C.). It had only one room, a small *cella* reached by a monumental stair climbing to a 10-foot-high podium. On this platform 30 feet wide was a deep Ionic portico two columns deep. As typical in Rome there was no peristyle, only a pseudoperipteral design with the five columns behind the portico and those at the rear three-quarters engaged so that the cella occupied essentially the entire width. The frieze carving and the empty pediment were chastely carved, more Greek than Hellenistic. It was altogether a handsome, even a refined, building until the Christians converted it into Santa Maria Egiziaca in A.D. 880, enclosed the portico, and inserted windows.

Pl. 169

The best-preserved example, one much beloved by Thomas Jefferson and influential on his designs, is the Maison Carrée at Nîmes. Its podium is 12 feet high. It is pseudoperipteral prostyle hexastyle in the Corinthian order and has a rich but restrained entablature. Nîmes is worth a visit for the Maison Carrée alone, but there is more there since the Pont du Gard is but a few kilometers away.

Pl. 167

My own affection for Roman temples (excluding the Pantheon) stops thus early, though one or two circular forms are delightful, such as the round temple of Portunus of 31 B.C. in the old Forum Boarium at Rome, which is closely related in its refinement to a Greek *choragic* monument, or the Augustan Temple of the Sybil, perched on the edge of a rocky prominence near Tivoli, circular peripteral with a peristyle of eighteen Corinthian columns. Both of these, it will be noted, are still very early.

Perhaps the quality of later Roman temples deteriorated in part because Romans were at once less religious and more tolerant of other religions. As Gibbon pointed out, "[T]he various forms of worship which prevailed in the Roman world were all considered by the people as equally true; by the philosophers as equally false; and by the magistrate as equally useful. And thus toleration produced not only mutual indulgence but even religious concord."[123] It also weakened architectural motivation to build a superior temple.

[123] Edward Gibbon, *The History of the Decline and Fall of the Roman Empire*, vol. I (New York: Harper, 1880), pp. 250–251.

It was not long after the early Empire moreover that the gods began to be closely identified with the state, the state with the emperor, and the ritual worship became an official act. The generally enclosed life of the Romans was changing to public display. The power of the state needed to be symbolized by greater size and, alas, by greater proliferation of detail. Thus the enormous ruins of the temples of Baalbek, Palmyra, or Antonius and Faustina or Saturn at Rome are impressive in scale, debased in detail, and I, for one, am happy that I do not have to see them as they probably once were.

Somehow the great structural achievements of the Romans, the vault and the dome, were never seriously applied to temples (save the Pantheon). Quite frequently toward the end of the Republican era, a domed, semi-circular apse was built into the back wall of some temples to receive the cult image, but this was either embedded in the wall or built independently inside, and thus not expressed on the outside. It was not until Diocletian built his temples and mausoleums in the Palace at Spalato (A.D. 300) that the vault was seriously[124] used in a Roman temple.

I suspect all this means that the heart of the Roman was elsewhere: in the courts or basilicas; in the life of the Imperial forums; in other practical things, the markets; in places of public amusement, the amphitheaters, the theaters, and the baths; and in places of private luxury, the villas.

TRAJAN'S MARKETS

The successful general, Trajan, was an equally successful builder, especially of socially useful structures suitable to a fairly moderate if definitely paternalistic rule. He built baths, aqueducts, markets, ports, flood-control works, administrative buildings all over the Empire; naturally he did not neglect Rome. The artificial harbor at the mouth of the Tiber that connected both to the river and the sea by canals was a terrific *tour de force*, but the remains of the buildings, nearly all of vaulted concrete, are hard to visit. His spacious baths, outdoing the modest ones of Titus and built over the Esquiline wing of the Domus Aurea, have left only a few fragments. But his great Forum, which we have already noted (pp. 81–82), was *Pl. 26* praised in antiquity by observers like Pausanias, Dio Cassius Marcellinus, by later visitors like Stendhal, and even much today. Less noted, save by scholars, less spectacular in its vistas but of great interest if you take the trouble to look, are the markets on the slopes above the Forum.

The Forum itself was monumental, classical, trabeate. It was made of noble stone and the only brick was at the libraries perhaps for the practical purpose of absorbing moisture.

In the markets, on the contrary, the trabeation, cased in colored mar-

---

[124] Despite such smaller examples as the vaulted sanctuary and possibly a coffered stone vault in the Temple of Jupiter, Baalbek (A.D. 273, that is, not much earlier).

ble, was replaced by concrete arches and vaults, faced with bricks, to produce plain and even austere effects.

They were probably finished shortly before the Forum was dedicated. Since then they have suffered many alterations, being occupied, built on or over by several parishes and other religious organizations of the Middle Ages, and thereafter by palace builders of the Renaissance (Ceva-Roccagiovani, Caetani). But when the Via dei Fori Imperiali was driven from the Piazza Venezia to the Flavian amphitheater (Colosseum) by Mussolini, the markets were cleared and much of Trajan's constructions were found intact. They have been shored up by tie rods and preservative masonry, and some of the upper walls have been built up to even levels to support new roofs. In the higher ranges the roofs are now of wood and tile replacing the original barrel vaults, long since decayed, but things are so arranged that even a nonarcheological visitor can get a good idea of an important aspect of Rome he might easily overlook.

Pl. 168

The markets, made up of streets, offices, shops, were surely part of a substantial urban redevelopment program, common in the second century as suggested also at Ostia, Timgad, Antioch, etc. These particular markets were certainly, at least in part, intended to replace the shops (tabernae) which had been demolished to clear the site for the Forum and the Basilica. How large they were we do not know, but today 170 rooms are either accessible or visible. The rock of the hillside is sometimes visible, but given Roman temperament, it must have been much shaped by Trajan's engineers so that the outline of the Forum rather than the natural contours of the hill determined the shape. The audacious design rises to six major levels above the Forum at methodical stages of about 20 vertical feet each. They take off at the base from a brick-faced concrete hemicycle set on the same axis but a different (more remote) centering. This hemicycle was repeated through the first three levels (up to the Via Biberatica), after which the design became less symmetrical. The restoration by Ricci, leaving the red-brown brick unclothed by stucco or marble, seems to have been an honest one.

Although as you wander around unguided through a plan contaminated by the passage of time and human affairs its clarity may not be self-evident, a little reflection will suggest that there was very careful thought as to circulation between streets and shops, where stairs and ramps were placed, how nearly every covered space was lighted and ventilated, how view terraces were provided, and so on.

We do not know how all the rooms were used. Perhaps those at Forum level were for the imperial cashiers; perhaps dole was distributed at the top, but this is speculative. No one seems to doubt that most of the rooms were for shops, but how distributed is less certain. Here and there are drains which may have been for fish or wine shops. Not many of the rooms are spectacularly different from the rest. An exception is the galleried room at the third level, which, in modern times, has been named the Aula Triana. This space is in excellent condition. A sort of classical galleria, it has a nave lined by rooms rising to three levels. The reason for the levels has been the subject of much speculation, but its aesthetic significance is unquestionable.

Roman architects had been fascinated by hill-side sites for a long time but their earlier designs were based upon axial balance and symmetry. At the markets the center-line of the hemicycle was not used to control the overall plan and no balanced rectilinear silhouette was attempted. There were no peristyles or courts because the markets existed for the life of shops and streets. The result, both visually and functionally, was an urban unit, a city quarter with an irregular skyline, curving and turning streets, changing vistas, and an elaborate internal communication system. An ascent from the street at Forum level reveals the directional flexibility implied by the curving sweep of the hemicycle facade. All straight lines are relatively short, either turned or intersected by other axes, branching away at various angles. Beside and opening onto these axes are clearly defined volumes, *places* that punctuate the potential of motion. The sense of motion is increased by the laconic treatment of vertical surfaces and the sequence of visual events works smoothly.[125]

Aula Triana shows all these characteristics: spaciousness, simplicity, clarity. Oblong bays are less static than square ones would have been. The vaults spring from well up on the second story and not from the pavement level, and this augments the sense of height in the central space. You can note that this effect is still further emphasized because the clerestory arches are stilted, rising from short piers at the impost level of the vault form.

The aula is a coherent whole, an entity in itself and this is character-istically Roman. The discipline behind the design is extremely strong—it provides a powerful sense of place, accentuating the difference between the sensation or knowledge of being in *a* place and the transient experience of passing one location to another. This Roman sense of place is almost overwhelming. Inside there is ideal human order undisturbed by any suggestion of movement between places. . . . The visitor is placed in a volume that is neither too great nor too small and is not interrupted by structure. Impressions of surface are heightened at the expense of mass. With its unencumbered, noble space, the *Aula Triana* belongs with the Pantheon in the very first rank of Imperial architecture.[126]

[125] MacDonald, *Architecture of the Roman Empire*, op. cit., p. 90.
[126] Ibid., p. 91.

The rest of the markets are less spectacular but consistent. You move in and out of doors in an appropriately Italian, indeed an appropriately modern way. It fits the climate, the sky, the way of light. You will not find the markets on many of the guided tour lists. But they are well worth a few hours of your time. They will give you a different sense—and possibly a better sense—of the nature of Roman life than the blood and sand of the arena.

THE ARENAS AND OTHER BUILDINGS FOR ENTERTAINMENT

Yet the arenas are there, built mainly to satisfy a sense of pageantry expressing a brutal and barbaric streak. Since no closed stage was required, an elliptical shape served best. The most magnificent of the arenas was surely the Colosseum, but it is just enough ruined so you can get a better sense of the spatial *enclosure* in the smaller amphitheater at Verona, just as the theater at Orange reads more clearly than the theater of Marcellus. But the Colosseum is unique because its very size and the necessity to build it on a plain and not against a side hill required new engineering of concrete, of corridors and cells beneath the arena, and of hundreds of raking vaults to form the foundations of the four tiers of seats. It is remarkable, stupendous, even magnificent. It compels awe and admiration for a people who could carry forward such a vast undertaking. But it commands more wonder than admiration, more admiration than affection. Unfortunately it is a little hard to say how much of this reaction is conditioned by aesthetics and how much by morality.

Pl. 171

I am afraid I feel much the same way about the Roman theaters. What was played in them was generally trivial and vulgar when not worse. The action, the technical needs of the *scaena* made demands far beyond those of the Greek tragedies so that the theaters became cluttered up as almost everything else did in Rome with too much architectural detail. The Greeks were content to use natural hill bowls and thus achieved the dignified and simple effect of such a theater as the one at Epidauros. But the Romans often built without the advantage of nature and thus had walls to decorate, beginning with the Theater of Marcellus, which they set about doing with a happy and profuse will. The Roman theater at Aspendos has a semicircular auditorium in place of the Greek two-thirds. This has been cleverly reconstructed, including a sloping wood canopy over the stage, perhaps both to protect actors from the weather and to improve the acoustics. The one at Sabrata, probably built by Septimius Severus, is big enough to seat 5,000 people. It has an awesome *scaena* wall with a three-storied colonnade. Though smaller ones like the one in old Pompeii (75 B.C.) were large enough to be completely roofed in, thus making *scaena* and auditorium in an integrated whole such as the Greeks had never attained (or presumably desired), larger ones such as the one at Orange (50 B.C.) were too big for this, and though the *scaena* had a wooden roof, the spectators, if protected at all, must have been sheltered as in the Colosseum by large awnings hanging from cables.

Probably the most dramatic ruin of a Roman theater from a strictly touristic point of view is the Augustan theater at Leptis Magna.

As you sit now in the much restored auditorium looking toward the sea, you have a dramatic and photogenic view through the grove of columns, but of course when the theater was operating these were walled to form a backdrop for the action. The auditorium, though, reveals the vomitories which led in; inscriptions in Latin and neo-Punic proclaiming the munificence of the citizen Annobal Rufus who gave the theater to the city in A.D. 1–2. You can see the semicircular *cavea* divided into three zones by two ambulatories, of which the lower reaches the street directly on the natural bank by vaulted passages. The central zone is on an artificial bank, the upper on a vaulted substructure incorporating staircases leading upwards from the street.

This structure may well be the most exciting Roman ruin in North Africa. It also carries an interesting reminder noted by Mortimer Wheeler.

> Two unusual features recall—what Romans were likely to forget—that the classical theatre was in origin a place for religious celebration. At the top of the auditorium were found remains, apparently of a small shrine dedicated to the goddess Ceres-Augusta by Suphunibal, daughter of Annibal Ruso, in A.D. 35–36 . . . . And beside the orchestra at the foot of the auditorium below the stone parapet which screens the five shallow lowest steps from the rest of the audience, an octagonal altar was set up by a Tiberius Claudius Sestius in A.D. 91–92; it stood in the midst of the movable seats which were placed upon these steps for notables on theatre-days.[127]

THE BATHS OF CARACALLA

There were no such reminders in the great baths (*thermae*) where people practiced private vices publicly, but personally instead of vicariously.

Public baths were ubiquitous in the Roman Empire. They could be found everywhere, in desert towns or on the left bank of the Seine in Lutetia (Paris). Of the 800 establishments in Rome, most were small, and such enormous establishments as those built in honor of Caracalla and Diocletian, accommodating 1,600 and 3,000 bathers, respectively, were the exception. However, to study such a large one as Caracalla, as we shall do, is not to make an unrepresentative examination since it simply reproduced on a more grandiose and opulent scale the necessities which were cared for also in the smaller establishments plus embellishments such as the Farnese Bull which the smaller ones could not aspire to.

Few of the baths were operated privately. Most emperors and other

Pl. 170

---

[127] Wheeler, *Roman Africa in Color*, op. cit., p. 64.

wealthy men had their own establishments, but there was more fun to be had at the public baths. Alexander Severus, Hadrian, Galba, almost all the emperors except Trajan, liked to mingle with the tumultuous mob. The moral emperors such as Marcus Aurelius and Hadrian established rules against mixed bathing, but like the Volstead Act these were evaded. Finally Alexander Severus recognized the facts and legalized mixed bathing. Then prostitutes and ladies, slaves and citizens, swindlers, pickpockets and their judges, debauchees and reformers mingled together, the dregs with the cream, all reduced in some ways to a common level by their common nudity. This was rather more than even an emperor or a Trimalchio could put together at home.

As you approached Caracalla's baths from the northeast, you saw a rather unpretentious arcaded facade of two stories, 1,100 feet long and 40 feet high. The lower floor of this facade which served also as a surrounding wall provided shops on the street. The upper floor was at the level of a great platform 20 feet above the street on which all the main buildings rested. Below the platform there was a labyrinth of vaulted corridors for service and storage purposes, lighted and ventilated by circular openings on to the platform, covered by bronze gratings. The rooms on the floor of the facade building at the upper level opened on the platform and were devoted to private bathing.

Pl. 174   The general impression on approaching the baths of Caracalla was not one of a towering monumentality such as the forum presented, not even one of profuse decoration. All this was reserved for the inside. The high vaulted roofs of the *tepidarium* soaring 80 feet or so above the outside might command the eye briefly, and the still loftier dome of the *calidarium* might have been barely visible from some points of vantage. But at best they could be seen only in part, and the visual impacts were all reserved for those who entered the baths. Nor did the colonnaded wall itself make much effort to impress. Later on, inside the baths, you would walk among and on opulent marbles and mosaics, elaborate and sumptuous, but the wall you first saw was merely covered with a fine stucco.

Entering the portico (which offered the only principal entrance) and ascending, you would emerge on the platform which was 1,100 feet on a side and 20 feet above the street. But even now you would not be aware at once of the colossal block of buildings rising from the platform directly in front of you. It was separated from you by a promenade 130 feet wide, laid out formally with alleys of trees. If you knew the baths well and had a specific purpose of bathing in mind, you might cut across this alley to one of the four doors on the north wall of the block leading into the baths themselves. Even then the way a Roman bathed was not standardized.

Romans bathed differently according to their medical needs and their individual tastes. A conventional man might begin by playing ball in the *palaestra*. After getting up a sufficient sweat he would go to the *apodyterium* or even the *tepidarium* where he would undress or be undressed, rub himself or be rubbed with unguents. Then he would go to the *calidarium* for another sweat, be rubbed again with unguents before going out into the street, a protection against the common cold which was a conventional ailment of the Romans, affecting even the emperors.[128]

Athletes might play in the *palaestra*, have the oil, dirt, and sweat scraped off with *strigiles*, take a cold plunge or swim in the *tepidarium*, get their coats of grease, and go. Others might omit the exercise, take a sweat in the *calidarium*, follow it only with a hot bath or a cold bath or even just have cold water poured over them as a preliminary to the universal unguents.

But if you were a stranger or a dawdler, you might skip the baths for a while, turn to the right or left and, following the trees, circle the main building block. Thus you could emerge at the rear behind the *calidarium* and find a large plaza 400 feet deep, 1,100 feet long. At the ends of this plaza you would see circular porticos enclosing rooms which have been thought by different authorities to have been libraries, lecture halls, *palaestrae* or exercise rooms, and the services therefor.

Anyway, it seems plausible that this was one of the places where the poets and orators held forth. Perhaps no one was talking, perhaps what he said bored you. Then you would pass through the gardens filling the park or *xystus* and come finally upon racing or other athletic contests. Behind the stadium and at the end of the enclosures was a series of two-story reservoirs which were fed in turn by the Marcian aqueduct.

Stone pines, imported cedars, olives, whatever the trees were, they were formally planted and trimmed and pollarded in keeping with the absolute and undeviating symmetry which prevailed throughout this establishment. The projecting hemicycles or *exedrae* at the east and west which enclosed the libraries and *palaestra* were elaborately colonnaded and carved.

Perhaps the races and exercises in the *palaestra* were as boring as the orations, and then the visitor would be drawn to go to the main block, which, after all, had been the justification for the whole ensemble. This block could be entered from any side through formal and monumental entrances, and our visitor would naturally have gone in from somewhere near the back. But we want to understand the system of the building, and this will be easier if we let our imagination carry us back to the north and come in, as a purposeful bather usually would, through one of the north doors nearest the center.

It is hard even to comprehend the size of this main block which covered 270,000 square feet and was bigger than the Houses of Parliament in London. A principal room of the establishment, such as the *tepidarium*, was itself 80 feet wide and more than 180 feet long and over 100 feet high,

---

[128] Much of the description of bathing techniques I owe to August Mau, *Pompeii: Its Life and Art* (New York: Macmillan, 1907), pp. 188 ff.

Pl. 170

yet a glance at the plan of the whole will show how little of the total space such a great room occupied.

When we look at the plan, we note that it is mechanically and axially symmetrical. The *tepidarium* occupies the central spot. The *frigidarium* is parallel to it at the north. The *calidarium* leads off from it to the south on the central transverse axis. These three main rooms are flanked to the east and west by peristyles, by training rooms for youths, called *ephebia*, and on the north and south by other baths, dressing rooms, foyers.

Giving up our view from above and returning to the pedestrian, we would pass first into an anteroom. To one side we could see through a colonnade the great open space of the *frigidarium*. On the other, by a less monumental and private entrance, we could pass to the *apodyteria* which were on two floors. We might pause here to disrobe, be given a preliminary oiling and sanding, and then go out, probably naked.

To one side of these peristyles and toward the exterior we could look into the *ephebia* where we might see youths training at various sporting skills or merely exercising; in the opposite direction we would see a high hemicycle in which a poet or orator might be declaiming. If he were not too popular (and few were), we might be able to shoulder through the crowd around him and thus come in at one end of the *tepidarium* into a great hall forming a sort of foyer or antechamber, which we might also have reached directly from the *apodyteria*. At this point we would have a vista through the *tepidarium* and beyond it to a room exactly like the one in which we were standing, a total view of more than 300 feet.

This vista would lead us naturally into the soaring space of the *tepidarium* so that we would have come imperceptibly from rooms of small scale and of increasing impressiveness into the climactic room of enormous scale which was also the most important one of the entire complex.[129]

Here we would first be assailed by the awesome scale of this enormous space—79 by 183 feet between its walls with three great vaults whose soffits were 108 feet above the floor. The whole length was divided into three bays. Each bay of the longitudinal walls contained an arch rising to the full height of the cross vault. A similar arch stood at each end of the hall. The thrust of the vaults thus fell upon four central piers and four end or corner piers. The central piers were 14 to 16 feet thick, 54 feet deep to the north, 80 feet deep to the south. But the depth of the south piers was relieved by arches forming the sides of the antechamber to the *calidarium*. At the corners the thrust was both longitudinal and transverse, and here it was carried by walls 108 feet long on the right and left and by piers of the same size as the other north and south piers at the front and rear. The

---

[129] It must be conceded at once that much of the designation of room purposes continues to be conjectural. Robertson puts the space usually called the *tepidarium* to the purposes of the *apodyterium* since it seems to have no heating arrangement but this would seem to be a clumsy piece of planning. [D. S. Robertson, *A Handbook of Greek and Roman Architecture* (Cambridge: Cambridge University Press, 1954), p. 260.]

spaces between these buttress walls were used to contain four tepid baths; the middle bays on the north and south provided monumental vistas into the *frigidarium* and the *calidarium*. The side and end walls of the *tepidarium* rose higher than the surrounding roofs, and so this great space had a brilliant clerestory.

Not only was there munificence in the scale of the room and the boldness of the structure, but every architectural and decorative detail was opulent. There were Corinthian columns of many sizes throughout the baths, and most of them were of marble. All the shafts were monolithic. The great columns of the *tepidarium* carried broken entablatures which in turn received the springing of the vaults. These columns were more than 5 feet thick and 38 feet high and were not of marble but of solid granite. The smaller columns standing in the niches were of red porphyry, of white alabaster from Asia, or of many kinds and colors of marble from the isles of Greece. The halls and courts were all paved with marble mosaics portraying gladiators and other athletes, nereids and tritons, surrounded by geometrical designs. The capitals, the steps, the linings of the baths, the *exedrae*, the entablatures were all of white marble. The walls were covered with colored marbles in panels to a certain height, and then white marble took over to the springing of the vaults. The vaults themselves had shallow panels, not deep coffers, and these were filled with glass mosaics. Color, structure, and scale all contributed to an effect which must have been imperial, not playful; overpowering, not intimate. These rooms had grandeur, they were rooms which might have given pleasure only when they were crowded. But this is not a criticism, for they were not designed for the solitary man of Chirico.

North of the *tepidarium* was the *frigidarium*, generally believed to have been open to the sky and to have offered an open-air swimming pool particularly attractive to the Romans in the hot and sultry summer months. Its north wall was unbroken as a barrier to the wet winds from that quarter. The area of the *frigidarium* was about the same as that of the *tepidarium* and it was similarly decorated except for the crowning glory of the vaults. Indeed the way these great spans were covered is a matter of speculation and even controversy, though there is evidence, both in receptors at the top of the walls and in the presence of tons of L- or T-shaped iron, to suggest a metallic frame. But the absence of vaults permitted an even greater unfolding of the entablature. Both rooms contained much sculpture of the monumental and confused type that was currently appealing to the Romans.

To the south of the *tepidarium* was a foyer with two baths in it, possibly of an intermediate temperature, and then followed the great, round hotbox, the *calidarium*, a circular hall roofed with a dome. In the middle of the floor was a circular hot bath. The dome may have had an open eye in it at the top like that of the Pantheon. Certainly the *calidarium*, in common with the other great rooms, had not only a sumptuous architectural

Pl. 173

sculptured and painted decoration, had not only magnificent vistas into the other great areas, but was also full of the fantasy play of running waters splashing from lions' mouths of marble or silver into handsome marble basins.

Special attention had to be paid to keeping such a room warm. Here we may again admire the Roman ingenuity. Ordinary Roman tiles about 2 feet square and a scant 2 inches thick were laid on a base of concrete 3 or 4 feet below the intended pavement of the baths. Then small piers 2 feet high were built on this base. These piers carried a concrete floor a foot thick. On the concrete floor the builders floated first a layer of pounded tufa and shards, then a thin course of marble cement in which the mosaics of the finished floor were laid. Thus when the furnaces were lighted at a lower level, the smoke and hot air flowed under the floor through the *hypocaust* and escaped through flues in the walls.

It is hard to read the plan of the Baths of Caracalla from parading around the ruins. Most of the rich decoration is gone, though here and there one may come on a piece of mosaic flooring. The opulence has to be recalled by drawings which may or may not be reliable. The architectural forms might until recently have been more easily imagined by a visit to the main waiting room of the Pennsylvania Railroad Station in New York. Going to see *Aïda* in the ruins will not help much. But prowling the ruins in daylight will nevertheless give an impression of Roman scale which is almost unique. The single more powerful impression of which I am aware is to be found in the great remnants of the vaults of the Basilica of Con-

Pl. 172

stantine/Maxentius just off the Forum Romanum, where all the grandeur of Rome is displayed simply and without compromise.

HADRIAN'S VILLA

But I would like to close our visit to Rome on a less grandiose note.

There was always another side to Rome than the side of Caracalla and Trimalchio—men who accepted Cicero's advice that you should eat to live, not live to eat. Many Romans preferred the country even when they had to live in the city, and believed with Horace that the true beauties were in the campagna, "That corner of the land beyond all others for me smiles, where heaven sends warm mists and a slow spring."

It was in the same vein that Livy wrote of the Roman campagna. "Where it is easier for the soul to become antique and contemporaneous with the monuments it gazes upon."

Pompeii was a very special and early type of Republican town for the wealthy, by no means a suburb of anything, and thanks to its protective destruction by the ashes of Vesuvius, it is the first historical demonstration we have of the private house as an important if small piece of Roman architecture. The privacy was complete, a microcosm of the complete state. Within its walls the family was supreme. Pompeii was done with elegance and taste, not often to be found in later Imperial Rome. There it was hard to achieve any kind of serenity in the city, and so those who could built suburban or rural villas away from the bad summer climate and the febrile life of Rome.

In principle the urban house was detached from the outside world. It offered no ostentatious facade to impress the stranger. It received little light from external windows. There was a symmetrical arrangement of rooms around a central uncovered court or *atrium* in the middle of which a tank, the *impluvium*, caught the rainwater. Behind this was an open living room, the *tablinum*, a peristyle surrounded by a colonnaded walk enclosing a garden with flower beds and fountains; and around the peristyle various apartments including perhaps a reception room, the *oecus*, dining rooms, *triclinia*, parlors (*exedrae*), a *lararium* for the effigies of the family gods, the *lares*. Such a house was already a large one. Most palaces were but enlargements and elaborations on this idea, although the late palace of Diocletian at Spalato was planned more like a camp. Save for some of the quite different and much smaller villas of Republican Pompeii, it seems to me that Hadrian's villa at Tivoli (118–138) is the most moving.

The life of the emperor "was a life of state from which there was only the illusion of escape."[130] The villa might offer to an emperor so-minded a genuine escape. The Spanish-born emperor Hadrian was such a man, sometimes magnanimous, as often jealous, an architect of skill who considered himself as good as Trajan's great professional architect Apollodorus. He was a brilliant dilettante in the best original sense of the word—in poetry, in philosophy, in contemplation, in government, in military skill, though accused of being languid about the latter. He was a compulsive but tasteful builder. To Rome itself he left her greatest building, the Pantheon, described in another context earlier (pp. 43–44). In his day, the surroundings of the Pantheon were elegant, the approach magnificent. Today these have much deteriorated, but not the building. The visitor can scarcely fail to sense that the Pantheon remains not only the greatest building in Rome but one of the certain masterpieces in all architectural history.

Hadrian's personal villa at Tivoli expresses all that was best about him, with its libraries, its *stoa* for conversation, its graceful communications, its enormous variety of vistas and places, never ostentatious, never vulgar, surely the noblest of the Roman villas. It may well be, as Frank E. Brown suggests, "an architectural portrait of the greatest individual of the Roman world."

Pl. 175

> Its sprawling fabric, flung impeccably over ridges and valleys, matched his every moment, mood and attitude with a space to fit it. Morning, noon, or evening, moated or towered solitude, free or formal society, repose, reflection, diversion, the prince, philosopher, poet, or poseur were alike caught in the villa's sensitive net. . . .

[130] Frank E. Brown, *Roman Architecture* (London: Studio Vista, 1968), p. 40.

Yet, for all its freedom, the emperor's whim and the emperor's architecture were bounded by the forms into which the Empire had crystallized all human experience. The villa might exhaust the vocabulary of forum and basilica, theatre and bath, halls of state and privacy. It could not go beyond it. . . .
On the one hand, ritual, this cosmos for which man was beholden to none but himself was his proudest creation, the monument of his supreme self confidence. On the other it was the measure of human frailty, of human inadequacy to support a burden of responsibility so crushing. It was the scene not only of man's proud self-reliance but of his frantic search for excuses, for the certitude he could not give himself. It could be lasting only because it was built in ignorance of the pressures it would have to bear.[131]

If three days or more are to be spent on classical architectural Rome, one should be devoted to Tivoli. A day for the forums, a day for Caracalla and Nero, the Flavian amphitheater, the Palatine and the Pantheon, and a day in the country at Tivoli with Hadrian. There are other things to see and do in Tivoli—the splendid fountains of the Villa d'Este, the temple of the Sibyl and a delightful lunch nearby under the arbor at the Sibilla, for which you should allow enough time. The usual order is fountains, lunch, the Villa. It should no doubt be reversed, if the fountains have not been turned off, for the Villa is of prime importance, and the reflections which it suggests are likely to be more meaningful before the wine. But I am not quite sure of this. The Villa is really at its best toward sundown and in the twilight. This is probably more than symbolic.

WHAT OF ROMAN ARCHITECTURE?

What, finally, shall we say of Roman architecture? It is a mixed bag as were the Romans themselves.

Was it as Faure has suggested that "in Rome the real artist is the engineer, as the true poet is the historian and the true philospher is the jurist"? There is no doubt the Romans were proud of their technical skill, always liked to make things bigger, liked to think of themselves as practical. Frontinus asked, "Who will venture to compare with these mighty conduits, the idle Pyramids or the famous but useless works of the Greeks?" With their engineering and their military mind went a half admiration for frugality and restraint; but Rome was schizoid in this and there was always a conflict between austerity and vulgarity; restraint never quite dominated the architecture of Rome.

On the one hand the Roman paid at least lip service to *gravitas*, *pietas*, *virtus*, to sobriety, dignity, sincerity, dutifulness, loyalty, honor. He had frightening energy, lacked interest in speculative subjects or any kind

[131] Ibid., pp. 42–43.

of theory, scientific, political, aesthetic or religious, perhaps even curiosity. Pliny remarked, "We are gluttons for the useful and the good."[132] The order of the words is significant.

But against these qualities there are those of savagery and brutality and coldness never missing even in the Republic. A Roman minded an unpropitious Caesar more than he did a bad one, and it was earthquakes and a defeat by Boadicea that angered him against Nero rather than the latter's murders and excesses. He could be and often was dissolute. But it is part of the conflict that even in the Empire the parade of the good alternates with the bad; gross Tiberius, insane Caligula, brutish Commodus will be offset by progressive Trajan, cautious, versatile Hadrian, contemplative Marcus Aurelius. All this somehow is suggested by the architecture.

As Muller says of the Roman, he was "incapable of understanding Plato, Archimedes and Christ alike—'he could only rule the world.'"[133]

H. G. Wells thought that the true symbol of the classical Roman attitude toward science was not Lucretius but the soldier who hacked Archimedes to death at the storming of Syracuse. There really was no Roman science, no physics, no chemistry. Even the doctors were Greeks, most of them slaves.

Romans had little curiosity about the human world, either. They did not discuss political science as a matter of theory or speculate about the principles of economics. They did not write psychological tragedies like those of Euripides, although Seneca could fill your stomach with the practical details of the plague that followed Oedipus. They were not even very much concerned about geography, which was of practical importance to them but about which they were abysmally ignorant.

To be sure, the Romans were practical enough to be adroit at exploiting to the full the technology they had, but their curiosity did not encourage them to fundamental discoveries which might have supported a newer and still more useful technology. They had no national organizations to support on practical grounds those essays in curiosity in which the Roman people as a whole had no interest or faith. To the taciturn and incurious Roman it seemed merely that the speculative Greek talked too much.

So the Romans made few innovations, but their energies and their realism did let them force the technological fruits of others' discoveries to the greatest possible size. They were magnificent civil engineers and lawyers but never natural or social scientists.

The Roman attitude toward science had its mirror in their attitude toward art. These hard-bitten realists, soldiers, lawyers, engineers, betrayed themselves in their portrait busts.

The artist held even a lower place in the Roman esteem than he did in the Greek. Even Vergil could say:

[132] Nostri omni utilitatum et virtutum rapacissimi.
[133] Herbert J. Muller, *The Uses of the Past* (New York: Oxford, 1952), pp. 208–209. (The inner quotation is from Will Durant.)

Others, I deem, shall work the breathing bronze to softer forms; others shall from marble draw faces to the very life; shall plead their causes with readier tongue; shall trace with the rod of wisdom the courses of the heavens and tell the risings of the stars; the Roman's heed shall be to guide the nations under his dominion, to set on the world the habit of peace, to spare the humble and wear down the proud.[134]

All these attitudes combine in what the Romans asked for and got from their art. First they wanted the luxury which Seneca deplored:

Today a man thinks himself poor and unclean unless the walls gleam with large and costly mirrors, unless Numidian inlay sets off Alexandrian marble, unless their surrounds are faced all round with intricate patterns with all the colour range of paintings, unless the ceiling-domes are a mass of glass, unless our swimming-pools are lined with Thasian marble (once a rare sight in any temple), unless the water is poured through silver valves. . . . So we progress; establishments which once drew admiring crowds are classed as antiques, once luxury has elaborated some new device, to her own defeat.[135]

Up to the time of Augustus the Romans may be said to have had a style, sober and dull and middle-class and imitative of the Greeks as it may have been, but:

When generals and Caesars rose from the lowest ranks of the army and the farthest corners of the provinces, when the most important religious movement of the time was a movement starting with the dregs of the people and gradually invading the upper classes, art also took on an increasingly popular and provincial guise, and little by little discarded classical ideals.[136]

But all this provincial art came to Rome and there it was mixed together. Now people of the same cultural class, the same economic and social level, demanded and got anything they wanted. To paraphrase a well-known architect of the 1920s, a Roman builder might have said, "We can do it in Greek, we can do it in Persian."[137] To copy masterpieces began on a large scale. Horace made no bones about it:

[134] Excudent alii spirantia mollius aera (credo equidem) et vivos ducent de marmore vultus; orabunt causas melius, caeliquue meatus describent radio et surgentia sidera dicent: tu regere imperio populos, Romane, memento (hae tibi erunt artes), pacisque imponere morem, parcere, subjectis et debellare superbos. [Translated by R. W. Moore in *The Roman Commonwealth* (London: English Universities Press, 1942), p. 178.]
[135] Ibid., p. 177.
[136] Arnold Hauser, *The Social History of Art*, vol. I (New York: Vintage, 1957), p. 119.
[137] At the Princeton bicentennial architecture conference of 1947 this man, then well known, now deceased, asserted that a competent architect could design a good Gothic, Renaissance, Georgian, or Greek building, according to his client's whim.

O ye, my Pisos, eager well to write
Turn o'er the Grecian models day and night.[138]

But when you copy masterpieces well enough, you may find it impossible to invent any of your own. This was the Roman plight.

So the great architecture of Rome rests in the straightforward engineering of its aqueducts and bridges; its early restrained copying, as in the Maison Carrée; its enormous scale; and above all no doubt in its management of space. Later more consciously monumental works deliberately sought splendor.

> This [Roman] love of splendor—this craving for the grandiose and feeling for the practical . . . [carried] the danger of lapsing into grandiloquence and pomposity, for the temptation to overelaborate was one the Romans found difficult to resist.
> The Greeks, even during the Hellenistic age, sought to make their buildings works of art by means of pure architectural form, by simplicity and breadth of style, but the Romans were easily seduced by decorative effects. . . . In Greek building, ornament is always organically related to the construction and often demonstrates unseen static forces. Even when used solely as decoration in frieze or molding, ornament is strictly controlled and never allowed to become obtrusive. Now the Roman love of flamboyance regarded ornament principally as a decorative adjunct with no deep significance. It would be applied where, for the Greeks, it would have had no justification. . . . It may be said without exaggeration that while the Greeks sought inner meaning, the Romans were content with outward appearance.[139]

It was the Roman arcuate and vaulted construction which provided the canon for the future of European architecture up to the Renaissance, and for a long time after that the Roman treatment of the pilaster and loggia and the idea of monumental axiality dominated. But there was something more. You see it in the Baths of Caracalla, Trajan's Forum, in the Pantheon, in Hadrian's Villa.

> [T]he Romans mastered a task the Greeks had never attempted: the enclosure and architectural modeling of space. The Greeks had always devoted their attention to the refinement of architectural forms and to the sculptural quality of their buildings, but the Romans were absorbed in the problems of structure and the creation of noble interiors. The spatial effects attained in the thermae and the great villas and palaces were unknown to the Greeks whose interest was centered on simplifying and perfecting the vertical and horizontal elements . . . with which they enclosed space without much concern for the quality of the space enclosed.

[138] Horace, from Alexander Murison's translation of *The Art of Poetry*, in Basil Davenport (ed.), *The Portable Roman Reader* (New York: Viking, 1951), p. 418.
[139] Bodo Cichy, *The Great Ages of Architecture* (New York: Putnam, 1964), p. 42.

This space was a mere foil for the architectural fabric. The Romans, on the other hand, ceaselessly and indefatigably took space itself as their medium, giving it a character dominating that of the enclosing shell. The Romans, who inherited a plastic architecture from the Greeks, transformed it into an art of space and so determined the role that it was to play throughout European history.[140]

While stands the Coliseum, Rome shall stand:
When falls the Coliseum, Rome shall fall;
And when Rome falls—the world.[141]

But it was not the colosseum by which Rome should be measured.

BYZANTIUM

It is a deceptive and superficial generalization that Byzantine architecture, the buildings of the Eastern or Greek arm of Christianity, was an architecture of the Greek cross plan and the surmounting dome or domes or half domes; whilst Romanesque, the early Medieval Western or Roman architecture, was an architecture of the basilican plan, the apse, the barrel, and sometimes the ribbed vault. Most of the churches to be found in the areas falling under these two ecclesiastical domains do indeed follow these respective patterns. But there are confusing and important exceptions both ways. In strictly Romanesque Aquitaine in the west of France, St-Front in Périgueux follows a Greek cross plan with domes; while the cathedrals of Angoulême and Cahors sport domes, though on a more linear plan. In Sicily during the period of Norman control San Giovanni degli Eremiti and San Cataldo are eastern domical, while distinctly Byzantine mosaics are the chief ornaments of the basilican Monreale and the Capella Palatina. On the other hand at the western outpost of Byzantium, Ravenna, at the very moment when the clearly Byzantine San Vitale and the Mausoleum of Galla Placidia were being built, so were the apsed basilicas of San Apollinare in Classe and San Apollinare Nuovo. Early and in a different context I have spoken of the frequent use of the basilican plan in Eastern churches up to Justinian (pp. 51–54). Influences passed both ways through what was after all a rather porous curtain.

BAPTISTERIES AND MARTYRIA

By the fourth century A.D. round forms were being used seriously in Italy and not only for the small pagan *tholoi* and the large pagan Pantheon. These forms did not serve well for the Western congregational rituals

[140] Ibid., p. 62.
[141] Byron, George Gordon 6th Baron, *Childe Harold's Pilgrimage*, canto IV, stanza 145.

which found the basilica in the end more suitable. But they were practical for baptisteries and *martyria*.

Until the Middle Ages baptism was generally by immersion, in groups, and only at one of the three great Christian festivals—Easter, Pentecost, and Epiphany. Usually there was only one baptistery in a city so it had to be large. And for a long time the baptistery could be quite independent of a church structure. The baptistery was always polygonal or circular in plan, centered around a large baptismal pool in which the neophytes were immersed, and provided with an annulus for the supporting congregation. The smaller Roman temple forms did not offer enough space; domes such as those of the Pantheon were beyond resource or need; and in adapting the Roman form the Christians found some difficulty in covering the space needed with a roof supported by the outside walls. A natural device was to make a circle of single or paired columns to support the central roof and surround it with a one-storied circular aisle enclosed by the outside walls. The earliest one extant, despite many alterations—a timber dome replacing the original one of stone, the aisle now flat-ceilinged replacing a barrel vault—is the Baptistery of San Giovanni in Laterano in Rome. A section and plan of the Baptistery at Nocera (A.D. 350) shows what this was like.

Pl. 176

Another natural use of the round form was for a *martyrium* or a memorial chapel. In these the altar or sarcophagus replaced the baptismal pool. One of the oldest and best preserved of these is Santa Costanza built in Rome by the Emperor Constantine (A.D. 338) in memory of his daughter. The building is circular, the central space domed. It is separated from the barrel-vaulted circular aisle by twenty-four pairs of Corinthian columns, each surmounted by a heavy broken entablature from which the arches of the circular arcade spring. As in most of the Western Christian churches the dome, which would doubtless otherwise have leaked, is capped by a flat conical roof. The walls of the aisle have no windows, all the light coming from windows in the drum supporting the dome, which might be conceived of as a circular clerestory. Instead in the walls of the aisles there is a system of niches, alternately semicircular and rectangular. They bear some traces of the original mosaics suggesting faintly the opulence that was once there. This memorial is one of the more attractive things to visit in Rome, doubtless overlooked by most tourists. It has however been discovered by the Romans and is very popular for marriages, which seem to be scheduled almost around the clock, so the architectural visitor has to sneak in between vows and kisses, so to speak.

Pl. 177

Pl. 178

A larger and later Roman example (A.D. 470) is San Stefano Rotonda, now in process of careful restoration. Here the central drum is supported by an annulus of twenty-two Ionic columns with polished shafts, and the architrave is continuous, conveying the impression of a peristyle. The exterior has the usual early Christian simplicity, though the continuous curvature of the aisle roof set well below the conical roof of the *naos* is effective. Arches can be seen in the wall of the aisle, leading to the conclusion that there was once a double ambulatory.

If by now you are avid to visit more of these circular buildings, you might try the rarely visited San Lorenzo Maggiore in Milan (360), a most unusual scheme with double arcades and projecting *exedrae*, a very interesting space. Since San Lorenzo has been much built on since and much restored by Martino Bassi in 1576–1619, you may have trouble getting your mind through the fact that he converted the original square of the central area to an octagon and replaced the original cross vault with a dome. But large two-storied *exedrae* project from the four sides to give a round appearance to the exterior, and by providing such a melange of columns, curving walls, arches, half domes, almost Baroque in feeling, the late architect enormously enriched the spatial effect. The original San Lorenzo predates the more famous San Vitale in Ravenna by 150 years.

Pl. 179

The architectures of both Byzantium and the West can be seen as a firm reflection of religious politics and liturgical necessities. For some time there were efforts to find a useful combination between the basilican plan and the central-domical one, though it is probably stretching things to suggest that the effort at Hagia Sophia was a symbolic reflection of Justinian's effort to reunite the Empire.

THE CENTRAL FORM IN BYZANTIUM

As a matter of fact, up until the time of Justinian (527) very few *churches* East or West had done more than ring changes on the basilican plan. But Justinian's builders turned decisively to vaulted centrally planned buildings with a central dome, which had been maturing in the secular architecture of the late Empire as palace churches or *martyria* and for which there may have been some latent pressure of Eastern tradition and taste.

The thrust toward the central scheme resolution was truly determined, in Krautheimer's opinion,[142] by the Aegean liturgy, the elaborate celebration of the Mass, the development of processional entrances, and the appropriation of the nave by the clergy. For such a service in which the performance of the Mass occupied the central area liturgically, it was essential that the architecture provide a center which might be regarded as a sort of theater in the round except that the spectators were not allowed to see many of the most important scenes. Why, is moot. The changing ritual asked for different space; and fortunately prototypes for adaptation were there to be seen even if, as in Hagia Sophia, the extrapolation had to be large.

BYZANTINE CONSTRUCTION

The conditions of terrain and materials had as usual something to say about construction. The geographical position of Constantinople put it at the

[142] Krautheimer, *Early Christian and Byzantine Architecture*, op. cit., p. 149.

crossroads of the great water route from the Black Sea through the Mediterranean and the land route of trade between Europe and the East. It had the Golden Horn—a deep, tideless harbor of great length. Strategically and commercially it was a better site than Rome's. It was also more beautiful, standing on seven hills fronting the Bosphorus and the Sea of Marmora. Its noninsular position made it possible for ideas about art and architecture to flow in and out as readily as corn and oil.

There was no good building stone nearby, and the local materials had to be clay for bricks and rubble for concrete. But the cement was not there and so the masons had to be called on for more skill. The monumental materials had to be imported; marble came from the island quarries and those on the eastern shores of the Mediterranean, and Constantinople became the main marble-working center and supplied all parts of the Empire. But no stone was quarried nearby. The sea made it possible to bring good-sized monolithic columns from abroad to such an extent that they were used even in the construction of underground cisterns.

Despite the possibility of importing stones, stereotomy did not reach the heights it did in the Transalpine West. It was easier to make a carcass of concrete and brickwork, to allow it to settle and then, when desired, to sheathe it in marble. Brick also permitted more freedom in decorative patterns or in the application of mosaic or fresco, and less freedom for the art of the stonecarver. The Byzantine bricks therefore were carefully made, ordinarily thin like Roman brick (about 1½ inches) laid in thick beds of very hard mortar. They could be laid over a wall core of concrete. They were laid in many patterns, meandering frets, chevrons, diagonally as well as horizontally to produce a wide variety of unfinished facades, sometimes ornamented by stone bands or blind arches. The domes too were often made of brick or light porous stone or even of pottery (San Vitale). Thus we come here practically for the first time to an architecture which is essentially not a stone but a brick architecture. I do mean to speak later and specifically of some other manifestations of brick architecture, but to defer Byzantine to that point would sacrifice clarity to rigid outlining.

JUSTINIAN

What suddenly erupted in architecture in Byzantium we surely owe to the powerful character of the Emperor Justinian the Macedonian (527–565), who came to power about seventy-five years after the Goth Odoacer deposed Romulus Augustulus, the last emperor of the West, at Ravenna, and a quarter of a century after Italy was united by Theodoric.

His policies set out to establish the absolute power of the emperor and the revival of a universal Christian Roman Empire. He sought to make the Mediterranean a Roman, not a Byzantine, lake, to "reconquer," so to speak. His funds and his manpower came from the Eastern provinces; he ruled from Byzantium but he still thought of the Empire as centered around the Mediterranean. Hence he visualized Ravenna as a subcapital, subject to

Constantinople but vying with it in splendor, and Rome was to be a spiritual center balancing the see of the Patriarch in Byzantium.

To do this he used arms to quell inner unrest and to take large parts of the Empire from the barbarians, to secure the frontiers; he developed a nearly bribe-proof civil service; established great universities at Constantinople and Beirut; reestablished religious orthodoxy, eliminating heresies and compromising less dangerous views; reorganized the law into a uniform code; used grand propaganda schemes to promote his own glory; established a well-planned publicity campaign aimed at the intelligentsia and carried on by the sycophantic court historian Procopius and the court poet Paul the Silentiary. He established a trade in luxury goods from as far away as China, India, Abyssinia; he began a grandiose building activity, mainly in the capital, designed to impress both the intellectuals and the populace and to provide employment for the masses.

Most of his accomplishments survived his death by little more than fifty years. The Lombards (Longobards) took over Italy except for Ravenna and the far south in 580, fifteen years after his nephew Justin II had seized the imperial power. The Holy Land and large parts of Asia Minor were overrun by the Persians in 614 and lost for good to Islam in 636. The Slavs got as far south as Corinth by 577, and the Bulgarians crossed the Danube in 680.

Yet there were great residues. In Justinian's time there were the architectural glories of Hagia Sophia and Ravenna. Later on, despite the vicissitudes of political power and the violence of theological quarrels, not even the Iconoclastic movement of the eighth century halted the building of excellent if smaller churches in much of the East, and this continued with no serious abatement well into the sixteenth century.

Hagia Sophia

But first there was Hagia Sophia (532–536). I have already said some things about its engineering and its space (pp. 44–45) but since it is one of the greatest buildings in the world, more must be said.

The first basilica was built in 360. There were the usual vicissitudes. It was remodeled in 415, burned out in 532. It was then that Justinian decided to do the unbelievable. He took columns from Rome and Ephesus as a matter of course but brought fresh marbles as well, not only from the Aegean but, so it is said, even from the Atlantic coast of France. The logistics performed by Anthemios were prodigious, the cost perhaps 250 million 1975 dollars.

Like Baron Haussmann later, Justinian found the conventional master builders inadequate. So he turned to theorists, men called by their contemporaries *mechanopoioi*, that is, scholars who knew the theories of statics and dynamics and were well versed in mathematics. Anthemios of Tralles had written a book on conic sections and was an expert in projective geometry. He was also an inventor of repute said to know the principle of steam power and of the "burning mirror." His partner Isidorus of Miletus had taught stereometry and physics at the universities of Alexandria and Constantinople and had written a commentary on an older treatise on vaulting.

These engineers contrived a bold but simple structural system based on a huge rectangle 230 by 250 feet. Inside they placed four huge piers on the corners of a 104-foot square. From these at a height of 70 feet they sprung four arches, those to the north and south embedded in the nave, those to the east and west freestanding. From the apex of the arches and the four connecting pendentives, they sprung a shell dome with 40 ribs and 40 curved webs, buttressed on the outside by 40 closely spaced short ribs framing small windows. They put protruding towers on top of these buttresses perhaps to help to weigh them down. They also made a further effort to counter the longitudinal thrusts by two large semidomes opening east and west resting on the main piers and on two pairs of subsidiary piers, but it is doubtful that these did much good since they were too thin to exert much counterthrust and their apices have in fact collapsed several times. Not much more bracing, if any, was provided by the smaller conches which opened on diagonal axes of the bays of the half domes, or the barrel vaults which projected on the central axis from the half domes. Pl. 179

This core is an inner core of a double shell—hazardous in its statics, really standing free in space, not really involved with the ancillary spatial structures or they with it.

The construction was certainly simple and bold. The building methods followed suit. The eight main piers *were* built of large ashlar blocks. But the walls are made of thin bricks set in 2¾-inch mortar beds interspersed with limestone course. The bricks of the vaults are not radially placed but are set on their sides in very thick mortar beds, in an inferior version of Roman concrete.

Inferior structural materials, inferior details, reckless construction, "Defying all laws of statics, shaken by successive earthquakes, collapsing at its weak points and being repaired, the Hagia Sophia stands by sheer miracle."[143]

And it has had difficulty standing. We do not see today the Hagia Sophia which was consecrated on 27 December 537. The first dome, which was very flat, collapsed in 558. A steeper ribbed one replaced it in 563 on a base which had been deformed by the thrust of the first dome so that the piers and buttresses tipped backward, the east and west arches expanded, and the lateral arches bent outward. More or less patched up, the western portion of the new dome nonetheless fell in 989 and an Armenian architect replaced it. Then the eastern part collapsed in 1346 and was rebuilt. The Turks came along and conquered and in the middle of the fifteenth century planted minarets at the four corners, clustered mausoleums around

[143] Ibid., p. 155.

the blanks of the structure. Inside they covered the mosaics with yellow paint,[144] filled the windows with stucco gratings, hung four enormous shields with verses from the Koran. This has marred the vision of course but not destroyed it. The sense of mobile space earlier referred to remains one of the greatest sensations to be experienced in any building interior in the world. The frequently quoted observation by Procopius is indeed true. The main dome hovering over all with not much apparent structure, seeming more like a canopy than a structure, does appear "as if suspended by a chain from heaven."

It is hard to explain the nonspatial aspects of the decoration even with many colored pictures, to say nothing of words. Krautheimer has done as well as anyone.

> The term solids—in this architecture at least—is a misnomer. The piers are massive enough if seen from the aisles; but they are not meant to be seen. Their bulk is denied by their marble sheathing. The column shafts are huge, measuring two and a half to three feet in diameter, but the colourful marble counters any feeling of massiveness. Precious materials, subtly graded, shimmer over the interior. From the dark grey marble plaques of the pavement rise high grey marble pedestals carrying columns of green marble with large white veins—both on the ground floor and in the gallery arcades. Reddish porphyry columns stand in the conchs that flank apse and entrance. The piers and walls in the nave are covered by marble plaques in three zones: first, green marble slabs flanked by yellowish plaques with purplish veins; above, porphyry slabs enclosed by dark bluish marble with yellow veins; finally, a third tier repeating the first. Slabs have been sliced in two and the sections fitted together so that the veins form a symmetrical pattern along a centre axis. The capitals of the 107 multicoloured columns are all overspun with foliage, their shiny marble leaves and branches standing out against the deep shadows of the ground. A lacework of tendrils overlays the spandrels of the arcades; . . . delicately undercut by drills . . . elsewhere, white mother-of-pearl rinceaux are inlaid into black marble. Silver, gold, and mosaic are joined in this wealth of colours and shades. Silver sheathed both the *synthronon*, rising in three tiers in the apse, and the column screen of the chancel, the latter projected westward from the arch of the forechoir and continued by the long *solea*. Golden lamps dangled in the intercolumniations, others rose from the trabeation of the chancel screen. Domes and half-domes, vaults, and soffits gleamed with mosaic. A few fragments survive: golden tendrils on a bluish-green field, purple crosses on a gold or silver ground. Figurative mosaic was apparently missing.[145]

The exterior is more or less familiar to anyone who has ever looked at a picture postcard or seen a colored slide of Istanbul. Along with the

Pl. 180

[144] Some of which they are now removing to reveal the mosaics.
[145] Krautheimer, *Early Christian and Byzantine Architecture*, op. cit., pp. 157–158.

Taj Mahal, the Parthenon, the Houses of Parliament, the National Capitol in Washington, and the Eiffel Tower (not all necessarily of equal merit), it may be one of the most famous exteriors in the world.

> To design a shockingly bold interior was, no doubt, the primary concern of Anthemios and Isidorus. Yet the exterior is equally impressive. The volumes are stacked on top of each other and the eye is led subtly towards the forechoir, from there towards the eastern half-dome, and finally up towards the dome. Surrounded by palace buildings to the south and east and by city buildings to the north and west, the Great Church towered above the city and the Sea of Marmara. With this picture still vivid, the visitor entered the atrium to be enclosed by porticoes in which one pier rhythmically alternated with two columns. Finally, after passing through the transverse barrier of the long but shallow esonarthex, he entered the church proper through one of five doors, the royal gate in the centre. Only then did he see the nave revealed, focused on its huge dome and half-domes, and only then did he understand as relations in space what had been but half-intelligible from the outside.[146]

Outside of Constantinople there was only one building to compete with Hagia Sophia. In Constantinople, Hosios Sergios and Partehos was second in prestige but was inferior to the smaller San Vitale in Ravenna, where we should now go.

RAVENNA

To understand the curious shifts in the architecture of Ravenna we need to know a little of its history. It is hard to realize now that it was once an imperial city, first Roman, then Byzantine. In A.D. 420 the Roman Emperor Honorius (395–423), long wholly under the influence of his Vandal general Stilicho,[147] whose daughter Maria he had married, disturbed by the frequent invasions of Italy, moved the western capital from Rome-Milan to Ravenna. Built like Venice on piles, Ravenna was relatively safe from the barbarians and it had a good port at Classis, six miles to the south, which had been founded by Augustus. On the death of Honorius his beautiful, pious, adventurous sister Galla Placidia essayed to govern the Empire in place of her son Valentinian III. She and her successors were quite unable to fend off the Ostrogothic invasions, first of Odoacer (476–493) and then of Theodoric (493–526). Theodoric became a Christian and began to embellish the town. But following his death almost simultaneously with the accession of Justinian (526), Ravenna soon fell to Byzantium (540) and was then made the subcapital of the Eastern Empire.

The oldest of the four Ravenna buildings we shall note is Sant' Apollinare Nuovo (493–525), built by Theodoric as a Palatine church. It was

---

[146] Ibid., pp. 158–159.
[147] Whom, however, he caused to be murdered in 408.

long called San Martino in Cielo d'Oro but was renamed for Saint Apollinaris when his relics were moved here from Classis. The original building was early Christian from the West, a strictly formal five-aisled basilica which had to be sure, a spacious and well-lighted interior and twenty-four Greek marble columns.

What we see now except for this interior is almost all much later. The round detached or almost detached bell tower (campanile), however fine, belongs to the tenth century and is one of the earliest detached belfries which were so popular in Italy throughout the Romanesque and into the Gothic. The portico is sixteenth-century Renaissance built then to replace the old *atrium*. The two large windows in the west wall are also Renaissance.

What is important to us is that Sant'Apollinare Nuovo ushers in, in their full splendor, the period of the Ravenna mosaics. From Sant' Apollinare Nuovo to the sixth-seventh-century mosaics of Sant' Apollinare in Classe, these are surely the finest in Europe, surpassing what was done contemporaneously in Constantinople or much later in Palermo and Venice. Dante praises their "symphony of color" in the *Commedia*. The *tesserae* are small, brilliantly bright in color. The pictures are clear, harmonious, sad—but not so sad as the Russian icons or the paintings of Rouault, despite the fixed dark eyes ringed with black. They use symbols freely but also deal with reality.

The array of mosaics at Sant'Apollinare Nuovo, whether or not the oldest in Ravenna, is in any event interesting. The left side of the basilica bears on its frieze twenty-two holy virgins leaving the town (and the port of Classis) to follow the Magi in offering crowns to the enthroned virgin, and the right frieze depicts twenty-six martyrs leaving the palace of Theodoric to carry crowns to the Christ in Majesty who is encompassed by the four evangelists.

The next building in time, and certainly the most important building in Ravenna and the second most important in Byzantine architecture, is San Vitale. Its dates are probably 526–547. The latter is firm since it was then consecrated by Archbishop Maximian. It is popular to attribute it to Justinian as a commemoration of his recovery of Ravenna, but that was not until 540. Certainly when completed it was fully a part of the Imperial Court—the mosaics of Justinian and Theodora alone would attest to that. But it may well have been started by the Ostrogoths.

It is a very original building. Its materials and its craftsmanship are clearly local but not provincial although column shafts and capitals were certainly imported from the workshops of Constantinople. The bricks, burned locally, are thin and long like those of Constantinople, not like the higher, shorter ones of Northern Italy of the time. The vault (it is really that rather than a dome) is built differently.

The plan is simple. An outer octagon 118 feet across is concentric to *Pl. 181* an inner octagon about half the size (54 feet, 9 inches). The eight piers of the inner octagon rise to support an eight-sided cloister vault on squinches, which looks like a dome. This vault is made of earthen pots nested into each other, and the construction thus becomes so light as not to need much in the way of buttresses, though they are there in a subtle system which carries the thrust down at an angle to the ground.

The ambulatory and the galleries were not vaulted until the Middle Ages so that originally we would have felt more emphasis on the core, but it is still very evident. The apsidal chapel opens smoothly enough from one side of the inner ring opposite the entrance. The other seven bays all have open semicircular niches providing great unity to the design. These carry the circular gallery which was much desired in the Eastern churches of the day.

The exterior of San Vitale is aggressively simple, made up only   *Pl. 182*
of beautifully laid brick. But there is a sensitively proportioned array of masses. The polygonal apse is flanked by low circular chapels, each of which has a lower rectangular absidiole and a higher rectangular turret. Ascending from the apse, the eye then meets roof after roof, each beautifully related to the next, the gallery, the chancel, and finally the central roof. It is a composition excelled only by some of the great apse combinations of the French Romanesque or the buttressed absides of such French Gothic cathedrals as Bourges or Paris.

But the church is inside. And here the restraint turns to splendor. The splendor comes from the concentration in central baldachino and chancel   *Pl. 183*
of the *opus sestile* pavements, the elaboration of the capitals, the veining   *Pl. 185*
of the marble on the piers, and the mosaic decoration. But there would be another richness, the richness of varying space, even if all the opulence were stripped away.

> As contrasted with the sister buildings of Constantinople, the design
> seems simplified. But this seeming simplification is counter-balanced both
> by greater clarity of articulation and greater complexity in the interlock-
> ing of volumes and spatial vistas. . . . As the visitor passes through the wide
> square quadriporticus of the atrium and into the long shallow narthex,
> he is unaware of the anomalous position of the narthex. Standing off-axis,
> it touches only a corner of the outer wall of the structure. It com-
> municates with the ambulatory through subordinate triangular spaces,
> the one to the left leading into the bay opposite the chancel, the other
> leading into the adjoining bay. Thus the vistas become immensely complex,
> and the visitor standing behind the convex screens of the niche arcades
> remains uncertain of his true position with regard to the chancel and
> altar—eager to clarify it by proceeding to the core of the structure.[148]

But the opulence is there too and particularly the opulence of the mosaics. Those of the chancel and the apse date from 546–48. Green, blue,

[148] Krautheimer, *Early Christian and Byzantine Architecture*, op. cit., p. 170.

Pl. 184

Pl. 186

and gold dominate the coloring. On the sides and end wall of the chancel are Old Testament scenes of Abraham, Isaac, Abel, Melchizidek; inside, the Empress Theodora and her suite offering the Wine of the Sacrifice; on the other side the Emperor Justinian with his court including Bishop Maximian bearing the Eucharist. The figures are life-size, the raiment contemporary and dazzling. The details are careful and moving. The Empress bears the gift of the Magi on her cloak; ducks, herons, moorhens abound in a leafy landscape. And at the center of the apse at the ceiling there is the commanding figure of Christ in Majesty. He sits on an azure globe; he holds the Crown of Life and the Book of the Seven Seals. Beside the throne are two angels, below them Saint Vitalis and Bishop Ecclesio, the founder of the Church, who does not fail to show off a model of the building.

These mosaics are superior in color, elegance, and power, if not in human sentiment, to those which other Byzantine mosaicists installed at Monreale several centuries later. Also the mosaics in Sicily tend to overpower the architecture while those at San Vitale are fully attuned. I think you will never really forget a visit to San Vitale. And this can truly be said of only a score or so of buildings still standing.

It was not forgotten by Charlemagne when he built his royal mausoleum 250 years later in faraway Aachen (Aix la Chapelle), which is interesting to compare despite the many intrusions and modifications of later centuries. Though the Palatine Chapel at Aachen is well worth a detour, it is heavy and austere as compared with the elegance and lightness of the forms at San Vitale, so if only one can be visited, by all odds let it be San Vitale.

Let us now stop just over the way from San Vitale at a small and unpretentious building, the so-called Mausoleum of Galla Placidia. It is sometimes alleged to be the oldest building in Ravenna, which it may be if it is indeed her tomb and was built during her lifetime or soon after it. The sarcophagus at the far end is rumored to contain her body, but this would not mean much. The date assigned by many scholars is circa A.D 425, but others put it a century later.

What is important to us about this small building (39 feet long and 35 feet wide inside) is that it is probably the first extant cruciform plan, almost Greek but becoming Latin by some four feet. Each of the square arms is covered by a barrel vault. Over the crossing is a dome of the same hemisphere as the pendentives. The plan is one which, reduced to a symmetrical (Greek) cross, we shall find used over and over again with modifications and accretions in small post-Justinian Byzantine churches.

Unlike the Byzantine churches none of this shows outside. Here we are presented with uncompromisingly rectangular wings, their walls relieved by blind arcading. Their vaults are concealed by pedimented gable roofs. The central dome is encased in a square wall looking like a tower and capped by a pyramidal roof!

But the inside is thoroughly Byzantine, heavy with mosaic. The lower walls are lined with red-orange marble slabs. The mosaics, predominantly deep blue, cover everything else. On the reverse of the entrance is the Good Shepherd. At the far end over the sarcophagus is Saint Lawrence walking on the gridiron of his martyrdom along with a bookcase holding the Gospels, a thoroughly ungainly composition. In the other tympani are stags symbolically (souls) drinking from the Fountain of Life. On the dome are a cross and the evangelical symbols.

Pl. 186

At Sant'Apollinare in Classe, six miles out of Ravenna and the latest of these buildings (534–549), we return again to the basilican form and an almost perfect and beautiful example, although it was begun just shortly before the fall of Ravenna. It has magnificent mosaics, concentrated on the triumphal arch and chancel, where the green fields and the sheep of the apse are enormously moving, even though they are of the sixth or seventh century and somewhat less powerful than earlier ones.

Pl. 16

Pl. 17

BYZANTINE ARCHITECTURE AFTER JUSTINIAN

After Justinian's death the Empire fell apart rather suddenly and thereafter suffered its ups and downs until the final conquest of Constantinople by Mohammed the Conqueror in 1453. Much of the time it was reduced precariously to its Greek speaking core centered on Constantinople and the Aegean. But its religion and its architecture were more stable. Even the Iconoclastic movement which raged in the third decade of the eighth century affected the decoration of the architecture rather than its forms. It destroyed much art and briefly prevented figurative representations, until the second Nicene Council (787) decreed them again permissible if they were not regarded as more than representational, not divine in themselves. Though this still forbade religious sculpture, mosaic and fresco could come back, and they had always been more important in Byzantine architectural art.

More important was a gradual change in the liturgy—a growing emphasis on the "Great Mystery," the Mass, in which God revealed himself through the actions of the priesthood. This required in turn the provision of larger and larger spaces to the officiating priests which became the very focus of the church. Naturally then the domed center bay where the great Mass was celebrated should become the nucleus of the entire building. All attention was drawn to it; it was therefore entirely logical that the characteristic plan of the eighth and ninth centuries should have been a Greek cross with a main dome over the crossing, and sometimes subsidiary ones over the arms.

This however was not so much a spectacular change as the natural development of an idiom already latent in the great churches of Constantinople. There was not so much space, there was much less money, so spectacular things were not made, the scale was more modest, that is all.

The church survived military vicissitudes. Even when the armies were defeated, the churches were carried to Kiev, Vologda, Novgorod; to lower Saxony; Byzantine mosaicists went to Monte Cassino; a Greek architect designed the Duomo at Pisa, while the Caliphs of Cordova called for mosaic workers from Constantinople.

It was, of course, extraordinary (one is tempted to say, typically Byzantine) that Hagia Sophia, the greatest example, came at the beginning of a style and not as a culminating masterpiece.

It was followed by more sober and perhaps sounder methods of building, although the technique of thin brick shells on slender supports with quite weak curtain walls between them was developed and exploited not only in churches but in cisterns and later on in mosques. Out of this have come a considerable variety of small churches which are worth collecting as one goes by and a few which are worth seeking out.

Given the small church, the usurpation of the crossing by the clergy, evidently the laity would be outside the *naos*, in the porticoes, in the narthex, or just outdoors. The *naos*, interpreted as heaven, had to be inaccessible to laymen during services; nonetheless laymen could enter between services.

> [S]mallness, intimacy, and subtlety are basic stylistic concepts of Middle and Late Byzantine architecture. A wealth of decoration designed to overwhelm the visitor would be crowded into the tiny space of these churches: marble sheathing and precious tapestries on the walls and mosaics or murals in the vaulting zone; icons and reliquaries of gold, enamel, and glass, such as have survived in the treasure of S. Marco in Venice.
>
> From the late ninth to the eleventh and twelfth centuries, then, church building in the capital and throughout the Empire continues to be immensely fertile. New types are established, and a highly developed and sophisticated Middle Byzantine architectural style is evolved.[149]

Naturally the richest churches were in the rich centers, but everybody tried, and I am not going to take you through all the pleasant small Byzantine churches that are to be found and easily reached in Greek and closely adjacent territories. A short list may be enough. It would have to include the Kapnikaris (875) in Athens; and San Eleutherios, of about the same date and also in Athens, very small, very typical, with its dome pushed up higher above the roof line by an elongating octagonal support.

My two favorites among the easily visited small Greek Byzantine churches are not far from Athens. The Katholikon at Daphni dates from the ninth century; the Katholikon of Hosios Loukas of Stiris in Phocis[150]

---

[149] Ibid., p. 248.
[150] Hosios Loukas was a monastery. To western eyes accustomed to monasteries of the Cluniac size (1,200 residents) it seems small, but for the Byzantines it was large. The biggest convent in Constantinople had a congregation of 50 nuns. Monastic sanctuaries to accommodate memberships of eight were not uncommon.

is later, say 1020, and its exterior form is less gracious than that of Daphni because it is attached to another church. Each has an octagon-supported dome rising from a Greek cross plan; the cross is in each case enclosed in a rectangle which starts as a square and is then made a rectangle by the addition of a narthex. Each has splendid mosaics. The interior spaces, though small, have a subtle splendor. They are impressive examples of the Middle Byzantine plan.

Still in Athens there is San Theodore (1049) and the Little Metropole (1250), which is no doubt the smallest church in the world with the title of cathedral. Its exterior dimensions are 25 feet by 38 feet; the drum of the dome is only 9 feet in diameter, little more than an enlarged, if elegant, cupola.

Also in Greece a visit to Salonika is rewarding on several counts. Most notable is the Church of the Holy Apostles, which various authorities date in the tenth or twelfth or fourteenth centuries, while it is also alleged to have ninth-century mosaics!

Be that as it may, the exterior is one of the loveliest examples extant of the way the Byzantines used architectural forms to break up and embellish their exteriors while leaving the inside walls unbroken so that their flat surfaces were hospitable to fresco and mosaic.

The walls are faced with alternating bands of red bricks and light stones on thick mortar joints. The principal decorative feature is the arcading, which relieves the flatness of the walls.

Though this effect was common to most churches of this type, it was done with special skill here so that the masses build up as beautifully as the finest absides to be found in the French Romanesque—but here there is no abside.

The charming little church of Saint Panteleimon near Nerezi in Macedonia despite its late date (1164) seems to come right out of the ninth century, and there are countless curious variants in Bulgaria, Serbia, Croatia, Yugoslavia, Romania,[151] indeed throughout the Balkans, Mesopotamia, and of course Turkey.

BYZANTINE ARCHITECTURE IN SICILY, FRANCE, AND RUSSIA

Let me close the Byzantine chapter with a look at what happened when Byzantine architecture spread into Sicily, France, and Russia.

Sicily's link to the Christian East, which might have fostered Byzantine development there, was severed by the Arab occupation in 827. The Normans conquered it in 1091, and by the end of the twelfth century the Norman court there had reached a high level of contemporary refinement.

---

[151] The curious Romanian deviants in Moldavia may be particularly picturesque. These are late (fifteenth and sixteenth century). They have icons around the *outside* walls, unusual vaulting, conical roofs as, for example, at Voronet. See *Time*, August 10, 1970, pp. 48 ff.

Generically these were the same Normans who had built the handsome but austere, clearly proto-Gothic Romanesque churches of La Trinité and St-Etienne at Caen in Normandy between 1060 and 1140; or the marvelously massive round columns and the daring vaults of the nave at Durham in 1093. But by the time they built in and around Palermo 50 years or so later, these Normans were no longer Vikings; they had tasted the East. The Norman kings and the Eastern emperors were in constant touch with each other, often exchanging presents. But the religion was after all Western Catholicism. So the traditions of church planning came from the basilicas of Rome and their evolution in France; the mosaic workers were called to Palermo from Greece but especially from Constantinople, while much palace architecture and decoration rested on the Islamic residues. The blend, not so much eclectic as composed, had a fantasy no one forgets who tarries in Palermo. For example, there are the La Martorana (1129–1143), San Giovanni degli Eremiti (1132), and San Cataldo (1161), each interesting but especially perhaps San Cataldo, whose three red domes rise without compromise in a line to cover the nave. Or, perhaps the most ingratiating *Pl. 195* of all, St. John of the Hermits, with its later thirteenth-century Gothic cloister.

The most beautiful and interesting things, though, are in the Palazzo dei Normanni in Palermo and the Benedictine Abbey Church of Monreale a few kilometers away on a hill overlooking the "Conca d'Oro" (Golden Conch Shell) of Palermo.

The Norman Palace was built by the Norman King Roger II, though little on the Baroque outside would tell you so save the Tower of Ninfa, which is in Pisan style. Inside, the palace, which has been remodeled so many times, has a seventeenth-century courtyard of modest quality and is principally occupied by the Sicilian Parliament. Ascend however to the first *Pl. 187* floor and you will find the glowing, genuinely magnificent Capella Palatina built between 1132–1140 by the same Roger. It is in the fabric of the building and so has no visible exterior. The plan is Western. Ten old columns collected from here and there support a nave and two narrow aisles. The arches are somewhat stilted, an Arabic effect, but the voussoirs have Byzantine mosaics. There is a clerestory also covered with Byzantine mosaics on gilded backgrounds, which also cover the apses and the upper part of the altar wall. But the ceiling is stalactite in the purest Arabic form and so is the geometric decoration of the lower half of the sanctuary. Seen in the right light, which is the light of a thousand candles, this can well be called fabulous.

The Cathedral of Monreale (1174–1232) offers a quite different experience. Its exterior is of no particular interest save for a few details of *Pl. 188* the blind arcades on the apse ends, interlaced arches, and richly colored mosaics. It has also one of the finest cloisters anywhere. But the glories of Monreale are inside.

The order of the interior is directed by the simple basilican plan. The beautiful eighteen columns of the arcade seem identical, though drawn from various Roman temples, and carry the eye down the nave in a smooth, uninterrupted rhythm. The arches themselves are slightly stilted and pointed in the Saracenic mode. Above the clerestory is a simple Romanesque wall with semicircular arched windows, one to the bay. The ceiling of the nave is of wood with an open gable of elegant simplicity and cross timbers whose soffits and sides are elaborately painted. But you have probably come to Monreale primarily to see the handsome mosaics rather than the Arab-inspired multicolored marble designs or the sweeping inlay of the floor. These mosaics do not light up with the Eastern brilliance of Ravenna or the Capella Palatina until you reach the apse, which is normally pretty dark even when the sacristan turns on the lights (what it needs, of course, is the blinding flicker of myriads of candles and *flambeaux*). In the apse there is a gigantic Christ Pantocrator in the best Byzantine tradition—others above the episcopal and royal thrones show King William II, the Norman founder of the Abbey, offering the cathedral to the Virgin and receiving his crown from Christ.

But much the most interesting mosaics adorn the walls of the nave. Here viewed from right to left and from top to bottom you can read *seriatim* the complete cycle of the two Testaments. Armed with binoculars you should probably read this visual text seriously and sequentially; the colors are appropriately sober and serene and the pictorial quality remarkable.   *Pl. 190*

You should not leave Monreale without going into the cloisters to the right, since they are among the most beautiful to be found anywhere. The   *Pl. 191* columns are paired and in enormous variety, some with plain shafts, some fluted, some covered with Norman chevrons or Saracenic arabesques or geometric mosaic inlays. The stones are of many colors. The capitals are sculptured with remarkable freedom from almost classic acanthuses to the Biblical stories, parables, and symbols we shall find so richly in the French Romanesque. They too are worth reading, one by one. The arches are stilted and pointed and slightly Saracenic. Here is a case where the overall composition is excellent and so too the details, and no harm is done to the spirit of the former by close attention to the latter. It is perhaps symbolic of the whole situation in Sicily and certainly of the "Norman" architecture there that the fountain in the center of this cloister is pure Moorish!

Sicily was obviously a marvelous crossroads. It has beautiful Greek temples (Segesta and Agrigento), fine Roman remains (Syracuse and the mosaics of Piazza Armerina), but nowhere else is this particular blend of Islam, Rome, and Byzantium to be found so frequently and so handsomely. It is a unique situation and result and one almost beyond "style."

The last flurry of Byzantine architecture in Western Europe is San Marco in Venice (1042–1085; consecrated 1093).

How it came to be is not hard to understand. The Venetians had had complex if not always friendly relations with the East at least since the ninth century when they stole the relics of Saint Mark from Alexandria and built their earlier cathedral to house them. When this burned down in 976, there was time for another look. At this point the Venetians had long escaped active Byzantine rule but their growing and always practical, even venal, mercantile republic had maintained close diplomatic ties with the Byzantine Empire, while Venetian businessmen were well established in the ports of Greece. The Byzantine oligarchy wanted a palatine church. The doges were eager to build a gorgeous monument to compete with the Pantheon and Hagia Sophia.

So they elected to build San Marco on the model of one of Justinian's great sixth-century churches. What they got was in general Byzantine, and certainly the most important Byzantine church of the Middle Ages; but Venice was not Byzantium, and what they got was not a natural product of Byzantine art.

The model more or less closely copied was that of Justinian's Apostoleion in Constantinople, destroyed by Sultan Mahomet II in 1463 to make way for a mosque, but the design is perhaps reflected about as closely in Justinian's Church of Saint John at Ephesus, which, almost entirely ruined, was being rebuilt in 1965.

Pl. 192

The plan reads clearly enough. It is almost a Greek cross with two side aisles in each arm. There is an apse in one arm and side chapels at the ends of those side aisles. Great piers (28 by 21 feet) carry the central dome and the front one of the same size. The lateral domes and the one in front of the apse are of smaller diameter. Still the essence of good Byzantine design is suggested by the plan.

How it was carried out was a somewhat different matter. Walls and piers were quickly finished and the first consecration occurred in 1073. But the decoration dragged on for centuries, with corresponding style changes all Western in character combined with loot from Constantinople or Nero's triumphal arch.

Timber domes were added to cover the brick ones in the thirteenth century and then gilded. Altogether San Marco may be the largest conglomeration of looted objects and looted ideas to be found anywhere in the world of architecture.

Pl. 194

Though this cathedral has the largest and finest *atrium* in the world in the Piazza San Marco, its famous exterior really is "boisterous," as one critic has put it. Inside Krautheimer finds the space sense appropriate to Middle Byzantine, but even if this is so it cannot compare with the great feeling of the Pantheon or Hagia Sophia. I personally find it junky, even though there is some pleasure in picking your way along the narrow galleries, stumbling over iron reinforcements as you go. The interior, I feel, relies not on great *architectural* arrangements, which seem heavy as compared with the bubbles of Constantinople, but on what magic there is in precious materials, brilliant colors, gold mosaics not arrayed with a maximum of skill or sensitivity. In short it is as vulgarly ostentatious as many other things in Venice, from the guests at the Royal Daniele to the strands of the Lido.

Given the position of Venice these vagaries were natural. But natural or not, this does not make San Marco into great architecture, however spectacular. Simpler and more important and at bottom more beautiful things were going on all over Europe—in France above all, but in England, Germany, and Italy as well. Eclecticism may not always be as evil as its enemies proclaim. But its success certainly depends upon the discrimination and taste with which you borrow. Wunderkammer architecture is unlikely to be great architecture especially in vulgar hands.

A more unusual application of Byzantine occurred in Romanesque Aquitaine in France, where its most complete example is the cathedral of St-Front in Périgueux (1120).

The plan of St-Front is a Greek cross with five domes, an apse, and a narrow narthex. Like San Marco it is almost identical with the plan of the Apostoleion, but unlike San Marco it has been kept clear of clutter.

Pl. 193

It is noteworthy that it is bare of all decoration. The simplicity of the wall surfaces emphasizes the grandeur and purity and force of the structure. Some find this plain interior to be a good demonstration of how poor Byzantine churches would have been without mosaics. I am not sure it does not prove the contrary.

The five domes, all of the same diameter, rise on pendentives over each arm and over the crossing, and since they are uncamouflaged outside, they do provide an appearance more Eastern than Romanesque. But inside, except for the plan, St-Front is utterly un-Byzantine. The semicircular arches which carry the domes are sprung from very heavy piers and indeed are so wide they look like short barrel vaults, so that each bay seems like a separate compartment.

The strength of undecorated domical interiors seems to me even more clearly shown at St-Pierre in Angoulême (1105–1130). But this church, despite the domes, is patently Romanesque in its plan, the powerful plain piers and arches, the severity and perfection of the masonry construction, and in most of its details. If the dome ever came from Byzantium, it would not be obvious from the line of four stretching down the aisleless nave.

Some eighty examples of domed naves have been noted in Romanesque areas of Aquitaine centering mostly around Perigord but extending to Fontevrault on the north and St-Vicente de Cordova on the south. Some have only one at the crossing, others a few more along the nave, and there is the Greek cross plan of Périgueux. How or why this Byzantine form was popular for a time in Aquitaine in southwest France, so far away, has really not been answered, although naturally a consistent use of domes to cover each nave bay, the crossing, and even the aisle bays was one logical way to solve the problem. What we do know is that they soon died out and gave way to the vault all over Western Europe.

The most durable and colorful extensions of the Byzantine right down to the sixteenth century occurred, as a matter of fact, in Russia. I have not seen them and can judge only from pictures and plans and other people's notes so am reluctant to say much about them. What you can see now evidently is not earlier than the eleventh century because the earlier wooden churches, which may or may not have had some similarity to the stave churches of Norway, have not survived. The oldest masonry church is St. Sophia at Kiev (1018–1037), though Cichy says the Destiatisnaya Church in Kiev dates from 991. Much of the influential prototype architecture evidently came from Novgorod, which was never run over by the Mongols. After this there was an enormous proliferation of church building. Greek architects, German architects, Lombard architects were imported but followed the Byzantine ground plan, and became so Russianized that their origins could be detected only in their details. This applied even to the Bolognese architect, Ridolfo di Fioravanti, imported to build the Uspenski Cathedral at Moscow, which still followed the Byzantine tradition.

Pl. 198

Pl. 197

But Slavic taste had an effect. Domes multiplied to seven, nine, thirteen. There are fifteen on St. Michael at Kiev. They were pushed higher and higher on their supporting rings. They ripened into bulbous forms. Inside, the decoration became mural painting rather than mosaics, the spatial unities disappeared. It all culminated, I suppose, in the extraordinary St. Basil in Moscow (1555–1560), which is like some giant hopak of the Bolshoi. This was built by Ivan the Terrible after he had conquered the last Tatar stronghold, Kazan. Eight chapels surround the central area which is a diagonally placed square inside an outer square. The plan itself is easy to read but the exterior expression is not. The chapels linked to the center by low passageways were crowned with towers and the bulb domes— fluted, twisted, scalloped, reticulated, gilded, painted—were added in the seventeenth century. "Like candle flames [they] circle the tent shaped central tower that reaches high above them."[152] Gone is the Byzantine. We have here met romantic Slavonic architecture in full cry.

Pl. 196

It is wild and fabulous and I should like very much to see it. But I am much too old to face the discomforts of Russia now. So you must go and tell me about it.[153] Meanwhile let me take you back to a place and a time which I do know well—and love well—to Romanesque France.

ROMANESQUE

The conditions under which Romanesque architecture developed were generally the opposite of those for Byzantine architecture. Centralized power was absent, growing rather than declining. It was in the hands of the clerics rather than laity. The great buildings came at the end, not the beginning. Major influences were regional, not centralized. Though both architectures

---

[152] Bodo Cichy, *The Great Ages of Architecture* (New York: Putnam, 1964), p. 151.
[153] The best preparatory books with which I am familiar are George H. Hamilton, *The Art and Architecture of Russia* (Baltimore: Penguin, 1954), and Krautheimer, *Early Christian and Byzantine Architecture*, op. cit.

were fundamentally religious, though both reached back to Christ, though both had elaborate rituals, the churches of the West were designed for congregations as much as for the celebrants of a very different Mass.

The great Romanesque architecture is of the tenth and especially the eleventh century and the early years of the twelfth. It did open a new era in Western history but was not a miraculous awakening followed by a startling efflorescence. All the forces which brought it about had been developing over some hundreds of years.

But there was a convergence of these forces about the year 1000. The barbarians had become stabilized and were members of the Christian community; the Normans were becoming feudal and orderly and abandoning piracy as their main business. Islam was receding and Spain being reassimilated into the Western system. "The Mediterranean was becoming once more, if not a European lake, at least a natural channel for travel and interchange of ideas."[154]

The trade between Byzantium, Genoa, Venice, and Pisa carried more than goods. A comparable development occurred in the Baltic between the Flemings and Prussia and Russia. Two important political conformations were emerging—the Holy Roman (essentially Germanic) Empire and the Capetian monarchy of France. There was an increase of population thanks to a relative political stability, the beginning of a renewed urban life, and an important addition to feudalism and monasticism, namely the genesis of an urban-mercantile civilization beyond the Alps.

It was a time of enormously energetic and powerful churchmen—great abbots, monks who were church builders, monastic reformers and prelate-politicians. "These grandiose figures loom at the entrance to the century like the stone precursors of the church portals."[155] The kings who were seeking to centralize power were at this time no match for the prelates, and such offset as there was came from strong feudal dukes in Normandy, in Burgundy, in Poitou, and Aquitaine.

Although cities were beginning to be re-formed on old sites or arising fresh on new sites, the total situation was still more rural than urban. Carolingian cities were small, running from 5,000 to 10,000 in Germany; Rome had only 10,000; London but 25,000; whereas contemporary Constantinople may have boasted a million. Nonetheless, if there was only one church in a town, it might have to be very large, where there was only one religion and most people practiced it. Thus the Ottonian Cathedral of Mainz (987–1036) could crowd in 15,000 people. Politically, as the central power of Rome declined, it was often the urban bishop who became the man of power.

But the main thrust came from the monasteries. They belonged to several different orders to be sure. The Benedictines who had been domi-

[154] Henri Focillon, *The Art of the West in the Middle Ages*, vol. I, *Romanesque Art*, Jean Bony (ed.) (London: Phaidon, 1963), p. 26.
[155] Ibid., p. 27.

Pl. 199

nant in architecture in the days of Monte Cassino (529) were somewhat in decline. But they were enormously benefited by Charlemagne and his successors. Their monastic churches in the Carolingian period were at a scale comparable to an urban cathedral such as Mainz. They had extensive requirements for choir space; they wanted an impressive setting for processional liturgies, so the buildings were much like the cathedrals of a metropolitan city, with the important difference that they were located in a totally planned community. If the groupings were picturesque, they were nonetheless ordered—an organic distribution of functional elements, strongly articulated in plan. The Benedictines accounted for the older monasteries in England, such as Canterbury and Westminster, and especially St. Gall in Switzerland.

It is probably risky to try to characterize the orders too sharply. The Benedictines were the chroniclers, perhaps the most learned. The Augustinians were preachers, fond of disputation. Cistercians were reclusive, interested in agriculture. Cluniacs were studious, artistic, perhaps the most worldly. Carthusians were ascetic. Of these it is not surprising that the Benedictines and the Cluniacs were the most concerned about architecture and exerted the greatest influence upon it. The Cistercians built too but with greater austerity. One of their number, Saint Bernard of Clairvaux—best known to history as the instigator of the Second Crusade, for the establishment of the rules of the Knights Templar, the condemnation of Abelard, and for his preaching of lost causes—is a byword among observers of Gothic architecture for his moral-aesthetic contests with the Abbot Suger over the opulence of the Abbey Church of St-Denis, and indeed his general aversion to the Cluniac attitudes toward food, dress, and architecture. Other orders which seriously influenced architecture came much later. The Society of Jesus, for example, was not founded by Ignatius Loyola until 1540, as part of the Counterreformation.

Whatever the order, the monasteries were central to the four bases of medieval civilization. They had much to do in influencing the economic revival, in fusing the Latin and Teutonic peoples, in developing canon law, and even in affecting how the feudal system developed. They were the centers of stability but also of innovation—of education, of art—and it is hardly surprising that they had so much to do with the transition from the Early Christian Roman basilica to the vaulted church and the revival of masonry vaulting (now without the benefit of pozzolana cement) on the grand scale which had become lost through disuse after the fourth century.

In France, where the Romanesque architecture had its finest and most varied flowering, the Cistercians and the Cluniacs led the way, but especially the latter.

[T]he monasteries were not only the refuge of exemplary Christians, detached from the life of their time, nor mere centres of meditation and culture, nor yet—in accordance with the spirit of their first foundation, renewed by the Cistercians—agricultural stations set up near a source of water for the purpose of tilling the virgin soil of desert places. For besides being planned, as they already had been in the Carolingian era, on the scale of towns, complete with schools, industrial and artistic workshops, scribes, blacksmiths and masons, they also intervened powerfully in the temporal destinies of the world, they cast a fine-meshed net over all Christendom, they were an organizing force and a focus of action. . . . in the Romanesque period, the political and moral stature of Cluny was outstanding. It was a monarchy of monks, a monarchy of the spirit, ruled over by the abbot of Cluny, the abbot of abbots, whose moral authority was effective even beyond the organization of which he was head. The greatest of these abbots were both saints and leaders of men. Their community gave the Church several popes, numerous theologians, and a number of those great figures who, like St. Odo and St. Hugh, epitomize and at the same time transfigure by their virtues, the age in which they live. [In our time it is a role which university presidents might have played but for a complex of reasons usually fell short of—jeb.] Cluny, said Emile Mâle, was the greatest phenomenon of the Middle Ages. The modern development of orders vowed to contemplation or charity, and lying rather aside from the main current of spiritual action . . . provides no basis for our understanding of this immense priestly organization and its relations with the kings, emperors, and popes, whom it often welcomed and entertained within the walls of its principal house. These great abbots were artists, not after the manner of princes enamored of pomp and architectural splendour, but in a more profound and fundamental way. They loved music so greatly that when they came to decorate their church they caused the capitals of the sanctuary to be carved with figures symbolizing the various modes of plainsong. They loved nobility and dignity of form even as embodied in corruptible flesh, and one of them extolled a predecessor for the perfection of his beauty. These men stand in the foreground of the history of Romanesque art, not indeed as initiators of its morphology and style, for the roots of those lay deeper, but in the capacity of organizers. They it was who chose the sites of its activity, or at least it was they who animated the roads along which stand its most important monuments.[156]

Very little of the great monasteries remains to be seen, save in suggestive ruins. Generally in resentment against their power but sometimes for other reasons, they were destroyed. Some, like St. Gall, remain only in the records of historians; others, like Cluny, offer small fragments. Glastonbury and Fountains in England offer picturesque ruins through which it is possible to wander and dream up some idea. But the record of ruin for the great monasteries, for Citeaux, Cluny, Fontevrault, Jumièges, Rievaulx, Jedburgh, Tintern, Glastonbury, Fountains, St. Gall, and so on, is almost unmarred, although at every one save St. Gall there is something medieval worth seeing and some like Fountains and Glastonbury are more than rewarding.

Moreover the scholars have preserved for us and recreated for us

[156] Ibid., pp. 63–64.

quite reliable documentation of what these monastic communities were physically like, helped sometimes by complete plans left by the monks. There was a monastic church situated in a courtyard and so arranged that it might, when desired, be open to the public. Attached to this was a cloister court which led to the chapter house, the sacristy, the dormitory (with a stair into the church for early matins), and underneath the dormitory often the cellarage for the storage of oil, wines, and beer. The cloister also led to the refectory and kitchens which, being smelly and noisy, were on the side away from the church. The lavatory was also usually in the cloister walk. Beyond this an inner court might contain an infirmary, a guest house, a library, a scriptorium for writing and illuminating and, oddly, a servants' hall. Then another court, the common court, approached through a gateway to the outside world which let in carts, was surrounded by granaries, bake houses, stables, storerooms, servants' rooms, tribunal, prison, the abbot's lodgings, and the barns. Farther afield there might be mills, workshops, gardens, orchards, fishponds. Obviously there were differences from monastery to monastery—some things omitted, some added, some more emphasized here, less emphasized there. But the abbey church was a constant.

Pl. 199

The manuscript plan of St. Gall (820) shows an almost military arrangement. A long entrance approaching the west apse of the abbey church passes at the left the coach house and at the right a series of stables each designated, one for sheep, one for goats, one for pigs, one for cows, and one for mares, and in the corner of this group the servants' house. To the right of the church one encountered first a pilgrim's hostel and its kitchen, this separated by walls from the storehouses and the cloisters. The cloisters as usual led to the refectory and its kitchen, the dormitory, the lavatories, and the baths. Still further to the right was an array of service buildings, more stables and cowsheds, workshops, a fruit press, mills, a brewery, and a bakery (connected to the refectory kitchen), then the craftsmen's house, the granary, poultry yards, and the kitchen garden with houses for the keeper of the poultry and the garden.

At the left of the church were quieter quarters, a guest house and an annex for it, a school, the abbot's house connecting into the church, and the library which was in the church fabric. Behind this came the medical services, a bleeding house, a house for the doctor, a medicinal herb garden, a hospital with its own bath and kitchen, a school of novices balancing the hospital and hard by the cemetery. No layout could be more considered, more orderly, more functional.

But we cannot see this and when we want to visit actual existing churches, we have to turn to and be thankful for the pilgrimage routes.

Cluny organized the pilgrimages, and thereby became the moving spirit of that nomadic Middle Age which rolled in wave after unceasing wave down the roads which led towards Santiago de Compostela and the oratory of San Michele on Monte Gargano. This does not mean—far from it—that Romanesque art is exclusively Cluniac and that its leading features are to be traced back to Cluny itself, nor even that it was strictly dependent on the geography of these far-flung routes. The significance of the pilgrimage roads lay in the fact that they traversed various regions, beckoning always towards foreign horizons and intermingling the sedentary and the travelling populace; while acting as channels for the propagation of artistic types, they also attracted to themselves the forces and traditions of the localities through which they passed, and these tended both to swell and to modify the character of the waves of influence. At the stages of the journey they fostered the dissemination of the *Chansons de Geste*, and in doing so they mingled one aspect of the Middle Ages with another. They magnified local saints into saints venerated throughout the Western World, and by permitting the transmission of images over great distances, they enriched the universal language of iconography. The old Roman roads had been instruments of Roman penetration. The pilgrimage roads had a twofold action. They may have contributed to the unity of Romanesque art, but they also ensured its variety.[157]

There were many reasons for becoming a pilgrim, some perhaps better than others. One might be votive, a thanksgiving "that holy blissful martyr for to seke, that hem hath holpen whan that they were seke."[158]

One might be to seek pardon for some sin or to gain indulgences for future sins. One might be judicial, a form of penitential punishment meted out by a confessor or even a clerical court. One might be even, I suppose, just the satisfaction of wanderlust, a way of carrying on trade or selling a song, or just to be able to say to the boys back home that you had been there. Whatever your purpose, if you were a serious pilgrim you wore a recognizable garb, you carried a priest-blessed scrip and staff, and frequently on the way back you bore a badge of the shrine on your hat. Leading thinkers of the church supported the pilgrimages as good and useful but had no delusions about them. Thomas à Kempis in the *Imitation of Christ* remarked: "They that go much on pilgrimage be seldom thereby made perfect and holy."

Be that as it may be, there is no doubt that the routes, partly laid out for safety and ease of travel which still offered little of safety or ease, and partly, no doubt, connecting places which already had surfaced as places of sanctity, created new places along the way and aggrandized those that were already on it. Although the end goal contained the most important relics to be courted, it was just as well if lesser relics could be lauded along the way. So since pilgrims had to rest somewhere and tended to worship wherever they rested, it is not surprising that so many of the churches of the pilgrimage routes were much larger than the resident population would have supported.

The terminus of a pilgrimage was a site where important relics were

---

[157] Ibid., pp. 64–65.
[158] Geoffrey Chaucer, "Prologue," *Canterbury Tales*.

reputed to be. The most important was naturally Rome where one went to worship, not the Pope, but the relics of Saint Peter. The route was long from France—crossing the Alps by the great Saint Bernard or Mont Cenis passes, joining the Emilian way via Modena, passing through Piacenza, Fidenza, and Parma thence southward to the Cassian Way at Arezzo, and reaching Rome by Orvieto and Viterbo. But this was a long and costly pilgrimage from England or France, and few could manage it. (The pilgrims of Chaucer going to Canterbury to visit the remains of Saint Thomas Becket are, of course, much later since Becket was not murdered in the Cathedral until 1170.) For the French there were several places of pilgrimage—to Saint Michael of the Mount, to Tours, where Saint Martin was supposed to lie, or Conques, the shrine of Sainte Foi, or Amiens, where it was reputed the head of Saint John the Baptist was available for inspection and veneration. But the leading goal (after Rome) was not in France at all but on the northwest coast of Spain at Santiago da Compostela, which claimed to have the remains of Saint James the Greater.

A diagram of the main routes from France to Santiago will show how many of the principal Romanesque monuments lie along them. Despite some changes in scenery south of the Pyrenees, it is not surprising that the

Main French Pilgrimage Routes to Santiago da Compostela

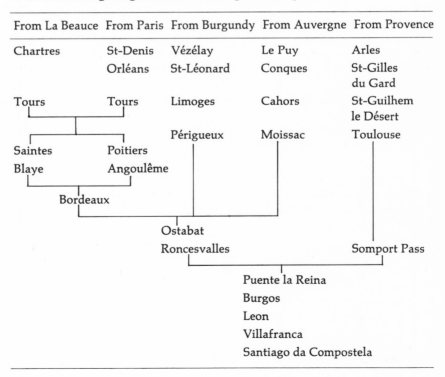

From La Beauce	From Paris	From Burgundy	From Auvergne	From Provence
Chartres	St-Denis	Vézélay	Le Puy	Arles
	Orléans	St-Léonard	Conques	St-Gilles du Gard
Tours	Tours	Limoges	Cahors	St-Guilhem le Désert
		Périgueux	Moissac	Toulouse
Saintes	Poitiers			
Blaye	Angoulême			
Bordeaux				
		Ostabat		
		Roncesvalles		Somport Pass
		Puente la Reina		
		Burgos		
		Leon		
		Villafranca		
		Santiago da Compostela		

architecture of Burgos, Leon, and Santiago seems almost more French than Iberian.

There were many architectural sources which came together to make the Romanesque of the pilgrimage routes. There were obviously and most directly the Roman basilica, arch, and vault. There were contributions from Byzantium and the Arabs which are quite evident when they appear as, for example, Byzantine short columns and basketweave capitals, Arabic iconography, especially in the bestiaries, but these are only the most obvious. There were early Lombard experiments with stone barrel vaulting as early as the ninth century and also with blank arcading for decorating facades. You can see some remnants of this at San Pietro at Agliate near Monza (875), close by Milan, now most famous for its automobile race, or at San Pietro at Toscanella (founded 628, altered 740, 1040) where the stone barrel vault and the blind arcading can still be picked out from the later elaborations, although much damaged by recent earthquakes.

What finally emerged as Lombard Romanesque, charming as it is, owes less to these original Lombard inventions than the churches of France do. But the journey was evidently not direct but rather by way of Spain, where the claims made by a Spanish scholar, Puig-i-Cadafalch, that the small churches of Northern Spain were indeed not local but first Romanesque, are now taken seriously by many. If you want to see an example in Spain, you could visit San Miguel de Lino (848) or the magnificent small-stone vaulting, squinches, half domes, and dome of San Pons de Corbera in the mountains of Garraf northwest of Barcelona. At Oliba's Ripoll, descending from the Col de Puymoren, the seven apsidal chapels are half cylinders suggesting an array of silos. Indeed there are very good reasons, not all historical, for prowling around the little Romanesque churches of Catalonia culminating with a visit to the magnificent collection of early Catalonian art in the Museum at Barcelona, but this is a detour. I must no more than hint, despite the fact that Barcelona is one of the most charming and underrated cities of the world and would be even if Antonio Gaudí had not worked for the Guells there. If you want to see this Lombard Spanish strain without moving out of France, you can do it in the *Pl. 200* marvelous nave of St-Martin du Canigou of about 1009.

There is one other important source, which came from the Teutons and which manifested itself principally in the Carolingian and Ottonian architecture of Germany which preceded the Romanesque. We have already spoken of one manifestation of Carolingian building aspirations in the royal Mausoleum at Aachen. There was little invention in that and it had nothing to say to the Romanesque. But the great Carolingian Benedictine monasteries like St. Gall did. Their church plans often had large apses at the west as well as at the east and even sometimes transepts at both ends, as though two churches had been joined. The idea of symmetric apses was not in itself new—it appeared, for example, in the Basilica Ulpia at Rome—but the use in churches was, the Western apse being designed to take care of new cults which might arise. It was an idea also which lasted a long time and was used over and over again without much new imagination in the great churches of the Rhineland at Worms and Speyer, of which I shall talk later.

A more important Carolingian invention, perhaps more French than German, was the idea of prolonging the side aisles. Formerly these terminated in chapels. Now they were carried around the sanctuary and radiating chapels led off them. This was a very important idea.

But the Carolingians at best laid some groundwork. They left untouched the problem of vaulting the great naves in stone, the problem of abutments, and the problem of lighting. Also there was no anticipation of Romanesque decoration so delightfully integrated to the structure—Carolingian decoration remained veneer to the end.[159]

How much credit you want to give to the Carolingians and the Ottonians in germinating the Romanesque may depend entirely on how much of a Germanophile or Germanophobe you are. I, for example, have paid too little attention to the westworks, which Cichy thinks the most important invention of Carolingian religious architecture. These were antechurches usually with three towers. From them, he says, came the great towered west fronts of Romanesque cathedrals. Certainly the massive westwork of Minden Cathedral where the side towers are not developed is exceptionally impressive. Certainly the west front of Marmoutiers in Alsace of the twelfth century is also impressive and does repeat the Carolingian disposition of ninth and tenth century westworks with the larger central tower set back from the flanking ones and square while they are octagonal. This is a very beautiful arrangement of mass, density, pilasters,

Pl. 202

Pl. 203

Pl. 201

[159] The fullest realization of Carolingian work surely came in Germany, due to the emergence in 962 of an energetic political-religious system. This Ottonian architecture used the arcades and bands of "first Romanesque." Probably three different regions can be identified. In Saxony there are St. Michael at Hildesheim of the early eleventh century (1001–1033) and Gernrode Abbey Church of 961. The best example of one of the three types of Ottonian work is St. Michael at Hildesheim (1001–1033). At first glance Hildesheim certainly looks very much like a basilica. But the heavy arches on all sides of the crossing define the principle of carrying a tower there. More significantly the central nave is divided visually into three square compartments by square piers, between which run the columns in the nave arcades. Thus the interruption of the even flow of the basilican schemes where arcades were carried on identical supports throughout can be imagined as the first stage of an evolution leading to a situation where the nave walls would be articulated by vertical shafts, so that finally the whole structure would be divided into separate vaulted compartments (bays). The bronze door reliefs of Hildesheim (ca. 1015) now on the cathedral are also remarkable in the depth of their modeling and an exception to the general stricture about Carolingian and even Ottonian decoration, the heads in very high relief being reminiscent of the doors of San Zeno Maggiore in Verona.

A second section of Ottonian work, classified as the Imperial region, centers around the old (1009) Cathedral of Mainz and a third, around the area of Cologne-Werden, of which a typical example is St. Aposteln (1035–1220). But by now the architecture, as in the Kaiserdom at Speyer (1030) and the Abbey of Maria Laach (1093–1156), was in a time when Romanesque was developing well in the rest of Europe, and I would rather discuss them later as the German version of Romanesque.

blind arcading, and well worth a visit, as is the westwork of the former
Benedictine Abbey at Corvey.

Pl. 206

Given all this rich trove of tentative solutions, what were the problems the Romanesque builders had yet to solve, or the adaptations they
had yet to make? As noted earlier, there were problems of the transept
which provided additional capacity on both sides of the choir platform and
problems of how to handle the crossing. There were problems of changing
the apsidal relations from apses in echelon to chapels in ambulatory. There
were problems of developing masons, not all of whom could be imported
from the Comacine brotherhood.

Pl. 204

Pl. 205

There were two other major problems, the problem of the towers and
the problem of the roofs.

In the beginning the tower was ancillary even if it did help to establish the verticality which later became a trademark of the Gothic if not of
the Romanesque. Sometimes, surely, the tower served as fortification or
observation post since the church, usually the strongest building in town,
was normally a refuge in times of violence. The tower might be used as a
lantern at the crossing to admit light to space above or near the altar. Such
lantern towers, for practical reasons of structure, should be low. A third
purpose was to house bells, and this made no requirement that the tower
be attached to the church building at all. Some of the early buildings proliferated towers the way late Turkish Sultans proliferated minarets. Abbot
Angolbert's monastery at St-Riquier (about 790 and now destroyed) boasted
nine. Seven were planned for Cluny and Laon, at least six for Chartres,
and as many for St-Bénigne, Santiago. How strong this might have looked
you can guess from the four towers of Lincoln Cathedral or many-spired
Tournai.

The belfry was another matter. If you wanted a bell large enough to
be heard at a distance, it would have great inertia and could not safely be
rung from a tower at the crossing. You might also like to have it high, and
on both counts the idea of detachment was natural. Many of the early
belfries, starting probably at Ravenna, were round, as of course was the
famous one at Pisa. But it was not long before the Lombard belfries became square though still remaining detached. They became familiar at
Cluny through Abbot Odo and his successors. In France they were soon
incorporated into the western facade, which was easier now that they were
square, but certainly not impossible when they were round, as for example at Notre-Dame-la-Grande in Poitiers. Later in the Gothic the attached towers became useful as buttressing, but that is jumping ahead.
Meanwhile in the Romanesque the use or nonuse of west towers, crossing
towers, transept towers, and how conspicuous they were to be if they
existed at all came to be enormously a matter of choice and a fairly good
identifier of a particular regional style.

The roof problem was the most difficult. Somehow, although persistent in the East, Roman engineering skills had been lost in the West and

had, as it were, to be rediscovered. Except for a few small churches in the South and on some short spans as in crypts, most of the roofs of the West before the eleventh century were of timber.

The first new stone experiments occurred, naturally enough, over the easier spans of the side aisles. This resulted in a four-point support, and it was natural to think of repeating this articulation in the nave by carrying the shafts of the piers right across the clerestory wall and up to the foot of the roof. This made no structural sense since, when the pier arrived at the roof line, it had nothing in particular to support and the wall itself would have carried the flat roof without any help from the pier. Its early use was therefore visual. It did begin to divide the *appearance* of the nave into bays.

The problem of vaulting the wider nave with something other than the barrel vault was tackled in the North rather than the South (although some say Lombardy). There seemed to be three problems: sagging if the span was considerable; adequate support at the sides for the thrusts; a problem of elevation induced by the fact that if both sections were kept semicircular, the diagonals would rise higher than the transversals and a flattened diagonal was undesirable. The last problem was solved by making the transversal pointed (ogival) while keeping the diagonal semicircular. It is not safe to say whether this was done first at Speyer in Germany, at Caen in Normandy, or at Durham in England, or more or less spontaneously and simultaneously at all three. The solution came in the ribbed vault—ribbed arches were built both transversely and diagonally in each bay to form a frame a little like an umbrella. Then the interstices were filled in, certainly adding strength as well as closure. This leap forward in the Romanesque opened the way for its brilliant exploitation in the Gothic.

These ribs, of course, concentrated the thrusts at the side walls and they had to be contained. Normally buttressing was provided by the cross vaults of the aisles, by external buttresses, or (as at St-Etienne in Caen) by semi-barrel vaults over the triforium gallery supporting the whole length of the nave wall.

It seems fairly certain, though the reasons are obscure, that the first true ribbed main vaults in the history of architecture were made at Durham. In the choir, instead of barrel vaults over the aisles, the Norman builders placed oblique transverse arches against each of the vaulting piers; in the side aisles of the nave were the first flying buttresses, so noble a feature of later Gothic exterior. These were quadrant arches rising against the wall buttresses in the triforium and transmitting the thrust of the nave vaults down to the outside wall. At Durham and elsewhere where they appeared during the Romanesque they were concealed in the triforium by the slanting roofs.

Can we now say what is Romanesque? It begins with almost basilican plans and flat roofs; it ends with elaborate apsidal arrangements, vaulted naves, nascent flying buttresses. Can it then be defined so sharply as, for example, the Classic Greek temple? The answer surely has to be no, although by some strange chemistry and after only a little experience you can identify most Romanesque churches as Romanesque.

The classic definitions do not help much. The French term *roman* was probably coined by a Norman antiquary, M. de Gerville, who, in December 1818, wrote a letter to a friend, Le Prévot, about some Norman churches.

> It is universally agreed that this heavy, clumsy architecture is *opus romanum* distorted or gradually debased by our rude ancestors. At the same time, from a singularly mangled Latin, there was emerging a Romance language (une langue romane).[160]

The judgment is not unlike that pronounced by the Italians of the Renaissance when they contemptuously coined the term "Gothic." But both judgments were wrong. As Focillon remarks, "The term is more valuable than the doctrine." But the term is not self-defining, nor is it usefully descriptive.

Kenneth Conant tells us that the record of Romanesque times is a synthesis of traditional forms, culminating at Cluny and Citeaux, the flowering of many and varied regional styles, some of them carried forth by missionaries and colonists as the Romanesque area expanded into Spain, the Holy Land, Middle Europe, and Scandinavia. We have been talking of the elements of this synthesis, to be sure, but not noting clearly enough perhaps that few Romanesque churches, if indeed any, show all the elements of the synthesis unless we are to settle for the proto-Gothic churches of Caen as representing a culmination. This would leave out too many favorites to suit me.

Indeed, as Focillon points out in his discussion of dating, "Styles do not succeed each other like dynasties, by the death or expulsion of the last male heirs."[161] In the single country of France in the twelfth century Romanesque was moving into the full bloom of its classical period south of the Loire and north of it engaging in the "precocious experiments" which would lead soon to the fundamental Gothic program. Meanwhile Romanesque persisted well into the thirteenth century in Germany, and perhaps even longer in Spain and Italy. In the eleventh century, then, Romanesque had taken on that part of its "characteristic form marked by the systematic use of wall-arcades and flat pilasters,"[162] but it was developing the apsidal arrangements of the plan, working on towers, and especially on roofs, so that everything was in a state of flux. In its moment of stylistic maturity in the last third of the eleventh and first third of the

---

[160] From Ch. Gidon, "L'Invention du terme d'architecture romane par Gerville (1818)," *Bulletin de la Société des Antiquaires de Normandie*, 1935, cited by Focillon, *The Art of the West in the Middle Ages*, op. cit., p. 29, footnote 1.
[161] Focillon, *The Art of the West in the Middle Ages*, op. cit., p. 9.
[162] Ibid., p. 62.

twelfth centuries, there was the great outpouring of magnificent architectural sculpture in France, but this was either less noteworthy or absent in other countries of the Romanesque; and even in France the churches of Normandy and Aquitaine were austere while those of Burgundy, Poitou, and Languedoc were rich.

Certainly in the Romanesque there is the first Western study of structure as a problem of equilibrium in three dimensions as opposed to the classic, and especially the Greek, use of gravity only vertically. But this will not define Romanesque either since it was also the concern of the earlier Byzantine and the later Gothic builders. Not much more can be done by using the study of light as a reference point, although Romanesque churches were as traditionally dark as Gothic churches were light.

Romanesque is then elusive to define sharply by a period of time, by an area in which the building took place, or by a consistently used system of structure. It was almost universal that the Romanesque builders had great respect for the wall of relatively small dressed stones often with blind interlaced arcades; that their churches usually had transepts and apses; that the windows were sparing; that arcades in the nave were common and that the piers of the arcades were usually impressively thick and strong looking; that arcaded triforium galleries were common; and that the overall effect was one of serene and powerful, sober and dignified, well-grouped masses accented by the picturesque grouping of towers and apses. But an exception to each of these can be found somewhere in a church which is unquestionably Romanesque and also unquestionably excellent.

As compared with Gothic the churches are substantially lower in feeling, and inside one is more aware of the walls and less of the articulated skeleton, and they are *usually* darker. That is about the best I can do. If Romanesque Modena seems to you to have little in common with Romanesque Caen or Durham, you are probably right.

It *is* possible to be more specific if we are talking about one highly important, but only one type of church, the pilgrimage churches of France.

Looking at the plans of five of these, stretching from Tours to Santiago de Compostela, we can see how remarkably alike they are. All the naves have side aisles, some two and some four, and these are all groin-vaulted. There are substantial differences in the west tower arrangements and whether the church is entered directly, through a tower, between towers, or by a more sharply defined narthex. Almost all the naves are long; all are roofed with arches, and/or barrel vaults. Each has a transept, each a well-defined crossing. Each has a clear sanctuary terminating in an apsidal wall which has openings into a groin-vaulted ambulatory. All but one have five chapels radiating from the ambulatory, though their shapes sometimes vary from the usual semicircle. Each has chapels on the east wall of the transepts. Clearly this is all one style and will remain so however the massing of the elements and their height affects the exterior appearance. The reason for this plan we will remember is to provide queue lines for the mass of pilgrims to permit uninterrupted circulation inside from the west front to the apsidal chapels and back, since the relics of the saints are mostly in these chapels, though occasionally in the crypt. At Tours, Toulouse, and Santiago one could follow a continuous aisle down the nave, around the transept arm, around the ambulatory, around the other transept, and so back to the west front by the other aisle. But the transepts usually also provided controllable auxiliary entrances or exits.

All this is very orderly and much the best arrangement for circulation. But let us not grasp too rapidly at the idea that the radiating chapel plan defines the Romanesque. Another whole family of churches, in a scheme known as the Benedictine or Berry plan from that province, to which it was not confined, disposed the chapels of diminishing scale in echelon at the ends of the aisles with the central apse much the most important. Not as good for circulation, this plan was better for presentation.

If I tried to take you through all the best examples of the Romanesque, including France, Germany, England, and Italy, I would have to discuss at length at least eighty fascinating monuments. It is obviously too much. Let me try instead to mention some of the best of each of the Romanesque components, indicating some of the major pleasures of each of the regional architectures.

FACADES (WEST FRONTS)

Let us begin with Romanesque facades. Because of their great variety from region to region, they are quite good indicators of regional Romanesque style. Romanesque west fronts, even when limited to France, have an enormous basic variety long before you get down to looking at tiny details. In Provence, *provincia nostra*, not strangely, they harked back to Roman triumphal arches. A good example is St-Gilles du Gard (1140–1160). What we see now looks like the lower part of such an arch, a wide central opening flanked at some distance on each side by another arch, each covering a portal. The arches fill the height of the story, and they are very Roman looking, with fluted pilasters, elaborate late classical capitals, wide string courses, all approached by a monumental stairway extending across the entire width. The square towers way out at the flanks, much hacked up by the Protestants, seem almost irrelevant. The arch post was probably originally surmounted by a great triangular gable as in most churches of the area, but this is long gone, and what we see now, fortunately well to the rear, is an ugly end wall of the nave, the disgraceful product of some eighteenth-century clod of a restorer.

Pl. 210

I hope you will remember Marmoutiers in Alsace, which I have mentioned already (see Plate 203). Here is a case where the suggestion of towers is absorbed into the wall. Despite the great beauty of its central three arches, its blind arcades, and its three gables, it is suggestive of a fortification. Not nearly so handsome but in the same vein is St-Philibert of Tournus (950 on) in Burgundy. The towers merge into the wall; they are very military looking, with the whole facade covered with blind arcades and Lombard bands, with narrow slits for the few windows, with a parapet cornice fitted out with machicolations and a central door which looks as though it had been punched through the wall and into the narthex as an afterthought.

Pl. 213   St-Pierre at Angoulême (1130) in Aquitaine has some suggestions of Marmoutiers but has been much elaborated into something that no longer has the appearance of a fortress. In fact it is a great decorative frontispiece with the towers emerging as units in themselves only when they rise above the gable since down below the arcature does not sharply mark them. It is a very beautiful Poitevin facade, one of the finest of the Romanesque to look at, but it offers no expression of the interior which, you may remember, has an aisleless nave roofed by a line of domes. The well-proportioned tower, two-thirds of the facade, a little wider than it is high, is divided into five vertical bays, two on each side being arched at the top and enframing what looks like an arched doorway at ground level. But all this arcading is blind and contains sculpture which increases in quantity and complexity as the eye moves upward and to the center. The wider central bay first enframes the arched portal and then, after a well-proportioned piece of flat wall, an arched window almost as large as the portal. Above this arch, carving occupies the area up to the string course.

Above the string course the lateral horizontal rhythm changes; at the flanks are a pair of voussoired blank arcades, and toward the center itself a single voussoired arch. But the center continues its own verticality which has already contained the portal and the window to terminate in a great arch whose crown rises above the level of the story. In the wall contained by this arch is a sculptured portrayal of Christ and the symbols of the four Evangelists as described in Revelations. Now the towers emerge, the paired open arcaded belfries relating to the paired blank arcades below, capped with a balustrade and the "fish-scaled" conical or beehive roofs characteristic of the region. It is only these roofs which rise above the large and sophisticated gable artfully indented by the five bays of blind arches in ascending array (raking arcade). It is a most satisfactory composition.

Pl. 212   At St-Nicolas at Civray in Poitou (twelfth century) there are reminiscences of Angoulême, but something different is beginning to happen. Here the facade has become very low and rectangular, almost a wall of two nearly equal levels, capped by a parapet and flanked by relatively anemic, three-quarter-engaged round buttresses which rise uninterruptedly from bottom to top. The lower stage of the facade has three equal voussoired arcatures. The flanking ones frame paired blind arches, the center one the portal. In the upper story three further arches are now separated by engaged round pilasters smaller than but mirroring the flanking "buttresses" and rising from a molded architrave corbel course, looking almost machicolated, such as was used in Roman triumphal arches between the arches and the attics. It is almost but not quite as though one St-Gilles facade had been laid atop another. The side arcades are wildly sculpted; the center is open to provide a window flanked by two archaic statues that rise as high as the column capitals from which the arches spring. Above this stage is a repeat of the arched corbel and then a flat undecorated parapet. Peeking up from behind are two little tourelles bearing beehives. If you can half close your eyes at Civray, you can see that the composition is very direct and simple.

But at Notre-Dame-la-Grande (1130–1145) of Poitiers in Poitou, gen- *Pl. 209* erally praised as being one of the best Romanesque facades, it is quite hard to close one's eyes enough to let only the composition show through. If you can manage it, you will note a lower three-arched facade much like that of Civray, flanked by considerably more impressive round-buttress towers. The upper stage is, however, completely different, retaining large central arched windows but flanking them with two levels of blind arcades, four at the lower, three at the upper. Finally there is a substantial gable where at Civray there was none. It is a considerably more dynamic composition and it is extremely busy with sculpture and decorative carving. Almost no surface of column, of extrados, of intrados, of voussoir, of spandrel is left untouched, save the gable which has abstract circles in its lower section and diagonally placed squares in its upper but which is pierced by an enormous, deeply cut, aureole also containing sculpture. The sculpture of Notre-Dame-la-Grande is lively, often wittily grotesque, and examining it in detail may turn out to interest you more than a detailed study of the facade, despite the round flanking towers.

Another way to provide a west front would be simply to make it all out of a single centrally placed western tower. This is what one might call the solution at St-Benoît-sur-Loire (1060–1130), which has a massive squat *Pl. 219* single tower only two generous stories high, or you might prefer to call it a great porch three bays deep. Whatever you call it, it is powerful and impressive. At the first level four forceful buttresses rise to the top; the outside ones start from the ground; the inner ones ascend from the capitals of the massive, three-quarter engaged round columns, from which also are sprung the lower-story arches. From the buttresses at their top, after a narrow supporting molding, the upper arches spring. These openings are much more elongated than those of the lower stage. All of these arches frame inner narrow open arches except in the middle bay, where a ridiculous lancet window was inserted later. This porch, one of the strongest forms extant, is probably older than the nave. Though it looks squarish, it is actually an irregular trapezium. The central door is not on the axis of the nave. The rather heavy pavilion roof does not improve the overall appearance. Again here you are likely to become engrossed by the sculpture of the capitals which engage themselves in a welter of subjects from the Evangelists of the Revelation and the Last Judgment to scenes from the lives of Christ or Saint Michael to mysterious animals straight out of the bestiaries.

More towerish is the western front of St-Savin-sur-Gartempe (first half of eleventh century). It is a beautiful square tower which was originally freestanding, but it was connected to the church and turned into a porch when the nave was extended at the end of the eleventh century. It now appears in five stages including the high spire, which was a fourteenth-century addition, rebuilt in the 1880s. The lower two stages are the old ones, a rather squat base story now partly underground and a much taller one ending in a modeled cornice. On each face of this story are two elongated blind discharging arches framed by the corner buttresses and a central pilaster; it is pierced by very few and very narrow windows. The two next levels are still old, of the first quarter of the twelfth century and in the same style, with open arches and a surmounting parapet. When the tower was turned into a porch, the first level was vaulted and the entire area covered with interesting frescoes which are quite rare in the French Romanesque. Indeed most will visit St-Savin for the frescoes, which also adorn the tribunes, the inside tympanum of the west wall, the pilasters, and the ceilings of the nave.

Pl. 10

A third central tower facade appears at the Abbey Church of St-Pierre in Moissac (twelfth century). It would not be distinguished save for one thing. It too serves as a porch for the church, but instead of a portal only at the west, it also has one at the south. And it is this portal which has on its tympanum the magnificent Enthroned Christ of Revelations, which may well be the finest product of Romanesque sculpture and certainly is the greatest Romanesque treatment of that particular subject.

The future, though, lay in none of these but in the emergence of the towers from the wall to become powerful flanking elements, as important perhaps as the central wall, portal, and gable. One might have decided to keep the towers low and let the gable reach well above them, and this was more or less the Italian choice. We see the French choice emerging in the two great Norman churches of Caen. They are of about the same age, though Matilda's church, La Trinité (L'Abbaye aux Dames, 1062–1140), took longer to build than William's St-Etienne (L'Abbaye aux Hommes, 1064–1077).

Pl. 208

The towers have not really yet emerged from the wall at St-Etienne. The lower wall is almost square and is separated into three parts, narrower at the sides, wider at the center by prominent buttresses running uninterruptedly almost to full height. Three small portals correspond to the nave and the two side aisles. The second and third stages gently separated by string courses carry single arched windows on the sides and three in the middle. The culminating gable is piddling. Then the towers seem to take off from the top of this wall although their inner edges do line up with the outer edges of the inner buttresses. Their first stage has seven narrow, tall blind arcades; their second contains five somewhat less elongated arcades of which the second and fourth are pierced by slit windows. Above that the final Norman stage has paired arches, each enclosing slit windows separated by a column. We have here a clear example of how knowledgeable the Romanesque builders were about expressing the fact that as you went higher in a masonry tower you needed less masonry (though a more graceful and imaginative example is to be seen as I have said at the campanile of the Abbey of Pomposa on the Adriatic not far from Ravenna). Even the Norman part of the towers are perhaps out of proportion to the nave and gable section at St-Etienne, and if they were not, the thirteenth-century additions of flèche and tourelles certainly made them so.

Though again not particularly graceful, the emphasis on the towers becomes more explicit at La Trinité. Here they clearly start from their own base, the ground; they are larger and are themselves buttressed; their appearance of strength is emphasized by the preponderance of blind arcading, whereas the nave wall is pierced by many and generous windows. The three portals clearly express the aisles and nave behind them. There is a little sculpture on the tympanum, but the Normans generally did not have the same desire for it as the builders of Burgundy or Languedoc.

But except for the austerity of the unsculptured walls, these churches were pointing the way the French west front would be going by the time the Gothic came along. It was the going thing at Cluny, at Paray le Monial, where the crossing tower joined the chorus and exploded at many-towered Tournai (1066).

Does the fact that this facade arrangement did prevail later in France (if not in Italy, or Germany, or very consistently in England) establish it as the genuine French Romanesque? What do you want to say is typically Romanesque? Conques, St-Gilles, Marmoutiers, Tournus, Angoulême, Civray, Poitiers, St-Benoît-sur-Loire, St-Savin-sur-Gartempe, Moissac, Caen, Paray le Monial, or Tournai? They cannot all be typical. And how much more difficult would it be to isolate "Romanesque" if we tried to include in one rubric the multiple open arcading of twelfth-century Cremona; the Italian churches where the gable rose well above the flanks, such as San Pietro of Toscanella (seventh-eleventh centuries) with its triumphal arch and blind arcading and the large circular window in the gable, San Zeno Maggiore in Verona (1070), or the duomo of Modena (1099–1120) with its *Pl. 211* five firmly marked bays and the dominant central gable sporting an enormous rose window; many-marbled San Miniato in Florence (1013); the extraordinary combination of Norman, Byzantine, and Muslim put together on the front of eleventh-century San Rufino at Assisi with the sculptures of the four Evangelists projecting from the wall around the rose window; *Pl. 207* the flat simplicity of San Michele, Lucca (1188–1213), so much like Pisa *Pl. 214* with its fantastic five stories of colonettes and arcades; or the commodious loggia of the atrium of Sant'Ambrogio in Milan (1140). Then if you add *Pl. 217* in German examples like the double-ended churches which have no fronts, only apses, or the great westwork of Minden, where will you be? *Pl. 202*

LATERAL VIEWS

Let us leave the multiplicity of front facades and look for a moment at some lateral views, which can occasionally be excellent. Without study and from memory, I can recall the climax of the design of the south elevation of the Church of the Apostles at Cologne as it used to be before we bombed it, and some overly contemporary restoration was done. Here the high western tower introduced us to a long barnlike set of high roof and two sets of lower roofs interrupted near the beginning by the equally simple projection of the west transept and then exploding into richness at the east with the octagonal galleried lantern over the crossing, the apsed transept end, the two octagonal conically roofed towers, and the triumphantly finishing east apse. Or there is Angoulême, whose west wall leads to the firm nave with the three domed bays before the crossing, each separated by a wide, firm, full-height buttress, and each containing a pair of large well-proportioned arched inset windows with several layers of reveals, culminating toward the east with the short projection of the transepts which lets the dome over the crossing stand out. There is, of course, the Cathedral of Pisa whose south elevation is very consistent and effective;

Pl. 219

but most of all there is St-Benoît-sur-Loire. Here the low tower-porch starts off the design by projecting slightly beyond the nave to form a firm accent, but its roof does not rise above the ridge line of the nave save for a modest cupola. The benign consequence is that we do not begin with something that sets the tone too high, as anything looking like a Victorian locomotive smokestack would do. Then there is the long line of the nave, ridge, and simple sloping roof, the many bays of the nave wall with strong separating buttresses, and a single ample window—and low down the shed roof of the aisle, complementary to the nave roof. This is broken finally by a transept which is just properly assertive, firmly projecting its simple gable end with two flanking cylindrical towers with conical roofs and a large arcuate central window. The accent here is the strong tower of the crossing sitting so well on the roof, rising just the right amount above it when crowned by its pyramidal roof and its aspiring flèche. East of the crossing the simple ridge line of the choir steps down and projects a considerable distance to end in a large apse and its half-cone roof. It is the best Romanesque lateral facade I know of and gives the impression of being all of a piece, although it has been the subject of many reconstructions.

Pl. 216

Then there is the graceful north facade of the Cathedral of Cremona, simpler and perhaps handsomer than the west front, which has suffered from Renaissance and Baroque improvements of the gable. The north facade has three almost equal bays sharply marked by continuous buttresses, its pointed arch and blind arcades containing three openings at the sides and four in the middle, the central point rising slightly higher than the sides. It has three round windows, the central one a little larger and centered a little higher than those of the sides; and a modestly pitched gable with an open raking arcade, with three octagonal tourelles having open pavilions at their tops sitting at the corners and astride the gable.

So we should always take a look at the sides, and may occasionally reap a rich reward even if only in a detail, as for example, the stone mosaics on the south side of Clermont-Ferrand's Notre-Dame-du-Port (eleventh century), or the charming lions and porches, *regia* and *pescheria*, on the south and north sides, respectively, of the duomo at Modena. Anyway you have somehow to get to the rear, or east front, which is often the most rewarding elevation of a Romanesque church.

REARS (ABSIDES, EAST FRONTS)

The Romanesque rear is generally a consequence of the adoption of the ambulatory with radiating chapels. But even given this plan, much depends on how the builders chose to treat the chapels as to height, as to external shape, as to fenestration and columniation, as to roofs, as to masonry, as to decoration. Thus the mass effects, the shadow effects, and the color effects may vary enormously from church to church, but the designers seldom stuttered, and there are very few Romanesque churches whose backs will be viewed in vain.

It is neither hard nor unpleasurable to go around France collecting absides though not all of them may seem beautiful. St-Philibert at Tournus displays a very clumsy arrangement of three rectangular chapels set much too high on the ambulatory wall with windows uneasily inserted between them, their sawed-off ends with buttresses stopping in a strange way, and a most unfortunate terminating pediment.

At St-Savin-sur-Gartempe you will see only two levels, the huge choir-apse and the silolike attachment of five apsidal chapels almost touching each other as they meet the wall of the choir-apse.

At very old Germigny-des-Prés (806) you can see what things were like before the invention of the radiating chapels, where there is a single strongly stated but enormously simple choir apse, almost basilican, butted against the end wall of the nave but talking harmoniously with similar apses which terminate the transepts.

Pl. 215

The backs of the Auvergnat churches are particularly interesting. At Issoire's St-Paul (eleventh century), for example, the transepts are carried to a much higher level than the choir or the nave, so that the entire apsidal arrangement is terminated abruptly and firmly by a wall towering above it. This high transept is typical of Auvergne.

Pl. 218

At St-Julien, Brioude (twelfth century), there is the lovely rhythm of the arched windows of the choir apse, arranged in sets of three, of which the flanking ones are set lower than the center, the handsome inlaid decoration above, the strong bracketing for the cornice and the graceful comb on the ridge.

The east end of St-Nectaire (twelfth century) has an even more elaborate decoration of the frieze of the choir apse, the more evident because of the contrast with the light spandrels immediately below and the dark austere sobriety of the radiating chapels. Here again you can see the effect of the characteristically high Auvergnat transept.

Over in Burgundy at Paray le Monial's Notre-Dame (1109), we would notice the effect of the undulating profile of the roof tiles, the angularity of the polygonal ambulatory, the unhappy consequence of a rectangular apsidal chapel on the center line, and the exaggerated banding over the apse chapel windows, which was handled so skillfully at St-Nectaire.

Pl. 224

Finally if you should wander around to the rear of the Abbaye-aux-Hommes (St-Etienne) at Caen (1064–1077), you will find an impressive and enormous scale of three concentric circles, the great arched, only slightly convex, curved chapels, the big round windows of the ambulatory fighting to be seen at their bottoms, and the narrow ogival windows of the choir-apse, but both the ogives and the flying buttresses should tell you that this back is not Romanesque but of a later date.

You can collect good Romanesque apsidal arrangements farther afield than France. I know of none in England, mostly because of the quite different development of the plan east of the altar, partly because before this occurred the Normans seem generally to have had less interest in the apse, and partly because even if they did build any the English urge to redo the Norman work in newer styles eventually eliminated the originals. But there are riches in Germany and Italy and of quite a different sort from those of France.

In Italy most of the churches continued to have either a single apse raised very high against the nave wall and possibly arcaded in two or even three stories as at Pisa (ca. 1250) or more felicitously with two side chapels, extending from the side aisles but subsidiary to the apsidal extension of the nave. Ignoring some unfortunate changes which have been made over time, one can see a good example at Cremona. The side chapels are of nearly the same diameter as the central one but flatter in curvature. The choir-apse chapel begins its curvature about where the side chapels abut it and carries up very much higher. All three are sheathed in marble up to the stilted arch arcaded galleries which go around them in strong contrast to the pink-red brick which is the dominant building material of the duomo (except for the west front) and indeed of the city of Cremona itself. All butt against the gabled brick end of the cathedral with the walls especially prominent above the side chapels.

Pl. 225

But surely the design of Modena is the most consistent, the most harmonious, the most elegant, and the most beautiful. It is all of stone. Three half cylinders rise side by side, the flanking ones much smaller and skillfully proportioned to the center one. The side ones correctly are lower than the center and their cornice lines coincide approximately with the parapet line of the arcade of the central cylinder. The side apses are backed by a plain and again well-proportioned wall which might have been better aesthetically but perhaps not functionally if a round window on each side had been left out. The center apse cylinder whose roof line is at about the level of the roofs of the walls at the sides is in turn received by a higher wall with two small flanking towers, which have open arcades and pyramidal roofs and between them a simply gabled roof. The overall proportions are fine and quickly comprehended.

But notice that the detail is equally careful and sophisticated. Save for necessary changes in scale, it is identical for all three of the apsidal elements. Extremely elongated, three-quarter-engaged column bases rise almost to the roofs, dividing each half cylinder into three equal curved bays. The column buttresses support relieving arches whose crowns reach near the cornice. The cornices are firm but made of three simple bands simply built out from the walls. Within each of the enframed curved walls there is a semicircular arched window near the bottom, then a substantial rise of unadorned and unpenetrated wall, then a narrower window, also semicircular, also arched. Above this a range of blind arcaded corbels support a simple banded parapet. From this rises a pair of columns supporting a trio of arches to provide a final embellishment and an interesting walkway. There can be few peers to this back of Modena in the grace and absolute consistency of the design.

But perhaps the most impressive of the apse treatments are to be found in Germany, where at times they dominate the overall design. This is not very much the case, for example, at Maria Laach (1093–1156), where the apse is relatively small and the three towers clearly overwhelm it. It becomes a little more evident at Worms (1110–1181), where the apse has grown and acquired an open arcade. It is still more forceful at St. Aposteln in Cologne (1035–1220), where the brick of the three-staged apses has taken charge. But it is most attractive in my opinion when it is dominant but not authoritarian as, for example, at the riverside of the Kaiserdom Speyer (1030). Here the single apse with high blind arcades, like those at Modena but not rising to enclose the open arcade, is topped by a continuous cloisterlike open arcade, and then a half-conical roof meets a high gable with a steep raking arcade and blind arched corbels; all of this is topped by the flanking towers, which, very plain and only slitted by windows, begin their journey toward increasing lightness only at about the level of the ridge (or slightly below).

ROMANESQUE INTERIORS

Romanesque architecture, cursorily summarized, might be said to be a progression first from solid lateral walls into which various arcades and embrasured windows seem to have been punched (Nevers, Winchester), the wall supporting transverse arches or simply a truss across the nave. Then it moved to a breaking up of the wall into bays by columns, attached to piers, which rose all the way to the cross arches to support them, and articulated with other shorter columns, also attached to the piers, to support the arcades (Poitiers, Vézelay), coupled with a shift from flat ceilings to tunnel vaults running continuously (St-Savin). Finally the vaults evolved from barrel vaults between transverse ribs (Poitiers), to pointed cross vaults between transverse ribs (Vézelay), to hexpartite ribbed vaults which, however, did carry the weight of the infilling (St-Etienne, Caen). Occasionally, especially in the Loire region, there was a system of freestanding columns running all the way to the vault to support either a continuous tunnel vault (St-Savin) or in Burgundy, transverse arches (Tournus).

There are, needless to say, many other delights to be found in the interiors of French Romanesque churches. I have been much pleased by St-Savin-sur-Gartempe, so very colorful and elegant. It has two very narrow aisles almost as high as the nave and thus no clerestory side lighting. The columns of the nave are very tall and very rich stone, quite freestanding, highly veined and polished, and they carry an arcade high up in the church from which a continuous tunnel vault springs covered with an interesting fresco. The color and the freedom and the unbroken perspective right down into the apse are very effective.

In the same vein of freestanding columns, in this case sober round ones of brick, is St-Philibert of Tournus. But now the columns support transverse arches, separating the barrel vault into bays.

St-Etienne (Nevers) has great interest in its side aisles. In most Romanesque churches these short spans are cross- (groin-) vaulted, but at Nevers the upper parts of the side aisles are half arches springing from the summit of the outer wall and butting against the high walls of the nave. These have been called "flying buttresses in embryo."

The interior of Notre-Dame-la-Grande at Poitiers is a delight (1130–1145). Like many of the others it is three-aisled, with a barrel-vaulted central nave, but it is much more fanciful (and complicated). The piers are square and bear four half-round shafts on the aisle side to carry the cross vault laterally, to spring the arches of the arcade, while the tallest ones, facing the nave, soar to the spring lines of transverse arch ribs which compartmentalize the barrel vault. The columns are heavily adorned with painted geometrical forms in great variety which spill over on to some of the wall surfaces. [There is a great deal of quite different painting at St-Paul at Issoire (eleventh century), but the unpainted Auvergnat naves seem preferable to me.]

Pl. 222
I believe that my greatest favorite of the French Romanesque interiors is that of La Madeleine at Vézelay (1104). It has one feature which I do not like. The main engaged columns running up to support the transverse arches have their verticality interrupted by molded string courses and imposts (very popular with late English Gothic) at the level of the springing of the arches of the ground floor arcades and again at the beginning of the clerestory wall with its deeply embrasured windows. These designers always had a problem of how much emphasis to give to horizontality and how much to verticality. But my own personal taste says that the horizontality is well enough cared for by the various levels of galleries and that the articulation of piers, each sweeping uninterruptedly to support whatever each is going to support, is the better way. But in all other respects Vézelay is tops. There is an uninterrupted view to the choir apse. The effect of the transverse arches in dividing the bays is countered by the reassertion of the perspective through the alternating pink and gray courses of the transverse arches and some of the columns. Vézelay has no tribune

or triforium but does not suffer from that. Between its transverse arches is not a barrel vault, but pointed cross vaults, this being probably their first use in a French nave.

There are curiosities along the way. At Neuvy's St-Sépulchre (1045) there are clear evidences of the Crusades. There is Islamic influence in the trilobed arches of the east end of La Charité-sur-Loire (late eleventh century). At St-Lazare, Autun (1130–1140), you will notice that the barrel vault and the transverse arches are *pointed*, thus interrupting the smooth movement of the semicircular arch from pier to pier. The men of Autun may have been on the verge of discovering the system which was later exploited in the Gothic, but nothing of that was realized here.

At the journey's end you will, I suppose, have to go to the galleried basilica of St-Etienne at Caen (vault ca. 1110). Here, having quite fully developed the vertical division and articulation of the nave walls, the Normans went the logical step further to provide vault compartments, using strongly molded transverse and diagonal ribs continuing the line of the wall shafts. This was done in hexpartite form, that is, a cross-rib at every pier but diagonals spanning to every second pier (in quadripartite vaulting each pair of diagonal ribs is contained within a pair of transverse ribs). This innovation of ribbed vaulting was certainly an advance over the cross vaults of Vézelay and Speyer, even if the ribs do not carry the interfill as they do in Gothic but apparently were added mainly for aesthetic reasons.

Pl. 223

So if you are studying the steps toward Gothic, you must, as a matter of duty, go to Caen, and once arrived you may in fact declare the two churches there as the paladins of French Romanesque and be in excellent company. But I find them less warming than several of the other Romanesque churches I have been describing or, among the Norman work, than the great nave of Durham, or the transept of Winchester, both in England.

And as for the other high spots of Romanesque interiors: in Germany there are surely Hildesheim and Speyer. The nave of Hildesheim, St. Michael's (1001–1033), gives a strong impression of basilica, with its relative low arcade; it has heavily decorated voussoirs, intrados, and spandrels, a large expanse of blank walls, and then the clerestory above and its painted flat roof. But the Romanesque structural principles are there, the strong arches on all four sides, to emphasize the crossing of transept and nave and to carry a crossing tower; and the use of the module of the crossing for the division of the nave into three bays by the piers which interrupt the customary previous unbroken even flow of the earlier basilican arcades. It is attractive, but its interest may mainly be that of an anticipator.

Pl. 201

In Speyer, on the other hand, whether in the nave or the transepts (omitting later changes) or the high-ceilinged crypt, we are in space which might be French—with bays well marked by columns engaged to the piers, the verticality interrupted by imposts, but finally reaching the transverse arches in the usual way. And the end wall of the north transept is very Romanesque, divided in two equal parts by an enormous pier, and each division carrying a strong array of deeply embrasured arched windows.

The Architecture of Stone 367

In Spain the little churches of the Catalonian mountains seem to me the most rewarding, perhaps even including the famous Mont Serrat but certainly including the pieces which have found their way to the museums of Vich and Barcelona, but I suppose if you have become entangled with the pilgrimage routes, you will want to visit Santiago da Compostela (1075–1122). You may find it disappointing. It is on the whole more French than Spanish, though there are hints of Spanish futures in the details of the Puerta de las Platerias. Inside, though, the nave is quite standard, having high arcades at the first level with considerable stilt to the arches, coupled arches at the tribune, articulated columns attached to the piers, broken by imposts, and strongly accentuated transverse arches. Except for the height of the arcade, which lends a certain feeling of loftiness, several of the French examples I have cited have more appeal to me.

Appeal is perhaps the right word to use for the "Romanesque" interiors of Italy. Way up on the Lakes from Como north, in such places as Piona or Gravedona, and in Como itself, there are a number of small examples suggesting that there once was in Lombardy a genuine belief in Romanesque architecture, so many of the principles of which are alleged to have begun there. But later on it seems to me the Romanesque men of Italy were not taking these principles seriously, but using them like playthings when they chose, a sort of anticipation of attitudes which would become more transparent later on when the Gothic dawned.

The most obvious examples are around Florence, and a distinguished example, consistent inside and outside, is San Miniato al Monte (1140–1180). Stripped of all the decoration both the outside and the inside proclaim that we are looking at a basilican church. Outside there are the high central gable and the two sloping side-aisle roofs. Inside there is the arcade and then the clerestory wall and the trussed wood roof. The columns are beautiful classic Corinthian marbles. Even the semicircular apse could easily have come from a basilica.

But we cannot, of course, ignore the decoration, which is very assertive. Gone are the sculptures and the lively interplay of light and shade which are so characteristic of both facades and interiors in the Roman north. Here everything is smooth and flat, made of marble inlays, usually of white panels defined by black bands. It is completely two-dimensional, quite unplastic. It is set within the framework of the main architectural elements, to be sure, but it bears no explicit relation to arch, column, or cornice. When it is as well done as at San Miniato, it certainly has its own kind of charm, but it is a foretaste of the Renaissance, not a product of the Romanesque.

In San Miniato we will also note a new arrangement by which the choir is raised well above the nave atop a heightened crypt to which one descends by twin stairs at the end of the nave while ascending to the choir by twin stairs at the ends of the side aisles.

It is not surprising, I suppose, that the nearest things to true Romanesque in Italy (aside from the detached campaniles) are to be found in

Lombardy. Many of the churches with the happy exteriors we have looked at earlier have been so fixed up inside that the Romanesque residues are hard to decipher, as, for example, in Cremona's cathedral. But Sant'Ambrogio (Milan), San Zeno Maggiore (Verona), and especially the Duomo at Modena have something to offer.

My own taste at Sant'Ambrogio (1140) is best satisfied at the exterior with its beautifully arched and walled *atrium,* and its two-decked, four-arched, single-gable-ended facade. Indeed the *atrium* is, I believe, unique among Romanesque churches.

The interior has all the right components if you are content merely to list them: vaulted nave and aisles, octagon overcrossing, triforium gallery, raised choir over crypt, apse. But the ribs of the cross vaults are very wide and squat, and though it was once claimed that these were the first weight-bearing ribs in history (as opposed to purely decorative adjuncts to a self-supporting vault), now they are shorn of whatever enthusiasms you may be able to muster at seeing a first. The general feeling of lowness impressed by the transverse arches of the nave is reinforced by the low springing of the wide arches of the triforium. There also may be more decoration than you will care for. But whether first or not, whether squat or not, whether overdecorated or not, Sant'Ambrogio is definitely Romanesque.

San Zeno Maggiore (1139) of Verona has a wonderfully simple, even stern, facade of Italian Romanesque elements, a single elegant projecting porch on two columns rising from the backs of the crouching lions, which are so ubiquitous in this area, a semicircular arch, and a gabled roof. The side aisles are well expressed by the sloping roofs and the nave by its high gable, below which is the large wheel window to light the nave. (The church tower is to the right as you face it, the one at the left being part of a house of the German emperors on which you can note the Ghibelline merlons.)

Inside, however, there are disappointments. There is a great deal of wall and no triforium, only a clerestory. The nave ceiling is of wood. There is the Romanesque separation into bays by alternating columns reaching to the ceiling. The seven-aisled crypt is of some interest.

Whatever reservations I may have about Sant'Ambrogio and San Zeno, I have none about the Duomo of San Geminian in Modena (begun 1099), which seems to me pure Italian joy. It belongs to Emilia, not to Lombardy, but it is akin and was designed by the Lombard architect, Lanfranco. A cold statement of its structure would cause no heart to leap, and black-and-white photographs do not reveal its warmth either. In them we see the German separation into bays each containing two fairly standard Romanesque arcade elements, each square nave bay corresponding to two of the aisles on either side, wall shafts going up, uninterrupted by strings or imposts, to support heavy transverse masonry arches which originally supported a wooden roof. Now there are cross vaults which were added in the twelfth century. The transepts do not project from the church—the raised choir and depressed crypt are well integrated to the whole interior.

Pl. 226

The Architecture of Stone   369

But if this sounds cold and hardly worth mentioning again, the impression is altogether different once one has entered the church. This is partly because there is really an enormous feeling of plastic space moving around and through the arches and even more because practically all the structure is of beautifully colored, beautifully executed brick masonry. Only the intermediate columns of the arcades are of stone, offering a pleasant contrast to the prevailing tone and texture. Then the stone floor is laid out in broad transverse bands of pink-red and grey-white, with more elaborate mosaics in a few critical spots. The approach to choir and crypt is also elegantly conceived as a porchlike rood-screen raised on slender marble columns, rising sometimes from crouching lions and in a few places from curious human figures. The capitals are carved in the best Romanesque tradition. Then they are capped by a broad frieze-parapet adorned with some of the finest Romanesque sculpture to be found in Italy, the panorama of the Last Supper filling the center, Christ and the Evangelists of the Revelation at the left, and scenes from the Passion at the right, all executed, together with most of the masonry, by the *maestri campionesi* from Campione on Lake Lugano. Except perhaps for fifteenth-century and later artwork in the apse, Modena can be given only the highest marks and placed high on the list of architectural monuments not to be missed while in Italy.

The Normans built a great many remarkable Romanesque cathedrals in England, but the energy of a whole succession of later bishops and deans and their desire to be absolutely courant with respect to "Early English," "Decorated," or "Perpendicular" Gothic led to the destruction of much of it, or the covering over of it, or at least to the juxtaposition with it of confusing new motifs such as the lierne vaulting of the nave at Norwich. Nonetheless there are notable bits and pieces to be looked for as you journey around, such as:

Bristol—chapter house
Canterbury—choir (1096–1126); rebuilt (1174–1185)
Carlisle—two bays of nave
Chichester—nave
Durham—nave
Ely—nave and transepts
Hereford—choir
Norwich—nave, transepts, and choir
Oxford—nave and choir
Peterborough—most of church
Rochester—crypt, nave, west doorway
St. Albans—choir, transepts, most of nave
Winchester—north transept
Worcester—crypt, transepts, chapter house

But most of this needs some detection because of later juxtapositions. Of the above, Durham, Ely, and Peterborough come through most strongly. Each is worth a visit on the Norman count alone, while for a variety of later reasons most visitors to England are unlikely to omit Canterbury, Norwich, or perhaps Hereford, Oxford, Rochester, St. Albans, and Worcester. There are some additional strong Romanesque vestiges at Winchester, Southwell, and Durham.

I have a particular affection for the north transept of the Cathedral Church of the Holy Trinity—Saint Peter, Saint Paul, and Saint Sarthun—at Winchester, where Bishop Walkelyn's work (1079–1093) stands substantially as it did when it was consecrated. The south transept, otherwise much the same, was altered by the addition of two later chapels, while nave choir and everything else have been changed by subsequent bishops, especially William of Wykeham (1367–1404). But the north transept gives a clear notion of how powerful the whole original church must have been and how simple. The piers of the lower arcade are very broad, the arches very wide. The columns, attached to the piers at every bay which has therefore a single arch at ground level, rise uninterruptedly to the roof. The bay thus created carries two arches well set back from the plane of the wall within a sustaining arch at the gallery level, while at the clerestory the single deeply embrasured window in each is flanked by small arches. It is reminiscent, I think, of the nave of the monastery church of Mont St-Michel which is essentially contemporaneous, but the triforium and clerestory details and proportions are more carefully worked out. The stonework is firm, as positive as the forms.

Pl. 228

The naves of Gloucester, Southwell, and Durham all have the sturdy, squat, freestanding round columns which lend such force to the impression. Of these, Gloucester's are the tallest, Southwell's the shortest. Gloucester, unfortunately, has additions of Early English rib and panel which are confusing.

Pl. 227

Southwell Minster (eleventh century), a "village cathedral," has a very simple open Romanesque wall construction quite undivided into bays, almost as though you had turned a Roman aqueduct into a wall. The openings rise above each other in a one-to-one relation. The ground floor's freestanding round columns are very short and hence seem extremely sturdy. They rise from simple plinths with simple annulets for capitals to support wide and deep semicircular arches, with some geometric ornament but none on the spandrels. Above, narrow clerestory windows on center with the arches below pierce the wall. Wooden beams cross the nave and above them in a wooden barrel ending against a triumphal arch, whose springing is a little above that of the arches of the second story arcade. It is all very direct and very impressive. The columns of Tewkesbury Abbey Church (1088) are equally so.

But Durham Cathedral (1093) must be the favorite of everyone who has seen it. It is at once more complicated than Southwell and more innovative. It separates the bays by unimpeded engaged columns rising to the

Pl. 229

springing of the nave vaults. It has pointed ribs in the transverse arches of the nave vaults, which are generally accepted now as being the first. It has what could be the anticipators of flying buttresses, but they are located in the tribunes and so are not visible from the outside. In each bay at the first story are a pair of compound deep semicircular arches supported by a sturdy freestanding column. These columns are unforgettable, both for their size, almost equaling the openings between them (as indeed the piers do), and for the carved decoration of chevrons, flutes, and drapery changing from column to column. This powerful nave, coupled with other later details which do not belong here and the splendid location on a rock frowning down on the town, makes a visit to Durham an unforgettable experience.

CAPITALS

Pl. 220
Pl. 221
Pl. 231
Pl. 232
Pl. 233

Capitals were an integral part of Romanesque architecture and do not gain from being displayed in a lapidary collection or being converted into a baptismal font, much less as an object in your drawing room. The question of how many capitals there can be available for sculpture naturally hinges on the nature of the architecture as well as, of course, on the desire and the fiscal and artistic resources. Since it is the wall which typifies the Romanesque, as Von Simson has said,[163] then there could not be many columns. But we have seen how Romanesque developed from basilican wall to something at least as open as Caen and Durham. And in the process columns multiplied and there was ample opportunity on their capitals for sculptors who had anything to say. The question scarcely arose as to whether there was anything to say. There was so much to say. There were the conventional old forms of capitals, local leaves and flowers, beasts real and conjured from Pliny or the bestiaries, scenes of country life, the zodiac and works of the corresponding seasons, the virtues and the vices, historical events from Charlemagne to the latest Crusade, the lives of international and local saints, the stories of the Old Testament, the parables of the New, the birth, the life, and the Passion of Christ, scenes of the Apocalypse and the Last Judgment from the Revelations. Where these came from, how they were modified, interpreted, and portrayed over the centuries in medieval France has been brilliantly told in three volumes by Emile Mâle.[164] There could be no better preparation for a comprehension of Romanesque sculpture, and I am not going to repeat any of it here. The smaller scenes never got on the tympani and the larger ones were not limited to them. In later Gothic days a wider range of surfaces were available to the sculptors. In the French Romanesque, next to the tympani, the capitals were the most

---

[163] Otto Von Simson, *The Gothic Cathedral* (Harper Torchbooks, New York, 1964). Originally published by the Bollingen Foundation in 1956.
[164] Emile Mâle, *L'Art Religieux du XIIe Siècle* (Paris: Colin, 1924). The other volumes deal with the XIIIth century and the end of the Golden Age, respectively.

promising place. They were used most profusely in the central to southern parts of France, in Burgundy, Poitou, Auvergne, but only in Normandy were they sparse. There is some of this sculpture in Germany and England but not a great deal, only a little more (aside from the lions of Lombardy) in Italy, and the work was at its richest in France, for example, at St-Nectaire, Souillac, Saulieu, Issoire, Moissac, St-Gilles, Poitiers, Vézelay, Autun, Paray le Monial, St-Benoît-sur-Loire, Tournus, even early Germigny-des-Prés. This is, of course, not an inclusive list.

Any inventory of the "greatest" capitals in France must be personal and probably also not very useful. About the worst way, at least for a traveler, is to work through capitals, checklist in hand. It is better to browse with the binoculars and let serendipity fall where it may. So let this list simply note a few excellent ones to give some idea of their range and distribution.

Baalam and his ass—Nave of St-Andoche, Saulieu

First temptation of Christ in the desert—nave, Saulieu

Flight into Egypt, detail—south side aisle, Saulieu

Saint Martin—St-Benoît-sur-Loire

Raising of Lazarus—crypt, Saint' Isodoro, León

Acrobats—archivolts, Vézelay

The Last Supper—Issoire

The Mystical Mill—Vézelay

Despair—Vézelay

Legend of Saint Theophilus—Souillac

Eve—Autun

Suicide of Judas—Autun

Last Judgment—St-Nectaire

Works and Days—Baptistery, Parma

Miracle of the Loaves—St-Nectaire

The wheeled cart—Bronze door, San Zeno Maggiore, Milan

Temptation of Saint Anthony—Vézelay

Horsemen of the Apocalypse—St-Nectaire

Adam, Eve, and the Serpent—St-Benoît-sur-Loire

One other aspect of Romanesque carving not to be overlooked are the Last Judgments on the portals of Vézelay, Autun, Moissac, and Conques. The portal of Conques, representing the Last Judgment, is one of the most considerable monuments of Romanesque sculpture. It is in perfect equilibrium, with Paradise to the right of Christ and Hell to the left. In the center, and dominant as always in these compositions, the Christ Judge sits in a large aureole which is floating on naively sketched clouds and stars. But there is nothing naive about the nobility and gravity of his features, his beautiful beard and moustaches, or the fall of his hair to his shoulders. His raised right hand indicates Heaven, his lowered left Hell. The robe partly falling away reveals the wounds of the Calvary. Angels carry phylacteries with mottos of love and of condemnation; above, other angels hold the cross, an iron lance, a nail; others signify the sun and the moon. In the corners of this upper level two angels blow the trumpets of the Last Judgment.

On most medieval Last Judgments after the angels have blown their horns calling to the Judgment, we see on the lower ranges the dead lifting the lids from their tombs and moving toward the Judgment, some with gloomy foreboding, others with serene, even smiling, anticipation. This part is omitted from the Conques tympanum. Instead, we proceed at once to the weighing of the souls by Saint Michael flanked by a watching angel at his right and a devil at his left. In numerous Last Judgments, the latter frequently tries to weight the scales against the defendant by various tricks such as tossing a toad into the left-hand pan.

Here Michael is located just below Christ; he holds the balance of which we see no more than the pans, facing a demon. Behind him one of the damned is projected into the vestibule of Hell through a trapdoor, just as he would have been in a mystery play. But before we descend to the two vestibules, we should notice an unusual arrangement of people who have been consigned to Heaven or Hell and now occupy this upper register. To the right of Christ are all the great figures from the history of Conques, bishops, benefactors; at the left are anonymous denizens of Hell, and here the artist has filled every cranny with them, subtly indicating the punishments appropriate for the various sins.

In the lowest register at the lintel, an angel stands before the door of Paradise to receive the blessed who then pass into arcades carried by colonettes, in the center one of which Abraham holds the just souls in his bosom, a standard representation; at the left the devil stuffs the damned into Hell through the maw of Leviathan, pushing them (including monks) to the feet of Beelzebub, who assisted by demons, presides over the torments. Many of the sins are here symbolized: pride fallen from his horse, usury with the miser hanging from a tree with his money bag dangling from his neck. The condemned have their tongues torn out, their brains, their eyes, their shoulders; they are quartered, strangled, whipped, mutilated, kicked, disemboweled, roasted on spits, beset at every point by devils, toads, snakes—and through this, appropriate Latin inscriptions meander along the lintel: "The thieves, the liars, the deceivers, the misers, the ravishers are all condemned as well as the profligates."

Naturally the tympanum was often tempting to the Romanesque

sculptors and it was often occupied with Apocalyptic scenes from the Revelations. Nor was the Last Judgment ever far from the mind of a religious medieval man, Gothic or Romanesque. Nonetheless although scenes from the Last Judgment appear on capitals now and then and elsewhere too in Romanesque churches, they are seldom on the tympani as they are at St-Lazare at Autun (1130–1140). The other great tympani are devoted to the Christ as Judge to be sure, and a terrible one he is at La Madeleine in Vézelay (1104), where he is the Christ of the Pentecost charging the Apostles with their missions, while a benign one at St-Pierre, Moissac (twelfth century), where he is shown with the Evangelists and the twenty-four Elders. We cannot say indeed that large-scale subjects are general on the tympani of even the French Romanesque churches and particularly not the Last Judgment, which came into its own on Gothic west fronts, though not universal even there. So we need make no great detour here. Look for yourself at the tympani of Autun, Vézelay, and Moissac and in detail. They are as fascinating as Hieronymus Bosch and better composed.

Pl. 230

Pl. 234

Pl. 235

After the Norman Romanesque buildings of France, French architecture moved smoothly into the Gothic. By any absolute standard the Gothic has to be regarded among the two or three greatest periods of European architecture, whether religious, as I will emphasize here, or secular. In some it will arouse sentiments of admiration rather than affection, and even seem cold as compared with the simple, dark, more primitive, Romanesque. There will also be those who find Romanesque depressing, as well as those who, like me, find it the most moving of all architectures. But on the great scale of monumental, perfected architecture, and regardless of personal taste, all will have to agree that the classic Gothic wins hands down over the premonitory Romanesque.

GOTHIC

Looked at one way, all the ingredients necessary for Gothic had been illustrated at Durham, Caen, or Vézelay. Though not as simple as it sounds, all that remained was to put them together—but this would require desire and perhaps imagination. It is rare in architectural history that the new comes like a thunderclap, and it was not so in this case.

Nonetheless historians and, I suppose, the rest of us are happier when we can identify at least turning points, if not the dawning of new eras. Scholars argue gently about what was "first" Gothic. Some, for example, talk about the abbey church of Morienval, Dagobert's old foundation in the diocese of Soissons, which, around 1122, obtained the relics of Saint Annobert and rebuilt the sanctuary and east end to accommodate them; in the choir they did use a ribbed vault. And Morienval is in the Paris region where the greatest Gothic explosion occurred. But unless Gothic is only a vault rib, Morienval can be taken as nothing more than a precursor—in most respects it looks very Romanesque.

A much stronger case, and the usually accepted case, can be made for the abbey church of St-Denis, then just outside of Paris. This church is still standing and can be visited, but the once royal church of France is now in a sorry district and in sorry condition itself so that a sentimental journey is doomed to disappointment, and only scholars can read it against Abbot Suger's text, which is the most complete treatise on a Gothic building we have from a contemporary source.

The entire memoir has been brilliantly translated, edited, and annotated by Erwin Panofsky[165]and makes very good reading as revealing of one of the great and fascinating prelates of ecclesiastical history as of the building itself. In it you can find marvelous accounts of the quarrels between the proud and worldly Suger and the austere Bernard of Clairvaux, of the numerous miracles alleged during the construction, of the dedication of the church in 1140, and so on. This rich and ambitious abbot, the sage adviser of kings, was a dedicated officer of the church, no doubt, but an admirer of opulence and probably a snob of the first order.

He was trying to build and succeeding in building an innovative church which would surpass anything in Byzantium, and encountered all the usual objections in the fulmination of the Cistercian Bernard of Clairvaux.

> In fine on all sides there appears so rich and so amazing a variety of forms that it is more delightful to read the marbles, than the manuscripts, and to spend the whole day in admiring these things, piece by piece, rather than in meditating on the Law Divine.[166]

Some of his own monks criticized his lack of taste; his more sophisticated friends called the work ostentatious and flamboyant. There were those who objected to tearing down the old Carolingian structures, in the name of sacred tradition; and always there were those, including Saint Bernard, who shuddered at the enormous expense.

But Suger persisted and always defended his actions on the four same grounds: that the old church was simply too small and too much in need of repair; that he did not undertake the work until after due deliberation with the brethren; that he scrupulously saved as many stones as possible from the old fane treating them as though they were relics; and that the work must have been approved in Heaven in the light of the many miracles which attended its construction.

[165] *Abbot Suger on the Abbey Church of St-Denis and Its Art Treasures*, edited, translated, and annotated by Erwin Panofsky (Princeton, N.J.: Princeton University Press, 1946).
[166] Ibid., p. 25.

The abbey church of St-Denis stands at the crossroads of an architecture which in the century between Morienval and the great churches circling Paris was to become one of the finest the world has ever seen.

If we are not to visit St-Denis but wait to examine the monuments of the Classic Gothic, is it possible before making the main visit to see if we can establish the main principles of Gothic, about which, as you may imagine, some arguments have swirled?

There are first of all the Romantic views, a great confused idea of the total nobility of the Middle Ages expressible in Crusades, courtly love, chivalry, a benign feudal system, manuscripts, costumes, but particularly in cathedrals. Depending on who is writing this sort of thing, whether Ruskin or Henry Adams or Ralph Adams Cram, the Gothic turns out to be picturesque, vegetal, infinite, and much to be emulated in principle, if not in detail. It leads to the sort of statement made by Victor Hugo in *Le Jongleur de Notre-Dame*. *"Au moyen âge, le genre humain n'a rien pensé d'important qu'il ne l'ait écrit en pierre."* Thus the cathedral becomes the supreme book, even the encyclopedia, of the time through a combination of architecture and sculpture. There is something in this but not enough.

One can explain it in terms of functional planning. The clergy grows and becomes more demanding, and so the choirs must be enlarged (lengthened); the cult of relics becomes less important, and at the same time relics are placed at the altars instead of in the crypts; and once the crypts are abandoned the nave and choir can be at the same or nearly the same level; the important churches are now urban, not monastic, particularly in France, and so the needs of the lay parishioner must be reconciled with those of the clergy; the priests must pray seven times a day and should not be disturbed at their prayers, hence rood screens (screens dividing choirs from aisles), infringing even on the nave in England and Spain; the custom of putting women upstairs disappears and with it the need for wide tribunes, hence the narrow triforium gallery to replace the tribune or even the elimination of the gallery altogether; increase in clergy and in private devotions and ceremonies stimulates a demand for more chapels; the liturgical great processions call for weather protection, hence porches, even at the transept ends, a solution made more possible through the elimination of the cloister, which, at the same time, produces a proliferation of pendant sacristies, chapter houses, and so on. All this is true but it is not sufficient to explain or even to define Gothic.

A common way to get at it is to state it as a combination of critical structural elements, notably the vault rib, the articulated pier, the flying buttress, the elimination of the wall and the entering of light into the building, coupled with its manifest visual verticality.

Obviously we would not have Gothic without the vault rib, the distribution of thrusts, the subdivision of the vaults, and the independence of parts, but we must not press this too far. On the one hand, there are those who say it is nothing more than a visual formality, conveying the illusion that shafts and ribs are essential, while in fact they are quite unnecessary since the thrusts were already concentrated at the corners of the vault severy by groins and needed no further support.[167]

Certainly most critics would accept the functional view of Henri Focillon rather than the visual view of Pol Abraham. The argument can be found fully joined in Focillon's work on the medieval art of the West.[168] But that the rib is only structural is not Focillon's conclusion.

> The cathedral, however, was not a conception only. It was not an inference from the drawing board. It was an intellectual order, but it addressed itself to the sense of sight, and the vault rib also was intended to be seen. It replaced an apparently undifferentiated system, equilibrated by its mass and weight, by a complex visible skeleton, and relationships of light and shade which tended to become increasingly graphic. The germ of the linear architecture of the *Rayonnant* style was already present in Saint-Denis, Laon and Noyon. To disregard the part played by the formal elements—and the illusory effects—would be an error as serious as the definition of a building by its plan alone. The vault rib is *a constructional, a structural,* and *a visual* factor.[169] (Italics mine.)

At the decline of the Gothic it became almost exclusively visual.

The formeret or wall rib came early. The groined vault could work once it was built without transverse arches and so the arched rib could work without the formeret. But if you wanted a great deal of window above, as at Chartres, the formeret supplied an upper termination and had more than visual meaning.

The flying buttress came more slowly. The original equilibrium was like that of the Romanesque. Rib-vaulted tribunes opposed the arches of the nave with a system of lateral arches. In turn they were opposed by quite massive buttresses, often with several offsets. But this meant that the upper walls could not have large openings, and the critical points of main thrust were not adequately served by the tribune arches. First these were stiffened by buttress walls in the tribunes pierced by narrow doors. The invention was to conceive of this buttress in arch form, whether or not it was revealed.

> From that moment the structure was complete. The flying buttress rose higher with the naves, it met the thrusts at their point of impact, or rather it sought for it empirically or developed double flights, and linked them together like the spokes of a wheel. . . . These remarkable systems

---

[167] The view of the rib as the essential element of rational Gothic structure was held by Viollet-le-Duc and Choisy; that it was purely illusory has been advanced most sharply by Pol Abraham.
[168] Henri Focillon, *The Art of the West in the Middle Ages,* vol. II, *Gothic Art,* Jean Bony (ed.) (London: Phaidon, 1963).
[169] Ibid., p. 11.

of external struts, which are themselves upheld and counteracted by enormous free-standing buttresses, attained colossal development, so that the cathedral naves are surrounded by a kind of secondary volume, a sort of cage, in which both the oblique and the vertical directions are strangely stressed.[170]

And highly visible, too.

This opening up of the wall, the increasing ascendance of void over solid often thought characteristic of the art of architect Pierre de Mon-tereau, tended to reduce the structure to a system of arches and supports to a cage in which wall-masses gave way to windows, seen at its most extreme in the upper chapel of the Ste-Chapelle and in all the rose windows of the great cathedrals as a consequence. The cathedral now replaces its walls of stone with walls of light. Many scholars regard this as the greatest distinction between the Gothic and the Romanesque.

> But it was in this very triumph that the danger lay. Architecture must have mass, and it must even impress us, though not overwhelm us, with the evidence of its weight. The just ratio of solid and void had been overstepped. Everywhere that the wall could be replaced by the coloured light of stained glass, the wall disappeared. . . . Light falling from the transept triforium, light from the enlarged clerestory windows, light from the rose windows of the transepts—except for the rigid bone structure, the whole building is as if dissolved in light.[171]

While the early Gothic churches grew large and rose high, even to four stories (Arras, Laon, Paris), the emphasis was one of horizontality as though main arcades, tribune arches, galleries of colonnettes and cleres-tories were laid on top of each other, each strongly stressed, each of equal importance. But after the example of Chartres, the multiple stories were abandoned; great clerestory windows extended from support to support; tall arcades rose through the old tribune level; nothing remained between arcades and windows except a narrow triforium eventually absorbed. Now the interiors led the eye upward along the formerets to the vault ribs, and when to this was added the greater height of the naves as related to their ribs there is no question that the Gothic cathedral had verticality.

Ribs, flying buttresses, verticality, masonry cage filled in with light-transmitting glass; these are certainly all characterizers of the Gothic, but even these seem too limited as a definition. There is something more mysterious here, something ineffable. This leads us naturally to symbolic explanations.

Abbot Suger said, for example, that the twelve supports in the choir

---

[170] Ibid., pp. 12, 13.
[171] Ibid., p. 43. Not everyone would agree with Focillon's *obiter dictum* about mass and weight, e.g., Mies van der Rohe or R. Buckminster Fuller. It seems to me a good general principle applying to most architecture but short of being a universal.

of St-Denis stood for the twelve Apostles; and the twelve in the ambulatory for the twelve minor prophets, but nobody seems to have known this except Suger and Pierre de Montereau. Anyway two others were added presumably for architectural, not symbolic reasons. It is easier on the whole to give credence to symbols found in painting or sculpture than in architecture. For instance, the most obvious possible symbol in Gothic churches might be the cruciform plan, but the evidence is that that was not the reason for adding transepts. And though this symbol was about as powerful a one as could be found in Christendom, its significance being widely understood, it is hard to see how it could have been widely symbolic when it was so much suppressed or interfered with by other constructions in so many leading cathedrals. Laon is moderately cruciform; Amiens and Chartres can at best be called borderline cases, while Reims, Paris, Beauvais, Bourges, and Sens are clearly not cruciform at all. In our century a church architect used the fish, a strong Christian symbol, for his plans, but since no user ever sits in a position to look down on a plan, the whole idea seemed to need too much literary exegesis. There is a forest of writing about Gothic architectural symbolism, and I do not propose to lead you into it or through it or even very close to its edges. A certain suspicion attaches to any *ex post facto* explanations; and of course a symbol is not much use unless it is widely understood, something our contemporary artists, each hoarding his own private symbols, decline either to recognize or to admit. Surely the most credible of all these analyses, something a little different but definitely related to symbolism, is that provided by Erwin Panofsky, who has worked out a complete Thomistic system,[172] as though to demonstrate the validity of Gottfried Semper's epigram, "Gothic architecture is scholasticism in stone." You ought to read the whole closely reasoned and carefully documented argument for yourself, and I can only harm it by trying to summarize it here; let me instead pluck two or three points bodily and without the argument.

On this theory the multiform articulations of the Gothic cathedral are not accidental, nor are they merely those needed to make the building work technically. They required collaboration of artisans with a scholastic adviser. The latter defined the controlling principles according to those principles which reached their climax in the formal scholastic writing of Aquinas in the *Summa*. The first principle was *clarity*, involving a system of homologous parts and parts of parts, with sufficient articulation and interrelation of these parts. Certainly this principle does appear in the High Gothic and not in the Romanesque.

The second principle was one of *transparency*. Since pre-Scholasticism accepted the insulation of faith from reason by an impervious barrier, it was reasonable for the Romanesque to provide a space which was determinate and impenetrable whether you were standing inside or outside of

---

[172] Erwin Panofsky, *Gothic Architecture and Scholasticism* (New York: Meridian, 1957).

it. But while high scholasticism might sharply limit the sanctuary of faith from the sphere of rational knowledge, it insisted that the contents of this sanctuary be clearly discernible. So in the Gothic cathedral the interior volume, though still delimited from the exterior space, had to project itself *through* the encompassing structure. This was seldom a matter of literal transparency. It would do, for example, if the cross section of the nave could be read from the facade, and so on.

Totality implied for the High Gothic an effort to develop a perfect and final plan, which is why we can think, partly at least, of *the* Gothic Plan. For the iconography it meant that the church would try to become an encyclopedia of Christian knowledge—theological, ethical, historical, natural. In structure it implied a synthesis trying for perfect equilibrium and the elimination of elements which threatened it—thus, for example, the search for only tripartite naves, the uniform bay, or complete analogy between nave, transept, and chevet.

A third principle, that of *distinctness and deductive cogency,* limited the otherwise theoretically limitless fractionalization. The individual element had to establish its clear identity, shaft from wall or pier, vertical support from arch, and at the same moment have an unequivocal correlation with the other elements. Thus the "postulate of mutual inferability" meant in the classic doctrine not only that we must be able to infer the interior from the exterior but, carried to the extreme and in the mind of a knowledgeable person, that the cross section of a single pier would imply the organization of the whole system.

In examining this elaborate theory of the Thomist Cathedral, it must always be borne in mind that the *Summa* of Saint Thomas was not a rule book for Gothic architects. All the great Gothic cathedrals of the Île de France were well under way before the *Summa* appeared. To the extent that the French Gothic cathedrals were "scholastic," it is more a matter of *Zeitgeist* than of direct instruction.

Panofsky asks whether the Gothic style, measured by its own standards of perfection, fulfills itself only when the wall *is* reduced to the limit of technical possibilities if, at the same time, a maximum of "inferability" is reached. This might be so in the Ste-Chapelle. But many call Ste-Chapelle a betrayal of the highest point of Gothic, which they claim is found in the naves of Reims and Amiens.

All this, then, may be Gothic, the romance of the Middle Ages, functional planning to meet late twelfth- and thirteenth-century liturgical and congregational needs, a handful of critical structural innovations, reduction of the barrier of the wall, the suffusion of interiors with light, an aspiring verticality, a rich iconography essentially encyclopedic, many levels of symbolism, and even "scholasticism in stone." The ingredients manage to produce, at least in the North, and particularly in France, a style that is unmistakable and identifiable at a glance.

It seems to me unarguable that the supreme examples of the High

Gothic cathedral are all to be found in France and in a radius of about 100 miles from Paris.[173] This could be contested, I think, only by someone overly moved by provincial or chauvinistic feelings. It is not, perhaps, an accident that the Île de France should have been such a center. For one thing it was an area which had not developed an established Romanesque style of its own which would have had to be overthrown. Its experiments carried on in the narrow boundaries of the royal land could readily react upon one another. The great pilgrimages were dying away. The great abbeys were beginning to lose out to urbanism, although of course just as there were great Romanesque cathedrals so there were great Gothic abbeys, and indeed the first stage of Gothic art involved the abbeys from Morienval to St-Denis. But the future lay with the towns and the cities, with the bishops rather than the abbots. And although the Capetian monarchs had by no means consolidated the unity of their dominions or completely subdued the rivalries of Burgundy, Aquitaine, and Normandy, it was becoming quite clear that the Capetians were there to stay, that the royal city was to be Paris, which would be the first city of the land, and that the Capetian Île de France would be the leading province.

So absence of inhibiting tradition, proximity of communities, the rise of cities and especially of Capetian Paris, coupled with the increase of Capetian strength and the energy of highly competitive, albeit supportive bishops, worked to the one end.

Whatever the reasons, the consequence is clear. The French cathedrals are the greatest exposition of Gothic. The English bishops were too busy remodeling from one fashion to the next; the Germans dallied with the Romanesque too long; the Italians never liked Gothic anyway long before Petrarch and others had uttered contemptuous words about it beginning around 1350. Petrarch himself did not use the word "Gothic" but had a theory that everything good had come from Greece and especially from Rome, and that everything bad had come from "barbarians." This barbarian theory was adopted by the humanists, who held that architecture had been decadent from the end of the Roman Empire to Brunelleschi (1419). Filarete (1460) wrote, "cursed be the man who introduced 'modern' [i.e., Gothic] architecture. I believe it can only be the barbarians who brought it to Italy." Alberti talked about "rustic and coarse like the Goths."

[173] For example:

	Miles from Paris
Laon, 1160–1225	88
Soissons, 1160–1212	67
Paris, 1163–1235	—
Bourges, 1190–1275	141
Chartres, 1194–1260	60
Reims, 1212–1300	103
Amiens, 1220–1288	93
Beauvais, 1225–1568	49
Ste-Chapelle, 1244–1247	—

Then Vasari (1525) picked out the specific barbarians, coined the expression *"stile gotico,"* i.e., the Goths, ignoring the inconvenient fact that the great development had been in France.

To be sure these were all Renaissance men, but they did not have to fight hard in Italy for their revolution. Long before them the "Gothic" architects of Florence and Orvieto and Siena were demonstrating either that they did not understand Gothic principles or that they did not adhere to them. Gothic was simply not natural to the Italians even in its great days elsewhere in Europe.

In Spain the principles of French Gothic prevailed, though less purely, in such northern cathedrals as Burgos, Leon, and to some extent Salamanca, but from Toledo south the architecture was heavily overcast with Moorish influence.

The fact that the three largest Gothic cathedrals are those of Seville (1401–1520), Milan (1385–1485), and Cologne (1248–1880), is not really relevant to these conclusions. The distinction of these never equals their size and Milan and Seville are really very late while the main design of Cologne was not finished until 1880.

The Low Countries, following a path somewhere between German and French Gothic, provided splendid towers as at Tournai, but otherwise their most notable Gothic buildings were secular.

In France itself the greatest cathedrals all appeared in the narrow area described and over a brief time span from 1160 when Laon and Soissons were started to 1244 when the Ste-Chapelle began. The time stretch for completion was more varied, but except for Beauvais, which had a complicated history, and the Ste-Chapelle, which was finished in three years under royal urging, the time required for the main achievement of each cathedral ran around seventy-five years.[174]

There are many other interesting Gothic cathedrals in France: at Toulouse, at Rouen, Bayeux, Coutances, le Mans, Noyon, Strasbourg, and so on, and at Soissons and Sens in the orbit of Paris; but consensus focuses quite generally on a big seven: Laon, Amiens, Reims, Beauvais, Paris, Chartres, and Bourges. Is it possible to say that one of these is the greatest or even the most typical? Each has characteristics within the general style which makes it the most popular with one or another person. Mâle typified some of these cathedrals in terms of their iconography: Chartres the encyclopedic; Amiens the messianic and the prophetic; Paris the ubiquitous Virgin; Laon the erudite; Reims the *nationaliste*—French not universal, that is, catholic; Bourges the virtuous and saintly. These generalizations are really too broad, however convenient.

We shall say little of Laon with its atypical square Cistercian end, or of unfinished Beauvais. If we examine the plans of the remaining five side by side, Bourges and Paris in principle look almost identical. There are two

Pl. 238
Pl. 242

---

[174] Laon, 65; Chartres, 66; Amiens, 68; Paris, 72; Bourges, 85; Reims, 88; Beauvais, 343.

aisles on each side of the nave and all carry around the choir apse forming a two-aisled ambulatory. There is no transept as such, the naves have sexpartite vaults, and additional width has been obtained by building lateral chapels between the buttresses. At Paris the five apsidal chapels are also between the buttresses, while at Bourges the five apsidal chapels are semicircular and independent of the buttresses. Bourges has the correct five doors on the west front to reveal the nave plan, Paris violates the rule of transparency with only three.

Pl. 236

Pl. 239

Amiens and Chartres, though the latter is broader, have essentially the same elements. All the vaulting is quadripartite. There is only one side aisle on each flank of the nave, extending to make the ambulatory. Chartres has five radiating chapels, Amiens seven. Each has a clearly stated transept with north and south portals. In each the inner bays of the transept are extended for three bays of the choir, but at Amiens they stop at the apsidal chapel line, whereas at Chartres they carry around, forming with the nave aisles' extensions a two-aisled ambulatory. The Chartres plan is somewhat confused by the sacristy at the second north bay of the choir and the adjacent chapelle of Notre-Dame du Pilier outside the transept wall, and even more perhaps by the fourteenth-century St-Piat chapel southeast of the ambulatory. Similar additions occur at Amiens. The three west doors at Amiens are a clear scholastic expression of the interior plan; but at Chartres the provision of chapels under the west towers interdicts this and creates a serious imperfection as at Paris, if scholastic expression of transparency is to be taken seriously, or unless the narthex be taken as the thing to be expressed.

Pl. 237

Reims is very direct. The two side aisles of the transept are carried directly around the choir apse so that the transept is melted into the choir. The two side aisles of the nave are correctly expressed by the portals of the west front.

Now if we were to add to these minor differences other differences of comparable spread in sections, in rib and arcade details, in rose windows, and so on, it is evident that while all five are unmistakably Gothic, at the same time each is unmistakably itself.

That being so, which should be chosen for our walk around? The arrangement of Reims is too special. The broadening out of the eastern end was done because for so long it was the coronation church of France and this gave space for the coronation ceremonies. Moreover, though Reims may once have been "the shrine of religion, the pride of France and a treasure house of Art,"[175] it has been assaulted by the Germans in two wars and much mutilated thereby. The restoration has been skillful but you sense the mutilation just the same, and a visit to Reims does not seem to me to be the happiest one to be made in France.

Bourges is one of my great affections, but it is not quite typical

[175] Sir Banister Fletcher, *A History of Architecture* 17th ed. (New York: Scribner, 1961), p. 485.

enough with its extra aisles, its hexpartite vaulting, its two-leveled galleries, its clumsy west front (despite the great Last Judgment on the principal tympanum).

In popular terms surely one might have to choose Paris or Chartres. Paris is probably the best known. It has been more readily accessible to more people than any other of the big five. It is well located for viewing, the back from the Île St-Louis, the south elevation from the banks of the Seine, and the west from the controversial parvis created by Viollet-le-Duc, so that it is only to the north that it is hemmed in by a characteristically medieval ambiance. It has a noble appearance. And it has been well publicized by novelists like Victor Hugo, who did rather too much favor to the gargoyles in *Le Jongleur de Notre-Dame,* and more recently in Allan Temko's brilliantly written, extended, ecstatic essay, *Notre-Dame de Paris.*[176] It is perhaps partly because it is so well known that I do not choose it here. There is another reason. It is that, though the church of Maurice de Sully is very good in almost every way, it is never the best; its west front is surpassed by those of Amiens and Reims; its abside by that of Bourges; its towers by those of Chartres; its porches by those of Chartres and Amiens; its sculpture by that of Chartres, Amiens, and what is left of Reims; its stained glass by that of Chartres and Bourges.

Pl. 240

Chartres offers comparable questions. It too is amiably located and quite easily viewed. Except for tourists, its town does not press upon it. It has great serenity in its sculpture and great simplicity in its vault ribs, and, best of all, it has magnificent glass. It has also had a very good "press," headed, of course, by Henry Adams and his influential work, *Mont-Saint-Michel and Chartres,*[177] but aided by Samuel Chamberlain and other men of good will and honest sentiment. So without any statistics, I would guess that it is the second most visited cathedral of France—at least by Americans of good taste who would prefer it to the atrocious Sacré Coeur on Montmartre or the nondescript later vulgarities of Lourdes, and are not concerned about the redolence of history in St-German-l'Auxerrois.

Nonetheless, and again partly due to its familiarity and partly due to one or two real deviations from the Gothic norm, I have concluded not to use Chartres either. Notre-Dame d'Amiens has the greatest homogeneity of any of the five and is more expressive of the central principle of High Gothic architecture while offering adequate and sometimes superior examples of most aspects of High Gothic art. It has suffered little from the vandalism of internal revolutionaries and external enemies and no more than others the mutilating "embellishment" of the eighteenth-century canonical tastemakers. It does suffer more than Paris, Chartres, Bourges, and Beauvais from its drab urban environment.

[176] Allan Temko, *Notre-Dame of Paris: The Biography of a Cathedral* (New York: Viking, 1959). Copyright © 1952, 1955 by Allan Temko.
[177] Henry Adams, *Mont-Saint-Michel and Chartres* (Boston: Houghton Mifflin, 1963).

A WALK AROUND AMIENS

The history of French cathedrals of the Île de France, allowing for changes in the names of the *dramatis personae*, is much alike from cathedral to cathedral. An early church on the same site, possibly a Gallo-Roman work, is destroyed by the Normans. Not long after a Romanesque basilica is built. The one at Amiens was consecrated in 1152. The cathedral receives some important relics. Those at Amiens were very important. They were relics of Saint John the Baptist, found in the ruins of an old palace in Constantinople, brought and given by Walon de Sarton, canon of Picquigny, in 1206. They remained a cause for important pilgrimages well into the fourteenth century. Then the Romanesque cathedral burns up. This was before 1220 at Amiens, probably in 1218. Immediately they decide to rebuild and if possible to outdo the neighbors. The neighbors for Amiens were not only the neighboring episcopates of Paris, Laon, Noyon, Senlis, but also the basilica at Reims. There is always a bishop of high birth and great intelligence. For Amiens this was Evrard de Fouilloy. There ought to be an illustrious theologian at the head of the chapter. Here it was Jean de Boubers, alias Jean Allegrin, alias Jean d'Abbéville, who later became a cardinal and a confidant of Pope Gregory IX. There ought to be a talented architect who sometimes can be named. At Amiens it was especially Robert de Luzarches who planned it, and later Thomas de Cormont and his son Renaud.

And, of course, there had to be money—lots of it. Amiens at that time was a prosperous textile manufacturing and commercial center. The King, Phillip II (Augustus), nearing the end of his reign, was happy to be a principal benefactor. Then there were the powerful local seigneurs and the profits from the pilgrimages.

Amiens was abnormal, though, in that so much was done in one period ending not later than 1269, in other words, within the reign of Louis IX (Saint Louis; 1226–1270). The only exceptions were the last stage of the west towers and the roof covering of the nave, and the fact that the first flèche was of wood not stone. All this too was completed by the end of the century. This explains the unusual homogeneity of the cathedral.

Then, as everywhere else, things were added, almost never improving anything. Chapels were inserted between the buttresses in the fourteenth century when the west towers were slightly altered. There were various restorations in the fourteenth, fifteenth, and sixteenth centuries. In the early part of the sixteenth century, before the disasters of the Hundred Years War, the capital of Picardy was very prosperous, and great collections of art were conferred on the cathedral with a special society of friends and masters created to help along under the name of Puy-Notre Dame, which lasted until the Revolution. Among the great additions of this kind was the wood carving of the stalls (1490–1531).

As in most of the other cathedrals, Amiens had misguided friends in the eighteenth century who, at least at Amiens, left the architecture alone and lavished most of their bad taste on the furnishings.

The Revolution had no use for cathedrals, not even the much advocated Cathedral of Reason. But except for the treasure which was dissipated and which mostly disappeared, the melting of some bronze and copper fonts and tombs, and a few mutilations of the stone story of Saint Firmin on the north door by some volunteers from Lille, the Revolutionaries did little harm at Amiens, less than some of the early restorers of the nineteenth century such as Caudron, who replaced things gone with arbitrary fancies, although the brothers Duthoit treated the sculpture with an artistic sensibility very rare for the period. In 1849 Viollet-le-Duc came along. He may have been too absolute in his conceptions, although his laudable and overriding purpose was to strip the building of late additions and restore it to its original state. The changes for which he is most blamed are the arcade of the King's Gallery on the west front, changing much of the balustrades to more flamboyant detail, and the redoing of the top of the north tower. This is remarkably little damage to have done.

Some Kilroy kings and queens passed through Amiens now and then to be married, to receive homage, to ratify a treaty, to celebrate a recapture of the town from the Spaniards, and so on, but I will not plague you with these. They have left no scars on the cathedral, and it is not walked by the ghosts of Ingeborg of Denmark, Edward III of England, Charles the Dauphin, Joan of Arc, Isabel of Bavaria, Henri II, and Henri IV, the cardinal legate Alexander de Medicis, archbishop of Florence, or Henrietta of France, wife of Charles I of England.

Nor did the two wars on the Western Front have much effect. In the first one the Boches occupied Amiens so quickly and held it so securely and so decently that the cathedral did not suffer at all, though it was briefly threatened during the 1918 retreat until it was spared on the orders of William II of Hohenzollern.

In the second war it surprisingly survived intact among the great ruins of the town caused by the Luftwaffe's fire bombing of May 1940 and again by Allied bombing in 1944. So it has come down to us in wonderful condition, threatened now perhaps more than any time in its prior history by the pollution of industrial atmosphere which is steadier and less capricious than a Huguenot, a Montagnard, or even a Dr. Strangelove at the stick of a bomber under any flag.

Amiens is not an attractive city. It is all pretty gray and the cathedral does not loom up much from most of the quarters. There are quais on the banks of the Somme, whence the view up the slight rise to the north elevation ought to be better than it turns out to be. If you are stopping in one of the better hotels, which are marginally satisfactory, you may sleep quite near the cathedral but you will not see it; when you walk to it, you will come in at a south angle. So since the quarters are fairly narrow, not permitting a comprehensive view of the south elevation without ascending to some roof, you will make your way without much enchantment to the west front. But when you get there, you will face the greatest facade of any Gothic church in the world.

Pl. 243

We should look at this facade of Amiens the first time around in terms of its main elements only, and with a half-shut eye we can see that they are very clear and well related. Vertically two lateral sections flank a wider central section. They are clearly separated from each other by buttresses, and the buttressing is prominent enough when combined with the verticality of all the ornament and the sculpture to give the whole facade a clearly vertical cast. Nonetheless there are four horizontal levels, of which the second has two parts, so you might speak of five levels if you prefer. The first level and the tallest contains the portals which essentially fill it. The lower part of the second level is an arcade corresponding to the level of the triforium gallery inside and continuing it, so to speak, around the outside; the upper part of the second level is an arcaded gallery, the Gallery of Kings, with the statue of a king under each.[178] The statues of the kings are much larger than we would imagine; those of Amiens are more than thirteen feet tall, which gives some idea of the size of the whole facade. The third stage is that of the rose window, right under the vault of the nave and flanked laterally by a pair of arches in the towers; the fourth stage is that of the tops of the towers and the screen which connects them and hides the roof.

This facade has not escaped criticism. The gables of the side portals either conceal too much or too little of the sustaining arches behind them which brace the towers; the towers are rectangular in plan rather than square with the unfortunate result that though they look massive from the front, looked at from the sides they convey a little of the impression of an American Western false front. There was a reason for this, that of avoiding cluttering the nave with the necessary heavy supporting piers under the inner corner of the tower, so that once one has passed the portal he sees the nave without any sense of the towers inside. There are some alternatives in architectural design where compromise is not really workable and where choice of one diminishes the other. The towers were never really finished, and they have been criticized as not rising high enough above the nave to have achieved good proportions and not having been sufficiently disengaged from the facade.

But the principal criticism is leveled at the superposition of the two galleries below the rose, which bear down a little heavily. But the architect had a problem here imposed by the great height of the nave vaults.

Until Abbot Suger built St-Denis, the west facades had been pierced by normal shaped windows. But Suger adopted the round window, possibly excited by the example in the north transept of St-Etienne at Beauvais.

---

[178] The facades of Reims, Chartres, and Paris also each contain a Gallery of Kings, though not always in the same place—at Chartres at the very top, above the rose, at Paris right above the first level and just under the rose and running right across the buttresses, at Reims also above the rose.

The adoption was not easy. If you kept the diameter of the rose small, then you left an awkward space of wall beneath it and between it and the buttresses. If, as was more seemly, you made it as big or almost as big as the full width of the nave and therefore filled its stage of the facade from buttress to buttress, there were conflicts inside between its round shape and the ogival shape of the nave vaults; and outside, because you needed such a wide space between the end buttresses of the nave that you tended uncomfortably to narrow the space available for the side portals.

Beautiful as the rose is in form and elegant as it became in its tracery and its colored glass, this isolated circular unit did conflict with the general ideas of Gothic taste and ran directly against the idea that the facade should represent the interior.[179]

The architect of Amiens wanted a very high and narrow nave, and he wanted the rose window high, almost tangent to the ogive of the vault. For this he had to pay the price of a considerable band of wall below the rose and above the portals inside, and a way to treat the same expanse outside, for which he used the device of the pair of galleries, one superimposed on the other.

There is more to a rose window than its size and location. There are

---

[179] The Normans and the English with very few exceptions simply did not adopt the rose window; they merely enlarged a traditional lancet window until it filled the available space of the west wall of the nave. There are good examples at Bath, Winchester, Worcester, Westminster.

Pl. 240

The Italians already had brilliant examples of "wheel windows" from the Italian Romanesque in such buildings as the Duomo at Modena. So the Italians greeted the idea with enthusiasm and simply stuck the round window somewhere high in the facade (Orvieto, Siena, Santa Croce, Florence) abetted by the facts that sometimes the naves were not vaulted anyway and that they did not worry about how much a facade might be merely a mask.

Pl. 248
Pl. 247

But the architects of Picardy, the Île de France, and Champagne could not lightly abandon a motif sanctioned by the authority of St-Denis, nor could they lightly leave unresolved the question of exactly where to put it.

At Laon and Reims the choice was to put the rose low just above the portal. At Mantes and Paris it was to put it in the middle with one gallery intervening between it and the portals. At Amiens, Bourges, and Chartres it was put high, which was best for the interior, I believe.

Pl. 241

The middle-ground solution of Paris probably produced the best proportioned facade, but to make it work, the architect had to tell a lie by making a tripartite facade before a quinquipartite nave. This gave him lateral sections that were so wide in comparison to the middle section that most of the problems dissolved. The Bourges "solution" was clumsy. Chartres dismissed the problem by putting all three doors in the middle bay under the rose and getting the rose up high enough by imposing a story of arched windows a little taller than the portals between them and the rose. This too belied the expression on the outside of the aisles of the nave, but it did free the towers so that they became quite independent in plan as well as in appearance, framed the central element of the facade, and were finally tied together at the top by the Gallery of Kings.

Pl. 244
Pl. 246

What is often said to be the "final" solution was reached in 1340–1350 by the school of Reims on St-Nicaise. The rose was inscribed within the pointed arch of a huge window. This made the location of its center flexible. It could be lowered not to conflict with the vaults. The whole could reflect the cross section of the nave, yet the rose remained a rose. This solution, nearly English, was provided by Hugues Leibergier, and Panofsky calls it a genuine reconciliation of a *videtur quod* with a *sed contra*.

questions of the tracery, the colors of the glass, and the stories they may tell, all of which are more perceptible inside than out. But we should postpone this while we are examining main elements, just as we should say nothing more about the decoration than to note how remarkably well integrated it is over the whole facade.

The bounteous carving of the west front of Amiens is tempting, but for the moment, let us start going around the building.

Since we cannot easily see the side of Amiens clearly, let me not try to describe its south side but turn instead to Paris, which is the easiest French side to see and certainly as good as any. It was probably still stronger before chapels were built between the nave buttresses and also those of the choir, but these are a minor disturbance. The only serious disturbance is the construction east of the door of Saint Etienne. Otherwise everything moves harmoniously from the apse and choir of 1163–1182 past the great door of Saint Etienne opening into the transept (1250–1270) to the nave and west front of 1180–1200 in what is probably the handsomest south side en masse of any cathedral anywhere. You see the big divisions of the west towers, the seven bays and their separating buttresses and flying buttresses of the nave, the great south portal with its rose and gable. The nave and choir roof line itself and the roof area are, however, unifying factors of great importance accented at the back by the flèche at the crossing, the stretch of five bays of the choir, and then the curve of the ambulatory with its powerful double flying buttresses.[180]

These are the main elements of a south facade. The lateral buttresses of the west towers, the roof tiles, the balustrades, the compact buttresses of the nave, the far-thrusting buttresses of the abside, and the details and sculpture of the porch are matters for inspection later.

Now we ought to wander down to the abside of Amiens and then return to look at some of the details of the transept ends, either the north porch or the south porch or both as our taste in sculpture and zest for it might dictate. Before we leave the side we should look at the flèche. The flèche is small at the crossing of Paris, but it is even smaller at Amiens, in sharp contrast with the monumental and central spire of Salisbury. (Though none has aspired so high as Salisbury's spire, many English cathedrals have large ones at the crossing.)

Now if you were to follow my *ex cathedra* program of visit literally, we would have to go around the north side of Amiens and so back to the west front, where we would enter the cathedral. But I must be more flexible than that for my own purposes, and I know you will not let yourself be so rigorously bound anyway. An important thing on the way back will be one of the porches which are part of the facades of the transepts in fully de-

[180] The only competitors might be the south side of Amiens or the north side of Reims, but they are more complicated and less clear and much less easy to see. Despite the elegance of the north and south porches of Chartres taken by themselves, Chartres is still more cluttered.

veloped French cathedrals to the point where they offer most of the elements that are offered on the west fronts.

Sculpture is usually better when modeled by light, west fronts are better in afternoon, south fronts in the French latitudes at any time, and north fronts not very often, although some, like that of Chartres, cannot be missed. The end of the south transept at Amiens is considerably more interesting than the north, so let us go there. It is not really a porch as the north and south porches of Chartres are. It is, in fact, a facade of three parts framed by buttresses—in the first lowest part, the portal of the Vierge dorée; in the second, the middle, a pair of arcades and the rose window; in the third, the top, the gable. This will be the first time we have looked at a Gothic portal carefully, and it will save us time if we acquire a small glossary of terms. I have used some of these casually before, but it will help now to be more precise about them.

Portals are the major doors to a great Gothic cathedral, whether at the front (i.e., west) or lateral (at the north and south ends of the east transept). In general they play three roles aside from the obvious task of offering an entrance.

1. As an important part of the elevation working with other details, such as the King's Galleries, the rose windows, the gables, the screens, or the great lancets of England. Indeed in England that is about the only role they do play.
2. As things in themselves which can figuratively be plucked from the facade and examined separately.
3. As places to which sculpture could be applied, profusely in high French Gothic.

A west front might have as many as five portals, rarely fewer than three. The portal starts with a *plinth* or base of one or more levels. (A plinth may also be the base of a single element.) It then springs into an arch. The arch may take one of a great many shapes, of which an equi-pointed was customary in the French Gothic.

The springing does not occur directly from the plinth but from an intermediate columnar or pilaster arrangement, of which there are usually several. These "colonettes" may offer niches between them which can be filled with statues. If so, sometimes the statues stand on projecting supports, pedestals standing higher than the plinth and called *socles*, and may have a canopy over their heads, altogether forming a *tabernacle*, or the canopy itself may be so-called. Each colonette carries a deeply modeled arch arranged in a series of recessed planes corresponding to the recessing of the colonettes. These are called the *archivolts*. *Voussoirs* are any of the separate stones between the springing and the keystone of the arches.

The portal thus enframes rectangular doors usually paired. When paired, they are separated by a post called the *trumeau*. Above the doors is a flat area called the lintel. Above this, constituting the curved part of the spandrel between the archivolts, is the *tympanum*. All these elements and surfaces can be and usually are covered with sculpture. Along the plinths there may be abstract designs or a series of medallions: square, diagonal, round, trefoil, quatrefoil. These may contain a series of messages: works and days, virtues and vices, Biblical sequences, such as the life of Noah. The socles may be abstract or represent a symbol of the statue above or something it would be appropriate for him to tread upon, such as Saint George upon the dragon or Christ upon the lion, the aspic, and the basilisk. The large statutes are usually of a group: prophets, apostles, saints, Old Testament or New, arranged in a hierarchic order. The archivolts above may have floral carving or angels, archangels, and so on, in that case arranged in ascending hierarchical order from outside to center, or occasionally may carry spillovers from the story of the tympanum. The tympanum usually does tell a story in several layers: a Last Judgment, a scene from Revelations, the Assumption and Coronation of the Virgin, the life of a saint. The trumeau is reserved for a statue of the most important person on the portal: Christ, the Virgin, Stephen, or occasionally a particular local saint.

All this is carried on in enormous variety, not only of sculptural treatment, but of where things are located.[181]

This sculpture is all so marvelous that it is easy to get lost in it, and though I recommend that you do when you visit a cathedral, let us not do it here. Accordingly let me take you back momentarily to one by no means minor point of architectural detail—the profile of the moldings. If nothing else, they may help you to know what century you are in.

If we look now at the south facade of the transept of Amiens, we will note that it is well contained and well composed, but we may not like all the details. The gable end may have too many crockets, too many tabernacles, and some prominent vertical members which seem not to mean much. We may prefer simpler or more complicated tracery in the rose window. But if we look more closely at either of these, we may note something of further interest up in the tabernacles of the gable: eight people are ascending toward the height of the circle where a man is sitting with a dog at his feet. But the other eight are descending in increasingly dangerous positions, so that we have here a presentation of a fairly popular subject of the day, the wheel of fortune.

While we are looking at the rose window, which is flamboyant style and later than the main cathedral, we might reflect how the rose window really presents itself to us in two quite different guises—from the outside

---

[181] The statuary, generally executed before it was installed, was once entirely painted and gilded according to the current medieval practice. Moreover, some faintly visible traces of this coloring remain.

we are primarily observant of the design of the stone tracery; from the inside we are struck by the intensity, the quality, and the color of the light, and perhaps by the iconography as well.

Now our eyes drop down to the portal of the gilded Virgin. (Some of her gilt still clings to her.) She stands on the trumeau and is very famous or so became after Ruskin called her the "Picardy soubrette," but I think I do not like her very much. Perhaps she looks too smug or too sly, too worldly, too human, too coquettish. Beneath her in slightly recessed niches are bishops and other clerics bearing books, censers, candlesticks. Above her on the lintel are the twelve apostles. Flanking her in the four tabernacles on each side are two angels and six saints, mostly unidentified. There is a break in the continuity with which they reach the archivolts necessitated by the desire not to confuse the scene on the lintel with side issues, and then the archivolts take off for the peak. The carvings on these archivolts are very delicate and well worth scrutinizing, even if you are not fascinated by their subjects, which fall into one of four categories: (1) angels with censers or crowns; (2) scenes and people of the Old Testament metaphorically relating to the Messiah and involving such persons as Adam, Melchisidech, Noah, Isaac, Job, Moses, Aaron, David, Judith, and so on, each doing his familiar thing; (3) the four great prophets and the twelve minor ones of the Ancient Law with scenes from their lives or of one of their prophecies. The Old Testament figures run from left to right: Hosea, Joel, Amos, Obadiah, Jonah, Micah, Daniel, Jeremiah, Isaiah, Ezekiel, Nehemiah, Habbakuk, Sophonia, Hagia, Zacharias, Malachi. These ancient Jewish prophets are often seen on the French cathedrals as precursors of the Christ but also as "prophets of the ancient law." They are generally relegated as at Chartres to the north or cold and sunless side for symbolic reasons. (4) The fourth category is apostles, evangelists, and female saints. Some of these at Amiens have not been identified. The five registers of the tympanum, well carved but by no means telling as interesting or as familiar a tale, are mostly dedicated to events in the life of Sainte-Honoré, although the lowest register shows the apostles conversing in pairs as they set out to carry throughout the world their holy mission.

Let us now go back to the west front of Amiens to pick up a few other samples of cathedral sculpture before leaving the subject grossly unfinished. It cannot, however, be left out without leaving out something vital to the architecture. Frankl has tried it in his classic work on Gothic architecture, and I have seen students try it in their history drawings. But the omission is too crippling. The Gothic architectural sculpture is more than mere sculpture.

The great west triad of Amiens is splendidly framed and integrated *Pl. 243* by four buttresses of equal size, each ending in a steep crocketed pinnacle surrounded by eight smaller arrangements of columns and pinnacles on a small frieze. Again the spandrels of the paired blind arcades on the buttresses' quatrefoil openings reflect the quatrefoils which are used over most of the plinth; an array of statues standing on socles and under tabernacles runs all across the front, turning in at each door recess. At the doors themselves there are three statues on each side and three corresponding archivolts on the lateral doors and eight on the central door. All of this is free of a certain dryness that I detect, for example, at Paris. Like many other medieval sculptures it was painted and here, too, you can still see traces of the polychrome. Individual pieces are generally inferior to those to be seen at Chartres or Reims, but the ensemble is one of the best of the Gothic era. It was all done rapidly, in a single burst under one direction and inspiration in the period between 1220 or 1225 and 1236. It is very simple, the treatment in large planes, the clothes wide and simply draped. The left-hand door is dedicated to Saint Firmin, first bishop of Amiens, who appears on the trumeau in one of Amiens' most celebrated statues, and most of the surrounding iconography relates to him and kindred bishops and saints. The right-hand door is dedicated to the Virgin and bears her statue on the trumeau. She is quite stiff, even Byzantine, and better Virgins can be found elsewhere. Below her in the quatrefoils are scenes from the life of Adam and Eve, and these are of great interest as are other appropriate Old Testament scenes under each of the big flanking statutes which recall events of the Virgin's history: the Annunciation (the Virgin and Gabriel), the Visitation (the Virgin and Saint Elizabeth), the Presentation at the Temple (the Virgin and Simeon), the three Magi offering gifts to the Virgin on the trumeau, Herod dispatching the Magi, Solomon and the Queen of Sheba, the last because the Queen's visit to Solomon was often taken by medieval theologians to be a prefiguration of the visit of the Magi.

The tympanum has three registers: people of the Old Testament identical with those of the north door of the west front of Paris; the Death and Assumption of the Virgin; and the Coronation, which is copied on the tympanum of the north portal of Chartres. This tympanum at Amiens, like the other two here, is quite inferior in execution to the great ones at Bourges and Paris and Chartres. The voussoirs have angels, kings of Judea who were ancestors of the Virgin, and ancestors of the Virgin who were not kings.

Pl. 282

The most interesting of the three portals is the central one devoted to Christ, whose statue, "le Beau Dieu," is again one of the most famous of all the cathedral statues of Christ and justly so. It stands at the trumeau, and beneath Christ are the lion, the dragon, the aspic, and the basilisk signifying his triumph over Satan, Antichrist, the god of death and sin. The flanking statues are of the twelve major Christian apostles (Peter, Andrew, James, and Paul, John, Thomas, James the less, and so on), six to a side, and the four great Jewish prophets Isaiah, Jeremiah, Ezekiel, and Daniel, two to a side. The twelve lesser prophets also are displayed in threes on the faces of the buttresses. Finally the tympanum and six of the eight voussoirs are devoted to scenes from the Last Judgment.

Before stopping this inventory, I want particularly to call your attention to the quatrefoils of the plinth. We have already noted that those of the side doors bear relation to the subjects of the doors to which they lead. The ones at the great central door are by far the most interesting; they are unexcelled by any anywhere, even those at Paris, from which they were copied. I mention them so specifically because they are slightly below eye level and seem on a superficial quick glance to be merely decorative, and are often overlooked by visitors.

Here we find two series of quatrefoils. Those beneath the apostles, a dozen in number, show the virtues above and the corresponding vices below. The virtues are represented by women holding shields with a symbol of their virtues; thus Courage, a lion; Patience, a cow; Humility, a dove. Not all of these symbols are animals. Thus Faith has a calyx surmounted by a cross, Chastity a phoenix and a palm. Like almost all portrayals of the good in all times, these tend to be a little static and even dull. On the other hand, the corresponding vices below, figures in action, are full of excitement and interest. A cowardly knight runs from a rabbit; Rebellion shows a young man raising his hand against a bishop; Pride shows a man falling from his horse.

The other set of the main portal beneath the prophets not unnaturally contains scenes from their lives, but they are less interesting to me than one final group at the Saint Firmin portal where the Christian Georgics, or the works and days, are portrayed also in a dozen pairs, one pair for each month. Above, the signs of the zodiac are used, often very gaily; below, an appropriate human activity is shown, usually that of a peasant. Under the Pisces of February, a man warms himself before a fire and grills a fish; under the Ram of March, he cultivates a vine; under the beautiful Gemini of May, he sits beneath two flowering trees; beneath the Lion of July, he harvests the grain. It offers great pleasure to examine each of these in order (and perhaps even to photograph them) and later on to compare them with their opposite numbers on other cathedrals.

Here we finish a cursory leafing of the sculptured encyclopedia of Amiens, to which there are comparable collections at Paris, Reims, Chartres, and Bourges. No one cathedral has a monopoly on the best.

But it is time to go inside the Cathedral of Amiens, for there is what it is really all made for.

The raison d'etre was, of course, the high altar that stood in the sanctuary or presbytery of the choir. This is why the choirs were so often built first.

In the French cathedrals one can circle around and behind the sanctuary, using the side aisles and the ambulatory, and this is the situation at Amiens. Our view of the interior begins with the uninterrupted sweep from narthex to altar made possible when the canons tore down the jubé (see page 416). (The old glass of Amiens, which would have changed the light and color effects so much, has unfortunately disappeared, and so the light is of

Pl. 267

one quality.) Amiens' grandeur is certainly partly a matter of its enormous height, accentuated by the articulation of the piers so very vertical in their aspiration and starting clearly from the ground, as I think they should, and as they do also at Bourges, definitely do not at Paris, and do not very explicitly and categorically either at Reims or Chartres.

But by now we have talked enough about studying a bay so that you should be able to look at a bay of Amiens to see how it works and to compare it if you will with a bay at Chartres, Paris, Bourges, or Reims—to note how high the triforia are in comparison with the clerestory and the primary arcade, and what the effect of this is, especially in the extreme examples of Paris and Bourges or the middling example of Chartres. And you can do the same thing with the arcature and the treatment of the aisle and clerestory windows—as much as you like. But we are not going to do it here. Drawings of a typical bay of each of the five when juxtaposed will make it instantly clear why Amiens is the aspiring one, although it cannot add the additional verticality produced by the narrowness[182] and the height of the nave, transept, and choir.

Pl. 261

But you need no such intellectual guidance. You can see all this upthrust the minute you enter the nave. It cannot be long before your eyes will irresistibly be drawn upward to see the culminating glory of the cathedral, the high ribs of the vaults. The appearance of a single quadripartite bay is exciting, but when you move down to the choir and see one or more of these stoutly diagonated rectangles in juxtaposition to the vaulting of the crossing or to the six radiating ribs of the choir, you have seen the apogee of the architecture of the cathedral.

A great many Gothic choirs were outfitted with wooden stalls in their west parts. Usually there were two rows on either side, the upper for the canons or their vicars, the lower for the choristers. Two or three return stalls against the jubé were reserved for higher ecclesiastics. In England, at least, each canon or his deputy had to read the part of the psalms set on a tablet in his stall. Each stall had a tip-up seat or *miserichord* and an arm rest; on the under side there was a projecting ledge to permit a half sitting position so that the clergy could more or less comfortably comply with an ancient rule that enjoined standing during offices in the choir. The wood was always a fine one like oak or chestnut and the carving often very skillful and beautiful, or humorous.

The stalls at Amiens are among the finest in the world, considerably younger be it said than the cathedral since they were all executed in the decade between 1508 and 1519. Some of the carving is purely floral, geo-

[182] It is actually not narrower than the others; it only looks so. Key dimensions are:

	Width of nave, feet	Length of nave, feet	Height, feet
Paris	40	433	117
Chartres	49	433	122
Reims	55	462	127
Amiens	55	445	141

metric, bearing symbols of royalty or the church. But much more of it deals with religious and secular subjects, the same stories of the Old Testament, the Nativity, and later events in the life of Christ. These were often carried over on to the arm rests and the miserichords in the French cathedrals. One at Amiens, for example, shows Joseph hiding the cup in Benjamin's sack. Another, also from the life of Joseph, shows him at the feast prepared by his brothers. Of equal vigor are the building of the Tower of Babel or one of the sacrifice of Abraham.

One thing that is to be noticed in these woodcarvers' scenes is that they have a much more lively feeling of ordinary human life than was present in most of the stone carving. If Noah can be shown gloriously and happily drunk and no doubt modeled after one's neighbor, it would not be much of a step to put an apothecary or a notary at least on a miserichord, to become jovial or satiric about the subjects, to indulge in caricature and ribaldry or even gentle pornography. Some of this happened in France, but it was developed with even less restraint in England where, taken together, the miserichords offer a quite complete picture of ordinary life in the Middle Ages—of ploughing, sowing, reaping, of sports, of trade, of strange creatures from the bestiaries, of domestic scenes, pleasant and unpleasant, serious and whimsical. It would obviously be impractical to try for a catalog of the best of these, Romanesque or Gothic, but you can while away many happy hours turning up the seats to see what is there. I know you can find very good ones not only at Amiens but among the 2,000 or more that are known to exist in England, of which 700 or so are in the cathedrals, and some of which have been discussed already.[183]

WEST FRONTS

In looking at great French west fronts other than Amiens, you will perhaps note that Reims has much more elaborate decoration and wonder whether the extra gable ends and the half tourelles that rise above them are not unnecessarily fussy, whether the snaking of the King's Gallery around all the projections is such a good idea, although the location of the gallery is superb, and you may wonder whether the rose is not really rather suppressed in its low position; but you can hardly let these reservations blind you to the magnificence of the whole composition.

Pl. 241

If you prefer sobriety, you are obviously going to be much happier at Paris or Chartres. The elevation of Paris is most explicitly clear despite the fact that the Gallery of the Kings runs right across the buttresses. The rhythm of the four horizontal stages is appealing. The great width of the

Pl. 244

[183] Of these, one of my favorites is the tale from Chester of the knight who has seized a tiger cub and laid it across his saddle. He is pursued by the tigress, and to delay her he drops mirrors on the ground. When she sees herself in a mirror she takes it for her cub and stops to lick it, and so the knight escapes. This is a warning to a Christian not to let frivolous temptations or delusions divert him from his quest for salvation.

side bays, making an almost equal division into three parts, and the way the towers above the sides ride free are very pleasing as long as you can forget, and doubtless you should, that in scholastic terms it is a blatant lie.

Pl. 246

At Chartres, saving the top part of the north tower, the simplicity is even greater. I myself find it neither admirable nor appealing, with a good deal of failure in integration of details of the towers with those of the central portal section and something unhappy about the triad of arched windows below the rose. On the other hand, if you are primarily a tower man, you may be happy to see the towers of Chartres so prominent and such independent members of the facade, not only framing the central portal elements but actually dominating it, even though historical circumstances have made the two towers quite unlike and one much superior to the other.

In England there is no such thing as a typical west front, since even the enlarged lancet window is to be found on only a few of the churches. The most noteworthy of these are no doubt Rochester, Westminster Abbey, Canterbury, Norwich, Winchester, and York. Westminster is quite French except for the lancet, the screenlike portal, and the ascent of the towers, but lacks zest. Much the same can be said of Canterbury. Norwich

Pl. 240

is little but window. The Winchester design is exceptionally weak, York is the finest, but if the enormous west lancet were replaced by a row of kings, a rose, and a gallery, only the big lancets and the fine towers would tell you that you were not in France.

The most interesting English Gothic facades follow rather vagrant ways and are to be found at Ely, Peterborough, Lincoln, and Wells, where they are all in effect screens.

Ely might have been quite imposing if the north half had not been destroyed. A Galilee porch stands in front of the enormous west tower, and flanking west transepts lead at the south and did lead at the north to a pair of rounded towers at each end.

Pl. 245

Peterborough is very forceful. It is really a superb triple-arched deeply recessed Gothic portico of colossal dimensions flanked by two narrow towers, with the side arches wider than the central one, producing a rhythm something like 2:4:3:4:2. But it also has a horizontality reminiscent of several other important English "screen" facades (Lincoln, Wells, Exeter). But here the whole wall is the screen. Although the flanking ogival frames are wider than the central one, the springing line is the same, so that the side ogives are flatter, just as their crowning gables must be if all three gables are to peak at the same level. The effect is marred by a rather trivial porch of clumsy proportions and unfortunate detail installed in front of the central ogive. The central recess is indeed so narrow that the impression is one of a most effective duality, save for the wonder why the designer, obviously no Thomist, elected to reverse the actual dimensions of the nave and the side aisles. But the cavernous shadows *are* dramatic and the whole facade *does* have cohesion.

Pl. 253

Lincoln's famous west front is especially well composed and especially strong. It is essentially a composition of an enormous several-storied blind arcaded screen terminated by tourelles at the edges, pierced by an enormous ogival portal running full height, capped by an arcaded gable, enclosing also Norman doors of normal height, and flanked by two deeply recessed and tall recesses capped with semicircular arches. The flow from austerity to luxurious arcading is well managed, and the whole is climaxed by the two great towers which rise behind it.

Ripon is early English of an excellent austerity. Two large square battlemented four-storied towers flank a wider central section with a gable. The tall ogival arches in the center are five in the main two tiers and three in the gable. The second tier is taller than the first (also in the towers) so that the arcades become more elongated as the eye rises. One could look on the ten lancets of the center as a window of ten lancets, of which the lower five are of identical height and the upper rise to the center to follow the contour of the nave ceiling. This is how Canon Wilkinson would like us to see it.[184]

Then it can be interpreted as an older relative of the famous "Five Sisters Window" in the north transept of York Minster. Both were indeed built by Archbishop Walter de Gray. But the ten separate lancets of Ripon are quite widely spaced and there is no framing element to contain them all. Moreover the York window has five lancets, only a single row, of the same size, and these are attenuated to a marked degree. According to a seventeenth-century print, which does not look very reliable, the Ripon towers once had enormous and ugly spires which were removed as a precaution in 1664 after the fall of the spire on the central tower in 1660. Fortunately for Ripon they have never been put back, although it does produce an effect vaguely un-English, which even more vaguely recalls some of the Cistercian results in Germany.

Perhaps the most interesting of all the English west fronts is to be found at Wells. The facade has gone beyond a screen to become a gallery of tabernacled sculpture, for which the best theologians at Wells were instructed to set out the stories the sculpture was to tell, to name the saints who were to be represented, and to order their position. The north and south towers were located so as to increase the width of the screen and designed to contain tabernacles of their own. The width of nearly 150 feet is divided into five unequal divisions by six enormous buttresses with three superimposed tabernacles on the face and sides of each.[185]

Pl. 250

The two buttresses nearest the center support the nave arcades. The pairs of buttresses on the sides, extending higher than the nave buttresses,

---

[184] Canon W. E. Wilkinson, B. A., *The Pictorial History of Ripon Cathedral* (London: Pitkin, 1965), p. 20.
[185] All these tabernacles manage to house nearly 400 figures: the Lord, the Apostles, the nine orders of angels, the Resurrection groups, martyrs, virgins, saints, confessors, kings, bishops, warriors, scenes from both Testaments, many VIP's such as Solomon, Becket, or the Queen of Sheba.

are supports for the towers, which also have lateral buttresses, thus further extending the width and providing further tabernacles. This whole rests on a solid plain plinth rising to the height of the aisle doors. The central portal is twice as high but still low by French standards. Above the plinth and reaching high above the central door is a band of gabled niches or framed windows. Then the verticality takes charge, emphasized between the buttresses by paired elongated Gothic arches and in the center by three elongated lancet windows, and particularly by the buttresses themselves.

Even a superficial study will show that there are enough common features among the facades of the great French cathedrals so that we can reasonably speak of a "French" facade, while in England there is so much diversity as to make this impossible. Are we to explain this diversity of forms by some vagary of the English temperament incapable of constructing architecturally as rationally as the French? There is something in this no doubt, but it is not enough. Nor is the also defensible view that the English have on the whole been more successful in the use of words than in the visual arts, including architecture. But there was probably more to it than that.

The French cathedral was becoming urban, communal, unmonastic, unprivate, standing among the people in the crowded street. It should appear to welcome all; the west front and the majestic portals were intended to offer a splendid invitation to enter the House of God.

In England, on the contrary, the cathedral still stood in a walled precinct; it was still principally a church for the chapter, not a fane for the people. Laity other than pilgrims might even be regarded as intruders. That is why so many of the facades are unimportant. Monks themselves seldom enter by the front door. When facades become protective screens, there is little reason to try to indicate the internal order behind them.

If there is a good characterizer for the best English cathedrals, it is in the composition of the masses dominated by powerful and usually high central towers in a way only distantly related to the continental types. Now the screen can be distorted or stretched at will. At Peterborough the towers are minimized to enhance the portal; at Lincoln the portal is nothing but a vast frontispiece for the towers.

In Spain the most interesting of the west fronts is undoubtedly in Burgos, in northern Spain. It clearly starts out from French premises, but the great openwork spires are in the spirit of the German Gothic and indeed were executed by a German, Hans of Cologne. The paneling and the tracery are all elaborations from the north. It does not show the decorative forms of later Spanish Gothic, *Estilo Plateresco*, or silversmith style, of the mid-fifteenth to mid-sixteenth centuries, although there is some inside. Plateresque is, of course, purely decorative, lacks any architectonic quality, and is a melange of Moorish, flamboyant, and other late Gothic forms plus intimations from the Renaissance. If you care for this sort of thing, and it certainly has some weird attractions, you probably ought to go to Valladolid and see the main doorway of San Pablo which goes from *Pl. 252* ground to gable in one vast leap of decoration, flanked by two absolutely plain, well separated, and not very high towers. But Burgos is the more beautiful, the more romantic, and surely the greatest piece of Gothic architecture to be found in Spain, where much is baroque.

German Gothic is even more dominated by the great spire than English is. There are, naturally enough, a considerable number of German Gothic churches which look like less good French; and the Romanesque traditions persisted well into the Gothic period in Germany. Among the outstanding Gothic cathedrals of Germany, the west front of Ulm is in *Pl. 254* effect only a single marvelous tower-spire. Another dramatic west front in Germany is that of the Cistercian Abbey of Chorin (1273–1334). The great verticality, the powerful shadows cast by the buttresses, the attenuation of the three narrow central windows, the general austerity and even sparseness of the decoration and the quality of the brickwork all add to a handsome, even solemn, monumentality, possibly more reminiscent of the Romanesque than of the Gothic. Not all this may have been a matter of choice. The Cistercians began by having an austere attitude toward architectural expression. Stone was scarce in North Germany, and the choice of brick may have been a forced one. It is not easy to do intricate carving in brick even if one wants to, while the North German architect-masons either could not imagine or did not desire to perform the tricks with bricks which were taken for granted by the masons of Islam. At any rate the slender unrelieved buttresses, the low-relief blind arcades, the blind rose with its three inserted cusped circles, a few string courses, a good many crocketed gables and roofs combine to make this simple building far more interesting than its detail or its history would suggest.

THE PROBLEM OF SEEING A GOTHIC BUILDING

We have already referred to the problem of seeing the west front or, for that matter, any other part of the exteriors of most French Gothic cathedrals. The reason we can see the front of Paris well is because Viollet-le-Duc cleared away a lot of ancient if unimportant buildings so that a good view was possible; some had been cleared away earlier on grounds of sanitation and crime prevention. The reason you can scarcely see Strasbourg or Bourges at all is because the old buildings still stand on the other side of the street. The question is, was Viollet-le-Duc right or wrong? A man like Arthur Clennon in *Little Dorrit,* whether he was or was not interested in Viollet-le-Duc's reason, might well have approved simply because, like Nathaniel Hawthorne, he abhorred the past, and when describing one of the great streets of "melancholy stateliness" at the top of Oxford Street, wished them silently all down.

On the other hand, no architecture is fully seen out of its ambiance, and for historical architecture this produces some dilemmas. We can feel sorry for the blindered aesthete who is able to go to Ry-o-an-ji and see only the nine stones while ignoring the uniformed but giggling and many more than three little girls from a Japanese school; or the Hall of Justice at Chandigarh, oblivious to the squatting beggars. But these are contemporary situations. What is one to do about retaining an ambiance from the past around a distinguished historical building? Auguste Renoir thought that Viollet-le-Duc was wrong to have torn down anything. But he started by disliking architects in general (many painters at least mistrust them), and in particular he disliked Viollet-le-Duc. His dislike was so unreasoned that once he nearly vacated a most desirable apartment which he had located only with difficulty when he discovered that one of its facades fronted on the Rue Viollet-le-Duc. He was very angry at Viollet-le-Duc for tearing down the buildings on the Ile de la Cité to create the parvis of Notre-Dame, but not because a parvis had been made such as no man of the Middle Ages had ever seen. He was not interested in that lapse from historical truth. What he regretted was the consequent "absence of life" which thus came about.

But did it thus come about? This great painter, loving life, would never have lived in one of the old buildings or stayed there for longer than the picturesque moment demanded before he headed for the boats of Batignolles. And this was not unreasonable. The buildings that Viollet-le-Duc tore down were foul and the life lived in them was impossible for those who lived there. At most Viollet-le-Duc destroyed a visual reminder of the Middle Ages in which the life bore no resemblance whatsoever to the life of Paris in the days when Notre-Dame was made by Bishop Maurice from Sully-sur-Loire. Should he then have kept the buildings, cleaned them up, installed apple-cheeked and honest boys and girls in the costumes of pimps, prostitutes, cutpurses, innkeepers, clerics, and students to help out the tourist photographer on a sunny day? Should he have found a way to establish a new Villon, as poet-in-residence? This would have been a travesty as serious as those of Williamsburg or Sturbridge Village. Yet when the houses came down, a little of Notre-Dame came down, too. Obviously the problem of retaining an ambiance for historical architecture, unless everything around is quite good and worthy of saving in its own right, is thorny.

In fact, there are not many clear views of the sides of Gothic cathedrals. Even the secular architecture was seldom freestanding, although the manor houses set in country parks are an exception, or occasionally a small installation like the Market Hall in Ledbury Square can be seen in the round. However, many, whether guild houses, burghers' houses, or town halls, offer no exterior to see beyond a facade; a few have a corner position (Louvain) and thus show a front and a side; in such cases the side is normally in the same style as the front without the emphasis of entrances, and its inspection does not add much to the experience. An exception is the Doges Palace in Venice.

The cathedrals pose the same problem. Except in England, they were generally urban. Stemming from the Middle Ages they were generally in a cathedral square of some sort, but this was usually not large, while the buildings were. It was therefore hard to get far away from the long side before being arrested by buildings on the other side of the street so as to view the side as most facades may be viewed (exceptions are Strasbourg and Bourges). Consequently most of the photographs you will see of cathedral sides are deceptive. Look at them closely and you will see that the position of the camera is high so that the picture has been taken from another building and some distance perhaps more than a block away with a telephoto lens. If you could locate such a vantage point, and beg access, and be provided with telephoto or binoculars, you might then examine the side facade. This is hardly a "real" "fact of life" position, and the side facade viewed as a whole may well not be that rewarding.

There are a few exceptions in France and more in England. Albi is on a hill above a river. Bourges is open all around. Amiens is very tight except from the northwest. Paris and Chartres are easy from the south, especially Paris, thanks to its location on the Seine, and half of the north of Chartres is open; Reims and Soissons are possible from the north, and Laon for two-thirds of its stretch.

On the face of it, the English monuments should be more approachable because most of them are set away from the town, but here the various other clerical buildings and closed precincts do not make matters as easy as one might expect them to be. The north side of Salisbury is readily approachable by a diagonal path across common land, but the west half of the south side is covered by the plumberies, cloister, and garth (an eminently appropriate thing since the viewing of sides as facades is not a primary purpose for the building of a cathedral), and the east half of the south side can be viewed only from a distance and over the rather high walls of the school. Lincoln is quite satisfactory especially at the north; York is quite cramped. Wells is generously viewable except from the rear, and so it goes. But even when I say generously viewable, it seldom means that the panoramic view is possible. For the most part one must be content to prowl among the details, often quite exciting or even of major interest but to be put aside until later in this account. Moreover, with a little politeness and resourcefulness one can sometimes be allowed briefly into private quarters whence more is to be seen.

But the failure to be able fully to view many of the Gothic sides is less penalizing than might appear. As we have noted in the Romanesque, sides are not designed as facades. They come much more naturally from the plan and are less likely to be seriously dressed up to conceal it. The plan is asymmetric which in itself is not bad, but asymmetric designs to be successful must still convey some impression of equilibrium by the proper placing of weighting elements. A great central tower might be such a weighting element. But the central tower is not located where it is in order

Pl. 251

to punctuate the facade of the side. Instead it has to rise over the crossing and therefore must be over a transept which again was not located with the equilibrium of the side elevation in mind as a main consideration. Finally the ends of the French churches are usually absidal so that that part of the side elevation (east end, for example, of the south side) curves away amid a web of flying buttresses. The English churches with their square ends would in theory offer a better chance to close the side elevation, but again this was not a prime consideration in designing of the retrochoirs and the lady chapels.

Pl. 249

It is rare, therefore, that a contemplation of one of these sides, even when possible, is a major experience in itself. It should be tried, however, as part of a complete understanding, and it may be the most revealing evidence on the site of what the plan is.

TOWERS

The fact is that in the evolution of French cathedrals the central tower over the crossing was not a major feature of design, but only a punctuation mark. Thus at Amiens the flèche, though elegant, achieves its elegance through style and not by size. Such towers as were important in the French Gothic were normally only a special sort of buttress on the west front. The towers of the west front of Amiens rise barely above the facade itself.

The freestanding campaniles which I have already mentioned had only to take care of their own internal structural problems. They needed walls thick enough to carry their own weight and that of any floor; they needed to be broad enough so that they could not be tipped over by such lateral force as the wind might generate. And they needed to rest on foundations which would not permit them to settle indefinitely or to settle unevenly. Often the latter condition was not met. The leaning tower of Pisa is but the most spectacular example of an inclination from the perpendicular due to subsidence, but there are countless other examples, such as the tower at Modena, which is noticeably out of plumb.[186]

But the problems of the isolated tower are relatively simple. They begin to mount when the tower is attached to a building and asked to serve nontower purposes, for example, as a buttress. They reach a crescendo when there is an attempt to support a large tower not directly on the ground but high up in the air using other members to get the weight and the overturning moments safely down to terra firma. This is the problem of a high tower over the crossing.

You will remember that the interior arches of a vaulted structure counter-balance each other's thrusts just as the cross-vault ribs do. But the arches which come to the end of the building or its side do not meet a counter-

---

[186] There are other reasons for tipping, for example, earthquakes or disturbing of the supporting layers of earth by later construction nearby.

vailing force. At the sides this is provided by lateral buttresses, whether solid or flying. This can also be and sometimes was the solution at the west end. But developments led to some replacement of the west end buttressing by paired towers. In some special Gothic situations, mostly but not always late ones, a single tower could stand at the west end of the nave and serve the same purpose, although this required either additional buttressing at the edges as was provided at Ulm or a very heavy west wall such as existed at Albi. The ends of the transepts offered a similar problem, of course, and many plans were made for substantial towers at the ends of the transepts which, at Laon, for example, provided seven towers altogether (two on west front, two on west and two on east transepts, plus one at crossing). But these schemes were rarely realized and the transept towers are normally less conspicuous than those of the west front. This points up a principle. A tower acting as a buttress would need to be heavy enough one way or another to withstand the thrust of the arcades without tipping over. The fewer the openings, the more solid the construction of the tower, the less tall it would have to be. But another principle was taking hold, a principle not of engineering but of aesthetics. The towers were to act not only as buttresses, perhaps not even principally as buttresses, but as a centrally significant component of the facade, and, if high enough as a beacon of God, across the countryside.

Nothing could make this clearer than the will of Louis d'Amboise in 1485. By this time the Cathedral of Ste-Cécile in Albi had been standing securely for almost a century. Its squat west tower had held the building secure. But he wrote as follows:

Pl. 256

> Je veux et j'ordonne, dit-il, que l'on fasse un pinacle, c'est-à-dire une tour
> où l'on placera les cloches. . . . Comme il est fort nécessaire qu'il soit
> visible à *tous les yeux*, il s'élèvera de vingt-cinq cannes au-dessus de
> l'édifice.[187]

Thus three new stages were added to the three of the old for quite strictly visual purposes. The extreme of this was reached at Ulm where a magnificent openwork western spire attains a height of more than 529 feet.

Of the six great cathedrals of France, only Chartres has blatantly noticeable towers. Those of Amiens barely rise above the top arcade of the west front; those of Bourges are nondescript. The towers of Paris rise only slightly higher above the facade than those of Amiens. The towers of Reims do run higher and are an integral part of the facade. Take the spires off Chartres and they would be in about the same relation as those of Reims. There has been much speculation as to whether spires were intended for the others; if so and if built, the impression would have been very different. But as things are, we must stay with what we can see. Sav-

---

[187] Jean Laran, *La Cathédrale d'Albi* (Paris: Laurens, n.d.), pp. 39 ff.

ing Laon and Bourges the west towers of the great French cathedrals are integral parts of the facade framing the central bay and the rose window and in every case making their principal contribution in this integrated way. At Paris, Amiens, and Reims they are, in fact, so integrated that they are part of the portal arrangement at ground level.

Essentially similar arrangements exist in those English churches which roughly followed French arrangements, such as at Ripon (very low), York (moderate), and Westminster (very tall), although in the English cases the framed center features an enormous ogival west window, and at Westminster and Ripon there is no portal in the towers. But generally speaking the English tower arrangements are very special partly because the English facades which were screens did not accommodate themselves well to integration of towers and partly because the English were preoccupied with towers in a way the French were not, so we shall have to consider them separately. Meanwhile the French tower arrangements appeared elsewhere, in Spain for example, in such an ornate version as that of Burgos.

Pl. 257

Except for Giotto's tower in Florence, the greatest Gothic towers in Italy may well be secular, as for example, the campanile at the town hall in Siena, and this is true as well for the Low Countries where the belfry in Bruges exceeds in size if not in elegance the mature Flemish spire of the cathedral at Antwerp or the western towers of St. Gudule in Brussels.

The other and quite different use of the tower may occur at the crossing. If the ridges of the nave and the crossing are at the same height, there is obviously no problem. It is the problem often met in ordinary houses where two hip roofs join and can be solved by a simple valley arrangement. No tower is required at all and there is no physical reason to mark the crossing at all if you do not want to. Thus it was that at Chartres and at Bourges nothing marks the intersection (and indeed there is not even an intersection at Bourges but instead a firm sweep of roof from front to chevet). On the other hand, there is a small capping at Reims simply providing a wall for the nave and transept gables to butt against, although since their ridges are of the same height this is structurally unnecessary.

At Amiens and Paris, however, the choice was made to emphasize the crossing by the brilliant arrowlike spires (flèches) previously mentioned. Such a flèche is not difficult to support on the substructure.

If the ridge lines of transept and nave are of different heights, a central tower is, however, needed to provide a stopping place for the lower of the two gables. So far as the work it has to do is concerned, it need be no higher than the higher of the two ridges, but this will look strange, so it is natural to push the crossing tower somewhat higher. How much higher becomes a matter of appearance (and engineering hazard). The central tower now may offer three further advantages. You may wish to bring light into the crossing by putting windows into the tower. The French did this occasionally and to great advantage when, for example, the central tower at Coutances was made into a lantern in the last part of the thirteenth century. Aside from the light, however, this was not needed to provide a pleasant look upward, as the vaulting of the crossing at Amiens would amply demonstrate.

Up to a point, a central tower offers weight to hold down the piers at the crossing against the thrust of the nave and transept arcades. But if you get ambitious about central towers and try to make them higher and higher, you make difficulties for yourself. They begin to weigh more and more and to offer difficulties for the piers at the crossing, especially if these were not originally designed to support the weight of these new ambitions as was often the case. Probably worse than that, as they go higher they begin to catch the wind. Then they sway. And as they sway, they impose still heavier loads on the leeward columns while lightening those on the windward columns with a tendency toward tension which masonry is not designed to stand. Thus the four major piers try to bow outward and a dangerous situation occurs. All this is beautifully described in the previously mentioned perceptive novel, *The Spire*, by William Golding.[188]

The French did not go so far with the dangerous towers. After the fall of the nave at Beauvais, no important innovations in cathedral design were made in France and this happened at about the end of the thirteenth century. The French had serenely and clearly solved their problem and few great cathedrals remained to be built. The problem now was to maintain and to preserve. But the builders of England were more restless, less satisfied with what they had done, more prone to style changes, more interested in thinning down and thinning down again, perhaps even beyond any cautions of logic. The history of the English tower is, therefore, more complicated than that of the tower in France, and the English central tower is generally more interesting than the lateral ones.

Almost every English cathedral has an important central tower, although some, like those of Rochester (spired), Winchester, and Peterborough (flat-roofed), are squat with only one row of windows. At Selby and Ripon and Bristol the western towers form an equal triad with the central tower in harmonious agreement. This is generally true at Lincoln, too, although the crossing tower offers a slight though acceptable dominance in what provides a remarkable triad. At Canterbury, the western towers remain respectable though the big central tower is now clearly in charge.

Two special arrangements need to be noted. Peculiar to Exeter are mighty transeptal towers, all that remains of the Norman church begun in 1111; in 1285 they were incorporated into the Gothic cathedral then being erected and converted into transepts by opening up the inner walls with lofty arches.

Winchester and Ely had single towers at the west as well as at the crossing. The one at Winchester is gone, although the original Norman scheme would have called for a total of six, two at each of the transept

[188] William Golding, *The Spire* (New York: Harcourt Brace, 1964).

angles and one at crossing and west. The powerful west tower at Ely remains flanked by two of the four tourelles of the west transept in what would have been a magnificent, even a belligerent, composition, while the central one was replaced by the spectacular octagon, of which more later in the fourteenth century.

Southwell is the only English cathedral retaining its complement of three Norman towers. Durham's central tower was ruined by lightning in 1429.

In the rest of the cathedrals the central tower begins to take command in a way that was impossible with Norman construction. The central tower of St. Alban's, built mainly of Roman brick, has no eleventh-century peer. It has no competition from the later Victorian facade. It is the central tower which offers the important vertical element at Chester, Wells,[189] Hereford, Worcester, Tewkesbury, and Gloucester, and these have much affected derivative American collegiate architecture. Of these, Worcester, Gloucester, and Wells are perhaps the most aspiring.

Pl. 259

But the most clamant for attention are the spires of Norwich and Salisbury. At Salisbury, in particular, the pyramidal culmination in one ensemble with the great spire has few rivals in any place or any time or any style for sheer architectural grace. Since even many lesser English churches have fine central spires, England offers a wealth of experience for the tower collector, including such fine examples as the Boston "Stump" of St. Botolph's and the spire at St. Andrew's, Heckington.

Pl. 258
Pl. 264

If the great contributions of the French cathedrals to the architectural literature of the world depend upon their supreme organization of space, their marvelous balancing of thrust by thrust through the flying buttress, the brilliance of their apsides, their glass and their sculpture, British achievements of equal weight rest on their fanciful later ceiling vaults and their inspiring central towers. Yet the latter always gave trouble, and fell with monotonous regularity, Winchester's within fifteen years after it was built.

At Lincoln, for example, in 1239 one of the canons was preaching a sermon denouncing the masterful Bishop Grosseteste, then at loggerheads with the chapter—"Were we silent and the very stones would cry out for us"—when the central tower fell with a crash killing three people and causing such damage to adjacent bays of the choir and transept that immediate restoration was necessary. The piers at the crossings were reinforced, new arches and stouter walls were put up to carry the present tower, which was completed about 1310, but it had to be grouted in the twentieth century through the persuasiveness of Dean Fry and the generous funds of Albert Farwell Bemis.

Ely owes its magnificent and unique octagon to the collapse of the

---

[189] The peculiar composition of the west front at Wells conceals the quality of the towers. The southwest of these can best be seen as a tower from the cloister garth.

Norman tower about 1322. You can see at Canterbury, Salisbury, and Wells how strainer arches were inserted by medieval masons to brace the piers of the central towers as they began to lean. At Wells these scissorlike arches are quite ungainly and belittle the architectural character of the nave and transepts.

Pl. 266

Until 1330 Salisbury had a squat central tower. Certainly the original builders did not have the present spire in mind at all or they would have provided much thicker columns and piers at the crossing and sturdier foundations below. To meet the requirements of Bishop Wyvil during 1334–1365, the great architect Richard of Farleigh and his fellow masons exerted all their energy. To achieve this towering stone spire, 404 feet high, in spite of the slender available support, they made its walls as thin as possible. The bottom courses of stone were only 2 feet thick, those at the top a mere 9 inches thick. The walls were tied together with iron bars—flying buttresses were put up at the external angles and others were erected in the triforium, and clerestory of the nave, transepts, and choir immediately adjoining the crossing. They also inserted a strong stone vault at the crossing of the nave below the tower. Above this the timber scaffolding inside was allowed to remain to provide greater rigidity. Nonetheless there were great apprehensions during a storm while construction was going on and again when the final few feet of solid stonework and the capstone were installed.

Pl. 262

Despite these precautions and while construction was proceeding, the imposition of the new 6,000 tons caused the columns to bend. By the fifteenth century Bishop Beauchamp noted further signs of instability and caused two great stone masonry arches to be added at the entrances to the main transepts between the piers supporting the spire at the crossing. These, in the Perpendicular style, were much more handsome than the earlier double arches erected in the fourteenth century to strengthen the main walls which were being pushed outward.

All these precautions worked somehow, and the tower and spire settled with a further displacement of only 3½ inches. But the bend of the piers can be plainly seen and the spire has a declination of 29½ inches to the southwest. This was determined in 1688 when Sir Christopher Wren was called in to survey the cathedral and strengthen the tower with iron supports and ties and bands. Again in 1737 a small brass plate was inserted in the floor of the nave to mark the spot touched by a plumb bob suspended from near the top of the spire. Once more in the nineteenth century Sir Gilbert Scott and Arthur Bloomfield added further iron.

In 1951 when the plumb bob was used again, it was found that there had been no further movement. But, alas, it was also found that the iron bands of Wren and Scott had rusted and the stone of the uppermost 30 feet was so decayed that this section of the spire had to be rebuilt completely. At the same time, aided generously by the Pilgrim Trust, the rest of the spire was repaired and it should give no concern at least before the next inspection. This is the history, not abnormal, of the third highest spire in Europe, the highest in England, and possibly the most beautiful anywhere.

Back in the early days, as early as the fifth century, the towers, first appearing in Italy, were intended to hold the bells. Not the least of the ironies of the great new central towers of England was that it was much too dangerous to submit them to the strains of heavy swinging bells. So it became quite common to build bell towers hard by and these were often called *campaniles*, though the term strictly means only an unbuttressed tower. Today the only remaining old detached bell tower in an English cathedral is at Chichester.

The Germans built some of the most beautiful towers, though not as a rule over crossings. The best examples are the central west front towers at Freiburg and Ulm, and the tower of St. Stephen in Vienna which is at the south end of the transepts, this having been made into the principal entrance. The florid northwest tower and spire at Antwerp is impressive, and you will certainly find the Giralda at Seville interesting, starting as it does as a minaret and ending after many accretions of time with a large Christian statue on its top.

Pl. 254
Pl. 265
Pl. 260

Pl. 255

THE ABSIDE

On the whole, Romanesque absides with their many combinations of radiating chapels and varied roof lines are better composed than those of the Gothic; and German, English, Spanish, and Italian Gothic examples cannot compare with them. This is true also of most but not quite all of the French Gothic.

But there was a new element in the Gothic apse and chevet, i.e., the flying buttress, and when they are well related to the apsidal chapels and especially when the chapels are understated so that the great flying buttresses radiate majestically, then the French Gothic chevets are simply terrific. This was managed in ascending order of excellence at Reims, Amiens, Paris, and Bourges. At Reims the overall effect is very strong, but the curve of the apse retains the inner curvature of the five apsidal chapels at ground level, and the prominence of the windows and especially the high arcaded gallery above the windows of the chapel, bearing grotesque dogs on its rail, and most particularly the overly tall tabernacles at the ends of the buttresses with their steeply pointed roofs (even if their height or most of it is needed to receive the buttresses) all tend to confuse and certainly to detract from the sweep of the double flying buttresses. Finally there is an ill-proportioned blind arcade at the top of the apse.

Pl. 263

At Amiens the chapels are very high and thoroughly dominant and the bridging of the double buttresses, though interesting in itself, detracts from the harmony of the whole. Certainly one cannot deny the majesty of the back of Amiens, but for clear and simple exposition the palm must go

Pl. 270

to Paris or Bourges. At Chartres the arched buttresses sloping down from one another are indeed outstandingly structural, but the high and heavily buttressed apsidal chapels, close pressing one on the other, are the primary and almost the only thing we see. It could, of course, be argued in favor of Reims, Amiens, and against Bourges or Paris that in a liturgical sense it is the chapels that are important and not the buttresses and that when the buttresses become the center of interest, the design has taken a wrong turning.

Paris and Bourges have much the same apsidal plan in that the circular line which inscribes the main buttresses is the outside line *for everything*. Between the buttresses Bourges permits small circular chapels to extend in the middle third from the wall of the chevet, but these are not conspicuous and perhaps even enliven the circle a little. This containment of the chapels within the walls of the apse of course operates at once to let the buttresses run clear. At Paris those supporting the upper vaults ride in one great arched leap to the buttresses-piers that receive them, while the lower flying buttresses engage that same buttress-pier at a slightly lower level. This makes the upper buttress dramatically prominent, perhaps even a little too important.

The most beautiful solution seems to me to have occurred at Bourges. There are in reality three sets of buttresses here. The tops of the highest, supporting the vaults of the choir, do run in a straight line to the outer piers as in Paris, thus establishing a firm line and at a steeper angle. But they touch down at an intermediate point, the piers separating the two aisles of the ambulatory, joining there the shorter-span arched buttress from a lower point of the choir. Then a still lower arch-buttress from the vaults of the apse terminates as does the higher one in a very deep rectangular buttress which looks sturdy enough, as some of those in the other cathedrals do not, to resist any overturning imposed by the arch buttresses. (The two little clochetons atop each buttress, applied in 1835, are not in keeping, but hardly matter.) It is a dramatically successful solution, and the absides of both Paris and Bourges, but especially Bourges, can be seen beautifully from the ground. It was a solution possible only with a two-aisled ambulatory and a containment of the radiating chapels within the walls of the apse.

Pl. 268

Looking at the absides has emphasized the importance of the flying buttress in French Gothic design. But you really will never see many of these fully until you go aloft. Going aloft is not hard to do.

Thousands, of course, take the elevators to the top of the great sun deck on the roof of the cathedral of Milan. Many hundreds toil up this or that tower of this or that cathedral to overlook a city or, as in Paris, to stand on a balustraded parapet and photograph a few gargoyles or one's spouse with the Tour Eiffel dimly if at all perceived in the hazy or smoggy background. But I am speaking of a more extensive and rewarding high road. It used to be readily arranged in most French cathedrals, and I

The Architecture of Stone 411

expect it still is. You find the master maintenance mason who is almost always working around except for a fortnight or so in August, and persuade him to take you around and fee him generously at the end.

The journey has no perils, though it may induce minor fears. I have been scrambling around mountains for almost my whole life without fear, but I had one or two moments of anxiety in Bourges forty years ago. You climb up inside, of course, and you come to the first triforium gallery and later the second and higher one which runs all the way around the church. They are much wider and much more even underfoot than a mountain ledge, even of so tame a mountain as Katahdin in Maine. They do not have rails but there are visual boundaries supplied by the arcading, and though there are substantial gaps between them you really could not fall off unless you tried to. Nonetheless and for some weird reason, possibly imposed by the nearness of the ceiling over the void pressing down on me, I felt some sense of uneasiness as we completed the trip. I mention this merely as warning and I suspect it is an experience that befalls very few of the visitors who go high in the cathedrals. And even if it does occur to you, too, it can be fought off. Your guide is aware of such difficulties and if, when walking around outside, because you can do this, too, you encounter a hole in the parapet where the wall has fallen away and where, perhaps, he was working when you summoned him, he will bridge it with his body and spread his arms out protectively. And at the end after you have wandered over the leads and along the edges of the roof, he will take you to a flying buttress which has steps cut in it and, holding onto a cable which guards one side, you will walk down and into the supporting buttress and so safely to the ground.

I do not propose you do this merely as an adventure that most cathedral viewers do not experience. It has much more to offer than that. It is the only way you can successfully read the windows of the upper stories; it will give you an entirely different impression of columniation and vaulting; and it is really the only way you can collect buttresses in the fullest sense; moreover you can really do it only in France.

BUTTRESSES

You will soon note that although the function of the buttress is simple, the execution varies. It begins at the wall with the simplest increase in thickness where the vaults rest, to stepped buttresses, to diagonal props, to single half arches, to double half arches or a combination of proplike upper chord and arched lower chord and then unhappily to a change from simply expressed stone forms to more and more elaboration of details until the original engineering purposes are, to say the least, overclouded or even denied by the forms. You will find more than one type of flying buttresses in a single cathedral, but no one cathedral of which I am aware offers the whole gamut. The outside arch-buttresses of the nave at Noyon are good simple ones to begin with. Here are manifestly simple half stone arches overlaid with a masonry wall.

At the upper level of the choir buttresses at Chartres there is a lighter treatment of the same idea, there being almost no stone above the arch as it starts from the vaults, but a heavy concentration, for equilibrium purposes, as it turns into the receiving vertical-pier buttress. Another version is seen at the nave of Strasbourg where the weight of masonry above the arch of the buttress is relieved by punching a substantial circular hole through the fabric near the clerestory wall of the nave. The elegant buttresses of the nave of Paris narrow the arch rib at its half-crown to the thinnest possible dimension while increasing the thickness substantially at the vaults and at the support. This type, though less fined down at the crown and therefore less daring, can also be seen in the nave buttresses of Amiens. It is carried to its ultimate in a double form at Reims where the buttresses are so slight that they scarcely seem to be made of stone. *Pl. 269*

Pl. 272

Pl. 275

Pl. 274

Pursuing the ultimate along the lines of the Strasbourg gambit, we come to the "cartwheel" buttresses of Chartres where practically all the masonry between the upper straight rib and the lower arched rib is left out and replaced by an ogival arcade with holes in the spandrels, the columns of the arcade being disposed as though they rested on radii projected from the center from which the curve of the arch was swung. Not dissimilar are the buttresses of the choir and abside of Amiens, except that now the columns of the arcade are vertical, stepping down in height, and the pointed arches contain alternating pairs of ogival arches and of trefoil arches with suitable openings in the spandrel. *Pl. 273*

This was about as far as a sensible flying buttress could go, but that does not mean you cannot find fancier ones if you move later into history. The builders of La Trinité at Vendôme in 1500 felt like hanging crockets from otherwise fairly reputable buttresses. At St-Maclou in Rouen about 1500–1514, the arcades became even more ornate. You can go still further and find still worse, but I am not going to help you. Everyone will have his own taste in this, but mine says that buttresses like poets are at their best when they mean what they say and say it so clearly they feel no necessity for fancy dress.

PORTALS

The greatest achievement in portals was, no doubt, at Chartres, whose south porch is far more elegant architecturally than the somewhat clumsy north porch, while it is moot which has the greater sculpture. Each of these porches has a three-bay portal equivalent to that to be found on a west front. *Pl. 279*

At the south, at Chartres, the central trumeau is occupied by an imposing Christ. At his sides in the tabernacles are the twelve apostles. In the tympanum Christ sits between Mary and Saint John the Evangelist, angels carry the instruments of the Passion, while the lintel and archivolts are peopled with bas-reliefs which, in a strange way, show the Last Judgment, the Resurrection of the Dead, and the Nine Choirs of Angels. This set of portals at the south is then totally Christian. At the north, on the other hand, the Hebrews take over, though not totally. The trumeau is occupied by Saint Anne. But the twelve magnificent flanking statues in the tabernacles are of David, Samuel, Moses, Abraham, Melchisidech, and Elisha on the right; on the left are Isaiah, Jeremiah, Simeon, St. John the Baptist, Saint Peter, and the prophet Eli. These are among the most moving sculptures from the Middle Ages.

SCULPTURE

Pl. 283
Pl. 280

Pl. 293

After seeing Amiens and to round out a French Gothic sculpture experience you would still have to go to Bourges to see the greatest Last Judgment, to Chartres for the statues of the Prophets of the Ancient Law and the Christ Enthroned in Majesty of the west tympanum; you can have endless and unresolved disputes about which have the greatest Christs or Marys. Obviously we cannot wander into this enchanting wood here. For what it is worth, I have appended a list of some of my greatest favorites, but it must be remembered that this is a highly personal taste.

Column bases	Chevet chapels, Paris
	Ambulatory, Le Mans
Foliage capitals	Ambulatory, Sens
	Choir and nave, Paris
	Transept, Laon
Virtues and vices	Plinth, Paris and Amiens
	South porch pillar, Chartres
Works and days	Baptistery, Parma
	Plinth, Paris and Amiens
	Peasant in winter: rear door, north portal, Chartres
Other secular life	Student life: quatrefoils, Paris
	Liberal arts: Aristotle, voussoirs of right door, royal portal, Chartres
	Violante of Aragon: cloisters, Burgos
	Saint Louis: buttress, Reims
	Oxen: tower, Laon
Old Testament	Noah spandrels on west front of Bourges plinth
Saints	Joseph: center door, west front, Reims
	Theodore: west door, south portal, Chartres
	George: south door, Chartres
	Stephen: south door tympanum, Paris

Life of Christ	Adoration of Magi: choir closure, Paris Annunciation, Visitation, Presentation: south door, Amiens; west portal, Reims
Christ	Trumeau, Santiago da Compostela Le Beau-Dieu: central west trumeau, Amiens
Virgin	Resurrection: left west portal, Paris
Angels	Smiling angel: west front, Reims; chevet, Reims
Apocalypse	Tympanum, south portal, Le Mans
Last Judgment	Tympanum, north door, Reims; west front, tympanum, Paris; west front, tympanum, Bourges
Miscellaneous	Donkey playing lute: south face, south tower, Chartres Fantastics: Paris, upper exterior gallery Prophets of the Ancient Law: north portal, Chartres Four Evangelists: west front tympanum, Chartres

It is hard to leave a few out of the text: the Angel and the Joseph of Reims, the Saint Theodore of Chartres, the Uta of Naumburg; but such an enumeration would soon become endless and meaningless too.

If these great combinations of architectonic sculpture appeal to you, you will have to do practically all your viewing in France. There are individually good pieces in all the other countries, but the exceptional ensembles, such as the kings of the choir screen of Exeter, the many-peopled niches of the west front of Wells, the Florentine baptistery door of Pisano, the works and days at Parma, or a number of excellent Italian tombs are rare. In Spain there are a few serious efforts to emulate the French. You might care to look at the Puerta de Sarmental at Burgos Cathedral to conclude how far they have succeeded.

INTERIORS

The English cathedrals normally have side aisles, like those in France, leading to a *retrochoir* behind the high altar. This was usually a chapel for the shrine of a local saint with an ambulatory to assure free movement; it led at the extreme east to a lady chapel for the veneration of the Virgin Mary.

Pl. 284

The situation as to the *visual* accessibility of the choir was quite different in France, after the liturgical reforms tore down the *jubés*, than it was in England and Spain where the closure was very firm indeed, especially at the front where a choir screen in some cases became a stone wall, often with intricate carving, called a pulpitum. There was no great consistency in these. The west wall of the choir of Ely is of much-perforated wood and relatively easy to look through. The high altar at Lincoln has four columns supporting a solid roof over it, and curtains were hung between the pillars to conceal the place where the Eucharist was being offered rather than to reveal it to the public, a practice long since discontinued. But actually most English choir screens present a more or less solid front to the nave, whatever the pulpitums may be made of, though most are stone. The organ was often above the pulpitum, and from the loft, on Sundays and festival days, the Epistle and Gospel were read. This practice, recorded in the fourteenth-century *Customary* of Salisbury, came from its predecessor, Old Sarum, and was observed in the other secular cathedrals, such as Lincoln, but not in the monastic cathedrals.

Many of the medieval pulpitums of England have disappeared. Exeter and Southwell offer outstanding examples of early fourteenth-century open arcaded fronts. On the other hand, the pulpitums of Canterbury, York, Lincoln, and Ripon are frankly solid screens bearing tiers of niches for figures of saints or kings, many of which were removed by time or the Roundheads. The array of royal statuary at York is impressive.

If the screen did not stop all passage toward the east, it might have side gates, usually iron grills, and when pilgrims were let through them to visit the sainted relics behind, they had, naturally, to be kept out of the sanctuary so aisle screens had to be provided to close off the sides of the sanctuary. This was a favorite place to insert the chantry chapels of bishops, other ecclesiastics, or nobles.

In the early days the French choirs *were* enclosed by similar high stone screens. The pulpitum was called a *jubé*. Like the English screens, they were two walls of stone carrying a loft on which stood the nave rood, the choir organ, and a great lectern. The lower stage was an arcade in the center of which was the choir door and to the right and left were nave altars. They were much carved and decorated, as were the sides. Traditionally scenes of the infancy and public life were carried on the north wall; the Passion, Crucifixion, and Resurrection on the west wall. The south wall was somewhat more freely ordered, although it often included the various appearances of Christ after the Resurrection. It was undoubtedly remarkable work as we can conjecture from a few museum pieces and a few vestiges of the side enclosures at Paris and Amiens. These walls were ruthlessly mutilated during the Protestant uprisings of the sixteenth century, and received some reconstruction and repainting in the seventeenth only to find the canons of the eighteenth century busily engaged in tearing down both the jubés and the choir walls in an excess of revolutionary and egalitarian liturgical change.

Though obviously a great loss of sculpture, the results have some architectural visual values. At Reims the choir is completely visible through the high arcades, and the barrier is only a thin-railed iron fence. At Chartres one can see the whole length of nave and choir right to the apsidal windows, although there is a sculptured stone wall around the choir begun in 1514 by Jean de Beauce. At Bourges there is no closure save a low rail.

At Paris you can see through the arcades of the ambulatory and can search out only two sets of bas-reliefs, one at the north and one at the south. The closure is in slightly better condition at Amiens, where the first three pillars of the choir at the north and the south are connected by stone walls depicting the history of Saint John the Baptist, at the north and at the south the life of Saint Firmin. Even these, though not pulled down, were much mutilated during the Revolution and are heavily restored.

Now this solid enclosure of the choir was a very important element in the appearance of a Gothic cathedral interior, as is immediately apparent in England or Spain. Its absence in the great cathedrals of France make it certain that we really cannot see a French Gothic interior as it was, and to get a notion of what pulpitums or jubés are like you must visit England or Spain where the designs are unlikely to be very French.

One compensation is that we can see the whole great French interior in one sweep, and very impressive it is.

SPECIAL ENGLISH FEATURES

After the high period of vaulting in France and particularly in England, experimenters produced more and more complicated and less and less functional rib-vault systems, which often are very interesting, curious, pretty, and occasionally more than that.

One of the great English contributions to cathedral complexes, both important and common to all monastic houses, secular cathedrals, and collegiate foundations of the English Middle Ages, was the chapter house. A visit to the local chapter house should be on the agenda of a visit to almost every English Gothic establishment.

In cathedral priories the chapter of monks convened daily in the morning before the celebration of High Mass; in the secular cathedrals the canons sat weekly in chapter. Whatever the shape of the building they sat on stone benches built into or against the outside wall. When possible the chapter houses were entered from the east walk of the cloister, but when there was no cloister, as at York, Lichfield, or Southwell, they would be detached. In almost all cases after the Norman period, the construction was independent of other elements.

The English chapter houses gained their greatest architectural expression in the thirteenth century when their shapes became polygonal. Lincoln's decagon was built in 1230, Westminster's octagon in 1245, and Salisbury's in 1265, while Worcester's original circular plan was made decagonal about 1400. Standing free of the cloistered buildings, the walls could have large light-giving windows. Most of them were roofed by ribbed vaulting radiating from a central pier which afforded an opportunity for an architectural tour de force that probably anticipated the complex rib structures in other parts of the later Gothic cathedrals, either originally or by conversion.

Pl. 286

Even when they began to elaborate the tracery and other similar details in the late Flamboyant period, the straightforward French did not go in for fancywork in their major central supporting elements. They moved quickly from the early hexpartite systems of Laon, Paris, and Bourges to the final quadripartite solutions of Amiens, Reims, and Chartres. Only at the crossing did they try anything more. Where the main aisle of the transept was about the same width as that of the nave, the geometry was not difficult and the problem was solved directly and simply by diagonal ribs springing from the four columns defining the crossing. This was the solution at Chartres. At Laon the builders elected to add ribs running from the cross arches, so that when we look up we see a more complex but still simple ceiling. The extreme of this, still quite straightforward and certainly very beautiful, was at Amiens where bracing ribs were added to make a four-pointed star.

But English medieval art was shot through with the desire for originality, innovation, experiments. It could not long be satisfied with the original Cistercian import or its survivals, or adhere to the rigorous French logic of structure and arrangements. Soon the English vaults included subsidiary members, ridge ribs, and tiercons which are secondary ribs in a vault running from the main springer to a point on the ridge rib. They were intended less to brace the ridge than to subdivide the large interstitial surfaces which may have been difficult to construct, although these actually dangerous auxiliaries of the rib were not developed until near the end when structural logic was beginning to weaken. The first English tiercons were in Hugh's choir at Lincoln and they were soon popular. The still relatively simple lierne vaults of Norwich were, as Frankl says, marking a time when "the rib is becoming again what it was at the outset; an architectural member having a purely aesthetic function."[190] The Norwich liernes, it should be noted, sprang from a Norman underpinning.

The liernes are not genuine tiercons. About two-thirds of the way up to the ridge they bifurcate into two short ribs which run not to the ridge rib but to the diagonals, thus heading for a star shape.

Then the tiercons began to multiply in the lateral severies as at Exeter, producing in effect something like that of a fan vault but really a star vault. From these developed a variety of additional forms especially on the Teutonic part of the continent, and, in Spain, net vaults and other even more "baroque" forms. It would be important for a student of architectural history to classify these, to seek their origins and the stages of their development, but I do not mean to subject you to this.

The fan vault, on the other hand, was not a development from regular rectangular bay vaults but rather a transfer of the form from the single

[190] Paul Frankl, *Gothic Architecture* (Baltimore: Penguin, 1962), p. 146. Copyright © 1962 by Paul Frankl.

central column of the chapter house to the side columns of a nave or choir to produce a series of concave-sided funnels terminating in central tangential circular ribs.

There is no doubt of the beauty of some of this precocity, a move to replace a primarily structural architecture by one of effect. Some English critics still think the French Gothic was too skeletal, intellectual, even arid. The later French experiments with flamboyance were less convincing than the English, probably because they did not really believe in it.

You can find fan vaults in many English churches, but the most notable examples are at King's College Chapel, Cambridge, and in the Henry VII Chapel at the end of Westminster Abbey, where a magnificent set of fan vaults support hanging gilded bosses, the whole enriched by the many-colored banners of the Knight's Grand Cross of the Most Holy Order of the Bath. Some prefer one, some the other, but both are marvelous visually.

Pl. 285
Pl. 287

No one can deny that many of these extravagances are pretty—some perhaps even beautiful. But it is a laid-on beauty for beauty's sake, a toying with structure such as might sometimes happen in the Renaissance and certainly in the Baroque. If the Gothic was not quite dead (and it well may have been), it was certainly very near to its last breath.

In general, looking at English Gothic cathedrals, rather than churches or chapter houses, is made particularly difficult by the necessity of going through the dreary exercise of separating out the differences between the various English style periods: Early English (thirteenth century), Decorated (fourteenth century), Perpendicular (fifteenth century), and Tudor (first half of sixteenth century), and wondering why the various overly ambitious English prelates and overly affluent English patrons and their architects swung so violently from one fashion to another, even to the point of doing whole sections of churches over, and who did what where.

Salisbury is unusually consistent because it was pretty much all at one time, a thing made possible by abandoning the old site at Old Sarum completely and moving to the new site to build from the ground up. It was built in a very short time (1220–1258), almost entirely in the Early English style, and has not been much mucked up since, except for the fourteenth-century Decorated vaulting under the crossing, the bending of the columns by the overly ambitious tower (with the ensuing fourteenth- and fifteenth-century strainer arches, different in form, at the main transepts and the choir transepts), and for relatively minor potterings about by the later restorers, the egregious Wyatt and the more thoughtful Scott. We might have examined whether this cathedral, almost exactly contemporary with Amiens, was as typical of High English Gothic as Amiens was of France. We would have been able to detect the major differences in English and French planning and see how different characteristic naves were in the two countries; to decide whether the horizontality of Salisbury results from the fact that none of the supports of the vaults spring from the floor but instead all rise from the spandrels of the ground floor arcade. Then if "typicality" mattered to us, we should have had to decide whether Salisbury was typical. It ought to have been, of course, but the builders of other churches did not know, on the one hand, what to do with their extensive Norman remains (absent at Salisbury) or how to resist the enticements of later fashions, so that though Paris, Chartres, Amiens, Bourges, Reims, and a number of other French cathedrals can be said to be basically alike and one or another chosen as a type if not an archetype, the paradox of England is, on the one hand, that "typical" Salisbury has no genuine English counterparts, and on the other, that many other of the more wayward and less typical English cathedrals are warmer and altogether more pleasant to visit, including Canterbury, Westminster, Ely, Lincoln, Wells, and doubtless some others beside the very Norman ones.

THE PAINTER'S ART—STAINED GLASS

We shall have to leave the Gothic without reference to its many minor art treasures, the enchanting details of furniture that lie around cathedrals: altar plates and other liturgical instruments, vestments, tombs, chantries, other chapels, reredoses, predellas, cloisters, banners, brasses, bishops' thrones, reading desks, fonts, retables and their panels, crypts, ceiling bosses, and so on. But we cannot leave it without mention of the stained glass.

Although we saw some frescos in the Romanesque where there were walls to bear them, it is not surprising that, as the walls vanished in the Gothic, painting became less significant as a companion of architecture (save that most of the sculpture was tinted), though there are fragments of frescos to be seen at Bayeux, at Clermont-Ferrand, at Coutances by those who want to poke around.

The searcher for painting can do a little better in England; reconstructed pieces of a series of murals painted about 1500 and devoted to the various miracles of the Virgin can be seen in the Lady Chapel at Winchester; at St. Alban's, there is a handsome painting of William Fitzherbert, Archbishop of York, on the arcading east of the shrine, long bricked up after the Dissolution and thus quite well preserved now; there is a wheel of fortune dating from the reign of Henry III in the choir of Rochester; and in St. Saviour's Chapel at Norwich there are some fine paintings, comparable to good Italian work dating from 1381 to 1430 and serving once as a retable or part of a chancel screen or altar piece in the Church of Saint Michael at Plea.

But these and a few diptychs in France simply reinforce the generalization that

> during the Gothic Age wall paintings in France and Britain never assumed the same importance as in Romanesque times and they were far less numerous or extensive than in contemporary Italy or the Byzantine world

where the small windows always left considerable surfaces to be decorated.[191]

To realize the depth of this we have only to think of Giotto's *Marriage of the Virgin* in the Arena Chapel in Padua, or Lorenzetti's fresco, *Good and Bad Government*, in the Palazzo Pubblico of Siena, or Cimabue's *Crucifixion*, now destroyed by the flood, in Santa Croce, Florence, or the frescos which cover all the inside walls of the baptistery at Parma.

Sometimes even the French cathedrals had excellent *detached* paintings, such as the Titian, the Tintoretto, and the Zuccari in Reims, but an examination of these would become a search for painting rather than for architecture, even though they do hang in chapels, even though their subject matter is appropriate, even though, as rarely, they were painted for the particular place and not purchased afterwards by some devoted donor. Ferret them out if you will, but leave me out of it because I do not like to think of a cathedral as a badly lighted art gallery.[192]

A little more can be said of tapestries, of which there are a good many at Reims, though they are all late and most of them are from the Renaissance. There were presumably more in the Middle Ages, but we are really left with the glass windows, the consequence of the opening of the wall, as the nearest expression of the painter's art in the Gothic cathedrals, even though it was transparent rather than reflective. Everybody knows that it was a very generous legacy and anybody who has seen any of it knows that there is no adequate way to describe it either in words or paintings or colored photographs and strangely enough not in transparent slides either, so the only significant description must be "go and see for yourself."

Most of the important cathedrals have fragments of their erstwhile glass, but what can richly be seen is limited to York, Chartres, Bourges, and the Ste-Chapelle. Indeed almost nothing remains of what must have been the fenestral glories of Paris, Reims, and Amiens. The dramatic extremes are shown by two important but abnormal French churches—the all-brick, roseate, fortlike Ste-Cécile in Albi and the almost all glass Ste-Chapelle.

In his significant book, *The Gothic Cathedral*, Otto Von Simson bases his long essay on a clear hypothesis that Gothic architecture, to be understood, must be understood as "the representation of supernatural reality. To those who designed the cathedrals, as to their contemporaries who wor-

---

[191] William Richard Lethaby, *Medieval Art: From the Peace of the Church to the Eve of the Renaissance, 312 to 1350*, 3d ed. (New York: Philosophical Library, 1950), p. 172.
[192] I do not want to overstate the case. At Albi, where the walls were favorable, it was possible, as I have noted above, to impose the enormous fresco on the inside west front, much of which was lost, and the most important central part, when the wall was pierced in 1693 and again in 1736 when a new organ was installed. And at Cahors there are some colossal figures of prophets, fifteen feet or more high, painted on a bright red ground probably in tempera, probably dating from about 1300, and certainly adorning the dome there.

shipped in them, this symbolic aspect or function of sacred architecture overshadowed all others."[193] I hope you have deduced this without having had it underlined from what has gone before in this text and from your own observations about the structure, the plan, the iconography. But it need not follow from this that the diaphanous quality of Gothic architecture is the only important thing to differentiate it from the Romanesque.

The Gothic window has to be considered as a very special kind of painting. It is true that there is little space for mural painting in a Gothic church, but this is not a matter of accident. It is because the Gothic clients and their artists willed it so. The Romanesque wall was almost entirely a surface to be adorned with mosaic or fresco. These brought color to the interior, to be sure, but it was the color of reflected light, coming from small sources, not the incident light flowing into the Gothic cathedral. Romanesque and Byzantine wall art, and especially mosaic art, is best seen by the artificial light of myriad candles. Gothic wall art is essentially invisible except by day. Romanesque art is easily reached by the eye, among other things, because of its scale. Gothic stained-glass art is small in detail, often very far away, much harder to study carefully than Gothic sculpture, which is so often at eye level or nearly so. Both the Gothic sculpture and the Gothic glass are didactic and based on the same iconographic symbolism which is evolving. But with the Romanesque the detailed symbolism comes first, and with the Gothic glass the detailed symbolism comes last. The approach to the glass requires a different priority. First we need to sense the total effect of the light and the color on the larger volumes and the smaller volumes of the interior, and, second, the general outlines and tracery of the windows themselves, recalling as they do to the details of the other stonework. Finally we can, if we will, and there is pleasure in it, follow the tales of the individual windows.[194] As we do we might wonder how this was done by the humble worshipper who, no doubt, understood the symbolism better than we, even when we are armed with reliable guidebooks, but who was not armed as we are with a powerful miniature binocular made in Japan. It is a considerable mystery and one worth reflecting upon.

The simplest example to begin is "The Five Sisters" window in York Minster. The Cathedral of York does not, in most respects, offer the most exciting exemplars of various parts of English cathedral architecture, although it is by no means particularly inferior in any. Its greatest single glory is, although very few English churches contain more than a fragment of their original stained and painted glass, that there is a great deal at York.

---

[193] Otto Georg Von Simson, *The Gothic Cathedral* (New York: Harper Torchbooks, 1964), p. xiv.

[194] Not everyone would agree with this order. Von Simson, for example (ibid., p. 122), says: "Suger was the first to conceive the architectural system as but a frame for his windows [he did not invent the stained-glass windows—jeb], as translucent surfaces to be adorned with sacred paintings."

Elsewhere much was destroyed during the Reformation; often the broken glass was later replaced in small pieces to offer colored but not iconographic light. Again it was even removed and buried as at Salisbury and replaced with modern glass.

At York, on the other hand, some 117 windows, many almost complete, possess a very large proportion of their original twelfth-, thirteenth-, fourteenth-, and fifteenth-century glass. All in all, York has perhaps more than half of the old English glass which has survived.

The Five Sisters window, so named for a legend which has no historical foundation, occupies most of the north wall of the north transept and dates from the thirteenth century. The rectangular wall is filled by five lancet lights, each 50 feet high and 5 feet wide. (The glass in the gable is modern *grisaille*.) The subdivisions are geometrical throughout, except for the bottom panel of the center light. There is, thus, essentially no iconography. Nor is there a very strong color note in this admirable example of *grisaille*. The groundwork of such glass is gray in color; on it is painted an outline leaf pattern in brown enamel. In this groundwork are inserted geometrical patterns of colored glass, repeated in each panel. Only the lowest center panel contains a circular medallion of late twelfth-century glass, which has survived from the twelfth-century choir and which represents the visit of the prophet Habakkuk to Daniel in the Lion's Den. This is the only medallion comparable to those in the great French windows. The great *grisaille* of York is abstract, devoid of iconographic messages. Its colors do not have the elan, the glow, the excitement of Chartres, Bourges, or the Ste-Chapelle. Most of the time they are gray in the gray light that is the most usual in York. But the window is subtly beautiful; it is not inferior. It is one way the men of the Middle Ages could go, though not their usual way.

It is difficult, when looking at a great medieval window, to take one's mind off the color long enough to ponder the structure of the window (that is, the stone tracery) or the symbolic messages which parallel those of the sculpture, but both efforts should be made.

In the tracery there are enormous variations. Consider that of rose windows alone. For example, there are the simple almost primitive circles and half circles of the west front of Laon; the beautiful but plainly organized circles of the west front of Chartres, the equally simple but more sophisticated radii of the west front of Paris, similarly treated but more gracefully at Reims; the richer elaborations of the same theme in the transepts of the same church; or the quite different treatment of a similar theme at St-Ouen in Rouen; the swirling motifs of the thirteenth-century rose in the north transept of Chartres; the flamboyance of the south transept window at Amiens; or its given greater elaboration in the south front of Sens. Obviously you will encounter not only great beauty but great variety. It may even become difficult for you to remember which appeals to you most.

Among the cathedral windows of France, Chartres is the epitome, perhaps even the exaggeration, of the way the French would usually

Pl. 281
Pl. 277
Pl. 278
Pl. 276

choose to go when they had a choice of talent and material. It has been the subject of so many encomiums, loud and gentle, ecstatic and reflective, that it is tempting to ignore it. But it is the Grand Canyon of the glassmaker's art and it cannot be ignored. Nor can it be typed by a single example like the Five Sisters of York.

The people of the Middle Ages loved bold primary colors much as we do now, and the nostalgic "subtle" colors we see today are largely the consequence of age and fading. The reds and blues of Chartres recall the truth as their many pieces sparkle or grow dim according to the position and the quality of the sunlight.

The subjects are variously treated depending on their position. At the top level of the clerestory, the figures of the Prophets, the Apostles, the Martyrs, and the Confessors, to be seen from so far away, are gigantic figures. (This does not fully solve the problem of visual angle; in-tipped windows would have served better but only in this respect.) Their eyes immeasurably open, their contours strongly accented, lend them an expression of strange rudeness and of savage grandeur. In the side aisles the treatment is different; the windows are divided by elegant iron armatures into a certain number of medallions on which are painted little legendary scenes borrowed from the Bible and above all from the lives of the Saints. Here is the story of Saint Lubin, Bishop of Chartres, alongside that of Noah; of Saint Eustache alongside of Joseph. The window of the Good Samaritan and the Prodigal son is alongside of Saint Nicolas and Sainte Madeleine. The images follow each other in each window from bottom to top and from left to right.

One cannot always know what the compositions meant to the artists inspired by whatever pious recitations were in vogue—despite all reliances on Vincent de Beauvais, etc., and later interpretations by Emile Mâle.

Something the same must be said about the donors. They are usually shown in the medallions at the bottom of the windows or even in the roses of the high windows. They belong to all social classes: kings, seigneurs, members of the clergy, representatives of workers' guilds—the first indicated by the arms of the family, the latter by attributes of the profession. Even then among the noble persons and rich ecclesiastics who gave most of the windows of the choir and transept there are often doubts as to the actual donor, though the kings of France and Castille, the duke of Brittany, the counts of Champagne, Boulogne, Chartres, and Beaumont, the heads or the cadets of the families of de Montfort, de Courtenay, and de Montmorency are all specified on this or that window, and it is easy to make out in the naves and side aisles how patriotically liberal the medieval laborers were as represented by clothiers (or drapers), jewelers, shoemakers (or cordwainers), tanners, butchers, bakers, carpenters, masons, stonecutters, etc., all in the period between 1215–1240.

Chartres has more windows of the thirteenth century and Bourges of the fourteenth and fifteenth. At Bourges there are especially fine windows of the Nouvelle Alliance and of the Apocalypse. The rose windows of

Chartres are, of course, incomparable. In Paris the Ste-Chapelle, nearly all glass, is an inspiration in light and color, if not in drawing, with the maximum of glass and a minimum of structure. Also at Ste-Chapelle is a greater variety of the arrangements of the medallions. The rose offers a vast illustration of the Apocalypse centering on Saint John, and all the iconography is very carefully worked out. When we look at it today, we will have to have almost as much admiration for the scholarly restorers of the nineteenth century who have so well mixed old glass with new, so fully organized the 414 scenes that are new with the 720 that go back to the thirteenth century, that most of us will never know the difference even after we have made repeated trips to the Cluny Museum to see originals in a better state of preservation.

The Ste-Chapelle offers another remarkable experience in the extreme contrast between the almost glassless, low-vaulted, brilliantly painted lower chapel, and the high-ceilinged, slender-fingered, glass cage of the upper chapel.

Pl. 290

To enlarge on all this becomes very tempting. I cannot blame you, unless I am prepared to blame myself, for trying to compare the old glass of the Cluny Museum with the new glass of the Ste-Chapelle, for chasing down the stories of the windows of Chartres or speculating about the butchers of Bourges. But it is probably the small way of going about it and may conceal the important truths in a welter of minutiae.

André wrote: "The saint is a being of light." This is the big message from the Gothic, of which the light through the windows of Chartres is but the most emphatic part. It does not seem extravagant to say that there is no message of comparable force in today's buildings. The closest resemblances are probably to be found in the abstractions of Perret's Notre-Dame de Raincy or the still more abstract "betonglas" of Strifler's Trinitätskirche in Mannheim.

You can make what you like of this. I am afraid it is because the things we do in our great modern buildings are just less significant, so that there is nothing significant, let alone transcendent, their art can say. Religion or at least faith has failed, but nothing has satisfactorily replaced it. We do not believe in saints—or heros. Even the villains are mediocre. It seems that light has somehow gone out of the human world. Has it? If it has, why? This is a question Chartres or Amiens can legitimately ask you, one you should not dismiss too lightly.[195]

[195] I am, of course, aware that I have left out some very admirable nonecclesiastical examples of secular Gothic—castles, palaces, walls, gates and cloth halls, town halls, law courts, hospitals. When these buildings were planned to be symbols of civic dignity or commonwealth, truly Gothic forms were used and not alone for their decorative facades, interiors, courtyards, but actually to vault the main rooms. But the plans and sections were for specific and definitely nonliturgical forms, whether the end result was the clearly Gothic Town Hall in Brunswick, the brilliant exterior of Louvain, or only the Gothic forms as in the house of the wealthy merchant of Bourges, Jacques Coeur.

Pl. 288

CHAPTER SEVEN

THE ARCHITECTURE OF BRICK

The last structural material we should consider is burned brick. In a structural sense brick belongs in the family of masonry. It has roughly the same advantages and disadvantages as stone, some exaggerated, some muted. It has strength only in compression; brick structures are averse to being tipped. The brick by itself can span no further than its length and has to be supported either by another material sufficiently resistant to bending to act as a lintel, or to cooperate with other bricks through arcuate, vaulted, or domical action.

Bricks cannot individually be made very large for technical reasons since they have a tendency to warp or check if the clay slips are too big. Hence brick can be regarded for structural purposes as a special kind of small stone.[1]

But there are interesting differences from natural stones. Bricks are generally more brittle, and it is easy for a skilled mason to break them as he wishes, which assists in making patterns on the site. The mixture of clays used for the bricks and the nature of the burning permit a range of colors from pale yellows to deep mahoganies and even purples; if sand-lime combinations are used, grays, or grays flecked with black, are possible; while if the bricks are enameled or the basic brick wall is covered with glazed tile, almost any color, and durable color, can be invoked.

[1] In modern times there have been experiments with prefabricating brick panels held together with reinforcing metal, and this has been satisfactory for quite limited applications.

The economics of bricks, on the other hand, is such as to require most of the time that the clays used come from relatively local sources. From this, characteristically regional properties follow, and this seems to me advantageous rather than not.

Although bricks are generally small by force of technological circumstances, the range of the smallness within its own framework is substantial. A standard ordinary brick may run about 2 by 4 by 8 inches. But a "Roman" brick is much flatter and longer (say, for example, 3 by 12 by 18 inches) and a "Jeffersonian" brick much thicker and bulkier (say 3 by 4 by 9 inches). The visual effect of each of these is substantially different from the effect of the others.

These possibilities are much enlarged by the mortar joints which are, as a rule, more noticeable in brickwork than in stonework, if only because there are more of them and because their dimensions are almost certain to be greater in relation to the brick dimensions than is the case for most stonework. This can be made into an asset in design. The joint can be quite thin or quite thick relative to the brick; it can be of different thickness in the horizontal joints than in the vertical joints. It can be flush with the brick surfaces, recessed (raked), or protruding, and the choice makes more difference than one would expect in the texture and the shadow lines of the wall. And it can be varied in color.

There are still further freedoms of choice. Bricks may be made with quite smooth finished surfaces or with heavily "tapestried" ones. Whatever the choice, bricks do not emerge from the kiln absolutely uniform in size, color, or texture, even in a single batch. If they are used as they come, the wall will have more accidental variation in color, in texture, and in joint thicknesses (the mason's compensation). At greater cost, naturally, the bricks may be selected—usually to achieve greater uniformity, but for some tastes, less popular now than thirty years ago, to increase the randomness in a search for romantic "rusticity." This has been carried to the point of imitating variations which earlier builders were unable to avoid through skintling, or incorporation of some secondhand bricks, or pieces of bottle or glass cullets, or other ceramics, or even building the whole wall of secondhand bricks. Some of these devices may seem to you, as they do to me, to have passed over into the "corny."

Not all these alternatives are open to every local architect once the idea of importing bricks has to be abandoned. In a given place the local brickyard may have a limited number of standards to offer. To contemporaries who welcome the limitations of standards as a modern version of the "freedom of necessity," this will seem a boon. Others will envy the freedom the great Finnish architect, Alvar Aalto, is said to have of being able to find a kiln master ready, even anxious, to make bricks to his specifications.

Finally, brickwork offers great freedoms in the choice of bonding system. One way to lay bricks is simply to put them down one above the other (*a*). This makes a simple and orderly appearing wall, and tends to be popular today because of its plain geometry. Then a designer might choose to stagger the vertical joints in alternate courses; this is called *common bond* (*b*). Naturally it requires the use of some half bricks at door or window openings. At the corners the apparent half brick might be a *header*, that is, the end of a brick. (A *stretcher* is the long side of a brick.)

Pl. 312

If the wall is two or more layers thick, it is desirable to tie the layers together with something more than a sheet of mortar. Metal ties can be and are used. But the bricks too may be used as ties by laying some of them across the wall. This automatically introduces some headers into the face of the wall, and now the way you choose to alternate headers and stretchers provides an almost infinite potential variety. Diagram (*c*) shows the simplest form in which alternate headers and stretchers in each course are arrayed above each other. If you use all headers in one course and all stretchers in the adjacent ones and stagger the vertical joints (*d*), you have *English bond*. If you use alternate headers and stretchers in each course but stagger the joints (*e*) so that a header is always above the center of a stretcher, you have *Flemish bond*. If you use two stretchers and then a header whilst staggering the joints (*f*), you have *double Flemish bond*. From here on by doubling, tripling, by setting some bricks on end (*g*), you can produce great variety, including basket weaves (*h*) or herringbones. Not everything you can do will be equally practical or sturdy, it must be said.

You can find almost all the combinations shown in almost any town. How many have you noticed as you go about? How many more simple combinations can you dream up for yourself? How often have you paused to examine the brick pattern of a piece of architecture unless it seemed very fancy—for example, like that on the facade of the Greek Orthodox Church in Copenhagen?

Of course it can become very fancy. People have used different thicknesses of brick in different courses, different colors, different textures. They have recessed some and protruded others, either in an overall pattern or in panels. They have made pilasters, and string courses, and niches, and blind arcades. They have laid in bands of color. The abstract painter, Joseph Albers, made a mural in bricks for the Harvard Graduate School designed by his friend and Bauhaus colleague, Walter Gropius.

Out of this rich potential, rich crops have been harvested. In numbers the great buildings of brick are not to be compared with those of stone, but in almost all periods some brick buildings can be found to match those of stone, while now and again brick construction has been dominant.

In the matter of delight we recall San Vitale in Ravenna, the Earl's Barton Tower, the Romanesque Abbey Church at Jerichow in Saxony, the array of beautiful Lombard work from Piacenza, Cremona, and Crema, to Parma, the amazing fortress cathedral of Ste-Cécile in Albi, the north German brick architecture of Lübeck and Königsberg, many secular buildings of the Middle Ages, later English town and country houses, the mer-

Pl. 313

Pl. 308

chants' houses of the seventeenth century in the Low Countries, much of English Georgian, Jefferson's Monticello, Byrd's Westover in our own country, and in our own day the sensitive use of brick by Alvar Aalto. But if I were limited in choice to one brick, the richest architecture, exploitation of brick and other ceramics, it would have to be the architecture of Islam.

The total architecture of Islam was naturally much more than a brick architecture and much more important than Western observers have yet to grant it. It was truly a world architecture spanning more than a millennium of remarkable work and extending geographically from Agra in India to Toledo in Spain. It is a religion we do not know enough about.

It started with Mohammed who was born in A.D. 570 and began his prophetic career in 612. Before Mohammed's time Arabia had been inhabited by nomadic pastoral Semites in the deserts and traders on the coast, falling considerably under Greek and Jewish influences. In 622 following his flight (Hegira) to Medina, Mohammed organized the commonwealth of Islam after great struggles.

Mohammedanism has six ineluctable requirements of belief in:

1. God, that is, Allah
2. God's angels
3. The prophet Mohammed as the *last* of the prophets
4. God's revealed books of which El Koran is the *last* and the only indispensable one
5. The resurrection day
6. God's predestination (Inshallah) which predetermines men's actions and their outcome

It demands only six duties:

1. Recitation of profession of faith
2. Attesting to the unity of God and the mission of Mohammed
3. The five daily prayers
4. Observance of the feast of Ramadan
5. A pilgrimage to Mecca
6. The holy war

In various times and in various places Mohammedans have been as diverse in their observance and application of these beliefs as Christians have in theirs; they have been rational and emotional; austere and exuberant; sincere and hypocritical. Sometimes their wars have been bona fide crusades, sometimes outright attempts (often successful) at conquest.

They have been brutal and gentle, warlike and peaceful, barbarous and civilized. Their architecture has borrowed from others and been innovative; now traditional, now evolutionary.

The spread of Islam and Islamic architecture from the Dome of the Rock of 643 to the completion of the Taj Mahal, more than 1,000 years later in 1653 and half-way around the world, and under a variety of leaders —Omayyads, Abbasids, Fatimids, Seljuks, Almohads, Ottomans, Moguls— has certainly been seen and reported on by many European writers from Marco Polo on, but more often than not through romantic glasses, such as those of Burton, Fitzgerald, or Washington Irving. In structural expressions, its concepts of interior space, its innovations in new ways of treating large wall surfaces, especially in Iran, have too widely been overlooked in the Christian West, so that, for example, the architectural encyclopedist Sir Banister Fletcher called it a "non-historic style." *Pl. 316*

There has perhaps always been a Western hostility among Europeans and European descendants toward Mohammedanism and Islamic architecture, and this traces back to viewing the Moors as enemies in Europe during the Crusades (not finally expelled until 1492). In European history courses the seamy sides of the Crusaders have been steadfastly understated. For a long time, too, mosques were not open to Christian visitors. And finally and perhaps most important, there has been since Victorian times what Donald N. Wilber calls "negative Orientalism,"[2] which thought of the Orient as "luxurious, picturesque, exotic, and erotic," a home of "mystic cults, sensuality, cruelty, dazzling colors and elaborate ornament."

It is possible that Islamic architecture can be viewed by us objectively in terms of its *appearance*, its forms, proportions, colors, but only if we do not overcast this viewing with value judgments or emotions. It has been called irrelevant, unexperimental, unprogressive. Actually it was imaginative and daring. It used all the arch, vault, and dome forms very early and in very experimental ways. The decorative treatments which so sharply excite our Western attention never really overpower the basic architecture. The brick arches of Iran explored all the possibilities, and you can see many of them in a single mosque in Isfahan. Though there was a great respect for tradition over the 700 years of work on the Iranian and Anatolian plateaus, there were evidences of quite different cultural approaches, of climatic or technical differences, or those of regionally available materials. Though changes were slow on modern time scales, actually Islamic architecture went through stages of experiment, development and overdevelopment, and decay quite comparable to analogous stages in the West. Although toward the end decoration tended to obscure the most blatant expressions of structure, it was always more than the decorative style

---

[2] Sonia P. Scherr-Thoss and Hans C. Scherr-Thoss, *Design and Color in Islamic Architecture* (Washington, D.C.: Smithsonian Institute Press, 1968), p. 16.

which it has so often been accused of being, and in its highest periods there was no more compromise with mere prettiness than there was with the dominance of structure.

All this is too vast a record for me to attempt to set straight here, both because of the limitations of space and time and because of the extent of my ignorance. I shall deal too cursorily with most of the great Muslim works, notably those of Egypt, North Africa, Spain, India, and most of Turkey.

As in most Western architectures, the principal buildings of Islam have been devoted to religious functions.

These include mosques (masjid, cami, mescet); religious schools (madrasa, medrese), often but not always attached to the mosque; convents (khanagah, tekke); shrines and mausolea (mazar, imamzada, gunbad, turbe); minarets (minar, minare). In addition there were palaces, forts, hospitals, caravanserai (khans, hans), bazaars, bridges, fountains.

The palaces were generally elegantly decorated and supplied with delicate comforts in the form of gardens and brooks running through their very interior but, save in India, were usually carelessly built and few have survived. This can generally be said of the secular buildings, except the bridges and inns. Of the latter, an excellent example can be seen no further away than Granada.

Shrines and tombs were very common and resulted in some elegant architecture. In Anatolia and Iran the interred was usually buried in a basement crypt above which rose octagonal or square tomb towers—some were supplied with interior and exterior domes or a polyhedral roof. In India the Mogul emperors began a tradition that the son should erect a noble tomb for his deceased father and these, more like buildings than like tombs, enclosed the central envelope with corridors and walls, corner towers, gardens, pools, exterior walls, and entrance gates in an increasing profusion of elegant detail from Humayun's tomb in Delhi (1560) and *Pl. 314* Akbar's in Sikandra, to the Taj Mahal in Agra where the tradition stopped (1632–1653). From Humayun on, the basic pattern was about the same. Each of the four sides has an enormous arch set in the rectangular wall (much like the developed eyvans of a mosque). On the corners are tall octagonal towers capped by arched balconies and canopies. The central area beneath which are the bodies is crowned by a huge bulb dome raised on a drum. When the Shah Jehan planned the Taj Mahal for his most beloved wife, he created in white marble one of the unquestioned architectural marvels of all time. He intended that his own tomb should be across the river and of contrapuntal black marble. But he did not reckon with the condition of the exchequer he would leave to his son Aurangzeb; he vastly overrated it, at the same time underrated the piety, austerity, and frugality of his son, who, when he spent money at all, disbursed it for mosques and not for palaces or tombs. So the Shah's tomb never came into being and he lies in cramped quarters beside his wife in the Taj Mahal.

But the principal requirement of Islamic architecture was the mosque, whose basic program was unusually simple. A mosque has the following minimal requirements:

A central area where the faithful can prostrate themselves in prayer. This may be open to the heavens or roofed over depending upon the requirements of the climate. If the central area was open, it was often lined with arcades behind which were small prayer halls. In general the Iranians liked to supplement the great open court with small high chambers to offer privacy and seclusion to the individual worshipper, while proposing nobility for all by the aspiring dome. If roofed over, it may be cut up by hundreds of columns as at Qairawan or Cordoba, or a single great space as in the larger mosques of Istanbul.

A *mihrab* or prayer niche placed so as to indicate the direction of Mecca. The mihrab could be simple or ornate but usually had the richest decoration in the mosque. In Iran it was always approachable. Decoration was often principally familiar passages from the Koran executed in handsome calligraphy with much variation in the script. But elsewhere the area in front of it was sometimes treated as a sanctuary and was made into a special dome-crowned square room, often very elegant. Indeed the enclosure, screened under the argument of protecting a governor or a sultan while at prayer, might become very private indeed.

A *mimbar* or pulpit adjacent to the mihrab. This often had an ornate staircase and might or might not be canopied.

A *minar* or minaret from which the muezzin would call to prayer. A mosque needs but one. However, minarets were sometimes proliferated to as many as six, either for reasons of symmetrical design or as a status symbol for the builder, although the erection of more than one was only a royal prerogative. They showed great variety in shape, in the number of circumferential balconies, in the treatment of the top, and in the austerity or lavishness of the decoration of the walls.

An ablution basin or tank or fountain for ritual washing prior to prayer. This, too, might be simple or complicated, provided with still or running water, open or surrounded by an arcaded canopy. There were large options as to where to place it.

In addition to these requirements, other things were common enough. There could, for example, be a desk for reading from the Koran. This was often a handsome stone table supported on columns.

The treatment of the entrance portal leading to the central area might be simple and unpretentious or lofty. The little and early Ottoman mosques of the fourteenth and fifteenth centuries preceding the monumental Ottoman mosques of the sixteenth and seventeenth centuries often had preliminary porches, usually but not always of five bays, and again with great variations in relative proportions of height and width. The mosque might be combined in a single complex with the bath (hamam), the convent (zaviye), the school (medrese), and the public kitchen.[3]

The section before the sanctuary mihrab, or indeed containing it, called the eivan, ivan, liwan, eyvan, might be vaulted (usually barrel) or domed (on squinches from a square base). In Iran a portal of great proportions, leading from the outside into the large, arcaded, rectangular open court, was soon provided in the wall opposite the entrance opening into the sanctuary, designed in scale and appearance much like the eyvan itself, and in the culminating "standard" Iranian plan, there was an eyvan portal in each of the sides of the courtyard wall. The Ottomans, on the other hand, concentrated on producing a high thrusting, stately mass which was basically a large dome starting from four or eight piers under which a large crowd could assemble. Sometimes there were two or four half domes thrusting against the main dome, all deriving, it is to be supposed, from Byzantine Hagia Sophia and preceded by an open forecourt.

It must be evident that there was nothing like a standard mosque plan, and if you feel this needs emphasis, you can find it in the plans of early Ottoman mosques provided by Aptullah Kuran.

It should also be evident from the foregoing that by choosing, as I have, to limit this treatment of Islamic architecture to some very fine examples of ceramic materials principally in Iran and Anatolia, I am leaving out a great deal of magnificent Islamic architecture which any architectural tourist ought to seek out.

This would include:

Pl. 316

The earliest extant Islamic work, the Dome of the Rock in Jerusalem, which was begun in 643 and is a rotunda form, very rich, clear, distinguished and definitely Islamic, though obviously owing much to Byzantine predecessors.

The survival in the stone mosque at Damascus (begun 707) of the pierced stone windows which, although also an extension of a Byzantine idea, became one of the great ornamental glories of Islamic architecture everywhere but notably in India and Spain, reaching their culmination perhaps at the Taj Mahal.

Other important brickwork, such as the colossal mosque at Samarra (842), or the brick walls of Calif Al Mansur, Baghdad (begun in 762).

Pl. 317

The Ibn Tulun Mosque in Cairo (878), a noble product of the Abbasid dynasty whose enclosure arcades and east end are of bricks. The arches, which are elegantly pointed, spring from couples of engaged

---

[3] An excellent and interesting treatment of the variations in early Ottoman mosques is provided by Aptullah Kuran, *The Mosque in Early Ottoman Architecture* (Chicago: The University of Chicago Press, 1968).

round columns. As in most early Egyptian mosques, the brick was covered with stucco, paint, and gold to produce a sumptuous surface treatment altogether different from the Byzantine tradition of marble and mosaic or the later Iranian use of glazed tile. Here we could have noted as well how the pointed Islamic arches and domes probably derived from corbeled bricks rather than segmented stone.

Examples of cruciform plans of mosques developed under Saladin to care for the four sects or cults of accepted Islamic orthodoxy.

The marvelous Qairawan mosque built in North Africa about 670. This mosque has plain exterior walls, but inside there are sixteen aisles in which brick arches rest on columns taken from ancient classic sources. The tie bars which absorb the thrust of the arches were used with admirable "honesty" from the very beginning. The arches are of a characteristic "horseshoe" shape, a clear precedent for the great mosque at Cordoba even to the provision of some scalloped arches.

The elegant Great Mosque of Cordoba (786) on the Qairawan plan. With double interlaced, highly decorated arcading with a magnificent mihrab and a dome over the eyvan before it, this dark and mysterious interior with its striated stone arches is in sharp contrast to the sun-drenched, austere forecourt and its unembellished enclosing wall. It is one of the great buildings of the world. (Parenthetically, those who object to the modest depredations of the Muslims in modifying Hagia Sophia for their religious purposes should contemplate with greater horror the obscenities of the indifferent but obtrusive Catholic Church planted in the midst of this grave Islamic forest.) *Pl. 319* *Pl. 318*

The Alcazar of Seville and the Alhambra of Granada, in which the delight of Moorish ornament, script, cusps, stalactites, mosaic, lobate arches, fountains, and pools were carried to their highest point—indeed to the point where the structure is lost in the decor. Since the structures are in fact so indifferently wrought of mud brick with burned brick facings, a wooden roof with plaster revetments, all encased in plaster and tile pilasters and ornaments, this may not matter much. Though justly famous and obviously known to any well-read Westerner, they are not really among the most distinguished pieces of Islamic architecture. The Alcazar, formerly the palace of a Umayid commander of the twelfth century, is somewhat older than the Alhambra, which was commenced in 1230 and is, in my opinion, marginally more distinguished. *Pl. 320*

The great work of the Moguls in India and Pakistan. There is the city of pink sandstone built by the third Mogul Akbar (1556–1605), and the "forts" at Agra, Delhi, and Lahore, which are so much more than forts. In Jehangir's ensemble at Lahore there is the lacy pavilion, the Duvan-e-Aam, of which three sides are open arcades of wide pointed

The Architecture of Brick 435

arches supported on free-standing coupled columns; the Dewan-e-Khas with its five wide bays of flattened cusped arches supported on bulbous capitals; Jehangir's quadrangle of low pavilions grouped around a parterre of grass and pond on which the deer feed and the peacocks spread their plumes; the magnificent Shish-Mahal with its fantastic ceiling, its squinched frieze, and its dazzling wall panels of glass mirrored mosaics penetrated here and there by windows with marble screens; and the Naulahka pavilion with its convex roof and its cusped main entrance flanked by marble and mosaic patterns. All this was done for Jehangir by imported architects and is firmly Islamic, even Persian, in its spirit, certainly not Indian. Further to the south there are the distinguished tombs of Humayun at Delhi, Akbar at Sikandra, and, culminating all, the Taj Mahal, adding up to the greatest architecture of India, though the work of conquerors.

Finally there are the great Ottoman mosques of Turkey, especially those of Istanbul and Bursa, among which it would be hard to pick a best one. There are the delicately painted tile panels of the Rustem Pasha Mosque (1574), still linear, still floral, but in a wider range of colors and with less stylization than heretofore to be found, both on the outside walls of the mosque and the head of the mimbar; the Mihrimah Mosque (1540–1555) with its unusual fenestration, its sloping buttresses around the dome, its strongly balanced composition disturbed only by its single, very slender, very high single minaret; the Sokullu Mehmet Pasha Mosque (1571–1572), free on the inside of any structural divisions where a hexagon inset in a rectangle provides the transition to a dome, abetted by six spherical pendentives and four half domes filling the corners of the rectangle; the sedate highly vertical entrance to the forecourt of the Suleymaniye (1556–

Pl. 321

1557), which itself is an orderly complex of mosque, school, library, haman, and almshouse, all arranged in a rigorous geometry around the focal monument, the mosque; or the Sultan Ahmet (Blue) Mosque (1609–1616), with its skyward-reaching four minarets, each with three annular balconies, very sharply pointed conical roofs, building up through lower towers and shallow domes to smaller cupoles, then larger half domes "rising wave upon wave to the summation of the dome."[4]

Evidently to omit so much is to be guilty of the same offense, or something like the same offense, of which I have accused my predecessors. But space offers no alternative so let us press on to the brickwork of Iran.

Although the Iranian builders used stucco, enameled tiles, and stone as well as brick, and other Islamic builders used brick, the art of bricklaying as developed in Iran and to some extent in Afghanistan was carried

[4] Scherr-Thoss, *Design and Color in Islamic Architecture*, op cit., p. 298.

to a very high point. There the bricklayers learned to create striking patterns and textures which were, nevertheless, subtle, even before they combined the bricks with tiles and other more highly colored ceramic elements. In admiration of the beauty which they created with their ceramic overlays, it is quite easy to forget that the brickwork started by being structural.

How structural it was is revealed in early examples of almost every kind of masonry structure. Consider, for example, the massive walls of the Masjid-i-Ali Shah (1312–1322) in Tabriz. The side walls of fired brick were 34 feet thick, laid very carefully with very fine joints and with almost no attempt at texture. The forecourt may have been paved with marble, the walls with faience. The columns in the portico may have been of almost translucent marble, the arches adorned with gold, but the wall stands there as a clear reminder of the beauty of a simple but noble material used straightforwardly.

Where is there a finer tower anywhere than the great Gunbad-i-Kabus (tomb tower of Kabus) in Gurgan (1006–1007)? Even the famous Lombard *Pl. 322* brick tower of the Abbey of Pomposa, mentioned earlier, is scarcely a competitor. It appears with a truncated conical base from which the unrelieved radial buttresses rise tapering slightly to an inverted truncated cone at the top. The intersections of these planes, top and bottom, are remarkably impressive when combined with the strong shadows cast by the bold projections of the buttresses. The roof is capped by a brick cone made of specially shaped bricks. The bricks of the main tower are square, measuring a little more than 8 inches on a side and 2 inches thick, and are so hard that they ring if struck. According the old tales, the coffin of Kabus was suspended high up so that the sun could shine upon him through a small window. This does not have to be true to confirm the conclusion that in this 56-foot-diameter, 200-foot-high tower we behold a masterpiece of brick monumentality.

Mention of the size of the brick calls to mind that the Iranian masons were using different bricks from those to which we are accustomed, in general harder fired but also of quite different sizes and shapes. Principally they were square up to 25 centimeters (10 inches) on a side and relatively thin, 5 centimeters (2 inches). In making patterns where the full width was not desired, the "standard" bricks were either cut to the right size or special shapes were struck before the bricks were laid. Since the big monuments used the same local clays as the lesser buildings, they harmonized readily, at least in color, with the ambient architecture.

The bricks were laid from scaffolding which could be used as well for the decorators applying the last layers of bricks in patterns as for the basic structural wall. Some of the patterns were laid up by the masons *in situ*, others by the assembling of precast sections. The art of patterning was carried to a high degree of skill and beauty before colored backgrounds, glazes, enamels, and mosaics were introduced.

Shadow lines were provided by the treatment of the joint, by moldings, by laying panels in relief, by the insertion of brick end plugs, by blind arches, raised brick tracery, or brick ornaments placed in high relief. In the pre-Seljuk and Seljuk periods (1037–1194) brick was used both for structure and decoration, and in this so-called "naked brick" period many patterns were developed, some very bold, some minutely intricate. Only rarely were a few colored tiles employed to accent some element of a facade, but they did not, at this time, play anything like a major role.

At the Seljuk tomb tower in Demavand, for example, the octagonal structure is faced with three panels on each face different from face to face and from level to level, in diagonals, chevrons, herringbones, crosses, eight-pointed stars. Some of the crossed diamond forms are in high relief, some in low; some are in positive, some in negative expressions of the diamonds. The engaged columns at the corners have very wide interstices and deeply recessed bonding in which, moreover, the texture of the mortar bed is made still more forceful by impressing it with the fingers while wet.

At Kharraqan two other octagonal brick tomb towers, in one of which engaged arches, divided into two major panels separated by a band of three small blind arches, occupies most of each of the eight sides, while on the other there are simple engaged arches, nonetheless employing about seventy different brick layouts. Whole and half bricks provide an unusual arrangement of opposed diagonals. There are wheels, interlaced stars, some designs which at first glance seem very free. Later on and still without the use of color, brick end plugs made of carved or stamped hard plaster broke up the patterns of otherwise symmetrical brickwork, as in the mausoleum of Chelebi Oglu at Sultaniyah (1310); and when the use of plaster became still more common, incised abstract patterns suggestive of brickwork were often very effective as in the Kufic inscription on the mausoleum of Pir-i-Bakran at Linjan (1303). But even before the advent of any plaster, any tile, any color, the variety of brick patterning developed can only be described as amazing—and beautiful.

The quality and variety of pure brick structural elements is not less amazing. I have already spoken of the arch and the unusual shapes it could take since the bricks were used more as corbels than as segments. But the Islamic builders soon graduated to vaults and domes. The vaults they built in a variety of forms unimagined in the West where, a good solution having been found, it was little tampered with thereafter. On the other hand, in the Masjid-i-Jami in Isfahan (the Friday Mosque), you can see an array of vault patterns juxtaposed to each other such as probably can be found nowhere else in the world.

Pl. 323
Pl. 324
Pl. 325
Pl. 326

There are, for example, the library vaults built between 1121 and 1175 in such variety that they were numbered by Herzfeld, and whose imaginativeness and beauty can be conveyed only in part by photographs. It was the small size of the brick that made the variety possible, and it was the skill and taste of the Iranian builders that kept the possibilities well disciplined, so that great diversity was achieved without fragmenting a fundamental unity. Some of the vaults seem but an array of squinches, but a subtle array; others are clearly ribbed. Though the ribs almost always cross each other or interlace, they are working ribs. Repairs to library vault 60 in Isfahan's Masjid-i-Jami requiring removal of sections between the ribs demonstrated that the ribs were self-sustaining.

In Islamic work vaults moved rapidly into domes, for it was the dome that was the usual desired outcome. Originally intersecting arches were used to reduce the square floor plan to an octagon, and then the dome was corbeled inward from that. How this worked out in its simplest form appears in the northeast dome chamber of the same Masjid-i-Jami (1088) which has withstood severe earthquakes and other destructive forces for nearly a millennium. Here the array of columns and arched niches on a square plan rise to the arches which change the plan to an octagon, succeeded by squinches, until the dome floats on the collar of the cupola.

> The tall Kufic inscription is so conceived so as to continue the strong vertical character of the lower chamber. Like the ultimate chord in a symphony, the dome is the final solution of the structural drama. Here sophisticated design challenges interpretation. Vertical motion ceases; the area of contemplation has been reached.[5]

In this great work, what begin by looking like ribs turn into a series of triangles which develop into and interlace with five pointed stars.

The earlier Iranian domes were usually single shells which, seeming quite high in the relatively small interior space, tended to look squat on the outside. They offered another problem of appearance. Since they needed to decrease in thickness toward the crown, the base might be three or more bricks thick and the summit one to one and a half. To cover the steps thus produced on the exterior, the surface was smoothed out with dressed brick; ultimately the covering was faience in Iran, lead sheets in Turkey. A good example of how the single shell dome looks is afforded by the Masjid-i-Shaykh Lutfullah in Isfahan (1601–1618), which I think to be one of the most beautiful mosques in the world. But the Iranian builders did not see it that way, and long before this mosque was built had set their course toward achieving more imposing exterior heights. Threatened now with destroying the interior scale, they solved this problem along with that of the exterior surface by resorting to the double dome, which permitted, among other things, the extreme bulbs to be seen outside of Iran. (Even in Isfahan there are much higher domes than that of the Lutfullah mosque.)

The squinch, meanwhile, beginning as a working part to offer a transition from one shape of the plan to another, soon developed its own personality as a decorative item. It could be subdivided first into quite large pieces making up most of the form of the enormous eivan portals or prayer

[5] Ibid., p. 44.

Pl. 328

places, such as the northwest eivan of the Masjid-i-Jami in Isfahan (1121–1122, redecorated 1700–1701).

Pl. 329

Pl. 330

Pl. 332

Broken up still more into what are usually called "stalactites" but could more descriptively be called honeycombs, the deep recess of a large squinch was reduced as in the Madrasa in Khargird. By the fifteenth century this device had become very popular with architects, and the honeycombs began to be smaller and smaller until, as at the Masjid-i-Shah's entrance portal in Isfahan (1612–1638), the tiered squinches fill the entire arch and transform it into an enormous geometric apse. By this time the desire for decoration by faience, by mosaic, by inlay had reached its peak so that the combination is brilliant and unforgettable. Similar attitudes had become applied to the once simple minarets so that those of this same mosque not only show a great spiraling of blue tile on their shafts but a repetition of the stalactite motive in the projected arches which support the annular muezzin's balcony near their tops.

Long before these developments in the decorative use of structure, the simple early brick patterns had given way to more elaborate and versatile arrangements. The use of plaster was the first of these. Colored to match the color of the brick, it could then have simulated brick patterns scratched into its hardened surface, but of course the carving could also be done to produce freer forms, including the cursives. The plaster could be precast, in which case its use on the buildings was no longer really plastic; or it might be carved *in situ*, with or without stencils, which were also used when the plaster was painted after application. When this was done on very hard white plaster, large areas might be left unornamented with dramatic effects such as the Spaniards used later in another context in some of their Baroque cathedral facades.

It was not long, though, before enameled tiles, faience, superseded plaster. Small pieces of color accent had been used quite early, as in the Gunbad-i-Surkh in Maragha (1147–1148). But as skill in faience and affection for it grew, it was not long before all the surfaces of the monuments were covered with faience mosaic, as brilliantly, even fantastically, revealed in Isfahan in a way which we tend to associate, rightly or wrongly, with the apogee of Iranic architecture. At the beginning the mason or mosaicist used square brick-sized tiles glazed in single colors of which a small variety, dominated by dark and light blues, offered his palette. He had a pattern at full size either on paper or scratched into a bed of white plaster. He used small hatchets to cut the basic tiles into the needed shapes, which he laid face down onto the pattern. Then the backs were coated with plaster. When this had set, he had a panel which he lifted off the pattern and installed on the building. This, of course, took a great deal of time and was therefore costly. But the effects were marvelous, enhanced by the unevenness of the handwork so that the surfaces showed subtle contrasts of shade and reflection.

Gradually more efficient methods were developed, culminating in *haft rangi* (seven colors). Here standard square tiles were simply painted to the design with the appropriate one of seven colors, and the tiles were fired all at once. Some of this work is excellent and hard to tell from mosaic; it offered opportunities for refined treatments quite impossible in true mosaic, but like so many technological "improvements" before and since, on the whole, it was accompanied by as marked a deterioration of craftsmanship and even of design as we may expect when sonnets are printed out by computers manipulated by linguists or intellectuals rather than poets.

It was not long before the walls were fully covered with decoration and the structural fabric was no longer directly exposed, although it was never positively concealed either.

There were some self-imposed limitations on the subject matter of the decoration. It is commonly believed that Islamic doctrine prohibits the portrayal of living creatures. There is, in fact, no such injunction in *El Koran*, though it does appear in the writings of the prophet Mohammed. Living forms are common in miniatures from many times and places and not only in those devoted to secular subjects, and they appear sometimes in architecture, especially in the Safavid buildings of Isfahan, but they are still comparatively rare and usually floral; so that it is true that geometric forms or script predominate.[6]

In these circumstances, it is not surprising that Islamic sculpture did not attain the status of a major art, comparable to and the peer of architecture, as was true both in India and the West with consequent advantages of richness and problems of competition. On the other hand, calligraphy and carpet weaving did. Some of the handsomest faience motifs are highly suggestive of carpets woven at the same time.

But even more important than carpet designs was the work of the calligraphers which appears throughout Islamic architecture from Arabia to Spain. Many of the calligraphic inscriptions in Arabic were intelligible only to a handful of religious scholars and could appear to most worshippers only as decoration. Others were the most familiar 99 sayings of the Koran. The first centuries favored the beautiful Kufic script, but later other versions came into vogue and passed away. Whether chiseled in relief, executed in mosaic or in paint, whether slender or blocky, horizontally or vertically emphatic, flowing or rectilinear, abstract or concrete, clearly legible or confusingly interlaced, the calligraphy was an important part of architectural decoration to an extent never realized before or since, and always was in harmony with the structural surfaces. It demanded the attention of the greatest calligraphers. The inscriptions of the Masjid-i-

Pl. 333

[6] Among the notable exceptions in Isfahan are the birds, animals, and huntsmen portrayed on the painted tiles of the spandrels of the outer blind arches of the Hest Behest [itself, of course, a royal palace and therefore secular, and also late (1669)], the birds of the ceiling fresco of the main reception hall of the Ali Kapu [also an official and secular building], and the paired peacocks on the portal of the Masjid-i-Shah, which, though royal, is still a mosque.

Pl. 331 Shaykh Lutfullah, for example, were made by the most eminent calligrapher of Safavid times, who worked most of the time at the small scale of the manuscript. Calligraphy was used freely wherever a linear surface encouraged it, on lintels and jambs of doorways, on frames of entrance portals, at the top of panels, on friezes, on the collars of domes, both inside and outside, and on secular as well as religious edifices.

To understand the full richness of Islamic work, you will have to go to the Soviet Union, Spain, to North Africa, to Egypt, to India and Pakistan, to Syria and Iraq, and Turkey, among these most particularly Spain, India, and Turkey. The very special and wonderful case of Iran which I have singled out will require of the avid collector considerable and not always convenient travel with more or less marginal gains at least, say, to Tabriz, Maragha, Sultaniya, Demavand, Gurgan, Gunbad, Nayin and Kharraqan, and Meshed. But more than in the case of many architectures a very good collection can be made in a single city, the beautiful city of Isfahan, one of the few fairy-tale urban collections of the world, clustering around

Pl. 315 the Maidan Square but including at least the marvelous and diverse mosques, the Friday Mosque (Masjid-i-Jami), the Masjid-i-Shaykh Lutfullah, the Masjid-i-Shah, the Ali Qapu palace of the Shah Abbas, the Chahar Bagh Avenue with its lovely trees and its destructive motor roads, the damaged forty Pillars Palace, the Chehel Solun, and the still more ruined Hesht Behest, the Madrassa Chahar Bagh (royal Chahar Bagh School), the historic bridges, the "shaking minarets" of the Monar Jonban. A list of the ancient monuments in Isfahan, regardless of their state of repair, runs to eighty-six items. Many are in good repair—a half dozen are magnificent.

Agra, Delhi, Lahore, Granada, Seville, Toledo, Damascus, Istanbul, Cairo, Baghdad, Tabriz, Isfahan—these are urban names to conjure with. Some of them, like Cairo and Istanbul, are greater cities and contain a wider range of history and of historical architecture than Isfahan. Of them all, Istanbul is certainly a totally more beautiful city. But for a sheer display of Islamic architecture at its finest, there is nothing to compare with Isfahan. It is indeed a Xanadu but finer than Kublai Khan (or Coleridge) ever imagined.

CHAPTER EIGHT

THE DEPARTURE FROM TOTAL ARCHITECTURE: THE RENAISSANCE

Certainly if one looks at late Islamic architecture with a fishier eye than I have brought to the viewing, he might say that the ornamentation *had* overwhelmed the structure and that something had perhaps gone wrong. My mind tells me that this may be so, but my senses reject the finding.

But my attitudes toward the architecture of the Italian Renaissance, from Brunelleschi's Foundling Hospital in Florence of 1419 to Palladio's Villa Capra outside Vicenza of 1567, are less waffling, saving some exceptions, such as Michelangelo's pre-Baroque Campidoglio in Rome, Alberti's Rucellai Palace in Florence, and a half dozen others. Here my mind has managed, I think, to understand what these Italian designers were trying to do and to appreciate how well, given their premises, they achieved what they set out to do. This is one level surely at which architecture ought to be judged. But there is another and more personal level, that of delight. As I have perhaps overstressed earlier, this need not require any intellectual rejection of the premises on which an historical architecture rests, or any moral condemnation of the uses to which an architecture was put;[1] it may be no more than the fact that one derives no particular pleasure from looking at it or of being in it. This is my problem with Renaissance architecture, though not Renaissance painting. However, I do not intend to

---

[1] For our own times, a moral judgment seems to me essential.

condemn categorically the Renaissance because of my blind spot. Nor do I mean to insist that an architecture which uses structure and materials and function "sincerely," what might be called *total* architecture, is beyond doubt superior to the architecture of the stage set, or the architecture which puts all its chips on the aesthetic canons, however well conceived, of unity, rhythm, proportion, equilibrium, and scale. Whatever one's conclusions about the *superiority* of total architecture, however, it seems true that such architecture went into a long, if fitful, sleep in Florence toward the beginning of the fifteenth century and did not really awaken again until late in the nineteenth century, broken only by the brief experiments of the Baroque to which I will come later.

No doubt part of my aversion to the Renaissance stems from the way it was forced on us in architectural school as the only real model for our own work. Certainly part of it comes from dislike of the ubiquity of its colonial and eclectic translations. Practically all the important buildings that stood around us or were being built around us were eclectic, and rarely first-class, translations of old Renaissance or classic models. Moreover, the Renaissance models themselves were no more than eclectic derivations of what fifteenth- and sixteenth-century Italians had taken to be the architectural spirit of Imperial Rome. (In theory nineteenth-century eclecticism tolerated other models, especially Romanesque or Gothic, even Egyptian, Islamic, Mayan, but the preponderance of the eclectic choice remained Renaissance.) And underlying all of this resentment may have been my early attachment to the Gothic.

Whatever the reasons, it was a long time before I even deigned to look carefully at the buildings of the Renaissance. I know this to have been a very stupid attitude. Since then I have looked a great deal and read a great deal and believe I do understand the premises. I do appreciate the skill with which such men as Brunelleschi, Alberti, and Bramante built upon these premises and have even come to like some, if not many, of the buildings. Nonetheless I know that I will be at best a limping guide and will, therefore, devote only a modicum of space to the Renaissance, leaving the rest in other and more loyal hands.

Renaissance theory was anchored securely in the belief that the writing of Vitruvius was gospel. Especially influential passages were those relating the proportions of human figures to the proportions of temples, expressed visually by many drawings, of which Leonardo's is the most famous, showing man inscribed in both circle and square and to be taken as the "measure of all things."

The Italian Renaissance was not a universally classic spirit but only Roman. It looked not to Greece for its architectural inspiration, but rather to what Rome had made out of Greek elements. It was interested in Roman codes, in Roman scale, in Roman details, and in Roman space concepts when they were different from Greek. From Brunelleschi on, the study, preferably on the site, of Roman architectural antiquities was a highly valued part of an architect's training reaching toward indispensability.

From this study, Brunelleschi and his followers postulated that architectural art of the highest quality demanded a demonstrable and *recognizable* order. Taken as essential, symmetry offered the easiest path to attaining it. Since the functions of most buildings could at that time be conceived in symmetric arrangements, most of the difficulties an adherence to symmetry created for later eclectics did not arise in Florence or Rome. This recognizable order was also the result of solicitous care in the proportioning and balancing of spaces, the relation of similar parts to each other (e.g., rhythm and counterpoint of windows), clarification of stories, and the relation of objects to different objects, systematized, for example, as perspective.

The Italian urge toward this certainty derived in part from its Latin ancestry, but, I suppose, also because Italians had never been any happier about Gothic than serious admirers of Northern Gothic have been about Italian Gothic (Lombard Romanesque is quite another matter). You will recall that when Italians finally "accepted" Gothic, they ignored the most important Gothic structural principles and preferred to play with Gothic detail as a new fashion in decoration.

When the Renaissance began, Giotto's campanile hard by the growing Duomo was a prominent Gothic ornament of Florence. How Florentines took it I do not know, but it has confused Westerners who had come to admire the Lombard towers pierced only by small slits to achieve uninterrupted height, or the Roman campaniles with their strongly marked stories, or the skillful and functional gradation of fenestration as shown at the Abbey of Pomposa over near Ravenna. Though Giotto had not invented anything in this tower, he had expressed the elements very differently.

Pl. 257

> After all you could describe it as just a rectangular tower covered with white, pink, green and black slabs of marble.[2]

Ruskin was at first displeased by it but after living beside it for a long time had more favorable reactions. Later Somerset Maugham, at twenty, accepted the tower only because Ruskin had accepted it; forty years later he admired it without the support of Ruskin.

Now these were Northern admirers of true Gothic, wanting to like the Italian version and having difficulty in doing so. Brunelleschi, on the other hand, might have admired, as perhaps Alberti might have done, the very departures from Gothicism which most perplexed and troubled Ruskin.

Whatever the Florentines thought of Giotto's tower, the Italians were more than ready for change. Indeed, they soon enough coined pejorative words for the great medieval works. The *handle* for change was provided by the sudden interest in humanistic studies and classic literature, includ-

---

[2] Sean O'Faolain, *A Summer in Italy* (New York: Devin-Adair, 1954), pp. 119–120.

ing principally Latin literature, so that architects and artists followed each other in what became the much-traveled road to Rome.

Though Filippo Brunelleschi (1377–1446) is generally credited with having opened the Italian Renaissance, his greatest work, the dome of the Duomo, probably really belongs to the Gothic spirit in all but one respect. Alberti was describing his friend Brunelleschi when he portrayed an ideal architect as a man who "having meditated on the mathematical logic of the universe, creates marvels in the interest of the human community." Like most of the great Italian Renaissance architects, Brunelleschi began in a different field of art, operating as goldsmith and sculptor. He entered the 1401 competition for the bronze north doors of the Gothic baptistery, and his design, for example, of the reliefs of the sacrifice of Isaac, show how polemic against the Gothic tradition he was already prepared to be. But Ghiberti, who was content with the kind of gentle departures from formalism Giotto had introduced a century earlier, seeking only to enrich and develop it, won the competition, and Brunelleschi set out for Rome to study the classic monuments at first hand. The ground-floor Corinthian colonnade of the Foundling Hospital in Florence (1419) was one of his first buildings.

Pl. 292
Pl. 289

Thereafter he was all architect and no longer a multifaceted artist. He came to big fame when he won the competition for the dome of the Duomo (1420–1434) with what is clearly a miracle of design.

The problem began as a technical one. Over a hundred years earlier Arnolfo di Cambio had started the foundations of the new Duomo. In 1418 when the Florentines decided to finish the building, they found that the width of the drum inhibited the use of wood centering; meanwhile the essentially decorative nature of Italian Gothic had led to a loss of technical knowledge coupled with a decay of tradition through which specialized master masons had disappeared. Brunelleschi conceived a new form, a double dome with ribs which could be kept in an equilibrium of thrust and weights whereby the structure could support itself during construction. This was a new application of *Gothic* principles, and indeed the ribs are Gothic in appearance. But the spatial structure resulting from this articulated organism was not Gothic nor was the fact that this architectonic form acted as the central generator for the entire spatial interior. This is why Giulio Carlo Argan can call it an "essentially perspective structure" and say that "in realizing it Brunelleschi transformed the indefinite space of the Gothic cathedral into a rational system of relations."[3]

After Brunelleschi, impatient Italian time moved fast. Almost every day saw some new thing. The treatises on architectural theory built up and came to the attention of foreign rulers. The movement spread from Florence first, through Italy, and then over the Alps. And the movement was never static. Each idea exhausted itself rapidly. It was only eighty years

[3] Free translation from Giulio Carlo Argan on Brunelleschi in Pierre Francastel (directeur), *Les Architects Célèbres* (Paris: Lucien Mazenod, Editions d'Art, 1959), vol. II, pp. 58–59.

from Brunelleschi's Florentine Dome, only sixty from his San Spirito, to the beginning of the High Renaissance in Rome with Bramante's Tempietto there of 1502. Mannerism was in the saddle in Mantua with Romano's Palazzo del Té, less than another quarter century later, while Michelangelo gave hints of the Baroque in his Piazza del Campidoglio of 1536. Palladio's great works around Vicenza were about 1550, one hundred and thirty years after the work on the Florentine dome began. The portent of the triumph of the Baroque in Rome may have been in 1568 when the cornerstone of the Gesu was laid, but was certain by 1630. The boundless energies of Bernini and Borromini faded away with their deaths in 1680 and 1687 so that the entire span from Brunelleschi's first building to Borromini's last was little more than 2½ centuries. Thereafter the torch went elsewhere, but it was not reduced to flickering reminiscences for almost two centuries more.

I will not attempt to lead you through the main developments of the Renaissance which, in my hands, would result in an academically arid exercise. I do want to mention a few famous products of the Renaissance, and after that to say something about the cult of personality which is so dramatically illustrated in this time.

For example, there is Brunelleschi's Foundling Hospital in Florence of 1419. It has little in common with heavier Roman classic precedents and might even be denied by some to be truly Renaissance in spirit. But the loggia is delicate, clear, beautifully proportioned, and the separation of stories by the entablature is so explicit and the details so charming that it is a lovable building whatever may have been the experience of the foundlings who lived there.

San Spirito (1436) does not excite me as much as San Lorenzo (1420), even though I know the latter to be traditional and to owe most of its beauty to the serenity of its proportions, while the former, thanks to its central plan and equally focused elements, has been called, with some justice, "the clearest expression of the demonstrable order which the Renaissance valued so highly."[4] But for me there is no more here than an historical-intellectual appreciation and the church has no sensuous appeal—so it is simply not enough.

As for the great Leon-Baptiste Alberti (1404–1472), who, though not the first, may really be the central figure of the early classic Renaissance, there is no doubt about his admirable preparation in mathematics, music, law, and the writings and monuments of antiquity. His own writings were thoughtful and influential, though I think he erred in accepting the judgment of Vitruvius that Roman, not Greek, represented the culmination of the architectural art. But he built little and not much of that was great. Of his few extant architectural works, only the Palazzo Rucellai of Florence

Pl. 294

Pl. 295

[4] Norbert Lynton in Trewin Copplestone (ed.), *World Architecture* (New York: McGraw-Hill, 1963), p. 234.

in 1446 causes me much thrill. This is surely the finest of all the Renaissance Palazzi, because of the delicacy of its proportions, the distinction of its modules, and the abandonment of fortress feelings such as were perpetuated in the ruder Strozzi (Maiano, Florence, 1489); the Pitti (Brunelleschi or Alberti, Florence, 1458); or the lower portions of the Medici Riccardi (Michelozzo, Florence, 1440–1460). It is also historically important, since it is the great assertion of the system so generally adopted later of articulating the whole facade by the use of superimposed orders, as the Romans had often done before but never so discreetly or subtly. Seldom, perhaps never, elsewhere has the harmony of scale of the orders been so completely achieved, so that we sense genius here as well as system. On the other hand, I have almost a positive aversion to the facade of Santa Maria Novella (1456–1470). I do not understand why Alberti felt it necessary to put a new facade on a harmless old Italian Gothic church, although it was so much a Renaissance thing to do, a practice seldom honored in the breach. And granting that he had a facade problem of joining in a "classic" way the narrow upper nave and the wide lower stories, the enormous scrolls (also much copied later, unfortunately) which he used to solve the problem, much touted as they have been, seem to me absurd. We have now already come perilously near to unabashed "facade" architecture.

I can muster even less delight or affection for the Roman facades Alberti created for San Francesco in Rimini (1447–1455), San Sebastiano and Sant'Andrea in Mantua, regardless of how they may have been maimed by subsequent rearrangers. They are excellently proportioned, especially, perhaps, the Rimini Church. San Sebastiano and Sant'Andrea are not of that excellence outside. One of my troubles here undoubtedly is that I see no intellectual sense or visual delight in patterning the entrance to a Christian church of the fifteenth century after a Roman temple of more than a millennium earlier, especially if you modify the temple to make it seem more like a triumphal arch, say, the great one of Titus in Rome dating from A.D. 81, which turns up again later on at the Logetta in Venice (1540), or as at the Rimini church in the form of the Arch of Augustus in the same city.

Of Alberti, Vasari wrote later that although he had surpassed his contemporaries in theory, a great many excelled him in practice.

We should not hold it against him that he usually had others execute his work, since this was a common Renaissance practice. He did supervise and see achieved San Sebastiano. He watched Matteo de Pastis build the temple at Rimini and complained to his architect-builder that the changes made were discordant to all the architect's "music." Rosselino built the Rucellai palace for him and may have influenced the design. The first stone for Sant'Andrea was laid two years after his death and the building later completed by Juvara, a man of quite different taste.

I expect in the end Alberti was more influential through his writings on architecture. These were achieved in 1450, divulged in 1452, and printed for the first time in 1485, more than a decade after his death; they constituted the first serious writing on architectural theory since the Vitruvius of classical antiquity. The Renaissance would spawn much more before it was over—Serlio, Palladio, Vignola, and others—but none more significant than Alberti.

He echoed much of Vitruvius, including the architectural tripod of *necessitas, commoditas, voluptas*. But he was a brighter and more sensitive man than Vitruvius and much more candid. Utility and beauty, he proclaimed, did not always march hand in hand; the beauty of a building did not necessarily arise as the consequence of the perfect satisfaction of a given need. Each had its own laws, and as you reached toward one, you might well move further away from the other, a sort of Heisenbergian principle for architecture. On the other hand, superimposed ornament had nothing to do with architectural beauty, so you could not solve the practical problem first and then rely on embellishment to save the beauty. You had to achieve utility and beauty simultaneously, not sequentially, and there lay the rub. Architecture cannot really find its models in nature, but, if not copying nature, ought to take example from her (*veluti animal aedificium*). Here are premonitions of Frank Lloyd Wright. The plan is already an *oeuvre* and contains germinally the qualities and defects which the finished building will display. Here are premonitions of Le Corbusier. This is all very wise. The fault if any lay not in the theory but in the execution.

Alberti recognized and greatly that the placement of a single building must be part of a larger unity (although Sant'Andrea is not that considerate of the nearby older baptistery of San Lorenzo). This unity should provide a concord with a countryside or an urban assemblage. The building of a city ought to go beyond the material problems of circulation, hygiene, and the like, to include aesthetics. This is advice our present generation of young students and le Corbusian "urbanists" might well heed.

He was a towering figure of his day, and it is not surprising that his admirers spare little praise. "He was more than theorist, philosopher of architecture. Papini said he was the most Greek of the Italians."[5]

Here and there in the republican, mercantile, classic Renaissance spreading out from Florence and northern Italy, I have found moments of delight, such as Michelozzo's Portinari Chapel in San Eustorgio, Milan (1462). More often, however, come moments of respect, such as for the overly ornamented yet horribly influential Certosa di Pavia of Amadeo (1481); and especially the vestibule of Brunelleschi's Pazzi Chapel in Santa Croce (1430–1443), despite its unresolved problems and its relative lack of sophistication.

Pl. 296

When the scene shifts to Rome, Bramante, and the High Renaissance, my views become briefly more favorable. For at least a short time a great harmony was achieved in Rome following the capture of Milan by the French Army of Louis XII in 1499. The first great designer to emerge,

---

[5] Free translation of quotation of Paul-Henri Michel in Francastel, *Les Architects Célèbres*, op. cit., pp. 62–63.

The Departure from Total Architecture: The Renaissance 449

Pl. 304

Bramante, was a master of proportion and detail. The cortile of the Palazzo Cancelleria (1495–1505), whether or not by Bramante (the dates are not encouraging), is clearly ingratiating, with its two-storied vaulted gallery resting on old Doric columns taken from the ancient basilican church of San Lorenzo. I have less affection for what is often taken to be Bramante's masterpiece, "a perfect architectural gem," the tiny Tempietto (1503), the circular chapel in the cloisters of San Pietro in Montorio; perhaps this is

Pl. 291

because I do not attribute so much importance as some would to Bramante's unquestioned mastery of refinement in moldings, carving, and details, but more because it seems to me not to be so fine as the classic Roman circular temples which were its inspiration or so appropriate for its presumed purposes.

Saint Peter's is quite another matter. It is very important on any account and not alone for its associations. As we see it, it is the result of many successive architectural hands, some benign, some perhaps malign. It gains surely from Bernini's great Baroque colonnaded forecourt but not from the heavy columniation he imposed on the nave. It profits from Michelangelo's dome but not from the elongation of the nave by Maderna, the major deviation from Bramante's marvelous Greek cross plan. Many plans for the main envelope and the dome were proposed—by Sangallo,

Pl. 298
Pl. 299
Pl. 300
Pl. 301

by Raphael, by Peruzzi—and each of these had some magnificence. But none of them, including the realized plan, had the genius of Bramante's. This basic plan was proposed by Bramante in 1506 on the commission of Pope Julius II, approved and accepted but never executed. However, it influenced Michelangelo so much that we can take it almost to have been realized. Here in beautifully proportioned symmetry we find a basic square in which a Greek cross is partly inscribed and partly extended beyond. Between the arms, four smaller Greek crosses and four corner towers are all suavely fused. This was a masterful proposal, both functionally and aesthetically, although Bramante's simpler and flatter dome, had it been executed, would surely have been less impressive than Michelangelo's.

Aside from the plan of St. Peter's and other Bramante works, I like most from this high Roman period Raphael's San Eligio degli Orifici (1509), the first building done by him when he came to Rome and completed seventeen years later by Peruzzi. It is austere and clear, and I would like to believe Wittkower's thought that it epitomized the religious feeling of the Renaissance, such as it was.

The Roman climax was short-lived, and the degeneration into Mannerism came all too soon. The term *Mannerism* is slippery, and the complexity of the movement too dangerously elusive to simplify, but however it is bounded, and whether it is of the sixteenth or the twentieth century, it makes me uneasy. It is certainly easier to bear in "sublime" form, à la Michelangelo, but sublime or not, something is amiss in an artificial system in which *architectural* elements have no functional significance whatsoever, and personal expression is the main goal. This is still true under the severe

Pl. 302

discipline of Michelangelo's Laurentian Library (1523–1526) (at least so it seems to me), though the triple staircase (completed by Vasari in 1571) is much less offensive than the ridiculous Palazzo del Té in Mantua built by the painter Giulio dit Romano in 1526–1531.

I imagine that Mannerism in any form started out laudably enough by trying to break with established canons and to encourage innovation, soon seeking a personal and "expressive" art and bound soon to become at best idiosyncratic and at worst awful, especially at the hands of the non-geniuses who flock uncritically to a new standard which says that all things done one's own way have equal merit. When the beginning is touched with genius, it may initiate a great new thing also with standards, such as the Baroque of which Michelangelo's Piazza del Campidoglio of 1536 may be a herald (as some find even the Laurentian to be).

However, it is difficult to take a firm ground about Mannerist developments in, say, Venice. Sansovino's library (1556) is far from painful, and Sanmicheli's Palazzo Bevilaqua in Verona (1527) manages to resist the greatest excesses of Roman Mannerism. I suppose we owe some sort of debt to the candor with which Peter Lombard said in his Palazzo Vendramin of 1481 that it was all right to have an appliqued facade, i.e., one where the architectural embellishment stops at the corners of the front. Fra Giocondo's Loggia del Consiglio in Verona of 1476 is remarkably graceful, both in form and color. But if we are to reckon with the Venetian Renaissance, we must first and foremost come to an understanding with Andrea Palladio, surely the greatest architect of his immediate time (1518–1580), whose later influence has been among the largest and most durable. Despite the fact that most of his greatest work was outside Venice, especially in his native Vicenza, his influence was so great as almost to suppress the development of the Baroque in Venice and to make him the Virgil of the neoclassicists in the eighteenth century.

I used to be repelled by the formality of Palladio and plans like that of the Villa Rotonda (Capra), 1567, which then seemed to me to have no relation to life. With time I have come to realize and appreciate the perfection of this style, whether displayed in the facade Palladio imposed on the Gothic Basilica, Vicenza (1549); the Palazzo Valmarana in Vicenza (1566); the Palazzo Chiericati, also in Vicenza (1560); or even his two great Venetian churches, San Giorgio Maggiore of 1560 and Il Redentore of 1576.

Pl. 297
Pl. 307

Then on a quite different plane, I should suppose everyone should be interested by the innovative Teatro Olimpico in Vicenza completed after Palladio's death by Scamozzi in 1580 and Scamozzi's own theatre in the little Gonzaga town of Sabbioneta and its greatest treasure.

Outside of Italy, save for two French exceptions, the "pre-Baroque" Renaissance engages still less of my affection. Until they had created their own quite French version as stated, for example, in Pierre Lescot's wing of the Louvre (1546), the French, it seems to me, did import Italian advisers and artists but looked on the Italian Renaissance mostly as a stylistic novelty, to be applied when desired, for example, in combination with be-

Pl. 306

The Departure from Total Architecture: The Renaissance 451

loved medieval remains, free from principles and ideology. It was a rather splendid turning of the tables on the previously held Italian views of the Gothic, and a much more certain reading of the styles.

The French did not find it hard to add to good Gothic palaces without feeling the necessity of covering everything over so that vastly interesting and even romantic results were obtained in different ways at the transi-*Pl. 311* tional Château of Blois (1508), Azay-le-Rideau (1516), the much-altered *Pl. 303* Chenonceaux (1515–1556), and even to some extent at the Palace of Fontainebleau where the forests and the gardens and the furnishings are perhaps superior to the architecture. The chateaux certainly created a charming ambiance in the valley of the Loire but were neither quite Renaissance nor quite medieval. In the hands of a master like Pierre Nepveu, the *Pl. 305* Château of Chambord (1519–1547) looms as more important.

The two rectangular plans are unusual; the inner block, memory of a donjon and square like the keep of earlier English castles, is reminiscent of fortified days despite the elliptical barrel vaulting of the four contiguous halls. There is the famous double staircase, the two spirals within a stone cage on which people can ascend and descend without seeing each other. The many circular towers waste space when used to contain orthagonal rooms, but why should the affluent owner have cared? There are Gothic features and Renaissance details, Gothic verticality and conical roofs; and there is the skyline based on the high-pitched roof, the ornamented dormers, and the elaborate and high chimneys which became the characteristic of early French Renaissance buildings. When Fletcher suggests comparing it with Vignola's palace at Caprarola, he puts the academic Italian at a great disadvantage, however classic his book about the orders may have become. The symmetrical plan, the terrace, the details of the Renaissance plan may have stemmed from Italian theory, and the Renaissance decoration applied by imported North Italian masons, but the whole result has the beautiful and romantic simplicity in complexity that is characteristic of much early French Renaissance architecture.

This continued to be so even in such chateaux as Ancy le France (1546), but when the talented Philibert de l'Orme began the Château of Anet a year later for Diane de Poitiers, evicted from Chenonceaux, he produced something which again leaves me cold. His free use of Renaissance forms in the projecting entrance pavilion may well have been an anticipation of Baroque space modeling, and it *was* frequently copied later on throughout Europe, but though this may make it historically significant, it does not score highly in my book of choice architecture.

De l'Orme is, it must be said, an impressive figure, whether we like or dislike his work. He had great versatility in the styles, and thereby possibly no great convictions, save an insistence on high standards of workmanship. Anet not only uses Renaissance forms as freely as the Italian Mannerists did but suggests and anticipates Baroque ideas of space. Of his Palace of the Tuileries we do not know very much.

More sure-footed is Pierre Lescot's wing of the Louvre (1546), clearly derived from Italian palaces, using Italian details of columns and pediments. But by its roof, the lowness of its upper story, and its three slightly projected pavilions, it manages to be something that achieves that balance between verticality and horizontality which is characteristic of the French Renaissance, and quite missing in the Italian prototypes. From here on the French Renaissance went its own distinctive way.

German Renaissance seems to me to have been generally coarse and excessively "busy"; English Renaissance impresses me as consistently unimaginative and dull even to the point of dreariness. The Low Countries had many attractive mercantile and official houses in the sixteenth century, but most of the most cheering had Gothic, if not exactly ecclesiastical, undertones, even to the point of dominating the impression. In Antwerp, the Town Hall (1561–1563) does seem to represent a reasonable understanding of Renaissance ideas underpinned by French explications and commentaries, but save as a point of history, it seems to me not much more interesting than Longleat House, Wilts (1553–1568), which is often cited as being an important indigenous British application of Renaissance principles.

Pl. 309

Pl. 310

But enough. I feel I must stop, before you are totally convinced that I ought not to have written about the architecture of the Renaissance at all, and go on to a quite different issue, one which the Renaissance raised for the first time and which has been with us ever since—the cult of personality of the architect.

We need not settle here whether the cult of personality in architecture is a "good" or "bad" thing for architecture; or whether the Greek idea that it is the work of art that matters and not the name or personality of the artist is a better thing for the arts and the society that uses or enjoys them. Whatever the answer, the Renaissance puts the question spectacularly. Here, for the first time the name of the architect may be more easily remembered than the name of a building; the style more characterized by reference to him than by reference to his *oeuvre*.

It is not, of course, that there were no famous architects before Brunelleschi. In speaking of this cult of the individual, "one of the most pervasive of modern historical myths," E. H. Carr has pointed out that there always were individuals and that the men we bother to study were not acting in a vacuum but always in the context and under the impulse of their society.[6] But somehow the names do begin to throng upon us after the dawn of Renaissance and surely not only because our records are better. It must have something to do with what men of different ages have thought worth recording.

Even in these essays we have encountered a few individual architects and their patrons, for example, Imhotep, Amenhotep, and Senenmut for all of Egypt. Another twenty-five or so names of less importance have been identified. In the Christian East are Anthemius of Tralles and Isidorus of Miletus, Sinan, the great entrepreneur-architect of fifteenth-century Turkey,

[6] E. H. Carr, *What is History* (Harmondsworth: Penguin, 1964), pp. 32 ff.

and a half dozen other vague figures; among the ancient Greeks a flock of mythical or legendary precursors, the gods, the cyclops, Euryalos and Hyperbios, Daedalus, son of Eupalamos, who, with his son Icarus, perhaps built the labyrinth of Crete; Trophonios and his son Agamedes, who may have made the first stone temple of Apollo at Delphi. These are all very shady as are their works. Then there are a half dozen Ionian sculptor-architects of the archaic sixth century b.c. whose names, like those of Phoikos, Chersiphon, and Bathycles of Magnesia, are known only to scholars; the four architectural heros of the Pisistratids, whose names again are in questionable texts about the foundations of the Temple of Zeus Olympus in Athens. The urban works on Samos by Eupalinos of Megara are a little better known, but not much, and even less so are the six men who worked in Olympia. In the flowering fifth century most will be content with Iktinos and Callicrates of the Parthenon, Mnesicles of the Propylaea, Hippodamus the Milesean urbanist, and perhaps Callimachus, who may have invented the Corinthian column. There are another forty-odd lesser names. Of the fourth-century Hellenistic time few will have cared about Theodotus, who did the Asclepion at Epidauros; Polyclete, who made the Theater and the Tholos in the same city; Pytheos, creator of the Mausoleum at Hallicarnassus; Paeonios of the new temple of Artemis at Ephesos; and Archimedes of Syracuse, he of the levers and the bathtub. We know their works sketchily and them scarcely at all, and we may not even have noted that architects were then more often engineers than sculptors.

The Romans leave us fewer noted names: Vitruvius, Celer and Severus of the Domus Aurea; Apollodorus, architect of Trajan and enemy of Hadrian. There are, of course, more names, maybe forty, but I speak only of those whom a nonspecialist might recall if pressed. In the Far East a few stand out, but more are monks than architects.

There are few more associations in the Middle Ages and names can be attached in one way or another to many different buildings but in such different roles that it is hard to say what hand in the actual architecture such Romanesque figures had as Fulbert, Bishop of Chartres, Bernier, Abbot of Tournus, Begon, Abbot of Conques, Gislebert, monk of St-Ouen, or the several abbots of Mont St-Michel—Hildebert I, Hildebert II, and Roger II. Of the big names which come down we have not many more than Suger of St-Denis, Guillaume de Sens of Canterbury, Villard de Honnecourt of Reims, Luzarches of Amiens, Pierre de Montereau (St-Denis, Ste-Chapelle?), Jean de Chelles (Paris), Robert de Coucy (Reims), Erwin von Steinbach (Strasbourg). Not all these were necessarily architects; most indeed were clients.

To illustrate the magnitude of the change that occurred in the Renaissance I have provided some tables, including only the greatest names which have come down to us from Italy, England, France, Germany, and Spain in the fifteenth to eighteenth centuries. This highly selective list shows 26 Italians, 19 English, 30 French, 6 Teutonic, 4 Spanish—a total of 85 for the 450 years.[7] This is to be compared with 21 of comparable importance for all the previous 5,000 years.

There is something bewildering and risky about these Renaissance-Baroque architectural cocktail parties. The bewilderment rests in the number of names, almost a hundred, you meet so suddenly and the difficulty of disentangling them. And if you do it, what will it advantage you, aside from conversation or scholarly shorthand?

What shall you do with them? Buildings in those days were long in building. Architects died before the work was done, and it was finished by someone else, who, whether son or pupil or rival or stranger, did not always, indeed not often, elect to carry on without major changes. Or if the architect did not die, the patron might die, and contracts being what they were not in those days, the new patron might sack the architect in favor of one he liked better. Or, even if both the patron and the architect lived, they might fall out with the same consequences as though one or the other or both had died. In all such cases, whose building are you looking at anyway? Fontainebleau is there and Versailles and the Louvre are there and St. Peter's. Each of these has more than one important name attached to some part or another. Saint Peter's, for example, has at least five, and many more played some sort of role. Who did what is of considerable legitimate concern for scholars for reasons I am not going to explain here, but does it matter so much to you?

Further, there are many things in the lives of the architects which are amusing to know and some which are instructive as well—how architects have got jobs and kept them, what their origins and their training were and how much of this has varied from country to country and era to era, the sculptors and painters of Italy who became architects, the family monopolies of professionals of France, the bookmen and amateurs of England. It is sometimes important and often interesting to ferret out how original the individuals were, whom they borrowed from, how much or how little they changed their borrowings. Their position in society is far from trivial. And in such great encounters as those between Louis XIV and Colbert on the one hand, and Bernini on the other, there may be much food for thought, even as to architect-client relations in our own day. All this is certainly an important part of the corpus of architectural history, and it is not completely irrelevant, though surely not central, to architectural viewing either.

Certainly in the Renaissance and in the even more personal architecture of the Baroque, it is not really possible or sensible to leave out the names of the architects as though they really had not walked the streets of Rome or Paris or Vienna at all. And I have not tried. But I hope as we move through this broken field, we will not forget that it is buildings and groups of buildings which concern us more than an analysis, say, of why it was that Borromini committed almost accidental suicide.

[7] The lists of identified people number many more, as many as 300 Italians, and rather more French, for example.

	1400	1450	1500	1550

Visconti Control Milan   F. Sforza   L. Sforza

Cosimo de Medici   L. de Medici (The Magnificent)

Calixtus III (Borgia)   Pius II   Alexander VI (Borgia) 1492–1
Nicholas V   Sixtus IV   Leo X   Paul III   Juli
(Rovere)   (de Medici) (Farnese)

Charles VI   Louis XI   Louis XII   Henri

Charles VII   Charles VIII   Francis I
Henry IV   Henry VI   Richard III   Henry VIII   Ma
Richard II   Henry V   Edward V   Henry VII   Edwar
VI

Martin Luther

BRUNELLESCHI 1377–1446   VIGNOLA 1507–1573

Baptistery   Duomo   Pazzi Chapel in Sta Croce
Doors   Foundling Hospital
MICHELLOZZO 1396–1472   Portinari Chapel   PALLADIO 1508–1580

Pal. Med-Riccardi   Pal. C
L'Annunziata
FILARETE 1400–1469   SCA

Osp. Maggiore, Milan
ALBERTI 1404–1472   L

Rucellai Pal.
De Re Aedificatoriae
S. Maria Novella
S. Andrea, Mantua
FRA GIOCONDO 1435–1515

B DA MAJANO 1442–1497
Pal. Strozzi
BRAMANTE 1445–1514

Tempietto   Plan of St.
Pal. Cancelleria
SANGALLO 1445–1515

Sacristy, S. Spirito
AMADEO 1447–1522

Certosa di Pavia
LEONARDO 1452–1519

MICHELANGELO 1475–1564

Laurentian   Dome S
Library   Cam
RAFFAELLO 1483–1520

S. Eligio dei Orifici
SANMICHELI 1484–1553

began Pal. Grimani
SANSOVINO 1486–1570

Library (V
ROMANO 1499–1546

Pal. del Té (Mantua

1600	1650	1700	1750

V.

Urban VIII   Alexander VII
(Barberini)   Innocent XI

Louis XIII   Louis XV

Henri IV   Louis XIV

James I   Commonwealth   James II   Anne   George II

Charles I   Charles II   William   George I
                                              and
                                              Mary
                                    Peter the Great

ITALY

6

Olmpico, Vicenza (started by Palladio)

0

Pal. Borghese

NA   1556–1620

ade St. Peter's

BERNINI   1598–1680
Baldachino St. Peter's
              Piaz. S. Pietro
              S. Andrea el Quirinale

LONGHENA   1598–1682
        S. Maria della Salute
BORROMINI   1599–1687
        S. Ivo della Sapienza
        S. Carlo alle 4 Fontana
              JUVARA   1678–1736

                          Stupingi
                          FUGA   1699–1781

                          S. Filippo Neri (1780),
                          Naples
                          PIRANESI   1720–1778

1475	1500	1525	1550	1575	1600	1625	1650

NEPVEU 1470–1538

Chenonceaux   Chambord
SERLIO 1475–1553

Rigoles generale d'architettura
G. DELLA ROBBIA 1488–1566

Azay le Rideau
LE PRIMATICE 1505–1570

Fontainebleau
DE L'ORME 1505–1570

Ch. d'Anet
LESCOT   1510–1578

Louvre-Cour Carrée
GOUJON 1510–1568

J. A. CERCEAU Ier 1510–1585

J. BULLANT II   1511–1578

Chantilly
L. MÉTEZEAU 1559–1615

Place des Vosges
DE BROSSE 1571–1626

Pal. de Luxembourg
J. C. MÉTEZEAU 1581–1652

Charleville (Place Duc
LE MERCIER 1585–1654

Louvre-Pav. de l'H
N. FRANCOIS-MANSART 1598–

L'Hôtel Vril
Ch. de Mais
LE VAU 1612–1670

PERRAULT   161.

LE NOTRE   161

C
VA

L. I

J. HA

1700	1725	1750	1775	1800	1825	1850	1875

A. J. GABRIEL 1698–1782

Opera House, Versailles
Place Louis XV, Concorde

J. F. BLONDEL 1705–1774

Architecture Française
Traité de L'Architecture

HÉRÉ de CORNY 1705–1763

Pl. Stanislas, Nancy

SOUFFLOT 1713–1780

Ste-Geneviève, Panthéon

MIQUE 1725–1794 (guillotined)

Marie Antoinette's buildings at Versailles

LE DOUX 1736–1806

Barrières de Paris

PERCIER 1764–1838

FONTAINE 1762–1853

Pavilion of Louvre
Rue de Rivoli
Arc de Triomphe (1806), (Chalgrin)

Bib. Ste-Geneviève
(1843), (Labrouste)

Les Halles
Bib. Nationale (1861), (Labrouste)

F R A N C E

ade)

s; Tuileries
07

7

des Invalides; Place Vendôme
6

RT 1646–1708

s, Dome des Invalides

TTE 1656–1735

Ch. de Bühl

1500	1525	1550	1575	1600	1625	1650	1675

Burghley House, (Cecil)

THYNNE 1510–1580

Longleat House

R. SMITHSON 1536–1614

Hardwicke Hall

THORPE 1563–1655

Audley End
Hatfield House, (Lyminge)
Blickling Hall, (Lyminge)

INIGO JONES 1573–1652

Banqueting Hall-Whitehall Palace
Queen's House-Greenwich

WEBB 1611–1672

Greenwich Hos

PRATT 1620–1684

Coleshill House

WREN 1632

London
St. Pau

HAWK

VAN

1725	1750	1775	1800	1825	1850	1875	1900

SOANE 1753–1837
Bank of England
SMIRKE 1781–1867
British Museum
Coal Exchange 1846 (Bunning)
Crystal Palace 1851 (Paxton)

E N G L A N D

6
n's College, Oxford
6
im Palace
685–1748
Holkham Hall
1682–1754
St. Martin in The Fields
Radcliffe Camera
WALPOLE 1717–1797
Strawberry Hill
CHAMBERS 1723–1796
Design of Chinese Buildings
Civil Architecture
PAINE 1725–1789
Kedleston Hall
WOOD II 1727–1782
Royal Crescents, Bath
R. ADAM 1728–1792
Syon House
Adelphi Terrace NASH 1752–1835
Royal Pavilion, Brighton

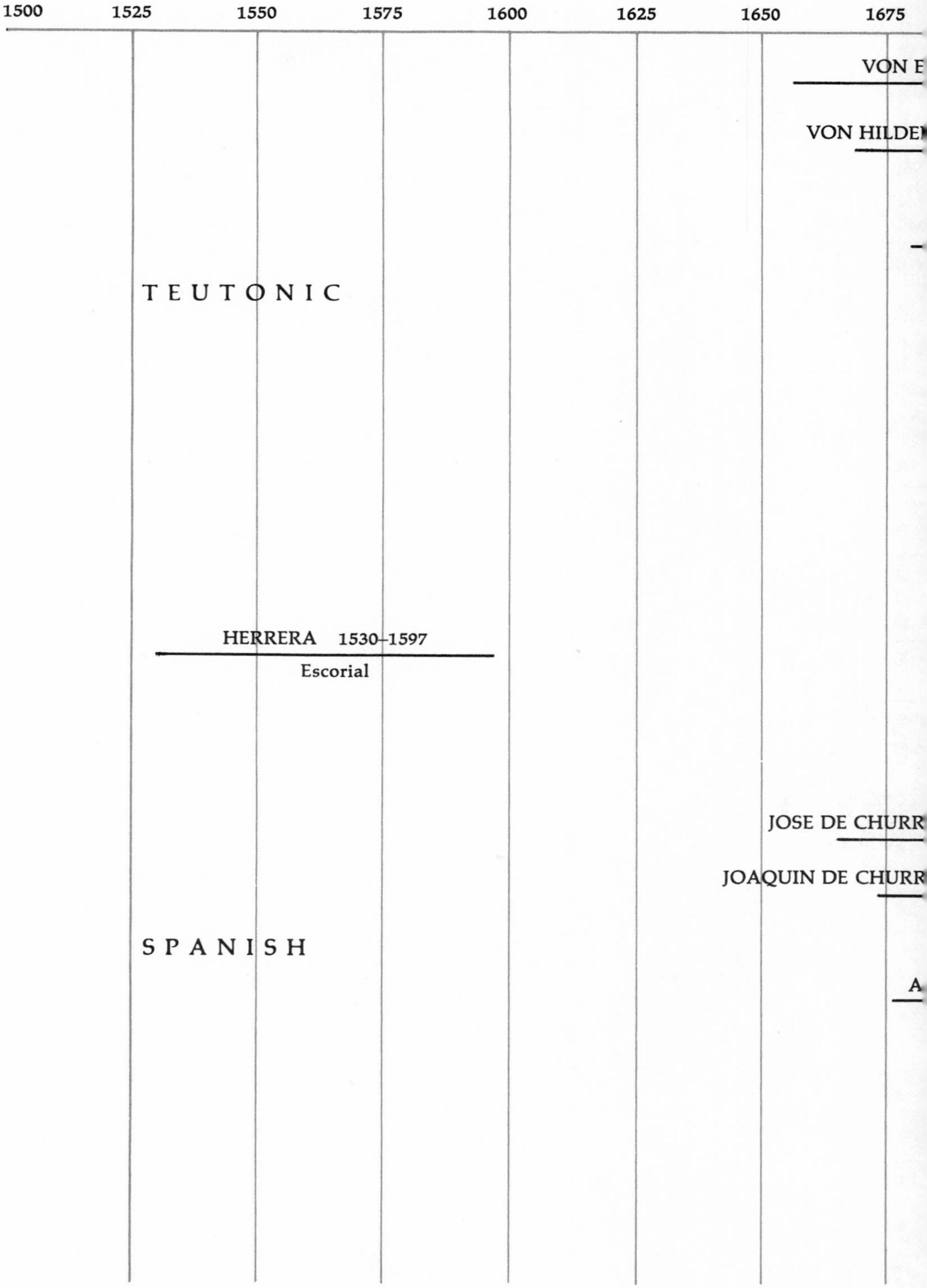

1500	1525	1550	1575	1600	1625	1650	1675

VON E

VON HILDE

TEUTONIC

HERRERA   1530–1597
Escorial

JOSE DE CHURR

JOAQUIN DE CHURR

SPANISH

A

23

aiserkirche, Vienna

'45

a Mirabell, Salzburg
lvedères, Vienna

MMERMAN 1680–1758

MERMAN 1685–1766

       Steinhausen
           Ottobeuren Kirche
            Wieskirche

LIÉS 1695–1768

           Residenz Theatre, Munich
                Theatinerkirche, Munich

ANN 1687–1753

         Vierzehnheiligen
   Palace Wurzburg

25

'25

and College de Calatrava
al Salamanca

RRIGUERA 1676–1750

aza Mayor Salamanca

CHAPTER NINE

THE ARCHITECTURE OF "GRANDEUR":
THE BAROQUE

There has for a long time been considerable unresolved argument as to whether the architecture from Early Renaissance to Rococo is one evolutionary development or more appropriately separable. Whether a building is High rather than Early Renaissance, Mannerist rather than High, Academic rather than Mannerist, may be a fuzzy question near the boundaries. Things do not change in architecture on a given day, if, indeed, they do in anything. People still quarrel as to whether Dante rang down the curtain on the Middle Ages or spoke the Prologue of the Renaissance. They can debate whether or not the Campidoglio left Mannerism behind to initiate the Baroque or whether we must say that Baroque began only with Bernini and Borromini. That is why many writers do not try for such clear compartments but let the Renaissance flow from Brunelleschi through Borromini to Juvara and Fuga. This, in general, it seems to me, is not the right way to go about it.

Fully developed Baroque architecture is unmistakably different from Renaissance architecture, and this difference is far more profound than would arise merely from a different attitude toward details. Baroque is certainly an extrapolation of the Mannerist departure from the strict architectural grammar of the High Renaissance, into something more personal and "expressive." It is perhaps, as someone has said, the most self-consciously symbolic architecture ever produced. It may be an exaggeration to assert that it is Gothic architecture using classical elements, but there is something in the idea. To say it is theatrical is to say the truth, but only part of it. Gone are the workshops of classicism, the pretensions of the humanists. The Baroque reaches out to create space and an enclosure which will transcend an architecture which boasts of its self-imposed limitation of being man-centered. It is something like the imperium of Virgil's Jupiter which was to know no bounds. Appropriately it began in Rome where some, but not all, of its greatest successes were scored.

Obviously, I might have included Baroque and Renaissance in the section on stone, but I have not done so because in these later architectures material and structure were taken for granted and other considerations were more important. It is not that the structures were inept. Brunelleschi's Dome, which ushers in the Renaissance, is a marvel of construction. The arch-baroquist of them all, Borromini, was, according to Tapié, more of a technician than a theorist.[1] He and the other leading architects of the Baroque knew how to balance thrusts and counterthrusts, how and where to hollow. If, as was the case with Borromini, they scorned to break up the flat surfaces of walls by superimposed decoration, they had to produce their desired undulation, their play of light on curves and planes, walls and cornices and columns, structurally. Though not proclaimed so categorically as in the Gothic, the brilliant structure is certainly there, although sometimes partly hidden by the superimposition of ground plans on each other, by the elimination of corners and unequivocal projections, and in the case of those who were less pure than Borromini by the concealing or at least muting applications of gilt, stucco, colored marbles, or *trompe l'oeil* painting. However, when the concern for proportion (Renaissance) or theatrical effect (Baroque) dominates to the point where structural elements can be used as decoration in places where they serve no structural purpose, when columns can be twisted (though not a Baroque invention) to the point where a structural engineer might be uneasy, when pediments and architraves can be frankly broken, a new set of principles are at work.

So we must concede that there are other ways of classifying architecture than by material. There are, for example, the space concepts of the late Sigfried Giedion announced in 1928 in his *Bauen in Frankreich*, refined and elaborated in his Charles Eliot Norton lectures at Harvard University in 1937–38 and published as the influential *Space, Time and Architecture*,[2] and fully worked out in his posthumously published work, *Architektur und das Phänomen des Wandels* in 1969.[3]

[1] Victor L. Tapié, *The Age of Grandeur: Baroque Art and Architecture*, translated by A. Ross Williamson (New York: Praeger, 1961), p. 46.
[2] Sigfried Giedion, *Space, Time and Architecture*, 1st ed. (Cambridge, Mass.: Harvard University Press, 1941).
[3] Sigfried Giedion, *Architektur und das Phänomen des Wandels; Die Drei Raumkonzeptionen in der Architektur* (Tübingen: Ernst Wasmuth, 1969). The English edition,

In this interpretation there have been (after purely primitive constructions) three periods of architecture. Each has involved a different idea of the relation of architecture to space. The first thought of architecture as sculpture, in which the building is fundamentally *surrounded by* space. This began with the architecture of Mesopotamia and Egypt and ended with the hegemony of Rome, including the Greek, as its last important Western example. The second thought of architecture as *surrounding* inner space. It began to show itself in Classic Rome. Now architecture enclosed space or, as it is put in the German text, involved the "hollowing out" of space while at the same time opening into it by windows. From the Roman Pantheon to well into the eighteenth century there was a steady extension and evolution, *thermae*, villas, Trajan's markets, the Flavian amphitheater (Colosseum), Romanesque, Gothic, Renaissance, Baroque, Georgian. In this classification Baroque space inventions and illusions were but a variant. The third concept combined architecture as sculpture and architecture as inner space, including the two necessities of isolation and entering, and added notions of transparency and interpenetration. It began more or less at the same time as the new technology of iron. Transparency is more than translucency, for the latter can, as the Gothic showed, continue to act as a separator. The new idea began, says Giedion, with painters of the late nineteenth century such as Th. Van Doesburg, the Cubists, the Purists, le Corbusier and Ozenfant and the Jugendstil, and suggestions can be found in such early buildings as Frank Lloyd Wright's Unity Temple built in Oak Park, Illinois, in 1905–06. Giedion adds that up to now there have been relatively few buildings in which this synthesis has been fully realized and puts forward as examples Jørn Utzon's Sydney (Australia) Opera House begun in 1957 and Kenzo Tange's Olympic Sports Hall in Tokyo of 1964.

If this theory of space concepts as the definer of periods is valid, then, evidently, we must regard the Renaissance and the Baroque as coming at the end of a period which includes the Gothic; the nature of the structure and materials used, even the question of decadence, may seem irrelevant so long as the space does not decay; separation of the Renaissance and the Baroque from the Gothic may seem superficial and little more than a matter of taste.

But though much of Giedion's theory seems to me plausible, I am not convinced that it is fully compatible with the facts of the Baroque and of the contemporary scene. Indeed the proof of the third concept may still hang in the balance. Such a building as Kallmann's Boston City Hall of

---

Architecture and the Phenomena of Transition, was published by Harvard University Press in 1971. Giedion wrote the Foreword to his last work at his mountain chalet in Amden, October 1967, and completed the German and English manuscripts together with the precise location of the illustrations on 8 April 1968, the day before he died while taking his customary walk in Zürich.

1969 or Johansen's Mummers Theater in Oklahoma City may seem largely, if not totally, to support it, but Breuer's Whitney Museum in New York of 1954 may be taken to contradict it. The returns are not all in and may not be for decades or even centuries. Moreover it is hard for me to accept the notion that the Baroque concept of space was not at least as revolutionary as the more Cartesian proposals of Theodore Van Doesburg, even to the point of anticipating the main point. The big innovation of the modern age would seem to me to be not spatial, which the Baroque had fully explored, but transparency, which many late contemporary examples seem to be abandoning.

Certainly there was a revolt against eclecticism, nascent by the mid-nineteenth century and full-fledged by the mid-twentieth; and certainly Baroque in its day also represented a revolt, at least against the firmly stated rules and conventions of the Renaissance, and I believe against more than that.

One can sometimes get a quicker idea of what a style was like from the fulminations of its critics than from the eulogies of its admirers. The Baroque has had more than its share of enemies, especially among northern "democratic" Protestants who were offended by exuberance, transcendence, or regal display.

Of the greatest and probably purest of all the Baroque architects, Borromini, Lynton reminds us that his buildings departed in so many ways and

> so radically from traditions of humanist architecture that they were denounced as bizarre and extravagant by contemporaries in Rome and by later generations elsewhere, until the name of Borromini stood for all that was against good judgment and taste.[4]

In our own day Sacheverell Sitwell tells us that the Los Aguas Palace in Valencia has "a distinct likeness in texture to almond paste," but hastens to point out that in a favorable light many fine marble buildings look "nicely edible."

So far the judgments quoted have been essentially visual and free from moralizing. The cup becomes more bitter when spite enters in. The Versailles of Jules Hardouin-Mansart is surely and despite its defects one of the architectural masterpieces of all time. Yet such was the hatred of Saint-Simon for anything connected with Louis XIV that his indictment is viciously false, despite the many unquestioned *aperçus*. It makes good but nasty reading.[5]

[4] Norbert Lynton in Trewin Copplestone (ed.), *World Architecture* (New York: McGraw-Hill, 1963), p. 271.

[5] Saint-Simon, *Mémoires*, A. de Boislisle (ed.), vol. 28, p. 160 ff. The translation here is from Lucy Norton, *The Memoirs of M. le Duc de Saint-Simon*, and is cited in Victor Tapié, *The Age of Grandeur*, op. cit., pp. 142–143.

It is not surprising that the men of the Enlightenment did not admire the Baroque. When Denis Diderot came to describe Rome in the eighteenth-century *Encyclopédie*, he wrote about it unfavorably as compared with Paris and London.

> The much vaunted palaces are not all equally beautiful and are poorly kept; the greatest part of the private dwellings are miserable. The paving is bad, the streets are narrow and only swept by the rain which falls very rarely. The city, swarming with churches and convents is almost deserted to the east and south. Its walls have indeed a circuit of twelve miles, but this circuit is filled by uncultivated land, and fields and gardens that are there called *vigne*. He was right who said that the seven hills, once the adornment of the city now serve as her tomb.[6]

This stricture is, on the surface, not explicitly a criticism of the Baroque, but since Rome was the ultimate creation of Baroque urbanism, fostered by a countless succession of popes, the criticism of the city must be taken as a basic criticism of the architecture, if not the art. And indeed it contained germs of truth. Our contemporary Paolo Portoghesi, whose enthusiasm for the Baroque can hardly be challenged, tells us that despite the grandeur of Rome under the Popes, it

> had, increasingly, become a city of pure show, a sort of gigantic, historical spectacle, in which the heterogeneous population recited its daily comedy, lacking both the cohesion and the political force of a community, as well as any real perspective for development or transformation that would allow it to fall into step with the developing European culture and technology; fatalistically the Romans awaited the succession of popes as the only concrete possibility of change.[7]

To grapple with the Baroque, one must, among other things, look upon it as an experiment in architectural urbanism. Papal concern with the improvement of Rome may be said to have begun with the plan of Nicholas V, Parentucelli (1447–1455), following perhaps a plan of Alberti. It lasted down to the end of the eighteenth century, though by then tepid and marginal. It reached crescendo under Clement VII, Giulio de Medici (1523–1534); Paul III, Alessandro Farnese (1534–1549); and Paul IV, Caraffa, (1555–1559); Clement established the famous trident, the fundamental structure of the urban expansion of the Campio Marzio, which urban model was widely imitated in Europe; Paul III supported Michelangelo's creation of the Campidoglio, that big "urban episode," "an ener- *Pl. 369*

[6] Quoted by Paolo Portoghesi in *Roma Barocca: The History of an Architectonic Culture*, translated by Barbara Luigia La Penta (Cambridge, Mass.: M.I.T. Press, 1970), p. 11. This is an invaluable and also a beautiful and highly controversial work fortunately now available in English, though expensively.
[7] Ibid., p. 11.

getic nodal point," multidirectional, spatially organized as compared to the continuous minute circulation of the connective tissue of the city,[8] while Paul IV opened up the Porta Pia, a firm and decisive point. It peaked again under Gregory XIII, Buoncompagni (1572–1585), and Sixtus V, Peretti (1585–1590). Gregory laid out important streets connecting important basilicas, such as San Giovanni in Laterano and Santa Maria Maggiore (Via Merulana), but more importantly issued the bull, *Quae publice utilia*, in 1574, "that was to remain with minor and secondary variations the building code of Baroque Rome."[9] It provided for opening new major streets, enlargement and straightening of lesser ones, eliminated the traditional narrow passages between houses, enlarged building nuclei by providing incentives to buyers and even some requirements for compulsory sale, and in particular, preserved the continuous wall surfaces that created street corridors by requiring owners of lots where demolition occurred to erect high walls on the new streets, thus tending to give to Rome through these perspective corridors the appearance of a wall-lined city in marked contrast to the abundant greenery on the periphery. Sixtus V may be considered as the last medieval urbanist or the first modern urbanist, but his Sistine plan was far from medieval. Though he had some interest in communal problems, his primary concern was with religion and ceremony, and he set out to connect the seven pilgrimage churches by large strategic avenues, at the ends of which two or more of these poles could be visibly perceived,

> thus ideally diminishing the distance between these glorious and revered ancient monuments of the church, that, in their dislocation on the periphery conformed to a now very remote urban structure, that of ancient Imperial Rome.[10]

The Sistine plan opened new areas on the periphery, created new directrices, reduced the necessity of transforming the medieval central city. But Sixtus has been criticized for concentrating on connecting the poles of religious and central interest while remaining quite indifferent to the poles of civic life and even to have impeded the "formation of a functional street structure related to the practical exigencies of the community."[11] Later popes were less urbanistically focused, continuing the tradition of adorning piazzas with fountains, often spectacular ones, but leaning toward colossal building projects of palaces separating the urban core from the country (especially under Paul V, Borghese, 1605–1621); or of restoring and modernizing ancient churches.

Urban VIII, Barberini (1623–1634), also transformed piazzas such as

[8] Ibid., p. 27.
[9] Ibid., p. 28.
[10] Ibid.
[11] Ibid., p. 29.

that of the Quirinale, the one before the church of Santa Maria Maddalena, and the Trevi Fountain, while his successor, Innocent X, Pamphili (1644–1655), completed the Campidoglio, made the Piazza Navona into one of the great urban nodes, restored the Lateran Basilica and the piazza before it. Following him Alexander VII, Chigi (1655–1667), started an impressive series of works, such as the piazzas of Saint Peter's, Santa Maria della Pace, and del Popolo. But even this ambitious prelate could not accept Bernini's proposal for moving Trajan's Column to the Piazza Colonna, alongside the Column of Marcus Aurelius, and filling the space with two large fountains which would make it possible to flood it on feast days as was already possible in the Piazza Navona. Since the Palazzo Chigi was on the Piazza Colonna, one can imagine Alexander's regret at not being able to match the Navona. He did, however, have a wooden model made of Rome and put it in the same room with a wooden coffin as a reminder that fame and death are inseparable. All of these achievements were by way of visual embellishment, "intervals for contemplation immersed in a continuous urban fabric," and under Alexander the technique of urban retouching reached its apogee, although Bernini and Borromini still had many years to live.[12]

After Alexander Chigi, there was a substantial slackening of building activity and even occasional critical reactions against it. Thus Innocent XI, Odescalchi (1676–1689), was possessed of such uncompromising morality and exemplary piety that he had little time or interest in being a building pontiff. In fact on January 28, 1679, he declined to build the third arm of Bernini's Piazza San Pietro, which has never been completed.

> His Beatitude has refused to give permission to the chapter of Saint Peter's to embellish the plaza by building the missing arm, since there reigns in the Pontiff no ambition to leave an eternal memory of himself but only of his piety and in this way fortifying the *camera* with money [that] funerals can be offered to those who to-day . . . are dying of hunger.[13]

Later still Innocent XII, Pignatelli (1691–1700), was more concerned with improving the public service, the administration of the state, and the elimination of nepotism than with architectonic grandeur. He set out, for example, to transform the Palazzo de Montecitorio which had been begun by Bernini in the reign of Innocent X as an aristocratic palace into something useful, the Curia Innocenzia. But so strong were the memories of the imperial papal Baroque that this pope had to reject Carlo Fontana's magniloquent proposal to embellish the plaza by the transportation there not only of Trajan's Column but also of the Trevi Fountain!

[12] Anyone interested in a more detailed description of what the popes did to urban Rome may find it in Portoghesi, ibid., pp. 26–39, from which much of the foregoing was drawn.
[13] Aviso of January 28, 1679, quoted in Portoghesi, ibid., p. 35.

There is little doubt that if we were today to make moral judgments about papal Rome, a good many of us might think more highly of Innocent XI and Innocent XII than of the great papal builders. Nonetheless it was the latter who made physical Rome what it is and their attitudes were more important to architecture than those of the later Innocents.

The papal hands did lay heavily on Rome for good and for ill, for good in producing the urban architectural masterpiece it became, for ill in fostering its feudalism, its parochialism, its provincialism, its maintenance of a privileged class contrasted with an enormously large destitute one without the mediations of a middle class, its rejection of scientific truth whenever it controverted dogma. It was the bad side which justified the diatribes of Diderot. But it is the good urbanistic-architectural side that we ought to examine here.

We shall not come close to understanding Roman Baroque architecture if we ignore the urbanism of Rome. Not all great architecture, not even all great urban architecture, is so intimately related to the urbanistic program of its city. But in Baroque Rome we shall go far astray if we insist on limiting our examination to the individual artifacts, isolated from the fabric of the city. This was the mistake I made when I first looked at and rejected the Baroque. I found its details repellent (some of them still repel me) and hence drew the wrong conclusions.

It took me a long time to recover from the midwestern Congregational version of Scotch-Presbyterianism in which I was reared. I could find pleasure in Baroque only later when I was able to see that Baroque was, for a time anyway, sincere in its enthusiasms and faith; that its urge toward inventiveness and away from arbitrary formality, its resistance to petrifaction, was good, not bad. I then recognized that, if anything, there was greater cynicism and indifference in revived classicism. So I can now agree with Tapié that Baroque had captured and expressed spiritual and emotional forces which prevailed, however historical events of seventeenth-century Europe might turn. It is much more than a "sacred dance," a cirticism once applied to Corregio's frescos of the Assumption of the Virgin in the Cathedral of Parma (1526–1530).

The term "Baroque" was derived from the Spanish *barucca*, meaning an unusual pearl of irregular shape, and was first used contemptuously by nineteenth-century historians to designate architecture of the seventeenth and first half of the eighteenth century, which they considered a degeneration of Renaissance forms and a denial of strict classical precepts to which their own century was returning. Indeed the term was not inappropriate, once you had defined the essential qualities of style as dependent, not only on order and harmony, but on *blatantly evident* order and harmony, producing an impression of serenity and restraint. Obviously profuse details, enormous scale, theatrical effects, "agitated movement," "tempestuous inner force" seemed the antithesis of this. But there was more to it than that. This becomes easily apparent even if one examines only the plans of characteristic Baroque churches, but especially if one compares Bramante's High Renaissance Plan for St. Peter's (1506) with the Baroque plans of Il Gesu (1568), Banz (1710–1718), Vierzehnheiligen (1743–1772), or Wies (1746–1754).

Pl. 334
Pl. 335
Pl. 336
Pl. 337
Pl. 338

The general political and economic situation in Europe was favorable to the birth of a new style. The Counterreformation was scoring triumphs; France was restored and ready for glory after the victories in the Civil Wars of the Fronde and the Spanish Treaty; Austria had lifted the Turkish siege of Vienna. England was experiencing a new prosperity after the Glorious Revolution of 1688.

After the sack of Rome in 1527 a new line of popes was avid to make it again a great city with something of its ancient grandeur instead of a badly laid out medieval town of 50,000 where pigs wandered through garbage-littered streets. The Medicis regained the power in Florence. The King of Spain established his supremacy in Milan and Naples. Venice was at her most gorgeous with Giorgione, Tiziano, Veronese, and Tintoretto working contemporaneously. None was to die until near the end of the century. The Pope was able to spend beyond his income by the issuance of *Monti*, or promissory notes, which were much in demand. Other governments as a matter of course and despite cycles of deflation spent well beyond their capital. Though private fortunes changed hands with various surges in the times, some individuals kept their wealth and became big spenders. The desire for grandeur was everywhere, and even the enormous numbers of the poor seemed to find, or were alleged to find, relief from their everyday distress in contemplating the pageantry of the wealth and in sharing vicariously this strange, magnificent world.

Historically, the Baroque came out differently in different countries and peaked at different times. There is no doubt that it started in Italy, was concentrated in Rome, and was at that point centrally religious.

When it started has been much argued by scholars and to little avail. Some would place it at the beginning of Il Gesu by Vignola in 1568, but this is almost certainly too early except for those who wish to stake their definition of the Baroque on its connections with the Counterreformation, and as an expression of the new importance to be laid on a concentration of view on the altar. A more plausible date is that advanced by Wölfflin in 1888. He set the beginning at 1580 in the papacy of Gregory XIII, Buoncompagni (1572–1585). This is six years after the bull, *Quae publice utilia*, which has already been mentioned as the cornerstone of Roman Baroque urbanistic principles. Michelangelo has completed his contributions to the Campidoglio and to St. Peter's. Giacomo della Porta (1533–1602) is in his prime and has completed the facade of Il Gesu. Within the decade he will have finished the dome of St. Peter's according to the plans of Michelangelo. Domenico Fontana (1543–1607) is a mature thirty-seven and is busily planting the obelisks in the squares. Carlo Maderna (1556–1629), the youthful nephew and collaborator of Fontana, has yet to fly on

The Architecture of "Grandeur": The Baroque   473

his own. The three greatest achievers of the Roman Baroque are yet to be born: Pietro Berretini da Cortona (1596–1669), more painter than architect; Gian Lorenzo Bernini, perhaps more sculptor than architect (1598–1680), quantitatively the most important and perhaps most influential in matters of scale; Francesco Borromini (1599–1667), all architect, the most rebellious, the most innovative, the Baroque of Baroque. Such a date may have to count on the Baroque as but an evolution from Mannerism.

But if you look at the Baroque as *revolutionary*, and, as I have pointed out, I can see no other plausible way to look at it, you may prefer to agree with Briganti who establishes 1630 as the decisive year.[14] It was certainly a seminal one. Borromini had not yet fallen out with Bernini and they were collaborating on the Barberini Palace and on the Baldachino for St. Peter's. Four years later each would get his first important solo commission, San Carlo alle Quattro Fontane for Borromini and the Capella Re Magi in the Palazzo di Propaganda Fide for Bernini. But this date is acceptable, as Portoghesi warns us,[15] only if we do not forget "the complex ferment of ideas and problems that occurred at the very end of the sixteenth century and beginning of the seventeenth century." Or that, though these artists were very personal and revolutionary, even the most rebellious of them, Borromini, did not advocate a complete break with the past or reject *in toto* the architectural contributions of such predecessors as Fontana, Della Porta, and, it goes without saying, Michelangelo. I do not feel the necessity here or anywhere else of deciding this matter. What is clear is that the Roman Baroque and probably all Baroque reached its high point in the period 1625 to 1675 when it was dominated by Bernini from Naples; da Cortona from Florence; and Francesco Castelli, called Borromini, from Lugano, all Romans by adoption. They came along at a time when papal patronage was generally munificent and ambitious both as to buildings and as to the urban plan for Rome. Sixtus V, who in a reign of only five years became one of the most famous of the "building popes," announced that Rome needed worldly beauty as well as spiritual power and divine protection.[16]

Tapié tells us that the Roman plebs were used to living a life of poverty surrounded by churches and palaces resplendent with gold and marble. He cites Marcel Reymond, who insisted that the Church was democratic in its sovereignty, even opening a view to all the riches of art and pageantry in its churches which previously had been enjoyed only by princes.[17]

This carries little conviction to me. Portoghesi goes to some lengths to say that though, perhaps, the patrons were not so concerned with the people, the artists were.

[14] Briganti, *G Milleseicentotrenta, ossia il Barocco in Paragone*, vol. II, no. 13, 1951.
[15] Portoghesi, *Roma Barocca*, op. cit., p. 50.
[16] Tapié, *The Age of Grandeur*, op. cit., p. 16.
[17] Ibid., p. 72.

The political program of the ruling class to distract the people with beautiful images of civic life became, in the linguistic effort of the artists, a desire for a universal communication, a discourse articulated on many levels of accessibility in order to preserve significance and meaningfulness for both the men of culture and the humblest observer, and often, within the limits of architectural expression, became the clear hypotheses of a different and more human society.[18]

He tells us how Bernini, in Paris, announced that if someone in Rome was unjust, it was not the people. It is perhaps so that Borromini cherished his modest background and, as so many architects before and since, liked the skills of the artisan. But this does not make him a friend of the people nor prove that he "actually aspired to an identification of the cultured with the popular tradition," even though it seems certain that he did "exalt the value of human work that becomes richness and vitality of form as opposed to the value of material that expresses merely the ostentation of the power of money." The latter can be seen by looking at the work and reading the contemporary accounts of how skillful he was at enlisting the best talents of the building craftsmen, resulting in "the fruit of that encounter between the workman and the revolutionary will of the architect." But it is less clear that the solutions were in fact of interest, "not to the critics and the sophisticated, but rather to the artisans and the workers,"[19] save perhaps for the skill of their execution. The plebs, alas, even the politically revolutionary plebs, perhaps the politically revolutionary most of all, have not been noted for their zest for revolutionary aesthetics. It seems patently true, as many critics have hastened to point out, that the great Roman Baroque architecture was for men of power and the architects did not disdain to get along with men of power and to accept the aspirations of these men. The public's share, where there was any, consisted in being allowed on the streets and in the churches where they might share in the art as they could not in a private collector's palace.

But it does not seem to me necessary to climb to such high and such shaky moral ground. The Baroque was a great moment in architecture. Can we then say with any precision what its basic principles were, without worrying longer about its morals? Here too there is no great consensus of learned opinion, and some of the definitions are pretty slippery. Some think of it as a sort of *Zeitgeist* which gradually recommended itself to artists; others put it as "a set of ideas, the creation of which may be traced historically, that move and transform a culture."[20]

It does not possess a unitary language but rather has a common denominator for a plurality of languages. "The beginning is nothing more than a mass of critical hypotheses."[21] The criticism may attack classical tradition

[18] Portoghesi, *Roma Barocca*, op. cit., p. 18.
[19] Ibid.
[20] Ibid., p. 22.
[21] Ibid.

at its roots, or be content to challenge the limitations imposed by a dogmatic insistence on adhering literally to that tradition.

I suppose if one were to try for a single valid generalization of the architecture of the Baroque (and it would be dangerous to do so), one would have to say that it was an experimentation with space and infinity. If so, some of the apparent continuities with Mannerism become trivial or disappear altogether.

Space in the Baroque view cannot be detached from infinity. It is the task of the architect or painter to create the *illusion* of infinity as well as he can with finite materials and finite dimensions. The word illusion is important. The philosophical writing which underlies this is benignly vague. Thus Giordano Bruno in the first dialogue of *De l'infinito, universo e monde* tells us that "Infinite space is endowed with infinite quality and in that infinite quality is lauded the infinite act of existence."[22]

There are perplexities in this infinity comparable to those Sir Arthur Eddington felt when he contrasted what his senses told him was a table and what physics said it was. They were voiced by Pascal in the *Pensées:* "Nature is an infinite sphere whose center is everywhere and whose circumference is nowhere. . . . It is indifferently large and indifferently small. . . ." The human body is imperceptible; it is also a colossus.

How might one go about expressing this in tangible architectonic terms? The single point of view, the axial dominant position, would surely not do. The differentiation between spaces would be too pronounced. The progression toward the infinitely small is marked with the volute, "a theme to which were devoted for more than a century both fantasy and exacting logic."[23] Three-dimensionally, it can appear in a helix such as Borromini used to cap Sant'Ivo.

Pl. 367

It is not, of course, that volutes and helices had been unknown to or unused by architects of earlier cultures and in many parts of the world but never before with a concern which was at once metaphysical and ecstatic. The metaphysics becomes dominant with the Baroque reduction of point to line, of line to surface, of surface to volume, and all of these to space with dicta on infinity by Bruno whereby point does not in the end differ from solid. Physically this calls for transitions so subtle as almost to go unnoticed, and it is coupled with the maximum of illusory techniques.

There was nothing like this in Thomism; nothing like it in the premises of Alberti. Given such cogitations and assuming them to have been taken seriously and not as a mere matter of genteel table talk, Baroque architecture had to be a revolutionary architecture in a degree to which the men of the Renaissance and their Mannerist successors not only never aspired but would have rejected had they been invited to do so. These men of the high Roman Baroque were deliberate and self-conscious revolution-

[22] Cited in ibid., p. 12.
[23] Ibid., p. 14.

aries, conciliatory as Bernini may have been, irredentist as Borromini may have seemed. Even here the philosopher gave them comfort. In *Eroici Furori*, Giordano Bruno has Tansillo say, "Poetry is not born from rules, except by the merest accident: rather the rules derive from poetry; and therefore the genera and species of true rules are as many as are the genera and species of true poets."[24] This obviously does not quite solve everything. Who are the "true poets"?

Yet these revolutionaries are not angry. Borromini expects that his recognition will be long coming. Bernini thinks his reputation will disappear within a century. They do not reject the continuity of the classical heritage but object only to being dominated by passive dogmatism, the unquestioning acceptance of traditional readings and design from crystallized formulas.

Can you enjoy or hate the Baroque without all this theory? Of course you can, because the details are so noticeable and so generally delightful or repellent. So it is easy to get no further than the details, as once happened to me. This is what Portoghesi warns against when he says, "to know, to study, to discover the face of the Baroque city for contemporary consideration means not to abandon oneself to the distracting charms of a few beautiful images; but to attempt to reconstruct a revolution that failed."[25]

And fail it did. It offered Italy, especially Rome and Turin and more lightly Venice, a glorious half century or so, and then architecture drifted back to classical romanticism or revivalism or classicism. It never really caught on in France, which was faithful to classic thought as it turned the Baroque into the charming but less strong rococo. It had another, exciting but quite different, later life in Germany and Austria and still another in Spain.

At the height of the Roman thrust, when the experiments were ever bolder, it worked with more details than I can enumerate, but among the larger ideas were the abandonment of the dominant viewpoint, acceptance of the visual lie, a desire to create illusions, especially inside. It dramatized the use of light and color, the effect of sinusoidal facades and sinusoidal interiors, of walls which flowed away and dissolved, of statue-crowned parapets. It engaged itself incessantly with volutes and spirals, and it related all this to an image of urbanism held in common with otherwise reactionary papal patrons.

In the abandonment of the single dominant viewpoint so precious to classic Romans and men of the Renaissance, the Baroque became as sculptural an architecture as the world has ever seen, sculptural in attitude rather than in detail, the converse in effect of Hindu architecture. It is natural for a sculptor to expect the observer to walk around his work, but

[24] Ibid., p. 12.
[25] Ibid.

it was truly a revolutionary idea for architecture that though there might be a hierarchy of axes, the central view at most served "only to give a unity to the various movements of a continual narration that unfolds along the entire structure of the surrounding walls and demands to be investigated and seen in its very slightest detail."[26] It was not a casual statement of Bernini's that "One of the most important things is to have a good eye for judging contrasting positions." Reciprocity of figure and background is essential to the Baroque. That is why it is perhaps the most modern of any historic architectures. But there is a great difference. The Baroque architect used every art to achieve his effects; the contemporary architect usually tries to go it alone.[27]

The Roman Baroque was not limited to churches, for there were princes in Italy in those days, priestly and otherwise, and they built palaces, but never in Italy so princely as the churches, large and small, prepared by some of the work of Michelangelo, announced by Vignola's Church of the Gesu, brought to a climax by Bernini and Borromini in Rome, by Longhena in Venice, and Guarini in Turin, resisted in Florence, attempted elsewhere from Naples to Milan and by many worthy names, but never with such force as in these cities and by these six.

If you want to find anything approaching this excellence albeit in quite a different vein, you will have to turn first to France and then much later to Austria and Bavaria. If Italian Baroque is above all the triumph of the triumphant churches of the Counterreformation, the great Baroque (or Classicism) of France is witness to the glory of triumphant despotism in the person of the *Grand Monarque*. The two great patrons of the architecture of the Baroque were secular absolutism and the Roman Catholic Church, the second in Italy and especially Rome, the first in France and especially in the environs of Paris.

It was not so from the beginning in France. The beginnings were in the church; Jacques Le Mercier's Church of the Sorbonne (1635), built for Cardinal Richelieu, and François Mansart's Val de Grâce of 1645. These churches, though clearly Baroque, are restrained compared with contemporary churches in Rome, from the beginning showing a taste for the classical which emerged with great clarity in Jules Hardouin-Mansart's beautiful, and essentially perfect, Dome for St-Louis des Invalides of 1680.

It was as though in architectural metaphor the French architects were asserting their ambivalence about the Italian exuberance, recognizing that their true contemporaries were Descartes, Corneille, Poussin, that they were more classically oriented, more analytical, colder, perhaps more logical, all national characteristics; they were capable of using Baroque elements *au choix* and with great skill, but without total commitment. In the end it fell to the king to commission the greatest monuments of Baroque

Pl. 343

Pl. 342

[26] Ibid., p. 15.
[27] See, for example, Moshe Safdie, *Beyond Habitat* (Cambridge, Mass.: M.I.T. Press, 1970).

France. The costs were certainly as high or higher than they were for the Church at Rome, and in the end they bankrupted France and hastened the Revolution. But at the time there was the same argument as we have met in Rome that lavish architecture somehow benefited the people. Now after Louis had called for oriental splendor reminiscent of Solomon, it was Bossuet who announced, "Expenditure on the magnificence and dignity of the King is no less necessary, to maintain his majesty in the eyes of strangers."[28]

If Tapié is to be believed, French peasants, at least for the time being, were as relaxed about the Pharaonic architectural extravagances of the Monarque as Italian peasants were about the extravagances of the Popes. France was still Catholic in word if not in deed, but certainly more skeptical than Italy. So long as Cardinal Richelieu remained, the contest was perhaps slightly loaded in favor of the Church. But as the inept plottings of his successor Mazarin failed, and as the King emerged victorious in the Wars of the Fronde, the balance shifted perhaps forever. The State and not the Church would determine the course of architecture in France.

There may or may not be decisive battles in history; certainly there are not many moments of decision in the history of architecture to seem as important as Hastings, Crécy, or Gettysburg. But if ever there was such a time, it may well have been the period when the greatest king in the world, Louis XIV, engaged the greatest architect in the world, Bernini, and after months, even years, of fascinated encounters, rejected his proposals and sent him back to Rome and entrusted the project instead to an eminent committee of Frenchmen.

Even if it was not quite as influential in the future of French architecture as I have made it sound, it is one of the great stories of architect-client relations from which contemporary reflections may arise. So I shall tell it here but perforce more tersely than it deserves.[29]

Louis the XIV and his queen took up their residence at the Louvre in the Summer of 1660. It was an incomplete palace, partly redecorated, too small for the court. It was uncomfortable, and much too hot in the summer. The king, who never liked Paris anyway, was tempted to transfer all his grandeur to Versailles, where a great deal of building would also have to be done, but which would be acceptably comfortable while the additions were being made.

Colbert, Louis' foresighted minister, feeling it essential that the principal seat of the crown be in Paris and not Versailles, worked very hard to see to it that Louis did not succumb to the temptations of being a suburban king. Large additions to the Louvre had been made principally by Le Vau between 1661–1663. They left unsettled how to complete the quadrangle of the Louvre and how to make the east front as imposing as every-

---

[28] *Politique tirée des propres paroles de l'Ecriture Sainte*, Tome X. Quoted in Tapié, *The Age of Grandeur*, op. cit., p. 77.
[29] A fuller account is to be found in Tapié, *The Age of Grandeur*, op. cit., pp. 110–131.

one thought it must be. Le Vau's solution was mainly to make the east facade rather higher than the rest. Foundations had been laid when it was decided that the east wing should be the main formal entrance to the Palace, to be grand and noble beyond anything proposed by Le Vau.

With this in mind a great competition of French architects was proposed with "advice" from leading Italians. In France designs were to be prepared by men of the fame of François Mansart, Houdon, and Cottart. In Italy approaches were made to Rainaldi and Bernini through the French Ambassador and a special envoy. On the fourth of May 1664, Bernini wrote an effusive acceptance, setting aside all other work, and on the twenty-third of June he sent a design to Colbert—not advice.

The role of Colbert from then on has been much debated. There seems no doubt of his determination to keep Louis XIV out of Versailles; there seems no doubt of his determination to provide an elegant surrounding for the King regardless of the state of the *fisc*, which was not good. I feel the evidence indicates that he had a genuine admiration for Bernini, thought him to be the authentic architectural genius of the day, was captivated, as was the King, by the idea of having the greatest architect of the day build the greatest palace of the day for the greatest monarch of the day, and that he labored hard to have this idea realized. Those who find conspirators in every bush have been able to find his performance hypocritical and aimed, if not from the outset, at least very soon, at protecting this important commission for an architect of France. There seems little doubt that a number of the French architects worked to such an end. Chauvinism in the selection of architects, local in San Francisco, for example, statewide in California, or on the national level when federal buildings are in question, is not uncommon in the United States of the 1970s.

Pl. 339

Pl. 340
Bernini's first proposal of which there are drawings was extremely bold, bold enough even to seem scandalous to some. A great semicircular piazza, offering implicit threats to the future of the much beloved and historical if undistinguished St-Germain L'Auxerrois, was to be matched by a huge concave facade and colonnade dominated by a projecting oval pavilion. The front loggia was in fact to be two, one above the other. Square end pavilions, an attic raising the height of the center, and a balustrade with statues completed the composition.

All the competing plans seemed tepid. Colbert called it a "superb and magnificent piece of decoration," but left little doubt that he felt Bernini's scheme had thought only of the facade. He prepared a long report which enumerated, item by item, the failures to deal with what he called the "sordid necessities" of light and circulation. He sent this criticism to Bernini asking him to review it. This leaves the impression that he thought Bernini's great talent would cope with the difficulties. The reaction does not seem to have disturbed Bernini either. During the winter of 1664–65, still in Rome, he made a second plan of which the only extant copy, and that dubious, is in the Stockholm Museum.

In 1665 Bernini obtained leave from Pope Alexander VII and travelled to Paris for a stay of several months. It was a luxurious, almost regal progression with honors at every stop as if the King "had the whim of treating 'the King of Art,' almost as an equal."[30] Well out of Paris he was met by a high-placed envoy, de Cantilou, Master of the King's Household, who was attached to Bernini, and visited him every day trying to smooth all difficulties. In his first audience with the King his famous phrase, "let no one talk to me of petty things," met with generous regal approval.

There were difficulties from the start. With his new scheme Bernini set out to show that he really was not going to do much harm to St-Germain l'Auxerrois. This was not convincing to many. In any event he called for a great deal of demolition causing Colbert to remark plaintively, "You can't just throw people out overnight." He was very critical of Paris as a city and this made him few friends. Colbert, who was trying apparently to help him to succeed, remarked, "If only he would spare others a little." Even the King acknowledged, "He doesn't praise many things."

Nonetheless a design of what was practically a new palace seems to have been accepted, and a foundation stone was laid on the seventeenth of October. But then the architect and the minister had a real falling out over Bernini's proposed location of the royal chapel as a sort of oval projection from the north. (Colbert was probably right, though he could scarcely have foreseen the future Rue de Rivoli.) This spat was patched up but there had been too many previous arguments. Colbert was dubious about a rough-rock base, but the King overruled him. Colbert worried about too much demolition, but the King said that though he would like to preserve the buildings of his ancestors, he would tear them down if necessary, adding grandly that money was no object. Let Colbert worry about where the money was coming from. (Napoleon was later to tell his architect that architects had ruined Louis XIV because he demanded no budget from them.) Colbert had indeed tempered Bernini's sweeping plans for demolition, reminding him that though beauty or comfort should override expense, a great architect ought to consider whether a particular great expenditure really did add much to the beauty or the comfort.[31]

Colbert thought correctly that the royal apartments would be too noisy. The criticism, though correct, would have applied to any arrangement of royal apartments in the east wing as opposed to the quieter, more beautiful, more secure southern exposure on the Seine. So, although the fault may have been in the program and not in Bernini, it does say something about what this great Baroque architect thought about royal comfort when it conflicted with royal display that he apparently made no proposals leading to greater amenity. In the end the Kings stayed in the comfortable central wing and no French ruler or President has ever taken up residence in the east wing.

[30] Tapié, *The Age of Grandeur*, op. cit., p. 116.
[31] Colbert, *Lettres et Instructions*, vol. V, p. 251. Quoted in *ibid.*, p. 117.

Colbert thought Bernini's kitchen facade was too tall, thought the great courtyard should remain square and not elongated as Bernini was determined to have it (even if this would put the center pieces and the dome off center). Yet it is probably evident that Colbert continued to admire Bernini since he asked for so many other designs by him for bridges, squares, the location of an obelisk, a chapel at St-Denis, all of which caused apprehensions not only among French architects but in Louvois, Le Tellier, Louise de la Vallière.

Bernini left Paris on the twentieth of October following ritual banquets, speeches of esteem, presents, rewards for his staff, a pension for him. Tapié dismisses the notion that all this was a polite court comedy of which even the laying of the cornerstone had been a scene, and that by the time Bernini left for Rome the decision to scrap his plans had already been made.

Colbert did have a problem. He did think the King needed to have one elegant residence and knew, as the King did not, or refused to admit, that the treasury simply could not support two, one at Versailles and one at Paris. He was certain that the choice had to be for Paris and thus decided that everything else should be subordinated to the completion of the Louvre.

Yet this aspiration was not enough. French architects had always thought Bernini a stage designer rather than an architect and had not hesitated to say so. The models made for Bernini and presented by Rossi in 1666–67 were not very convincing. Bernini's plan would take at least three years to execute. Meanwhile the King would be badly housed in Paris and constantly tempted to slip off to Versailles (which he did anyway).

Still Colbert wrote to Bernini on the eleventh of March that the project would forge ahead. Two months later on the fifteenth of May he wrote again to say it would have to be postponed because of the shortage of funds and uncertainties as to how long the costly wars of the Spanish Succession would last. Meanwhile the King had to have a palace so they were reverting to simpler early plans. This postponement was, of course, a polite way of ending the project. But at the same time he asked Bernini, now aged seventy, to come to Paris, pick a new site, and begin all over. Nothing came of this.

Tapié speculates as to what was going on behind the arras.

Was it that the Bernini proposals were in conflict with French taste? If so, why did it take Colbert two years to discover this? Was he finally convinced or just worn out by the French architects?

Was this victory of the French architects over foreigners a matter of personalities rather than style?

The King's word was presumably final. Was he too much influenced by Louvois, his Minister of War and a rival of Colbert, or his mistress, the Duchesse de la Vallière?

Was it really a straight matter of expense and time? Colbert had not been able to stop the King from aggrandizing Versailles at great cost, and the old plan for the Louvre was cheaper and would be quicker to build.

No doubt, as in most historical matters, it was no one of these causes but a combination of them.

In the sequel a committee was formed of Le Vau, Le Brun, and Claude Perrault, a doctor and amateur-architect. In those days, of course, amateur architects were not unskilled in the sense that "Sunday painters" are taken to be today. For the old plans Perrault designed the classic east facade which we see today. It is a beautiful and restrained achievement.

Pl. 341

Would it have been better if the die had been cast for Bernini? I think not. Tapié, I think, is regretful. He says almost ruefully that what was done was probably the best that could be done given the abandonment of the aspiration to build the greatest palace in Europe by the greatest architect. This is more favorable to Perrault than Boileau was, who called him an assassin, not as a doctor but as an architect. But it is nevertheless faint praise. So too is the comment that the decision was really a victory of common sense over imagination, rather than a victory of taste. Tapié insists that it was characteristic of the whole reign that it always wanted to make buildings prestigious to the monarch while knowing, down deep, that it could not afford them.[32]

He finds symbolic the fate of the equestrian statue of Louis XIV made by Bernini as a kind of final statement that he bore no ill will. It was much disapproved, ultimately ruined through changes imposed by Girardon, and finally erected as an ornament to a garden near the Swiss Lake, hidden away as though the French did not really want it and did not know where to put it, a sign that the Baroque held no further attraction to the French.

Though a slight overstatement, this is, in principle, correct. The caprice of a monarch, however powerful, cannot quite sway the whole tone of a nation. French academies, French artists and writers and philosophers, French attitudes which would prefer Poussin to Rubens, French rationalism, French skepticism about Rome, all were a part of it. But certainly the King could be a great fosterer and was. Versailles was now carried out with amazing speed, and after 1679, under the designs of Hardouin-Mansart, achieved its final form, which, despite the strictures of Saint-Simon, was in fact the marvel of the age and is still a marvel.

Pl. 345
Pl. 344
Pl. 346
Pl. 347

Hardouin-Mansart preserved the new palace of Le Vau and Lebrun built around the simple original hunting lodge of Louis XIII, enlarged and consolidated the terraces, erected the long wings which provide the horizontal emphasis, made a magnificent stairway of the Hundred Steps to run down to the Orangerie, and linked the two pavilions of the facade by the Galerie des Glaces. Everything in the palace harmonizes with itself and

[32] Tapié, *The Age of Grandeur*, op. cit., p. 129.

The Architecture of "Grandeur": The Baroque   483

with the garden compositions by Le Nôtre of sheets of water, terraces, parterres, and the broad canal which can themselves legitimately be called architecture; "the whole logical progression from the design in stone to the open countryside . . ." forms one "simple and clearly intelligible work of art."[33]

If the two great patrons of the period were the Church and the State, the Church's Baroque triumph in Bernini's great four-deep colonnade of St. Peter's Square, combined perhaps with his baldachino and St. Peter's Chair inside the basilica, themselves lifting sculpture to the level of architecture, is matched by the secular despotic triumph of the Palace of Versailles.

Pl. 348

Pl. 358

In England neither of these forces was so powerful, and English flirtations with the Baroque were tentative, awkward, and short-lived as the English preference for its own version of a return to Palladio took charge. Such Baroque as there was a kind of blend of tepid Mannerism and embarrassed Romanticism culminating in the heavy and clumsy, even amateurish, treatment of Blenheim Palace (1705) by Sir John Van Brugh. The refined work of Inigo Jones, the master of the masque, is simply not a part of this picture, handsome as may be the banqueting hall in Whitehall Palace.

Pl. 371

In Spain the austerities of Herrera's Renaissance Palace of the Escorial gave way to the Baroque fantasies of the Churriguera brothers. This version of a very special flavor, manifested in the Cathedral of Salamanca (1706), the Grand College de Calatrava (1717), the Plaza Major of Salamanca, or the Santa Tecla Chapel at Burgos, is not the most extreme or exuberant of the Baroque decorations of Spain and offers pleasurable viewing. But the fact is that both the Churrigueresque and the precedent Plateresque in Spain ignore structure and spatial organization in a way that the great Italian Baroque never did and become a sort of "decor suspendu." And when Spanish Baroque went colonial, as in the facade of the church at Tepotzotlán in Mexico, the confusion of tangled detail can only be compared with the crawling sculpture of the worst Hindu example.

There are said to be good examples of Baroque in Bohemia and Poland, but I have not encountered them and cannot speak of them.

There remains as important the final and quite different eruption of Baroque, both imperial and religious, around Vienna and in south and central Catholic Germany, principally Bavaria.

Baroque was brought to the Catholic countries of central Europe in the last decades of the seventeenth century mostly by second- and third-rate Italian designers, but it soon fell into the hands of some outstanding native architects. It reached its peak there in what is sometimes called Imperial Baroque following the defeat of the Turks, the liberation of Vienna,

[33] Ibid., pp. 141–142.

and the ultimate achievement by the Hapsburgs of great power which enjoyed at least forty years of uninterrupted success. The artists generally leaned toward Borromini rather than Bernini, were enchanted by Guarini's achievements in Turin, and were exposed, as their predecessors had not been, to the uses of *trompe l'oeil* painting in architecture, as so brilliantly manifested by Andrea Pozzo in his frescoed ceiling at Sant'Ignazio de Loyola of about 1685 and the altar in the Chapel of the Gesu of 1696–1700. Indeed, just as the Vatican had earlier given Bernini permission to go to Paris, so it loaned Pozzo to Vienna where he spent the last seven years of his life.

Roman Baroque, even at Borromini's most fantastic flights, never quite detached itself from antiquity and the Renaissance. Austrian Baroque perhaps felt more elation; it was perhaps more aristocratic than imperial; "the desire to astonish by sheer size is tempered by a wish to charm." It is a spirit which "often valued sensibility and taste above the rigorous demands of deductive reason or settled purpose." It *does* have something of *Rosenkavalier* about it, but it is that of the Marschallin, not of Baron Ochs.

The big Austrian architectural names are three. Johann Bernhard Fischer von Ehrlach (1656–1723), the Viennese who spent twenty years in Rome, was drawing master to the Archduke Joseph, and built palaces of Roman majesty (which repel me, though Schönbrunn is possible), and the fantastic Karlskirche (1715), which combines Baroque planning with a temple front entrance, flanked by imitations of Trajan's historiated columns, very theatrical, smelling more of the lamp of scholarship than of inventiveness or taste, though his later (1722) Hofbibliothek, also in Vienna, is more restrained. Johann Lukas von Hildebrandt (1668–1745) was also trained in Italy but with Guarini in Turin; he was more complicated, more vigorous, possessed of a more ingratiating style and later more imitated; he was more painterly and a skillful user of varied surfaces for his facades and rich interiors. His masterpieces are the Lower Belvedere (1714) and the Upper Belvedere (1721) in the suburbs of Vienna for the Prince Eugene of Savoy, following the Versailles idea of a palace set in a landscaped park but as a summer residence more deliberately willing to be romantic. The Upper Belvedere achieves a special charm from its roof line, which descends in steps from a tall central block and from its skillful articulation of what are essentially a series of pavilions. An example of fantasy is the use of statues as pedestals along the architrave, although they clearly are not supporting anything.

Pl. 351

Pl. 350

Pl. 349

The third of the great Austrian figures, Johann Prandtauer, served Austrian monasticism with his masterpiece Melk on the Danube (1702–1738), a remarkable fortress or acropolis of curved terraces, monastic buildings, hall, library, and the dominating church, the precursor of the more sinuous, more ornate, and generally more enchanting German Catholic churches of a quarter century or more later.

Pl. 352

Pl. 353

The Architecture of "Grandeur": The Baroque 485

Melk, one might almost say, requires music to complete its full beauty—transient melodies in a building which itself seems evanescent.[34]

Indeed from now on the *appearance* of the organ plays an important part in Teutonic church interiors.

The handsome German Baroque, centering around Munich but going southward to the Valley of the Inn and northward to Banz, displays a conflict in style between the classical style of Cuvilliés and the developments from the Austrian Baroque of the brothers Asam, Zimmerman, Baltasar Neumann, and J. M. Fischer.

Pl. 354

Pl. 355

Cuvilliés (1695–1768), who did important Residenzen, may have made his most charming building in the little Amalienburg in the Nymphenburg Park near Munich, but the important Electoral Residenz at Munich and the Residenz Theater there were also of high quality. Cuvilliés was born a Walloon, at Soignies en Hainaut, and was noticed by the Elector of Bavaria, Max II Emmanuel, when he was only eleven. The Elector, exiled because of his pro-French policy, took Cuvilliés with him, first to Compiègne then to his court at St-Cloud. Learned in French ateliers, it is not surprising that the tasteful work of Cuvilliés should follow classic French principles, whether in his remodeling of the Palace at Bruhl or in the examples previously cited. His one venture toward the Italian Baroque was in the facade of the Theatinerkirche in Munich (1765–1768).

The Amalienburg is no more than a *maison de plaisance*, that favorite Baroque luxury, built as usual in a remote part of a palace park. Its interior decoration is especially rich, based on French *rocaille* motifs but lacking, in its profusion of forms, the severity and restraint of the French forms. Despite its complexity there is an inner order, and the charm is much multiplied in small examples, such as this one, where everything is reproduced almost to infinity by a proliferation of mirrors.

Johann Baltasar Neumann (1687–1753) was descended from a family of drapers of Eger but based himself in Wurzburg. Also an engineer and military builder, he is generally considered to have been the greatest architect of his country in the eighteenth century, the incarnation of German Baroque in its most rococo aspects. His activities were prodigious in number and in range. The episcopal palace at Wurzburg (1720–1770) is generally taken as his *chef d'oeuvre*. It was intended to rival Versailles in magnificence if not in scale, a fusion of French rococo and Austrian Baroque. The rooms on the garden front are *in suite*, the facade punctuated by a strongly projecting central block and relatively modest end pavilions.

But I personally much prefer, and would rate as his greatest monument, the church of the Vierzehnheiligen near Banz (1744). There are other German Baroque churches of great charm, as at Ottobeuren (1748–1766) by Johann Michael Fischer (1691–1766), an inventive planner who

[34] Ibid., p. 219.

was skillful at combining central and longitudinal elements. Ottobeuren is on the so-called Vorarlberg scheme, thus named because the architects of Upper Swabia and Switzerland mostly came from Bregenz. Its interior is reminiscent of Il Gesu in Rome. The containing walls have become little more than massive piers, engaged columns, or pilasters joined by galleried chapels rising the whole height, so that the entablature winds around the many curves of the plan. The main nave and the side niches meet and interpenetrate, so that the spatial complexity is one typical of most highly developed Baroque. The decoration, the rioting stuccos and paintings, play an important role in the overall composition far exceeding the individual excellence or inferiority of the parts. The facade offers curves and counter-curves of pediments, cornices, hollowed-out surfaces, contained by symmetrical, highly modeled, and well-harmonized towers, such as were common in the monastic Baroque churches of the period.

Still more winning, no doubt, is the church at Wies by the brothers Zimmerman, simple local men, sons of a stucco maker. Dominicus (1685–1766) usually designed the churches after 1724, while Johann Baptist (1680–1758) decorated them as well as making the decorations for the Amalienburg, the Residenz Theater in Munich, Prien, and elsewhere. Someone has called them "superbly mad." We should remember, I suppose, that these men were the exact contemporaries of Bach, Handel, and Domenico Scarlatti. Their pilgrimage church at Wies (1746–1754), though simple on the exterior, is one of the most brilliant exemplars of the period. An extended choir has a two-storied ambulatory providing a sort of curtain of light behind its arcades so that, as Cichy puts it, it "takes on the appearance of a baldachino." Light is very important in all late German Baroque churches, but at Wies it plays an essential role in the composition, enhancing the pastel shades, glinting off the gold trellis work and the gilded capitals, and flowing everywhere through undulant windows into ecstatic apotheosis with sufficient *trompe l'oeil* so that the *putti*, who, in many places are so repulsive, seem to hover in the shadows of the columns, "transforming the choir into a magic world where nothing is at rest."[35] There are fascinating contrasts between the eight white pairs of freestanding columns and the saucer dome in which we see the iridescent splendor of a fantastic heaven.

Pl. 356

But on balance, I suppose, Vierzehnheiligen has to be judged the master work. It seems at first sight to have a simple plan, but it is in fact made up of overlapping ovals which, at vault height, are separated by transverse arches to produce the complex space modulations which have caused Neumann to be called the "hero of this spatial polyphony."[36] Again there are the flowing and interacting ellipses, welded together by other smaller ellipses whose major axes are transverse, so that the small transverse vaults are visible while the longitudinal vaults meet in the center.

Pl. 357

Pl. 359

[35] Bodo Cichy, *The Great Ages of Architecture* (New York: Putnam, 1964), p. 346.
[36] Copplestone (ed.), *World Architecture*, op. cit., p. 862.

The spatial effects are more spectacular than at Ottobeuren or Wies, and the curves of the facade more convincing.

Many of these later German Baroque buildings are frequently called rococo. It is a distinction I have not made here since it seems unimportant to our purposes, and I agree with Tapié that the shift to rococo is "more of a slide than a transition," or as Hans Werner Hegemann suggested, "not a fundamental change of style, like the change from Gothic to Renaissance; it is not something entirely new, but only a phase within the great epoch that embraces it."[37] The change is rather one of emphasis, the pursuit of grace and decoration at the expense of monumental overall quality.

I have spent so much detail on the Teutonic Baroque because it is less familiar than the Italian or French and has often been underrated. This does not mean that the Italian was not the most seminal and important.

To make a comparable quick tour of the main Italian examples progressively, you would probably want to begin by examining what prophecies were made by Michelangelo in the Piazza del Campidoglio (1536), to see the giant two-story pilasters that became a common motif of the Baroque used here for the first time, and, more importantly, for the sense of ascending movement, the balustraded stairway, and the use of building masses to define, limit, and forcefully shape an open space. You would then go to Vignola's masterpiece, Il Gesu of 1568, whose facade (not by Vignola) may seem to resemble Alberti's Sant'Andrea in Mantua, but where, contrary to the strong cross currents of light in Sant'Andrea, the chapels are small and dark and force the eye to the crossing and the light falling from the drum into the chancel.

Pl. 369

Pl. 365

Pl. 366

Following a chronological line you would look at Maderna's facade for St. Peter's (1606–1612), mostly for its scale, the upward thrust of columns and pilasters, and the powerful entablature and attic.

Pl. 362

You would enter St. Peter's to examine Bernini's great sculptural-architectural masterpiece done in collaboration with Borromini, the Baldachino of 1624–1633, noting not so much that it was the work of his first chance or that its columns were twisted or that the roof of the Roman Pantheon had been despoiled to furnish the needed bronze, but rather how he had succeeded in creating a masterpiece consonant in style and scale with the great dimensions of the basilica.

Then you would go to San Carlo alle Quattro Fontane, "San Carlino" (1638–1641), Borromini's first commission (the facade is 1665). Like most of Borromini's masterpieces it is tiny—it would fit inside of one of the piers of St. Peter's. Here you would find the first flowing sculptural quality of high Baroque construction and see how clearly Borromini had subordinated the rich sculptural ornament to the movement of the whole, how he had limited the light to one small source at the apex, leaving much of the dark

[37] Hans Werner Hegemann, *Deutsches Rokoko*, cited in Tapié, *The Age of Grandeur*, op. cit., pp. 222–223.

church in mystery, and how firmly he had expressed the opposing curvatures of the facade.

The first of his works, it may be his greatest.

> The sinusoidal profile that orients the wall mass along diagonal directrixes is the great linguistic achievement of the Roman Baroque which rarely reached the clarity of enunciation of San Carlino.[38]

Inside there is a completely organic continuity between the dome and the surrounding spaces dilating and contracting as they do and despite the energy with which Borromini employed "the entire gamut of diminishing tones from the full luminosity of the streams of light projected from the octagons at the base of the dome to the complete darkness of the deep recesses."[39]

But when you go to San Carlino, do not let the brilliance of the exterior and interior of this church cause you to overlook the nobility of the small cloister of the monastery or the simple, even austere, forms of the subterranean chapel.

This building caused a great stir, and drawings of it were demanded from all over Europe and even from India. It was even praised as being of low cost because Borromini understood how to get the best out of his artisans.

At San Carlino you may also note the brilliant effect of a combination of light and dark on monochromatic white stucco. It is in striking contrast to the later use of multicolored marbles, especially by Bernini, or the white, gold, and blue so much beloved later in Germany. The monochrome was general in the beginning, not only with Borromini and da Cortona, but even with Bernini, as in the Raymondi Chapel attached to San Pietro in Montorio (1638–48), where Bernini first displayed his consummate staging of "raking light" emanating from hidden light sources, which came to be known in Baroque days as *luce alla Bernina.* Later on, beginning with the Cornaro Chapel (1644–52), Bernini experimented with the use of many colors of stone but in a different way. In the past, such juxtapositions had underscored the design by contrast or by insets, but now Bernini used them "to fuse the contiguous elements into a powerful coloristic vibration, emphasizing the textural value of the veining and patterning . . . blending them, reducing the volumetric breaks, and overruling the linear design."[40]

Then you might pay a brief visit to the oratory and the house of the Filippini (1637–50) (House of the Oratorians of San Filippo Neri), which Borromini did by winning a competition. Here he provided dramatic areas in the collective and proselytizing rooms but modest, even intimate, ones for the daily life of the Oratorians themselves. The generally accepted im-

[38] Portoghesi, *Roma Barocca*, op. cit., p. 13.
[39] Ibid., p. 17.
[40] Ibid.

portant innovation here is the curved facade. There had, to be sure, been curved facades as early as the sixteenth century but never so bold and never with such an explicit allegorical intention. All doubt about this is resolved in Borromini's own *Opus Architectonicum* where he clearly states that he meant this to offer the welcoming gesture of outstretched arms.

Since we have already learned that treatment of materials matters, we will pause to admire how the architect combined the texture of thin ground brick in the center with a thicker unpolished brick on the wings, and to note the elegance of the concave corner angle.

But the oratory also offers a very clear example of the Baroque lie freely admitted in *Opus Architectonicum*. The problem was difficult because the functioning of the building required that the oratory be put, not in the center, but at the extreme corner of the lot. But a monumental door opposite the altar would have been unhappily eccentric on the facade. So Borromini put it in the center, let it open into a symmetrical loggia where you veer left to enter the oratory so that the noncorrespondence, something like that of the doors of Notre-Dame de Paris, is left evident only to the memory. Borromini saw no reason not to be frank about it.

> Actually this facade connects on the interior with all of the building and on the piazza only one side of it extends along the flank of the oratory. But it was deemed necessary to make it, because being called the Congregation of the Oratory, it seemed that this place [i.e. the oratory] for its many pious functions had to be more conspicuous than all the others and seen by everyone and thus it had to have a distinctive and particular facade.... I therefore decided to deceive the eye of the passer-by and make the facade on the piazza look as if the oratory really began there and had its altar opposite the door.[41]

How much do you want to sniff at this?

Pl. 367

Then you will certainly wish to visit Sant' Ivo della Sapienza (1642–1650), which Borromini inserted in a sixteenth-century courtyard, providing at the top a six-lobed drum, supporting a stepped conical roof leading to a tall hexagonal lantern, all of whose sides are concave and separated by coupled columns, crowned by a diminishing spiral "twisting up into the sky."[42] You would find the intersecting triangles of the plan allegorical to the Trinity scarcely less interesting.

But you will need to look more carefully at how the radiating substructure metamorphoses into the curvilinear-rectilinear perimeter; and how the dome does not rest on arches, which would have created minor distracting spaces, but emerges plastically from the complex perimeter into the perfect circle of the dome, the apotheosis of the Borrominian synthesis. You will probably no longer care that this too is a lie, that there

[41] Quoted in *ibid.*, p. 15.
[42] Copplestone (ed.), *World Architecture*, op. cit., p. 804.

is no correspondence between the exterior and the interior of the dome, that the six uniform panels of the exterior give no hint of the fluctuating forms of the six interior lobes or that the high drum of the outside and its stepped roof have nothing to do but hide the pointed curvature of the inner vault.

But whether you care for the symbolism of the triangular matrix or the iconological reference to wisdom in the seven columns of the *exedra;* whether you do or do not note how the fluted pilasters, the thin horizontal courses running all around the periphery, the slight projection of the entablature, the convergence toward the lantern of the thin ribs of the dome, and the decoration of the dome surface obey the laws of perspective diminution, you can scarcely be unmoved by this interior. You may or may not be so moved as to agree with Portoghesi that

> this great synthesis comprises in a single image classical serenity and Gothic tension, not as ingredients of a convenient compromise, but as profoundly relived moments of a history that may finally be reclaimed in its dialectical interweaving of human values.[43]

After Sant'Ivo you may or may not wish to add the anticlimactic footnote of Sant'Agnese (1653–1657), for which Borromini supplied the plan but not the decoration, before a quick look at Cortona's Santa Maria della Pace (1656), for its one scenic effect of contrasting curves in space.

Now you would return to see Bernini's throne of St. Peter's (1657), an enormous chairlike reliquary, colossal in size, yet light in appearance, made so by the device of putting everything into motion. The brilliant contrast between the gilded bronze of "the world of reality and history" and the angelic white stucco of the top offers the finest example of another aspect of the Baroque, requiring great skill, to be sure, in solving the problems of height, space, and depth and unifying them, but something more. It has been called a hymn to light. Tapié says that as a whole it is a "poem to the spirit."[44]   *Pl. 360*
    Pl. 361

You would then stay with Bernini to visit Sant'Andrea al Quirinale (1658–1670), also a small building with strong interior cross axes of the   *Pl. 368*
ovals. Bernini considered it his masterpiece. Despite the severely classical character of the inside elements, the dark marble bottom contrasts in a most unclassical way with the heavenly sphere of the dome, all gold and white. The hexagonal disposition of the minor chapels, leaving out the transverse chapels at the extremes of the major axis, is also interesting and serves firmly to strengthen the elliptical plan.

You would have to end this tour by standing in Bernini's Piazza of San Pietro, that majestic and all-embracing colonnade, enfolding with its   *Pl. 363*
284 Tuscan columns arranged in four concentric rows an oval 650 feet   *Pl. 364*

[43] Portoghesi, *Roma Barocca*, op. cit., p. 174.
[44] Tapié, *The Age of Grandeur*, op. cit., pp. 54–56.

wide, an arrangement of genius, one of the few world masterpieces of monumental planning and so well known that I shall say little about it.

Great solutions usually make the problems solved seem less difficult than they were. The limitations as to measurements and configurations imposed on Bernini by preceding constructions were imposing. There were visible errors in the alignments of the church which he made almost imperceptible by the skillful location of the *exedra* centers and the fountains (the internal radius of the hemicycles equals the distance between the fountains). The most impressive thing is, of course, the monotonous and heavy rhythm of the four rows of columns of the hemicycles and their brilliant spacing, altogether Baroque, by which there is a continual metamorphosis, and one is aware of constantly passing from an arrangement of complete opacity to an arrangement of complete transparency.

Pl. 370

You could do all this without leaving Rome and legitimately following the chronological steps Romans of the day were following closely, given the highly competitive attitudes of patrons and artists alike. And you could, in fact, stop at Rome, although it would be a pity not to visit Turin for Guarino Guarini's San Lorenzo (1668–1687). Guarini, a Theatine monk, was of a younger generation than the great men of Rome and a disciple of Borromini, but so far extrapolated the Borrominesque plans as to make his work almost impossible to describe. San Lorenzo's plan starts on a square; half-way up it turns into an octagon whose sides bend alternately in and out. You might call it an octagon with incursions, or a square with incursions, or a curvilinear Greek cross, but whatever you call it there is an excellent transition to the curved, intersecting, almost Moorish arches of the dome. The effect is well described by Norbert Lynton.

> Looking through this one gets an impression of network hanging in infinite space. The whole thing has been achieved architecturally, not as later, with trompe l'oeil painting.[45]

Pl. 372

And I would urge you to complete this superficial Italian Baroque tour with Longhena's Santa Maria della Salute (1631–1685), to whose richness and exuberance of forms I have already referred.

A similar adventure in France would no doubt start with de Brosse's Palace of the Luxembourg, begun in 1615, and then follow along with:

Le Mercier's Church of the Sorbonne, 1635

François Mansart's Town House, the Hôtel de la Vrillière, of 1635

François Mansart's Chateau de Maisons of 1642

The lower part of the Church of the Val de Grâce of 1645, also by François Mansart

[45] Norbert Lynton, in Copplestone (ed.), *World Architecture*, op. cit., p. 275.

Le Vau's Château de Vaux-le-Vicomte of 1657

Perrault's east facade of the Louvre, 1667

J. Hardouin-Mansart's Versailles from 1669–1708

J. Hardouin-Mansart's dome for the Church of St-Louis des Invalides, possibly his masterpiece, of 1680

J. Hardouin-Mansart's facades for the Place Vendôme, 1698

Gabriel's Place Louis XV (de la Concorde) of 1753 (completed and partially spoiled in 1836)

Gabriel's Petit Trianon at Versailles, 1762, Baroque in date but edging toward Empire

All of these, it will be realized, are in Paris or in the nearby environs. A visit to each will be rewarding. The outstanding ones in my book are Vrillière and Maisons, Vaux-le-Vicomte, Versailles, the stunning Dome of the Invalides, and perhaps the Petit Trianon.

What the Baroque was can be concluded from the examples described. It was, above all, an architecture of embracing plans, interpenetrated space, modulation of walls and surfaces with an emphasis on curvilinear forms, skillful and selective play of light and shade. Though many of its most famous results are monumental, not all are, and some of the greatest are quite small. You could say it did not fear to be monumental, but it did not insist on it. It did not hestitate to use any device to further its dramatic and theatrical ends—stairways, reredos, organs, screens, any kind of furniture, any kind of painting, good and bad, literal or *trompe l'oeil*, any kind of sculpture, good or bad, since it was the combination that mattered and not the detail.

It may have begun as a simple rebellion against both classic Renaissance rules and a realization that Mannerism was not enough, but if this is a partial explanation, it is incomplete. It may have been in its first ecclesiastical forms an effort to refocus man on the altar as a product of the Counterreformation and a denial of the freedoms of the Renaissance church plans, a kind of Jesuitical purpose in architecture. This theory has occasioned large treatises, but some of them deny the premises.

It certainly always sought to be an expression of grandeur—grandeur of a transcendent, ecstatic faith and a church triumphant, or the grandeur of a monarch, the more powerful, the more totalitarian the better, but it was not to be scorned or declined by ambitious lesser princelings. It thrived best, naturally, in seriously Catholic countries or those with strong-willed monarchs. But it was not Pharaonic or necrological; on the other hand, it breathed life and hope and as a rule gaiety as well, but it was never quite frivolous.

It cost a great deal and could be paid for only by the very wealthy or by those who were able to postpone the paying of enormous debts almost forever. And indignation as to its ethics or questions as to whether it was addressing itself to the "right" problems were reserved for a later day.

When the deluge came, when the real power passed from more or less Catholic kings to a more or less Protestant, or skeptical, more or less democratic, more frugal bourgeoisie, the Baroque and the Rococo simply faded away.

They had held center stage in one or another place, in one or another form, for at least two centuries, from Il Gesu in Rome to Wieskirche in Bavaria, and it would not be hard to stretch at least the beginnings back to the Campidoglio and the endings to the edge of the French Revolution.

It was not an architecture to which many can be indifferent, and in the Waspish West, no doubt, more were taught to hate it than were encouraged to love it. But it was the last *great* Period of Architecture until now, if now is a great period, as I suspect it has a chance to be, even if the fact cannot yet be confirmed.

CHAPTER TEN

ECLECTICISM AND THE MODERN "REVOLUTION"

The Baroque was followed briefly by gentle Georgian, but then came a century or more of indiscriminating eclecticism, against which a few men seemed to be struggling helplessly, until suddenly the new era promised by many isolated examples and seminal proposals swept in like a tidal wave at the end of the Second World War. Or at least so it seemed to the man in the street, though those closer to the situation were aware of a few men like Labrouste and Paxton of the nineteenth century and an increasing number of venturesome men in Europe from about 1910 on.

What the eclectic designers did was to use any form which pleased them, Egyptian, Islamic, Japanese, but these rarely; more often Gothic models; and most of all classic or Renaissance forms, but especially the Renaissance as reinterpreted by the French classicists. They chose a visual model which they liked, and shaped or misshaped it to suit a contemporary use. More often they kept the shape with some skill and put the use into the Procrustean bed.

It was an overlong and architecturally unhappy time, and I do not propose to give it much more attention here.

Any sort of innovation is not necessarily good just because it is new. If you are incapable of good innovation, there may not be any inherent evil in imitation. Some of the greatest architecture in history has come from the refinement of earlier invention. The eclectics of the nineteenth century, when they tried to improve the old styles or to toy with the details, almost without exception debased the architectural coinage. When, as in McKim's Boston Public Library, they produced an Italian palace more beautiful than many a real Italian palace, they achieved it only at the price of disastrous distortions of function.

Henry Hobson Richardson is often cited as one of the precursors of the architectural revolution, but with at least equal accuracy he could be classified as the leader of a Romanesque revival. In this garb his buildings are the better the more they look like the buildings of eleventh-century France. A similar statement could be made about the Gothic of Ralph Adams Cram and Sir Gilbert Scott, the Spanish of Bertram Grosvenor Goodhue, the Renaissance or classic of a long line of architects from Sir Charles Barry in England to Charles Follen McKim and Paul Philippe Cret in the United States.

Then after this disastrous century and coming to a peak about now, there was more than a stirring toward a new, total architecture. It was based on a new technology and a new set of purposes. A Henry Adams type of observer might legitimately remark that the technology held more promise than the purposes. The change began with a new iron (or perhaps more properly a steel) age. It soon saw a new ferro-concrete age which was slower in maturing but may turn out in the long run to have been the more important.

I shall say little about either of these ages despite what I believe to be their major and continuing significance. There are several reasons why I choose not to speculate much about our Brave New World. In the first place any reader can see as well as I its present versions almost anywhere he turns. In the second place most of the major landmarks of the transition have been identified and are still standing. These transitional buildings, as important as they may be to historians, indiscriminating local patriots, polemicists, or ideologues, are rarely handsome intrinsically. Few of them are really useful now. From now on it can be predicted that they will rapidly (and justifiably) be torn down despite the anguish of knee-jerking preservationists.

The older monuments such as I have been talking about for so long, whether in Europe or Asia, now more or less preserved by national and other trusts, are beautiful residues of a larger corpus of work of which the average was doubtless not so beautiful, although in the course of history some very remarkable buildings have been razed by war or revolution. Since these older buildings are so beautiful and so often are still usable, they can be legitimately cared for without having to invoke their significance as historical turning points. Looked at this way, it is all right that Notre-Dame de Paris should have survived well while St-Denis, abbey and all, has not been scrupulously resurrected, although the Abbot Suger's basilica is unquestionably of greater historical importance. In time, William Le Baron Jenney's Second Leiter Building in Chicago, a milestone of American development, will have to go, and it would be hard to shed many tears over it now that it has been so thoroughly documented.

That brings me to my third reason. The writing about the evolution of the iron, then the steel frame and its successive skins, has been thorough and complete even up to the point of diminishing returns, though no doubt there are some dusty corners in which Ph.D. candidates can continue to poke their dissertational probes. This has actually been so ever since Sigfried Giedion opened up the topic with his landmark work *Space, Time and Architecture* back in 1941.[1] Starting from his text several others have carefully amended any early errors. It is possible for you to read from more affectionate and more accurate examiners than I about the probable line of development from the Bibliothèque Nationale and the Bibliothèque Ste-Geneviève in Paris, through Bunning's Coal Exchange and Paxton's Crystal Palace in London, through the cast-iron buildings of New York and St. Louis (and for that matter Charleston, South Carolina, on the north side of Broad Street), through what I believe to be the important but over-emphasized contributions of the Chicago School (Jenney, Burnham, Root), or the underemphasized contributions of the Art Nouveau (Horeau, Gaudi, Sullivan), the innovations in education of Gropius and the Bauhaus, and in thought and deed of Le Corbusier, the promotions of CIAM and the Museum of Modern Art of New York, to the final crystalline distillation of Mies van de Rohe at Crown Hall in Chicago and the Seagram's Building of New York. All this you can do for yourself with only a few readily obtained and easily readable books and with only modest travel. I leave it here.

Pl. 379
Pl. 380
Pl. 374

Pl. 387

I leave the metal glass cage, however, needing to express the personal reservation that, exciting as it was in its moment, it is already somewhat passé. This is not just a matter of *déjà vu* and the necessity to find some new thing. Our world is one and is likely to stay so for some time where the delicate products of our inventiveness are precisely the most vulnerable to the uninventive acts of terrorists. Glass and height may already be too hazardous to venture. Someday too we can hope that the true values of urban real estate to people as opposed to speculators will become clear, that the absurdity of building higher and higher on a few feet of falsely valued urban land in the middle of a fetid megalopolitan jungle will become apparent to so many of us that we will stop creating urban anthills and perhaps desert the ones we have already created.

Pl. 382

And someday, if we have not already, we may come to realize that, however imaginative some of Le Corbusier's individual buildings may have been, his urbanism for the motor age, come to fruition or almost so in Brasília, was not prophetic of what *ought to be*, not foreseeing the impending obsolescence of the poisonous motor car, but, even worse, suggesting a

Pl. 384

Pl. 383

[1] Sigfried Giedion, *Space, Time and Architecture*, 1st ed. (Cambridge, Mass.: Harvard University Press, 1941).

totally inhuman way of life. It is to be hoped that we can realize this in time before we venture on more Brasílias (not one of the competitors proposed urban transit not based on motor vehicles) or move another step toward George Orwell's *1984* by bringing any of Paolo Soleri's theoretical *Arcology* into actuality.

The more strikes, the more power failures we encounter, the more clearly we will see the folly of living in a situation where the elevators may not run because of human or technological failures, where there is no place to put garbage even when the garbage collectors are working so that we are smothered in our own refuse, when the top halves of our mountainous towers are perpetually concealed in smog, when the lights dim and the air-conditioned, sealed spaces are insufferable in more frequent brownouts, when it is unsafe to reach our place of work or play even in the daytime on foot or by public transportation, while private transportation is so clogged as to be essentially impossible.

When we finally see this and understand that the choice is between living a twenty-four-hour life in a mile-high fortress (*vide* Soleri) or choosing something else, then we will finally know that these fortresses, even if far more sensitively wrought than, say, the Pan Am Building of Belluschi and Gropius in New York or Yamasaki's monsters of the World Trade Center in downtown Manhattan, are neither necessary nor desirable. At that point the development of metal-curtain wall (glass or not) architecture as we have seen it perfected (Dymaxion may be something else again) may reach an end since, measured either on economic or aesthetic grounds, it has no utility save for heights which are not needed and which we shall have rejected. For all humanly needed heights and sizes, ferro-concrete offers the greater versatility.

It did not look that way at the beginning or even in the very early days following the invention of Eisenbeton (reinforced concrete), often attributed to the French gardener, Monnier. A great deal of the most important development certainly occurred in Europe and not in Chicago, which may be why self-conscious American architectural historians have not yet elected to write as extensively about it as they have about the Chicagoans. One of the earliest important reinforced concrete buildings was Anatole de Baudot's Gothic style church, St-Jean de Montmartre in 1894, just about the time the Chicago School was beginning to recover from the World's Columbian Exposition of 1893.[2] Auguste Perret, also French, was an early pioneer of 1900, and two decades later Le Corbusier. Frank Lloyd Wright was almost the only important American to experiment much with concrete until after the end of World War II, when a new set of circumstances came into play.

[2] For earlier uninfluential American developments, see John Burchard and Albert Bush-Brown, *The Architecture of America: A Social and Cultural History* (Boston: Little, Brown, 1961).

As for ferro-concrete, I do not propose to explore the modern uses of this enormously versatile material at much greater length than I have the history of the evolution of glass and steel cage. But it must be said that in recent years the technological innovations in the various ways of using the material have been far more extensive than those in the art of building in steel or aluminum. This is no doubt due in part to the earlier evolution from cast iron to wrought iron to steel, to the processing of steel into standardized components for rolling, to the evolution from bolt to rivet to welding for connectors, and to the parallel evolution of the technology of drawing very large sheets of glass and to the provision of a number of different properties in glass, glass which resisted end rays of the spectrum, which could be tempered to become almost shatterproof, and so on. But in practical terms and despite the development of lightweight trusses for roofs and frames of lower building, the steel frame, with whatever superimposed fabric was most efficient when the building was high, came to fruition some time ago.

On the other hand, concrete long remained essentially a plastic material which was poured wet into forms, set there, and, after setting, was revealed through the removal of the forms. The other early development, of pouring the concrete into molds to produce building blocks, often with cinder aggregates, reduced it to the role of a rather inferior masonry material (Frank Lloyd Wright once told me it was a "bastard" material), neither very handsome, versatile, or much desired, and chosen only for partitions, or at best for low buildings where cheapness was the primary desideratum.

Now the ability to pour concrete into any or almost any shape opened up an enormous potential for achievement of a very wide range of forms, either unattainable in metal frames or only at the high costs inevitable in specially made or fabricated metal components. In Europe at this time materials were relatively costly and building labor relatively cheap and skillful while the opposite condition obtained in the United States. Hence in Europe great efforts could be made to refine the use of concrete to be poured *in situ* involving more complex forms and the use of less material. In consequence the great innovations, both of forms such as those of Maillart, Nervi, or Torroja, and of methods, such as thin shells, tetrahedra, folded plates, and the like, occurred in Europe and were not often, at the outset, even imitated in the United States.

Concrete, however, could be and was used as basic structure with standardized forms, and great ingenuity was exercised in the United States in the way of controlling the ingredients of the wet mix, including especially the water and the aggregates, so that the expected properties would, in fact, be realized and coupled with methods of hoisting other than on a hod-carrier's back. By these developments and the standardization of forms it was possible to make concrete competitive with steel as the ossature of a building up to a dozen or more stories but never at this stage competitive even for low skyscrapers. And since the skyscraper was the dominant American development, steel remained king.

Concrete, moreover, was not loved by Americans as a thing to touch. So it could have no popularity for low buildings where it might have been used either for houses or churches.

But there were many things to happen. Men like John Early in Washington, and others elsewhere, experimented with aggregates, with brushing the cement off them to produce colored variegated surfaces often of great beauty; they looked for linings for the forms which would produce almost glasslike surfaces on the finished concrete, or brush-hammered the concrete to make a rough, strong surface, overcoming the random defects left when forms were stripped, or introduced designed texture by the nature of the forms themselves. Others developed hardeners and ways of painting the cement surfaces.

Meanwhile in the concrete factories men were learning how to pour prefabricated parts far more sophisticated than mere concrete blocks, structural sections, sheets, all susceptible of far greater control than on the site, greater precision, greater refinement. Ultimately they learned how to "prestress" the reinforced members, that is, to induce stresses of the opposite kind to those they would encounter in the building, so that when they were erected and began to work, much of the stress could be canceled out. This led to still greater refinement of shape and diminution of size in the prefabricated parts.

In consequence of these and comparable innovations, it became possible to put together an orthogonal building of premade concrete parts in which the panels could act at one and the same time as structure and surface and could be assembled rapidly and with the aid of new, highly imaginative counterweighted derricks erected efficiently and economically to much greater heights. This has recently been one of the stylish and classical ways to build, and although it could not be done at extreme heights, it has, when combined with the limitless or almost limitless potentials of concrete as a "plastic" material, reduced the supremacy of the steel frame essentially to the very high building, i.e., the imperialistic and socially absurd skyscraper. In a very real sense reinforced concrete is now the king of building materials, offering enormous freedom of form and of surface. We should expect a considerable reign, I would suppose, since neither the Dymaxion antics of Buckminster Fuller nor the spatially more interesting and suggestive "tents" of Frei Otto are so relatively unrestricted in their potentials.

Pl. 373
Pl. 375

There are, however, some unresolved difficulties or perhaps some fundamental limitations. Every building material has some. Concrete is at bottom a kind of man-made stone. It has stone properties of hardness and coldness. It is not caressing or warm to the touch as wood may be. It is probably at its best when it is used forcefully and at its worst when the attempt is to achieve delicacy. No matter what is likely to be done to improve its properties, it will be stained easily and it will develop hair checks on its surfaces and irregularities of harmless but unsightly cracks at the joints. Every building material has comparable though not identical defects. But for most old materials the weathering itself is either graceful or is subject to repair. We do not yet know how concrete will age.

And in concrete design the temptation to overdo is great. Simply because enormous cantilevers are possible, there is no necessity to use them unless they serve some purpose. Because large hunks of wall can be left out and cavernous shadows created, there again is no necessity to indulge this. The first masters of forceful concrete forms, such as Le Corbusier, Breuer, Rudolph, Kallmann, may have flirted with such temptations but escaped the enticement. The masters of concrete unitary design, such as Ieoh Ming Pei and early Kenzo Tange, managed clear and handsome expressions. The masters of concrete free forms, Le Corbusier, the late Eero Saarinen, and again early Tange, showed another and good way to go. They made a major contribution when they restored light and shadows to architecture which had been bereft of it under extreme Miesianism. But there are signs of corruption, mannerism, Baroqueism, whatever you wish to call it, creeping in in such work as Tange's proposal for housing in Tokyo Bay, Johansen's Goddard Library in Worcester, Massachusetts, Moshe Safdie's Habitat '67 in Montreal. Time alone will tell, but it would *Pl. 378* be ironic if the very versatility of concrete were to cause concrete design to become decadent less than a century after it was introduced. Perhaps this is an inevitability of a time when change is seen as a value in itself and when ideas of all sorts are so rapidly and widely adopted and exhausted; and when perhaps society is in such a state of separateness that no common values and no common taste can act as a moderator and stabilizer. But I do not know that any of this is so and that is the reason I have chosen to talk in the main about works of other times where the ends of the dramas have been played.

You could no more quickly get an idea of the wide range of forms and materials which one or another of our leading architects finds worth exploring than to look at an issue of *Time* current at the moment I am finishing this first writing (September 21, 1970) illustrating Franzen's Agronomy Building at Cornell University, Pei's library and plaza at the State University of New York's Fredonia College, Roche's student union at Rochester Institute of Technology, Johansen's Goddard Library at Clark University, Obata's University Center at the Edwardsville campus of the University of Southern Illinois, Pereira's library at the University of California at San Diego, and Rudolph's chapel for Tuskegee Institute in Alabama. These are all university buildings. They are only a fragment of the architectural scene. Even more extravagant designs are those of the Shizuoka Press and Broadcasting Center in Tokyo (Tange), the new capital of East Pakistan (Kahn), the Oklahoma Mummer's Theater (Johansen), the *Pl. 377* extravaganzas of "esthetic of survival" structures (Knowles), or the "arcology" of Paolo Soleri. And you would certainly need to consider also the "pop architecture" of Robert Venturi. Not one can be said to represent the jelling of an architectural style on the part of its designer, let alone a social consensus. Some of the forms may become classic; some may be the passing fancy of an hour. It will be interesting to see what a similar portfolio ten years hence will show.

But however it may end, I believe that there may never have been a time, not even the time of the Baroque, when there was more exciting experimentation in architecture. I happen also to think that many of the works will stand comparison with the other great works of the architectural past. They lack certainty as to where they are going. The themes of the society are less well defined, less generally accepted. The desire of each man never to repeat much of anything he has ever done before, to avoid slow refinement of his own thing, has largely expanded. In consequence the work is nervous, even at times febrile. But it is never dull and is only occasionally truly eccentric. It might end rapidly by excessive mannerism or through the acceptance of the cult of the vulgarity of Las Vegas as advocated (perhaps tongue in cheek and I hope so) by Robert Venturi, but I think it will not. If not, it will be a great period for architectural watching, and I only wish I were going to be able to watch it for a longer time than actuarial probabilities suggest.

CHAPTER ELEVEN

ON PREPARATION

As we have gone along, I have from time to time made comments on whether it is better to approach a building in avid ignorance or stuffed with previously read, if not fully digested, information or misinformation. I have posed implicitly and explicitly the question of how much you really need to know.

Also, and again only from time to time, I have taken you "around" a building, notably at Zoser's complex and at Amiens.

This book is intended obviously not as a complete presentation of the history of architecture, chronological or otherwise, or as a descriptive catalog of all the wonderful buildings men have made, but rather possibly to help those who wish to see architecture in new and, I hope, exciting and even enlightening ways.

Therefore before I end with any conclusions I have about the present and future role of architecture in society, it may be worthwhile to backtrack a little and to recall some ideas that may allow us to "go about a building" in a way to maximize our chances for understanding and appreciation.

Let us begin with the matter of preparation.

In *The Pilgrims Progress* it is reported, "who that goeth on Pilgrimage but would have one of these Maps about him, that he may look when he is at a stand, which is the way he must take." Reading in advance of architectural travel is by way of making such a map in the mind.

A major risk might be that you may have learned too much about a masterpiece to enjoy it fully. Of many of my fellows who profess the humanities, I have come to feel that their knowledge has robbed them of whatever sensitivity toward or love for poetry or painting or literature or whatnot they presumably must once have had. Of course, they may never have had it. There is no magic in scholarship that will make a soaring bird out of a groundling. But even if once they were gay and loving, a hardness may have set in. This is what Samuel Johnson had in mind in his preface to *Shakespeare* when he wrote, "There is a kind of intellectual remoteness necessary for the comprehension of any great work in its full designs and true proportions; a close approach shows the smaller niceties but the beauty of the whole is discerned no longer." This is a risk to be guarded against—the risk of not being able to see the wood for the trees.

A somewhat similar risk is that the overly well read may come to find that the vicarious pleasures of the text surpass the real ones of the encounter. C. E. Montague has spoken of this in a somewhat different context in his splendid book of essays:

> All authentic affection rests upon vision. Vision, again, rests upon knowledge. But minerals will not turn into flesh without first turning into something vegetable: so a mere intellectual grasp of a country's physique will not, alone, engender love of it. Knowledge has first to pass into vision, the state of mind and heart which does not merely apprehend evidence but broods excitedly over some completed and transfigured image of an apprehended object. Once attain that condition, once make knowledge sensuous, and then none of nature's limitations on the ordinary reach of the senses need disable you. England, bewitchingly small, lies complete at your feet; she rides like a boat at her moorings, off Europe; all of her nestles below you like Macclesfield seen from the moors, or Florence from Fiesole. Then the grand passion may come, the love that can revel and dote on the very idea of the beloved. But vision comes first; the lover must see the beloved and not merely have read her biography, very well done, and a scientific account of her person.[1]

A possible disadvantage of reading and planning is that it may cheat you out of a measure of serendipity. We all in more or less degree cherish in our hearts the wish that some day we may step around the corner and encounter an unanticipated ineffable experience that no one has ever encountered before. Montague understood this, too.

> The true delight of travel, . . . seems to prefer to come as a thief in the night, and not at the hours you specially fix for its entertainment. You make an appointment, as did Leslie Stephen, to meet it at sunset upon the

---

[1] C. E. Montague, *The Right Place* (Garden City, N.Y.: Doubleday, 1924), p. 105. This fine and perceptive book, long out of print, is a boon to any traveler, and I cite it often and at length.

top of Mont Blanc; or on the roof of Milan Cathedral at dawn; or you take a gondola far out on the lagoon at Venice, to look up and see sunrise strike the whole chain of the Alps; and, after all, the wayward spirit may only come at some moment and place that have seemed, till he does come, to have little distinction about them. Like other brands of happiness, this one can only be caught by hunting something else. . . .

[T]he best-laid of holiday plans are rather like trees that you grow on the chance that a bird may sing, some day, on one of them.[2]

Yet we live in a world in which the probability of serendipity in travel is necessarily diminished. We can scarcely protect our precious naivete about faraway places no matter how we may try. Color pictures and stories in so many kinds of magazines, documentaries on film and television, advertisements from travel agencies have made everything familiar from the Galapagos or Bali to the Bering Straits, from living in a rock-cut cave in Cappadocia to hunting with a blowpipe in Arnhem Land. It is hard for anyone to come to anything with the pure uninformed mind, the *tabula rasa*, that presents him with the thrill of the totally unexpected. This is much more the case now than when Montague (or even I) was young.

Of course, Italian management being as it is these days, a little slap-dash, it is still possible to find on arrival and after countless planning that the right day is the wrong day after all. The palace manager may just have a longhand notice "Chiuso oggi" on the door and gone off fishing. If you cannot relax about such experiences in negative serendipity, you had better not travel at all. At least planning will have mightily reduced their probability.

One *risk* of arriving with the open (read "unprepared") mind is that you may miss things you would prefer not to have missed. Coming with this open-eyed approach you might elect to stop by Mantua on the ground that you had always admired the poetry of that greatest of Mantuans, Vergil. This is likely to be a disappointment, for neither the Via Virgilio nor the Piazza Virgiliana have much to add to the *Georgics*. What one could say, I suppose, is that caught on the right day, which should be misty and cloudy, a sensitive and possibly sensitized person might relate to the countryside around Mantua, to the melancholy of the Bucolics. But this is perilously close to the danger of seeing through others' eyes, so that Corot speaks to you more than Barbizon, Cézanne rather than Provence, Utrillo rather than an Italian village street. But of that, more later.

Well, if we admit the necessity of preparation, how are we to prepare? A visit to Mantua may gain but slender marginal profit from some advance untangling of the relations between the Viscontis, the Gonzagas, the Sforzas, the Medicis, the Borgias, the Scaligers, the d'Estes, the Monte-feltres, and so on, between the Guelphs and the Ghibellines, between the

---

[2] Ibid., pp. 23–24.

great condottieri, all of whom are central to much peopling of the squares and the buildings of Renaissance Italy. It is something less than enough to pick up what you can in a hurry after you have dismounted in the Piazza Sordello by a quick glance at your green Michelin. The green Michelin *is* a good *vade mecum*, its stars are usually not ill chosen, save in the opinion of any specialist-expert you might happen on; its historical information is normally enough in quantity and in reliability for the immediate moment. But it is not enough if you are to get much to remember out of the visit since you are trying to orient yourself, fend off street salesmen, find a place where you can buy the film you have just run out of, satisfy yourself that you are legally parked, and so on. The guide will direct you to the apartments of the Ducal Palace if they are open but will not tell you where to concentrate your interest if you are short of time and if you are to put the palace back in the context of Isabella d'Este instead of treating it as a museum in which you can see tapestries after Raphael, Greco-Roman sculptures collected by Isabella, or paintings by Greco, Tintoretto, and so on. Do you prefer rooms decorated by Guilio Romano or by Mantegna? How can you decide on the cast of an intellectual die or on the sayso of a guide coursing along in a language you only half understand (it will be better to encourage him to stay in Italian and not to venture into French!)? Will you try to spend more time in the Paradiso looking down the lakes imagining you are arm-in-arm with that much painted, beautiful, extravagant woman, Isabella d'Este? Shall you be your master or the servant of a guide?

The Michelin will direct you too to the facade of the Church of Sant' Andrea, one of the reputedly great works inside and out by the great Renaissance architect, Alberti, with a cupola by quite a different and later architect, Juvara of Turin, but what price such information unless you have some context for Alberti or Juvara? One of the most interesting things to do in Mantua for 10 or 15 minutes is to visit the interior of the rotunda of San Lorenzo, a very nice Romanesque octagon, recalling others of more importance elsewhere and open sparingly from time to time during most days. The green guide deals with it during its description of the charming Piazza delle Erbe (which, of course, you will encounter without preparation) in the following nonimpelling terms: "The rotunda (Church of San Lorenzo) is Romanesque." This is scarcely a clarion call to visit.

The more extensive and better organized *Guida rapida Italia settentrionale*, put out by the remarkable Touring Club Italiano to the utter shame of the publication of our lobbying automobile associations, has more to say. It affixes a star, it provides a date (eleventh century), it speaks of the splendid massive interior, with its deambulatory arcade running around the central space, and of the arcaded cupola. But this is still not enough to do much for the unprepared.

The baptistery does stand on the square at least and is obvious to the eye of anyone who happens by. And the interior is to be seen by anyone who elects to go in (during the short hours it is open), however unplanned or vagrant his motive. So to see it is not beyond the bounds of happy accident. What you make of it will still depend, I submit, on what sort of background you bring to it. If you reply that unless it is of interest itself without background about, for example, other comparable round churches, it may really be of interest only to the pedant or the collector, I cannot make much of a reply.

But if you can hardly miss being aware of San Lorenzo once you have penetrated the Piazza delle Erbe and will hardly fail to penetrate to the Piazza delle Erbe once you have come to Mantua at all, the same is not to be said of Sabbioneta, one of the charming towns of Italy which history has passed by. If you come quite unprepared to Mantua armed only with your green guide, you will read that a collateral branch of the Gonzaga family owned the duchy of Sabbioneta but that will scarcely be enough to send you scurrying through the pages of the guide to be told about one of the most interesting little walled cities of Renaissance Italy with its pleasant low-key ducal palace, an amazing octagonal church with *trompe l'oeil* painting, and an olympic theater by Scamozzi for comparison with the greater one in Vicenza which he finished after the main lines had been laid down by Palladio.

The chances of happening on Sabbioneta by accident are remote. The road that passes nearby and offers a modest sign toward it is not a principal route, so that you are unlikely to be passing by in your automobile, and if you do, you are unlikely to be turned aside from your destination by the discreet sign. Similarly what will prompt you to seek out or pause in Todi, Bevagna, Urbino, Gubbio, the bastide Monpazier, and so on?

Let me not press the search for the obscure very hard. There are Romanesque churches to see in Italy of far greater importance than any to be found on the Lombard Lakes, and north of the Pyrenees than the charming array of little ones in Catalonia. Collecting the hammer-beam trusses of Crunch and Cawston and Salle in Norfolk, moving as they are, is not as great an experience as the cathedrals of Norwich and Peterborough and Ely, which more or less encircle them. Sabbioneta is not a Niagara Falls of Renaissance town planning; and architecturally if you must choose between it and, say, Modena or Parma to the south and Cremona or Piacenza to the west, I should have to advise you to choose the last four. But perhaps the choice does not have to be made. Or perhaps you would choose Sabbioneta anyway. How can you choose it if you do not know about it? How can you wisely reject it through ignorance?

Actually, preparation works on two levels. On the one hand, it puts more and better information in your hands than the guidebooks will about even the greatest and most obvious monuments, and this may increase your yield when you make the visit; on the other hand, it may send you to places or things you would otherwise have overlooked. In this latter sense it is a little like turning over a furrow and scanning what is to be seen in the new clods; some things may then be discarded at once, some picked up, looked at, and tossed back into the furrow. Now and again something may be kept; it may even turn out to have been an antique of great value.

There is another value of preparation which is of quite different order. Supposing you plan for a trip and then do not go? Has all this work been a total loss? Quite to the contrary, I should say. There are joys in the planning itself—and memories, too. Long before we ever got to Egypt we thought we were going to and spent a summer and autumn in preparing. Then things turned about in our world and we did not go. When we finally did, the world was different, Egypt was different, we were different. The important things, the Nile, the Pyramids, the mastabas, the Temple of Luxor, and the tombs of Thebes had not changed, though alterations were occurring around Aswan which would affect adversely the inferior late temples of the Upper Nile. But in the years between the hope and the realization, the memory of the work done in consequence of the hope was far from profitless. Indeed, I could bring myself to urge preparation for voyages one knows in his heart he will never make at all. There are worse ways to spend a winter's evening.

Though I shall come down in the end firmly in favor of as much preparation as possible, it is only fair to point out that like any other worthwhile venture, it entails risks, and that these are not trivial.

Perhaps the largest is the one already mentioned—that somehow you will be unable to see with your own eyes. When M. Perrichon finally made his voyage to the Alps, he had read so much about Le Mont Blanc that he knew exactly what he had to say about it. He could have made his famous and banal apostrophe beginning, "Quand je survoye le Mont Blanc..." with both eyes blindfolded and without even being there.

If Goethe says to you, "You must think of the Lido as a dune,"[3] he is not saying much to hinder you in viewing the Lido differently, if indeed you should, and it is quite irrelevant that this was the first time he had seen the sea. But when Stendhal asserts that the awnings alleged to have covered the Colosseum could not have worked in the driving rains one suffers in Rome, or that Jews still avoided the Arch of Titus because of the victory it was supposed to celebrate,[4] can we escape the influence of this prejudiced, carelessly informed great writer? And can we ever look, for example, at the arch again in the same way as before? Again C. E. Montague sounds the tocsin for me.

> Still, it is into another's passion that you are admitted by art. Not what you ever felt for yourself when gazing out from Richmond Hill, but what the

[3] Johann Wolfgang Goethe, *Italian Journey* (New York: Random House, Inc., Pantheon, 1962), p. 82.
[4] Stendhal, *Voyages dans Rome*, in *Rome, Naples et Florence, en 1817*, texte annoté et présenté par Roland Bezer (Paris: Editions Juilliard, 1964).

spirit of Turner felt at the instance of that expanse of champaign and river; not your own inarticulate tumult of joy in presence of Tuscan vistas of cypress and poplar, but the serene, clear-running ecstasy of John Bellini before the same prospect, is what your mind apprehends and enjoys for some propitious instants. Quite distinct from that choice and fugitive experience is that which we commonplace people achieve for ourselves when confronted with nature herself. Each in his own poor way, we have to play Turner as well as we can, and make our delight or our awe articulate to ourselves in some selecting and composing reverie over such bits of the world as are ours to behold.[5]

It seems to me generally true that the observations of the great essayists and critics are more dangerous to encounter than the observations of the great painters or the great poets, although it may be wiser to encounter the rhapsodies of the giants of writing after we ourselves have visited the scene of the rhapsody. Precisely because of the formidable power of great artists, visual *or* literary, to fix impressions ahead of experienced events, it is better to meet them with such security as reasonable personal experience can provide.

You need perhaps to be especially cautious about what the great architects say. Lou Kahn, for example, is a contemporary architect to be reckoned with, but when he says, "Paestum marks the great event in architecture when the walls first parted and columns became,"[6] he is not telling historical truth or making a significant metaphorical observation. Our trade is full of fascinating stuff like that, fun to read and deserving as much attention as Shakespeare's tales told by an idiot.

There is another sort of writer though, competent, let us say, as a scholar, full of the enthusiasm and the fire of the poets, and possessed of an agreeable writing style. (Unfortunately not many scholars do write well though writing badly is not a guarantee that the scholarship is sound.) Such men by the very virtue of their enthusiasm and their knowledge may be dangerous for the unsophisticated, and for a first encounter with the actuality. But given the armor of other experience in the area of their interest, they offer among the most pleasurable and profitable experiences in architectural reading. I shall cite only one example, chosen because I happen to hold the writer and his work in substantial esteem.

With a very large understanding of and experience with Greece and its temples, Vincent Scully[7] has made a beautiful book which explores the mythology which caused the temples, many of the usual details of the temples themselves, but in particular for my purposes here concentrates a great deal of attention on the siting of the temples, and examines and presses with great vigor a particular thesis that these sitings are related to the points (male) and the breasts (female) in which the profiles of Greek

[5] Montague, *The Right Place*, op. cit., p. 47.
[6] Cited in Vincent Scully, *The Earth, the Temple, and the Gods* (New Haven, Conn.: Yale University Press, 1962), p. 66.
[7] Ibid.

mountains on the mainland, in the Aegean islands and on Crete and Sicily abound.

There are, as with many other architectures, valuable things the scholar can tell us about Greek architecture, and it is not easy to decide which of these one ought to know, or even is interested in knowing—methods and materials of buildings; nature of the desired use; how the sites *were* used, for processionals, etc.; how the Acropolis, for example, might have looked in its polychromatic heyday; what evolution there may have been; how much was original, how much borrowed; how far back did it begin; when did it culminate; did it degenerate and, if so, when and how and why?

The study of sources can soon get into matters more interesting and speculative than whether somebody else's megaron was the prototype of the Greek temple. It can begin to be involved in mystery and magic in questions, as Sigfried Giedion in effect put it, as to whether the past is actually The Eternal Present. Given such interest, such wonderment about Urmensch, and given the vagueness of all our knowledge, large speculations become possible. And so to understand Greek architecture you must examine not only the Greek architecture, you must examine also the Greek landscape, the nature of the Greek gods, and how the Greek citizens elected to recognize them, especially in respect to the landscape. And this is what Scully has done, from Paleolithic man onward, through Stonehenge, the English towns, the circular landscape of England, the oblong, unilinear, mountain-focused terrain of Crete to the specific Greek temple sites which he says were physically appropriate to the individual characteristics of their particular patron diety. He has put these broad conjectures together with erudition and has written about them beautifully.

It is the focusing of the Greek sites on the "slot of the horn mountain" and on the relation of these horns to other horns, such as those of Minos, to bull dances, to mazes, to holiness, that provides the thrust of this work. Out of it Scully has produced a remarkable *tour de force* based on much less concrete evidence than is available, say, for the Middle Ages, although the temples and the mountains are still sufficiently there.

This is not the place to examine the credibility of Scully's interpretation of the evidence, wild and inconsistent as some of it may seem. In any case, his hypothesis is not irrelevant. If the conclusion is valid, it should be an important factor in the judging of a Greek temple, just as it is well to understand the meaning of East-West orientation in Western Christian architecture of the Middle Ages, or of Mecca in the arrangements of an Islamic mosque. If the theory is false, the Greek temple remains to reverence—and enjoy.

In this case and in the case of many other important books involving enthusiastic interpretations which are controversial, what are *you* to do? They can neither be wholly proved nor wholly disproved as a rule, however reluctant you may be to impute to remote ancestors a wisdom and a philosophy and above all a systematic, rational, and orderly development of planning and architecture which any experience you may have with present-day architects and planners would lead you to deny. Surely they are not to be placed on some new *Index Expurgatoria* for avid collectors of architecture. But it may be fair to warn the wanderer in these morasses to carry before him the banner with the strange device, *Caveat lector*.

It might not matter too much when you go to Greece if you have swallowed Scully hook, line, and sinker, provided you have not become so intent on locating horns and double horns and rolling tetonic hillocks and engulfing wombs and the relation of temple axes and peristyles to these that you never really see the temples at all. On the whole it would be better to read Scully after you are back from Greece.

I have to warn also against full swallowing of the writings of great synthesizers and polemicists like Lewis Mumford and Sigfried Giedion. This is not because their conclusions are necessarily false or because their details are in error but because they have to be elliptical about their examples and have to assume in you their familiarity—just as Spengler and Toynbee and Pareto had to do in another sort of work. It is, of course, flattering to have it assumed that you know about buildings of which you have never heard, or about buildings which you think have seen or know and in fact have not really seen or do not really know. (Mumford is more guilty here than Giedion of not supplying collateral data.) But this nodding of the head at unknown or dimly understood references is an idle way to spend the time, and you will get more out of the great syntheses and the great hypotheses if you are able to encounter them with some ammunition of your own rather than entering the field armed only with their highly personal ammunition.

What then to do? It is tempting to turn to primary sources, however difficult they may be to comprehend when found, once you have become aware of the dangers of the secondary sources. But it is not quite that easy.

It is naturally hard to find the primary sources, even though a number of them have now been translated for us. It also implies more concentration on a particular historical time than you may want to give. But supposing you accept these limitations, the question remaining to answer is whether these witnesses from another day are telling the truth, the whole truth, and nothing but the truth. Why are you to assume that the bishops and clerics of another day were any more careful about exaggeration and half-truth and downright lies than leaders of the Pentagon and the State Department of the United States of America were in the 1960s and 1970s?

Nor do such "authorities" agree much with each other. One will say that the workmen in the great medieval cathedral were so spiritually moved that they were ready for any sacrifice, another that they had to be watched and sometimes even penalized severely. Leo of Ostia, who wrote about the building of the Abbey of Monte Cassino or Abbot Harmon of the Company of Saint Pierre-sur-Dives, who recounted the labor of the people of Chartres and "the Miracle of the Carts," seem to be writing about a different world than Gervase of Canterbury, who described the looting and pillage following the burning of Canterbury Cathedral in 1174 or the slightly later mason's record (after the Black Death) of how masons had to be impressed for the work on Westminster Abbey. Shall you find the truth by adding the legends and lies up and dividing by two? Is the Abbey Church of St-Denis diminished by disbelief in the miracles accompanying its building as recounted by Abbot Suger?

The documents are interesting, often fascinating. They may or may not give true insights into what the Middle Ages were like, but they give little insight about architecture itself, with rare exceptions, such as the debates over how to build the Cathedral of Milan.

So you select your documents and you read history as you choose to remember it. Chartres Cathedral is too great a human achievement to be much embellished or marred by errors about how the people acted or did not act in the building of it. More harm perhaps is done to the objectivity with which we judge our own times by our credulity with respect to the myths of another time.

And there is in them, sometimes, something credible and important in the sense of occasion they may truly convey even with wrong facts. This is, of course, what Thucydides meant when he wrote his famous words asserting his own theories as to the writing of history.[8]

He will recount the Periclean oration not from nonexistent documents but as a man like Pericles must have spoken on the occasion of the funeral oration, and he thus includes the praise which Pericles gives to Athenian public buildings, although he himself expresses elsewhere some personal reservations about the wisdom of the Athenian architectural achievement, made possible by extravagance. Unhappily there have been few historians like Thucydides, perhaps even no others.

On the whole, however, wherever documents exist and can be read with interpreters of the quality of Panofsky, it will probably be better to use them than the unvarnished imaginations of later observers, however more comfortable their styles may be. But this is not always possible. You might find it easier to guess about the purposes of a contemporary like Arthur Schlesinger, Jr., when he wrote *The Age of Jackson*, than about Procopius when he wrote *Periktismaton*,[9] though they also seem fairly obvious. But after you have got through worrying about the motives of the recorders, you still need to do some worrying about the qualifications of the contemporaries. The previously cited case of Garcilaso de la Vega will illustrate what I mean.

Problems of the sort raised by wondering about Garcilaso become more severe as you try to reach still further back into history.

---

[8] Thucydides, *The History of the Peloponnesian War*, Book I, paragraphs 20–22.
[9] Procopius of Caesarea, *Works*, vol. VII, *Buildings*, translated by H. B. Dewing with the collaboration of Glanville Downey (Cambridge, Mass.: Harvard University Press, 1940).

As Dinsmoor tells us:

> Historians and geographers of antiquity generally made only passing
> allusion to buildings with which their readers were assumed to be so familiar
> as not to require description; and when details or dimensions were given
> to emphasize peculiarities in size they were just guesses or approximations
> to start with and so garbled in the translations by medieval copyists as to
> be almost valueless; writings by professional architects and/or historians . . .
> have been totally lost apart from a few distorted reflections through
> Roman eyes such as the abstracts from a few art historians in Pliny's
> encyclopaedias (Historia Naturalis) and allusions in Vitruvius.[10]

Dinsmoor is speaking of the relatively recent architecture of classical
Greece of which we have many literary remains and reasonably complete
ruins. Yet until the serious archeology of the twentieth century, a Greek
bibliography might be made up of such items as travel writings by Ciriaco
of Ancona (1424–1447), badly copied by Giuliano da Sangallo in 1465,
and by Pierre Belon (1546–1550). Later King Charles I and the Earl of
Arundel (1621–1642) undertook, as Arundel put it, "to transplant old
Greece into England" by importing actual architectural marble from Delos
and Paros. Capuchin monks combed Athens in 1648; the Marquis de
Nointel, ambassador at Istanbul, had a staff drawing the Parthenon sculptures in 1674. For a time after 1690 Greece was closed to foreigners by
the Turks. In the eighteenth century other books began to appear, notably
by Wood and Dawkins in 1750 and Stuart and Revett (1751–1754). Soufflot
was the first French visitor to Paestum in 1750, which had been discovered
by Antonini in 1745, by Winckelmann in 1758, by Copley in 1775, and
engraved by Piranesi in 1778. This is but a partial example of how a bibliography accumulates. The titles are now of much interest only to scholars
and possibly more to those interested in the period of the writers than in
coming more fully to grips with classical Greece.

Certainly the documentary writings of contemporaries and especially of the principals are of great interest and of value to the curious.
Often they throw less light on the architecture itself than on those who
made it, but this of course helps, indirectly, to explain the architecture.
Yet how much are we to believe?

Patrons do not often write retrospective accounts of their intentions
and accomplishments. "From his point of view the work of art should
render praise unto the patron but not the patron unto the work of art."
Hadrian, Maximilian, Leo, Julius, Jean de Berry, Lorenzo de Medici "decided what they wanted, selected the artists, took a hand in devising the
program, approved or criticized its execution and paid or did not pay the
bills."[11]

[10] William Bell Dinsmoor, *The Architecture of Ancient Greece*, 3d ed. (London: Batsford, 1950), p. xviii.
[11] Erwin Panofsky, *Abbot Suger on the Abbey Church of St-Denis and Its Art Treasures* (Princeton, N.J.: Princeton University Press, 1946).

Where thy treasure is there will thy heart be also. A very considerable idea. Suger's work is a very considerable document about a very considerable building by a very considerable man. It does not have its equal in all the extant literature of architecture. There is little doubt what it says about Suger. The question is how much of it relates and how to your visual experience at St-Denis?

And the number of genuinely apposite and modestly credible other pieces among the primary sources is scanty. They are clearly not enough. Where then are we to turn? A hundred years ago the guidebook might have been taken seriously as a form of preliminary reading. This alas can no longer be said.

There is scarcely an important piece of historical architecture, particularly of the West, that has not been overinterpreted. Of these interpretations, particularly those dealing with works built before extensive written comments and records are available, the best that can be said is that many have been serious works of scholarly extrapolation. It cannot be said that they are true; it cannot be said that they are false. And scholars of equal ability and integrity may be quite at odds with one another. Publication under the imprint of a serious publisher guarantees no more than that the job undertaken was a serious one—it does not guarantee the truth of the theory advanced. These are therefore dangerous waters in which an amateur should be cautious about swimming. It is all too easy to pick up a book by a man of repute and to be convinced by it without knowing that somewhere else in the literature is an equally valid but not necessarily truer explanation of quite a different sort. This is especially so if the writing is charming, the illustrations handsome, the credits and the footnotes sufficiently generous.

It is not that this writing does not contain some important insights.

It is well to be reminded in the face of the fashion for sweeping generalizations that no period or style can really be neatly packaged. "Styles do not succeed each other like dynasties, by the death or expulsion of the last male heirs."[12]

It is well to try to think of the extent to which a period does or does not have a *Zeitgeist*. What may be claimed on this score, for instance, for the Middle Ages?

> The Divine Comedy is a kind of cathedral; the summae provided the key to medieval imagery—religious drama and carved and painted decoration exchanged resources.[13]

But medieval art was also encyclopedic. Since all things are in God, it took all things as its theme. The thirteenth century made it hierarchic.

[12] Henri Focillon, *The Art of the West in the Middle Ages*, vol. I, *Romanesque Art*, Jean Bony (ed.) (London: Phaidon, 1963), p. 9.
[13] Ibid., p. 3.

[But] Romanesque art had perceived them (i.e., the measureless diversity of created things) only through a mesh of ornament and in a monstrous guise. It had combined man with beast and beast with chimera. It had festooned the capitals of the churches with a fantastic menagerie and stamped the tympani with the seal of the Apocalypse—it seems not the created world, but the dream of God on the eve of the Creation, a terrible first draft of its plan. It is the encyclopedia of the imagination preceding the encyclopedia of reality.[14]

Unlike the Greek it does not "exist in the sphere of the incorruptible."

We need constantly to remember that we are susceptible to judging what we see either as myth of a Golden Age or in strictly contemporary terms. We need to remember of Francis I, of Saint Louis, of Louis XIV that admiration and nostalgia for any of their periods may increase and decrease with fashion, and with what we know about them. New information may change the color of an age from gold to black.

Yet you cannot visit the island of Cos and its temple of Asclepius, for example, without being affected and helpfully by the judgment of Lewis Mumford.

The physicians at Cos knew the healing qualities of seclusion and beauty, space and order; they set their sanatoria on a little island, famous for its grapes and mulberry trees, and its specially fine silk, with a wide view over the sea, a noble landscape freed from the clutter, the disorder, the smells and noises of the Greek city.

Perhaps no one has ever translated these ideas so effectively if quite unconsciously as Henry James did in his dream allegory, "The Great Good Place." People travelled hundreds of miles by land and by sea to be under the care of such dedicated physicians, bound by their noble oath, working in such a healing environment. By the very act of detachment through travel, the patient took his first step toward rehabilitation; and the psychosomatic discovery of the curative properties of a change of scene may have been a contribution of Hippocratic lore, based on improvements the physicians observed in newcomers even before they applied their positive remedies. Can one doubt that the order that came into the new cities of the fourth century registered, in collective form, some of the lessons that this great school of healers and hygienists applied to the individual patient? That sense of space and harmony, in nature and of nature and yet surpassing nature through man's own ordered effort, left its mark on later cities.[15]

Here Mumford makes the ruins of Cos relevant without ever once telling you what you are going to see.

[14] Ibid., p. 7.
[15] Lewis Mumford, *The City in History* (New York: Harcourt Brace, 1961), p. 137.

And Giedion, too, can help in advance:

The pyramids stand on the rim of the desert. Below them stretches the fertile valley, behind them a limitless waste of sand. Life and death, an exuberant fertility, and an equally sterile land, come together without compromise.
In one respect the pyramids are unique. No later period has ever attempted to make use of so subtle a simplicity to express its irrepressible urge to link human fate with eternity. It is this absolute simplicity and perfect precision that transforms the logic of numbers into enigma and mystery. The enormous, highly polished triangular planes repel any disturbance of the dead. The pyramids were undisturbable symbols, seats of the god-kings. Their huge immaculate surfaces formed a mirror for the ceaselessly changing atmosphere. They displayed what the eye only partially perceives. They reflected all that passes between earth and sky—all the infinite, delicate changes of the moving hours. They gather the light even today, though their surfaces are now rough and granular. The play of ever-changing light imbues them with eternal motion. Their color and form passes through every phase: almost complete dematerialization in the midday glare, enormous weightiness in the evening shadows, a black triangular plane soaring vertically upward in the starlit night.[16] [If only you can keep the infernal *Son et Lumière* turned off—jeb.]

An unbiased eye that had never beheld a pyramid—Riegl's observer, say—would not automatically compute its volume. The plane surfaces acquire an existence of their own. In reality, only one or at most two of the triangles can be perceived at one time. Through the changing light they somehow become detached from the solid body they form.

The Ka was, in a somewhat similar manner, thought to be independent of man. It was part of him and yet simultaneously apart. It could enter and leave his body. The upward-soaring triangles of the pyramid seem to possess this same independent entity.[17]

Thus Giedion is examining the pyramid as a prototype of modern form. To Mumford it is "a sacred form translated into a man-made pyramid to attest the Pharaoh's power."[18]

Either view lets you see the pyramid with your own eyes. If you are overly prone to moral judgments, Giedion's explanation will keep you freer to judge what you see.

Have you ever viewed architectural engineering as animate? This is how a poetic engineer at the University of Virginia does.

Nature, comprising the forces of gravity, wind, earthquakes, soil pressure, solar radiation, etc., is like a never sleeping giant relentlessly attacking Man's building. Sometimes it acts passively by resting on the Structure

---

[16] Giedion, *The Eternal Present*, vol. II, *The Beginnings of Architecture*, op. cit., pp. 504–505.
[17] Ibid.
[18] Mumford, *The City in History*, op. cit., caption to Plate 1.

with its dead weight, and at other times it strikes out violently with winds and quakes. Always there is the insidious eating away at weak spots by rust and corrosion. The Structure reacts to all this as a trusted servant, holding out the adversary as best it can so that Man can freely swell within. Its resources lie in the interaction of the strength of its sinews (steel, concrete, etc.) and the assumed configuration of its body (girder, arch, truss, etc.). Through the power of its braced shafts (columns and foundation) the hostile forces are eventually transmitted into the ground and dissipated.

The sympathetic designer feels for the Structure as it heroically carries its burden day and night, sometimes for centuries, complaining only occasionally with a creak or a crack. He sees the stress trajectories lying within the Structure as dynamic lines of life. As blood flows in a biological system, so too do stresses flow in a Structure. They enter the Structure at the point where the alien forces attack, and then proceed in generally parallel paths from beam to column to foundation until they are safely discharged into the all-absorbing parent earth. However, at clumsy connections or irregularities of shape, the sympathetic observer winces at the pain borne by the Structure in having its stress trajectories twisted and tortured in trying to negotiate these places. A smooth orderly flow generated by simple arrangements is a pleasure to bear and a delight to witness. It is like seeing a gentle fish swim gracefully around a bank, in contrast to seeing the brutal struggle of a salmon trying to jump a cataract.

Contrary to the belief of lay observers, Structures are by no means static inert substances. They are actually in motion, in some cases slightly and in other cases greatly, yielding under the action of outside forces ever-changing from hour to hour and day to day. As trees bend in the wind, so do buildings. A further look deep inside even a simple brick would reveal billions of atoms swirling dynamically with life.

So in truth, even so-called static structures are really quite dynamic and do indeed respond in many ways as living creatures.[19]

If you approach architecture with thoughts like these in mind, I do not see how you can fail to have a richer experience than if you had failed to encounter them. The gains are worth the risks. But the risks are not trivial. They can come from being overly embracive of the generalization so that you can think no other way but to see Hippocrates under every Aegean plane tree or the Ka stepping out of every Egyptian tomb or the swirling of the atoms in every architectural brick. Such extreme consequences may be unlikely.

But you may suffer from too much devotion to a special or even a narrow view; or from plain confusion about the uncertains, the speculations, and the out-and-out controversies in which the literature abounds.

Of uncertainties and controversies it may be necessary to say little

[19] William Zuk, "Join the Architecture of Movement 'Movement,'" in *Modulus*, student magazine of College of Architecture at the University of Virginia.

more than that they abound. Uncertainties dog us at every step in Micronesia to be sure, but in more explored areas as well, uncertainties about purposes as at Stonehenge, or the Labyrinths, uncertainties as to the errors of Manetho in his records of Egypt or Herodotus on Persia. How well does the internal evidence from the palace of Tiryns support the generally held view that it was either pedimented or corniced, and if so, which? Why really were the Minoan columns tapered downward? What were the Aztecs really like? Were they as vicious, brutal, and bloodthirsty as the friends of the Mayas want to think? If so, was there not an ambivalence between their vigorous, terrible sculpture and the poem of pessimism and anguish:

> We only came to sleep,
> We only came to dream . . .

Was it really "the rhythm of time" which enchanted the Maya? Such questions in greater and lesser degree plague every corner of architectural history, not always much illuminated by written documents. Were the satirists of Imperial Rome truthful recorders of what they saw? Would Abbie Hoffman's journal, or Bill Buckley's, be a sufficiently explanatory legacy for posterity, as reliable say as Juvenal, Martial, and Seneca?

Where there is uncertainty there are opinions and often heated controversy. Were Mayan corbels really vaults? What went on in Mayan "observatories"? What were their "corridor palaces" for? Which interpretation of the Middle Ages and Gothic is "right," Focillon's, Frankl's, Von Simson's, Panofsky's—let alone the older Ruskin's? The exploits of Theseus were in the flank metopes of what used to be called the Theseion of Athens, now known to have been the temple of Athena and Hephaestos mentioned by Pausanias. In what senses of the understanding of Greek *architecture* does this matter?

Yes, the reading of architecture is like walking warily over a bog. In the end, though, if your architectural encounters are to be rich, read you must. You may not care much or need to care much about provenance and prototype. Where the Mayans came from and why they fell apart may not concern you. You can get along without a parallel table of the Capetians and the Plantagenets. You may not even need to know about the monastic and lay derivations of the English cathedrals, of the role of the bishops in their governance, or of what Saxon fanes were torn down. You may not care for a Domesday register of architects' names or about the fall of Sejanus as recounted either by Juvenal, Plutarch, or Ben Jonson. But all these and more are somehow and in some way relevant. There are limitations in the theory of I like what I like, or History is what I choose to believe. So Dinsmoor is right to say:

> Architecture might be called the sheet-anchor of history, which without the everlasting testimony of the monuments would certainly become fluid and unstable.

But the testimony of the monuments if necessary is not sufficient, so Dinsmoor has to add:

> How much more is open to the student who examines architectural works with full mythological knowledge, or from the point of view of the trained philologist or historian.[20]

Yes. Read you must, if your architectural travel is to have rich rewards. To help where it may, I have appended an amateur's bibliography. Perhaps it is the wrong kind. It contains no poetry. So read in any event, the historians if you must and the poets if you will. But don't blame me if you read the wrong things; and particularly, do not blame me if you are too gullible.

REPRISE—HOW TO GO ABOUT A BUILDING

Many years ago I sat in the Guards Club in London with the then Tory Whip, the late Harry Cruikshank, who was preparing to introduce me to cricket at Lords. The point he said was to get there at the high moment. That would be when a famous batsman with many centuries to his credit came in. But to arrive earlier would be boring. So we sat in the easy chairs receiving timely bulletins from the steward until the moment arrived and we set forth. But when we got to Lords, we learned that the unexpected had happened. The anticipated champion had been bowled out as soon as he took up his stance at the wicket. There was nothing for it but to return to the Guards and the Scotch.

One can approach the arts the same way, and there is nothing wrong in being selective about them once one has a basis for selecting. Surely some of the Canterbury Tales will have longer appeal for any one of us than others, but it is a discourtesy to Chaucer and a disservice to ourselves if we try picking and choosing before we know the terrain. So the first time around it is better to begin where Chaucer intended we should begin and end where he wanted us to end. The greatest symphony is not made up of favorite bits and pieces. You will not get a great experience of Beethoven by playing sequentially the "best" movement of each type plucked from the garden of nine. When well informed, you might come late to a concert or leave early to avoid something you felt no need to hear again, but it might be better to have heard it more than once before deciding.

Most great works of art, at least up to now, have had beginnings and endings and their designers have consciously arranged this. It is not otherwise with architecture, and it is perhaps only in this sense that it really deserves to have been called "frozen music" (by August von Schlegel),

[20] Dinsmoor, *The Architecture of Ancient Greece*, op. cit., p. xvi.

although I suppose one can speak a little more than metaphorically of its harmony and counterpoint.

Indeed, there are analogies to be drawn between architecture and music that may be closer than with the other arts. Like music, architecture is something that has to be experienced through time. But this is true of other arts, too, clearly of theater and poetry and dance; and, though less obviously, of painting and sculpture as well.

Like music, the greatest architecture should not be entered at random. There is a significant sequence of events. This is true also of poetry, of drama, and so on. It is so whatever the new nihilists may bellow to the contrary. But the designer of the symphony, the opera, the ballet has the greatest control of where you choose to come in. So, too, the dramatist. There are few buildings, however, without side doors, and these days the main door is not always even open. The painter has no control of a positive sort over where you begin to look at his painting—he can use devices to catch your attention where he first wishes it to rest and others to distribute it in the directions he hopes it will travel. But he has no time control. In this sense painting and sculpture have no beginning or end, except for occasional rarities such as Mantegna's Procession in *The Triumph of Caesar*, and similar parades by Benozzo Gozzoli and others, or such narrative sculptures as Arajuna's Penance or the Fall of the Ganges.

The playwright loses some of his time control when his play is printed and read privately rather than performed publicly; the same thing happens to the poetry when it ceases to be sung; the novelist has never had this control. Some, though perhaps not many, novels may successfully be entered anywhere, forward and back. Joyce may suggest an exception, though the suspicion remains even here that Joyce had a better understanding than most of his readers and that the first time around anyway one would be well advised to begin at the beginning and end at the end. But the point is that the consumer of the art is free to choose, once the poem, the play, the musical score is put on a printed page, on the possibly risky assumption these days that the consumer is, in fact, literate.

What is said here has naturally no application to the habitual latecomer and early departer whose devotion to meals and tea conditions his behavior more than his devotion to the arts; and even less to some modern music and theater sessions involving "participation" where the idea of beginning or end has only disastrous connotations. (This is by no means the same thing as the tightly structured *Waiting for Godot*.) In these seances one can come in whenever one likes and leave whenever one likes and still have participated in the "dialogue" and "the mutual and meaningful experience." (Personally I like to leave such affairs before I arrive.)

Architecture is not a happening, thank goodness, and the very circumstances under which it is put together have contrived, at least so far, to keep it from suffering the gross indignities which have been heaped on the other arts by instant poets, instant actors, instant playwrights, instant painters, and skillful public relations people or dealers pandering on the one hand to pathetic adolescence which is not less *attistic* because it is bearded, and on the other to a few bored and overly affluent patrons. As someone has remarked about the "new poets": even Dante's laundry list would not have added much to the *Vita Nuova*.

Architecture, too, is best not encountered at the outset as though it had no beginning or end, but rather the intended sequence should be sought. Later encounters, as repeat engagements with any work of art, are quite a different matter. Then one can ignore all the rest of Westminster Abbey for a quick repeat of the delight of the vaults, or even the bosses or the banners of the Henry VII Chapel. One need not read all of *Antigone* every time one wants to think again about a favorite chorus.

But works of art are entitled to demand a first experience on their own terms. If, as John Middleton Murry wrote, "Great poets mean what they say," then they are entitled to be met at first on their own grounds and not in the dustbin of *Bartlett's Familiar Quotations*.

Architecture lies in an uneasy middle ground among the arts in this respect. The architect usually has less control than the composer of where the observer comes in and where he leaves. For example, you can shut your ears for a while to let them wait for a particular moment when you want to come in where Brahms did not plan for you to come in. But only with a prodigious musical intellect and then only intellectually can you play it backwards. But any fool can reverse the order of a building without even having to walk backwards. He has more control than the novelist or painter, and a well-designed plan will offer more control than may be apparent. Where it is possible without making the experience too bookish, it would be just as well on the first encounter to try to follow the planned path.

This will by no means be easy. One of the first questions surely will be, whose path? As I hope I have shown, from time to time most buildings have had multiple users. The Shinto priests in the secret recesses of their shrines have a different experience from the worshippers who toss coins in the buckets; the cathedral of the English chapter was not the cathedral of the English layman; Westminster Hall and the appended Houses of Parliament have a very different appearance and, I suppose, meaning to the Queen making her annual visit through the Royal Entrance, to a back bencher hurrying through passageways to a division, and to a loyal colonial tourist seeking to savor the whole thing. Whose approach is the just one? The answer must be all, but since one cannot be all, one has to choose or try to savor all.

The composer is at the mercy of the players every time his work is performed. The architect is at the mercy of the artisans, and a great one, though pressing them to the height of their abilities, will not ask them to do what they are unable to do. But unlike the composer, the architect is not at risk at every performance, only during the building. The architect cannot completely control the program nor the progression to it. Like the composer, he too cannot completely control the execution of the work. But unlike the composer, he is not vulnerable all the time. When the building is first made, he must depend on the skill of the artisans who can make or break him, and later on he has been much harmed at times by repairers and especially by restorers. And, occasionally, overeager hands can murder his design by ill-considered intrusions, as in the spectacular example of the Rubens in King's College Chapel, Cambridge.[21] But all this is pale compared with the mayhem which can be done to a composer's intentions by mediocre players, but even more especially by overzealous interpreters.

Like music, architecture cannot often produce the big climax, the immediate and explosive confrontation, without preparation, without lesser experiences on the way.

When you go up the cog road to Zermatt, you never see the Matterhorn until you have rounded almost the last corner. Here is the big climax without preparation. There is not much prelude before you walk into the impressive rotunda of the Roman Pantheon. But there is some, and you should not run past it too fast. In most architecture the prelude to the climax is longer.

So I suggest encountering the prelude and following the architect's plan, tentatively, as one sort of guidepost for a first encounter with a building.

You may not want to follow this program, and even if you do want to you may not always be able to. But given an ideal situation here is how I might like to do it. I would like to come upon the building from a distance, indeed from several distances, a kind of zooming in on it from varying points of view. If you think of Chartres across the wheat fields of La Beauce, you are understanding what I am driving at, but you should not forget that it offers an entirely different impression viewed from the little river, down among the washerwomen looking up the narrow picturesquely roof-tiled streets. The standard distant view of Mont Saint-Michel across the tide-emptied sands or the flats of water is quite different from the view at sea. Most of us will see Hatshepsut's Temple at Deir-el-Bahri from somewhere in the vicinity of the Nile, but those who know the temple well may tell you that it is most dramatic when you come down on it over the rocky palisaded backdrop. This experiencing of a variety of approaches could be called getting a full sense of the building simply as a mass sitting on its site. I suppose one of the views we ought to include now would be the view from the air, although almost no build-

[21] The college accepted the valuable painting, and unwisely the insistence of the donor, that it go in the chapel which had a complete and harmonious interior that could only be marred by an inappropriate painting, however fine the latter might be outside the chapel.

ing, not even a contemporary one, has been designed with the air view much in mind.[22]

This is only an opening gambit, of course, and one could easily overdo it coursing the countryside and boxing the compass of viewpoints so to speak. No one is likely to do this thoroughly before moving in on the building; for many buildings it would be quite impossible to find some viewpoints; and I suppose I am advising a kind of slow-take reconnaissance, if not today, why then tomorrow.

But if the building is a great one, it will be calling on us to stop this shilly-shallying and approach nearer. It will even cry to us to look at it alone, forgetting its urban context. But in the end this must happen. I think the preference should be to approach the building from the front if it is at all possible. Sometimes it will not be and occasionally we might need to be careful about what is the front. The Egyptian pyramids, though symmetrical, do have a front defined by the valley temples, the causeway, etc. The Parthenon's "front" is really its back. It is not what you see when your eyes emerge on the Acropolis through the guiding openings of the Propylaea. It would be absurd to put on a blindfold here and to make your way to the other end, which was the front where the outdoor altars were. One should not make a fetish of the frontal approach but just keep it in mind. But to follow the processional route would not be foolish.

This approach brings us near enough to some part of the building front or not so that it would be easy to let the eye get engaged in the details. If one can exercise enough self-discipline, I would hope that this could be avoided for the moment in favor of a broad-stroked comprehension of the main elements, the porch and dome of the Pantheon, the towers, the rose, the portals of Amiens with the tympani or the tracery of the rosace left in a kind of blur. Hence one might circumnavigate the building as far as the neighborhood arrangements permit. One will see the nave buttresses, the transept facades, the porches attached to them, the buttresses of the apse and the massing of the apsidal chapels, and so on, until he has worked his way around to the front again. At this point I would think it better to go inside and engage the interior in the same sort of encounter, noting senses of space and connection more, say, than bay details or the specifics of nave vaulting. This may take longer than the outside, for the interior spaces like the outside from a distance give very different impressions depending upon where one stands, and these changes in the impression of space are one of the most important experiences a great building has to offer.

After the largest overview and the middle overview, my own taste in

[22] Perhaps a caveat should be entered about this. It is a very common and generally useful practice of contemporary architects to try to help their clients to understand what the now as yet unbuilt building will look like through a carefully made presentation model. Unhappily this model is all too often viewed from above, that is, given an air view which it will seldom offer in practice.

looking over an unfamiliar building (of course, if it is thoroughly familiar, I may have come back for a single cherished reexperience; for example, I would probably return to the Medici-Ricciardi Palace in Florence only to ascend to the first floor and to look again at the Benozzo Gozzoli frescos) would be to study the larger rhythms, the greater articulations, the proportions, for example, a bay of the nave of Chartres or of Durham. It would be a matter of indifference to me whether these were outside or inside and the choice might be related to the time of day or the number of people around (not too many—have you any idea how heavenly the Sistine Chapel is before the tide of tourists has come flooding in?) or even the weather or whether I feel the need to sit down for a while. Only after that would I want to begin the microscopic search that is often so rewarding. Shall I dwell on the building materials and the craft and love which have been lavished on them? Shall I ponder the stone tracery of a rose window, the individual capitals of a Romanesque church, the great sculptures of the south and north porches of Chartres, the Last Judgments of Bourges, or Autun, or Moissac? Shall I read the marvelous story told in the serial mosaics of Monreale; the basement frescos or the Cosmati pavement marbles of San Clemente? Shall I read the stories of the windows of some of the French cathedrals, the prodigal son, the tree of Jesse, the *nouvelle alliance*? Shall I look down at the noble floor of Amiens before I look up at the noble vaults? Shall I collect the tradesmen's signs of many of the medieval windows, descend to crypts to visit treasures or ascend to the roofs to look at gargoyles or walk the leads? Shall I fasten on the rood screen at Exeter or study the many beautiful chantry chapels in which so many English cathedrals abound? Shall I turn up the choir seats at Malvern Priory to look at the wonderfully human and often hilariously secular misericords; or stand at the many royal tombs in Westminster Abbey or look at the banners unfurled there in the Henry VII Chapel or turn eyes upward again to try to make out the decoration of the bosses? Shall I go into the nearby museum whether on the Acropolis or in some ancient fane? Not all buildings offer such a range of excitement—not even all the great ones. But most of the great ones of the past have quite a lot more than meets the eye or the first quick survey—or than is to be found in many contemporary buildings, which, whatever their other merits, tend to be fairly antiseptic.

I realize how wooden I have made this sound and I do not intend it as a prescription or even a checklist for another traveler. I follow it myself only once in a while. And there is nothing to be ashamed of if you, for example, do not find the brass plates of memorial tombs in old British churches as fascinating as I or even the archaic painful capitals of Saulieu, though I hope I have persuaded you at least to look before you decide. (Looking at the brass may be difficult, so ubiquitous are the makers of "rubbings" these days.)

But there are the big principles of more or less keeping within the same scale during one sequence of time and not marching down one aisle and back up the other pausing faithfully at everything marked in the guidebook. You could do this in many situations and never experience the grandeur of a great piece of architecture at all because of your preoccupation with the angels' pinions.

There is a second principle I believe valid, and have discussed in more detail earlier, which is to have some conception of the plan of a great building or site before you are in it. This is less important for a simple building, such as the Pantheon, than for a complicated one like Canterbury Cathedral; less necessary for the Acropolis than for the Imperial *Fora* and less important for them, so orderly is their array, than for Hadrian's Villa at Tivoli, where, fortunately, you can examine a large model before getting lost.

Another basic piece of advice which may seem snobbish but is not is that you will not do very well with any really great building by a single visit—any more than you will have much grip on the Saint Matthew Passion or Hamlet following a single encounter. It is imperative to go back more than once during a single visit to the city which houses the monument and even more important to come again some other time. Great buildings are buildings for all seasons and they display themselves differently at different times of day, at different times of year, and under different conditions of weather and use. If you are very lucky, you may find them in a time of maximum use: the wedding of a mayor's daughter in the Capella Palatina in Palermo with every candle lighted, the mosaics agleam and reflective, a visitor's gallery in an important room of state, a great ceremonial parade toward and around a Japanese shrine. But even if this lucky chance does not befall, the repeats are more rewarding than the first visit—the masterpiece becomes a part of you.

This will not be the frequent lot of many of us. For most Westerners Agra and Isfahan and Ise are unlikely to be frequent ports of call. But Paris and London and Rome well may be. I suspect I am never in Paris without at least a short call at Notre-Dame. And as with the *Eroica* symphony, there is something new and rewarding on each encounter. You simply cannot respond adequately to the call of a great building by replying "but I have seen you."

And now for the hardest piece of advice of all but one of the best. Leave *all* your photographic equipment in your hotel room on your first visit unless you are sure it will be your last visit, and maybe even then. I say this as one who has been photographing architecture for years, whose slide collections are esteemed in at least three libraries, and who has for much of his life used his own pictures to illustrate lectures.

Now I am not urging you to stop taking pictures or to stop displays of home movies and home slides, though I hope you have the same distaste I have for shots of Miranda on a camel in front of the Sphinx, unquestionable as the testimony is that she was in fact there. Who ever doubted that, anyway? Or cared?

No, what I am saying is that photographs are one thing and seeing a building is quite another. Why should you, when blitheful in heart you enter the precincts of Delphi, carry all this weight on your back? Since at most places more than half of all the great architecture is inside, you cannot do much with architecture, no matter how steady you think your hand, without a minimum tripod, a reasonably long telephoto, and a reasonably broad wide-angle lens. You will always be changing film at a crucial moment. Worse, something may stick, especially in an automatic camera, and you may waste hours trying to find a dark room, for example, at Paestum, because you are not man enough to sacrifice all those potentially precious exposures already on the film. You will often be so angry because the light isn't just right or whatnot that you cannot see the beauty that is there. That is, of course, the real reason for leaving the camera aside on the first reconnaissance, which is the most critical one you will ever make. The better you are as a photographer, the more sure-footed you will be about sensing what will frame well. But what the camera frames, beautiful as it often is, selective as it can be to emphasize something that the wandering eye might pass by, it is simply not the same thing as the unencumbered eye and body can comprehend. You are not a camera; the camera's eye is not your eye, and I pray you to leave the camera on the shelf the first time around so that you will look at the architecture unencumbered by unnecessary restraints. After that, shoot as much as you like and I guarantee that your pictures will be more knowing and telling. And if by chance you never get around to the pictures, you should have memories fixed in your head that would never have been there had you submitted yourself from the outset to the tyranny of the camera. I know you will agree and then disobey the injunction. But isn't it worth thinking about? And why not try the experiment at least once?

The other bits of advice are more trivial. By all means, carry along a good pocket mirror if you are going to spend much time looking at ceilings; by all means, take one of those compact, light 6–8 power binoculars the Japanese make so well if you intend to study many capitals or stained glass windows. You will never realize how great a painter Corregio really was unless you visit his ceiling in the Duomo in Parma aided by these simple equipments. And, of course, wear comfortable, sensible shoes. There is really no way to examine great architecture except on foot. And if you must eat a gourmet lunch at noon, abandon the architecture and take a nap instead. It is possible to be to all intents and purposes asleep while strolling glass-eyed through the Ste-Chapelle after lunching across the Seine in that place of overly inflated reputation and carrying too many stars in its Michelin crown but still abounding in soporific food and drink.

CHAPTER TWELVE

ON DESECRATION AND DECAY

Through any account of an ongoing architecture, the historically conscious person will be aware of a thought which may pain him or please him—depending upon his mood: the thought that "this too will pass." It must cross our minds every time we encounter a ruin—but it will also occur to us when we engage an active, operating building, such as Notre-Dame de Paris or the Louvre, and know its history.

John Ruskin, who tended to be sentimental about many architectural problems, was realistic about this one. He recognized the pleasures of weathering and patina on the one hand, remarking that there were as many hues in a pink wall in Italy as there had been seasons to corrupt its matter. But at the same time, he was beset by the evils of change.

Seán O'Faoláin remarks that Keats, had he lived to Ruskin's day, "would probably have sighed for the perfection of the Rome of 1820; so small, a country town, with goats lying in the streets and cows being milked below the Spanish Steps." He quotes Ruskin who lamented the wiping out in Florence of the Via dei Calzaioli, the street of Bronzino, and Donatello and Michelozzo and the Or San Michele, which he reported as having been so altered as to consist "almost exclusively of shops of bijouterie and parfumerie"; who was legitimately wrathful at having to stand on a loom to see the frescos in the old refectory of Santa Croce, which had been turned into a carpet factory. In the second volume of *Modern Painters*, 1846, Ruskin burst forth:

> There is not a monument throughout the cities of Europe that speaks of old years and mighty people but is being swept away to build cafés and gaming houses.

But about all this O'Faoláin is more philosophical.

> Every age has changed and meddled with its inheritance, sometimes impairing it, sometimes enriching it. . . . Cities are not museums. . . . Cities must not only be seen to be believed, but felt as growing, living things. . . . It is as impossible to study cities out of books, as it is to study men, and neither can be ordered to stop growing.[1]

Change may be slowed down or accelerated, but it can no more be arrested than King Canute was able to arrest the incoming tide by ordering it to stop. The readiness is all. One might be underready and thus become an overzealous preserver and restorer of the obsolete; one might be overready, prone to regard rapid change and innovation as goods in themselves and thus become an overzealous demolisher. But even those who sit in the middle have to be aware that the current of the river of time, however much it may eddy, however much it may idle over oxbow shoals, sets in only one direction.

The solution is no doubt the unglamorous one of compromise. Do not assume that everything now is ipso facto better and that it is essential that everything be up to date in Kansas City. But on the other hand do not automatically applaud every preservation as ipso facto laudable.

One of these tides, however, which we ought to strive to resist with all our might and main is not urban at all. I have already referred to the flaws in the urban concepts of Le Corbusier as they appear in such new cities as Brasília. And there are very serious risks to some presently beautiful and pleasant older cities by the high-rise obsessions of some leading architects, potential Berninis of our day, and their avaricious entrepreneur clients (one is tempted to say customers).

But even more ominous is the slow but accelerating desecration of the world's most beautiful nature spots by such things as the condominiums and new resort hotels which have, like tent caterpillars in the woods, impaired the wonders of the European Alps from Innsbruck to the Val d'Isère, the Spanish Costa del Sol from Malaga to Algeciras, the west coast of Mexico from Acapulco to Puerta Vallarta, and the Hawaiian Islands, and which threaten a splendid isolated part of the High Sierra by Disney enterprises. The architects of these thoroughly mercenary ventures are by no means po-

---

[1] Seán O'Faoláin, *A Summer in Italy* (New York: Devin-Adair, 1950), p. 96. The Ruskin quotations are from O'Faoláin, p. 94.

tential Berninis. But things might be even worse if they were. The individual buildings might be better, as architecture, but the arrogant competitive ensemble might be conspicuously worse. To defend the remaining bastions will, I fear, be to fight a losing battle given population growth, human affluence, and greed. But at least the defense can slow the erosion. And it might work a miracle.

One of the great demolishers is nature herself, much as man may try to thwart her. Every day she insinuates herself against every building, eroding here by wind and rain, seeping in through the cracks to cause rot, sending armies of insects to riddle timber with their tunnels. No building material is immune to nature's toll, though some are more resistant than others—creepers and ice can split the hardest stone, and where stone does not fall, the jungle may soon overcover it and reclaim its own. Against this incessant attack, men are ambivalent. On the one hand they reinforce nature's forces with their own destroyers and eroders, on the other they fight both the natural and human forces with maintenance techniques which, when kept up, will generally prevail against the lesser legions of nature until the civilization collapses, maintenance ceases, and nature quickly reduces the abandoned building or city to a ruin or causes it to disappear altogether. Against the larger natural disasters, the earthquakes, the tornados and hurricanes, the volcanic eruptions, men's defenses are at best partial, and rebuilding is their only response; sometimes even this cannot be done—when, for example, as at Pompeii or Santorini, the site itself is contaminated beyond hope or totally destroyed, as it might also be in an atomic age or, in a more lingering way, by neglect of the facts of ecology.

But there are other forces at work to destroy or change architecture. They are strong forces, and from them a paradox arises. Most primitive builders use ephemeral materials that are carried away by the wind, washed down by the rains, trampled by elephants, consumed by fire almost as a matter of routine. The most convenient maintenance may be replacement of the whole. Here a conserving factor comes in. The life has been traditional, the building materials and methods traditional. Nothing has permanently been altered by the coming of the elephants or the winds. The loss is not looked upon as an opportunity for a long-desired change. So the new villages and buildings arise as they were before, very often on the same precarious sites, so that the most ephemeral of constructions become in effect the most durable in a tradition-bound society. On the other hand, to a change-desiring people, the very durability of buildings when married to the economic attitudes of overripe nations causes regret that buildings last so long and are so hard to demolish or to be permitted demolition.

Sometimes the decay of such buildings is in the people who use them.

There is first of all the corruption of the user. Once-primitive people find that "Yarn is much easier to work than hibiscus bark," and women tell an itinerant priest, who is also delivery boy for mail-order houses, that "it's not so scratchy to sit on." But the earlier lavas were more beautiful.

> Outer islanders forsake the clean uncluttered beauty of their islands for the crowds and squalor of Majuro and five other district centers. They hover like moths around the attractions of the settlements—government jobs, schools, hospitals, movies, high priced canned food and higher priced beer. They used to eat roasted bread-fruit, boiled taro root, fried reef fish washed down with water from green cocoanuts slashed open by machete, while they were garlanded with maramars, coronets of fresh wild flowers. It may be a poor trade-off for the purging of internal parasites and the elimination of tattoo.
>
> The clearest degradation, architecturally, is seen in the one room shack, a cabin built on a stone-base with siding and a corrugated iron roof, marginally cleaner, and infinitely uglier. Better than the transition but inferior to the old are the neat row of class rooms looking like some California subdivision with Venetian blinds built at Melekeiok Palau. . . . The Army may do more harm to civilized life when it settles down on a tight little island than when it burns a forest.[2]

It is this sort of attack rather than that of nature that the conventional primitive village is most vulnerable to, and the village is losing the struggle all the way around the world.

In more "advanced" societies corruption is more likely to be by the user rather than to him. Goethe was much concerned by the slobs he saw at work when he visited Vicenza.

> Looking at the noble buildings created by Palladio in the city, and noting how badly they have been defaced already by the filthy habits of men, how most of his projects were far beyond the means of his patrons, how little these precious monuments designed by a super-mind, are in accord with the life of the average man, one realizes that it is just the same with everything else. One gets small thanks from people when one tries to improve their moral values, to give them a higher conception of themselves and a sense of the truly noble. But if one flatters the 'Birds' with his lies, tells them fairytales, caters daily to their weaknesses, then one is their man.[3]

If people *are* swine and if architectural pearls are cast before them, you may expect that the pearls will be ground into the mire.

A somewhat different kind of human desecration occurs when too many transients swarm into anywhere and take over, whether it be New York or Charles Street, Boston, the Spanish Steps or Stonehenge, whether

[2] David S. Boyer, "Micronesia: The Americanization of Eden," *National Geographic*, CXXXI (May, 1967), pp. 702 ff.
[3] Goethe, *Italian Journey*, op. cit., pp. 47–48.

they be self-styled "beautiful people," hippies, or American Legionnaires on convention. They may leave no seriously unpleasant permanent residue on their leaving, if only they would leave.

Cook tells of the terrible use to which some of the English naves were put in the fourteenth century. Naves were used for trade or simple loitering. State councils were held in the nave of old St. Paul's Cathedral. People played ball there. Casks of beer, loads of fruit were carried through until this was forbidden by law in 1554.[4]

Doors in the aisles of the nave provided a short cut from the north to the south side of the building. In a different day a similar indignation had been expressed when the Colosseum in Rome was put to similar use.

Degradation seems to occur often just by the presence of more people than a place was designed for. If Abbot Suger is to be believed, this is what had happened to old St-Denis. It happens in the Sistine Chapel from time to time right now. We usually think of this misfortune and its consequences in terms of natural scenery and it is indeed a very serious problem for the modern world even in those natural spots which have been protected from greedy exploitation, but this is not primarily an architectural problem, though sometimes architecture abets the despoilation.

We feel much the same way when too many people come to a beautiful building that once was more lonely as we do when they pack Yosemite. We are right to feel aggrieved when people act like starlings. But there is not much we can do about it. It takes the utmost tact to keep onlookers out of the choir of an English cathedral during evensong, and they, in turn, usually resent it. There are many people who have become affectionately fond of the grime-washed Paris facades who are resenting bitterly the clean-up which perhaps makes the buildings look as they first looked—"*quand les cathédrals étaient blanches*," as Le Corbusier put it in one of his book titles. We are indeed conservatives in this sense. We are like Goethe's conservatives. "Though time changes everything, they cling to the form of a thing as they first knew it, even when its nature and function have changed."[5] The most "progress-oriented" of us still feels a pang when tomorrow morning he sees a hole where yesterday there was a building to which he was used even though he never quite loved it. This is what lies behind most movements to save the Penn Station, save the Bradbury building, save the Old Corner Book Store. Most of them are not only wrong in principle but they are, thank goodness, also mostly doomed to fail. There will, I suppose, in time, be a movement to save the Pan Am Building in New York, though this is now hard to imagine.

It is usually hard also to accustom one's habit to changes in the disposition of a building because of changes in the fashion of its use; or more often of changes in the style of new buildings as changes in attitude de-

---

[4] G. H. Cook, *The English Cathedral Through the Centuries* (London: Phoenix, 1957).
[5] Goethe, *Italian Journey*, op. cit., pp. 99–100.

mand. Usually these occur over a longer period of time so that they are not quite so noticeable to the man in the street as they are to the historian. Whether the result is progress or decay may often depend more upon taste than on fact. There are those who prefer Hellenistic sculpture to Archaic Greek art of the sixth century; and conversely there are those who prefer the National Gallery in Washington to the Whitney Museum in New York, both no doubt as to shell and as to contents. As we stand in our moment, it may be hard or impossible to tell whether our architecture is improving or decaying. What we do know is that unless it fails to follow all the precedent history of architecture, there will be a moment when it will begin to decay, whether it is apparent to contemporaries or not; for some men of today, no doubt the moment of glory is yet to be reached; for others we are well on the way down the slope.

Decadent or not, the changes will come. It came even to the Egyptians whose movement to change was so glacially slow that even the foundering occurred with a majestic slowness that required nearly a millennium for its consummation.

The Greeks, who were more agile than the Egyptians in all things, were naturally more agile in decay as well. This was partly, but only partly, a consequence of the change of power, the ascendancy of Macedonia after the battle of Chaeronea in 338 B.C. During the fourth century with rapidly changing political fortunes and gradual encroachment by the "foreign" Macedonians, the architecture of the mainland and the western colonies naturally diminished in importance. But in Asia Minor under the luxurious and relatively free Persian satrapy there was something like an Ionic Renaissance. "Alexander found many great projects underway and hastened to make them his own." But:

> Throughout the Greek world the fourth century marked the beginning of a decline from aesthetic perfection. The religious aspect, the chief inspiration of most styles of art, had reached its culmination in the Periclean temples and now began to be outweighed by secular elements, a stage of development which indicates that we have passed the crest of the wave of Evolution. [I am not sure that this can be taken as a universal—jeb.] From the temple which had previously represented almost the sole aim of architecture, attention was diverted to a great variety of structures, almost as many types of buildings as we erect at the present day. . . . And even in religious architecture the same striving for diversity and innovation is manifest in the increase of ornament at the expense of strength and dignity.[6]

Advance, retreat, side-stepping, revival. Even among the Mayas there was change, a chance for acrimonious debate about the state of the times as measured by the new noncornice.

[6] Dinsmoor, *The Architecture of Ancient Greece*, op. cit., p. 217.

And so it has always gone and no doubt will always go so long as men build buildings.

I need not multiply the examples further. You can find them in any style you will to study. The word "evolution" may not be exactly the right one. But the changes, whatever they may be, whether for the better or the worse or nonjudgeable, are the consequence of internal forces, and we have to learn to live with them. It is harder to be content with those which come from outside, especially those which are produced by humans rather than impassive nature.

Nature continues, of course, to threaten. Right at this moment Mohenjodaro, one of the most striking archeological monuments of the dawn of civilization, is threatened with final extinction by the same Indus River whose floods are supposed to have caused the people of their advanced city to abandon it about 1500 B.C. after a millennium of successful life there. Now the riverbed creeps slowly closer to the site. The sun draws up the salt-laden water into the brickwork, and as the water evaporates the salt remains to corrode the brick. "Today the walls of Mohenjodaro, kept intact beneath the earth for centuries, crumble away in fistfuls of red powder."[7] And the jungles constantly threaten ancient temples, whether in Guatemala or Ceylon.

The hand of man is faster, if less sure. Man has never been able to build anything that other men were unable to destroy. The tombs of Egypt were violated even in their heyday.

But if the vandals could not remove the frescos of Egypt or did not think them valuable enough to try, the humidity of hundreds of human breaths, exhaled by countless tourist visitors, can. Many of the greatest tomb murals in Egypt are deteriorating under this force just as the murals of the cave of Lascaux were, so that now visits to them either cannot be made at all or are heavily rationed.

There are other kinds of vandals, who may even seem respectable. Raphael and his papal patrons used the buildings of classical Rome as quarries convenient for their new projects, just as Abbot Suger had wished to do earlier for St-Denis. XIX-dynasty Egyptians, especially under Rameses II, looted the modest temples of the Middle Kingdom to get building materials for their more pretentious monuments.

This went on all over Egypt as it has everywhere else. The Gothic churches usually rest on crypts of Gallo-Roman origin. The pyramids of Meso-America conceal one or more smaller pyramids on which they were over-built. Only rarely does man's hopes that his name can be preserved in stone come true.

Today's vandalism of this sort is not for the reuse of materials but the reuse of land.

The destroyers may not be taking down the old for as gentle a pur-

[7] *The New York Times*, November 20, 1968.

pose as to build something new. Alexander perhaps burned Persepolis. Persepolis is a ruin defaced as well, until recently for most of us, by Greek anti-Persian propaganda as much as by Macedonian tinder and torch. Omar's lion is gone now, and the lizard scurries furtively from the footfall of the tourists who dismount daily from the agency buses or have spent the night in an adjacent modest caravanserai in order to see the ruins in a Persian dawn. They walk with vague impressions of Darius, of Xerxes, of Alexander, but no one fails to remember the experience as important. How much more impelling it must have been before the bitter night when Alexander broke in. The record of destruction or damage to distinguished buildings by military men is long, from Alexander and doubtless others before him, through Napoleon and William Tecumseh Sherman to the "Huns" of 1914 and the bombardiers of the Luftwaffe, the Royal Air Force, and the United States Air Force in 1939–1945, and again for long recent years in Asia.

Another sort of vandal of quite different purpose has been the religious zealot. The Roman Catholic burned the codices of the Maya or destroyed the beauty of the Great Mosque of Cordoba in making it, or part of it, into an inferior church. The Moslems plastered over the frescos and mosaics of the Christians. The Byzantines seriously damaged a Greek Temple at Agrigentum as elsewhere by poking windows through the walls of the *cella* and tacking on an apse at the eastern end. The Hugenots in France and later the despots of the Revolution of 1789 wrenched the sculpture from the Catholic cathedrals wherever they could reach it. The books about English churches are full of gruesome details of how the cathedrals were ruined first by the King's Commissioners of the Reformation then worse by the Long Parliament of 1641 and the coarse excesses of the Commonwealth troopers. Civil war may be more deadly to architecture than wars of conquest.

But the damage has also been done in nonviolent times and by earnest, if ignorant, men with what were possibly the best intentions in the world. These are the restorers.

Such a man was James Wyatt, whom Augustus Welby Pugin called "this pest of cathedral architecture." "Between 1787 and 1797 he ruined Lichfield, Salisbury, Hereford and Durham." To a less extent the more gifted and intelligent Victorian architects Pugin, Gilbert Scott, and George E. Street added details that if not unsightly were at least more Victorian than Gothic. France was somewhat more fortunate in Viollet-le-Duc, though not everybody says so.

Historians perhaps fear restorers more than vandals, because they cover up whatever clues might have remained. To those of us who are not historians, they may or may not give us false impressions of what the great monument was really like when it was great. When we go to a great historic cathedral today, or indeed to any building which has remained more or less in use, even a different use, we have to be conscious that we are seeing only a part of the original fabric, perhaps only a very small part. In a cathedral such as Bourges, a full-time mason who has put his whole life into it and knows the cathedral very well goes around its heights and its depths daily replacing here and there a corroded stone, and this has been going on for a long time. But here the grand design governs the detailed replacement, and the only deterioration is that owed to the inability of some contemporary stone carver fully to catch the spirit of the original of the piece of eroded carving he is now copying. (Modern air pollution is doing its best to see that soon the great medieval sculpture that stands outdoors will really be irreplaceable.) But aside from the cleanness of the new stones which make them stand out from the old fabric briefly until time quickly discolors them and blends them into the old, this maintenance restoration is about as harmless as any restoration can be and is essential if larger restorations will not be necessary later. And it is the larger restorations that are fraught with perils—from Williamsburg to Knossos.

When the well-known medieval historian, W. R. Lethaby, was made Surveyor of the Fabric of Westminster Abbey, a post he filled from 1906 to 1928, he wrote at the outset of his work: "Westminster Abbey and the King's Craftsmen." In it he said:

> The expert re-editing of old buildings, with all its pretensions to science, comes in practice to a muddling up of so much *copy* of old work, so much *conjecture* and so much mere *caprice* without leaving any record as to which is which. This actual obliteration of authentic remnants and evidence is what we call Restoration.[8]

Similar things happen when a relatively unimpaired building is refurnished. Jefferson's Monticello, for example, has handsome specimens of furniture such as Jefferson *might* have had but in many cases did not actually have. The whole place is also abnormally tidy. Does it or does it not then give a fair impression of what it might have been when Jefferson actually lived there? Does it inspire the sense of the shade of Jefferson hovering round its dim pilasters? Should it?

In addition to restorers there are the half destroyers, the remodelers. Sometimes it is necessary that they do this. To put a new museum inside the Sforzesca Castle at Milan may have been the only viable way to keep the whole thing; and this is surely so of some of the great palaces from Rome to Genoa. This, I think, we must accept with good grace as having saved for us the most important part which otherwise would have been washed away by the urgencies of our own day. We cannot afford many urban museums like Venice or to a considerable extent Florence—and certainly we cannot live in a world of urban museums. So we may consider ourselves lucky if we can still see the Tiepolo ceiling in the Palazzo Clerici

[8]William Richard Lethaby, *Medieval Art: From the Peace of The Church to the Eve of the Renaissance, 312 to 1350,* 3d ed. (New York: Philosophical Library, 1950).

in Milano on occasion since a small enterprise has made it possible by using the building to keep it from the demolisher's ball.

Another common type of remodeling is to make a building compatible with contemporary needs. We do this at small scale today. Gore Hall at Harvard with a fine old stone facade was gutted and brilliantly refitted with a contemporary interior by the Architects Collaborative, not for reasons of fashion but to make it possible for the building to serve Harvard's modern needs at all. Wurster, Bernardi, and Emmons converted an old candy factory on the San Francisco waterfront into a pleasant if somewhat "cute" mart called Ghirardelli Square, and Joseph Esherick did the same thing in different and, I suspect, less quaint terms with a complex called the Cannery. These saved the old facades and did what they did for the cityscape of San Francisco and simultaneously created new centers of contemporary urbanity. The task would have been harder or even impossible had the original buildings had more distinction, as for example, Frank Lloyd Wright's Larkin Building in Buffalo, long since gone, or his Imperial Hotel in Tokyo, now also demolished. A little imagination and zeal might have found a new use for the great steel and glass cage of the Penn Station concourse in New York City, if not for the Caracallan approach and waiting rooms. But this did not befall.

Another type of remodeling however has more to do with style than with use. When Bishop Walkelyn, the Norman, succeeded Stigand, the last Anglo-Saxon bishop at Winchester, it was only nine years later that he began the construction of a new cathedral. Fourteen years later, eighth April 1093,

> [I]n the presence of almost all the Bishops and Abbots in England, the monks came from the Old Minster to the New; on the feast of St. Swithun, they went in procession from the New Minster to the Old and brought hence St. Swithun's shrine and placed it with honour in the new building; . . . and on the following day Bishop Walkelyn's men first began to pull down the Old Minster.[9]

As a historian I might wish that the old church had been left there, but as a man of any sense at all I can see how impracticable that would have been for the bishop and the chapter.

I might wish I could see Bishop Walkelyn's cathedral intact. But his times were changing. It was more than fashion which asked that the old dark fanes be flooded with light. It is the people of the times who should have the say, not their dead forbears or their unborn successor-historians. I imagine, had I been in Winchester in the fourteenth century and had a vote, I should have cast it with the two Williams (or three if you include

---

[9] From a twelfth-century *Annals of Winchester* record as cited by N. Sykes, late Dean of Winchester, in *The Pictorial History of Winchester Cathedral* (London: Pitkin Pictorials Ltd., 1965), p. 4.

their master mason), and the event was, in any event, distinguished. We cannot say the same thing of the trivial shop fronts that are now being imposed on the lower floors of some of our good middle-aged office buildings. This is sheer and unnecessary desecration since retail trade could still thrive in a more responsive and sensitive attention to what was already there, as has occasionally been shown, for example, by Bonwit Teller in Boston, and quite consistently in London or Paris.

Out of all these human reasons, then, architecture is constantly being born, modified, destroyed. Analogies to a life process are a little too glib, and we can get along without them. As this process goes on, the death and destruction is pressed by those who have no affection for anything gone and for whatever motives, venal or spiritual, want to tear everything down and begin over. The pressures of these people are very strong and will in most circumstances prevail, sometimes unhappily. But they are not all Vandals. Only some.

At the other end are those who want to save everything. Perhaps they do not like the present; perhaps they fear the future. Perhaps they only have nostalgia for a time which may never have existed. They are the people who, in an extreme example, have marked 1,500 buildings in San Francisco as historic monuments to be marked for preservation, when any sober, objective valuation by an out-of-towner would be hard-pressed to find a dozen which warranted this protection. They include those who have managed to save in that same romantic, frontier, vigilante town Bernard Maybeck's Piranesian Palace of Fine Arts, designed by him for an exhibition and about which he himself had said it should not be preserved. At great cost they have not only kept it but have recreated it in permanent materials. Now they have only to find something to use it for, which is turning out to be very difficult. These are the sort of people who in Boston wanted to save a building where Garrison once printed the *Liberator* although it had no other distinction. These are the sentimental promoters of lost causes, most of which, though not all, should be lost. But just as the demolishers are not all Vandals, so the preservers are not all Luddites.

What is the right ground on which to stand on this issue? I have no doubt myself! If a building is totally or almost totally destroyed, be very cautious about trying to rebuild it in its former form. It will hardly ever work. Nor will a new stave church in the Dakotas, no matter how studiously duplicated.

If a building or a neighborhood is threatened with demolition, apply criteria such as the following to the decision.

Keep the building if it is of supreme architectural distinction. I am thinking in terms of Taj Mahals and Pantheons and not in terms of a Pennsylvania Station. There are not many of these supreme buildings in the world, and although there will be argument at the fringes of the list, they are resolvable. You should keep such buildings even if you can find no practical use for them other than to look at them (e.g., Versailles).

Keep buildings which are of unquestioned historical import for their genuine historical associations. Independence Hall in Philadelphia is such a building. The house in which some unknown sea captain in the China trade is said once to have lived on Russian Hill in San Francisco is not—nor is an imputed bordello on the Barbary Coast, or perhaps even an old absinthe house in the Vieux Carreé of New Orleans. In this area great defenses must be laid against the Kilroy-was-here type of preserver. When such buildings are kept, as much of the near neighborhood as possible should also be kept and restored with respect, and the whole made into a sort of historical museum. On the national scale in the United States only a few cities have such monuments of genuine historical importance. There are few Beacon Hills. But I would see no harm in keeping something of local importance in every city, pushing its local history as hard as it can without risking too much snickering from outsiders. I should think it reasonable to keep the strange old capitol in Guthrie, Oklahoma, for example, or the Old Main on many a college campus even though it may not be as elegant, say as Nassau Hall at Princeton.

In respect to a great many buildings which have some importance to the followers of architectural history and were very good in their day if not of absolute distinction over time, a different principle has to be applied. I am thinking of such different things as the old cast-iron Gantt building in St. Louis (now gone), the Pennsylvania Academy of Fine Arts in Philadelphia by Frank Furness, the second Leiter Building in Chicago by William Le Baron Jenney, or even the Monadnock Building in Chicago by John Wellborn Root, or most of Frank Lloyd Wright's earlier buildings. Here it is apparent that we have neither the funds nor the interest to justify trying to establish a sort of National Gallery of Architectural History which one would visit by touring from place to place. In time many of these buildings will turn out to be of such small interest to most people and of such minor importance on the scale of architectural history that to preserve them on such grounds will become ridiculous. Neither Wright's Unity Temple in Oak Park nor Maybeck's Christian Science Church in Berkeley are the equals in interest of Notre-Dame de Chartres or the Ste-Madeleine in Vézelay, and no amount of talking and writing will make them so. (They may be as important and interesting or may be even more so than a hammer-beamed church, say, at Trunch in Norfolk.) Churches, however, are the easiest to keep so long as congregations exist. But it is also true that Wright's Robie House is not the equal in interest of the house of Jacques Coeur in Bourges, or Sullivan's Wainwright Building to the Cloth Hall of Ypres; and we do not know yet whether the new

Town Hall of Boston will exceed the interest of the old Town Hall of Louvain or even the fairly recent eclectic Town Hall of Stockholm by Ragnar Östberg. Given this dilemma and retaining still a desire to maintain at least a visual thread of architectural history on the small as well as on the large scale of time (the large scale determined through unplanned destruction, the uncontrollable ravages of nature, of war, of bigotry, what we can visually remember), it seems to me there can be only one rational solution, using architectural criteria alone. There may be social criteria such as too long a lapse between extant but demolition-destined housing and its replacement, but that is a different problem. Aesthetically, we should earnestly try to establish for each of the worthwhile buildings which do not rise to the level of distinction set by criterion 1 or 2 (that is, absolute aesthetic or historic eminence) a new and viable use which is consistent with the arrangement and appearance of the building as it was. We should be very cautious, at the same time, in the way we go about "restoration."

This doctrine, if used unsentimentally, will certainly lead to the demolition or other loss ("desecration") of a great many above-average buildings. In the process some errors of judgment will be made and occasionally something of nobility and importance will be irreparably lost. But there is, I think, no other reasonable or even desirable alternative.

Goethe had it right.

The observation that all greatness is transitory should not make us despair; on the contrary the realization that the past was great should stimulate us to create something of consequence ourselves which, even when, in its turn, it has fallen in ruins, may continue to inspire our descendants to a noble activity such as our ancestors never lacked.[10]

This is easier to say than to act on when, with full respect and love for the past, we come upon a fine building which stands in the way of a major urban development, such as Richardson's Allegheny County Court House and Jail in Pittsburgh, or one which is functionally almost completely obsolete, such as McKim's Boston Public Library. How can we work around the problem if we do not take down and start over as the men of papal Rome did? If we add to the McKim Library more of the same, we will fail functionally and aesthetically. If we add a modern addition, we may succeed functionally but produce an aesthetic confrontation of the most disagreeable sort. Or, if lucky, it may turn out well at the hands of a sensitive modern architect who has also some respect for history. The Gordian solution, the move-on theory of Colonel Sellers and the

[10] Goethe, *Italian Journey*, op. cit., p. 143.

American West, the New Towns Movement which simply leaves the old behind to wither and die as gracefully as it may—none of these are quite responsible answers. There is no more difficult problem of contemporary architecture than that of creating something *now* which is a straightforward expression of what you believe *now* is and what *now* needs in a mood which has a decent respect for an architectural environment which belongs to *then*—not only respect perhaps but even love and regret that then is not now and never will be again. Once in a great while this is made to work at the scale of a single building and its neighborhood, or at a larger urban scale. But most of the time it fails—either from too much respect for the past, which weakens the present, or from too much respect for the present, which flaunts or at least ignores the past. Perhaps in most situations the choice has to be as sharp as that. When it does, it seems to me obvious that we have to opt for the present and stop regretting that Richard Nixon is not St. Louis the King, or George Schultz a Colbert.

Not too long ago I sent to my good and noble, now departed, friend Walter Gropius a statement on this subject by the partially romantic C. E. Montague. Gropius had not seen it before and liked it very much, which has encouraged me to believe that I was not wrong in thinking that it deserved to be liked—and heeded:

> But of all cities, London, after all, is surely the finest to look at. You find it out if you have lived there in your youth, and then been long away, but sometimes revisit the place. You see it then with effectually opened eye, as the man who has long been in some tropical wild sees rural England revealed while his train comes up from Plymouth through two hundred miles of trimmed, fenced garden, half-miraculous, half-laughable and wholly endearing. Fleet Street when the lamps are being lit on a clear evening; Southwark, its ramshackle wharves and mud foreshores, seen from Waterloo Bridge at five o'clock on a sunny June morning, the eighteenth-century bank of the river looking across to its nineteenth-century bank; the Temple's enclaves of peace where, the roar of the Strand comes so softened, you hear the lowest chirp of a sparrow, twenty yards away, planted clear and edgy, like a little foreground figure, on that dim background of sound; the liberal arc of a mighty circle of buildings massed above the Embankment, drawn upon the darkness in dotted lines of light, as a night train brings you in to Charing Cross; the long line of big ships dropping noiselessly down the silent river, past Greenwich and Grays, on the ebb of a midnight high tide—O, there are endless courses to this feast. And it changes incessantly. Westminster Hall and the Abbey may give you a faint illusion of permanence, just as the Matterhorn does, though it is falling down into the valleys all day. But quit your London for some thirty years and then come back and look. . . .
> Yet it is all perfectly right. Let everything—almost everything—change with a will, in any city that you love. People gush and moan too much about the loss of ancient buildings of no special note—"landmarks" and "links with the past." In towns, as in human bodies, the only state of

health is one of rapid wasting and repair. Wych Street, Clare Market, New Inn—they matter about as much as so many hairs or the tips of so many nails of some beloved person. The time for misgiving would come if the architectural tissues of London ever ceased to be swiftly dissolved and renewed. Woe unto her only when, like Ravenna or Venice, she buries no longer her architectural dead but keeps their bodies about her till they and she all mortify together into one great curio of petrifaction, like some antique mummy, a prodigy of embalmment. Kingsway, Aldwych and all the demolitions that made way for them were salutary signs of molecular activity in London's body. The Old Bailey was no bitter loss. Over Christ's Hospital itself the wise lover of London soon wiped away his tears. In the great ages of art, buildings have not been regarded as if immortality were their due. It is but an invalidish modern notion that any house which is handsome or has had an illustrious tenant ought to be coddled into the preternatural old age which the Struldbrugs of Gulliver found to be so disappointing. Cities whose health is robust are never content to live, as it were, on their funded capital of achievement in building or anything else; they push on; they think more of building well now than of not pulling down. And no cities are so excitingly beautiful as those in which architecture is still alive and at work, as it is in London to-day. Their faces are both ancient and young, without disharmony, for all good work, of any time or kind, can live at peace with the rest. The old looks and the young looks play a chequer-work over such faces; it may be as pleasant as any that patches of light and shadow make on the side of a hill on days of sunshine and blown cloud.[11]

Now that I am seventy-six I am more sure that this is so than when, at twenty-five, I thought, for a moment, that I, too, was a revolutionary. But I am more sure, too, that the work which replaces the demolished old good work, must itself be good. This, alas, does not come about as often as we should wish.

[11] Montague, *The Right Place*, op. cit., pp. 183–186.

CHAPTER THIRTEEN

THE URBAN AESTHETIC AND
THE PROBLEM OF URBAN JOY

I hope I have said it often enough along the way to make it clear that it is seldom sufficient to examine a building as an isolated object, shorn of context and of ambiance, whether the latter is the natural site or the man-made one of the city or town. A great many of the most important things we have been talking about are in fact groups, whether in a Greek precinct or in an English cathedral close, a Mayan ceremonial city or a great palace surrounded by parterre and lesser buildings. It is naturally easier for the designer to achieve a well-ordered composition when he has the whole thing to do, as in the Place des Vosges in Paris or the Place Stanislas in Nancy; or is able to impose a dominating design idea on what was already there, as Bernini was able to do at St. Peter's Square in Rome. It is also not too hard, perhaps, when the architecture of a time is well established as to principles so that conformity is not too difficult, at least among gentlemen. But not many top-drawer architects are in fact gentlemen. Each wants to design the ornament for the top of the tree or to have his lower-placed contribution outshine the topmost star. Beautiful Christmas trees are not measured by the brilliance of their individual ornaments any more than a tastefully attired elegant woman will allow her several items of jewelry to compete with one another. Yet sufficiently mediocre or bad taste on the periphery can destroy the topmost star or the loveliest bosom.

It has never happened that one master architect has been able to create a great city from scratch filled only with his own work (I said a *great* city), although occasionally, as in Paris and Rome, fairly large spaces have fallen under one hand. Nonetheless a few cities have achieved, how, it is not quite clear, a sort of overall architectural feeling no more disparate perhaps than the many elements of Canterbury Cathedral or the Louvre or St. Mark's Square in Venice, though naturally less internally consistent, say, than Palladio's Villa Rotonda outside of Vicenza.

Of these we can say, I believe, that there is a positive urban aesthetic, not unlike that of a work of architecture, very different and diverse in detail, not subject to so rigorous an analysis, or open to quite the same simple exploration; and possessed too of many stimuli beyond the formally visual which, though latent in a building, are much less central to the entire impression than they are in the great city.

It is of this aesthetic I now wish to speak. I know it is unfashionable to remind a suffering world which is terribly self-conscious about its suffering, and whose youth are given to extremes of self-pity and of self-righteousness, that there are amenities of life which are worth preserving and that some of these are aesthetic. But I do not apologize.

Nor do I apologize for resurrecting with some revision an essay on this subject which I wrote in 1957 on the S.S. *Kungsholm* on a long voyage home, because it has not really been widely published and because I could not say it as well now were I to try,[1] and because I really think time has not outmoded it.

The works of J. K. Huysmans are no longer fashionable, but makers of cities would do well to recall the experiences of his hero, des Esseintes. This man understood that the true aesthetic experience exacts the use of all the senses, not the optical alone; and that this experience is more sensuous than intellectual.

So it is for the city of today, even though architects and planners seem often to ignore it. The character of a fine or a mean city is composed of its smells, its noises, even its taste as well as its sights. Its sights include people, their clothing, their conveyances, their flowers, trees, fountains. A city has an unseen history which also forms its aesthetic. A city is not architecture alone, perhaps not even principally.

Cities have noises. There are the shrill engine whistles at the Gare St-Lazare, the chants of the street peddlers of Naples, the bells of the betjaks in Jakarta, the horns in the fogs of San Francisco Bay, the subterranean rumble of the subways of Manhattan, the unmuted Lambrettas on the Corso.

Cities have people and people have tongues. Street voices do not

---

[1] First published as "The Urban Aesthetic" in *The Annals of the American Academy of Political Science*, November 1957, pp. 112–122. I have deleted a good deal, not so much because I have changed my mind as because it seems to me not closely enough pointed at what I have in mind here.

sound the same even in a single country. The sharpness of Indianapolis is countered by the softness of New Orleans, the flatness of Omaha by the twang of Bangor, Maine. None is like the diapasons of Hamburg, the falsetto upturnings of London, the liquids of Rome or Helsinki, the wails or bleats of Bombay or Cairo. When they stop talking some people in some cities sing, some listen to sidewalk orchestras, some are silent. Thus cities do not sound alike.

Cities have smells. Wood smoke and manure provide the warm fall atmosphere of Bourges; coal gas cares for Lille, or Birmingham, or Washington, Pennsylvania; oil for Galveston; fish drying in the sun for Ålesund; coffee roasting for Boston and San Francisco; while, when the wind was in the southwest, Chicago used to know the sick sweet odor of drying blood and recently ardent flesh, although this has now gone into memory. Mainz is redolent with honeysuckle. Thus cities do not smell alike, although diesel exhausts tend to make them indistinguishable.

Nor are all the visual motifs of a city architectural. People wear clothes: the bizarre open shirt of Hollywood and Vine is not the careful gray flannel of Grand Central though it may be becoming so, or the big hat of Fort Worth, or the bowler of the City of London. The summer skirts of Stockholm do not resemble the kimonos of Kobe, or the saris of Madras, or the serapes of Bogotá.

People are carried about. Some cities have elephants, or camels or goats, many have mules and horses, some have rickshaws, some have sleds, and a few have sedan chairs even now. More have bicycles, and when you see many you can be sure you are in flat Amsterdam and not flat Chicago. Most common today, of course, are motorcars but even these do not look alike in every city; even the automobile scenery changes, though the smog spreads internationally.

Cities have history, at least great cities do, and historical spots have their own aesthetic. Some cities like Helsinki bear the formidable memories of many different occupations in architectural forms which have not been destroyed; some, like Athens and Rome, wear their proudest jewels in their magnificent ruins; some like Paris or London offer a wide canvas of relatively undemolished historical development. For many the historical aesthetic may be mainly an aesthetic of the memory: the door through which assassins sought to reach a Henry of Navarre; the ancient site of a wilderness fort such as Duquesne, or Dearborn; the pavement, long since replaced, on which a Crispus Attucks fell. Often the memory is served only by a plaque. But even such tremulous whispers from the past will cause the sensitive to prickle. Kilroy again!

Some cities have sidewalk cafés and some do not; some have awnings, or umbrellas, or arcades, and some do not; some are adorned with mosaic pavements and the result is different from that of cobblestones or asphalt. Some have pleasant street signs or street lamps. Some support flowers everywhere; some have rejected plants. Some are best known for their chimney pots. Some have amusement gardens, but a Tivoli, a Skansen, or a Liseberg is quite a different thing from a Disneyland or a Coney Island. Some have rivers, or canals, or lakes; some are moist with fountains; some are dry and hard.

All these things add to the aesthetic of a city. Most of them are the result of time and tradition. Few have been consciously created in a single moment the way a hotel manager might sprinkle an elevator in the Ritz-Carlton with perfume. Yet the city of the future will be incomplete if all these aspects of personality, while possible in an old economics of scarcity and overwork, are discarded as obsolete or impossible in the new economics of plenty and leisure. It would be ironic if the brave new city could sport no flowers because there is now no one left with time or inclination to tend to them or to replace the ones the flower children peacefully pick.

The city that we love or detest is the summation of all such things: of its smells, its noises, its people, its voices, its clothes, its vehicles, its animals; it is the sum too of its markets and its sidewalks, of its trees, flowers, water, and sculpture, of its clean or grimy air, of its abundant or covered sun, of the color of its sky, of its terrain, of a way of life, and a history. When the city is lucky, and this does not always happen, it possesses an architecture which has understood and loved all these nonarchitectural considerations. When we synthesize all these, the image of a given city springs quickly to mind as any exercise in calling names will prove. Most of us will have immediate and moderately reliable responses to names such as Bangkok, Benares, Hong Kong, Kyoto, Katmandu, Nuremberg, Florence, Venice, Athens, Cairo, Caracas, or Honolulu as well as to the great world capitals like Rome, Moscow, Berlin, Paris, London, Stockholm, Tokyo. In America a few cities evoke such images, but these are more likely to be New York, Philadelphia, Washington, Boston, San Francisco, or New Orleans than Houston, Kansas City, or Buffalo. We can even conjecture images of cities we have not seen, cities like Samarkand, Isfahan, or Leopoldville. Happy the city that proffers such a positive image. Unhappy the city that does not.

There has been a decline in the number of positive images. Newly created cities like New Delhi or Canberra, Chandigarh, Brasília, Islamabad need at least time. But the lesser and newer cities of the world look more and more alike every day, and, as we adopt each other's conveniences and inconveniences and merge them with our own, the same thing is happening to the greater cities, although at a slower pace. Whether or not it is better for French health that Coca-Cola replace Pernod, it is certainly not better for the French aesthetic, nor are the new high-rise centrally heated buildings in Paris. A slow leveling process is going on all over the world. Of course, it is theoretically possible to level up as well as down, but an improvement in standards of sanitation is not necessarily synonymous with an improvement in aesthetic standards, and urban-aesthetic leveling seems always to have been down. On the aesthetic side it may be that

Gresham's Law is at work in the world. The symbols of Western "progress," coveted in too many places, are not always pretty symbols. The symbols of the Soviet Union are no more pretty. Thus sanitation will remove the indigenous smells, mass production the indigenous costumes, mass communication the indigenous tastes, education the indigenous tongues, greed will demolish the beautiful old buildings. Easier transport will diminish the importance of indigenous materials. History cannot be expunged quite so easily, but many people would like now to forget much of their history, and not all peoples recall the past with pride. The camel will not survive forever on the streets of Tashkent, or the llama in Cuzco, or the water buffalo in Rangoon. Skylines will change, rarely for the better, architectural deviations will become less conspicuous. But even where the city centers that provided the character have been well protected, they become engulfed by the anonymous and expanding peripheral suburb.

The life of man in the large modern city has so changed that the visual aspects of the old city he may once have known and cherished can have only a tangential effect upon his life. Thus in his own impression, they are not at all as his memory might recall them even when they have not been physically changed. Nor do they look to him quite as they may to a stranger. Once this was not important, but in the modern world nearly everyone in a large city is, in a curious way, something of a stranger.

This is not to say that the city dweller thinks of himself as exotic. The exotic city so many of us want to visit is always over the range in Erewhon. We want to visit Erewhon and return to praise it, but the more important word is not "praise" but rather "return." In an increasingly nomadic world there can be fewer homes to return to, more determination to make every place like home, fewer exotic experiences. For the exotic and the indigenous are, naturally, the same thing only seen through different eyes. If the final world is to be one great Conrad Hilton chain or set of Army posts, this will have some effect upon the aesthetics of the cities. The quaint Alice Foote MacDougall repetition of the pretty picturesque will not do for modern man. We need not expect to hear muezzins calling from the minarets of Hilton-Mecca or perhaps even to buy Islamic food there. It is a shame if Harry's Bar has become the best Italian restaurant in Venice, which the Italian visitors know, as most of the Americans do not. I prefer a hamburger to a rollmop of an afternoon, but not in Alkmaar. But such news are out of date.

This leveling raises hard questions for the designer of new, as yet unbuilt, cities, perhaps even harder ones for those who will rebuild the old cities. Until recently, not many citizens were so proud of their historic center and as determined not to spoil it as the Parisians, but this battle too is being lost. The questions are humiliating if the urban designer whose heart does not leap up at the click of a computer is sensitive enough to understand them.

He must at once accept the fact, as the architect of a building must,

The Urban Aesthetic and the Problem of Urban Joy 547

that he cannot please all tastes. Probably more people would admire Paris or Venice than would admire Bakersfield or Shreveport, but even this will not be universally so. Hardly anyone, for example, finds it possible to be neutral about Valencia. Kenneth Tynan likes it but can quickly and with good humor quote some adverse verse.

La carne es yerba; la yerba aqua,

Los hombres mujeres, las mujeres nada.

The meat is grass; the grass water

The men are women, the women nothing.[2]

But if there are no guidelines, there are even worse difficulties.

The largest humiliation is that so little of the urban aesthetic is within the power of the designer to control, even if he has the capacity. He cannot write the whole symphony. He will not, perhaps fortunately, be able to design the noises, the smells, the costumes, the vehicles, even the major elements of the terrain. He can neither select them nor expunge them, but he will be a bad designer if he ignores them. He cannot be the choreographer but he ignores the chorus at our peril.

Nor can he remake or relive history. Yet he must be careful not to destroy it for there can be no great urban aesthetic which forgets history or tries to pretend that people have not trod the streets before. History offers particular pitfalls. It will not do, on the one hand, to wax sentimental about it and to create more Williamsburgs or Santa Barbaras. But it will not do to extirpate it either, and it will be wrong to destroy fine things for new projects. Boston without the old churches, the Bulfinch State House, Richardson's Trinity Church, McKim's Public Library, the Boston Common, and the Charles River Basin would not be much of a city, however dramatic its new City Hall. Solicitude for what has gone before cannot be limited to refraining from tearing them down. The designers of the two insurance buildings which destroyed the urban skyline of Boston were as much vandals as though they had torn down Trinity Church for a shopping center.

Cities are like human beings. They cannot void their past experience. This is a lesson better understood in Europe than in America. A primary and inexorable problem for the modern urban aesthetic is to respect and understand history without being servile to her. For us of today there is less risk of servility than there is of disrespect. We must never forget that there were brave men before Agamemnon—or Le Corbusier.

Many otherwise great designers have not possessed this sensitive understanding of history. They have been willing either to tear down fine old buildings, to restore them arrogantly, or to enter into an unfortunate and juxtaposed competition with them. But even if history is understood and appropriately revered, there remain other humiliating limitations.

[2] Kenneth Tynan, "The Judicious Observer Will Be Disgusted," in *The New Yorker*, July 25, 1970, pp. 33 ff.

The designer will scarcely be permitted, for example, to design whole cities except in books. Frank Lloyd Wright had to share Baghdad with Alvar Aalto and others, and in the end all was mostly "échoué," however much he may have protested;[3] this is probably just as well, no matter how towering the genius. Cities take a long time to make, and order or consistency are not the only ways to a fine urban aesthetic; they may indeed offer the most limited way. We should be nervous when whole cities are entrusted to mystics like Lou Kahn or technocrats like Buckminster Fuller, and even about Chandigarh and Brasília.

I have heard revealing debates about Broadway at night which will illustrate this point. Broadway is vulgar, strident, brassy, confused, and visually wonderful. Orderly minds perceiving the fundamental beauty wish that it might all be taken in hand by a single brain or at least by a group of sympathetic brains and brought into order, its colors subdued, its competitive excesses suppressed. Indeed my late and generally perceptive friend, Sigfried Giedion, used to argue with me that it should all be turned over to another great and talented friend, the painter Gyorgy Kepes. But this would, of course, have been exactly wrong. The greatness of this magnificent nocturnal honky-tonk is precisely that it is unbridled. There are other ways of using neon, as the basin of the Charles River at Boston, also unplanned, so different from Broadway or Ginza, will attest. But more liveliness on the Charles and more order on Broadway or in Tokyo would simply downgrade both.

This produces the rather negative conclusion that, though there are some fine examples of beautiful cities with master plans that have been observed, there are more examples of beautiful cities in which no such order can be found. The problem is then how to achieve the fine effects of laissez-faire without the disadvantages, disorder, and excessive competition; or how to achieve the fine effects of master planning without the disadvantage of stodginess or pedantry. This is an impossible question, but to me it seems that a city is too big a piece of sculpture for any one man to carve, and I am still more apprehensive about sculpture by a committee. I am even more apprehensive about turning it over either to sober sociological data-processing city planners or to leprechaun advisers in or out of the White House.

The architect-designer must face one further humiliation. Some cities are most famous not as cities but because they possess individual buildings of great consequence. But there are also cities of great beauty which own no buildings of the absolutely highest quality or in which the few such buildings as do exist have no dominant influence on the whole aesthetic. Two examples will suffice.

Old San Francisco from the Presidio to the Oakland Bridge used to offer one of the finest visual impressions furnished by any city in the

[3] At one point Wright asserted that Aalto would have approved turning the whole thing over to him, F. L. W. But Alvar has told me in his dry way that this was never actually the case!

world, an impression which could not be diminished by the less elegant ensembles of the surrounding East Bay, Peninsula, or Marin County. The streets were "badly planned" and marched their gridiron in defiance of the contours. The buildings lacked individual distinction with hardly an exception. Here there was no Louvre, no St. Peter's, no Forum Romanum, no Parthenon, no Hagia Sofia, no Taj Mahal. Not even the Coit tower or the belfry of the Ferry offered much punctuation. Anonymous and individually undistinguished buildings pushed their white walls up the hills to make one of the most beautiful cityscapes in the world.

The Götaplatsen of Göteborg, a handsome square, centers around one of Milles' finest fountains. As the Kungsportsavenyn slopes gently away from it towards the harbor, it leaves a square of excellent consequence, nearer to the Piazza San Marco than anything to be found in Stockholm, the so-called "Venice of the North." Yet not one of the three buildings which frame the square, not the City Theater, or the Art Museum and gallery, or the Concert Hall, adorns the square with a really fine facade. The facades, indeed, embrace great absurdities; but the relation of their walls, the rise of their steps, the quality of the pavements, and perhaps above all the tubs of flowers rising bank on bank combine to support the Milles fountain whose play of water on the colossal and archaic Poseidon and his humorous entourage produces a remarkable overall effect. Would the effect be greater or less had the enveloping buildings been made by greater geniuses, had they more brilliance in their own individual rights? One should not be too quick to say. What can be said with confidence and with no denial of the great quality of 860 Lake Shore Drive in Chicago is that such a Miesian building would be utterly out of place on the Götaplatsen, or the Place de la Concorde.

A great urban aesthetic arises not from a cluster of architectural *chefs d'oeuvre* but from a sensitivity on the part of each successive builder to the amenities that are already there. No good architect would really dream of destroying the beautiful natural terrain of an isolated site but would, instead, try to marry his building to the land and the vegetation and the water and the sky. It is easier to forget and it is common to forget that there is also an urban terrain and that this, too, is entitled to respect, even to love. Urban aesthetics are not to be made over as lightly as ladies' clothes.

The qualification must naturally be remembered that when we speak of the beauty of a city we speak usually of only a small part. Beautiful San Francisco does not include what has happened on the eastern and southern ridges of the Bay or down in the erstwhile walnut groves and artichoke farms. This is no different from Los Angeles or Atlanta or Needham, Massachusetts, or, for that matter, Paris. When we speak of the charms of Göteborg we are not talking about the brutal array of multistoried tenements that accumulate on its periphery, tenements with perhaps less to recommend them than the Dudok-influenced apartments nearer town and of an earlier day which it is now the fashion to repudiate. Beautiful Philadelphia is not West Philadelphia, and beautiful Sydney is not the string of abominable villas which line the coast for twenty-five miles toward the Pittwater.

A troublesome question arises here. As believers in the possibility of better things we have to admire the occasional efforts to do something fine on the periphery whether it be at Baldwin Hills Village or at Vällingby outside of Stockholm or Tapiola in Finland, and we must hope that somehow these advantages will do more than "filter down" when they are a little worn-out or unfashionable. The city of the poor should not be a city of fourth-hand Rios, although favas are written in the slums and not on the Copacabana. But when we are content not to be doctrinaire, we must also concede that even the best of these, as of now, have failed to achieve something that was implicit in the old city and that is too fine to give up without a struggle. In terms of superior safety, health, convenience, democratic standards, indeed in terms of most social standards which are currently accepted, they represent a considerable step forward and not only in comparison to the slum. But something is still missing from this new suburban aesthetic: something of beauty, something of humor, something of informality, something of surprise, something, in short, of nature.

No city is really beautiful, nor can any peripheral development achieve beauty, if nature is too much ignored. The hills, the rivers, the lakes, the sea, cannot be installed by man. But trees, flowers, fountains, pleasant pavements can. So can wide avenues, pedestrian walks, vistas, stopping points, other punctuation marks. New projects like Vällingby or even shopping centers like Northlands in Detroit have done fairly well with those things that can be made of brick, or stone, or glass. They seem to have tried, but in a pallid way, to introduce sculpture and painting; but either they have not spent enough for their art or not enough contemporary artists are ready for the challenge as, for example, the fountain makers of Rome, Nuremberg, Stockholm, and Göteborg were, each in his different day (or Lawrence Halprin in ours). Probably it is a little of each. The flower beds are not abundant enough and luxuriant enough, and they do not receive enough care; the trees are too few and too small; the water runs through spouts that are ungenerous. Meanwhile the parks of the old center where the grass is deep and green, the trees opulent—these are now too far away from too many people, and sometimes even too dangerous. Of course, new projects may mature with age, and, of course, it does take a longer time to make a tree than it does to make a flat; but when trees are destroyed in the making of flats, the pressures of obsolescence may see to it that a Vällingby never does mature. The suspicion remains that the tree, the moss, the fern, the flower, the water, and the sculpture are not greatly admired or coveted by the artists of the new complexes as they have ceased to be admired by most contemporary sculptors who may not be really competent now to produce a fine fountain if given the chance,

The Urban Aesthetic and the Problem of Urban Joy   551

and perhaps not very interested in the chance either. (There are exceptions like Halprin's fountain in Portland, Oregon.) It is also important, I think, to say that these "complexes" to which I refer may either be out of date for all of us save those with memories or at least for some newly emerging groups. I would like to see what would happen, for example, if the blacks of Watts were free to spend money at the level of the Götaplatsen; and if they did not elect for some focal point in their genre but really preferred to spread the manna too thin, this would itself be revealing. And if, having made it in high spirits, they let it go to seed in low spirits, that too would be revealing. But who should have the temerity to predict either revelation?

In more concrete terms let me suggest five specific problems of the visual aesthetic of the modern city, the problem of preserving or producing the gateway, the problem of preserving or creating magnets, the problem of accommodating to new time scales, the problem of aesthetics around the clock, and the problem of developing individuality and character in the periphery.

As we think of old—or even new—fine cities, we will often think of them in terms of major approach or gateway: the spire of Chartres across the wheat fields of La Beauce, the towers of lower Manhattan as one steams up toward the Battery, the air approach to Chicago across the false front of the skyscrapers of Michigan Avenue. There are cities of hills and sea: San Francisco, Rio de Janeiro, Lisbon, Sydney, Wellington, Oslo. There are cities that rise from the ocean: Boston, New York, Copenhagen. There are cities of the big rivers or estuaries: London, St. Louis, Rome, Paris, St. Paul, Melbourne, Vienna. There are cities of the plains: Isfahan, Salisbury, Lincoln in England or Nebraska. All of these, except perhaps the cities of the plains, have a particular appearance that must be seen from a particular direction, and historically there has been one dominating approach which has established the image of such a city. This overriding and individual image is not unimportant for the aesthetics of a city. The ancient approaches to such an image were leisurely and from the level of the high road or the surface of the sea or river, or now and again from a neighboring hill. One had time to see the image grow and change, to watch its details emerge from the mass. One looked up at the spires, not down. Each skyline had a regional and an identifiable characteristic. Thus the gateway to the city was visually as well as strategically important. As cities grew, they developed other approaches: those of the railroads were somber, dingy, and desolate; those of the automobile roads strips of chaotic vulgarity; those of the airplane utterly unpredictable and dependent upon the wind direction or the flight patterns at the time of arrival. Yet through all this, great cities possessed and still possess a dominant visual approach whether it is that of the Battery, the Great North Road, the Bois de Boulogne, or the Golden Gate.

Very often the most glamorous approach became the way of the visitor, not that of the native. But for a long time the native had his own, if more bucolic, way. We can see vestiges of these still in Philadelphia,

Boston, New York, London, or Paris. Here there was a continuous change of scale and pace and texture from countryside through village, to parklike suburb, here reaching some main theme of the city such as a great river or lake, then parks, boulevards, and thus to the heart of town which truly was a heart, not a series of disconnected and independent blood vessels. To be sure, this experience with its morning crescendo and its evening diminuendo might soon come to be reserved for the few who lived in the parklike suburb or even in the country. To be sure, the experience was quite different for the many who might have to approach Paris via the Porte St-Denis, or London via the Isle of Dogs, or New York across the petroleum-perfume of Bayonne and the piggeries of Secaucus. But this did not alter the fact that other approaches had been possible and might have been available to all. It did not alter the even more relentless fact that urban "progress" instead of making the best available to all tended rather to take it away even from the few. There is hardly a city in the world to reach which is not only a frustration to all of its citizens, but a visual abomination as well for all those who have not forgotten how to see, or in which one is not unceremoniously dumped by an access road from a freeway. Worse than the freeway, the doughnut stand, the drive-in movie, and the used-car lot have outmoded the tree—hardly a tribute to the aesthetic contributions of "small business." At a higher level Le Corbusier's written sketches for the boscage of Chandrigarh seem more literary than arboreal.

The question of the approach ought to be a dominant one today, complicated though it is by the fact that the approach must now be made from so many directions and at so many different speeds. A cityscape can no longer be a bas-relief; it must be a sculpture in the round, elegant from all points of view, from above as well as from below. It must be compatible with many speeds of approach and viewing, say from three miles an hour to more than three hundred. This means that scales and details have to agree on two quite different sets of coordinates. By a strange inversion, the gateway may even be within the city at a rail terminal, for example, or the impression of arrival may begin at the airport. If the experience of the gateway is to be satisfactory, the problem of reconciliation is gigantic, and it may be a small wonder that the failures have been Herculean.

Once one had reached the older city he found internal and localized satisfactions, usually, though not always, on a more intimate, more human and personal scale. These were the parts of the city I call magnets. Some of them might be for purely utilitarian purposes: markets, exchanges, public buildings, even the rostrums of Hyde Park or Trafalgar Square. Others served specific pleasures: concert-hall or opera-house squares, circuses, or specific spiritual needs such as the parvis of the cathedral. Some were for general recreation: a zoo, a botanical garden, a pond in the Tuileries for the sailing of toy boats, the lakes of Stockholm for grown-up boats, the promenades for strollers. We all know how fortunate is the city which has many such magnets, how dismal the city with none. They may be monumental like the Place de la Concorde, or of normal scale like the Place Vendôme, or intimate like Gramercy Park, open like the Green Park, closed like Grosvenor Square before the Americans came. Best of all the city could provide a range of scales. Not all these magnets needed to be important.

At the corner of Fifty-Ninth Street and Fifth Avenue in New York there was a tiny such square, hard by the Plaza Hotel, a kind of pendant period to Central Park. Surrounded by undistinguished buildings, adorned with small trees and benches, this square, principally this cube of open air, enriched a region of several blocks. Had such spaces been multiplied every five or six blocks throughout Manhattan Island how immeasurably finer the city would have been! Instead the little square has been overwhelmed by General Motors. How different and more gracious would have been the life of Philadelphia had the original scheme been followed and had it been studded with many Rittenhouse Squares! The Danes have understood this.

Our older central cities have many such magnets to be sure. Rockefeller Center is one, and Grand Central Terminal has been one, and perhaps Lincoln Center will be one; the Place de l'Opéra used to be. But there are not enough magnets at the center and almost none on the periphery. As the periphery swells, the central magnets become more remote and less adequate; the peripheral shopping center and local movie theater are hardly an adequate replacement. The problem here is whether magnets can successfully be invented or must rise naturally. What activates a magnet? Why are some parks visited and loved and others left empty? Such questions cannot be answered simply by reference to the transportation network or perhaps even personal safety. We need to find out how much and how effectively such magnets can be decentralized before we can tell how successful it will be to restore the central city as one great magnet, even if this is but a collection of lesser magnets in a central place. It is quite possible that new metropoli will consist of magnet ganglia connected by a network of fast transport. Such a solution is available to Dallas but not to New York, where the central investment is so colossal.

It must be suggested that, whatever their purposes, both the big and little magnets need much development. We need to be cautious lest certain simple amenities such as those of variety and surprise are not wiped out in the city as the store chain wipes out the boutique. This problem is particularly pressing in America where we so sharply separate our places of abode from our places of work, an Americanism which is violated only by the Chinese, some Italians, and a few artists, and now hopefully but not probably the blacks if they have a choice.

But whatever screen may represent the whole city and however the screen may be divided into neighborhoods, the problem of the two time scales will again arise—the scale of the vehicular, which is large, remote, and fast, and the scale of the pedestrian, which is small, intimate, and slow.

The problem of the changing time scale has perhaps been emphasized enough in the foregoing. There needs only to be this warning for those who identify technological change with progress. The new never quite expunges the old. The Olympian view from the airplane will not supersede all other views, nor will the restricted and truncated urban panorama permitted by the onrushing automobile window. There will still be those who must walk in the street or even want to. All the new urban design must not be for those who no longer walk or for those who prefer motion to repose. The city will still need places for people to sit outdoors and near to the ground. All the new beauties should not be out of their ken.

It is unnecessary to say much either about the twenty-four-hour city. Urban aesthetics cannot, as in the Middle Ages, content itself with a dayscape that vanishes at dusk. Indeed the most beautiful cityscapes of today may be those from airplanes at night. Then the defects of form and substance are mercifully obscured and only the lights remain. The individual excesses of the neon tubes are also concealed by distance and rapid changes of position.

But this is not the only night view of cities which are used more and more at night or were until they became too dangerous. For the man in the street the potentials for beauty in the electric light rest almost unexploited. We have our brilliant accidents like the accident of Broadway. We have our stereotyped floodlighting which simply pretends that a building designed for the day is actually being seen by day at 1:00 A.M., but which does not manage the deception very well. We have a few hints of how buildings might be designed in conjunction with streets so that their day aspect when lighted from without gives way to a quite different but equally charming night aspect when lighted from within. Such night lightings might produce design subtleties quite beyond those possible by day. The potentials exist even in old buildings as the illuminations at the Château de Chambord would suggest, but much wider possibilities for enchantment are contained in the modern modes. Combinations of lights—colored as well as white—of moving waters, of spot-lighted plants, not building by building but in urban groupings, could make the city of night even more alluring than the city of day. These things can come to pass, though, only if designers permit themselves more fantasy than their sobrieties now allow.

These considerations of day and night, of the new time scales, of the preservation and the extension of magnets and gateways are all important, but are overshadowed by the formidable battle against the plasmodial and anonymously ugly growth of the urban periphery the world over. A Vällingby or a Reston is not a great solution but simply much better than the things around it. How far it falls short of what is possible in urban planning becomes clear when we compare it with the refinement and repose of some of the diminishing best parts of any of the good old central cities, American or European. The modern world has much to recommend it, and anyway it is the only world we have, but it need not pay the price of abandoning refinement and repose.

There are two main theories as to how one might do better by those who live in the periphery, which means most of us. One might make the old center such a marvelous magnet and the approaches so handsome and convenient that we would always flock there for our leisure and be content with dormitories for the rest of the time. That is the implication of the projects of a Robert Moses although they are not so expressly stated. This somehow seems inadequate, perhaps even impossible.

The other and probably better way, which might have been the way of Los Angeles and which could still be the way of Dallas, was the way of Venice if we are to believe Sansovino:

> There are also, praise the Lord, on the island of the Giudecca several buildings of importance of which two, at the moment, seem more important than the others. The one at the near point of the island is the palace of Andrea Dandolo . . . the other almost at the other end of the island, of the Vendramin family. These and many other buildings nearby of more or less importance form a vast and great city which will appear to the subtle not as one but as many separate cities all joined together. If her situation is considered without the bridges, one will see that she is divided into many large towns and cities surrounded by their canals, over which one passes from one to the other by way of bridges, which are generally built of stone but sometimes of wood, and which join her various parts together. The shops which are spread all over the city also make her appear many cities joined into one because every quarter has not only one but many churches, its own public square and wells, its bakeries, wineshops, its guild of tailors, greengrocers, pharmacists, school teachers, carpenters, shoemakers and finally in great abundance all else required for human needs, to the extent that leaving one quarter and entering another one would say without doubt one was leaving one city and entering another—to the great convenience and satisfaction of the inhabitants and to the great surprise of strangers.[4]

This is the way sanity lies. The greatest lesson some European cities today could teach American city planners and architects—and traveling citizens—is that every pleasure does not lie at the other end of a ride in an automobile. The misfortune is that the lesson seems to be going the other way.

That the metropolis is necessary if only to support the great magnets like the symphony orchestra, the topflight opera, the diversity of tastes is evident. But that the periphery must supply the other magnets seems equally evident. It will not do to say that a varied personality on the periphery is impossible because the general taste craves uniformity, or because integration fosters it. History does not suggest that it was ever very different, and it is the task of the planner and the city designer not so

---

[4] Extract from "Venice, a Very Noble City" described by Mr. Francesco Sansovino, 1581. Translated by Giovanna Lawford and cited in Francis Henry Taylor, *The Taste of Angels* (Boston: Atlantic, Little, Brown, 1948), appendix C, p. 617.

much to dictate public taste as to seek incessantly to find the best of this taste and to encourage it to thrive in very diverse ways. The public taste is probably not so bad as hucksters make it appear to be, nor so uniform.

The new urban beauties will not be achieved by sociology; or by data processing; or by bureaucratic committees who are better at finding reasons to say "no" than courage to say "yes." The common quality of the new designers should be a respect, even an affection, for the past, an understanding of the present, and an optimistic solicitude for the future. The new beauties will not be created by copouts, whatever their avenue of escape.

The wise young men of our time will not be those who slavishly follow one great master, whether Mies, Wright, Le Corbusier, Aalto, or Kahn, Soleri, and Buckminster Fuller. If you think I have paid too little attention to Fuller's metropolis enclosed by a geodesic dome, it is because in my opinion it solves nothing and is strictly for birds rather than humans. And I have no confidence that the birds if polled would vote it a great aviary. The wise young men will be those who can see that these great men have in no case found a classic answer to our problems but have made enough suggestions upon which to build a great future, and that their ideas, moreover, are not altogether mutually exclusive. But equally essential will be a sensitive concern not only about one's own buildings but also about the buildings of the past, and so far as possible the buildings of the future, buildings of others. We shall need a new band of sculptors more interested in delight than in their own despairs, in the human condition more than their personal condition, more interested in materials other than metal, more interested in life processes as well as intellectual ones. We shall need designers who are not pessimists, who respect curves as well as straight lines, who can still see and admire and partly understand a sunset, the waving of a reed in a lake, the budding of a flower, the music of falling water, the sawing of the cicadas in the hot dusk at the close of a sultry day.

And we shall need imaginative clients.[5]

I have obviously been talking about the "beautiful" city in loose and essentially hedonistic terms.

There is nothing disgraceful or sinful about hedonism save for those who believe that man was created to mourn. The only difficulty is that we have to ask, whose hedonism? It cannot be the hedonism of the experts alone because they cannot always agree even about individual buildings. Elite consensus will be a little less capricious than one might imagine; nonetheless, it is not authoritative enough in a democracy to permit us to dismiss everything it rejects. General consensus is almost certainly even

---

[5] Here follow loose excerpts from another and more recent paper of mine. It is cited from "Design and Urban Beauty in the Central City," and was originally published in *The Metropolitan Enigma*, James Q. Wilson (ed.) (Cambridge, Mass.: Harvard University Press, 1968; Garden City, N.Y.: Doubleday Anchor, 1970).

less reliable. There must be a vast number of Americans who feel no active reaction of discomfort or displeasure as they use one of our strips of gas stations; fourth-rate supermarkets; used-car lots; hot dog, shrimp, and doughnut stands; inferior motels and other ugly examples of the degree to which frail and inexpert but quite uninhibited retail business can degrade the vision of the city. Is there not something symbolic about free fried chicken for all at a national political convention? If there were any active dislike amounting to a consensus, obviously these things could not endure. Does that mean they *should* endure?

Moments of great urban beauty have often, indeed usually, been achieved by dictatorial decisions. These produced the square of St. Peter's in Rome[6]; the Place de la Concorde and the Rue de Rivoli in Paris[7]; the Place Stanislas in Nancy[8]; and innumerable others. These were situations in which an autocrat with taste found an architect of genius to match his desires, and a great collaboration of client and artist ensued.

There would be little of beautiful Paris, perhaps nothing left, if we were to remove the works owed to Philippe Auguste, Maurice de Sully, Abbot Suger, Saint Louis, Charles V, Catherine and Marie de Medici, Louis XIII, Cardinal Richelieu, Madame de Pompadour, Louis XIV, Louis XV, Napoleon Bonaparte, Napoleon III, and Baron Haussmann—fifteen people none of whom were free from some taints of the autocratic. It is a vast understatement to remark that the democratic substitute for them is not easy to find.

It would be dangerous to trust the decisions of even thoroughly respectable groups whose primary missions and skills lie elsewhere, whether they be the PTA or NAACP, the DAR or the American Legion, the NAM or the CIO, the CIA or the FBI or the SDS, though doubtless none will fail to be vociferous. The justices of the United States Supreme Court might be no wiser (or the now popular "people" of the neighborhood). Even the consensus of the most relevant professional societies would almost by their nature be too conservative. Up until recently, the record of the AIA has been ultraconservative: and that of the AMA both as conservative and tasteless as the United States Corps of Engineers. Least of all can aesthetic decisions be trusted to the United States Congress,[9] or to an elected official, even a President. It is a puzzlement.

In the meantime a philosophy of hedonism drives us inexorably to the conclusion that a beautiful city, in a democracy at any rate, must have a

---

[6] Particularly under Pope Alexander VII and the Baroque genius Giovanni Lorenzo Bernini (1598–1680).

[7] Commissioned by Louis XV and executed by Jacques Ange Gabriel in 1755.

[8] Commissioned by Stanislaw Leszczynski, Duc de Lorraine, and laid out by Héré de Corny in 1753.

[9] This statement hardly needs documentation, especially so far as Congress is concerned. Witness, for example, the absurd hearings concerning the Air Force Academy and especially its chapel. Reflect on how the winners of the Smithsonian and the

variety of beauties appealing to a variety of tastes. It should not eschew monumentality because some liberals fear its symbolism. It should not tear down its Broadways or North Wells Street in Chicago because some thin-nosed people find them vulgar. It needs beauties of large size and beauties of small size, noisy beauties and quiet beauties, refined beauties and vulgar beauties. Jane Jacobs likes Madison Avenue because she finds action and "life" in the shop windows there and she thinks Park Avenue is "dead." That does not mean that Park Avenue should be at once converted into Madison Avenue. There are other equally tasteful people in New York, even in Greenwich Village, with quite different views.[10] Great cities have in fact offered great contrasts of beauty from the monumental to the intimate, from the classic to the romantic, from the urban to the bucolic, although the essence of any given city may be slanted one way or another. Paris, probably still the most beautiful of all, has great variety. It is fortunate that this diversity of components is an advantage; without it, it might be hard to accomplish anything. For components can be designed and can be preserved or changed, and so improvement is possible. Also, fine components can and need to be beautifully articulated with one another. This is a second element of urban design for beauty which is within the bounds of feasibility. To go beyond this, to seek a master plan for the total urban aesthetic, is to soar too near the sun.

The plain fact is that beauty and economy are not synonymous and that no urban beauty comes free.

It costs money to refrain from desecrating a coast or a river bank or a hillside, and a developer's private interests may too often appear to be consonant with the public interest in increasing tax revenues. It costs less, in the beginning anyway, to dump garbage in a harbor or on a piece of idle land than to dispose of its efficiently and cleanly. A town may lose some immediate advantage if it does not make some land out of an adjacent lake or harbor. A sand dunes park may seem an ideal location for a new and needed steel mill, and other locations may be more costly; but the dunes may be irreplaceable. More people, measured in numbers, will benefit from electricity supplied by new Grand Canyon dams than will be deprived of the erstwhile beauties of the undrowned or undried up river bottom. It costs more to plant a tree than not to plant it, to tend it than not to tend it, to cause flowers to grow in a bank or post office. At the

<hr />

Franklin D. Roosevelt Memorial competitions were swept under the rug. Observe how the Congress, under the lash of such connoisseurs as the late Sam Rayburn and his successors, supported a nonarchitect, the late George Stewart (who nonetheless was called Architect of the Capitol) in his expensive desecrations of a dignified and important piece of American architectural history.

[10] Jane Jacobs, *Death and Life of Great American Cities* (New York, Random House, 1961). This entertaining expression of a point of view had a more than transitory acclaim.

other extreme, magnificent buildings cost a great deal more than merely workable ones. Each and every one of these additional costs can be calculated and demonstrated by any half-way competent accountant. The liability column is easily verified. Unhappily the same thing cannot be said of the asset column. What is the monetary value of an urban tree; of the wading pool in the Tuileries Gardens of Paris; of the Mall in London; of an unspoiled Golden Gate? Disneyland may perhaps be measured in strictly box-office terms, but even when a charge is made, can this be said of the delightful San Diego Zoo, or the Children's Fairyland and Madison Square playgrounds in Oakland?[11] Various assertions can be made. It can be said that beautiful cities will pay for themselves because they will attract tourists. This was a common rallying cry in New York in the late nineteenth century. Beautiful cities *have* attracted tourists and that can be verified. But so have enough convention halls, large-capacity hotels, and bars, as witness Miami. The gross income the outsiders bring to a city can also be calculated. But where does the fiscal profit finally come to rest? Is the city better for its inhabitants when it is always full of conventioneers and tourists? The suspicion is that it is not. Even the economic case is not well established.

There are more elaborate defenses for building the beautiful city. For example, it is sometimes argued that intellectuals, and especially "productive" intellectuals like scientists and engineers, definitely add to the wealth of the community where they live. If it is also true that they will elect to congregate only in communities where cultural advantages and urban amenities abound, then should the city not invest in the production of these magnets? But is it true? And, if true, what are the economic details?

The fact is, of course, that convincing ones do not exist. Perhaps they could be arrived at, perhaps not. It is hard to believe that a lot would not have still to be left to faith. But it might be desirable nonetheless to have studies of this subject, though they will doubtless be historical and hence not completely convincing. Until they exist, it would be as well for the believers in urban beauty who feel impelled to defend it to seek other currencies. A common one is the soft currency of social benefit.

But even this soft currency may be hard to trust. It seems superficially reasonable to guess that, if one had to be poor, it might be more tolerable to be poor in Paris than in Lille, in London than in Sheffield, in Charleston than in Birmingham. But is this really so? We do not know. *We* can perhaps say that if *we* were poor we think we might have such preferences. But we are not poor. Moreover, we can judge only our own city from the point of view of a resident. What the city looks like to the tourist is quite a different matter. There may be compensations of other sorts in Glasgow

[11] The zoo is well supported, as it should be, by entrance fees for adults and by annual popular subscriptions. The free playgrounds in Oakland were both developed by the Park Department but with large contributions and impetus from private organizations such as the Lake Merritt Breakfast Club or The Lions' Club.

or Birmingham that do not spring up to pleasure the eye of the tourist who is always more avid in his quest for urban beauty when abroad than when at home. This is not to say that modern social scientists might not be able to find out some things about this question—to determine what kinds of measurable social benefits arise from urban beauty, and how much, if at all, they compensate for the failure to enjoy other social benefits.

But we do not have such studies today. We do not know how much edge would be taken off Watts if Copenhagen's Tivoli Gardens[12] or London's Green Park was near at hand. My suspicion is, not much. Indeed, beautiful cities of the past have been among the more turbulent, not among the more somnolent. Perhaps that is one of the reasons they became beautiful.

All one can say on present evidence is that urban beauty is probably worth something in a financial way and something in a social way and that it needs a less rigid definition in America to include nonarchitectural, nonhistorical, nonwhite notions of beauty.

Whether it is worth what it will cost is not possible to prove. In the end, and waiting much more study, cities will be beautiful if citizens, logically or illogically, want them beautiful and are willing to pay for it themselves. Handing the bill over to the federal government is no long-range answer. It is popular now because the remote federal government can collect taxes locally that local politicians would not dare to try to collect and because its credit is or seems more secure. But in the long run the federal government cannot collect more for urban development than cities can themselves provide. At most it can redistribute it. One of the weaknesses of this is that cities with no aspiration or taste for beauty will, willy-nilly, indulge in minor beautification at the expense of the great cities.

---

[12] Tivoli Gardens were started more than a century ago under a five-year concession from the King of Denmark to George Carstensen to build and operate a forty-acre pleasure garden just outside the city gates. Today these famous gardens, enveloped by the city, offer pleasure for young and old, cultural and popular amusements, food at the level of sausage and a dill pickle or a souffle or a *caneton rouennaise*, trees, paths, flowers, marching bands, fireworks in an array unequaled anywhere else in the world and perhaps not transferable. Admission is charged, ground rent is paid to the city, and the stockholders have for years received a dividend of 10 percent. Tivoli seems to be admired equally by Danes and foreigners. Efforts at something comparable but more firmly based in folk art in Stockholm and Oslo have fallen far short. The nearest approximation in the United States is perhaps the complex of buildings and activities in Balboa Park, San Diego, although, despite the Zoo, these are weighted heavily on the cultural and international side; or the more specialized Disneyland and the various Marinelands. One essence of Tivoli is that it is "downtown" and does not demand an expedition, so the visitor can go with or without children and for a "little" day as well as a "big" one. Not many American cities could offer comparable sites, although the Boston Common, part of Central Park, or lower Grant Park in Chicago might do. But Americans cannot be made into Danes quite so easily and the very Americans who patronize Tivoli every day they are in Copenhagen might never patronize a local Tivoli if they had one. Still it might be worth trying in some newly developing city if the design and management could be held to the standards of Tivoli.

Who in Monterey, California, would vote against a freeway tunnel at someone else's expense? Would a majority in Monterey vote for it if the money could be used for something else in Monterey? This is not an argument against the tunnel but merely a statement that the citizens of Monterey have been deprived of a free choice in the use of what was probably, at bottom, their own money. There will be no more national gain for urban beauty in such procedures than in any other kind of egalitarianism. Until a substantial amount of the revenues are fed back without strings to the cities which determine how much goes to relief, and how much to education, and how much to housing, and how much to roads, and how little for beauty, with rules for each of these, the particular aspirations of a city to be beautiful or distinguished in some quite different way will inevitably be subdued and the whole result cast in the image of what seems decent and desirable in Washington. There may even have to be subdivision within the metropole. There seems no real doubt that a large part of the federal budget earmarked for urban improvement of all sorts should go back to the cities to be foolish about in their own way. Then there may be some beautiful cities. Otherwise there may be none.[13] In the view of the General Accounting Office all the great and beautiful cities of history have been "foolish." Let then some of our cities be beautiful if they choose and let those who will, be wise.

Even so, the city would, of course, have very difficult decisions to make as to what to spend for beauty, out of a finite pot, when so many other things need to be done.

> The major problem facing the big cities of the world for the rest of this century is the improvement of the quality and meaning of life for the general population and especially for previously deprived sectors at the bottom of the social ladder, or off the ladder altogether.[14]

These are recent words of the San Francisco poet-journalist, Kenneth Rexroth. He was aiming his shafts first at the culture of the "establishment," which he says, rightly, does not touch enough people to matter much, and then at the bureaucratic, cautious, even censorious actions of most of those who run urban recreational facilities such as parks. The latter, says Rexroth, again with some truth, fear to let the parks be used for spontaneous neighborhood affairs.

> We need, as a first step, to open up to the widest, most varied, most intensive use the public facilities we now have which can enable us to

---

[13] How to distribute the funds fairly would not be easy to work out—but the notion is so logical and has been so often advanced that it needs careful attention by the bureaus in Washington, where its popularity is predictably doubtful, and by the Congress, who might understand the reasoning better.
[14] Kenneth Rexroth, "Arts for the Street Corner," *San Francisco Sunday Examiner and Chronicle*, July 3, 1966, section 1, p. 16.

stimulate and foster cultural activities at the grass roots, or rather, pavement and street corner level. . . . Both as to membership, personnel and function, all our city commissions dealing with cultural questions are obsolete.
The committee members are all living in a bygone age and the only power they have is to make mischief, to halt and hamper creative action.[15]

The target of this statement might have been a much larger one. It might have included urban beauty in the physical sense as well as the beauty of urban life in the quite different sense of pavement play. Both are presumably parts of urban joy.

To discuss them implies the assumption that a joyless city may be meaningless to its ordinary citizens, however well it serves as a fort, a warehouse, a production center, a place of pilgrimage, or a seat of government. Joy, of course, is not always a sufficient antidote to pain. There are surely some other urban problems that can establish some sort of priority over the problem of urban joy. A throbbing tooth may make it impossible to listen to a great performance of great music. If pain is incessant—the pain of poverty, of rejection, of starvation, of hopelessness, of fear, even the pain of hate—there may be no energy left to seek or relish urban joy. It may even come about that the only positive joy is that of defying the city, of desecrating its most cherished monuments, of destroying its most delectable beauties. I must then take it for granted that the urban problems of health, welfare, education, opportunity, public safety, and so on have to be at least partially solved before it can be reasonable to think about urban joy at all in any terms, much less the terms of urban beauty.

But there is a risk here. What do we mean by partially? Despite campaign oratory, the deep social problems will never really be solved for *everybody*. They do need to be solved for many more people than they now are; and they can be. But the solution will cost much more money and much more imaginative and experimental efforts than are being spent now and will take a much longer time than Americans like to allow for the solution of any problem. It will be tempting, therefore, to try to put all the money and all the imagination and all the effort into working on situations where the disease is self-evident and attracts more personal human sympathy than can be attracted to urban beauty. This in turn can lead to postponing any effort toward urban beauty to some later, better time. One might even feel quite moral about "putting first things first." This is a dangerous temptation.

The lesser danger is that we may be satisfied with trying for urban beauty on the cheap, in planting a few forlorn trees or indulging in praiseworthy but not very far-reaching neighborhood litter collection, to the obligato of an occasional speech from on high, usually by a President's wife. The greater danger is that the whole idea of urban beauty will be

[15] Ibid.

postponed to another day when the intervening corrosion and decay will be too much even for people as affluent as we to remedy.

The idea of postponing beauty has long had an appeal for Americans. John Adams in his frequent letters from France bewailed the fact that American culture would have to wait a few generations while other things were done. Shortly before he died a few years ago, a leading American board chairman asserted in full confidence that if Americans had wasted their money on fountains the way the foolish Romans had, there would not have been enough resource and power left in America to permit us to "save the world." More recently, in the presidency of Lyndon Johnson, Walt Rostow noted, after the usual perfunctory curtsey to urban beauty, that we might have to postpone any efforts in that direction for a long time in view of the necessities in Asia about the destruction of which he had no doubt.

Thus in the name of public health, of education, of welfare, of safety, of civil liberties, of balanced budgets, and all the way up to national security, it is easy for the practically minded to find excuses for deferring "extravagant" expenditures on urban beauty. Take no more land for parks, do not refurbish the opera house, build the cheapest possible freeway, commission no artists become watchwords so long as a single citizen lacks a hot meal or a hospital bed. This, of course, means forever. In such a view no urban beauty is as valuable as a rendezvous in space or a hollow military "victory" "with honor" in Asia. Whom the gods would destroy they first make mad.

Even if reform were to attain all its objectives, if there were no wars and no surveillance of citizens, if everyone were well fed, decently housed, healthy, gainfully employed, decently dressed according to his taste, sufficiently educated to use abundant leisure, and even if in the city there were no dark corner in which it was unsafe to be alone, and even if a few of the citizens were daily commuting to Mars or for that matter Pluto— the city might still be an unhappy city. For happiness is positive; it is something more than the state of not being unhappy. That is why one is tempted to paraphrase Vergil, *Quidquid id est, timeo censores et dona ferentes.* "However it may be, I fear the reformers when they come bearing gifts." The gifts are likely not to be generous enough and almost certain not to be amusing enough; they will not be designed for urban joy but only for the alleviation of urban pain.

I rest firmly in the premise that the pursuit of urban beauty cannot wisely be postponed; that it has pragmatic if unmeasurable value; and that major efforts should be made to foster it, enhance it, and achieve it at the same time that other, more humanely attractive and demonstrably useful projects are being vigorously executed.

There are risks in the notion of diversity in the city. Whose diversity? It must be everyone's. The old ladies of Rittenhouse Square must have the right to sleep their days away without being pestered by rock and roll just as the rock and rollers must have places to shatter their own eardrums but not everybody else's. No group must take over and reduce or elevate the whole urban scene to their standard. Probably it should be permissible to feed a pigeon somewhere, but please, not everywhere. All this is easier to say than to achieve, and it will not even be acceptable to those who insist on the right to do their own thing wherever they feel like it. There is an application of Gresham's law to urban beauty and urban joy.

We must also stretch urban boundaries beyond the central city. The periphery enhances the central city and vice versa, or at least it should be so. The problem is not the crass one of making the central city beautiful so that it can survive the hegira or turn the tide a different way. That may or may not transpire. The problem is for the whole metropolitan area to be beautiful. In this the central city can hardly fail to play a principal role— in communities where there really is one—because such centers have now so much of the greatest urban beauties. And if a modern city does not have a center, it will still have more or less to create one (or perhaps several). All this implies the assumption that the interdependence of the core and periphery must be more firmly established politically and economically than it now is.

It is something more than a metaphor to say that the professors in Berkeley ought to pay something to the city of San Francisco to help preserve the view which they hold in such esteem at the cocktail hour; or that the people of Marin County should pay to the same city to support the privilege of working in skyscrapers which they decline to permit to rise on their own terrain, thus getting the best of both possible worlds practically for nothing more than the discomforts of commuting—or so it seems. The assumption of necessity for some metropolitan governmental entities and some greater coordination I take for granted so far as urban beauties are concerned.[16]

The elements of urban beauty include the total cityscape, the approaches from which the resident may see it, a variety of middle-sized urban details such as great avenues, squares, and other open spaces, water and water fronts, gardens and parks, smaller backwaters, and finally an abundance of little details sometimes called street furniture. Evidently these are subject to an increasing amount of design as they become smaller, but that is no reason to despair of the big ones or to leave them to chance.

[16] The idea of super-metropolitan governments with large overriding powers is by no means universally accepted by scholars, let alone by politicians and suburbanites. See, for example, Martin Meyerson and Edward C. Banfield's position on this for Metropolitan Boston. "There is much to be said for letting people decide locally how much of each service they wish to pay for and consume.... Politics would not go out the window just because metropolitan government came in." [*Boston: The Job Ahead* (Cambridge, Mass.: Harvard University Press, 1966), p. 21.] But they concede certain metropolitan functions which do call for central management, such as real estate taxes, water supply and waste disposal, air pollution control, major outdoor recreational areas, and transportation. All of these bear on urban beauty.

It is possible in architecture for a great overall design to be ruined by unhappy details,[17] but it is impossible for even magnificent details to save a fundamentally bad design. This is also true for a city.

Architecture is only one of the details of a city; an important one but not the only one as I have remarked. The most totally beautiful cities undoubtedly will contain some great architecture. But it is theoretically possible to have too much. Restraint is as helpful to the beauty of a city as it is to that of a Christmas tree. That is why Architecture with a big *A* is stressed here mainly in the discussion of landmarks and the design of major spaces. Good architecture with a small *a* should pervade a beautiful city; and the small *a* will often, though not always, imply modesty, even neutrality. Look at Copenhagen some time, or think of how the Athenians spoke of their city and "its bright pellucid air."

It is, of course, still not quite enough. New York fails most as a beautiful city not because it lacks much fine architecture and art, in which it is in fact rich, not because of the hovels of many of its lesser streets, not because of its dirt and crime, but because too many New Yorkers act as though they hate each other. It is the urban joy and not the urban aesthetic that is missing, and this cannot be glossed over just by calling it "fun city." The solution of such an urban problem may outreach the capacities of a thousand Berninis. How or even whether it does is the query of our final chapter.

[17] This was unhappily the situation in Penn Center, Philadelphia. See Martin Meyerson, et al., *Face of the Metropolis* (New York: Random House, 1963), pp. 61–65.

CHAPTER FOURTEEN

BERNINI IS DEAD?

The architect has never accomplished his great works single-handed or as a master slave driver bending every helper to his will. Historically important architecture has required the collaboration of artisans, of engineers, and of artists, usually in the fullest sense.

The present organization of the building industry has made the relation of the architect to the master craftsman more remote and often nonexistent. The days when the architect was himself a master mason who therefore knew quite exactly and at first hand what a good fellow mason could reasonably be expected to do are long gone. The more recent days when the architect, no longer a building craftsman himself, still knew a number of such craftsmen whom he could assemble to collaborate with him on a job, he understanding them and they him, have practically disappeared. Vestiges of this process are seen at times when some architect and some general contractor have achieved a harmonious working relation. But the general practice of competitive bidding (mandatory in most American governmental work), with the necessary corollary of large quantities of working drawings and voluminous specifications; the rise of jurisdictional trade unionism and more recently antidiscrimination provisions, good in themselves and long overdue, but misused to produce incompetent craft, the antithesis of the relation between Borromini and his artisans; and the increased amount of prefabrication all off the site have taken most of the close

Pl. 385

personal relations out of this aspect of architectural practice to the loss, I happen to think, both of the most sensitive architecture and of some life values for both the architect and the builder. Henry Hobson Richardson used to say that many of the best results could be worked out only on the site, and it was a practice much employed by Frank Lloyd Wright, still to a limited degree by Alvar Aalto, and often in small domestic work where the old relations can still exist, although economics is firmly saying no to much small personal domestic work directed at first hand by personal architects. It is too bad, but it is hard to see a road back, and the problem is no doubt how to make the new system work better and more sensitively than it often now does without resigning ourselves to the conclusions of Bruno Taut, who proclaimed, forty years ago, in a stentorian and absurd Communist voice:

> Leadership has been transferred to other hands. To the hands of those who erect buildings, produce building materials, manufacturing them from raw materials, extracting them from pit or mine, and working them up in factories; to the hands of those responsible for installation and transport, to those who can, in short produce everything that everybody needs.[1]

The relation of the architect and the engineer is also slowly changing. No longer are they combined in one person. We have had in our day a few great engineers of building like Robert Maillart, Eduardo Torroja Miret, Pier Luigi Nervi, and Felix Candela. Their best work in my opinion has been without the collaboration of architects, though about this most architects, including the late Walter Gropius, would say the opposite. But they have shown now and again, especially Nervi working sympathetically with an architect like Marcel Breuer, that genuine collaboration is possible among peers. And there have been a few engineers like Fred N. Severud and Paul Weidlinger who have demonstrated their ability to comprehend what the architect sought and to help him to achieve his will. More often there has been a sort of contest which yielded bad results if either party froze too early in his opinions as to how something should be done. The problem of the relation between architect and engineer has become more complicated of late because it is no longer merely a matter of structure. Modern heating and ventilating systems, electrical systems, elevator and escalator systems often have more to say about what can be done in some of our most important building types than the structure itself. So the question of who controls what has become more subtle.

I do not want to say much about the quarrels between architect and engineer, the one thinking the other dull and tasteless, the other thinking the one flighty even to the point of being cavalier. Each has a role to play, and if he is to play it well must believe it to be the central role. Neither is

[1] Bruno Taut, *Modern Architecture* (London: Studio, 1929), pp. 140 ff., cited in J. E. Burchard and Bush-Brown, *The Architecture of America* (Boston: Little, Brown, 1961), p. 362. This was, in fact, more true in the Middle Ages than in the twentieth century.

a villain. The engineer is supposed to contrive things that will stand up firmly, be economically achieved, and will be finished on time. The architect cares about the same things but he is also trying, and most importantly, for something with a touch of Xanadu about it, and for this if he can manage it he will incur increased costs and delays in time. The results of this natural and legitimate difference in goals can be unfortunate if either gets out of hand. I think it not overoptimistic to believe that both parties are slowly learning to live and work with each other more constructively. In pragmatic America if the thing comes down to a public contest, the engineer will usually win, and this does not guarantee the best results or even promise them.

It is almost the opposite in respect to the other arts and architecture. You can rummage through the architectural past right down to the Georgian and dig out very few examples in which there has not been a manifest harmony of purpose between the architect, the sculptor, and the painter. Now and again we have seen a building in which there has been too much or too little art, the one overwhelming the architecture, the other leaving it impoverished. At times, as in the days of classic Greece, or medieval Europe, the artists have been greater than in other times, such as Imperial Rome or Baroque Germany. But the generalization is still good.

Today the situation is more cloudy. Artists have become far more personal, not quite capable of submerging themselves in an architectural and cultural ideal as they did, for example, in the north porch of Chartres. Not all architects really want collaborating art, and of these Mies van der Rohe was probably the leader when he said that it was hard enough to design a good building, let alone to embellish it satisfactorily with art. Some architects today will include a little art in their buildings, using it, however, as a sort of punctuation or underlining, but the budget for this is a separate item and is one of the first to vanish in a moment of financial stress, and the younger generations of architects are less interested.

There is a serious problem of what the art should be about in contrast to the highly religious or highly imperial, almost propagandistic, art of the "great days." What is the propaganda now to be about? What will be its credibility? How soon will it be quite out of date? How would you go about advising an artist to express the spirit of a cigarette company whose name adorns a building in Manhattan which is really owned by someone whose profession is speculation in real estate? Whose spirit is to be expressed? Would any of the parties be pleased if the expression took the form it would be likely to at the hands of a conscientious artist? God was presumably a longer tenant than Pan American Airways.

The consequence of all this is that we can find very few present-day buildings in which the art is integrally and inseparably a part of the architecture; and not very many more where the building and the sculpture or the painting genuinely enhance each other. I am not sure that it matters as much as my intuition tells me it does.

Bernini Is Dead? 569

The nineteenth-century eclectics made valiant efforts to emulate their predecessors in the skillful use of mural or even ceiling painting. McKim adorned the stairwell of his Boston Public Library of 1895 with murals by Puvis de Chavannes and what was then the card catalog room with scenes of the Quest of the Holy Grail by Edwin Austin Abbey. But most of such later efforts were unconvincing. There were no more Giottos, Mantegnas, Tiepolos, Michelangelos, Caravaggios, Benozzo Gozzolis, or Corregios. There were no great mosaicists at all. The subjects the muralists chose no longer seemed relevant.

Architectonic sculpture had long gone by the board. Efforts to revive it, whether at the Scheepvaarthuis in Holland or by Goodhue and Lee Lawrie in the State Capitol in Lincoln, Nebraska, were also unconvincing and little-emulated.

In Mexico there was a group of powerful revolutionary muralists, Rivera, Siqueiros, and Orozco, and they had some brief and startling successes in Mexican buildings on the outside as well as the inside. But when some of the artists were invited to the United States to provide murals for Dartmouth College or Rockefeller Center, they honorably declined to leave their anticapitalist convictions behind and, however skillful as paintings, the messages were inappropriate to the buildings they adorned. Even in Mexico where the themes were acceptable, the peak was reached on the facade of O'Gorman's University Library, and the movement soon died away.

Among the leaders of the Western architectural revolution there was more ambivalence toward the collaborating arts. Mies van der Rohe, as already noted, had the same aversion to the collateral arts as Frank Lloyd Wright had earlier had, thinking that architecture was enough. Le Corbusier believed that art was an important element of architecture but chose to be his own artist, designing bas-reliefs and inscriptions for exterior walls, using his own calligraphy, for example, for the murals and the glass of Ronchamp, and most particularly creating a sort of enormous nonobjective mural by the use of different colors in the recesses of the honeycombed terraces of some of his Unités d'Habitation. Only Gropius and the colleagues or products of his Bauhaus thoroughly believed in the collaboration of all arts in the making of a building. Gropius tried, not too successfully, to achieve this in the Harvard Graduate School, and Breuer, sometimes successfully, as often not, at Unesco House in Paris. Perhaps the most successful of these efforts was by Villanueva at the University in Caracas.

But the tide was against even these partial successes. The Légers, the Mirós, the Arps, who knew how to deal with a wall and cared to do so, were few and gradually they aged or died. The new architecture offered less wall for murals; and even when there was a large wall, the architects usually preferred to keep it plain or to design their own abstractions as Osterlen did successfully and Gutbrod less successfully, both in Germany.

The painters themselves, though they were seeking larger and larger spaces on which to say less and less, were not very interested in mural collaboration, and it was probably a good thing that they were not encouraged to embed their works thus securely for posterity to be confused about.

The next generation after Gropius, much influenced by his attitudes, whether or not they had studied with him, made modest tries to continue the marriage of art and architecture, but since their forms and spaces no longer were very favorable to murals and mosaics, the collaboration tended to be with sculptors of such different approaches as Moore, Calder, Epstein, Lipschitz, Bertoia, and Gabo. But these were free-standing pieces, rarely in scale with the enormous buildings they sought to improve. In the extreme case of the Picassos installed in Chicago, the relevance to the architecture was by no means clear—and in very few, if any, cases could these works be said to bear the positive relation to the buildings which was common to the metopes and frieze of the Parthenon, the statues of the Colosseum, the tympani and capitals of the Romanesque, the porches and windows of the Gothic, the walls and ceilings of the Renaissance, the Baroque baldachino and chair of St. Peter's in the great Roman basilica. Somehow the silver cord had snapped.

It remained for the youngest generation of contemporary architects to discard it altogether. The most blatant of these views has just been expressed by one of the cleverest, most persuasive, and most arrogant of the latest crop, Moshe Safdie, architect of Habitat '67 at the Montreal Expo and of subsequent later versions of it elsewhere.

> There is a pretentiousness in our culture. We ignore or degrade the things that should give art to our life [I assume he means manufactured things], and create a sub-culture of so-called art that is *irrelevant*. If we put our energies into thinking about the things that we really use in our lives we would be producing what we admire so much in other cultures.[2]

It is a curious interpretation of history. The Greeks, the men of the Middle Ages, the Japanese did have beautiful utensils, but that did not cause them to value "useless" art the less or to dismiss it from their buildings, although the greatest Japanese architecture was indeed unadorned save by craftsmen.

Safdie goes on:

> When I was doing Habitat I was bombarded by painters and sculptors who wanted the opportunity to do a mural here, a sculpture there. At first I just avoided them without really knowing why. And then I realized that most often when so-called fine art was put in architecture, it was like make up, compensating for the inability of the architecture to respond to life in such a way that it satisfied our emotions.[3]

[2] Moshe Safdie, *Beyond Habitat* (Cambridge, Mass., M.I.T. Press, 1970), p. 141.
[3] Ibid., p. 167.

This is so manifestly untrue historically as to be beyond argument. It may or may not be so today, but one should not be put off from wondering just because Safdie is still growing up, takes the satisfaction of his emotions to be the satisfaction of everyone's emotions, and falls back on "meaningful" statements like "responding to life" which really belong, so loose are they, in the glossary of current adolescent jargon.

> A total and comprehensive design will result in a place that does not have to be saved by art. Conversely, objects and places conceived in an integrated and unarbitrary way have the makings of what we sometimes call art. . . . Habitat is environment, not sculpture.[4]

Surely the architecture of the Baroque was a total and comprehensive design. The art *was* integrated, was part of the totality and the comprehensiveness, a contributor to but not the savior of the architecture.

> What saddens me is that I feel I am living in a society that has diverted much of its creative energies to the world of visual art at the expense of the art of life.[5]

Well, in other times visual art was part of the art of life. Whether much genuine creativity now goes into the visual arts could be argued. Safdie may quite well be right to think that visual arts (at least painting and sculpture—less certainly the arts of motion) have little to do with life today. He may be quite right that as art is now made, it has no contribution to make to architecture as it is now made. Indeed, if I were an architect, I know of not more than one or two painters and half a dozen sculptors whom I would let intrude in any way on my building.

We cannot beg the questions Safdie raises by pointing to his naivetés as when he claims that he was not allowed to build a Habitat near the site of the New York Stock Exchange because neither the Exchange nor its architecture wanted "mothers with baby carriages strolling in the stock exchange plaza at lunch time,"[6] pure corn of the type he would excoriate if it were used, say, by Spiro Agnew. We cannot explain it all away by noting that Safdie is a technocrat and a total functionalist (allowing his definition of function), arbitrary, insistent that satisfied function is automatically beauty. It will not do us much good to try to determine who is guilty, if indeed anyone is guilty, the architect or the artist. I happen to think that if anyone is guilty, both are guilty, the artists, however, to a much greater degree than the architects since the state of practically all current painting, and much of the farm-machinery school of sculpture, is despicable while this cannot be said of the state of current architecture. But perhaps no one is guilty. The consistent successful collaborations of

4 Ibid.
5 Ibid., p. 169.
6 Ibid., p. 191.

artists and architects throughout all previous great historical periods of architecture cannot be the balance in which our present situation is weighed and found wanting. One may regret the divorce or be gladdened by it. What is certain is that it exists. Whether the decree is permanent and final, who can know?

A major relation to which I think sufficient attention is rarely given is that between client and architect. It may actually be so that great results require a great client as well as a great architect, and this may be part of what Eliel Saarinen meant when he said that people got the architecture they deserved. Back in history we have noted a number of almost one-to-one relationships: Zoser and Imhotep; Hatshepsut and Senenmut; Pericles and Ictinus; Trajan-Hadrian and Apollodorus. The relations may not have been as easy as receding and telescoping history tends to make them appear—or as simple—but they were clearly there. They persisted surely down through the great merchant princes of the Renaissance and the all-powerful kings or popes who might command, for example, all of the time or almost all of the time of such a man as Le Nôtre. In our own day not many of the best architects would like to work all the time for a single patron, and not many of the best patrons, such men as Irwin Miller of Columbus, Indiana, think in terms of limiting their relationship to one architectural talent. But even now young talents may profit from such a relationship. Wright owed much to a few clients like the Coonleys and the Barnsdalls and later to the Johnsons of Racine; Gropius got a second start with considerable help from the Storrows, after Peggy Guggenheim; Mies from his faithful supporter, Herbert Greenwald; Ieoh Ming Pei for a time from his association with William Zeckendorf.

It is harder to find great patrons than it once may have been, if only because no patron has quite enough power any more. More and more architecture is institutional; within the institutions there is seldom a dominant voice expressing a consistent institutional will in the matter of patronage. More and more the direction falls into the hands of committees, which, on the one hand, makes it easier for the skillful architect-navigator to steer his own course, but on the other, deprives him of powerful and steady support in times of crisis. Again, I suppose, we have to admit that we cannot bring back the good old days. But it may be amusing and possibly profitable to remember some of the antics, old and new, by which architects have sought such patrons or patronage.

In insisting that more is owed to the patron than is usually admitted, even to the point of suggesting that the American Institute of Architects might sometime consider bestowing a Gold Medal on a great client, I am not attempting to establish a new pecking order. I am quite sure which comes first. A great architect may achieve without a great patron; a great patron can achieve nothing without a great architect. But one of the attributes of a great client is that he knows a great architect when he sees one.

All the great architecture we know in the world we owe to architects. This is true whether or not we know their names. It is true even if we have ascribed the wrong authorship to a building. (It is always tempting to downgrade the successful—and even the near-great.) The tale of the mythical office boy who really did the master's work turns up all over architectural history, and it may have been more valid when the master-apprentice roles in architecture were more general. But even after this had died away, the myth persisted. When I was a boy, there was a tale that the architect of Yale's Harkness Tower, James Gamble Rogers, had a talented sot in tow (probably an Eli) whom he kept in a garret and stuffed with booze and from whom he collected all the whimseys of New Haven Gothic. I refrain from citing familiar later examples.

As I have said above, there are, of course, many others who contribute to the making of architecture, and none of these is really indispensable. A great architect may occasionally transcend the limitations of his client. On the other hand, and Baron Haussmann to the contrary notwithstanding,[7] no great client was ever able to cause an architect to transcend his limitations as an artist. The best results have come about when client and architect were moved by common purpose, of course.

The architect himself is naturally replaceable in the sense that another man may be chosen to do the job. And since any first-class architect cannot safely be modest—and must believe in his superiority—it is not surprising that there has been fierce competition for jobs through most of history, competition one might say for the benefit of posterity as well as for the present comfort and prestige of the architect. It is fairly fashionable in these days for otherwise generously disposed clients to complain that architects are trying to build monuments to themselves. What else should they be about? If the whole thing comes off well, they may also succeed in building a monument to the client, as Palladio did for Capra.

In these efforts to get jobs, architects have been ingenious beyond all measure. One could start with Vitruvius. He was no great architect himself and Augustus Caesar understood that very well. So he wrote a ten-volume tome on architecture, dedicated to the Emperor.

Vitruvius was not only a mediocre architect but a bad Latin stylist. Most of his work consists of fairly dreary discussion of building practices (except maybe to historians),[8] and though it might have helped Augustan builders to change Rome from brick to marble, it did nothing to elevate

---

[7] When Haussmann had finally forced Baltard, the dogged classicist, to design Les Halles as "umbrellas of iron" which the Emperor desired, Louis Napoleon was delighted and demanded to see other work by "this great architect." When he saw it, he was disillusioned. But Haussmann remarked smugly that it had been a matter of the same architect but a different prefect. For more detail, see Joan Margaret Chapman and Brian Chapman, *The Life and Times of Baron Haussmann* (London: Weidenfeld and Nicolson, 1957).

[8] Albert A. Howard, Preface, *Vitruvius: The Ten Books on Architecture*, translated by Morris Hickey Morgan (New York: Dover, 1960), vol. V.

the imperial aspirations as Machiavelli's *Prince* set out later to do in another time and for a different purpose. Possibly conscious of this, Vitruvius devoted the Introduction of each Book to flights of literary, historical, and philosophical fancy, all modestly embarrassing. As Professor Morris Hickey Morgan indicated when he translated Vitruvius, the language of Vitruvius was scarcely Ciceronian, and he worked very hard to make it clear that there was no "conspicuous literary merit *in* the work."

Goethe discovered Vitruvius through Palladio and found him interesting, though less convincing than Palladio himself. Nonetheless the work of Vitruvius should still be of interest to architects despite its technological obsolescence. It raises many questions that are still unanswered today, notably those concerning the proper education of the architect. Here I want only to recount what this anxious man said about getting commissions. In dedicating his work to the Emperor, he praised the imperial intention to provide public buildings intended for utilitarian purposes, and in Book II he talked about how an architect might get a commission.

> Dinocrates, an architect who was full of confidence in his own ideas and skill, set out from Macedonia, in the reign of Alexander, to go to the army, being eager to win the approbation of the king. He took with him from his country letters from relatives and friends to the principal military men and officers of the court, in order to gain access to them more readily. Being politely received by them, he asked to be presented to Alexander as soon as possible. They promised, but were rather slow, waiting for a suitable opportunity. So Dinocrates, thinking that they were playing with him, had recourse to his own efforts. He was of very lofty stature and pleasing countenance, finely formed and extremely dignified. Trusting, therefore to these natural gifts, he undressed himself in his inn, anointed his body with oil, set a chaplet of poplar leaves on his head, draped his left shoulder with a lion's skin, and holding a club in his right hand stalked forth to a place in front of the tribunal where the king was administering justice.

This did attract the imperial attention to Dinocrates, who then announced that he was

> "a Macedonian architect, who brings thee ideas and designs worthy of thy renown. I have made a design for the shaping of Mount Athos into the statue of a man, in whose left hand I have represented a very spacious fortified city, and in his right a bowl to receive the water of all the streams which are in that mountain so that it may pour from the bowl into the sea."

Alexander was delighted with the scheme but found the site impracticable. Still he kept Dinocrates and ultimately ordered him to build the city of Alexandria.

This was how Dinocrates, recommended only by his good looks and dignified carriage, came to be so famous. But as for me, Emperor, nature has not given me stature, age has marred my face, and my strength is impaired by ill health. Therefore, since these advantages fail me, I shall win your approval, as I hope, by the help of my knowledge and my writings.[9]

The men of the Renaissance were most charming in their skull-duggery. The example of Tintoretto and how he got the paintings of the Scuola San Rocco in Venice is but the most dashing. It is too long to tell here and too good to be spoiled by abridgment.

A quite amusing volume of anecdotes of this sort could no doubt be compiled, but that is not what I am about here. Suffice it to say the practice has not died away. Not many commissions are obtained these days at the country club. But I have seen a well-known designer smell out the affection an American monsignor had for Rome and travertine and parlay this interest of an influential board member into an important commission for which I must hasten to say he was well equipped. I have seen a graduate of M.I.T. and Harvard, pursuing what he believed a client's disinterest, profess that he knew nothing about an important public square in Boston, while a rival from Italy had spent two days before the meeting wandering the square and its purlieus which seemed to him essential to what he had to say, as indeed it would have been in Rome or Verona. I have listened to a good architect who had liked the sobriquet "the quiet one" so much when applied to him that in his presentation he was as quiet as Miró, which means too quiet when selling is to be done. I have seen an urbane architect from San Francisco dressed to a part which did not fit him and unhappily did not fit Dallas, Texas, either, though he imagined it would. I have seen another distinguished firm with enormous work to its credit drown the selecting committee with too many slides of too much, making an unnecessary point, creating the restlessness with which one sees a friend's new slides from Celebes where Mrs. Friend is always taking the play away from the anog, and incidentally losing the job. I have seen a job lost because an able man had eaten too many oysters in Italy in hepatitis season and really could not bear down on his client-prey with any conviction. All this is simply by way of indicating how precarious the whole game is and how lucky the world has been then and now when a favorable concatenation of the stars comes about. One of the stars had probably better be a Bernini of the times.

All this naturally raises the question of whether architects have more foibles than you and I, the sober folk who do the world's work. To this my answer would be no, they probably do not have more foibles but they certainly have more colorful ones. They are in fact a fairly feline lot with

[9] Vitruvius, op. cit., vol. II, p. 36.

all the sensitivities that Montaigne properly attributed to cats—but they are feral felines.

If any of them should take this amiss, I might atone by adding that they are not less feline than critics, or less feral, but considerably more significant. In art critics, too, in addition to felinity there is a considerable femininity, not less in the males of the species than the females.

All these attributes of architects, admirable ones, I happen to think, although ridiculous to men of common sense and all too open to ridicule thereby, show up naturally when they are not soliciting as well as when they are.

In no city I know does this matter of the importance of the client appear with more clarity than in the architectural history of Paris and Rome, of which enough details have appeared in the text.

The title of this book and this chapter should read with the stress on the last word in the best tradition of Yiddish shading.[10] The man Bernini has, of course, passed away. Many wish he had no emulators today.

This Giovanni Lorenzo Bernini, of whom we have heard before, was born in Naples in 1598 and lived most of his life in and around Rome until he died in 1680. His life-span traversed nearly the whole of the seventeenth century. An architect and sculptor of enormous talent and scale and exuberance, he was the successor of the more restrained Michelangelo and the predecessor of his more effusive pupil, Borromini. The three of them were the producers of the great stage of the Italian Baroque.

The Baroque was, in architecture, sculpture, and painting alike, an art of "restless oppositions, uneasy equilibriums, violent clashes, polarities brought momentarily into precarious balances, and of passions brought briefly under control." This description by Professor William Coleman of Syracuse University was, you must remember, attached to the works of Bernini and his contemporaries and not to the Sydney Opera House, the Boston City Hall, the Yale School of Fine Arts, Habitat '67, or any of the unexecuted work of Robert Venturi. You may wish to reflect whether they could properly be applied today, omitting perhaps the references to passion—"an art of restless oppositions, uneasy equilibriums, violent clashes, polarities brought momentarily into precarious balances."

We have already encountered Bernini's misadventures with Louis XIV, and we must be aware that great as St. Peter's Square is, it is unconducive to a sense of comfort and ease in the mind of the small man, save when, multiplied, he congregates in hordes to pay obeisance to the Pope on the papal balcony.

In asking rhetorically whether Bernini is dead, I am not raising again the adventures of an architect with his client. I am not talking about the interesting question as to whether contemporary architecture has (again

---

[10] Familiar to most of us today. If the reader has doubt, he should consult a charming recent book, Leo Rosten, The Joys of Yiddish (New York: McGraw-Hill, 1968), pp. xvi–xviii.

metaphorically) entered its Baroque phase. I am not talking about the contemporary attitude toward profusion of exuberant detail (generally negative). I am not talking about whether the Baroque conception of architectural space and less importantly the undulant wall have had a favorable or an unfavorable effect or no noticeable effect at all on how contemporary architects think about urban space. I am not even thinking much of the revolutionary aspects of the Baroque to which there are current analogies. No, I am concerned primarily with the presumed attitudes of a Bernini-type toward practical considerations and especially nowadays toward the common man.

We cannot say of Bernini, I would argue, that he scorned the freedom of necessity in architecture. His clients were big, powerful, rich, and some of the restricting conditions were missing, to be sure. If you want to dismiss the big, the powerful, the rich, however defined, from the role of architectural clients in the last quarter of the twentieth century, you can bury Bernini now. I am not so anxious to run to that interment.

Bernini, as an aftermath of the Renaissance and its humanism, certainly would have accepted, and indeed did accept, some of the Platonic views of art, if not the one that the artist is by definition subversive since he appeals to the emotions and not the reason, and therefore ought to be controlled; or, perhaps, that the art is more important than the artist.

Sculpture and painting were not always deprived of the freedom of necessity which conditioned their finest hours. When the visual arts had living meaning, to serve as totems or taboos or as forms of productive incantation, they were not free. How to propitiate or bribe a god, how to guarantee procreation or fertility in the fields, how to fend off drought or flood or death, how to ensure success for the hunt or in battle, could not be trivial purposes. They could not be subject to the whim of the artist to decide what was important or even, save within quite narrow limits, how to depict it. Abstractions had to be comprehensible to all and not concocted in the private language of some individual who preferred to talk to himself. The artist had indeed to "be with it" and to "do his thing." But what he had to be with were the needs of his fellows which had to be met—hopefully they were his needs as well—and his thing had to be a thing that was meaningful to society and not something which would be more valued the more personal and the less universal it became.

When these arts ceased to be magical and became didactic, the same principles still held. Despite the enormous ingenuity and personal sensitivity of the artists of the Middle Ages, the sculptors and the glassworkers of the medieval cathedrals and the illuminators of the manuscripts were bound by canons established long before by the Councils of Nicaea. They were established beyond the caprice of the artist or, for that matter, of his client, the bishop. You could not reduce the number of the twenty-four ancients of the Apocalypse because some other number might compose better; for a symbol of the Resurrection you had to think of Jonah or

Daniel or the lioness breathing into her still-born cubs, and not of Salome or the aspic who might entrance you more. You had to force your work of art into places you had not chosen and into shapes you found difficult, since they had been determined by higher architectural and even liturgical considerations.

In general, similar limitations were imposed on any other historical art which was magical or didactic, whether it depicted the triumphs of Rameses or Trajan, the historical legends of Greece, the adventures of Rama, the astronomy or the rain god of the Maya. They applied largely even to the few early periods when the arts were less devoted specifically to magic or to teaching but, as in the Greek fifth century, were expected to provide hedonistic representations of the ideal human. Even then it was the ideal which dominated the artist, not the artist the ideal.

By Bernini's time the more stringent limitations on painters and sculptors were falling away. Magic was no longer their game, though illusion certainly was. Nor was education, at least as practiced by the iconographers of the Middle Ages. Bernini's statements in sculpture or particularly in St. Peter's chair are more nearly propaganda than education. And if you want to insist in the most modern fashion that the *Christ in Majesty* at Chartres is also propaganda or even that all "education" is "propaganda," including even African Studies, let us not waste time on that debate; let us only say that the propaganda had shifted its message from the ineffability of Christ to the omnipotence of the Church and its Chief Vicar, which is a shift of enormous magnitude. Bernini's architecture, especially the monumental envelopment of St. Peter's Square, is at bottom directed toward the same result, but it is still pro- and not antinatural, and it still believes in function and in the overall praiseworthiness of at least some parts of an establishment.

In the eleventh canto of the *Inferno*, Dante quotes Vergil's description of human art as the "grandchild of God" since art is said to copy nature and nature is the child of God. This seems to me on the whole more attractive than the converse view that nature copies art, or Paul Rudolph's statement that function follows form. As epigrams in the Oscar Wilde tradition they may cause us to smile at their brittle brilliance. But unfortunately their perversity is believed by those who ought to know better.

It should be apparent to anyone who looks at art journals or roams the art galleries today that sculptors and painters have largely loosed the bonds of necessity, even the necessity of clear communication, so that we do not often know whether they are for the establishment or against it or neutral, whether they are concerned only with their own insides, with the cynical collection of royalties, or simply with being noticed, which is easy over a short span. I do not propose to guess here whether this is a healthy or an unhealthy state of affairs—or whether it is a fundamental phenomenon or merely an ephemerality of fashion.

What I do wonder about is the extent to which similar aspirations on the part of architects can corrupt architecture, if "corrupt" is an appropriate term, as I believe it to be. It will not happen easily because architecture has always been bound more than the other arts by the freedom of necessity, and it still is. It has less chance to be revolutionary in anything other than style since its patrons are inevitably of the establishment; it can seldom indulge in satire or subversion; and even gentle humor is out of place in most situations. Oldenburg or Warhol are inconceivable as architects. All this *is* limiting. It is even more limiting that the building is put up to serve some human purpose which is not directly related usually to aesthetics, and if it fails too miserably to serve these purposes, as it often does, its artistry will be regarded as irrelevant or even condemned if it can be seen to be responsible for the functional failure.

It is only natural that some contemporary architects should be envious of the apparent freedoms of other artists and wish to break the shackles of need. They can score but limited successes in such endeavors, if only because of the size and cost of their artifacts and the justified unwillingness of the patron or client to give them ultimate freedom to make architecture into colossal urban sculpture. Some of our contemporary buildings which have been accorded the widest acclaim from critical claques whose judgment is based solely on form and space have been the most dismal functional failures. This has occurred when the visual imperiousness of the designer has been allowed to override all sensible, much less sensitive, consideration of other than aesthetic needs of the user. We should probably rejoice that clients still have reservations about the God-like attributes of architects, even the greatest ones, perhaps especially the greatest ones. So the architect, I happen to think to his advantage, is still considerably constrained and also supported by the freedom of necessity.

I need to be quite explicit here. The type of imperiousness to which I refer is exemplified by designs for a school of art in which the working conditions for the art students are impossible; or a set of laboratories based on the architect's notions as to how physicists ought to want to work; or causes so much money to be spent on the buildings of a research institute that the funds available to support research are seriously diminished. This much, if undesirable, does not represent a total loss since some adaptations and some uses can ultimately be made—and the major error is only in the overvaluation of form as the principal constituent of the design.

And certainly I am not talking of enormously innovative proposals and achievements such as those of Buckminster Fuller, Frei Otto, Moyshe Safdie, or Paolo Soleri.[11]

Some of these may never be realized; some may not work; some may even be Procrustean in their demands upon the user; but they are not

[11] For example, geodesic domes, tents, Habitat '67, all as shown at Montreal Expo 1967 in America's pavilion, Germany's pavilion, and Habitat '67, and Soleri's ideas in his suggestive book, *Arcology: The City in the Image of Man* (Cambridge, Mass.: M.I.T. Press, 1969).

disclaimers of the freedom of necessity. On the contrary they are trying to stretch the boundaries of these freedoms while recognizing them as real.

One of the haunting and perhaps unresolvable questions which arises about the relations of engineering to architecture I have hinted at before. Did the engineering come first as the solution, perhaps, to a problem which society had scarcely formulated, and was it then grasped and forced to greater heights by imaginative architects or others? Or did the social requirement stand there and demand that engineering find ways to meet it?

If we look at the question in modern terms and especially in the context of things other than buildings, we may find a clue. No one would insist, I suppose, that it was the desire of something called society or even of very many men in society to talk over long distances almost instantaneously, or to fly even short distances, and that these desires forced the inventions, however much they may have pressed later for more powerful solutions.

Indeed the conservative tendency of most people, their apprehension about the unknown, seems inevitably to produce resistance to change rather than demand for it and certainly guarantees that there will be no great demand for something new, the disadvantages of which are easier to imagine than the advantages, even if the disadvantages, imagined, turn out not to be real while others, unimagined, turn out to be serious.

In almost all cases of advanced modern technology we have to say, I think, that the desire of a few people to do something never done before, the restless urge to probe the unknown, often with very scant appreciation of or even concern about the ultimate consequences, must be the germ of change. Whatever the innovators may later rationalize in their autobiographies, their approach in the beginning must be analogous to that of Hillary who said he was impelled to try to climb Everest because it was there.

The old German proverb, *was mann hat gethan mann kann thun*, "what man has done man can do," is generally valid. The four-minute mile, once run, becomes common; Everest, once conquered, is more easily climbed again. Once man has flown at Kitty Hawk, many will fly. The extrapolations are often attended with great difficulties, of course, but the solution is more or less certain if the solution, now deemed possible, is wanted. But it is reasonably clear that the egg starts things if we can call the egg the idea.

In history there may have been few unique great ideas. Newton and Leibniz conceived the calculus simultaneously and without communication with each other. There were others trying plausible ways to fly at the time of the success at Kitty Hawk. But this is not important. The idea that something *can* be done rather than that something *ought to be done* is the first motivator for Promethean man who refuses to stay chained to his rock. The Promethean drive is likely to be individual.

After the thing *is* done, however haltingly, others may perceive things that *ought* to be done and press the technology to its limits demanding more than the inventors dreamt of and occasionally more than they can deliver.

I think the same sequence has been true in architectural engineering. Some Egyptian found out how to split stone, another how to move modest pieces, a third came upon and reported the marvelous pink granites of Aswan. Then a Pharaoh or his minister said, if that, why not this? Cut me a much larger piece of stone than anyone has ever cut before; bring it to me at Luxor; put it up for me before the pylon of my temple. And in the end it is done.

I am not tempted to assert that, vis-à-vis the innovators, architects have played a much more imaginative role than this in the development of architectural engineering, at least since the days when architect, engineer, and master mason may have been one. In general, architects have been users rather than inventors—Pharaohs, if you like, who have also asked of the engineers more than the engineers themselves might have dreamed of doing. There are some exceptions, of course, and Frank Lloyd Wright may be an almost contemporary example. Two other innovators of this sort, Frei Otto and R. Buckminster Fuller, are really engineers and not architects as will be seen if one examines closely the total consequence of their work.

Pl. 373
Pl. 375

But engineer or architect, the proposals of these men deserve the attention and applause they get. Very likely their proposals are less universal than they would like to think. Attempts at reuse of the Geodesic Dome at Montreal have proved awkward despite the fact that it is such a wonderful construction, so handsome in its transparency, whether the light comes from within to glow in the outer darkness or from without to bring the sky to the interior. But it ought also to be apparent that it is a very limited architectural solution, offering space which is really useful for very few purposes. Of course the purposes can be modified to suit the space at least up to a point, but that is scarcely the right direction for architecture which should be molded by people rather than mold them. It is also probably of limited advantage to have the sun, the sky, the wind, and the air only at second hand. There may be a human limit to the amount by which the elements can be ignored or the user be stretched on the Procrustean bed by design. Frei Otto's even more suggestive tents obviously have their difficulties too. But this does not really diminish their importance.

If Bernini were called in to award the Golden Apple, the Bernini Prize, so to speak, I suspect he would consider and approve the work of Kahn (Salk Center, La Jolla, California), Rudolph (Yale School of Fine Arts, New Haven), and Kallman (Boston City Hall), but end by awarding the prize to Fuller, Otto, or Soleri. But neither group would cause him to doubt that his spirit was living after him.

There is a challenge to Bernini, perhaps even an assertion, that he is dead or ought to be in proposals becoming more generally discussed since

1966 when Robert Venturi published his book, *Complexity and Contradiction in Architecture*.[12]

It is hard to describe what it is really about. It certainly derives in part from the earlier "pop art," suggesting again that at least in modern times the theoretical balance of trade favors the painters and not the architects. Venturi's theories seem to me not so much aesthetic as ideas of resignation. There is nothing as ironic in them as pop art was before people began to take it seriously. Venturi says truly that the Utopians, the great earlier architectural moralists, Gropius, Wright, Mies, Le Corbusier, have affected only a trivial portion of the modern city, that the Kitsch vulgarity epitomized by the Las Vegas strip is nearer to the overall reality. It is not only exciting but also not chaotic. Indeed it is functional; it expresses communication rather than form, is symbolic not spatial, informal, antiheroic, nonmonumental. It is anything but *"chôtic,"* and if we study it enough, we can learn something real—that "architecture is not enough." But since he is an architect, Venturi does produce a building now and then (he has had a few clients) and they, up to now, are "banality taken seriously" as contrasted, for example, with the whimsical if unimportant work of another maker of "nonstraightforward architecture," Charles Moore, which, at any rate, can make fun of itself.

Venturi's unrealized project for the National Football Hall of Fame does perhaps have in it a Bernini component. The functional building, a sort of archive and museum, is "dwarfed by the immense billboard whose 200,000 lights are electronically programmed to produce moving images, words and phrases, even diagrams of football plays. The billboard and its messages, visible across a broad parking lot, would not be mere adjuncts to the building, but an integral part of the whole enterprise" (which Venturi calls a "bill-ding-board"). Indeed they would likely be the central element, because, as Venturi says,

> Symbols . . . can evoke the instant association crucial for today's vast spaces, fast speeds, complex programs, and perhaps jaded senses which respond only to bold stimuli.[13]

Now Venturi's disenchanting statements about a McLuhanesque world which is full of vulgarity and cheapness may be too close to the mark to dismiss lightly. The disenchantment may be justified. Our world *is* for the moment at least skeptical about heroes, about universal truths, about beauty. If this is what architecture is about, then it may be hard to say we need architecture any more. But if we do live in an antiarchitectural

[12] Robert Venturi, *Complexity and Contradiction in Architecture* (New York: Museum of Modern Art and Graham Foundation for Advanced Studies in the Fine Arts, 1966). For an excellent article on this subject, see Franz Schulze, "Chaos as Architecture," *Art in America*, July–August 1970, pp. 89 ff.
[13] Ibid., p. 93.

world, it is hard to see what the Venturis are supposed to do. They cannot, after days on the boards, produce anything half so vulgarly exciting as the Las Vegas strip. If Venturi is right, then Bernini *is* dead and "none so poor to do him reverence." Long live Howard Hughes and Frank Sinatra.

The same sort of prediction which I believe to be a grim one for the future of architecture and consequently for the future of the good life may be implied by the far more serious Constantinos Doxiadis.[14] Doxiadis has a great concern for the human condition and is a reformer and a Utopian, unlike Venturi who simply wants to tell it like he thinks it is. I do not want here to express the reservations I have about what I believe to be the pseudoscientific approach of Doxiadis, but rather discuss his views, which are well stated, about the difficulties confronting a would-be Bernini who wanted to take charge today. The complexities of any large urban architectural problem (and only these are worthwhile) insist either that the architect continue to depend on the knowledge of others for many of his decisions, with the unhappy corollary that the body and weight of this knowledge is geometrically expanding so that such a decision means that the architect will have to let others decide for him how to locate his buildings best and what to emphasize in them in a degree never known by Bernini; or that he know a great deal more about more things, which will necessitate a redefinition of his role and his task and a decision as to how far he is prepared or should be prepared to go. Given the limitations of the human capacity, Doxiadis might have gone further and asked himself how this could be achieved since design as now conceived is something more than a full-time occupation. Doxiadis continues. I paraphrase.

In order to achieve his new goal the architect will have to understand that he cannot play God, as Socrates accuses him of doing in Paul Valéry's *Eupalinos*.

One of the common ways of playing God, even if innocently, is for an architect to attempt to solve a problem in his own individual way by projecting his own needs as the needs of the community. The results of this are far too apparent to be ignored. Often people have been "completely alienated" from the settlement in which they have been put because of the unfamiliar and unexpected and often inappropriate solution offered them by experts who, however well meaning they may have been, knew little about the lives and aspirations of those for whom they were designing. We should be wary of urbanists who live in the suburbs, of praisers of small towns who choose to live in a metropolis, of designers of new tenements who live on Park Avenue. Yet when the neighborhood is brought in, the dialogues tend to degenerate into confrontations and the program never seems to get very well articulated.

[14] Constantinos A. Doxiadis, *Ekistics, An Introduction to the Science of Human Settlements* (New York: Oxford, 1968).

Of course, one cannot play God if too many say no. Indeed the greatest threat to the future of Architecture lies not in the would-be-Olympians, or the pop-Venturians, or even in the anarchistic Abbie Hoffmans. It lies rather in the "no-sayers." Efforts to achieve neighborhood participation up to now have mostly foundered on the shoals of ignorance, inarticulateness, and cheap, local demagoguery. But the potential power of a minority veto is greater than that. It was bad enough when Senators and Representatives in Congress brought their collective aesthetic blindness to bear on national projects so that George Stewart's hideous rebuilding of the National Capitol thrived under the patronage of Sam Rayburn, while the Air Force Academy starved for trees, where the taste of current colonels' wives for pseudo or even genuine American antique furniture determined the residential taste at Colorado Springs, while the only interesting federal architecture had to occur far away in remote embassies which not many members of Congress would visit. The brilliant new Boston City Hall could never have been built save for the supportive courage of then Mayor John Collins, who turned a deaf ear to the dissenters in and out of government after the design had won a competition. Though these skirmishes on the wider terrain sometimes came out well, it is hard to be confident that any Architecture will survive a consistent application of the minority veto.

I think we may be unaware how much things have changed. Years ago there were straws in the wind: the deletion of Fagin from *Oliver Twist* lest the image of the Jews suffer, absurd rewriting of *Penrod* to spare some black sensibility; the banning of prayer, of flag salutes, of Christmas carols and Christmas decorations in public schools and other places because some minority wanted their children to be unexposed to these things. Thus the many were deprived in the interest of the few. Gradually serious organizations, engaged in generally good causes and now enjoying power almost for the first time, have been carried away into undiscriminating demands for the protection of civil rights or the conservation of nature. Observing what a minority can achieve if it is noisy enough, citizens' groups are now marched in against anything that comes up, and though their attention has not yet focused often on architecture, there is no reason why it should not be and will not be. Already such groups have prevented, for example, the building of a new department store on 96th Street in Manhattan which is cited not because it matters much but because it shows the power of a small but vociferous minority. But unless there is more resistance on the part of political leaders and more courage to build what needs to be built well and beautifully, things will get worse. Minorities on welfare might prevent the building of a major art center because they wanted the money for their alms-baskets; minorities in a neighborhood might prevent the building of any sort of a cultural enterprise until all their housing needs were fully satisfied; and beyond that, aesthetic censorship by such a stentorian small group is only around the corner.

The taste of the majority as represented by the Las Vegas strip and Venturi's embrace of it is less frightening than the censorious veto of tiny minorities in a land where the affirmative shout is seldom heard but the minority veto is becoming the rule. No modern Bernini can survive this continuing veto.

All this is discouraging and encourages the role of God-playing. We should probably face it that most of our famous form-givers are by no means loath to be Olympian. They might ask Doxiadis what the real alternatives are. In his Utopia architects are able, humble, and dedicated, and respectful of the knowledge of others. If this may be possible in Utopia, is it possible on Olympus or Parnassus? And if not, where is there a chair for Bernini?

Modern humanistic scholarship, with its analysis of a poem, say, by Matthew Arnold several times longer than the poem itself, with its apparent rejection of the simple truth once voiced by J. Middleton Murry, "Great poets mean what they say," such technicism among the "custodians of value" cannot help architects in their dilemma.

But there is another prong of humanism, if not of scholarship, which is worth keeping sharp—this is the eternal vigilance lest the individual be swept up in the mass. There always was in humanism a tacit assumption that its concern was wholly with man as an individual and not at all with man as a social being. Whether practiced by scientists or sentimentalists, this humanism (not humanistic scholarship) is the zealous guardian against the computer, against space travel, against atomic power plants on handsome coasts, against the corporate society, against the mob, against *1984*, against the Census, against the Pentagon, the FBI, the CIA. When the doctrine becomes exaggerated into the pathetic nihilism or anarchy of young people seeking an individuality they do not possess and are unwilling to work to develop, demanding, so to speak, an instant personality in adolescent tones, then we reject the consequences of overemphasis on the attistic individual. But it does not need to be expressed in such sniveling terms. Bernini never lamented his fate, at least in public, and the sadder Borromini only rarely, but they too were caricatures of exaggerated individuality, products of egocentric immodesty, unconcerned about the fate or even the presence of common men outside of St. Peter's Square and even then only as grains of sand to be dealt with on their and the Pope's terms. However, Bernini was no Uriah Heep—he admitted his purposes, and he did not suffer from the disease of self-righteousness.

But when we do come down to the individuality of the common man and how this does or does not conflict with the leveling forces of the common need, the great texts—*Lear, Antigone, Paradise Lost, The Commedia*—do not help us much. They offer no prescription for Watts, and neither do the Zoser complex, the Parthenon, the Pantheon, or the Cathedral of Chartres.

It is not so much that humanists care more about the fate of Hecuba or other Trojan women than about the women of Biafra or of Watts, or that they may promote individuality to the point of absurdity, but rather that they cannot supply the other ingredient to architecture to collaborate with the one furnished so well by engineers.

To whom then are architects to turn since they are right to sense that the engineering, the technological solution is deficient and even dangerous unless other factors are considered?

Scientists can offer them, along with poets, a sense of conscience, and perhaps, though not so certainly, some hints as to method. The social scientists can supply parts of the needed information, although their limitations are quite as evident as those of the humanists to which they are polar. In fact, a lot more could be said against the absence of aesthetic impulses in social science if I had time here.

We might be tempted to turn to the medicine men, thinking, for example, that if we were to throw a large enough geodesic dome over a large enough city, and, given levitation, spend our days in reading *Nine Chains to the Moon*, everything would be all right. But it would not be all right any more than it was on Laputa. We might let ourselves be spellbound by McLuhan who always seems to be saying more than he is and about whom it might be suggested that the massage is the message. Guides such as these are likely to be *fata morgana*, will-o'-the-wisps leading us into the swamp more deeply than we are but not getting us out. In this category I also place Venturi.

Ignoring the turgid details and the pseudoscientific charts, the homely and less spectacular and slower way generally suggested by Doxiadis is likely to be more productive. In the end we must rely, I expect, on a new kind of architect—modest, informed, sensitive to the totality of the problem, aware of how to put together a meaningful team. In every such effort there are conflicting priorities, and the resolution of these in a reasonable way is seldom an averaging way or an achievement of the least common denominator by insisting on consensus, which is almost certain to guarantee the most mediocre results. The hypotheses of Doxiadis may or may not stand up when they are tested, but it would be folly, because of reservation as to their details, to conclude that it is impossible to develop a science of human settlement in which, however, the sports are not exterminated by the rules.

This is where I think Doxiadis is on the right track. I believe he means what he says. He does believe that a science of human settlement is not impossible, even though, as it seems to me, his own concepts are presently at best in a primitive Linnaean stage. But he recognizes as well that if we wait for the proper

> development of a science of human settlements we may find ourselves overwhelmed by the rising tide of the problems. We may even lose the battle for such a science since humanity may find no use for systematic theoretical thinking in a period of panic tension.[14a]

[14a] Ibid., p. 15.

So we must use provisional systems and observe the consequences of their use more objectively and thoroughly than we have yet done even about the much observed settlements, say, of Chandigarh or Brasília.

But these systems cannot successfully rely on the intuition of one genius or near genius, says Doxiadis, even if he is Breuer or Rudolph or Kahn or Pei or Safdie; much less can they expect to rely on a consortium of genius operating in some sort of troika rig. What is obviously needed is the collaboration of many disciplines and of disciplined representatives of the appropriate disciplines.

To provide this is far more difficult than to arrange the collaboration of architect and engineer, which itself has been stumbling enough. The principal trouble has been that either the architectural or the engineering boundaries were too firmly set before the collaboration was attempted so that too many of the conditions were frozen. Collaboration to be really effective must begin at point zero and must give full weight to what each discipline has to say from the beginning—when the important decisions are actually made. This principle is more important than whether, in a given situation, the chairman is to be an architect or an engineer or even a sociologist (perhaps not an economist unless, like John Kenneth Galbraith, he is in some respects a bad economist and possibly a wiser man who knows when the stern voice of economics should not be taken to be the voice of God).

The chairman must not take himself to be always the wisest man in the room; but neither must he be a Caspar Milquetoast who sees as many shapes in a cloud as the tactful Polonius pretended to. He must be a leader more than a moderator, but not a man who makes all decisions while the collaborators tremble at his frown.

Architects may aspire to this role though they need a much broader and tougher preparation than they are now getting, and this has to be accomplished without stifling their visual creativity, a prescription that many think impossible. I happen to think it is not impossible, but it will not be easy, and it may be within the grasp of only the most highly endowed. This does not matter. But if it is not done, architects must be prepared to see other people calling all the important signals.

It is not easy to see Giovanni Lorenzo Bernini acting as a chairman, but I want to see his modern counterpart, with different goals, to be sure, acting with power in the final decisions about design. I do not want to see him catering to the mob taste as the so-called architect of the Las Vegas strip; or accepting the dicta of the pop or rock world simply because they come through so uncompromisingly or in so many decibels; I do not want to see him cowed by neighborhood committees even though he should listen to them more than he once did; I do not want him to accept the verdict that everything is rotten, that there are no heroes, that no monumentality is any longer real, that we live in a time of antiarchitecture. Of course, if asked to do all these things, he would probably reply, "Better I should be dead!" And he would be right.

The real fly in the amber is different from any of the things I have been discussing. Certainly there are at least a handful of contemporary designers possessed of the mettle of a Bernini or a Borromini. There are a few potential clients in the world with the foresight and means of the great builder-popes. It is not inevitable that we shall become a tasteless egalitarian society. The Supreme Court cannot declare one-man one-vote in matters of art. Our main problem is that our most talented architects do not engage themselves with the pressing needs of the day, which are not World Trade Centers or Hotels Fontainebleaux. We do not have nor do they try to design beautiful housing, hospitals, recreation centers for the poor, not even schools very often. That is not the way affluence or fame comes to the architect, and those who control the building of such things cannot afford them, do not seek them, and could no doubt advance persuasive reasons why they do not seek them. But excuses from either side are not good enough.

The Egyptian peasant needed the symbolism of the pyramid of the King-God, the Athenian the buildings which supported the Panathenaic festival, the Romans the confidence imposed by the Pantheon, the Japanese the natural serenity for contemplation provided by the Ise shrine, the medieval Frenchmen the cathedral of Chartres, the Counterreformation the majestic welcoming arms of St. Peter's Square. There was less social need for the Palace of Versailles and none at all for the Vanderbilt palace at Asheville. Today, about the last thing we need is the proclamation of the virtue of money or conglomerates. Yet in building such temples is where the "bread" is, and our name designers have their nostrils well tuned to the bakery. In some ways the great architects of our day seem to be suffering from a severe attack of the corruption from which none of us has totally escaped. Until this changes, even the worldly Bernini may well be dead.

I myself doubt that it is going to change. It will certainly not be changed by the young architects who abandon architecture to build bungling cabins in the woods.

Years ago it was the noble practice of distinguished doctors to charge some patients high fees and to do the same work for the poor for nothing. I have yet to hear of millionaire architects giving much of their time to comparable charity, and no doubt the trade-union rules of the AIA might even prevent it. I am not sure that the clients who cannot pay, receiving such proposals from the maestros, would even accept them, with or without gratitude. We can be sure, I think, that the great bureaucracy, public and private, which now makes the majority of architectural decisions, would be in solid opposition.

Charity or no charity, however, there will not be great architecture which is not made for truly significant social purpose.

In 1956, John Peter collected and recorded for The Reynolds Metals Company, *Conversations Regarding The Future of Architecture* which make humorous, if unhappy, listening only twenty years later. The participants were distinguished architects of their day: Mies van der Rohe, Walter Gropius, Eero Saarinen, Richard Neutra, Ernest Kump, Phillip Johnson, and Gordon Bunshaft (senior design partner in the New York office of Skidmore, Owings, and Merrill).

In these conversations the architects seemed to display a common agreement that in the "less is more" skeleton and glass construction of Mies the modern architectural revolution had found its classic expression and that the remaining aesthetic problem for years to come lay simply in the evolution of Miesian principles with perhaps small refinements. Of those recorded, the work of Neutra, of Gropius and his associates in The Architects Collaborative, and of Kump had never before followed these principles and did not afterwards. Eero Saarinen had used them seldom and not too happily and broke away from them altogether in his later and greater work. Phillip Johnson's abjuration came later but was complete when it came. Of all this famous crew only Gordon Bunshaft, and through him, his firm, remained and still remains largely but not totally committed. Another man of talent, I. M. Pei, has made several but not his best buildings in accord with these principles. Mies, himself, never deviated. A good many mediocre men jumped aboard this seemingly safe bandwagon, so that scattered around the United States there are a good many Miesian-type office buildings and high-rise apartments, although it is only in Chicago, where Mies lived and taught, that they preponderate to a sterile and monotonous degree. Even so early, primarily under the influence of Le Corbusier, dramatically opposed and much more versatile concrete style was developing in many buildings which were not high-rise and even a few which were. Other innovators were emerging with their own fine, if very personal, styles: Minoru Yamasaki for a short time, Eero Saarinen and Marcel Breuer always, and Pietro Belluschi in his smaller buildings, to name but a few.

Pl. 381
Pl. 386

From 1956 on, my own bibliography reveals, even from titles, that I was feeling a growing concern that the strong river of the architectural revolution, of which I had been a vigorous verbal supporter, was splitting into too many streams and fanning into a marshy delta of mannerism.[15] Not only did I write about the concern I had but I also delivered lectures in many universities in 1962 and 1963 on *The Unassimilated Past* and *The Evolution of Confusion in Contemporary Architecture.*

[15] "The Shape of an Architecture," *Architectural Record*, vol. 121, no. 5, pp. 183–189, 1957; "The Urban Aesthetic," *The Annals of the American Academy of Political and Social Science*, vol. 314, pp. 112–122, 1958; "A Pilgrimage—Ronchamp, Raincy, Vézelay," *Architectural Record*, vol. 123, no. 3, pp. 171–178, 1958; "Finland and Architect Aalto," *Architectural Record*, vol. 125, no. 1, p. 126 et ff., 1959; "Technology and The Architect," *The Canadian Architect*, vol. 5, no. 4, pp. 47–53, 1960; "Alienated Affections in the Arts," *Daedalus*, Special Winter Issue, pp. 52–73, 1960; "A Parable via Milano and Roma," *Architectural Record*, vol. 128, no. 1, pp. 123–130, no. 2, pp. 157–164, 1960; "Must Our Cities Be So Ugly?," *Saturday Evening Post*, vol. 234, no. 48, pp. 54–58, 1961; "Inurbanity in America: A Parable from the United States," *Casabella*, no. 265, pp. 2–26, 1962.

This concern peaked in 1962 when I made an extended tour in the Middle and Far East and was able to observe that, in their very different styles and in all their great periods, they followed a pattern of evolution paralleling that with which I was familiar in the Classic periods of Greece and Rome, the medieval Romanesque and Gothic, the Renaissance, and the Baroque. Each had reached a logical apogee and then died, either by dissolving into mannerism (everybody doing his own thing) or through revolution such as that of the Renaissance against the Gothic, or our own contemporary one against eclecticism. This trip so cemented my conclusions that, in 1963, I wrote and published two articles which sealed my position as of that time. I called these *The Fallen Pole* from Cleopatra's great speech over the dead Antony:

> "... O! See my women,
> The crown o' the earth doth melt. My lord!
> O! wither'd is the garland of the war,
> The soldier's pole is fall'n; young boys and girls
> Are level now with men; the odds is gone,
> And there is nothing left remarkable
> Beneath the visiting moon."[16]

In these articles I reached something approaching despair as to the future of contemporary architecture because I could see no emergent central purpose or theme. We seemed bound for mannerism at best and a final public repudiation at worst. But now, ten years later, I realize that, concerned almost totally with aesthetic expression, I was seeing in far too trivial terms. I was not taking Lewis Mumford's grim prophecies seriously enough. Within the limitations I was then thinking, it seemed entirely possible that a new and modern Bernini might emerge and even be recognized. Our problems as clients or critics would be those of identification, recognition, and support.

Recently Peter Blake, once a strong advocate of the contemporary movement, has published an article denouncing the failures of the contemporary dream.[17] This article, while correctly enumerating the many failures of "functional architecture" to be functional, still does not strike at the heart of the problem, namely, the almost total failure of the "form-makers" of our day to have any true concern for human beings and human scale. Turning a little land back to a city in the form of a windswept plaza, whether or not adorned with a little sculpture, a few trees, a mosaic pavement, or a pool or fountain, is simply not enough.

[16] Shakespeare, *Antony and Cleopatra* act 4, sc. 12, line 62 ff. The two articles referred to appeared under the title "Beneath the Visiting Moon," *Progressive Architecture*, vol. XLIV, no. 11, pp. 160–170; no. 12, pp. 126–131. How my appropriate title was changed to the meaningless one is a bitterly humorous story which is, however, irrelevant here.
[17] Peter Blake, "The Folly of Modern Architecture," *The Atlantic Monthly*, September 1974, pp. 59–66.

It is true that some lovely smaller buildings have emerged, usually in rural or semi-rural environments; examples would be Saarinen's administration building for the John Deere Company on the outskirts of Moline, Illinois, or Belluschi's library for Bennington College in Vermont. But the architectural problem today is basically urban, and here, viewed in the light of the urban ecology, the results have seldom been noble. Again it is true that there are occasional handsome urban enclaves of peace and human scale such as I. M. Pei Associates have created in the Christian Science Center in Boston, right in the shadow of the aesthetically abominable Prudential Center against whose ugly backdrop it glows all the brighter. Things like Ghirardelli Square in San Francisco or the new Boston waterfront are pleasant but serve trivial purposes. It is also true that a few big-name architects, when not indulging in the giantism of high-rise buildings, have built some, not many, distinguished buildings on appropriate urban sites. These would be like many of Marcel Breuer's buildings, the Boston City Hall of Gerhard Kallmann, almost everything by Eero Saarinen save the unhappy U.S. Chancellery in London, and almost all of Phillip Johnson's later work. Finally there are a few monsters such as Pei's glass icicle for the John Hancock Life Insurance Company in Boston or the braced behemoth tower for the same company in Chicago by Skidmore, Owings, and Merrill. These might be judged as intrinsically beautiful, taken only as themselves, and built on a different site. But each has been built in total disregard of the quality of the city in which it has been planted. The Boston building is a self-centered denial of all the values in the previous and distinguished low scale of its site on Copley Square. The John Hancock Tower in Chicago may be only the exclamation point to the brutal high-rise elements of the Lake Front which have taken Chicago's main beauty spot away from the people of Chicago, for whom the Burnham Plan intended it, and turned it over to a minority of the affluent.[18] And most of the time our urban urbanity has been gnawed into inurbanity by other high-rise buildings which lack even individual aesthetic distinction.

Pl. 376

But even individual distinction does not justify this disruption of once-livable cities which has occurred almost totally in New York and Chicago, disruption which, despite stalwart opposition, is slowly destroying the once characteristic charms of San Francisco, Boston, and Vancouver, British Columbia; which has encircled Paris with tasteless *banlieux* of which La Reserve is but the newest, largest, and most egregious; which is now massing its forces to destroy the center of the erstwhile most beautiful city of the Western world; and which has crept down the Thames in London to the edges of the Tate Gallery. We are fighting a losing game in the over-developed West if, indeed, the game has not already been lost.

One need not romanticize those leaders who built classic Athens, the

[18] For an especially insightful and scathing indictment of what has happened to Chicago, see Carl W. Condit, *Chicago, 1930–70* (Chicago, Illinois: The University of Chicago Press, 1974), especially pp. 73–78 and 110–114.

bishops who caused the Gothic to flower, the Florentine princes and those of Rome who supported the Renaissance, or the Popes, Teutonic prince- lings, and French Grand Monarques who were served by the Baroque and who, in turn, served it. They were human—wealth mattered to them and power, perhaps, even more. But they were clients of taste and had some other purposes. The powerful clients of today are usually tasteless money- makers and nothing more or politicians of the stamp of Robert Moses or Mayor Daley, also almost always tasteless. For such patrons most architects have become the servants, so that it may even be hard to say today that the practice of architecture is not more like a lucrative business than it is a profession or an art.

Pl. 388

So now, and at long last, I have reached the saddening conclusion that Bernini is, in fact, dead, at least in the West and in countries which have been too much influenced by Western values. There never was a chance that he could flourish in the dreary, gray life of the Communist countries where a Bernini would inevitably have ended in a Gulag. What might happen in the Third World is impossible to predict, but nowhere do I expect in my lifetime to see any Berninis. Nor, I fear, will you. For all of us, I am sorry to say, I think the answer to the question of my title is YES.

CRITICAL BIBLIOGRAPHY

Preliminary Note

A standard bibliography may contain a list of every book and monograph an author has encountered on the way to his own work presented alphabetically and without comment. Aside from what this may do to enhance the reputation of the thoroughness of the writer's scholarship, such a bibliography is of occasional use to another scholar preparing his own as a start on a book he projects to write. Since I have assumed my readers not to be scholars, I refrain from imposing so long and useless a list on them.

A second and shorter type includes only works cited in the text. If a work is cited several times and intervening references are to other works, then the standard *op. cit.* footnote references provide full bibliographical information only the first time the work is cited. This type of bibliography may save the scholarly reader some time. Again it does not seem to me very useful to the reader of this book as I visualize him.

Instead I have gone through my long bibliographical lists and plucked out works which I think will help my readers to encounter and often to read *in toto*. This is what follows.

General

By far the most impressive of the large general encyclopedias in English is specialized, the *Encyclopedia of World Art* (New York: McGraw-Hill, 1959; Italian edition 1958). These fifteen volumes are profusely illustrated and the text is very illuminating and detailed, though often requiring some cross-referencing. It is, of course, not bedside reading and one has to know what one is looking for. Much more than architecture is covered, of course, but if you can afford it this is a great addition to your library.

Strictly devoted to architecture and contained in a single heavy volume is Sir Banister Fletcher, *History of Architecture*, 17th ed. (New York: Scribner's, 1961). The style is deadpan, but Fletcher remains a classic reference work, not for cover-to-cover reading, but especially good for its multitudinous and revealing drawings and plans, all brilliantly drawn. The text is not always in harmony with contemporary scholarly opinion, as not enough revision has been done since the first edition of 1896. The coverage of English examples is excessive as compared with other architectures. But the great weakness is the parochial attitude which gives such scant space to oriental and Islamic architecture, or pre-Hispanic work in America, which often refers to such styles as nonhistoric and generally confines itself to European architecture with appropriate bows to Mesopotamia and Egypt. The treatment of all contemporary architecture is pathetically thin. After all the caveats have been entered, however, there is nothing to take its place, and it must be an early acquisition to an architectural library.

A book which should probably be a vade mecum for anyone seriously interested in architecture is *The Penguin Dictionary of Architecture,* 2d ed., by John Fleming, Hugh Honour, and Nikolaus Pevsner (Harmondsworth: Penguin, 1972). Much enlarged and improved over the first publication and its several reprintings, it is the work of a battery of distinguished and thoroughly reliable scholars. In addition to providing good definitions of all the technical architectural terms the general reader is likely to encounter and illustrating these by drawings where needed, the book provides brief bibliographies of leading architects from Imhotep to Paul Rudolph, enlarged descriptions of building types (e.g., amphitheaters), and illuminating essays on each of the principal world styles as well as essays devoted to the architecture of specific countries. It is convenient in size and price and deserves nothing but praise.

Some sets of monographs are of special value for special purposes:

There is the Penguin series *The Buildings of England,* by Nikolaus Pevsner (Baltimore, various dates depending on the shire treated). These many volumes, very careful and scholarly, offer a remarkable and detailed, if specialized, survey, shire by shire.

Almost all the important Romanesque and Gothic churches of France are to be found in separate volumes, *Petites Monographes des Grandes Edifices de la France* (Paris: Laurens, various dates, mainly the 1930s). Though illustrated, the pictures are more informative than glamorous. The scholarship is quite good, though most of the works were prepared by local *abbés, chanoines,* or *priests.* A few are out of print and so far as I know they are only in French. I have retained one example, *L'Eglise de Conques,* in the section on Romanesque.

The English *Pitkin Historical Series,* published by Pitkin in London at various dates around 1965 are often excellent for individual churches. They too were written for the most part by local canons, deans, and the like. They tend to be more anecdotal, a little less scholarly, and far better illustrated than their French counterparts.

Nowadays a good many English, French, and Italian monuments have beautifully illustrated local books which can be purchased on the site and possibly ordered from afar, though I have not tried this. I have included as examples the books on Vézelay and Modena, but there are many others. Principally picture books, these tell little that is not visual, but they might be critical in deciding whether or not you wished to visit the monument at all.

Penguin is publishing an extended list of books on the architectures of various styles and regions. The selection of authors has been impeccable, so that one can count on the reliability of what is said. The readibility is another matter and varies from the exciting to the dull. I have included in the various categories those in this Penguin series that are relevant.

The Italian Automobile Club has an excellent set of works on Italian architecture, arranged by periods.

Picture books are often as helpful as books with text. Three relatively new ones I list in what I believe to be ascending order of value.

Key Monuments of the History of Architecture, Henry Millon (ed.) (Englewood Cliffs, N.J.: Prentice-Hall, no date).
Very little text beyond captions and the number of buildings quite limited, probably due to some imposed quota. All pictures black and white which is as often as not more revealing than color if one wants to see the architecture apart from extraneous handsome surroundings. Though limited, the selection is good. However, the buildings have been selected with unusual perception, the photographs are uniformly good, and there are more plans, better related to the photographs, than in most other works.

Cichy, Bodo. *The Great Ages of Architecture* (New York: Putnam, 1964).
A handsome book with profuse illustrations—black-and-white and color. Sectioned by styles. The highly readable text for each period precedes the major illustrations. Good glossary. The weaknesses are that the title is a misnomer since it is limited to the architecture of the West and the German examples receive more attention that they deserve. Nonetheless, a good book.

World Architecture, Trewin Copplestone (ed.) (New York: McGraw-Hill, 1969).
The text for the various periods is by well-qualified specialists who write with varying degrees of charm but none distressingly. The illustrations are profuse, both black-and-white and color. The architectures of Islam and India and the Orient are fairly treated; pre-Hispanic Mexico and Peru are skimpily treated to the point where they might better have been ignored. Still, the best compendium of its kind yet to appear.

In addition to these texts quite comprehensively applied to architecture, there are a few other works to be recommended as general reading.

Bacon, Edmund N. *Design of Cities* (New York: Viking, 1967).
Beautiful treatment of the main lines of development of a great many famous cities, with clear illustration of the classic grand plan now deprecated by most socio-urban writers.

Francastel, Pierre (directeur). *Les Architectes Célèbres*, 2 volumes (Paris: Lucien Mazenod, Editions d'Art, 1959).
Interesting short biographies, especially interesting as to the different geneses of Italian, French, and English architects.

Giedion, Sigfried. *Architecture and the Phenomena of Transition* (Cambridge, Mass.: Harvard University Press, 1971).
Giedion is not always easy reading, but his works are knowingly illustrated and this work is the apotheosis of his space theories centering on Rome. It also contains material on Malta not readily found elsewhere.

————. *Architektur und das Phänomen des Wandels: Die Drei Raumkonzeptionen in der Architektur* (Tübingen: Ernst Wasmuth, 1969).
Original German text of book cited supra, much more accurate and generally better than the English translation.

————. *Space, Time and Architecture*, 1st ed. (Cambridge, Mass.: Harvard University Press, 1941).
The work by which Giedion first became well known, this was a landmark in its day. Much subsequent writing by others has not dimmed its account of the evolution of contemporary architecture and there are also good observations about the baroque. The numerous subsequent editions, often revised, have not materially added to the stature of the original.

Goethe, Johann Wolfgang. *Italian Journey* (New York: Random House, Inc., Pantheon, 1962). Translated from *Italienische Reise, 1786–1788,* by W. H. Auden and Elizabeth Mayer.
A handsome presentation with colored pictures, some by Goethe, of the journal which has served me so well in my text. Goethe was a very observant traveler.

Montague, C. E. *The Right Place* (Garden City, N.Y.: Doubleday, 1924).
The one book in this bibliography I wish every reader might encounter, though to some, more's the pity, it will seem a little old-fashioned now. It is not pointed especially toward architecture but rather at travel.

Mumford, Lewis. *The City in History* (New York: Harcourt Brace, 1961).
Peruse with caution, although this is a *must* book by one of our greatest polemical and critical historians. It concerns the city more than architecture, but has much explanation of the social conditions that produced the latter. It has traps for the novice and the unwary, but fewer than Spengler, Toynbee, or Pareto. Look at some cities and think about them before reading.

————. *Sticks and Stones,* 1st ed. (New York: Dover, 1954).
Mumford's best book on architecture.

Ruskin, John. *The Seven Lamps of Architecture* (New York: Wiley, 1849).
If you haven't read it already, it may be too late. I need add nothing to the spate of pro and con things that have been written about this architectural moralist.

Scott, Geoffrey. *The Architecture of Humanism* (Garden City, N.Y.: Doubleday, 1954).
Highly recommended for the perspective it throws on polemic faddism in architectural writing, with special reference to Ruskin but very applicable to much of today's writing.

Shirakawa, Yoshikazu. *Himalayas* (New York: Abrams, 1973; original Japanese edition, Tokyo: Shogakukan Publishing Co., 1971).
This mammoth book, mostly of full- or double-page color photographs by a brilliant mountain photographer, contains numerous demonstrations of my point that mountains are superior to architecture.

Zucker, Paul. *Town and Square: From the Agora to the Village Green* (New York: Columbia University Press, 1959).
A classic work on the urban aspects of architecture, more literal and factual than Mumford.

Ancient West Asian

Culican, William. *The Medes and the Persians* (New York: Praeger, 1965).
Offers a sound historical background.

Frankfort, Henri. *The Art and Architecture of the Ancient Orient* (Baltimore: Penguin, 1955).
A classic, and better reading than some of the other Penguins.

Giedion, Sigfried. *The Eternal Present*, vol. II, *The Beginnings of Architecture* (New York: Pantheon, 1964).
For comment see Giedion listing under Egypt, although this volume has a good deal about the Hittites also.

Kramer, Samuel Noah. *History Begins at Sumer* (New York: Doubleday Anchor, 1959).
Popular.

Woolley, C. Leonard. *Ur of the Chaldees* (New York: Norton, 1965).
A pioneering classic, now somewhat criticized for its overenthusiasm and here and there for its deviations from what later excavations suggest.

Baroque

Holt, Elizabeth G. *A Documentary History of Art*, vol. II, *Michelangelo, Mannerists, Baroque, 18th Century* (Garden City, N.Y.: Doubleday, 1957–58).
Quotations from men and documents of the times—a reference work rather than one for cover-to-cover reading.

Kaufman, Emile. *Architecture in the Age of Reason* (Cambridge, Mass.: Harvard University Press, 1955).
Another classic. Very scholarly and not quite bedside reading.

Portoghesi, Paolo. *Roma Barocca: The History of an Architectonic Culture*, translated by Barbara Luigia La Penta (Cambridge, Mass.: M.I.T. Press, 1970).
A beautiful, interesting book, containing as provocative pictures of the time as one could find. The text is as controversial as the illustrations are beautiful.

Tapié, Victor L. *The Age of Grandeur: Baroque Art and Architecture*, translated by A. Ross Williamson (New York: Praeger, 1961).
Clear, readable, and excellent. Probably the best single book on the Baroque for you and me.

Wittkower, Rudolf. *Art and Architecture in Italy, 1600–1750*, 2d ed. (Baltimore: Penguin, 1954).
Again a first-class work by a first-class scholar, but better for information than for excitement.

Byzantine

Hamilton, George H. *The Art and Architecture of Russia* (Baltimore: Penguin, 1954).
The standard work; straightforward.

Kostof, Spiro. *Caves of God: The Monastic Environment of Byzantine Cappadocia* (Cambridge, Mass.: M.I.T. Press, 1972).

About cave churches, and very well done. Shrewd insights and covers more ground, if tangentially, than the title suggests.

Krautheimer, Richard. *Early Christian and Byzantine Architecture* (Baltimore: Penguin, 1965).
Well written, scholarly, and clear. Also comprehensive, with more about outlying areas than most works include. Provides an excellent explanation of the evolution of the early Christian basilica and also a generous coverage of "little" as well as "big" Byzantine architecture.

MacDonald, William. *Early Christian and Byzantine Architecture* (New York: Braziller, 1962).
Well done, but, like most of this series, too brief.

Procopius of Caesarea. *Works,* vol. III, *Buildings* (Cambridge, Mass.: Harvard University Press, 1940). Translated by H. B. Dewing with the collaboration of Glanville Downey.
Well-known sycophantic classic about the deeds of Justinian. Not very amusing unless to scholars. Like many books written by men about buildings of their own time, it assumes on the part of readers familiarity with facts generally only a contemporary would know.

Egyptian

Breasted, James Henry. *A History of Egypt from the Earliest Times to the Persian Conquest* (New York: Bantam, 1964).
The classic work. Though contradicted here and there by contemporary scholars (it was first published in 1905) and later evidence, it is still generally sound and quite readable.

Drower, Margaret S. *Egypt in Color* (New York: McGraw-Hill, 1964).
Handsome color plates and interesting text.

Gardiner, Sir Alan. *Egypt of the Pharaohs* (London: Oxford, 1964).
Quite stiff going for the general reader, even though a classic and shorter than Breasted.

Gayet-Tancrède, Paul. *The Glory of Egypt,* translated by J. E. Manchip-White (New York: Vanguard, 1956).
Handsome pictures, rhapsodic and amusing text.

Giedion, Sigfried. *The Eternal Present,* vol. II, *The Beginnings of Architecture* (New York: Pantheon, 1964).
Concentration on Egypt, but much on Sumer and Akkad as well. Giedion spent a great deal of time with the French restorers of Saqqara and the work reflects this, with Giedion's personal enthusiasms often unproved. Excellent photographs, several by Giedion himself.

Posener, Georges, Sauneron Serge, and Jean Yoyotte. *A Dictionary of Egyptian Civilization,* translated by Alix Macfarlane (London: Methuen, 1962).
Really an encyclopedia rather than a dictionary, and the better thereby. A good work to own, and it may indeed be the best quick way for a layman to start on Egypt.

Ranke, Hermann. *The Art of Ancient Egypt* (Vienna: Phaidon, 1936).

Only fair, though good enough to be included here. More on art than on architecture.

Smith, W. Stevenson. *The Art and Architecture of Ancient Egypt* (Baltimore, Md.: Penguin, 1958).
Serious and reliable and thorough.

Wilson, John A. *Signs and Wonders upon Pharaoh* (Chicago: University of Chicago Press, 1964).
A history of the archeologists working in Egypt, and, as such, illuminating.

Gothic

Adams, Henry. *Mont Saint Michel and Chartres* (Boston: Houghton Mifflin, 1963).
A beautifully written, loving account, often apocryphal, of two of the great monuments of the French Middle Ages. Though it will seem romantic now, and even at times deceptive, it is a great classic and should be read.

Cook, G. H. *The English Cathedral Through the Centuries* (London: Phoenix, 1957).
Interesting narrative, blow by blow, church by church, with many details of medieval practice, religious and secular.

Coulton, G. G. *Medieval Village, Manor and Monastery* (New York: Harper, 1960).
More about the economic and social organization of the English Middle Ages than about the architectural achievements.

Cox, J. C., and C. B. Ford. *Parish Churches* (London: Batsford, 1961).
Accurate enough but only modestly readable. Inferior illustrations by today's standards.

Focillon, Henri. *The Art of the West in the Middle Ages*, vol. II, *Gothic Art* (London: Phaidon, 1963).
Perhaps controversial in part, but most distinguished and readable.

Frankl, Paul. *Gothic Architecture* (Baltimore: Penguin, 1962).
Highly serious and studious, fairly technical study. Much emphasis, perhaps overemphasis, on Gothic structure.

Golding, William. *The Spire* (New York: Harcourt Brace, 1964).
A convincing novel about the ambitions of a cathedral dean to build the highest tower in Christendom (Salisbury?), and those who were destroyed by it.

Harvey, John. *English Cathedrals* (London: Batsford, 1961).
Much the same comment as for Cox, supra.

Holt, Elizabeth G. *A Documentary History of Art*, vol. I, *Middle Ages and Renaissance*.
See *Baroque* listing.

Le Goff, Jacques. *La Civilisation de l'Occident médiéval* (Paris: Arthaud, 1964).
But Romanesque too. This is a remarkable and handsome book for those who can read its easy French. It provides a splendid background for the under-

standing of medieval architecture and other aspects of medieval life. The pictures are unusual—good quality and helpfully captioned. The subject organization is also helpful, and there are excellent chronological tables.

Lethaby, William Richard. *Medieval Art: From the Peace of the Church to the Eve of the Renaissance, 312 to 1350,* 3d ed. (New York: Philosophical Library, 1950).
Sound, but perhaps not ingratiating to a lay reader.

Mâle, Emile. *L'art religieux de XIIIe siècle en France* (Paris: Colin, 1925).

————. *L'art religieux de la fin du Moyen Age* (Paris: Colin, 1925).
These are the last two volumes of a great three-volume work which is almost certain to produce fans of iconography among those who can read French (which is not, by the way, difficult in these works). Unhappily, only the second volume (thirteenth century) has been translated, and this is a pity since, despite the elegance of thirteenth-century iconography, the archaic treatments of the twelfth century are far more powerful and exciting even though less refined as to their sculpture.

Panofsky, Erwin. *Abbot Suger on the Abbey Church of St-Denis and Its Art Treasures* (Princeton, N.J.: Princeton University Press, 1946).
A fascinating historical narrative about the creation of a single landmark building and its maker. Highly recommended.

————. *Gothic Architecture and Scholasticism* (New York: Meridian, 1960).
An intellectual analysis of great interest, preferably to be read after personal experience of some French Gothic. It is a full exposition of the Thomistic interpretation of French Gothic architecture, which is not so much an explanation of how Gothic came about as it is of how Gothic was related to the spirit of the philosophy of the times.

Temko, Allan. *Notre-Dame of Paris: The Biography of a Cathedral* (New York: Viking, 1959).
Derivative and overly in love with Maurice Sully, but good and useful reading, and written with enthusiasm and skill.

Von Simson, Otto Georg. *The Gothic Cathedral* (New York: Harper Torchbooks, 1964).
Another classic, most interesting for its theory of Gothic light.

Webb, Geoffrey. *Architecture in Britain: The Middle Ages* (Baltimore: Penguin, 1956).
A standard Penguin.

White, John. *Art and Architecture in Italy, 1250–1400* (Baltimore: Penguin, 1966).
A standard Penguin.

Greek

Anderson, William J., and R. Phené Spiers. *The Architecture of Greece and Rome,* 2d ed. (London: Batsford, 1907).
A very old classic, no longer of first priority for general readers.

Dickinson, G. Lowes. *The Greek View of Life,* 22d ed. (London: Methuen, 1949).

One of several very good interpretations of Greek life by English scholars, who seem to have had an affinity for it.

Dinsmoor, William Bell. *The Architecture of Ancient Greece,* 3d ed. (London: Batsford, 1950).
Still the best source for a comparative study of all the extant Greek temples.

Hamilton, Edith. *The Greek Way to Western Civilization* (New York: Mentor, 1948).
An extremely amiable classic by a Danaophile.

Kitto, H. D. F. *The Greeks* (Baltimore: Penguin, 1952).
Another of the English classics about ancient Greek life. Reliable but brief.

Lawrence, A. W. *Greek Architecture* (Baltimore: Penguin, 1957).
Reliable and dull. Standard Penguin.

Livingstone, Sir Richard W. *The Greek Genius and Its Meaning to Us* (London: Oxford, 1951).
Still another of the classic English interpretations of classic life—by one of those who loved it most.

Roebuck, Carl (ed.). *The Muses at Work* (Cambridge, Mass.: M.I.T. Press, 1969).
A scholarly account of the arts, crafts, and professions in Ancient Greece and Rome. Second-round reading.

Scully, Vincent. *The Earth, the Temple, and the Gods* (New Haven, Conn.: Yale University Press, 1962).
Well researched and interestingly written, but perhaps conceals some booby traps.

Zimmern, Sir Alfred. *The Greek Commonwealth: Politics and Economics in Fifth-Century Athens,* 5th ed. (London: Oxford, 1952).
Another of the great British commentaries, perhaps the best because of its sobriety, to be followed by Hamilton, Livingstone, Kitto, and Dickinson in that order. But all these tell us more about the people who built the temples than about the temples themselves, and for specifics Dinsmoor is still the main piece, with the obligatto by Scully.

Indian

Rowland, Benjamin. *The Art and Architecture of India* (Baltimore: Penguin, 1956).
The best of an unduly scanty literature. Better reading than the usual Penguin.

Islamic

Hill, Derek, and Oleg Graber. *Islamic Architecture and Its Decoration* (Chicago: University of Chicago Press, 1964).
Detailed with pictures of many remote and much-damaged Islamic monuments.

Kuran, Aptullah. *The Mosque in Early Ottoman Architecture* (Chicago: University of Chicago Press, 1968).
Interesting, providing many insights into Islamic architecture, even that which is not Ottoman. Provides abundant well-drawn plans.

Scherr-Thoss, Sonia P., and Hans C. Scherr-Thoss. *Design and Color in Islamic Architecture* (Washington: Smithsonian Institute Press, 1968).
Probably the best book to start with. The text nearly matches the beautiful photographs. The emphasis is on decorative treatments rather than on plans and structure, but it remains an elegantly useful book to look at or to own.

Japanese

Fukuyama, Toshio, and Noboru Kawazoe. *Nihon no Yashiro: Ise* (Tokyo: 1962).
Means "Japan's Shrines: Ise." Not translated, but it is such a classic that I dare not omit it lest there be a Japanese reader in the house.

Hearn, Lafcadio. *Japan: An Attempt at an Interpretation* (Rutland, Vermont: Tuttle, 1965).
A famous American classic from an earlier time.

Kojiro, Yuichiro. *Forms in Japan*, translated by Kenneth Yasuda (Honolulu: East-West Center Press, 1965).
Interesting thesis and beautiful pictures. The "forms" are of all sorts of things ranging over a wide field of subjects.

Maraini, Fosco. *Meeting with Japan* (New York: Viking, 1960).
The book is thoroughly personal but very insightful, and even better than the same writer's account of the Italian ascent of K-2.

Noma, Seiroku. *The Arts of Japan, Ancient and Medieval*, 2d ed., translated and adapted by John Rosenfield (Tokyo: Kodansha International, 1968), vol. I. Photographs by Takahashi Bin.
Handsome and informative. Fine pictures, suggestive *aperçus*.

Sitwell, Sacheverell. *The Bridge of the Brocade Sash* (Cleveland, Ohio: World, 1959).
Another sensitive traveler who writes well, but with a little less feel for Japan than Maraini.

Statler, Oliver. *Japanese Inn* (New York: Randon House, 1961).
Good reading and something more.

Tange, Kenzo. *Katsura* (New Haven, Conn.: Yale University Press, 1960).
Beautiful pictures and adequate text.

———— **and Noboru Kawazoe.** *Ise: Prototype of Japanese Architecture* (Cambridge, Mass.: M.I.T. Press, 1965). Photographs by Yoshio Watanabe.
A great book, well written and beautifully illustrated. The best introduction to the Ise shrines.

Warner, Langdon. *The Enduring Art of Japan* (New York: Grove, 1952).
A well-established classic.

Modern

Chapman, Joan Margaret, and Brian Chapman. *The Life and Times of Baron Haussmann* (London: Weidenfeld and Nicolson, 1957).
A clear and consistently interesting narrative about this fabulous builder of Paris in France's Second Empire.

Doxiadis, Constantinos A. *Ekistics: An Introduction to the Science of Human Settlements* (New York: Oxford, 1968).
An important if unproved theory for our day by a serious man who is also a successful entrepreneur. At its best when least technical, but is often technical with bold extrapolations.

Giedion-Welcker, Carola. *Park Guell de A. Gaudi* (Barcelona: Ediciones Poligrafa, 1966).
A handsome treatment of one of Gaudi's most ingratiating achievements.

Hitchcock, Henry-Russell. *Architecture: Nineteenth and Twentieth Centuries* (Baltimore: Penguin, 1958).
Hitchcock is a scholarly authority, and this is a better than average Penguin, though stronger on the buildings themselves than on the social climate which brought them into being.

Jacobs, Jane. *Death and Life of Great American Cities* (New York: Random House, 1961).
Interesting and fresh but very personal and opinionated. Antimegalopolis, written in praise of the neighborhood. Possibly Utopian in its extrapolation of satisfactory urban enclaves to provide patterns for all modern cities.

Jeanneret-Gris, Charles Edouard [Le Corbusier]. *My Work,* translated by James Palmes (London: Architectural Press, 1960).

————. *Oeuvre complète, 1952–1957* (New York: Whitten Born, 1957).

————. *Quand les cathédrales étaient blanches: voyage au pays des timides* (Paris: Gauthier, 1965).
A consequence of Corbusier's first visit to America.

Madsen, S. Tschudi. *Art Nouveau,* translated by R. I. Christopherson (London: Weidenfeld and Nicolson, 1967).
Very good on a special, important, and not very long-lived moment in the modern movement.

Musgrave, Clifford. *The Pictorial History of Brighton* (London: Pitkin, 1964).
A good example of the Pitkin Pictorial series, and an excellent introduction to the Royal Pavilion at Brighton.

Safdie, Moshe. *Beyond Habitat* (Cambridge, Mass.: M.I.T. Press, 1970).
Easy to disagree with, but provocative.

Schuyler, Montgomery. *American Architecture and other Writings,* William Jordy and Ralph Coe (eds.) (New York: Atheneum, 1964).
Originally published in two volumes, but abridged by Jordy, this contains the best essays on premodern American architecture.

Soleri, Paolo. *Arcology: The City in the Image of Man* (Cambridge, Mass.: M.I.T. Press, 1969).
An imaginative, elaborate, well-illustrated development of a dubious theory as to what future cities should be like, with which one must be familiar to be *au courant,* even though it may make him wish for the return of Thoreau.

Venturi, Robert. *Complexity and Contradiction in Architecture* (New York: Museum of Modern Art and Graham Foundation for Advanced Studies in the Fine Arts, 1966).

Amusingly written balderdash, much praised by the avant-garde at Yale. The author has built so little that it is hard to tell how far his tongue is in his cheek, but one guesses regretfully that it is not there at all.

Note: There is really no good book on the modern movement since the dissolution of the Bauhaus, now more than thirty years ago, though there have been serious tries. Perhaps it is still too soon. Giedion's *Space, Time and Architecture* cited *supra*; the personal writings of Frank Lloyd Wright and Le Corbusier; Carl Condit's post-Giedion work on Chicago; and the enormous and expensive book on the Bauhaus published by the M.I.T. Press cover well enough the period until the dissolution, although there are countless other writings by men like Eliel Saarinen, Richard Neutra, Bruno Taut, Russell Hitchcock, and many more.

For our last quarter century one would do best, until the right book is written, to examine the back files of architectural journals, to keep abreast of the criticisms provided by Wolf von Eckhart in the *Washington Post* and especially by Ada Louise Huxtable in the *New York Times*, and to keep one's own eyes open as one goes about. Some additional light may be thrown by the monographs about individual modern architects in the Braziller series, although naturally these date very rapidly and unfortunately not all reach the quality of Norma Evenson's books on Brasília and Chandigarh.

Pre-Hispanic America

Bernal, Ignacio. *Ancient Mexico in Color* (London: Thames and Hudson, 1968).
Handsome and authentic. The carefully selected color plates are illuminated by brief but penetrating comment by a great and devoted authority.

Bingham, Hiram. *Lost City of the Incas* (New York: Atheneum, 1963).
A romantic tale of discovery worth a winter's evening, but not to be swallowed whole.

Bushnell, G. H. S. *Ancient Arts of the Americas* (New York: Praeger, 1965).
Very handsome treatment by an authority and, followed by Bernal (supra), a good starting work.

————. *Peru* (New York: Praeger, 1957).
A good starting work.

Caso, Alfonso. *The Aztecs: People of the Sun*, translated by Lowell Dunham (Norman, Okla.: University of Oklahoma Press, 1958).
A very popular account of a complicated people.

De Castillo, Bernal Diaz. *The Discovery and Conquest of Mexico* (New York: Farrar, Straus & Cudahy, 1956).
A very readable account by a man who was there.

Covarrubias, Miguel. *The Eagle, the Jaguar, and the Serpent* (New York: Knopf, 1954).
Handsome, enthusiastic, and informative. Goes well beyond architecture. Time has altered some of the views expressed.

De la Vega, Garcilaso. *The Incas*, Alain Gheerbrant (ed.) (New York: Avon, 1961).

Highly readable, though *cum grano salis,* by a man who was around at the time, but very young. The work is full of hearsay and the writing was done in Spain nearly fifty years after the author had last seen Spain.

Kidder, Alfred II, and Carlos Samayoa Chinchilla. *The Art of the Ancient Maya.* (New York: Crowell, 1959).
A studious work much referred to in other scholarly texts but also containing perceptive insights transcending the scholarly.

Kubler, George. *The Art and Architecture of Ancient America* (Baltimore: Penguin, 1962). By an established authority. Thoroughly sound and much more readable than most of the Penguins.

De Landa, Diego. *Yucatan Before and After the Conquest,* translated by William Gates (Baltimore: Maya Society, Johns Hopkins, 1937). (A more recent and scholarly translation was edited by Alfred M. Tozzer, *Peabody Museum of American Archeology and Ethnology Papers,* vol. 18, Harvard University Press, Cambridge, Mass., 1941.)
Landa was a Spanish bishop of Merida at the time who admired the achievements of the Mayans yet burned nearly all their codices in his determination to Christianize Yucatan and extirpate all "idolatrous writings."

Mason, J. Alden. *The Ancient Civilization of Peru* (Baltimore: Penguin, 1964).
A good Penguin.

Morley, Sylvanus Griswold. *The Ancient Maya* (Palo Alto, Calif.: Stanford University Press, 1946).
A respected scholar.

Prescott, William H. *Conquest of Peru,* revised and abridged by Victor W. Von Hagen (New York: Mentor, 1961).
A well-known classic.

Proskouriakoff, Tatiana. *An Album of Mayan Architecture* (Norman, Okla.: University of Oklahoma Press, 1963).
Good drawings of hypothetical reconstructions.

Rivet, Paul. *Les hauts lieux de l'histoire,* vol. IV, *Cités Maya,* Albert Champdor (ed.) (Paris: Albert Guillot, 1962).
Very French and very interesting, though perhaps apocryphal in spots.

Stephens, John L. *Incidents of Travel in Central America, Chiapas and Yucatan (1841)* and *Incidents of Travel in Yucatan* (Norman, Okla.: University of Oklahoma Press, 1962). Introduction and notes by Victor W. Von Hagen. Steel engravings by F. Catherwood.
Amusing account of a visit by an observant man long before the archeologists had gone to work. Amusing drawings characteristic of book illustration of the time and better than most.

Vaillant, George C. *The Aztecs of Mexico* (Baltimore: Penguin, 1955).
Well written.

Primitive

Allen, Edward. *Stone Shelters* (Cambridge, Mass.: M.I.T. Press, 1969).
Highly recommended as introduction to its subject.

Atkinson, R. J. C. *Stonehenge and Avebury and Neighboring Monuments* (London: H. M. Stationery Office, 1959).
Clear exposition of *one* of the prevailing theories.

Giedion, Sigfried. *The Eternal Present,* vol. I, *The Beginnings of Art* (New York: Pantheon, 1962).
This interesting volume relates largely, though not wholly, to the art of the Cave Periods, with special emphasis on Lascaux and Abbé Breuil.

Mission d'Enquête sur l'Habitat au Cameroun. *L'Habitat au Cameroun,* prepared by Jean-Pierre Béguin et al. (Paris: L'Office de la Recherche Scientifique Outre-Mer, Éditions de l'Union Française, 1952).
A handsome and informative book.

Newall, R. S. *Stonehenge, Wiltshire,* 3d ed. (London: H. M. Stationery Office, 1959).
To be used with, and sometimes against, Atkinson. I have omitted from the bibliography later texts advancing very controversial interpretations of what Stonehenge was for, but the reader who cares for bitterly antagonistic scholarly speculations can find much in the Stonehenge literature.

Renaissance

Burckhardt, Jacob. *The Civilization of the Renaissance in Italy* (New York: Phaidon, 1950).
Still a classic.

Holt, Elizabeth. *A Documentary History of Art,* vol. I, *Middle Ages and Renaissance.*
See *Baroque* listing.

McCarthy, Mary. *The Stones of Florence* (New York: Harcourt Brace, 1959).
Well-written bittersweetness by a woman who likes Florence more than she cares to admit.

——. *Venice Observed* (New York: Harcourt Brace, 1963).
Not quite as lovable as the book on Florence.

Morris, James. *The World of Venice* (New York: Pantheon, 1960).
Better than McCarthy on Venice, though quite reportorial.

Summerson, John. *Architecture in Britain, 1530–1830* (Baltimore: Penguin, 1954).
Distinguished work by a distinguished historian.

——. *Georgian London* (Baltimore: Penguin, 1963).
One of Summerson's most interesting works.

Vasari, George. *Lives of the Artists,* abridged and edited by Betty Burroughs (New York: Simon and Schuster, 1946).
Not as rewarding as the fame of its author would imply.

Wittkower, Rudolf. *Architectural Principles in the Age of Humanism* (London: Tiranti, 1952).
A classic for intellectuals.

Roman

Africa, Thomas W. *Rome of the Caesars* (New York: Wiley, 1965).
Popularly written.

Beyle, Marie Henri [Stendhal]. *Rome, Naples et Florence, en 1817,* texte présenté et annoté par Roland Beyer (Paris: Editions Julliard, 1964).
Personal views of a great writer who went to Rome time after time and wrote about each voyage, interestingly if from a French point of view which could never concede quite enough excellence to the Italians of any period.

Brown, Frank E. *Roman Architecture* (New York: Braziller, 1961).
Too brief, but reliable and readable, by a distinguished British authority on Rome.

Carcopino, Jérôme. *Daily Life in Ancient Rome,* translated by E. O. Lorimer (New Haven, Conn.: Yale University Press, 1965).
Good and reliable reading for general background.

Dill, Samuel. *Roman Society from Nero to Marcus Aurelius* (Cleveland: World, 1964).
Very substantial; a little harder going than Carcopino, q.v.

Gibbon, Edward. *The History of the Decline and Fall of the Roman Empire* (New York: Harper, 1880).
If you haven't read this by now, you probably never will. (Few *have* read it from cover to cover.)

MacDonald, William L. *The Architecture of the Roman Empire,* vol. I, *An Introductory Note* (New Haven, Conn.: Yale University Press, 1965).
First class in every way. It deals with only a few buildings, notably the Golden House of Nero, the Pantheon, and Trajan's Markets. It is so civilized in its coverage and so interesting that it is surely one of the first books to be read about Rome.

Mau, August. *Pompeii: Its Life and Art* (New York: Macmillan, 1907).
A much-referred-to classic that is also good reading.

Vitruvius. *The Ten Books on Architecture,* translated by Morris H. Morgan (New York: Dover, 1960).
I cannot say that this is really an earth-shaking book and in the Latin, at least, it is awkwardly written. But it has been one of the most influential books in architectural history, of interest now probably only to professionals and by no means to all of them.

Wheeler, Robert Eric Mortimer. *Roman Africa in Color* (New York: McGraw-Hill, 1966).
Wheeler is a distinguished authority who writes well. The colored pictures are spectacular. It is by far the best introduction to Roman North Africa and will probably make you want to go there at once, despite warnings in my text not to go before you have visited Rome itself.

———. *Roman Art and Architecture* (New York: Praeger, 1964).
Another attractive and useful book by this British authority, not primarily a picture book but good illustrations to illumine an interesting text.

Romanesque

Aubert, Marcel. *L'Eglise de Conques.* Petites monographies des grands édifices de la France (Paris: Laurens, 1939).
One of the many French monographs mentioned earlier. Listed here because of its long treatment of Conques, though better French monographs are perhaps those on Chartres, Bourges, Amiens, and Laon.

Barbier, Georges. *Martyre de Saulieu (Saint-Andoche)* (Paris: Zodiaque, no. 24, January, 1955).
Excellent photographs of most of the sculptures of Saulieu, notably the capitals.

Craplet, Chanoine Bernard. *Auvergne Romane* (Paris: Zodiaque, Special Christmas number, 1955).
Illuminating about one regional phase of the French Romanesque.

Conant, Kenneth John. *Carolingian and Romanesque Architecture, 800–1200* (Baltimore: Penguin, 1959).
About as good a book on the special architecture of this time as you will find. You may have to go to a library, but it is worth the trouble.

Deschamps, Paul (dirigeur). *Vézelay* (Paris: Editions Tel, 1952).
One of the very best monographs, with good illustrations dealing with one of the greatest French Romanesque churches.

Focillon, Henri. *The Art of the West in the Middle Ages,* vol. I, *Romanesque Art,* Jean Bony (ed.) (London: Phaidon, 1963).
Perhaps controversial in part, but a most distinguished and readable, even poetic, work. I would start my reading about the Romanesque with this work, but many would disagree, some, for example, preferring Conant for his sobriety and his rejection of aesthetic philosophical flights. It *is* strong against the defenseless. The same comments apply to volume II, on the Gothic. Bony's introduction is superb.

Horn, Walter, and Ernest Born. *The Barns of the Abbey of Beaulieu at Its Granges of Great Cornwall and Beaulieu-St-Léonard's* (Berkeley, Calif.: University of California Press, 1965).
A distinguished monograph by an excellent scholar and an excellent illustrator. Though apparently very specialized to the barns of Cistercian abbeys, it is so well written and so beautifully presented both in photographs and drawings that it will be a delight to the general reader and offer him a clear understanding of the wooden truss systems which culminated in the hammer-beams.

Kelly, Amy. *Eleanor of Aquitaine and the Four Kings* (New York: Vintage, 1957).
Excellent reading for general atmosphere.

Mâle, Emile. *L'art religieux de XIIIᵉ siècle* (Paris: Colin, 1924).
Detailed, fascinating explanation of iconography and its sources. See comments under *Gothic* listing.

Quintinalle, Arturo Carlo. *Il Duomo di Modena* (Florence: Sadea, 1965).
Another outstandingly handsome monograph, beautifully illustrating in color one of the greatest of the Italian Romanesque buildings, Emilian, not Lombard.

INDEX
PART I: PERSONS

- Aalto, Alvar, 61, 64, 96, 123, 428, 430, 549, 557, 568
Abbey, Edwin Austin, 570
Abelard, Peter, 346
Abraham, Pol, 378
Adams, Henry, 4, 69, 377, 385, 496
Adams, John, 564
Aegisthus, 246
Aeschylus, 167, 246
Agamemnon, 18, 246, 249, 276, 548
Agnew, Spiro T., 572
Agrippa, Marcus Vipsanius, 296
Akbar, 432, 435
Akhenaton, 254
- Alan of Walsingham, 118
Albers, Josef, 429
- Alberti, Leone Battista, 92, 169, 443–449, 469, 476, 488, 506
Alcibiades, 296
Alexander III of Macedon (the Great), 216, 224, 265, 295, 532, 534, 575
Alexander VII, Pope (Chigi), 471, 558n.
- Amadeo, Giovanni Antonio, 449
Ambrose, Saint, 56
Amenemhet I, 254, 255
- Amenhotep, 254, 257, 259, 453
Amenophis III, 257–260
Anacreon, 273
Anderson, William J., 299n.
Angelico, Fra (Guido di Pietro, dit), 39
Anne, Queen, of England, 119
Annobal, Rufus, 315
- Anthemius of Tralles, 44, 330, 333, 453
Antonius Pius, 309
- Apollodorus of Damascus, 321, 454, 573
Apuleius, Lucius, 296
Aquinas, Saint Thomas, 381

Archilochus, 273
Archimedes, 323, 454
- Architects Collaborative, 536
Argan, Giulio Claudio, 446
Aristophanes, 269
Aristotle, 280
Arnold, Matthew, 68, 586
Arp, Jean (Hans), 570
Artaxerxes I, 187, 265
- Asam brothers, 486
Asklepios, 209, 271, 515
Assurbanipal, 42
Atkinson, R. J., 158n.
Augustus, Caesar (Gaius Octavius), 284, 298, 303, 304, 324, 333, 448, 574
Aurangzeb, 432

Bacon, Francis, 1
Bach, Johann Sebastian, 487
- Baltard, Louis-Pierre, 574n.
Balzoni, Giovanni, 186
Banfield, Edward E., 565n.
Barnsdall, Aline, 573
- Barry, Sir Charles, 496
- Bathycles of Magnesia, 454
Beatus of Gaul, 46
Beauchamp, Bishop, 409
Becket, Saint Thomas à, 19, 25, 26, 350
Beethoven, Ludwig van, 519
Begon, Abbot of Conques, 454
Bellini, Giovanni, 27, 509
- Belluschi, Pietro, 498, 590, 592
Bemis, Albert Farwell, 408
Bernal, Ignacio, 172, 215, 226, 227n., 233, 235n., 243n.
Bernard, Saint, of Clairvaux, 346, 376

NOTE: *Persons* index includes clients, critics, and painters. The symbol • indicates an architect.

611

INDEX
PART II: BUILDINGS AND PLACES

Fontainebleau, Palais de, 124, 452
Fontevrault, Abbey, 343, 347
Fori Imperiali, Rome, 525
Fortuna Virilis, temple, Rome, 310
Forum Boarium, Rome, 310
Forum of Julius Caesar, Rome, 82
Forum of Trajan, Rome, 24, 81, 303, 311, 313, 325
Forum Romanum, Rome, 16, 24, 301–303, 307, 320, 550
Fountains Abbey, 347
Fredonia College, Library and Plaza, 501
Freiburg-am-Breisgau Cathedral, 94, 410
Freudenstadt, 66
Fuggerei, Augsburg, 66

Galla Placidia, Mausoleum of, Ravenna, 326, 336, 337
Gantt Building, St. Louis, 538
Geodesic domes, 37, 67, 92, 250, 580n., 582
Germigny-des-Prés, 363, 373
Gernrode, Abbey, 352n.
Ghirardelli Square, San Francisco, 536, 592
Giotto's Tower, Florence, 406, 445
Giralda, Seville, 410
Giudecca, Venice, 556
Glastonbury Abbey, 87, 347
Gloucester Cathedral, 22, 179, 371, 408
Goddard Library, Clark College, 501
Golden Gate Bridge, San Francisco, 552, 560
Golgotha Church, Jerusalem, 53
Gore Hall, Harvard University, 536
Goreme, 192
Götaplatsan, Göteborg, 550
Graduate School, Harvard University, 429
Gramercy Park, New York, 554
Grand Central Terminal, New York, 554
Grand College de Calatrava, 484
Grant Park, Chicago, 561n.
Gravedona, Italy, 368
Gray's Inn Hall, London, 117
Greek Orthodox Church, Copenhagen, 429
Green Park, London, 554, 561
Greensted Church, Essex, 111
Grosvenor Square, London, 554
Grotto of Lascaux, 182, 533
Guggenheim Museum, New York, 59
Gunbad-i-Kabus, Gurgan, 437
Gunbad-i-Surkh, Maragha, 440
Gwalior, temples, 189

Habitat '67, Montreal, 67, 541, 577, 580, 582
Haddon Hall, Derbyshire, 117
Hadrian's Villa, Tivoli, 301, 305, 320–322, 325, 525
Hadrian's Wall, England, 296
Hagia Sophia, Istanbul, 21, 44–46, 88, 90, 92, 93, 95, 328, 330–333, 338, 342, 434, 550
Halebid, Hoysalesvara Temple, 189
Hallidie Building, San Francisco, 62
Hampton Court Palace, 27, 38, 118
Harkness Tower, Yale University, 574
Hatshepsut, temple, Deir-el-Bahri, 39, 184, 187, 246, 256, 262–264, 522
Henry VII Chapel, Westminster Abbey, 22, 86, 179, 419, 521, 524
Hephaesteion (Theseion), Athens, 87, 268, 290n., 518
Hereford Cathedral, 22, 370, 371, 408, 534
Hesht Behest, Isfahan, 441n., 442
Hildesheim, Knockenhausern Amsthaus, 121
Hildesheim, St. Michael, 352n., 367
Hofbibliotek, Vienna, 485
Holborn, Staple Inn, 122
Ho-ry-u-ji monastery, Nara, 133, 147, 190
Hosios Demetrios, Salonika, 54
Hosios Loukas (Katholikon), Phocis, 192, 265, 338
Hosios Sergios and Partehos, Istanbul, 333
Hôtel de la Vrillière, Paris, 492
Hotel Fontainebleau, Miami, 589
House of the Filippini (Oratorians of San Filippo Neri), Rome, 489, 490
House of Jacques Coeur, Bourges, 425n.
Houses of Parliament, London, 317, 333, 521
Humayun's tomb, Delhi, 432, 436

Ibn Tulun Mosque, Cairo, 434
Il Gesu, Rome, 447, 473, 478, 485, 487, 488, 494
Imperial Hotel, Tokyo, 536
Inari shrine, 132
Independence Hall, Philadelphia, 538
Insulae, Roman, 66, 303
Ise shrines (Nairu and Geku), 6, 21, 30, 40, 110, 128, 136, 138–147, 189, 525, 589
Islamabad, 501
Ixworth, Norfolk, 116
Izumo shrine, 128, 140

ABOUT THE AUTHOR

JOHN BURCHARD was Dean of the School of Humanities and Social Science at M.I.T. from 1948 to 1964 and is a Fellow and former president (1954–1957) of the American Academy of Arts and Sciences and an honorary member of the American Institute of Architects. He has been visiting professor and later acting dean of the College of Environmental Design at the University of California, Berkeley. Among his many awards are the Presidential Medal for Merit (1948) and the Thomas Jefferson Medal in Architecture (Monticello, 1969); he was decorated as an Officier de l'Ordre des Arts et des Lettres (France, 1964). His articles on housing, library planning, architecture, urbanism, and cultural and educational subjects have appeared in such journals as *Architectural Forum*, *Architectural Record*, *Arts and Architecture*, *Casabella*, and *Daedalus*. Previous books include *The Architecture of America* (with Albert Bush-Brown), *Mid-Century* (ed.), *The Historian and the City* (with Oscar Handlin), and *The Voice of the Phoenix: Post-War Architecture in Germany*. He now resides with his wife, Marjorie, in Boston.

1 Taliesin West/*Hedrich-Blessing*

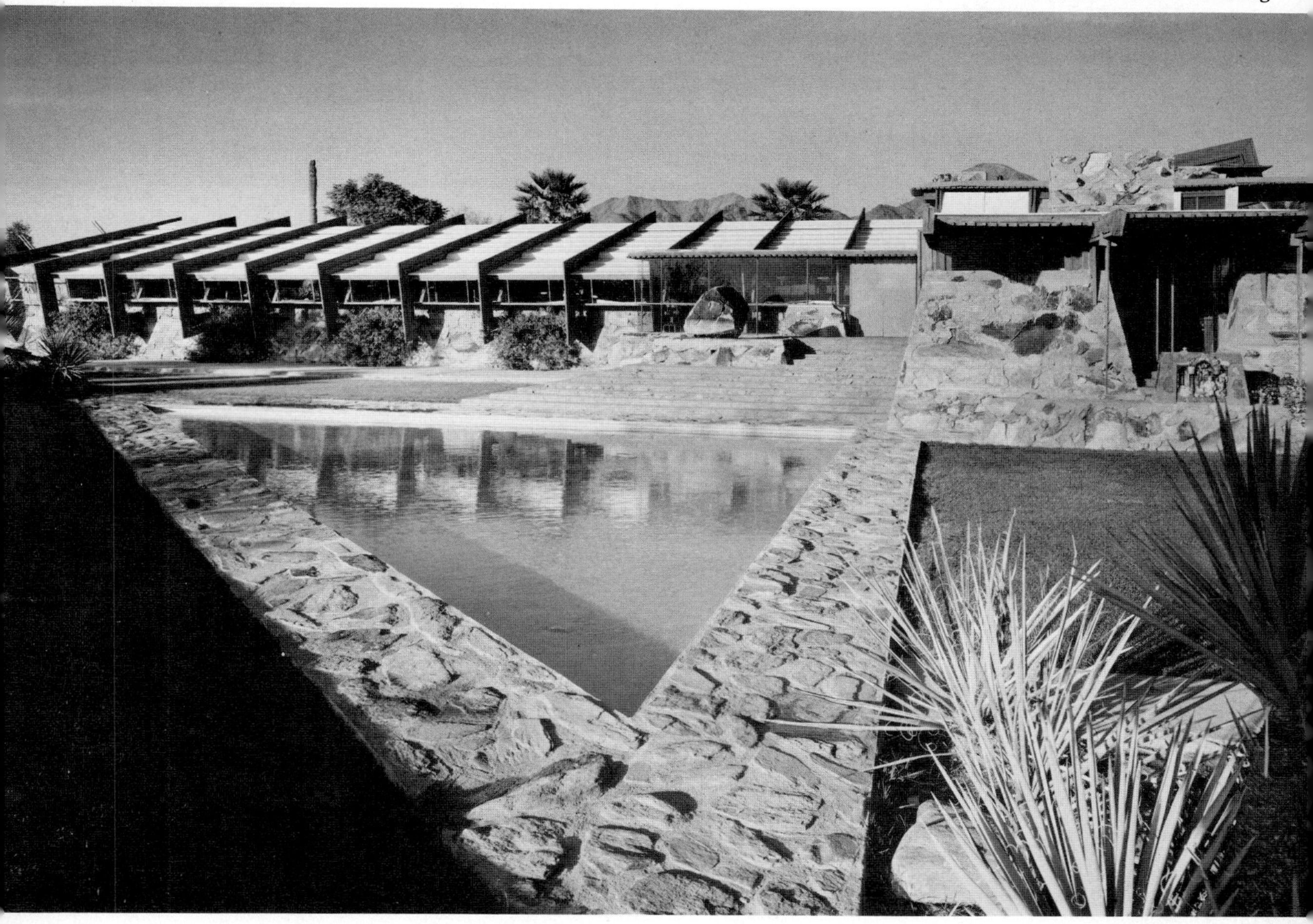

2 Canterbury Cathedral, plan
Fletcher 361B

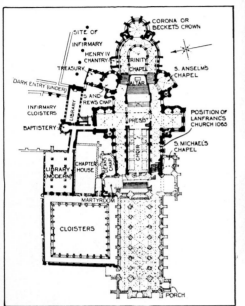

3 *"Falling Water"/Hedrich-Blessing*

4 Farm near Cisternino/*Edward Allen*

5 Royal Pavilion, Brighton, kitchen
OMIKRON

6 Royal Pavilion, Brighton
Mark Hewlett from OMIKRON

7 Stonehenge/*Mark Hewlett from* OMIKRON

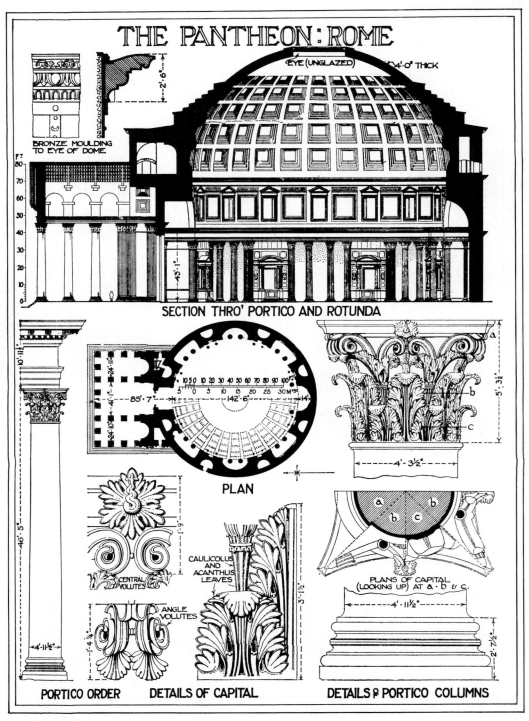

THE PANTHEON : ROME

EYE (UNGLAZED)   4'·0" THICK

BRONZE MOULDING TO EYE OF DOME

SECTION THRO' PORTICO AND ROTUNDA

PLAN

PORTICO ORDER   DETAILS OF CAPITAL   DETAILS OF PORTICO COLUMNS

CENTRAL VOLUTES

ANGLE VOLUTES

CAULICOLUS AND ACANTHUS LEAVES

PLANS OF CAPITAL (LOOKING UP) AT a·b & c

8 Pantheon, Rome, plan, section/*Fletcher 161 A,B,C,E*

9 Pantheon, Rome, interior
Tod from OMIKRON

10 Moissac, south portal
Caisse Nationale des Monuments Historiques

11 St-Etienne, Bourges, west portal, detail/*French Cultural Services*

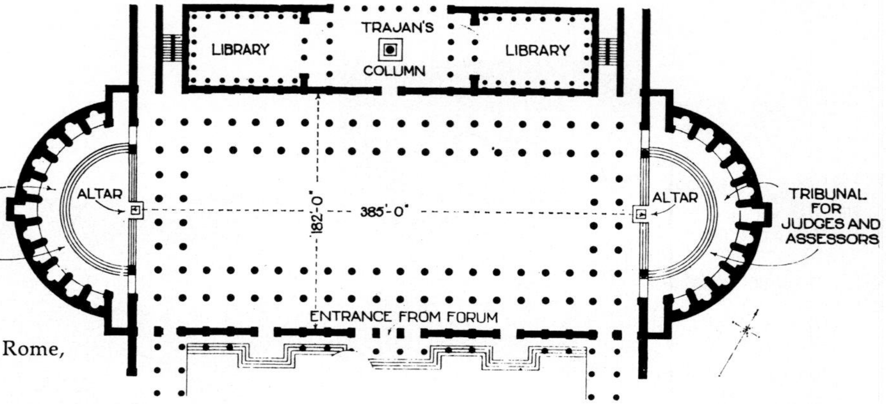
LIBRARY
TRAJAN'S
COLUMN
LIBRARY
TRIBUNAL FOR JUDGES AND ASSESSORS
ALTAR
182'-0"
385'-0"
ALTAR
TRIBUNAL FOR JUDGES AND ASSESSORS
ENTRANCE FROM FORUM

12 Basilica of Trajan, Rome, plan/*Fletcher 165B*

13 San Paolo fuori le Mura, Rome/*Fletcher 219D*

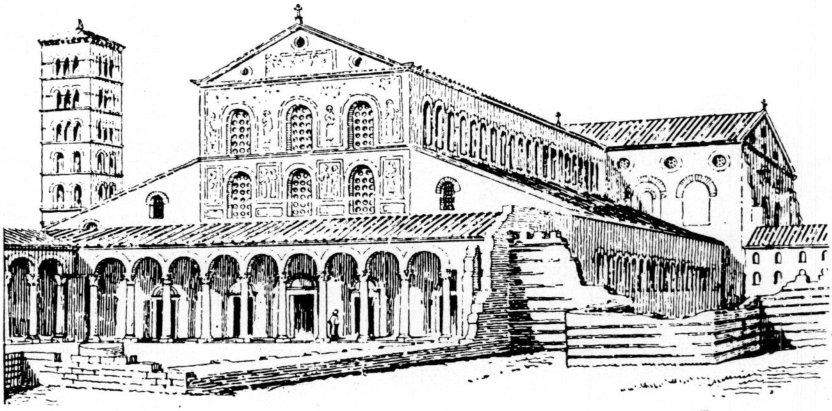

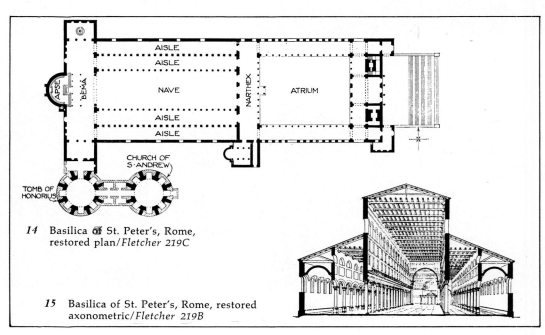

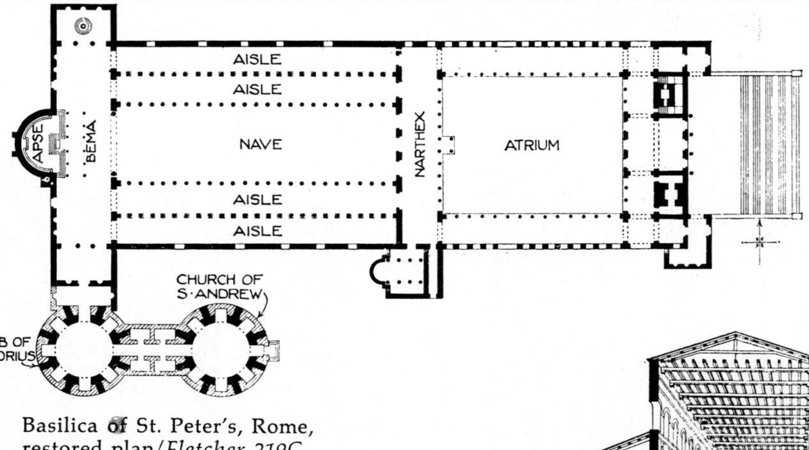
AISLE
AISLE
APSE
BEMA
NAVE
NARTHEX
ATRIUM
AISLE
AISLE
CHURCH OF S·ANDREW
TOMB OF HONORIUS

14 Basilica of St. Peter's, Rome, restored plan/*Fletcher 219C*

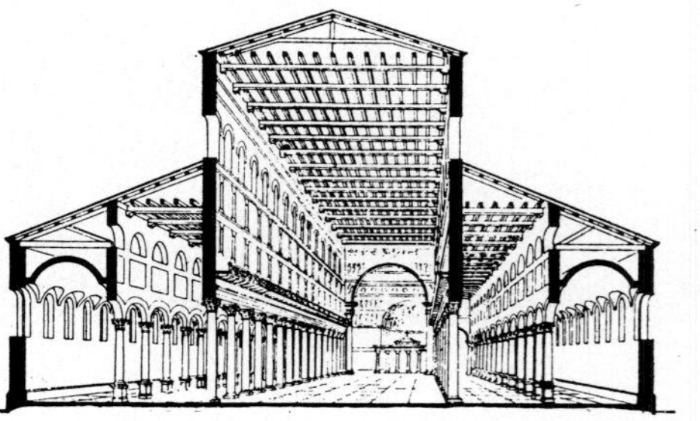

15 Basilica of St. Peter's, Rome, restored axonometric/*Fletcher 219B*

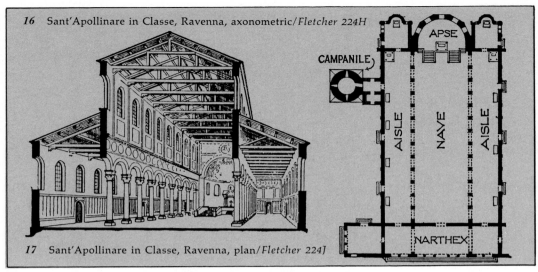

16 Sant'Apollinare in Classe, Ravenna, axonometric/*Fletcher 224H*

APSE

CAMPANILE

AISLE

NAVE

AISLE

NARTHEX

17 Sant'Apollinare in Classe, Ravenna, plan/*Fletcher 224J*

18 San Paolo fuori le Mura, Rome, axonometric
Fletcher 219F

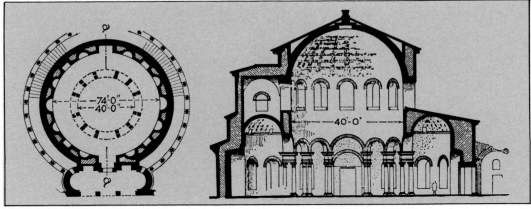

74'-0"
40'-0"

40'-0"

19 Santa Costanza, Rome, plan
Fletcher 233D

20 Santa Costanza, Rome, section
Fletcher 233B

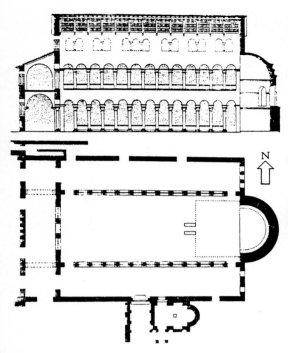

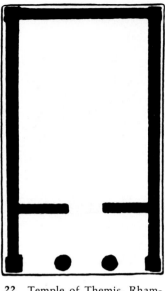

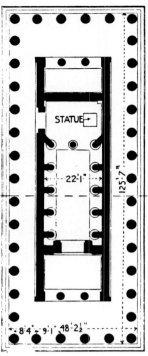

22 Temple of Themis, Rhamnus, plan/*Fletcher 82A*

21 Church of the Acheiropoeitos, Salonica, plan and section/*after Orlandos*

23 Temple of Apollo Epikourios, Bassae, plan/*Fletcher 97E*

24 Santa Sabina, nave/*Tod from* OMIKRON

25 Parthenon, Athens/OMIKRON

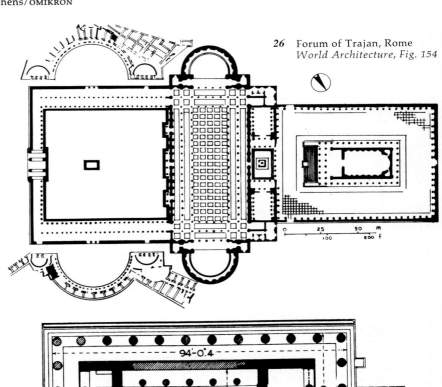

26 Forum of Trajan, Rome
World Architecture, Fig. 154

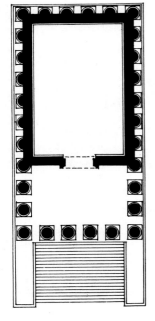

27 Maison Carrée, Nîmes, plan
World Architecture, Fig. 167

28 Temple of Aphaia, Aegina, plan
Fletcher 92H

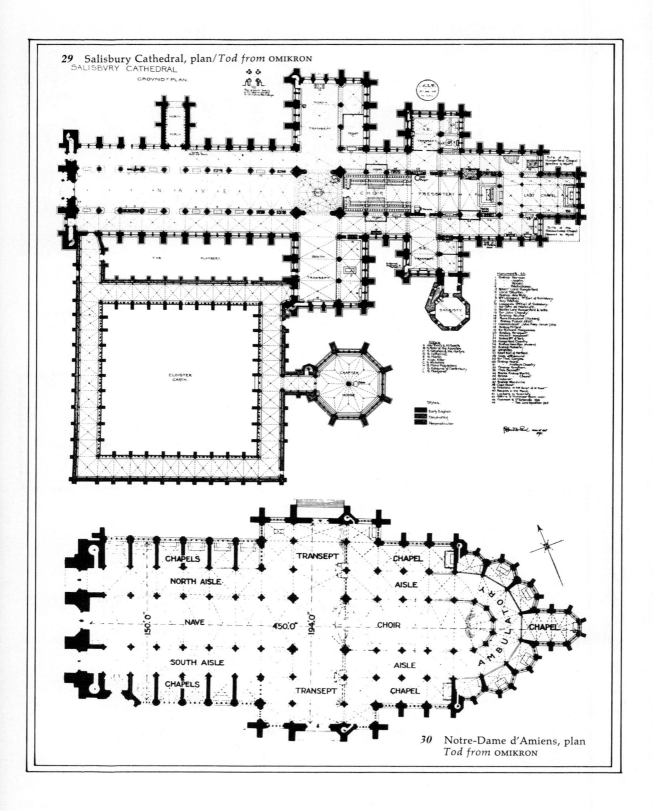

29 Salisbury Cathedral, plan/*Tod from* OMIKRON

30 Notre-Dame d'Amiens, plan
Tod from OMIKRON

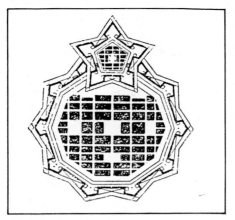
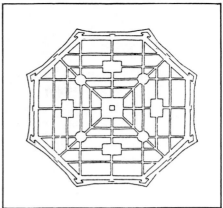

31 Plans of four "ideal" Renaissance cities
from Paul Zucker, Town and Square, Columbia University Press, 1959

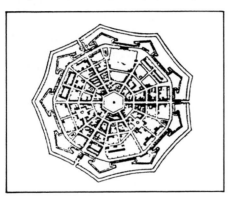
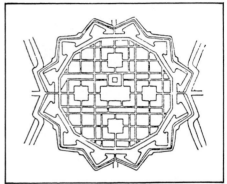

32 Parthenon, Athens. Half transverse sections through parthenos,
half through naos/*Fletcher 93F*

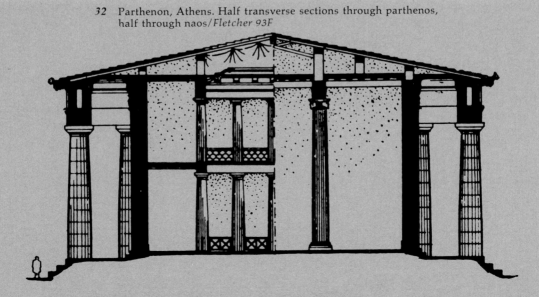

33 Ely Cathedral, interior bays, choir *Fletcher 442F*

34 Ely Cathedral, interior bays, presbytery *Fletcher 443K*

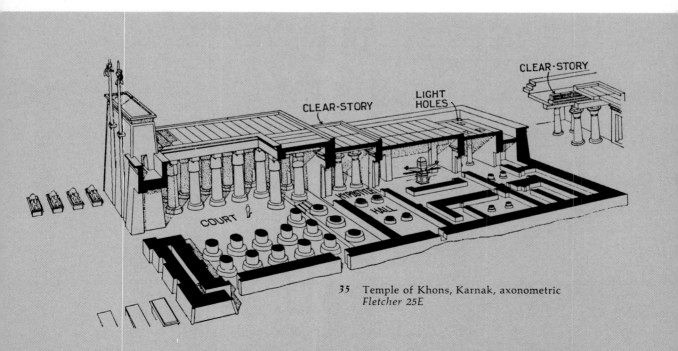

35 Temple of Khons, Karnak, axonometric *Fletcher 25E*

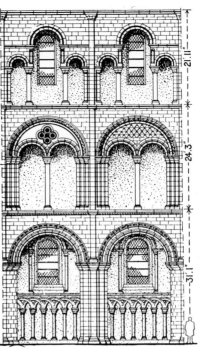

36 Winchester Cathedral, interior bays, nave/*Fletcher 443M*

37 Peterborough Cathedral, interior bays, choir
Fletcher 442B

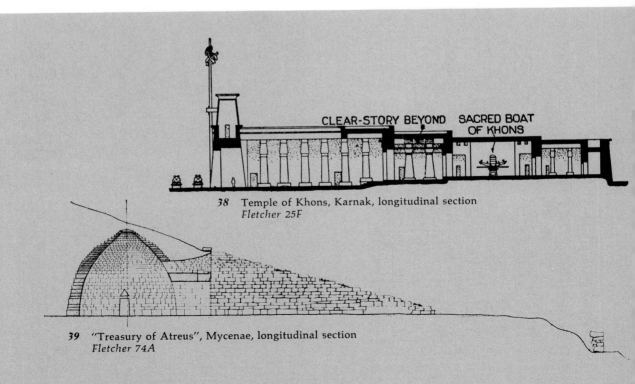

CLEAR-STORY BEYOND   SACRED BOAT OF KHONS

38 Temple of Khons, Karnak, longitudinal section
Fletcher 25F

39 "Treasury of Atreus", Mycenae, longitudinal section
Fletcher 74A

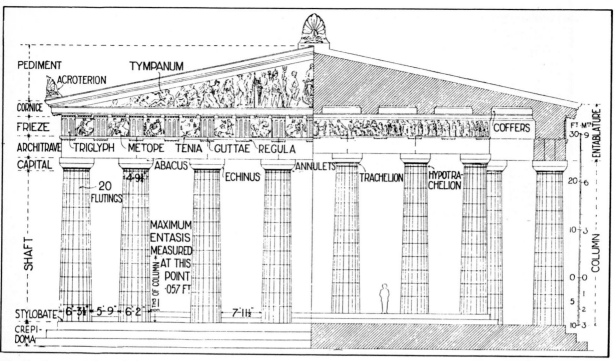

40 Parthenon, Athens, half elevation, half section
through portico showing elements of Doric order
Fletcher 85A,B

Opposite: 44 Stave church, Borgund/OMIKRON

42 Stave church, Urnes, carving older door/OMIKRON
41 Stave church, Hylestad, detail portal carving
OMIKRON

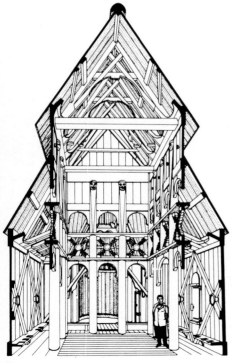

43 Stave church, Borgund, transverse section
World Architecture, Fig. 544

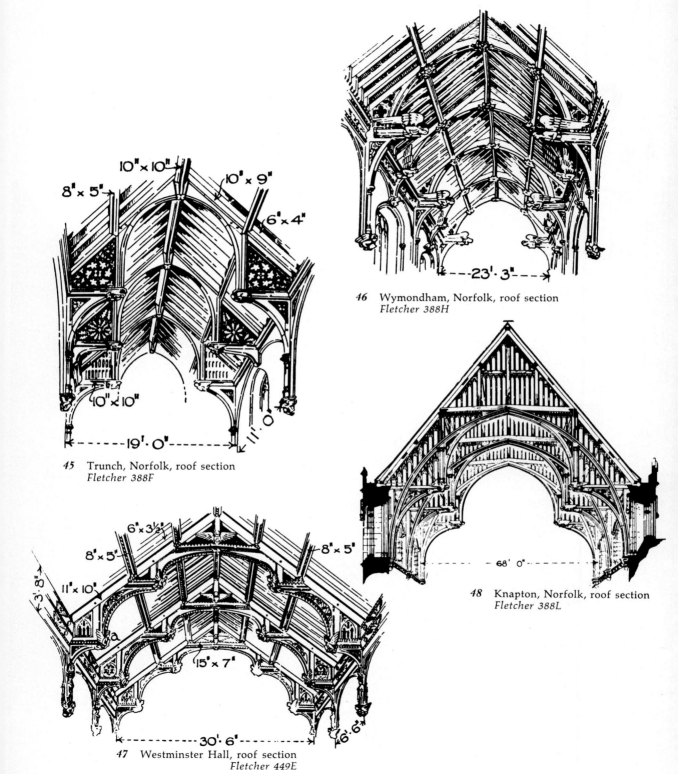

46 Wymondham, Norfolk, roof section
Fletcher 388H

23' · 3"

8" × 5"   10" × 10"   10" × 9"   6" × 4"

10" × 10"   19' · 0"   11' · 1"

45 Trunch, Norfolk, roof section
Fletcher 388F

68' 0"

48 Knapton, Norfolk, roof section
Fletcher 388L

6" × 3½"   8" × 5"
8" × 5"
3' · 8"   11" × 10"
15' × 7"
30' · 6"   6' · 6"

47 Westminster Hall, roof section
Fletcher 449E

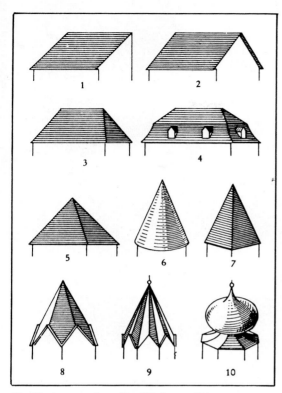

49 Various roof profiles/*Cichy, p. 424*

50 Eltham Palace, Kent, roof section
Fletcher 449G

36' 3"

51 Middle Temple, London, roof section
Fletcher 449H

40' 0"

53 Town Hall, Michelstadt/*Bildarchiv Foto Marburg*

Opposite: 52 Ely Cathedral, interior, octagon/OMIKRON

54 Queen's College, Cambridge, President's Lodge/*Royal Commission on Historical Monuments (England)*

55 Maison Kammerzell, Strasbourg
French Government Tourist Office

56 Rathaus and Stadtweinhaus, Münster
Bildarchiv Foto Marburg

57 Chinese frame construction/*World Architecture, Fig. 223*

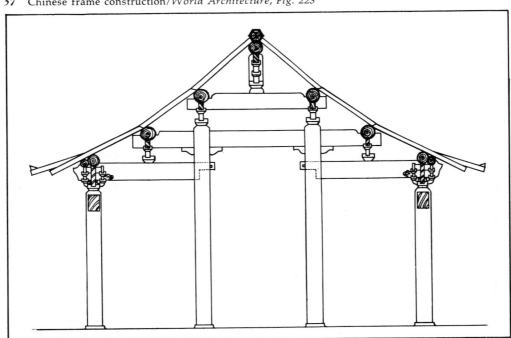

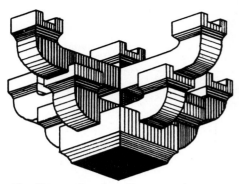

58 Chinese "tou-kung" construction
World Architecture, Fig. 227

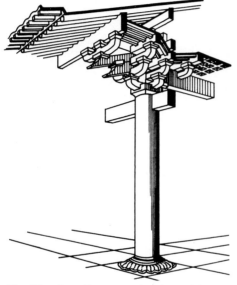

59 "Tou-kung" construction in position
World Architecture, Fig. 228

60 End wall, Chinese
World Architecture, Fig. 229

61 Ki-yo-mi-zu temple, Kyoto/*John Burchard*

62 Mo-mo-ya-ma carving, Nikko/*John Burchard*

63 Torii, Inari shrine/*John Burchard*

64 Japanese pagoda/*John Burchard*

65 Torii types
from Meeting with Japan by Fosco Maraini.
New York: Viking Press, 1960

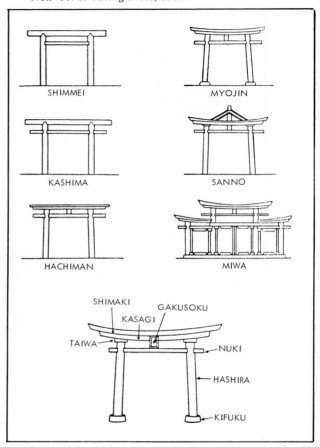

SHIMMEI

MYOJIN

KASHIMA

SANNO

HACHIMAN

MIWA

SHIMAKI
KASAGI
GAKUSOKU
TAIWA
NUKI
HASHIRA
KIFUKU

66 Naiku shrine, Ise, air view/*Yoshio Watanabe*

67 Naiku shrine, Ise, main sanctuary
Yoshio Watanabe

69 Naiku shrine, Ise, four fences/*Yoshio Watanabe*

70 Menhir, "The Monaco" near Modugno
Edward Allen

71 Dolmen, "Tavola dei Paladini" near Bari
Edward Allen

72 Inca wall, on Via Loreto, Cuzco
Roger-Viollet

74 Stonehenge, plan
*Department of the Environment,
Hannibal House*

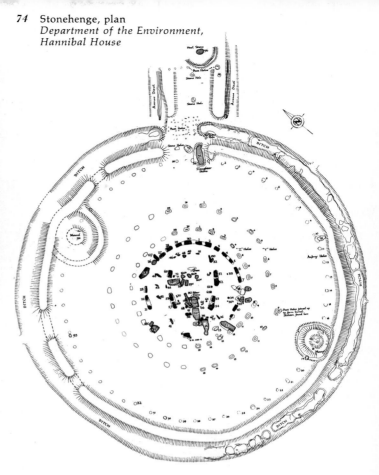

73 Stonehenge, lintels/*Royal Commission on
Historical Monuments (England)*

75 Stonehenge, replica/MEDIA FEATURES

76 Saccsihuáman, Peru/OMIKRON

77 Saccsihuáman, Peru/MEDIA FEATURES

78 Machu Picchu, Peru/OMIKRON

80 Polygonal terrace wall, Delphi
Tod from OMIKRON

79 Kenko, Peru
MEDIA FEATURES

81 Palazzo Strozzi, Florence
Italian Government Travel Office

82 Propylaea, Pinacoteca/*Tod from* OMIKRON

83 Area around ziggurat of Ur
OMIKRON

84 Zoser complex and pyramid/HIRMER FOTOARCHIV

85 Palace of the Nusta, Machu Picchu, windows/OMIKRON

86 Lion Gate, Mycenae
National Tourist Organization of Greece

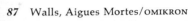
87 Walls, Aigues Mortes/OMIKRON

88 Walls, Avila/OMIKRON

89 Walls, Avila/MEDIA FEATURES

90 Krak des Chevaliers, Beirut
Tod from OMIKRON

91 Santa Maria Novella, Florence
Tod from OMIKRON

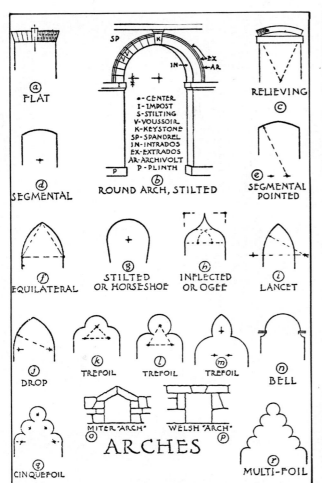

FLAT (a)

ROUND ARCH, STILTED (b)

- • — CENTER
- I — IMPOST
- S — STILTING
- V — VOUSSOIR
- K — KEYSTONE
- SP — SPANDREL
- IN — INTRADOS
- EX — EXTRADOS
- AR — ARCHIVOLT
- P — PLINTH

RELIEVING (c)

SEGMENTAL (d)

SEGMENTAL POINTED (e)

EQUILATERAL (f)

STILTED OR HORSESHOE (g)

INFLECTED OR OGEE (h)

LANCET (i)

DROP (j)

TREFOIL (k)

TREFOIL (l)

TREFOIL (m)

BELL (n)

MITER "ARCH" (o)

WELSH "ARCH" (p)

ARCHES

CINQUEFOIL (q)

MULTI-FOIL (r)

92 Profile of various arch forms *from Dictionary of Architecture by Henry Saylor. Copyright 1952. John Wiley & Sons, Inc. Reprinted by permission of John Wiley & Sons.*

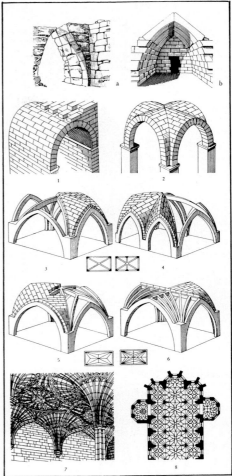

93 Development of vault/*Cichy, p. 429*

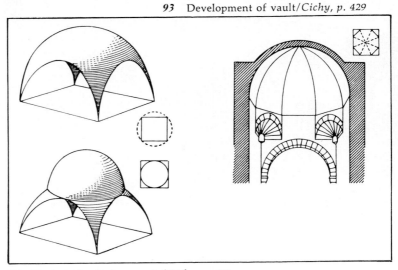

94 Various domical supports/*Cichy, p. 411*

95 Abu Simbel/OMIKRON

96 Sculpture of gate, Sanchi
Government of India Tourist Office

97 Lingara temple, Bhuvaneswar
MEDIA FEATURES

98 Varadararajaswami temple, Kanchipuram
MEDIA FEATURES

99 Durga sculpture, Kanchipuram
John Burchard

100 Chaitya hall and Vihara, Bhaja, plan and section/OMIKRON

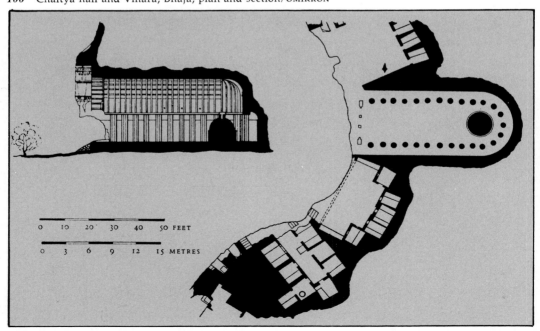

0 10 20 30 40 50 FEET

0 3 6 9 12 15 METRES

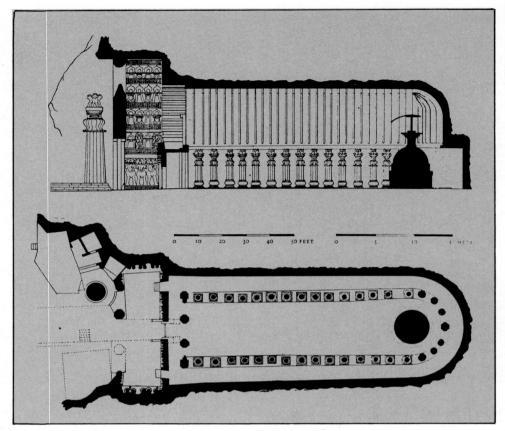

101 Chaitya hall, Karli, plan and section/*Tod from* OMIKRON

102 Chaitya hall, Karli, interior
Tod from OMIKRON

103 Preaching hall, Ajanta cave xix, interior
Roger-Viollet

105 Kailasanath temple, Ellora, plan
Benjamin Rowland

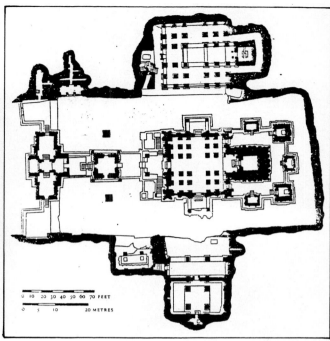

104 Raths, Mahabalipuram/OMIKRON

106 Kailasanath temple, Ellora/MEDIA FEATURES

109 "Fall of the Ganges",
Mahabalipuram, detail
OMIKRON

108 Ziggurat, Ur-Nammu, reconstruction model
Tod from OMIKRON

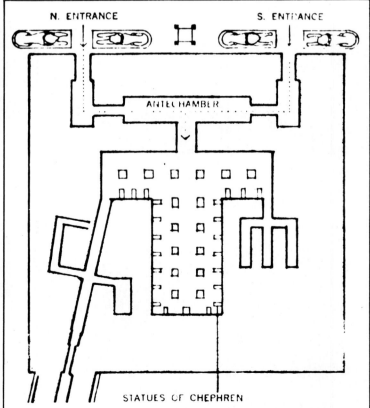

110 Chefren valley temple, Giza, plan/*Sigfried Giedion*

N. ENTRANCE   S. ENTRANCE

ANTECHAMBER

STATUES OF CHEPHREN

107 Typical entrance to chaitya hall, Ajanta
MEDIA FEATURES

112 Zoser step pyramid, Saqqara
World Architecture, Fig. 41

113 Zoser step pyramid, Saqqara, cross section
World Architecture, Fig. 40

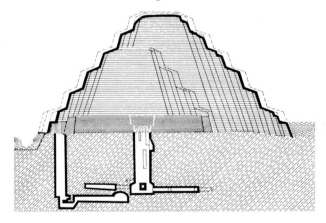

111 Zoser complex, Saqqara, Hebsed race relief
HIRMER FOTOARCHIV

114 Zoser complex, Saqqara, axonometric/*World Architecture, Fig. 36*

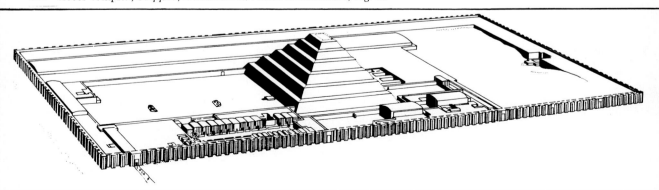

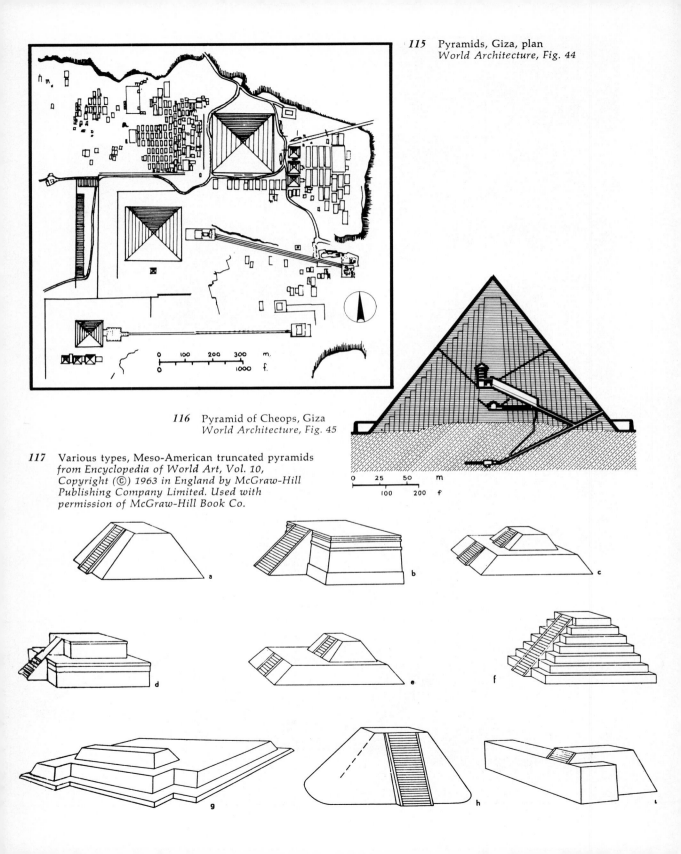

115 Pyramids, Giza, plan
World Architecture, Fig. 44

116 Pyramid of Cheops, Giza
World Architecture, Fig. 45

117 Various types, Meso-American truncated pyramids
*from Encyclopedia of World Art, Vol. 10,
Copyright (©) 1963 in England by McGraw-Hill
Publishing Company Limited. Used with
permission of McGraw-Hill Book Co.*

118 Temple of Quetzlcoatl, Teotihuacán, sculpture
Mexican National Tourist Council

119 El Castillo, Chichen-Itzá/*Den Hanna from* OMIKRON

120 Street of the Dead, Teotihuacán/*Lee Boltin*

121   Pyramid of the Moon, Teotihuacán/*Mexican National Tourist Council*

122   Platforms, Monte Albán/*Mexican National Tourist Council*

123   Conjectural restoration, Copán/*Peabody Museum, Harvard University*
124   "Nunnery", Uxmal, northwest corner of quadrangle/*Mexican National Tourist Council*

125 Pyramid of the Magician, Uxmal/MEDIA FEATURES

126 Palace, Sayil/*Tod from* OMIKRON

127 Governor's Palace, Uxmal, detail/*John Burchard*

128 Citadel, Mycenae/*J. Powell, Rome*

129 Chichen-Itzá, Chac-Mool sculpture
OMIKRON

130 Chichen-Itzá, Temple of Eagles, entrance detail
John Burchard

131 Tula, Atlantes and square columns of temple/*Walter Aguiar*

132 "Treasury of Atreus", Mycenae, ceiling
Edward Allen

133 Zoser complex, Saqqara, Processional Hall
OMIKRON

134 Conoid houses, Alberobello/*Grace Swayne from* OMIKRON

135 Temple of Horus, Ed-fu, portico
Tod from OMIKRON

136 Bases, Papyrus-bud columns, Medinet-Habou
Ministry of Tourism, Egypt

137 Great temple of Amon, Karnak, plan
Fletcher 26G

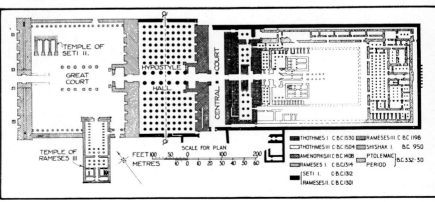

138 Preparatory Corridor of Amenophis, Luxor/*Tod from* OMIKRON

139   Temple of Karnak, hypostyle hall
Tod from OMIKRON

140   Hatshepsut's obelisk, Karnak
Tod from OMIKRON

141   Temple of Luxor, inner court
Tod from OMIKRON

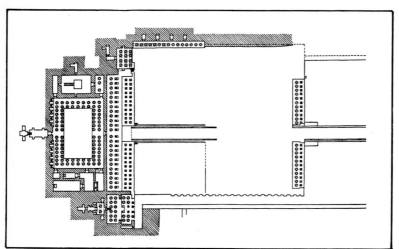

142   Temple of Hatshepsut, Deir-el-Bahri, plan
Lange-Hirmer

143   Temple of Hatshepsut, Deir-el-Bahri/*Tod from* OMIKRON

144 Palace of Darius, Persepolis, symplegma detail/*John Burchard*

145 Palace of Darius, Persepolis, north staircase/OMIKRON

146 Palace of Darius, Persepolis, bull's head gateway/MEDIA FEATURES

147 Palace of Darius, Persepolis, great stair entrance *John Burchard*

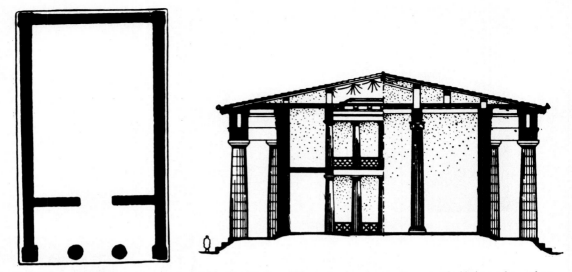

148 Plan, minimal Greek temple, distyle in antis
Fletcher 82A

149 Parthenon, Athens, transverse section, one-half through parthenos, one-half through naos/Fletcher 93F

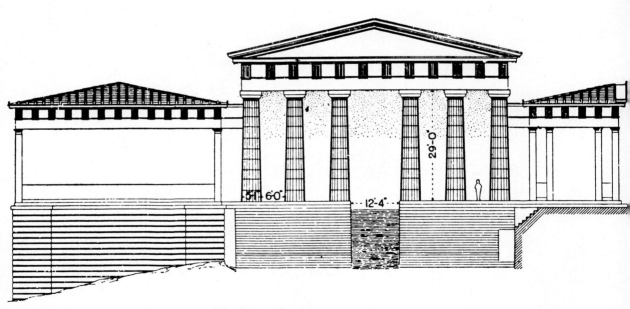

150 Propylaea, Athens, west elevation/Fletcher 116A

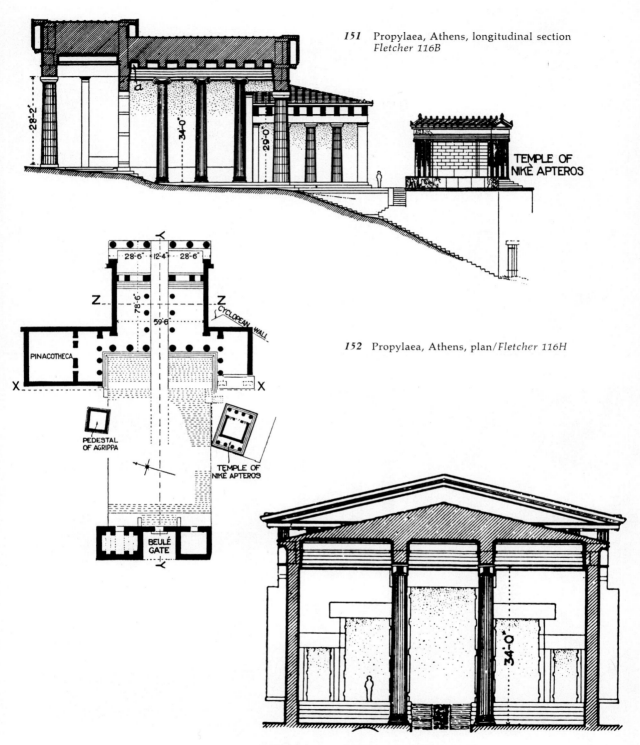

151 Propylaea, Athens, longitudinal section
Fletcher 116B

TEMPLE OF
NIKE APTEROS

28'-2"

34'-0"

20'-0"

28'-6" 12'-4" 28'-6"

78'-6"

59'-6"

CYCLOPEAN WALL

Z — Z

X — X

PINACOTHECA

152 Propylaea, Athens, plan/*Fletcher 116H*

PEDESTAL
OF AGRIPPA

TEMPLE OF
NIKE APTEROS

BEULÉ
GATE

34'-0"

153 Propylaea, Athens, transverse section
Fletcher 116C

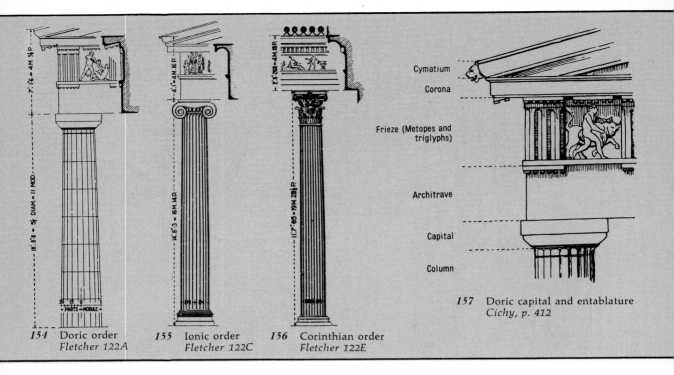

154 Doric order
Fletcher 122A

155 Ionic order
Fletcher 122C

156 Corinthian order
Fletcher 122E

Cymatium

Corona

Frieze (Metopes and triglyphs)

Architrave

Capital

Column

157 Doric capital and entablature
Cichy, p. 412

158 Parthenon, Athens, triglyphs and architrave/MEDIA FEATURES

160 Metope, lapith and centaur
British Museum

159 Panathenaic Frieze, detail/OMIKRON

161 Panathenaic Frieze, detail/*British Museum*

162   Flavian Amphitheater (Colosseum), Rome/OMIKRON

164   Arch of Titus, Rome
Italian Government Travel Office

163   Trajan's Column, Rome, detail
        John Burchard
165   Porta Nigra, Trier/MEDIA FEATURES

167 Temple of Portunus, Rome
Italian Government Travel Office

168 Trajan's Market, Rome/*Grace Swayne from* OMIKRON

169 Maison Carrée, Nîmes/*Tod from* OMIKRON

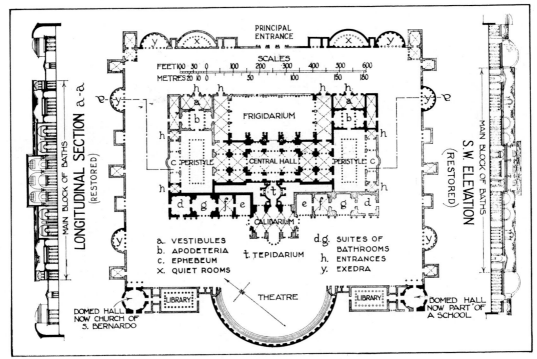

170 Baths of Diocletian, Rome, plan and sections/*Fletcher 169D*

171 Roman Theater, Orange/*John Burchard*

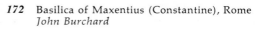

172 Basilica of Maxentius (Constantine), Rome
John Burchard

173 Santa Maria degli Angeli, Rome (converted by Michelangelo from Frigidarium, Baths of Diocletian)/*Tod from* OMIKRON

174 Baths of Caracalla, Rome
Italian Government Travel Office

175 Hadrian's Villa, Tivoli, detail/*Italian State Tourist Office*

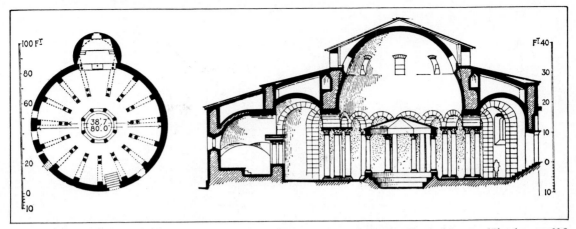

Top: 177   Santa Costanza, Rome, plan
              World Architecture, Fig. 461

Bottom:178   Santa Costanza, Rome, exterior
              World Architecture, Fig. 463

176   Baptistery, Nocera, plan and section/*Fletcher 230H,J*

179   Hagia Sophia, Istanbul, plan/*Tod from* OMIKRON

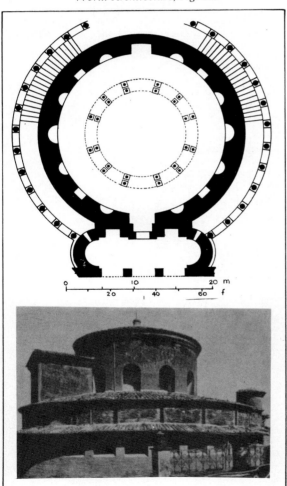

180 Hagia Sophia, Istanbul, exterior/OMIKRON

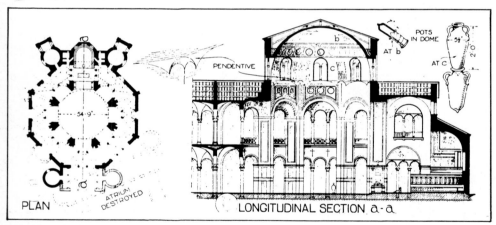

181 San Vitale, Ravenna, plan and section
Fletcher 249C,D

182 San Vitale, Ravenna, exterior
John Burchard

183 San Vitale, Ravenna, interior
Italian State Tourist Office

184 San Vitale, Ravenna, Justinian mosaic
Italian State Tourist Office

186 San Vitale, Ravenna, Theodora mosaic
Italian State Tourist Office

185 San Vitale, Ravenna, interior
Tod from OMIKRON

187 Capella Palatina, Palermo/OMIKRON

188 Monreale, apse exterior
Grace Swayne from OMIKRON

189 Typical Byzantine Crucifixion mosaic
OMIKRON

190 Monreale, nave mosaics/*John Burchard*

191 Monreale, cloister/*Grace Swayne from* OMIKRON

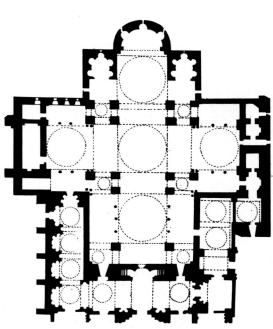

192 San Marco, Venice, plan/*Tod from* OMIKRON

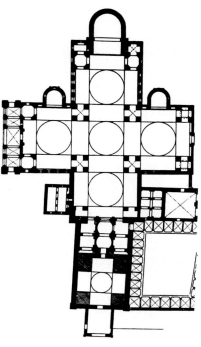

193 St -Front, Perigueux, plan
Tod from OMIKRON

194 San Marco, Venice, front/*Italian Government Travel Office*

195 San Giovanni degli Eremiti, Palermo
John Burchard

196 St. Basil, Moscow/OMIKRON

197 St. Demetrius, Vladimir/INTOURIST

198 Santa Sophia, Novgorod/*Robert J. O'Reilly*

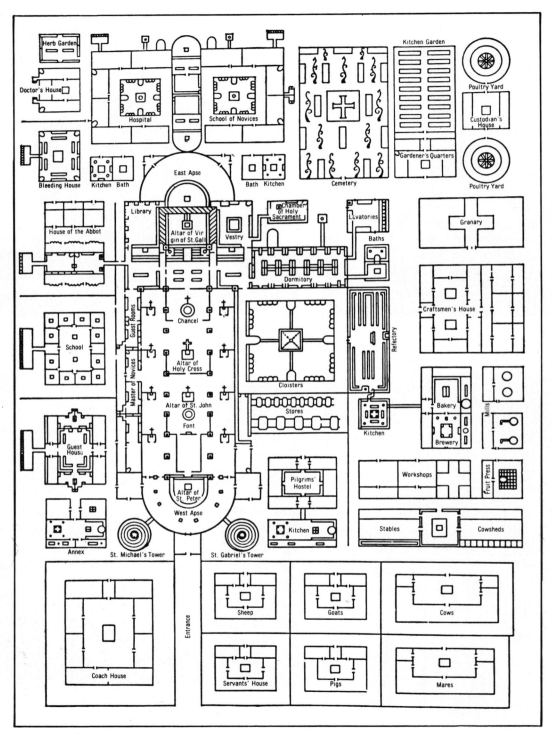

199 Monastery of St. Gall, plan/*Cichy, Fig. 56A*

201 Hildesheim, nave
Landesbildstelle, Hanover

200 St. Martin-du-Canigou, nave/*Tod from* OMIKRON   **202** Minden, Westwerk/*Bildarchiv Foto Marburg*

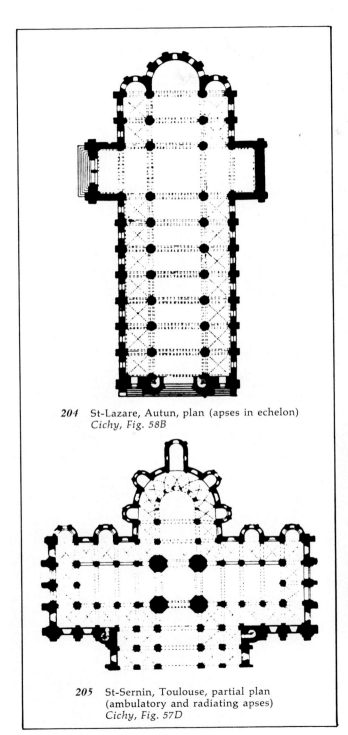

204 St-Lazare, Autun, plan (apses in echelon)
Cichy, Fig. 58B

205 St-Sernin, Toulouse, partial plan
(ambulatory and radiating apses)
Cichy, Fig. 57D

206 Corvey, west front/*Tod from* OMIKRON

207 San Michele, Lucca, west front
Grace Swayne from OMIKRON

208 St-Etienne, Caen, west front
Den Hanna from OMIKRON

210 St-Gilles-du-Gard, west front
Jean Roubier

209 Notre-Dame-la-Grande, Poitiers, west front
French Government Tourist Office

211 Duomo, Modena, west front
Italian Government Travel Office

212 St-Nicolas, Civray, west front
Tod from OMIKRON

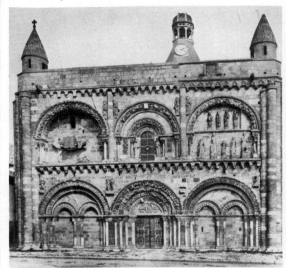

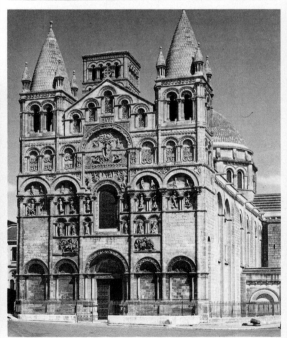

213 St-Pierre, Angoulême, west front
French Embassy Press & Information Division

214 Duomo and Campanile, Pisa/*Grace Swayne from* OMIKRON

215 Germigny-des-Prés/*French Government Tourist Office*

216 Facciata Cattedrale, Cremona
Den Hanna from OMIKRON

217   Sant'Ambrogio, Milan, atrium
     Italian Government Travel Office

218   St-Paul, Issoire, apse/*Tod from* OMIKRON

219   St-Benoît-sur-Loire/*Jean Roubier*

220 Romanesque capital (French)
John Burchard

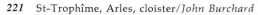

221 St-Trophîme, Arles, cloister/*John Burchard*

223 St-Etienne, Caen, nave/*Tod from* OMIKRON

222 Ste-Madeleine, Vézelay, nave
French Cultural Services

224 St-Etienne, Caen, apse/OMIKRON

225 Duomo, Modena, apse/*John Burchard*

226 Duomo, Modena, interior/*Tod from* OMIKRON

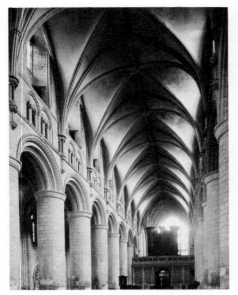

227 Gloucester Cathedral, nave
Royal Commission on Historical Monuments (England)

229 Durham Cathedral, nave
Royal Commission on Historical Monuments (England)

228 Winchester Cathedral, north transept
Royal Commission on Historical Monuments (England)

230 St-Lazare, Autun, west portal, Christ Judge
Den Hanna from OMIKRON

232 Romanesque capital (French)
*French Embassy Press &
Information Division*

231 Romanesque capital (French)
*Royal Commission on Historical
Monuments (England)*

233 Romanesque carving, pier of
southern inner portal,
Vézelay/*French Embassy
Press & Information
Division*

234 Ste-Madeleine, Vézelay, central inner portal
David Davis from OMIKRON

235 Moissac, south porch
French Government Tourist Office

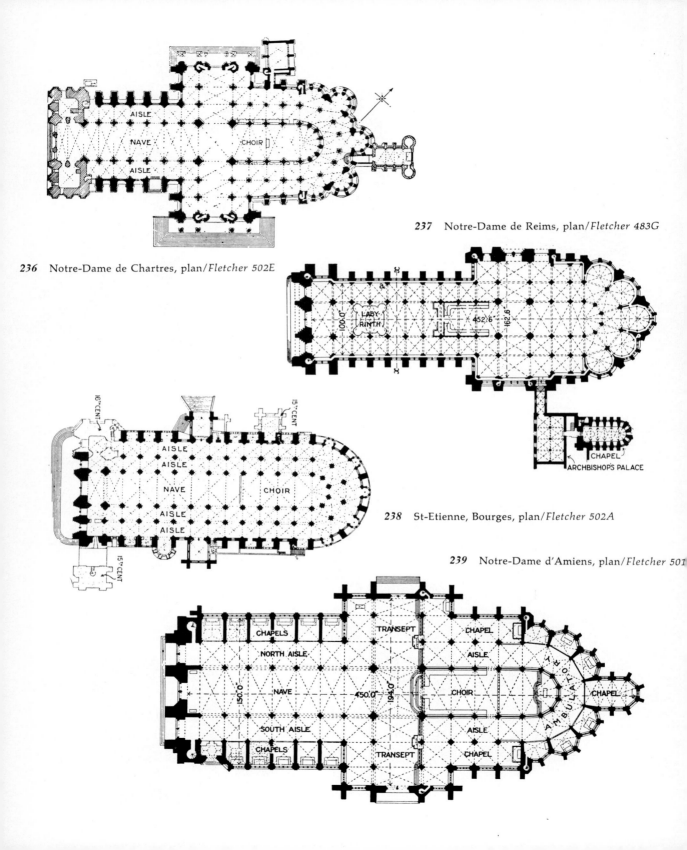

236 Notre-Dame de Chartres, plan/*Fletcher 502E*

237 Notre-Dame de Reims, plan/*Fletcher 483G*

238 St-Etienne, Bourges, plan/*Fletcher 502A*

239 Notre-Dame d'Amiens, plan/*Fletcher 501*

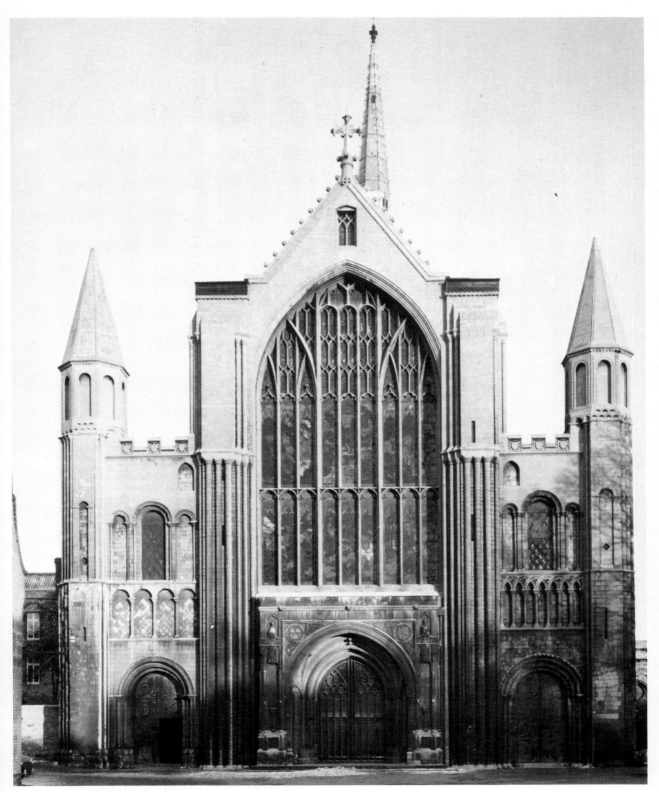

240   Norwich Cathedral, west lancet
Royal Commission on Historical Monuments (England)

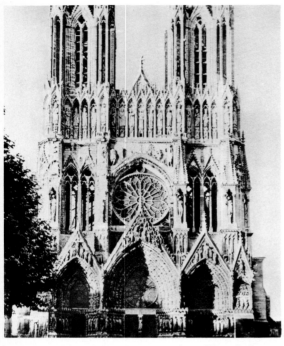

241   Notre-Dame de Reims, west front/*French Government Tourist Office*
243   Notre-Dame d'Amiens, west front/OMIKRON

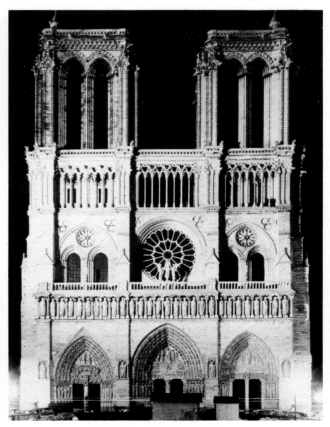

244   Notre-Dame de Paris, west front/
French Government Tourist Office

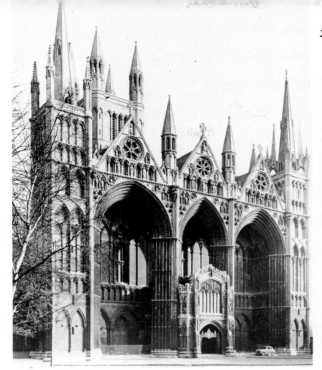

245 Peterborough Cathedral, west front
Berris Barrow from OMIKRON

246 Notre-Dame de Chartres, west front
French Embassy Press & Information Division

248 Duomo and campanile, Siena
Grace Swayne from OMIKRON

247 Duomo, Orvieto, west front/*Grace Swayne from* OMIKRON

250 Wells Cathedral, west front/OMIKRON

249 Le Mont-St-Michel
MEDIA FEATURES

251 Notre-Dame de Paris, east end from Île St. Louis
John Burchard

252 College of San Gregorio, Valladolid (now Town Hall)
Spanish Tourist Office

Opposite: **253** Lincoln Cathedral, west front
Mark Hewlett from OMIKRON

254 Ulm Cathedral, west front tower
Tod from OMIKRON

257 "Giotto's Tower", Florence
John Burchard

255 Belfry, Bruges
Belgian National Tourist Office

258 St. Botolph, Boston, England,
"Boston Stump" tower/OMIKRON

256 Ste-Cécile, Albi
Tod from OMIKRON

259 Wells Cathedral, south west tower/MEDIA FEATURES

260 Antwerp Cathedral, spire
Belgian National Tourist Office

261 Notre-Dame d'Amiens, cross vaulting
at crossing/*Jean Roubier*

262 Salisbury Cathedral, spire/*Mark Hewlett from* OMIKRON

263　Notre-Dame de Reims, abside
French Embassy Press & Information Division

264　St. Andrew, Heckington, spire
John Burchard

265　St. Stephen's, Vienna, tower/OMIKRON

266　Wells Cathedral, "scissors vaulting" at crossing
Royal Commission on Historical Monuments (England)

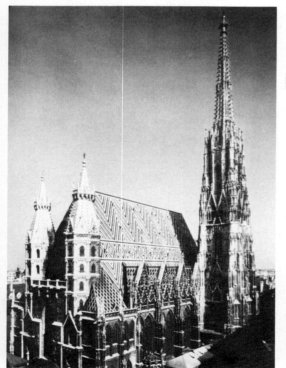

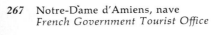

267 Notre-Dame d'Amiens, nave
French Government Tourist Office

268 St-Etienne, Bourges, abside/*John Burchard*

269 Notre-Dame de Chartres, choir buttresses
Tod from OMIKRON

270 Notre-Dame d'Amiens, abside
French Government Tourist Office

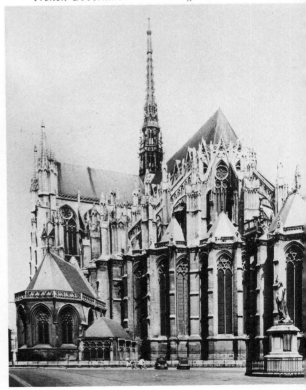

271 Notre-Dame de Reims, choir buttresses
Tod from OMIKRON

272 Strasbourg Cathedral, nave buttresses
Mark Hewlett from OMIKRON

273 Notre-Dame de Chartres, nave buttresses
Tod from OMIKRON

274 Notre-Dame d'Amiens, nave buttresses
Tod from OMIKRON

Opposite: **275** Notre-Dame de Paris, nave buttresses
J. Jangais from OMIKRON

276
Notre-Dame de Paris, rose window,
south transept, from inside/OMIKRON

277
Notre-Dame de Paris, rose window,
south transept, from outside/OMIKRON

278
Notre-Dame d'Amiens,
window of west front/
John Burchard

279   Sens Cathedral, south front/*French Government Tourist Office*

280
Notre-Dame de Chartres, west front,
sculpture central portal/ OMIKRON

282 Notre-Dame d'Amiens, west front, "Le Beau Dieu" *J. Jangais from* OMIKRON

281
Notre-Dame de Chartres, rose window, south transept/OMIKRON

283 St-Etienne, Bourges, west portals/MEDIA FEATURES

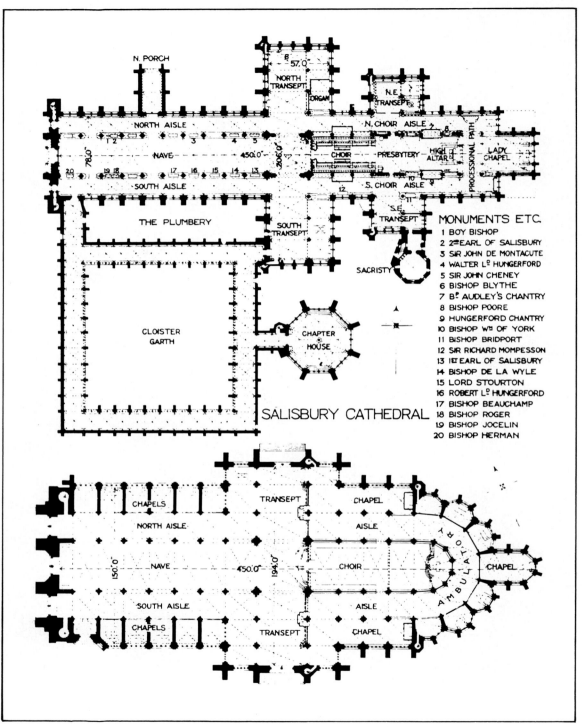

SALISBURY CATHEDRAL

N. PORCH

57.0"

NORTH TRANSEPT

ORGAN

N.E. TRANSEPT

NORTH AISLE

N. CHOIR AISLE

NAVE 450.0"

CHOIR PRESBYTERY HIGH ALTAR LADY CHAPEL

PROCESSIONAL PATH

78.0"

SOUTH AISLE

S. CHOIR AISLE

THE PLUMBERY

SOUTH TRANSEPT

S.E. TRANSEPT

SACRISTY

CLOISTER GARTH

CHAPTER HOUSE

MONUMENTS ETC.

1 BOY BISHOP
2 2ᴺᴰ EARL OF SALISBURY
3 SIR JOHN DE MONTACUTE
4 WALTER Lᴰ HUNGERFORD
5 SIR JOHN CHENEY
6 BISHOP BLYTHE
7 Bᴾ AUDLEY'S CHANTRY
8 BISHOP POORE
9 HUNGERFORD CHANTRY
10 BISHOP Wᴹ OF YORK
11 BISHOP BRIDPORT
12 SIR RICHARD MOMPESSON
13 1ˢᵀ EARL OF SALISBURY
14 BISHOP DE LA WYLE
15 LORD STOURTON
16 ROBERT Lᴰ HUNGERFORD
17 BISHOP BEAUCHAMP
18 BISHOP ROGER
19 BISHOP JOCELIN
20 BISHOP HERMAN

CHAPELS

TRANSEPT

CHAPEL

NORTH AISLE

AISLE

150.0"

NAVE 450.0" 194.0"

CHOIR

CHAPEL

AMBULATORY

SOUTH AISLE

AISLE

CHAPELS

TRANSEPT

CHAPEL

284 Salisbury Cathedral and Notre-Dame d'Amiens, comparative plans
Fletcher 501A,B

285 King's College Chapel,
     Cambridge, vaults *Royal Commission
     on Historical Monuments (England)*

286 Salisbury Cathedral, Chapter
     House vault *Royal Commission on
     Historical Monuments (England)*

287 Westminster Abbey, Henry VII Chapel/*British Tourist Authority*

288 Town Hall, Louvain/*Belgian National Tourist Office*

289 Santa Croce, Florence, neo-Gothic facade/*John Burchard*

290 Sainte Chapelle, Paris, interior, upper chapel
J. *Jangais from* OMIKRON

291 Tempietto, Rome/*R. S. Friend from* OMIKRON

292 Duomo, Florence, dome/*John Burchard*

293 Notre-Dame de Chartres, north porch sculpture, Prophets of the Ancient Law/*Tod from* OMIKRON

294 Ospedale degli Innocenti, Florence/*Tod from* OMIKRON

295 Palazzo Rucellai, Florence/SCALA/*New York, Florence*

296 Pazzi Chapel, Santa Croce, Florence
Walter Newman from OMIKRON

297 Villa Rotonda (Capra), Vicenza, exterior
Italian Cultural Institute

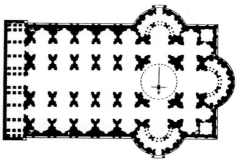

298 St. Peter's, Rome, Raphael's proposed plan
Fletcher 646E

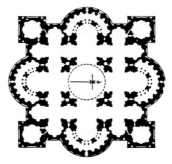

299 St. Peter's Rome, Peruzzi's proposed plan
Fletcher 646F

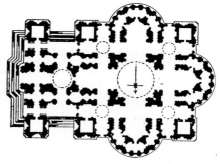

300 St. Peter's, Rome, Sangallo's proposed plan
Fletcher 646G

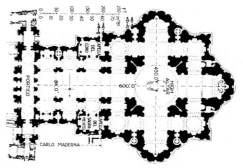

301 St. Peter's, Rome, plan as built with
modifications of Bramante's original
plan by Maderna and Michelangelo
Fletcher 649G

302 Laurentian Library, Florence, staircase
Tod from OMIKRON

303 Chateau de Chenonceaux
MEDIA FEATURES

304 Palazzo Cancelleria, Rome,
cortile/*Tod from* OMIKRON

305 Chateau de Chambord/*French Cultural Services*

306 Palais du Louvre, Paris, Lescot wing facing La Cour Carrée
David Davis from OMIKRON

307 Villa Rotonda (Capra), Vicenza, plan and section
from Key Monuments of the History of Architecture,
Henry Millon (ed.). Prentice-Hall, n.d.

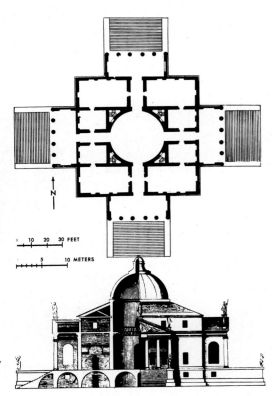

308 Westover, Virginia/OMIKRON

310 Longleat House, Wiltshire/*British Tourist Authority*

309 Town Hall, Antwerp/OMIKRON

311 Chateau de Blois, courtyard facade
French Cultural Services

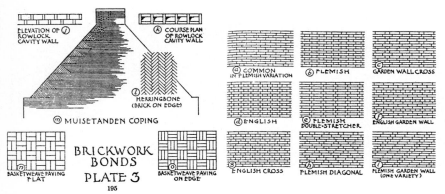

ELEVATION OF ROWLOCK CAVITY WALL ⓙ

ⓚ COURSE PLAN OF ROWLOCK CAVITY WALL

ⓛ HERRINGBONE (BRICK ON EDGE)

ⓜ MUISETANDEN COPING

ⓝ BASKETWEAVE PAVING FLAT

BRICKWORK BONDS PLATE 3
195

ⓞ BASKETWEAVE PAVING ON EDGE

ⓐ COMMON iN FLEMISH VARIATION

ⓑ FLEMISH

ⓒ GARDEN WALL CROSS

ⓓ ENGLISH

ⓔ FLEMISH DOUBLE-STRETCHER

ⓕ ENGLISH GARDEN WALL

ⓖ ENGLISH CROSS

ⓗ FLEMISH DIAGONAL

ⓘ FLEMISH GARDEN WALL (ONE VARIETY)

312 Various brickwork bonds/*Saylor, p. 195, plate 3*

313 Holsten Gate, Lübeck/*German Information Center*

314 Taj Mahal, Agra/OMIKRON

315 Maidan Square, Isfahan/MEDIA FEATURES

316 Dome of the Rock, Jerusalem/OMIKRON

317 Ibn Tulun Mosque, Cairo/*Tod from* OMIKRON

318 Great Mosque, Cordova, interior before mihrab/*Tod from* OMIKRON

319 Great Mosque, Cordova, interior/OMIKRON

320 Court of Lions, Alhambra, Granada/*Spanish Tourist Office*

321 Mosque of Sultan Sulayman
(Sultamaniyeh), Istanbul
OMIKRON

322 Gunbad-i-Kabus, Gurgan
H. C. Scherr-Thoss

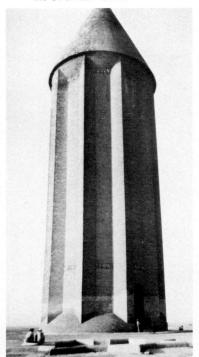

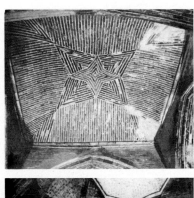

323, 324, 325, 326

Masjid-i-jami (Friday mosque), Isfahan,
various brick vaults in library
H. C. Scherr-Thoss

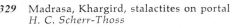

331 Masjid-i-Shakyh Luftfullah, Isfahan, interior
H. C. Scherr-Thoss

332 Masjid-i-Shakyh Lutfullah, Isfahan, stalactites
on portal/*H. C. Scherr-Thoss*

333 Calligraphy used in Islamic decoration/*John Burchard*

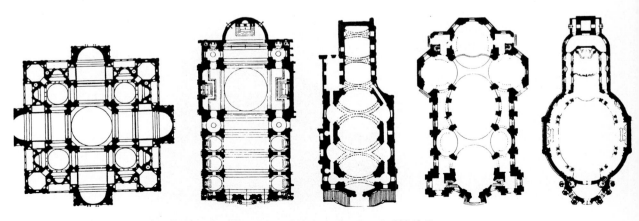

Left to Right 334 St. Peter's Rome, Bramante plan/*Cichy, p. 328, Fig. A,* **335** Il Gesu,
Rome, Vignola plan/*Cichy, p. 328, Fig. B,* **336** Banzkirche, plan/*Cichy, p. 328, Fig. C,*
337 Vierzehnheiligen, plan/*Cichy, p. 328, Fig. D,* **338** Wieskirche, plan/*Cichy, p. 328, Fig. E*

339 Palais du Louvre, Paris, elevation, Bernini's first proposal for east facade
Caisse Nationale des Monuments Historique

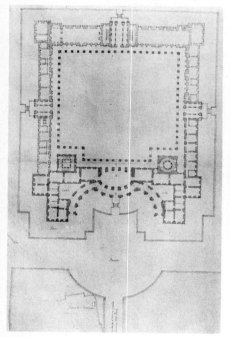

341 Palais du Louvre, Paris, east front, by Claude Perrault
J. Jangais from OMIKRON

340 Palais du Louvre, Paris, plan, Bernini's first proposal for east facade
Caisse Nationale des Monuments Historique

342 Val de Grâce, Paris
French Embassy Press & Information Division

344 Palais de Versailles, air view
Circadian from OMIKRON

345 Palais de Versailles, garden front/ *French Embassy Press & Information Division*

346 Palais de Versailles, Grand
Trianon/*French Embassy Press &
Information Division*

347 Palais de Versailles, Galerie des Glaces
French Government Tourist Office

348 Blenheim Palace, Oxfordshire/*A. E. Kersting from* OMIKRON

349 Summer (upper) Belvedere, Vienna/OMIKRON

350 Karlskirche, Vienna, interior
Austrian State Tourist Department, London

351 Karlskirche, Vienna, facade
Austrian National Library

352 Abbey Church, Melk/*Austrian National Library* 353 Abbey Church, Melk, interior/*Austrian National Library*

354 St. John Nepomuk, Munich, interior/*John Burchard*

355 Amalienburg, Nymphenburg, Munich, interior/*Lester Hult from* OMIKRON

358 Greenwich Palace and Hospital/*Mark Hewlett from* OMIKRON

Opposite: 357 Vierzehnheiligen, facade
Fremdenverkehrsband
Nordbayern

359 Vierzehnheiligen, interior
Fremdenverkehrsband Nordbayern

361 St. Peter's, Rome, St. Peter's Chair
E. Boudot-Lamotte

362 St. Peter's, Rome, Maderna facade and
Michelangelo dome
Italian Government Travel Office

363 St. Peter's and Piazza San Pietro, Rome/*Jack Marco from* OMIKRON

364 Piazza San Pietro, Rome, Colonnade/*E. Boudot-Lamotte*

365 Il Gesu, Rome, facade
     Italian State Tourist Office

366 Il Gesu, Rome, interior
     Italian State Tourist Office

367 Sant'Ivo della sapienza, Rome, cupola
Tod from OMIKRON

368 Sant'Andrea al Quirinale, Rome/*Alinari*

369 Piazza del Campidoglio, Rome
Italian Government Travel Office

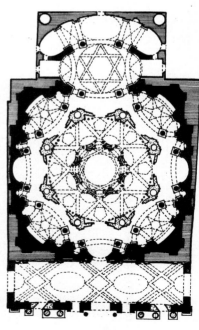

370 San Lorenzo, Turin, plan
Tod from OMIKRON

371 Church, Tepotzotlan, facade
Mexican National Tourist Office

372 Santa Maria della Salute, Venice
SCALA/*New York, Florence*

374 Schauspielhaus, Berlin (Poelzig)
Landesbildstelle, Berlin

375 West German Pavilion, Expo '67,
Montreal (Otto)
German Information Center

376 New City Hall, Boston, Massachusetts (Kallmann)
Chamber of Commerce, Boston

377 Mummers Theater, Oklahoma City (Johannsen)/OMIKRON

378 Habitat '67, Montreal (Safdie)/*City of Montreal*

Opposite: 379 Sagrada Familia, Barcelona
(Gaudí) OMIKRON

380   Park Guell, Barcelona (Gaudí)
John Burchard

381   Dulles National Airport,
Washington, D.C. (Saarinen)
MEDIA FEATURES

382   Exhibition Hall, Turin (Nervi)/*Grace Swayne from* OMIKRON

383 Houses of Parliament, Brasilia (Niemeyer)
OMIKRON

384 Unité d'Habitation (Le Corbusier)
French Embassy Press & Information Division

385 Civic Center, Saitsuna (Aalto)
Finnish Tourist Board

386 St. John's Abbey, Collegeville, Minnesota,
     bell tower (Breuer)/*St. John's University, Minn.*

387 Crown Hall, Chicago (Mies van der Rohe)/OMIKRON